Reviews

I thought the book was great. It is very detailed and excellent citations to back up your conclusions—a huge amount of work! Hopefully other people are reading it, also—it is a valid world view but one foreign to most people.

Professor David Shubert, Salk Institute, USA

I really think you hit on the major issues in a very thorough and comprehensive manner. The book is encyclopaedic in the very best sense - a complete overview with well integrated and synthesized chapters on each topic. Congratulations.

Joel Bakan, Professor, Allard School of Law, University of British Columbia, Vancouver, Canada

Unhealthy

Betrayal

How the Manipulation of Science and Politics by Corporate Interests Destroys Health and Threatens the Future of Humanity.

Andrew Burgoyne

Preface

A significant amount of this work is based on papers, scientific articles, and books, based on the US experience and is therefore in US spellings. I have used both US spellings and English spellings interchangeably, generally using US spelling when dealing with American works and UK English spellings when dealing with UK works.

Warning

This book raises a number of controversial questions regarding health treatment in our society; it also questions a number of beliefs about the cause and treatment of disease. It is purely intended to provoke debate and air what in my view, are important questions regarding our health and the health of our children.

It is not intended as advice for any health conditions or treatments. Anybody with health concerns is recommended to seek advice from their doctor or health professional.

Acknowledgements

Whilst I may not have directly quoted many of the works I refer to in this present volume significantly, I have relied on the volumes of others to provide the background to much of this work, such as Gary Taubes for the background on the whole carbohydrate issue, Ellen Hoddgson Brown on some of the monetary history, Catherine Caufield on the early background on the chapter on radiation etc. Due to the size of this volume there are too many people to thank personally, but let me say here that this work would not be possible without the information provided by the numerous authors that I refer to in this volume. So let me say here a great thank you to all the people who I have referred to in this work.

There are, however, a number of people who have given specific permissions that I would like to acknowledge. Professor Edwin Gale, I would like to thank for the information on the Troglitazone story and diabetes drugs. I am also indebted to Dr Mercola for being able to quote from Professor Don Huber's interviews with Dr Mercola on the Glyphosate/Roundup story.

Contents

INTRODUCTION

INTRODUCTION

Introduction

How healthy are you? What expectations do you have for your health, and that of your children?

Why are most Western healthcare systems facing collapse and serious health conditions such as cancer, heart disease, and diabetes endemic, and even on the increase?

What do you believe is the reason our health systems are failing us?

These are important questions, and questions we intend to answer.

Most recent reports on cancer suggest that the chances of contracting cancer are increasing, so-much-so that Cancer Research UK, now predicts that 1 in 2 people will develop cancer in their lifetime.[1] They also inform us that 28 percent of all deaths in the UK are due to cancer.

Aside from the terrible personal and emotional costs of this health disaster, healthcare financial costs have soared globally, particularly in Europe, the UK, and even more so, in the USA. In 2009, healthcare spending in the USA reached $2.5 trillion—which actually was the lowest increase in health spending for many years—but nevertheless represented 17.6 percent of the entire gross domestic product of the USA. In 2009, this represented more than half of the entire Federal revenue (54.2 %)—a phenomenal $8,086 per person. However, according to the CDC, during 2015, health expenditures *further increased* per-person to nearly $10,000 on average, with total expenditures reaching the immense sum of $3.2 trillion or 17.8% of the entire gross domestic product of the USA. [2]

This suggests an appalling scenario for our future, and in my view an unnecessarily unhealthy one. Is this really the best we can do? Not in my book, read on...

The Rise of Corporate Dominance

The last century has seen a dramatic development in the industrialisation and globalisation of human activity on this planet. In terms of our history it can be considered 'recent' development. This globalisation has brought massive changes in the structure of our socio-political systems—and the emergence of ever larger corporations has led to the development of powerful corporate influence over all areas of regulatory, economic and political life in an unprecedented way.

Accompanying this development has been a radical change in our agricultural system and massive transformation of our food supply, whereby the vast majority of food production is developed and controlled by large corporate interests that are increasingly global in their influence.

Concurrent with this development have been huge changes in technology and science, bringing with them very significant exposure to ever increasing levels of chemicals in our food, water and air, with little or no effective monitoring or oversight.

We reveal how organisations such as the U.S. Environmental Protection Agency, originally set up to monitor and protect the environment and our health, have failed in their mission, and simply have come to represent corporate interests—a betrayal of both our trust, and our health.

We find that many of the corporations that are responsible for polluting our food and water also profit from supplying drugs—offered as the treatment of choice—in response to the appalling health consequences of their pollution of our food with chemical cocktails of food preservatives, plasticisers, pesticide residues, and a whole host of chemicals that we now know are dangerous to our health.

We reveal studies that have examined human blood and tissue, of adults and infants that have revealed alarming levels of chemicals that were previously unknown to us. In one study, Dioxin, arguably one of the most toxic elements known to man, was found in the breast milk of all mothers examined. The same researchers found in excess of 250 man-made chemical contaminants in our body fat. To date there are few studies done to see what the effect these chemicals have on our bodies, either alone or in combination, as a cocktail effect. What we do know for a certainty, is that some of the chemical combinations are significantly more dangerous to us than anybody previously realised.

A System Based on Deceit

Unhealthy Betrayal, assembles a large and diverse body of evidence that can help you make sense of the health crisis we are facing, and suggest ways that we can address the critical issues that confront us.

We reveal ways that corporate interests serve to distort and manipulate evidence, to deceive the public to serve their own interests, which generally means, they put their profits before your health, and not just your health, but that of your children. What we now know is that the health effects can also have transgenerational effects that can affect our children's children, and even future generations—all passed on *via toxic exposure to just one parent.*

We are supposed to swallow the idea that they are acting for our benefit, that their obsession with using high levels of toxic chemicals, is the only way to produce 'cheap' food. But is it? When you add up all the costs; the healthcare costs, the clean-up costs, the lost days of work, the loss of a member of the family, the main bread-winner perhaps; the question has to be asked 'cheap' for who? This simplistic ideology is as economically-bankrupt as it is scientifically-bankrupt, as you will discover.

As regards to my qualifications to write this book, I am an independent researcher. I have followed a line of research that has looked at both writers from the past and current people who have become aware of the shortcomings of modern regulatory practice, and found troubling information. I tend to use the term 'we' when I am writing because I am reporting from the knowledge base of a very significant body of writers that I refer to, by people, from different disciplines, who grasped some of the simple truths that others either missed or chose to ignore, and who were not afraid to air their views. From these different writers I have assembled a bigger picture that reveals the reasons for our dysfunctional healthcare and economic systems.

If you have not already come to the realisation that it is time for change, and concluded that simply ignoring the crisis we are facing is not a sensible option—this volume should help you.

When enough people realise how we have all been manipulated, and deceived, simply to feed corporate profits at the expense of our health—then this will generate momentum for change.

Real change will come when enough of us arrive at the realisation that health is created by generating wholesome food, free of man-made poisons, not by creating impoverished chemically-laden foods that make us sick, only to be 'treated' with yet more man-made chemicals, drugs that do not treat the true cause of our malady.

Reading this book should help you see through the slick industry propaganda, and see it for what it is—mostly deceit, and enable you to see a way to better protect yourself and your family, and even set us on a path to restore the health of the environment we all live in.

Chapter 1
The Western Disease

Billions of public dollars are being misspent in an ill-conceived "war on cancer"—a war we are losing because we are not addressing the increasingly carcinogenic environment that man has created. We have introduced these creations into our water and air, our food chain, our habitation, our workplace, and into the products produced there.

In failing to allocate these resources for prevention, we are fighting the wrong war.

Quentin D. Young, M.D.

President, American Public Health Association [3]

Cancer incidence in the UK in 2007 was 297,990 new cases for the year which translates to one person every two minutes. Worldwide in 2008 it was estimated at 12.7 million new cases. It is further estimated 1 in 3 of us will get cancer and it is the cause of 1 in 4 deaths.[4]

This is a disease that is endemic in our society and affects a huge number of families and causes immense suffering.

According to Cancer Research UK, up to half of all cancers are considered preventable by making lifestyle changes, such as giving up smoking, reducing alcohol consumption, eating a higher fibre diet including more fruit and vegetables, and reducing saturated fat and red meat consumption.[5]

Vast sums of money have been spent on researching cancer, not just in the UK but globally. We keep reading in the press that they have a new wonder drug that is set to crack the problem; I have lost count of the number of times I have read about this. After a decade or so it wears a little thin.

UNHEALTHY BETRAYAL

With this background in mind, I came across the work of Ralph Moss PhD who used to be science writer at Memorial Sloan-Kettering Cancer Center in New York, considered one of the most prestigious cancer research establishments in America. In his book *'The Cancer Industry'* [6] he reveals research into Amygdalin sometimes referred to as Laetrile a chemical that is commonly found in plants, particularly in apricot kernels. This study was carried out by a researcher called Kanematsu Sugiura a well-respected scientist.

Sugiura ran a number of trials on Amygdalin, found it to be a promising compound for the treatment of cancer and studied it for a number of years on mice with tumours. At the time of his study there was already some hostility to the compound which was being used throughout America. According to Moss, there were a number of alternative therapies that were showing promise which were hounded by the Federal Drug Administration (FDA) considered to be in the control of big business—and these treatments were forced to either quit, move or go underground. In his book he investigates in depth a number of the promising alternatives.

However let us focus on the story with Amygdalin which is a compound found in certain easily available foods. Eventually Memorial Sloane-Kettering Cancer Centre (MSKCC) decided to hold a press conference (June 1977) to release details confirming the 'ineffectiveness' of Amygdalin. However at the press conference, which was attended by almost a hundred reporters and five film crews, the question was put to Sugiura "Do you stick by your belief that Laetrile stops the spread of cancer?" His reply was "I stick". It was the last time he was allowed to make a statement about the Laetrile/Amygdalin topic—and a few months later he was dead.

Moss's belief is that there was a genuine success with Amygdalin that could have threatened the vast profits made by the Cancer Industry. In his book he lists further alternative treatments including Vitamin C treatment.[7]

The controversy with Amygdalin however did not stop with Sugiura's demise. In 1952 Dr Ernst T Krebs, Jr., a biochemist in San Francisco advanced the theory that Cancer was a metabolic disease, primarily a deficiency disease much like, scurvy, pellagra, beriberi or rickets. He identified this compound as part of the nitriloside family which occurs abundantly in nature in edible plants. It is particularly prevalent in the seeds of the fruits in the *Prunus Rosacea* family (bitter almond, apricot, blackthorn, cherry, nectarine, peach and plum) but is also contained in grasses, maize, millet, apple seeds, linseeds and many other foods that are not used widely in the modern diet.[8]

Metabolic diseases, for those who are not familiar with the term, refer to diseases of the metabolism of the body, which basically means diet—everything the body has to metabolise through the normal bodily processes. The dictionary definition is:

THE WESTERN DISEASE

The sum total of the chemical processes that occur in living organisms, resulting in growth, production of energy, elimination of waste material etc. [9]

I highlight this definition of metabolism because it will come up later in the book in reference to a number of other conditions.

Cancer—A metabolic Disease

Krebs Jr, came from a family background of physicians. His father was both a graduate pharmacist and physician, practicing in Nevada. He discovered that the native population of Washoe Indians were remarkably free of respiratory ailments and that their native remedy for such ailments was the use of a plant known botanically as *Leptotaenia Dissecta*. He experimented with the plant and extracted the active ingredients which were found to have antiseptic properties. This discovery was put to good use in the great flu epidemic of 1918 which took the lives of over 10 million Americans. Dr. Krebs Sr, was able to save almost 100% of the hundreds of patients that came under his care. Thus Dr. Krebs Sr, was regarded as one of the first people to introduce an antibiotic into modern medicine.[10]

It was with this background in mind that Krebs Jr., who was familiar with the Trophoblast theory of cancer proposed by Professor John Beard, decided to look for a nutritional compound hinted at by Beard's work. By 1950 he had distilled a compound that he termed Laetrile. He labelled the active molecule as B_{17}.

The B_{17} molecule contains two units of glucose, one of benzaldehyde and one of cyanide interlocked together. It is believed that this structure can be unlocked by exposure to an enzyme called *beta-glycosidase* which is found in abundance in cancer cells but not in any harmful amounts in normal cells. When benzaldehyde and cyanide combine they work 'synergistically' which simply means that the combined effect of both substances is more effective than when used singly (in this case 100 times more powerful).

Normal human cells contain an enzyme called *rhodanese* which breaks down both benzaldehyde and the cyanide into useful by-products. However cancer cells do not possess this enzyme, so are vulnerable to attack from B17 for this reason.[11]

There is a considerable controversy about the use of B_{17}. The FDA in the US banned its use in America. Nevertheless there is still huge support for it, and there are many people who feel that there is need for further research into it. It is available in most countries outside the USA.

3

It is worth at this point mentioning again the Trophoblast theory of cancer proposed by Professor John Beard, professor of embryology at the University of Edinburgh. He discovered there were no differences between cancer cells and certain pre-embryonic cells that were considered normal cells in the early stages of pregnancy; he termed these cells Trophoblasts. He proposed the theory that cancer was in fact natural human cells that were employed for repairing the body but which, for one reason or another, grew out of control.

Apparently this action was influenced by the hormone oestrogen. This connection is significant in that there has been a lot of research since Professor Beard's work linking oestrogen and cancer[12] [13] [14]

It is not in the scope of this work to go into any real depth about B_{17}, or indeed any other of the subjects that I raise, I would refer you to the afore mentioned works for further information on this topic, and the references attached to each topic.

It is not the purpose of this book to offer solutions to health problems but to raise the possibility that some conditions including cancer, have a connection with metabolic problems and, by association, diet and food consumption. Personally I believe the use of Amygdalin will continue. I consume apricot kernels on a daily basis (apricot kernels are one of the richest sources of Amygdalin) as a preventative measure, a ridiculously cheap insurance policy.

The Link with Health, Cancer, and Essential Fatty Acids

Over the course of over 60 years of research Nobel Prize winning physician and biochemist Otto Warburg discovered what in his view was the primary cause of cancer. Whilst there are many toxic chemicals and products that are known to cause cancer in humans, these in his view are all secondary type cancers. What he found was that if a cell was shown to be deficient in oxygen it would become cancerous, if it dropped below 35% capability.[15]

He discovered that cancer cells were anaerobic and produced three to four times more lactic acid per molecule than benign tumours. He found cancer cells loved sugar and that sugar stopped normal respiration. There was unimpaired glycolytic activity in each case. I can recommend the book *The Hidden Story of Cancer* [16] as a good place to start for understanding this aspect of the metabolic nature of cancer, and its implications for us all.

THE WESTERN DISEASE

This discovery brings into question what the cause of low oxygen in human body cells is? Exercise and breathing are the obvious ways of bringing oxygen into the body, but it is the mechanism that brings oxygen into the actual cells that is the critical factor.

This mechanism involves the bi-phospholipid layer of the cell wall itself which is suggested to have broken down. This membrane is made from essential fatty acids (EFAs) which are converted to the phospholipids through the normal metabolic processes of the body. Phospholipids are highly oxygen absorbing, and enable both the transport of oxygen into the cell and the removal of carbon dioxide from it. If there were a shortage of phospholipids or if damaged EFAs were supplied to the body, this could compromise the ability of the body to maintain healthy cell walls, and of oxygen to reach the cells.

I have worked for a number of years as a nutritionist and one thing that concerned me was how little people actually knew about nutrition and the link with health and disease. Most people have heard about vitamins and minerals, but the subject of EFAs was severely lacking. Today, there is far greater awareness of 'omega threes' two of the best known EFAs, omega-3 and omega-6.

The most important thing to understand about EFAs is that they are *essential*, they cannot be manufactured by the body. The next important thing to understand is they are very reactive, particularly to heat, light and oxygen but also to other body processes. This is the beauty of them, but it also creates problems when you try to process them, as in the food industry. This subject will be discussed further in the book as it is relevant in many other health conditions, and I believe it to be a very important topic as regards to the long term health of all people.

However, for now, let's discuss the implications for cancer; there are two main ways that we can have a problem with EFAs. If the body is low on EFAs this can have serious health issues resulting in the compromised ability of the body to function. Secondly if damaged EFAs are introduced into the body, this can seriously impair many body functions, including the ability of the cells to import oxygen.

We cannot address the lack of EFAs without firstly looking at the source and quality of them. A fresh mackerel just out of the sea would be an excellent source of EFAs, as would any other oily fish like salmon, as long as it was free-range and hopefully swimming in un-polluted water. Other sources would be fresh nuts and seeds that have not been de-hulled or removed from their protective coatings. Flax seed is, for example, an excellent source of omega 3 EFAs. However as soon as you introduce, storage and processing of any kind, then you introduce potential for harm.

UNHEALTHY BETRAYAL

The Degradation of Essential Fatty Acids

One of the problems with EFAs is they can get damaged easily, and go rancid. This is the case with most vegetable oils; oxidation and the consequent rancidity can render the taste and smell of some foods unpalatable. In many ways this is helpful, as it protects us from ingesting damaged fats. But unfortunately, the food industry has found a way around this problem—which raises a number of issues with our health. The oil industry processes oils on a large scale. To maximise profits the oils are extracted in significant volumes through large expeller presses at high speed which can reach temperatures as high as 500 $^\circ$ F / 260° C. Once pressed at these kinds of temperatures, oils smell and taste rancid and burnt, so they are generally bleached and deodorised to compensate. This processing can cause the oil to foam, so anti-foaming agents are added and finally the product is often 'stabilised' with hexane (which is a component of petrol). The product now has little odour or taste. You could put this product in direct sun for twenty years and it would not change taste or smell significantly. The problem with this oil is that most of the life-sustaining nutrients have been destroyed. Now it contains damaged fats which cause free radical damage to the body if ingested. It can also contain trans-fats which are even more dangerous.[17]

Most margarine made from 1950 to 1990 was made from partially hydrogenated vegetable oil which generally means they contain *trans* fatty acids. One of the leading researchers in the field of lipids (fats & oils) who has done a lot of research into *trans* fatty acids is Mary G Enig Ph.D. She published an excellent book called '*Know Your Fats*' that I would recommend to anyone interested in researching the subject.

There is a significant list of adverse symptoms from consuming *trans* fats, and I will list just a few. For a more comprehensive list please refer to the above source.

Conditions include the following:

- Lowers the 'good' HDL cholesterol level in a dose response manner. (the higher the *trans* level in the diet, the lower the HDL cholesterol in the serum)
- Raises the LDL cholesterol level in a dose response manner.
- Raises total serum cholesterol levels 20-30mg%
- Causes a dose response decrease in visual acuity in infants who are fed human milk with increasing levels of *trans* fatty acids.
- Associated with low birth weight in human infants

- Increases blood insulin levels in humans in response to glucose load, increasing risk of diabetes.
- Affects immune response by lowering efficiency of B cell response and increasing proliferation of T cells.
- Decreases levels of testosterone in male animals, increases levels of abnormal sperm, and interferes with gestation in females.
- Decreases the response of the red blood cells to insulin, thus having a potentially undesirable effect in diabetics.
- Causes adverse alterations in the activities of the important enzyme system that metabolises chemical carcinogens and drugs (medications).
- Causes alterations of physiological properties of biological membranes including measurements of membrane transport and membrane fluidity.
- Causes alterations in adipose cell size, cell number, lipid class and fatty acid composition.
- Adversely interacts with conversion of plant omega-3 fatty acids to elongated omega-3 tissue fatty acids.
- Escalates adverse effects of essential fatty acid deficiency.
- Increases peroxisomal activity (potentiates free radical damage).
- Precipitates childhood asthma.[18]

As you can see from some of the above, the potential to interrupt oxygen transportation could be a serious concern with *trans* fatty acids, as well as the other types of damaged fats with free radical damage. This also gives rise to other possibilities affecting cancer proliferation in the body.

Modern Western diets are exposed to a large number of sources of damaged EFAs. When you consider that all vegetable oils react to heat, light and oxygen, you have to question why all products that contain vulnerable EFAs are not stored appropriately. The answer is probably twofold—cost and ignorance. Vegetable oils should not be kept in clear glass containers in a warm environment as they are on supermarket shelves. Quality un-refined vegetable oils need to be in opaque containers, refrigerated and stored for as short a period as possible to minimise damage.

It is not just the food processing industry that affects our uptake of EFAs; feeding cattle on grain instead of grass for example changes the balance of EFA makeup in the meat.

Industrialisation of the food industry has introduced new hazards into the food chain. Hydrogenation of vegetable oils was introduced in the US in 1910, but it wasn't until the 1950s that hydrogenated vegetable fats became seriously marketed to the baking and snack food industries. In the late 1950s Ancel Keys announced his belief that the coronary heart disease (CHD) epidemic was caused by hydrogenated vegetable oils—after previously pointing the finger at saturated fats. According to Mary Enig, the industry mounted a campaign to stave off a threat to their profits by offering to only partially hydrogenate their oils although there was little change in the levels of *trans* fats. A campaign was mounted to convince the world that the real culprit was saturated fats from animal and dairy sources—and polyunsaturates were represented as health giving.[19]

The American Heart Association (AHA) changed its recommendation for reducing the intake of hydrogenated vegetable fats, and they removed any negative reference to *trans* fatty acids in their revised statement in 1965. They continued to promote hydrogenated fats throughout the 1970s and 1980s as long as these contained double the amount of polyunsaturated fats to saturated fats.[20]

Vitamin D and its Role of Prevention in Cancer.

Recent studies have shown a remarkable benefit in taking vitamin D for the prevention of cancer. Theories linking vitamin D deficiency to cancer have been tested and confirmed in more than 200 epidemiological studies, and understanding of its physiological basis stems from more than 2,500 laboratory studies. Vitamin D has shown preventative benefits for many diseases, including heart disease and diabetes, and can even reduce chronic pain.

One noteworthy study by Lappe and others in 2007, on a group of menopausal women, achieved a 77% reduction in the incidence of all cancers across the board, after only four years. The women were given enough vitamin D to raise their serum levels to 40ng/ml, which is regarded as a relatively modest level. Many other studies suggest a more optimal level could be 50-70 ng/ml. Dr Mercola reports studies with a response of 90 percent. [21]

Environmental Factors and Cancer

In the year 1900 the death rate in the US for Cancer was 64 people per 100,000 and cardiovascular disease stood at 345.2 per 100,000. By 1960 the cancer rate had risen to 149.2 and cardiovascular disease reached 521.8 per 100,000.[22]

No discussion about cancer could be entertained without looking at the politics behind the problem—whether it is related to the primary causes or to all the other causes of this illness.

THE WESTERN DISEASE

Whilst this subject will be dealt with more extensively later in the book, I feel it appropriate to introduce this important topic now. I can think of no better place to start than with a quotation by Samuel S. Epstein M.D. It appears on the cover of his book 'The Politics of Cancer *Revisited*';

"The National Cancer Institute and the American Cancer Society have misled and confused the public and Congress by repeated false claims that we are winning the war against cancer- claims made to create public and Congressional support for massive increases in budgetary appropriations"

Samuel S. Epstein, M.D. is professor emeritus of Environmental and Occupational Medicine at the University of Illinois School of Public Health, and Chairman of the Cancer Prevention Coalition. He has published some 260 peer reviewed articles, and authored or co-authored 11 books including: *The Politics of Cancer.*[23]

Whilst some of the increase in cancer and heart disease can be directly related to our poor dietary habits, and the industrialisation of our food supply, a significant proportion can be attributed to chemicals and other hazards of the environment. We have a long history of exposure to hazards in the workplace, for example, that has resulted in certain cancers being described as "prescribed diseases", entitling victims to possible compensation. Occupational cancers in this category include skin cancer caused by exposure to coal tar and soot (1921); lung cancer caused by exposure to nickel compounds (1949); bladder cancer caused by aromatic amines in chemical dyestuffs & in rubber production (1953); mesotheliomas caused by exposure to asbestos (1969); adenocarcinoma of the nose caused by exposure to wood dust (1969); angiosarcoma of the liver resulting from exposure to vinyl chloride monomer (1976) and cancer of the navel cavity contracted in the manufacture and repair of footwear (1979).[24]

Since 1979 there has been a huge increase in the number of chemicals introduced into the environment. In the USA where figures are more easily available than in the UK, the Environmental Protection Agency's (EPA's) state-wide Toxics Release Inventory (TRI) admitted 6.5 billion pounds of toxic chemicals, including nearly 100 million pounds of carcinogens, are discharged into the environment annually. These figures are likely to be even higher than stated, since the report examined only a limited number of sites. The EPA also acknowledges that, of the 75,000 listed chemicals in their inventory, only 2.6% have ever been tested for carcinogenicity. Of this small number of studies, only 900, according to the International Agency for Research on Cancer (IARC), had been re-evaluated (since 1970) and 50% of the studies did not meet basic scientific requirements.[25]

According to the National Institute for Occupational Safety and Health (NIOSH) in the USA, some 11 million men and 4 million women are involuntarily exposed to a wide range of occupational carcinogens, representing the single largest cause of avoidable cancer. A report by the American Industrial Health Council, the chemical industry's trade association, was leaked to the press. This admitted that exposure to occupational carcinogens was responsible for at least 20% of all cancers, and that it posed a 'public health catastrophe'.[26]

Cancer Politics

Cancer is increasingly seen as a preventable disease and is caused by the way we live and work in our environment. For this reason there is much criticism of the approach of the cancer industry to rely solely on the treatment protocols that involve drugs, surgery and radiation. One of the main criticisms of the cancer charities, too, is their blind focus on supporting the pharmaceutical industry's approach, and their almost complete lack of interest in funding research that looks at the effects of the chemicals that we pour into the environment. They are further criticised because, in many cases, the pharmaceutical industry's powerfully invasive treatments have limited success— and in many cases reduce the quality of the patient's remaining lifespan.

Information about the environmental causes of cancer is very limited in much of the mainstream press. Much of the industry's stance is that the environmental causes of cancer are due to poor lifestyle choices such as smoking, inactivity and eating a high fat diet. This was promoted by two researchers, Richard Doll and Richard Peto, two influential epidemiologists who published *The Causes of Cancer* (1982).[27] Industry sources have relied on the work of these two men for a considerable time. According to Dr Epstein their analysis was based not on actual data, but their 'guesstimate' of a figure for lifestyle factors being responsible for 90 percent of cases. The other 10% they relegated to occupation, pollution and "industrial products". Dr Epstein further noted that their 'guesstimate' failed to include any consideration of the mortality of people over the age of 65, or Black Americans, both of which groups are disproportionately affected by cancer incidence. They further excluded recognition of the significant evidence that exists revealing the extensive range of occupational carcinogens that are responsible for many cancers, particularly lung cancer.[28]

THE WESTERN DISEASE

More recent estimates for occupational exposure concluded that they contribute approximately as much as ten percent of cancer incidence mortality—and this is considered a conservative estimate.[29]

The Radiation Link to Cancer

According to the late John Gofman, M.D., Ph.D., Professor Emeritus of Molecular and Cell Biology, University of California at Berkeley, the single biggest cause of cancer, that of radiation has been seriously overlooked. He has published numerous works on the subject of radiation and its effects on health. He was encouraged by the late Glenn T. Seaborg, then Chairman of the Atomic Energy Commission (AEC) to start a biomedical division at the AEC's Livermore Radiation Laboratory to study the effects of ionizing radiation on human health. In the years that followed Gofman came to the conclusion that radiation, even in low-level exposure, was far more dangerous to health than anybody realised. Gofman would not be silenced by the AEC for his views, so they cut off his funding. Gofman and one of his students, Arthur Tamplin (who co-authored the book *Poisoned Power—The Case Against Nuclear Power Plants Before and After Three Mile Island)*, campaigned against project Plowshare, which was designed to use nuclear bombs, for amongst other things, building canals such as a new Panama Canal. They also campaigned against the rush by the US government to build 1000 new nuclear plants in the USA. [30]

Gofman was aware of the dangerous effects of radiation, and came to the conclusion that there was no such thing as a safe dose. Using the available epidemiological data (statistical data) and his understanding of radiation and track analysis (that is of the tracks made by high energy particles) he discovered that even at the lowest doses, damage occurred to living tissue. In his book *Radiation Induced Cancer from Low-Dose Exposure: An Independent Analysis,* he details the effects of low-level radiation and their health effects on a cellular level, and states that there is no comparable mechanism for causing cells to mutate than ionization. Ionization can be considered as simply the knocking of an electron out of its orbit around its normal path around the nucleus of an atom. In the case of human tissue, the results are very unpredictable and not immediately noticeable. He discovered that the dangers were more apparent at low doses than at high doses, which is contrary to orthodox opinion—that is to say industry funded opinion. [31]

Gofman was one of the first people who drew attention to the effects of medical radiation via x-rays, fluoroscopies and later CT scans and their effect on health. He studied the effect probably more than anyone else and came to the conclusion that medical radiation exposure from X-rays (including fluoroscopies and CT scans) was a highly important cause of cancer mortality, probably the principal cause of cancer mortality in the USA. Over the years further research only further confirmed his views. In 1999 he published *Radiation from Medical Procedures in the Pathogenesis of Cancer and Ischemic Heart Disease: Dose—Response Studies with Physicians per 100,000 Population*. According to this research, he estimates that medical radiation was responsible for fifty percent of all deaths from cancer in the US. With regard to breast cancer, he puts the figure even higher at seventy-five percent. In later years, he revised this figure upwards. Gofman, in this study (of more than 700 pages), indicated that there could be a synergistic relationship involved—this is where the combination of two or more inputs create an effect that would not occur singly.[32]

Because of the seriousness of this issue, and its effects on health this will be further discussed in chapter 17, the chapter devoted to radiation. There will also be more on Gofman's work with regard to heart disease, and its connection with radiation, in the next chapter.

In the Annual Report by the US President's Cancer Panel of leading scientists, they expressed clearly what some of the key issues were, that needed to be addressed:

> Issues impeding control of environmental cancer risks include those related to limited research on environmental influences on cancer; conflicting or inadequate exposure measurement, assessment, and classification; and ineffective regulation of environmental chemical and other hazardous exposures.[33]

Cancer, and its many suspected causes, will be discussed throughout the book, and we will show similar links and connections between this insidious disease and some of the other metabolic disease conditions that exist in western men, women and children.

Chapter 2
Have a Heart

*"If people let the government decide what foods they eat and
what medicines they take, their bodies will soon be in as sorry
a state as are the souls of those who live under tyranny."*

—Thomas Jefferson (1743–1826)

I n our society, what captures the public imagination—and the subsequent effect on public policy—sometimes has more to do with public perception and political expediency than with actual science. The role of the media, the influence of political lobbying, and the part played by corporate interests, can have a significant effect on what becomes 'official policy'.

Heart Disease Theory

Heart disease in America significantly rose after the Second World War to the point that it was officially considered an 'epidemic'. The American Heart Association (AHA), which formed in 1924, was originally a private organisation of doctors. It re-established itself as a national volunteer health agency in 1948; its members hired a public relations agency, held its first nationwide funding campaign, and raised nearly $3 million. The same year U.S. Congress passed the National Heart Act, which created the National Heart Institute (NHI) and the National Heart Council (NHC). The administrators of the NHI had to lobby Congress for funds educating its members about the nature of heart disease. At the same time publicised to the wider population that heart disease was the number one killer of Americans. Prior to that time, public funding for heart disease research was insignificant—but by 1949 the NHI had achieved a budget of $9 million for research—and by 1960 this had increased six fold.[34]

Gary Taubes credits Ancel Benjamin Keys in his book, *The Diet Delusion*, with being one of the primary researchers to promote the theory that cholesterol levels predict heart disease, and that high levels of dietary fat were what caused them. In 1961 he made the front cover of *Time* magazine for promoting his theory that a low fat diet could eradicate heart disease.

Keys was at the time a physiologist at the University of Minnesota. He had a Ph.D., in oceanography and biology and a Ph.D., in physiology. He ran the Laboratory of Physiological Hygiene which, he claimed to *Time* magazine, was "to find out why people get sick before they get sick." He also was famous for developing the "K" ration for troops during World War II. Some say the "K" stood for "Keys". He also undertook a major study called *The Biology of Human Starvation*, that ran to fourteen hundred pages. He started his crusade against heart disease in the 1940s, back in the time when many physicians believed dietary cholesterol was the main culprit—and that people ate too many eggs and too much meat that, in theory, raised our blood cholesterol levels and caused heart disease.[35]

Previous research in 1937 by David Rittenburg and Rudolph Schloenheimer had demonstrated that the levels of cholesterol in our food did not directly reflect the levels of cholesterol in serum (blood). In Key's own study in which he fed men for months on diets that were both high and low in cholesterol, the results unfortunately did not support his theory. Keys nevertheless refused to accept defeat, and cited research into the fact that heart disease was reduced in many countries during the Second World War; (in Sweden, Finland, Norway, Holland and Great Britain), when levels of fat intake were known to be reduced. The trouble with this claim however, was that although fat intake was reduced during this time, so was that of sugar and refined flour which many people believed to be much more significant players in the progress of both heart disease and diabetes.

According to the United States Department of Agriculture (USDA), consumption in the USA of animal fats (such as in milk, cream, lard and butter), decreased after the end of the war, and consumption of margarine, vegetable shortening, salad and vegetable cooking oils increased. Vegetable fat consumption increased from 28 pounds to 55 pounds per capita during the thirty years from 1947 – 1977 and animal fat consumption decreased from 81 pounds to 71 pounds. This was during a time that was considered an 'epidemic' of heart disease.[36]

During this period, the World Health Organisation (WHO) called its first expert committee on the Pathogenesis of Atherosclerosis (in 1954) to address the increase in coronary heart disease and heart attacks. Ancel Keys addressed the conference, and reiterated his theory for heart disease. He was interrupted by Sir George Pickering from the U.K. who asked what his best piece of evidence was to support this theory. Apparently Keys was taken aback by this blunt request and offered only one piece of evidence which was summarily dismissed by Pickering and his fellow peers.[37]

In 1956 Keys launched the Seven Countries Study with Public Health Service funding of $200,000 per year—which in those days was considered a huge sum. The study assessed thirteen thousand middle aged men in mostly rural populations in Yugoslavia, Italy, Greece, Finland, Japan, the Netherlands and the U.S.A. It assessed their health at the beginning of the study, and re-assessed it periodically. The first results were issued in 1970, and subsequently at five yearly intervals. The mortality rates from heart disease varied wildly—from 9 per 10,000; in Crete, to 66 per 10,000 in Japan, to 992 per 10,000 amongst the farmers and lumberjacks of Kerelia in Finland. Keys insisted that there was a proven direct relationship with heart disease, saturated fat levels and cholesterol levels. The study was criticised by many for his choice of countries. It was well known for example that countries such as France and Switzerland have high intakes of saturated fats, yet relatively low incidences of coronary heart disease, and that countries like Japan have a very low fat consumption, but higher heart disease than say Crete.[38]

In 1965 a British study was undertaken to assess the effect of a low fat diet on heart disease rates. The fat intake of a group of men who had previously had heart attacks was restricted to 1.5 ounces—roughly a third of the normal amount. Their diets were reduced to half an ounce of butter a day, three ounces of meat, one egg, two ounces of cottage cheese and two ounces of skimmed milk. Yet, after three years, there was no difference in the recurrence of heart disease—and the authors concluded "A low fat diet has no place in the treatment of myocardial infarction."[39]

This prompted further trials in which, instead of reducing the fat content, the saturated fat content of the diet was replaced with polyunsaturated fats. One of the most publicised trials was the Anti-Coronary Club Trial in the late 1950s launched by Norman Jolliffe, director of New York City Health Department. The study involved eleven hundred men who were given what was called a "prudent Diet". They were allowed poultry and fish anytime but were restricted on meats such as beef, lamb or pork, to three times a week. At the same time, they were asked to consume one ounce of polyunsaturated fat each day. The proportion of saturated fat to polyunsaturated fat was four times smaller than the average American diet. Initially the results seemed favourable, but in

November 1966 they had to report that eight members of the study group had died of heart attacks, while none of the control group had.

A further trial was undertaken in 1969 by Dr Seymour Dayton professor of medicine at the University of California, Los Angeles to look into the effects of a low fat diet on death and disease among 850 residents of the local Veterans Administration hospital. The diet replaced the saturated fats of butter, cheese and ice cream with safflower, corn, soybean and cottonseed oils. Their cholesterol count dropped 13% lower than the control group, and only sixty-six died of heart disease, compared to ninety-six people in the control group on the standard American diet. However thirty one of the low fat group died of *cancer,* compared to seventeen in the control group. [40]

Political Intervention in Heart Disease

There were further studies done but none achieved results supporting Key's hypothesis. However, there was a big campaign by the margarine and vegetable oil industries, supported by the AMA, to win support in the general population for Key's theory. In 1977, the case for condemning saturated fat reached a new high when Senator George McGovern announced the publication of the first *Dietary Goals for the United States,* which was the first attempt by the Federal Government to promote dietary guidelines. It was produced by Mc Govern's Senate Select Committee on Nutrition and Human Needs, which had been originally formed in 1968 and given the task of eradicating malnutrition in America. It had manifestly failed in its task, and it was suggested in some quarters that it was facing downgrading which may have influenced its move at this stage. They nevertheless produced a report with some *dietary goals*.

- The first goal was to raise carbohydrate consumption until it reached 50 -60 % of the calories consumed.
- The second goal was to decrease fat consumption to 30% of all calories with less than 33% being supplied by saturated fats.

They suggested to achieve these goals that consumption of meat and dairy products would have to be reduced. The goals also suggested eating less salt and sugar, and more fruit, vegetables and whole grains.

The guidelines were badly received at the press conference, uproar ensued. This prompted Mc Govern to hold further hearings.

HAVE A HEART

One eminent cardiologist, Sir John Michael, from the University of London, testified that he thought the guidelines were irresponsible and premature. Even the American Medical Association argued against the proposals. There was of course, intense opposition from the beef and dairy industries.

The committee revised the guidelines later that year. The first guideline was changed to avoid weight gain, and they replaced the advice to reduce meat consumption (and animal fat) and to choose fish, chicken and meats that reduced saturated fat intake instead. What Mc Govern succeeded in doing was to turn the whole issue into a political issue, instead of keeping it simply as a question of science.[41]

Soon, other government agencies felt compelled to get on the band wagon. Administrators for both the Department of Agriculture (USDA) and the National Academy of Sciences (NAS) entered the debate. Carol Foreman of the USDA believed it was their duty to turn Mc Govern's recommendations into official government policy.

The NAS was formed in 1940 and advised the government on nutrition. They determined the Recommended Dietary Allowances (RDA) of vitamins and minerals for a healthy diet.

Due to all the disagreement and controversy around Mc Govern's report, many viewed it as a political statement, so it was eventually agreed that the USDA and the Surgeon General's Office would draft official dietary guidelines. Carol Foreman of the USDA hired Mark Hegsted, a Harvard trained nutritionist who had advised Mottern on the original *dietary goals* document. He was known as a supporter of Keys. He worked with J. Michael McGinnis from the Surgeon General's Office.

They were advised for their report by a committee of the American Society of Clinical Nutrition. Although there were significant differences of opinion within the committee, Hegsted and McGinnis nevertheless produced the *USDA Dietary Guidelines for Americans,* which was released in February 1980. It became the official government statement on the dangers of fat and cholesterol.[42]

Conflicting Opinions on Cholesterol

Since that time there have been numerous further studies on diets promoting lower cholesterol levels. One study involving over one million people before the introduction of Statins, found that the highest mortality rate was represented in the group with the *lowest* levels of cholesterol.[43]

Another study undertaken in Austria, involving 150,000 men and women over a 15year period, revealed that low cholesterol was significantly associated with all-cause mortality, showing significant associations with death through cancer, liver diseases and mental diseases.[44]

Much of this evidence challenged our 'official advice'.

So it's is time to consider some of the confusing information regarding cholesterol. Firstly, to talk about 'good' or 'bad' cholesterol is misleading. All types of cholesterol are manufactured in the body mostly by the liver for the benefit of the human body. But the idea that eating eggs, which are high in the kind of cholesterol that benefits the growth of young chickens, results in the same uptake of cholesterol into the human body, is not entirely accurate. Ancel Keys himself eventually conceded to this point in 1997 with the following statement:

> *"There's no connection whatsoever between cholesterol in food and cholesterol in blood. We have known that all along. Cholesterol in the diet doesn't matter at all unless you happen to be a chicken or a rabbit".*
>
> *Ancel Keys,Ph.D., Professor Emeritus,* University of Minnesota 1997 [45]

Cholesterol is actually a high molecular weight alcohol molecule. It is fat soluble, not water soluble, so it has to be transported around in a carrier called a lipoprotein, which has a water soluble exterior and a fat soluble core. This is to enable it to be transported in blood serum which is water based. It basically comes as four main types; chylomicrons, very low-density lipoproteins (VLDL), intermediate-density lipoproteins (IDL), low density lipoproteins (LDL), and high-density lipoproteins (HDL).

Cholesterol is essential to life; it is the basic building block for many processes in the body, from building hormones to supporting and repairing membranes. Our brains are composed of mostly water saturated fat, and cholesterol.

The largest lipoprotein, the chylomicron is manufactured in the gut. It absorbs fats as triglycerides (and some small amounts of cholesterol as part of the digestive process), and delivers these to fat cells in the body where they can be further broken down into Adenosine Triphosphate (ATP) the final energy molecule. The next size down is the VLDL lipoprotein, which is manufactured in both the gut and the liver, and transports triglycerides from the liver to other cells. The intermediate density lipoprotein (IDL) is simply created when the VLDL lipoprotein loses its triglyceride load and shrinks in size. The LDL lipoprotein is a smaller version of the IDL (this is the one that is called 'bad' cholesterol). The HDL lipoprotein is the smallest of them all (and is commonly referred to as 'good' cholesterol). HDL is assumed to be manufactured in the liver. Finally there is one other lipoprotein called Lp(a) which is another form of LDL but with a slightly higher density. This lipoprotein increases in volume when *trans* fats are ingested, and decreases when essential fatty acids (EFAs) are taken up. So this lipoprotein is, in fact a significantly more important marker than the ones most people make a big fuss about.[46]

I will report on a few more studies, not because I want to bang you over the head with even more low fat or cholesterol theories but because hopefully they will reveal the difficulty with accepting the current stance taken on cholesterol by orthodox medicine.

In the early 1970s the NIH decided that instead of doing one big study they would undertake six smaller ones. The results of these studies were released between 1980 & 1984 and showed the effects of fat in diets in populations in Honolulu, Chicago, Puerto Rico, and Framingham, Massachusetts. Apart from the Chicago trials, these studies all showed that low cholesterol limits were linked with *higher risk of cancer* (my emphasis). That link had been noticed in the VA Hospital study in Los Angeles, and it was suggested by Dayton and others that polyunsaturated fats used to lower cholesterol, could be the culprits. This was further confirmed by Swiss Red Cross researchers in 1972. Numerous further studies in the 1980s confirmed the link between a low fat diet and cancer. The Framingham study, which is still on-going, noted that men who had total cholesterol below 190ml/dl were more than three times likely to get cancer.[47] The Framingham trial studied research involved the consumption of the kind of mass-produced polyunsaturated oils that would have been available at the time, which would have been significantly damaged during the manufacturing process. So this confirms the information already noted about bad fats. One of the major problems with these types of study is they fail to acknowledge that some fats can be healthy and beneficial— *but only when they are not destroyed or damaged by over-processing*. There is a significant difference between organic un-refined oils that have been cold pressed, and the highly refined oils. In the case of flax oil, for example, when it is for human consumption, the best quality oils are organically produced, slowly pressed in darkness in an oxygen free environment, and then stored in non-light-emitting containers that are inert chemically, do not react with the oil, and are generally nitrogen filled. Nitrogen in this case acts simply as an inert gas. This is not a cheap process. The oil is then consumed without heating, and should be kept refrigerated at all times—as should any quality oil to help preserve its freshness.

UNHEALTHY BETRAYAL

It is worth, at this stage, looking briefly at what *trans* fats are—and what the likely effect of consuming them would be since we are widely exposed to them: they are created in the manufacture of margarines, in the high temperature industrial production of cooking oils, in the manufacture of shortenings and in the production of partially hydrogenated vegetable oils. Conversion into a *trans*-fat from a fatty acid involves in a very slight change – the rotation of the molecule around a double bond twists a fatty acid from its natural *cis*-configuration into un unnatural *trans*-configuration. This change can have major implications for biological systems, as listed in the previous chapter—but some additional adverse effects are listed here:

- Raises the atherogenic lipoprotein(a) (Lp (a)) in humans—whereas saturated fatty acids lower Lp (a). This is the lipoprotein that is linked with increased risk of atherosclerosis, and increased levels are associated with the damaged *trans*-fats.
- Lowers the available cream volume in milk of lactating mothers.
- Causes a dose response decrease in visual acuity in infants who are fed human milk that contains increasing levels of *trans* fatty acids. This can extend to 14 months of age.[48]

Further problems can occur with oils that are damaged by over processing at too high a temperature, the burning of oils, and the over-use of cooking oils. Any of these can produce a number of substances such as oxidised sterols, peroxides, acrolein, hydrocarbons and aromatic compounds that are not safe to ingest. It is further believed that free radical damage can be caused in human systems by bad oil and inadequate dietary protection—such as the anti-oxidants, vitamins A, C, E, selenium and the other body anti-oxidants.

The National Heart, Lung, and blood Institute (NHLBI) funded two large studies. One was the Multiple Risk Factor Intervention Trial (MRFIT) set up to encourage the participants to reduce smoking, to lower their blood pressure and lower their cholesterol levels. Twelve thousand men were studied over a seven year period against a control group, at a cost of $115 million. The treatment group were advised to quit smoking, take medication to reduce blood pressure where necessary, and eat a low-fat, low cholesterol diet. This included skimmed milk, margarine instead of butter, only one or two eggs a week, and the avoidance of red meats, pastries, puddings and cakes. One half of the group were given a cholesterol-lowering drug, cholestyramine, and the other half (the control group) were simply given a placebo pill.

However, in October 1982 the Trial collapsed when it was discovered that the death rate was significantly higher in the treatment group than it was in the control group.[49]

HAVE A HEART

The Lipid Research Clinic (LRC) then undertook a second trial—but this proved inconclusive.

So the NIH held a "consensus conference" to air the conflicting views that prevailed over both the low fat hypothesis and such studies. They invited twenty speakers, and included three sceptics. The 'official' view was that a low fat diet would afford significant protection against heart disease. The sceptics, who included Michael Oliver a cardiologist with the Medical Research Council in London, argued that the benefit of a cholesterol reducing diet couldn't be decided by a single drug experiment which produced borderline results.[50]

The NIH declared that there was at last a consensus about the low fat theory (even though this was not the case), and the effect was to solidify opinion. In 1986 they established the National Cholesterol Education Program (NCEP) which began in 1987. Its advice was to reduce cholesterol below 200mg/dl by either diet or the use of cholesterol reducing drugs. This was followed by the 700 page Surgeon General's *Report on Nutrition & Health* which was released in July 1988, and which promoted the reduction of fat levels. Coming from such an August source, this had the effect of quashing any divergent opinion particularly in the mainstream media.

In 1984 the American Cancer Society (ACS) issued a report suggesting a lower fat intake would reduce the incidence of cancer. They cited a comparison with Japan where there were fewer cases of breast cancer than America—which has both a higher fat intake and a higher incidence of cancer. Also quoted was the fact that fat consumption was rising in Japan—and so too was the level of breast cancer. However, this stance conflicted with the evidence from places like Copenhagen which had an incidence of breast-cancer four times higher than neighbouring Denmark, but where fat consumption was fifty percent lower. It also conflicted with numerous other large population studies in Framingham, Honolulu, Sweden, Georgia, amongst many others.

This controversial finding prompted NCI and NAS to provide funding to try and resolve the question. The program, called the Nurse's Health Study was led by the Harvard epidemiologist Walter Willett, and looked at diet, lifestyle and disease in approximately eighty nine thousand nurses in 1982. Over 600 cases of cancer were discovered in the first four years. The report was published in the New England Journal of Medicine in 1987, and showed that the lower the intake of fats, the higher the incidence of cancer was. Eight months later it was followed by a further NCI study which showed a correlation between cancer incidence and the intake of both fat in general and saturated fat in particular, in reducing cancer incidence. The Nurses study was reviewed in 1992 and 1999, and continued to link lower levels of fat intake with a higher incidence of cancer which by 1999 had reached three thousand cases.[51]

The original research, that had prompted Keys and others to jump on the cholesterol band wagon and the low fat theory for better health was based on animal research. Rudolf Von Virchow, a German pathologist in the mid-nineteenth century, noted thickened plaques in the arteries of some of his animal subjects—and he discovered that cholesterol was one of the components. Years later, a Russian doctor called Nikolai Anitschov fed rabbits a high cholesterol diet which also produced thickened arteries with lesions that were partially composed of cholesterol. Fat was also dumped in the muscles of some rabbits. Numerous studies were done on a multitude of animals, and produced similar results. The fact that the animals tested would not be exposed to such fats in their natural habitat did not seem to concern the researchers. This was the 'evidence' that inspired Ancel Keys' original conviction that a low fat diet was a better diet.[52]

Adding fats to the diet of lab rats also induced cancers, and enhanced the growth of tumours. Significantly it was found that the most potent fats for this carcinogenic effect were *refined polyunsaturated fats* However it was also found by David Kritchevsky, one of the authors of *Diet Nutrition & Cancer,* that low fat high calorie diets promoted more carcinogenesis than low fat low calorie diets. If rats were given only 75% of their daily calorie requirement, they could eat five times as much fat as usual, and still develop fewer tumours. [53]

In the late 1970s the World Health Organisation (WHO) launched a research project called MONICA which monitored cardiovascular disease in thirty-eight populations in twenty-one countries. This was the biggest international cardiovascular research project to date. By the late 1990,s it had reported 150,000 heart attacks and looked at 180,000 risk factors. It concluded that heart disease rates were falling globally, this was not as a result of reducing cholesterol levels, smoking or blood pressure. [54]

In Japan, where hemorrhagic stroke was almost as common as heart disease was in America, Japanese physicians were advising patients to *raise* their cholesterol levels, because lower levels were linked to strokes and a shorter life span. After more than 30 years of research by the Framingham study, it was discovered that the people whose cholesterol levels had fallen over the first fourteen years were more likely to die prematurely—and of cardiovascular disease.[55]

This research prompted NHLBI to host a workshop to discuss the finding. Researchers from nineteen international studies met in Bethesda, Maryland. Both high levels (above240mg/dl) of cholesterol and low levels below 160mg/dl were associated with an increase in mortality. The higher group had a higher incidence of heart disease, and the lower group a higher incidence of cancer, respiratory and digestive diseases and trauma. It was found that for women the higher their cholesterol level the longer they lived.[56]

If you are confused by so many studies seeming to make a mockery of a high fat diet being bad for you and a low fat diet being good for you, you're not alone. But stay with us and some clarity will prevail. Just remember to keep in your mind that it's the *quality and type of fat* that is being added to the diet that is significant. As previously stated, there is a major difference between unrefined oils and over-processed oils—and there are polyunsaturated oils. Udo Erasmus was one of the researchers who tried to draw attention to the difference between good and bad fats with his book *Fats That Heal, Fats That Kill* (1993). Lipid research (the study of fats and oils) has come on leaps and bounds since then and there is now a considerable amount of research that turns the idea of saturated fats being bad for you on its head. One of the leading lipid researchers in the field, particularly in the study of *trans fats* is Mary G Enig PhD. Her book, *"Know Your Fats"* is a primer for the general public which I highly recommend. She discusses the benefits of saturated fats, such as coconut oil, which she considers very beneficial (when, of course not over-processed) as well as the issue of animal fats. She also reviews some of the erroneous research in her book such as the talk by Ernst Wynder M.D. of the American Health Foundation. He presented a slide show which was supposed to demonstrate a correlation between animal fat consumption and colon cancer in many countries. In fact the correlation represented mostly processed vegetable fat in these countries (i.e. damaged vegetable fats).

She states "And now more than three decades after the initial fraudulent report, the anti-animal fat hypothesis continues to lead the nutrition agenda. It was a false issue then, and it remains a false issue today." [57]

One researcher on the topic of Cholesterol is Uffe Ravnskov, MD, PhD who wrote the book *"Fat and Cholesterol are Good for you!"* In this book he reviews evidence for and against cholesterol—and the use of statins to 'treat' high cholesterol levels. He starts with a few pertinent facts which I will share with you now.

- Firstly cholesterol is not a poison but a vital substance created by the body and is vital to the cells of all mammals.
- It is the major component of the brain.
- The body produces three to four times more cholesterol than is ingested with food.
- People with atherosclerosis can have low cholesterol as much as high cholesterol.
- High cholesterol is not a risk factor for women.

- High cholesterol is not a risk factor for people over the age of 65 years, although this is the group of people that are most likely to have heart attacks.
- High cholesterol protects you against infection.
- Old people with high cholesterol levels live the longest.
- Many of the cholesterol-lowering drugs are dangerous to your health and may shorten your life.

Bending Science

Ravnskov complains that scientific studies are poorly carried out, are filled with biases that make them almost worthless, and that the conclusions drawn do not truly reflect the findings in the study. Further, that the abstract that is given for the study inaccurately reflects what the study reveals in many cases. So unless you read the actual study for yourself and are able to unravel the data, you will not get the true picture. Many of the studies he looked at were purposely skewed to portray a picture that did not represent the true picture—a common complaint from many of the researchers mentioned in this book.[58]

One obvious fact is that younger people have lower cholesterol, and are less atherosclerotic, than older people. If you were to draw a graph showing atherosclerosis without allowing for age you would show a relationship that links atherosclerosis with cholesterol, but if you denote the ages the relationship does not exist. Also distorting the facts is a condition called familial hypercholesterolemia. This has an inborn error of cholesterol metabolism that affects less than one percent of the population. Carriers of it always have high cholesterol levels (greater than 300), and have significant vascular changes in their bodies. They should always be excluded from these studies, but far from being excluded they are frequently over-included to skew the results in some of these studies. Ravnskov lists a number of such transgressions.

One of the things that interests Ravnskov is what the true cause of heart disease might be. If the whole cholesterol theory is wrong, which some of the evidence seems to confirm, then what is the real cause of it? One of the unfortunate consequences of ignoring the ever-increasing message of true science is that there will be significant loss of life and suffering world-wide until the real cause of heart disease becomes common knowledge.

Ravnskov himself believes there may be a link with infection. He noted that patients with severe chronic heart failure have high levels of endotoxin, and various types of cytokines, in their blood. Endotoxins are toxic substances that are produced by bacteria, and cytokines are hormones that are secreted by the white blood cells to fight infection. That their presence in the human body is significant suggests there must be an infectious process in progress in some areas of the body. Supporting evidence for this theory comes from Dr Donna Vredevoe from the University of California in Los Angeles (UCLA), who discovered, in one study that she was evaluating, that more than half her patients with severe heart-failure had anergic immune systems. Anergy is a condition where the immune system is compromised—which means that sufferers from it with are very susceptible to infections. She further discovered not just that mortality was higher in the people who were anergic, but also that mortality was higher in the subjects with the *lowest* cholesterol.[59]

Cholesterol is Good for You

One piece of information that seems to elude many doctors and researchers is the simple fact that lipoproteins eliminate micro-organisms and their toxic products from mammals—including the so called 'bad cholesterol' LDL. Dr Sucharit Bhakdi and his co-workers from Giessen, Germany, was one of the first researchers to study this phenomenon. Alfa-toxin, for example is a seriously poisonous substance that is produced by staphylococci bacteria, and which can destroy cells. When alfa-toxin was added to red blood cells dissolved in a saline solution they burst. But when purified LDL was added to the red blood cell solution, the cells were unaffected by the alfa-toxin. [60]

There are in fact a number of studies that show how cholesterol prevents disease; here are one or two examples:

- Researchers from the Netherlands, working with mice, found that if they injected bacterial toxins into mice with reduced cholesterol, they died. But if they added an injection of human LDL before they added the toxins, they survived. [61]
- It has also been discovered that children with allergy problems, such as asthma and hay fever, were found to have lower levels of cholesterol than healthy children. In a Finnish study, which followed the health of 200 children from birth to the age of 20, it was found that children with allergic disorders had lower levels of total cholesterol in their blood and lower levels of LDL. [62]
- Another English study looked at the health of 3000 people with familial hypercholesterolemia over a number of years. This is the condition with an inborn error of cholesterol metabolism, in which sufferers always have cholesterol levels greater than 300,

and in which some have vascular changes from a much younger age. In the study, they analysed the data on mortality, and compared this to a healthy group of the same age. They found that although a few more died from heart disease, fewer died from cancer and other diseases.[63]

There are a number of doctors in the USA and in Europe who have gone against the 'official policy guidelines' and have suggested a diet that replaces dietary carbohydrates with foods rich in fat—for both weight reduction and the treatment of type two diabetes. This diet avoids potatoes, bread, cakes, cookies, candies and soft drinks, and has produced incredible results. No adverse symptoms or effects on the blood lipids were noticed and the levels of both total cholesterol and LDL were unchanged. At the same time, the triglyceride levels went down substantially. This was found even when 20-50 percent of calories were taken as saturated fat—which is more than the official guidelines by a factor of six times. [64] The topic of diabetes will be discussed in greater depth in chapter four.

The cholesterol levels in our bodies sometimes seem to bear little relationship to the levels of cholesterol that we consume. The body uses carbohydrates as a starting point for the production of cholesterol, not fat. As previously stated the myth that eating cholesterol rich eggs will increase the serum levels of cholesterol in the body is not based on fact. Ravnskov actually did an experiment on himself to prove this, and the detailed results were published in his book.[65]

The Danger of Statins

The cholesterol theory, as promoted by the major pharmaceutical industry, has prompted a whole range of drugs called statins to be produced. Their purpose is to reduce the 'high' cholesterol levels—which is fine if that's what you want to do. But unfortunately statins have side effects—which are not publicised anywhere near as much as the drugs themselves.

Ravnskov reviewed the first mega trial of cholesterol lowering drugs, the *Coronary Drug Project*,[66]-in which five different cholesterol lowering treatments were studied. He noted that three of the five were stopped prematurely when it became apparent that the levels of mortality were higher than in the untreated control group. The other two groups continued but, at the end, the number of heart attacks (106) was the same in the untreated group. The drugs studied were clofibrate (Atromidin ®) and nicotinic acid, and Ravnskov described the many side effects of these as "*horrendous*"[67]

HAVE A HEART

Clofibrate was also used in a further trial, a larger WHO study. Although non-fatal heart attacks were reduced by the drug, the number of fatal heart attacks increased (128 in the treated group compared to 87 in the untreated placebo group). [68]

Ravnskov discusses a further trial, the *Helsinki Heart Study* which was undertaken in two parts.[69]

The more 'successful' part of the trial involved 4000 healthy middle-aged men with high cholesterol. Each of the participants was encouraged to lose weight, stop smoking and exercise more. Half were given a placebo drug and the other half were given gemfibrozil. There was a significant reduction in non-fatal heart attacks, but slightly more people died in the treated group. There were, however, side effects; 83 people were operated on for gastro-intestinal ailments, compared to 53 in the control / untreated group.[70] Ravnskov asks what would you prefer, a non-fatal heart attack, or to be on the operating table for some gastro-intestinal procedure? Fortunately, as will be revealed later in this chapter, there are alternatives to both those outcomes.

The second part of the trial seems to have escaped the notice of a lot of people—probably because it was published five years late, in a more obscure journal. After five years, seventeen of those who took gemfibrozil in this second trial died of a heart attack, compared to eight in the untreated group.

Ravnskov elaborates with a number of other pertinent facts:

- That more than twenty five percent of statin users may become weak, dumb or impotent.
- That pregnant women could give birth to severely malformed children if they take statins whilst pregnant.
- That lowering cholesterol in women does not prolong their lives at all.
- That lowering cholesterol only benefits a very small minority of people.

How can this be I hear you ask? Why are we spending a fortune on medications that are so pointless (even more pointless than I have revealed here so far). Who does it benefit? Well the pharmaceutical companies benefit, which brings me to the part where we can give some explanation to how 'scientific' papers are produced to show results that the industry wishes us to hear. As Ravnskov observes - many scientific papers are not written by the eminent researchers whose name appears on the top of the paper, but by professional writers hired by the industry. In many other cases the conclusions drawn do not fit the evidence. In many cases the abstract of the paper does not reflect the evidence in the paper. In many instances researchers only read the abstract, and therefore are unfamiliar with the contents of the article. The way an article is written and presented also affects the interpretation on the study. More examples will be given of studies that are cited by supporters of various industry positions—but which actually show a negative result when examined with a critical eye. Many of the writers I cite are the very people who have uncovered many of these manoeuvers, and have made it their business to give a more accurate picture of what is really going on, what the whole story is.

It is time to introduce you to Duane Graveline M.D. a former USFA flight surgeon, former NASA Astronaut and retired family doctor. He has written a number of books about statins and the damage they can do. These were prompted by his own experience when he was given a statin called Lipitor, which triggered a transient amnesia episode in him. He had been taking Lipitor for only three months on a relatively small dose (10mg or less). At first, he did not believe that it could be the statin causing his amnesia, but he stopped taking it—just in case. His amnesia ceased, but when he reintroduced it he had another episode in which he reverted to a mental age of 17. He did not recognise his wife or even remember he was married; nor did he recognise his home. He, of course, stopped taking Lipitor but when he recovered he made it his business to find out more about statins to see if he could discover what had caused his memory loss. His research lead him to a discovery that was to change the whole understanding of the cholesterol theory, and of the way statins work in the body. It also raised a number of unbelievable issues.

Before we take a look at that, though, we need to take a look at the amazing way cholesterol is created by the body. Firstly, the building block of cholesterol is glucose, which is manufactured by plants that we ingest—as mentioned earlier the link is carbohydrate. It is then processed through glycolysis to produce acetyl coenzyme A (acetyl-CoA). The next step is the conversion of three molecules of acetyl-CoA to form hydroxymethyl glutaric acid which is part of the intermediate complex known as HMG-CoA. And this is the weak point in the chain of events which forms the basis of statins, and is where the pharmaceutical industry has intervened.

The next step towards cholesterol production involves an enzyme called HMG-CoA reductase, which converts two molecules of HMG-CoA to melavonic acid. This step was found to be easily inhibited—and suddenly a multi-billion dollar business was born. The trouble with this pathway is that it leads to a number of other pathways that have unforeseen consequences. It is a bit like treating a tree with many branches. You have an infection in one area of the tree, some infection in the leaves of one twig in a branch. So what do you do? You cut down the entire tree of course, no-one will notice! At least not for a while! You think I am exaggerating? Wait and see and you tell me. What follows is an incredible story. There is no need to read fiction when reality reads like this!

One of the problems of cutting down our 'tree' is that one of the branches happens to be the pathway that creates Ubiquinone, a coenzyme that gets its name from the fact that it is widely distributed (ubiquitous) throughout the body. It is lipid soluble, and is incorporated in the lipid protein complex of the mitochondrial membrane (the powerhouse of the cell). In its general structure it has a side chain of isoprene units. The most commonly occurring one has ten units, and is designated as Coenzyme Q10 (Co Q10). I give this piece of the story first as its ramifications are so profound for our human systems. Co Q10 is a readily available supplement that has significant uses in many areas of the body, not least in the brain.

Ubiquinone levels plummet when statins are introduced to the body and cause mayhem. Let me quote Doctor Graveline:

> "Such side effects as congestive heart failure and chronic fatigue, reflect ubiquinone's important role in energy production. Hepatitis, myopathy, rhabdomyolysis and peripheral neuropathy reflect ubiquinone's role in cell wall integrity and stability. Ubiquinone's role in the prevention of somatic mitochondrial mutations is also of critical importance and introduces a vast area of concern." [71]

Ubiquinone is crucial for energy production. Energy cannot be produced without it. It is of course, particularly important in the muscle cells, where it is needed the most—according to Ravnskov muscle complaints are the most frequent side effects from statin treatment. The problem is, there is very significant under-reporting of the side effects of statins. For example liver damage is considered to be another one, but it is only reported when liver enzymes in the blood are more than three times higher than the usual upper limit, and only if it has been reported twice. Similarly, when muscles are damaged, the concentration of an enzyme called creatine kinase (CK) becomes elevated in the blood. It is regarded as a warning sign of muscle damage of both skeletal muscles and the heart (which is after all a muscle too). Unfortunately, trial directors of statins tell us that this affects less than one percent of patients and will not acknowledge the situation until the CK levels are elevated at least ten times higher than normal, with two successive determinations. The problem with this approach is that there is significant research showing damage, even when the CK levels are considered normal.[72] Further, there are studies of muscle tissue using electron microscopy which reveal muscular abnormalities in patients without any presenting symptoms. [73] Just a few years after the introduction of Baycol (Bayer's statin drug), fifty patients receiving the drug died from renal failure—and Bayer was forced to withdraw the drug from the market. According to Ravnskov more than 100 patients were reported to have died from kidney failure on this drug.[74]

Whilst on the subject of the effect of disrupting the normal functioning of Co Q10, we have to address the important effect on the brain—which led Dr Graveline's amnesia. Deficient cholesterol manufacture in our glial cells disrupts synapse formation and the functioning of our brain cells. The ramifications of this barely bear thinking about. These are the very neural pathways of the brain that send crucial messages, and communicate from one cell to another. That was discovered in 2003 by Pfrieger, and explained the reports of amnesia, confusion, disorientation, forgetfulness and aggravation of pre-existing senility. [75] It seems this problem is being missed by a great many people, according to Muldoon, who with the right type of testing has found cognitive dysfunction in 100 percent of statin users. [76]

If that was not enough of a problem there are other branches on our tree that have been severely compromised. One of the curious factors about the whole statin issue has been the discovery that, whilst statins do reduce cholesterol, they also increase the risk of heart attacks and strokes. Yet it has been found that this is not due to the cholesterol reduction but due to another effect entirely. This factor is nuclear factor-kappa B a transcriptase that is prevalent throughout our immune system. This finding has been shock to the industry. Since nuclear factor-kappa B is involved in the suppression of inflammation, then the industry has the means to profit by potentially confounding our whole immune defence system

Let us look at one more aspect of our tree felling exercise, that of the effect of dolichols. Suppression of cholesterol with statins also suppresses dolichol expression which, in turn, affects neuropeptide formation. This is serious; neuropeptides are chemicals that regulate life processes on a cellular level throughout the entire body. Whilst they are primarily produced in the brain, they are messenger molecules that are involved in communication throughout our system—in the form of linked peptides travelling from the brain to receptor sites on cell membranes just about everywhere in our bodies. It has been suggested that every thought, sensation, and emotion that we have ever felt, or are likely to feel, is dependent upon the expression of these peptide communications. No wonder there is some disorientation experienced by statin users. There is a considerable body of opinion that suspects that disruption of this system is responsible for the depression, irritability, hostility, aggressiveness and road-rage type behaviour that have been reported. Disruption of neuropeptides has also been linked with proneness to addiction—and to suicides after statin drugs have been started.[77]

Rhabdomyolysis deaths still occur in statin users as they all disrupt the Ubiquinone pathway as Baycol did but there are further complications, such as cancer. Researchers Thomas Newman and Stephen Hulley from the University of California did a comprehensive study on animals treated with statins, and came to the conclusion that statins produced cancer.[78] In the first two simvastatin trials, *4S* and *HPS* more patients in the treatment groups got non melanoma skin cancer. Whilst the numbers may not have leapt out as being significant in each separate study, they became far more significant when judged together.[79]

In the *CARE* trial, thirteen women got breast cancer in the treatment group, but only one in the control group which Ravnskov suggests was *"highly statistically significant"*. The authors of the report, however, suggested that this could be an "anomaly". In the *PROSPER* trial of patients over 70 years old with cardiovascular disease (CVD), or a raised risk of CVD, all patients were treated with pravastatin. Whilst there was a slight reduction in death by heart attack, this was offset by an increase in mortality from cancer. [80]

A group of Japanese researchers in five different hospitals decided to look into the issue of cancer and statin use to investigate any significant connection between the two. They selected patients with various lymphoid cancers, and control patients of the same age and sex who had been admitted with other diseases during the same period. They found that there were almost twice as many cancer patients who were, or had been, on statin treatment, as hadn't. [81]

Skewed Science

There are numerous other adverse effects attributed to statin use that I have not listed here. My purpose is to report just enough of them to show that this is a serious issue which deserves a wider audience. However to show there are two sides to the story, I will discuss some of the statin trials a little further through the eyes of some of their more critical reviewers. One such person is Joel M Kauffman, Ph.D., in my view a serious scientist, a professor of chemistry. He was involved in 10 years of exploratory drug research at the University of Sciences in Philadelphia, and has numerous patents to his name. He has written over 80 papers on chemical and medical topics, but has decided to turn his attention to exposing fraud in medicine. In his book, *Malignant Medical Myths,* he first goes through the common methods that the Medical industry sometimes uses to conceal the true facts, and to create the illusion, for example that statins are good for us and that everyone should take them. He shows how various trials are biased and misrepresented and discusses the results of the trials from a far more rigorous scientific perspective.

Here are some of his views on the subject of statin trials. One of the ways that trial results are skewed to show a good result is when the authors discus the 'relative risk'. For example, let's look at his views on the *WOSCOPS* trial—where half the 6,595 men aged 45-64 were put on 40mg of pravastatin (Pravachol™) daily, and the other half were put on a placebo (-a look-alike non-reactive substitute). Their progress was studied for 4.9 years. Results in the Abstract included the statement:

"We observed a 22% reduction in the risk of death from any cause in the pravastatin group (95% CI=0-40%, p= 0.051)" (Shepherd et al 1995)[82] That sounds good, and Kauffman was pleased that they even gave the mortality rate—which they often omit, particularly when there is news they would rather we didn't see.

The confidence index which, in this trial, was given as 95%, gives the range that the data should fall into if the data followed a bell curve or normal curve. That basically means there was a 95% chance (19/20ths) that the 22% reduction in the risk of death from any cause in the pravastatin group was actually somewhere between 0% and 40% based on the laws of chance. It also means there was about 1 chance in 20 that there was no reduction in mortality due to the use of pravastatin, but that the reduction happened by chance. The p-value of 0.051 was supposed to show that there were only 5.1 chances in 100 that the actual RR of death did not fall between a 0 and 40% reduction of RR by chance alone rather than due to the drug. By convention this would be called "barely significant". There has been a convention since 1920 to determine results with a p-value of under 0.05 as "significant" but as Kauffman states this is purely arbitrary.

However one of the more pertinent statistics to get to grips with is the "Absolute Risk". The absolute percentage of men alive after 4.9 years in the pravastatin group was 96.8% and in the placebo group it was 95.9%, an absolute difference of just 0.9% which works out to simply 0.18% per year. Kauffman gives the "number needed to treat" (NNT) by obtaining the reciprocal of 0.18% which gives the figure of 556, which is the number of people you need to treat for one year to prevent one death for a year. For the trial duration this works out that you have to treat 111 people who had no benefit of not dying to prevent one death for one year with all the cost and side effects as stated above.

Kauffman goes on to review a large number of trials of the various statin drugs, and puts in the figures that he feels are relevant, the absolute risk figures of all-cause mortality and puts the whole lot in a nice table for those who would like to see what is really going on. He reviews the figures with the following comments:

"The benefits of the statin drugs in reducing mortality are exaggerated, being only 0.3% per year from the most favourable trials reported. This is not as great as the benefits of omega-3 supplements. Indeed lovastatin (Mevacor) increased the all-cause mortality rate in its two reported trials."

Statin Side Effects

He goes on to state that up to 75% of people stop taking statins presumably because of the side effects.

Peripheral neuropathy and amyotrophic lateral sclerosis (ALS) were reported by the World Health Organisation's Vigibase as being excessive in statin users worldwide. The drug companies have listed peripheral neuropathy in their list of disclaimers posted in the physician's desk reference (PDR). Graveline relates in his personal experience that they don't tell you the damage is most likely *permanent*. Nor do they tell you that the symptoms may not show up whilst you are taking the statin but, manifest sometime later. In his case, his symptom of amnesia disappeared once he stopped taking the Lipitor, but he later experienced problems with his muscles that have continued to this day. He also feels it has aged him significantly. He personally knows of some 250 statin users in walkers and wheelchairs because of the collateral damage to the nerves and muscles of statin users. He has a website for people to contact him and has numerous stories of the carnage that statins can cause. [83]

Ravnskov reviews a number of trials trying to show the way the research has been miss-represented. In the *MRFIT* trial for example, one of the trials that is often quoted to support the cholesterol hypothesis, [84] there is graph showing a straight line for mortality and cholesterol values, which gives an apparently positive correlation. However, if smokers are excluded, the correlation disappears and is insignificant.

In the famous Framingham study, if you look at all the men over forty-seven the cholesterol levels became totally irrelevant, they did not affect life expectancy at all. Those with higher levels fared just as well as those with lower levels. If the majority of heart attacks are in patients over the age of forty seven cholesterol levels become an irrelevance. Furthermore Ravnskov established from the Framingham data that if cholesterol levels decreased by themselves the risk of dying *increased*. He also goes on to cite numerous examples of populations with high cholesterol levels who are healthy, even protective. In one study that followed the health of 1000 elderly people living in the Bronx, New York for four years, he found that twice as many people with low cholesterol had a heart attack, or died from one, compared to those with the highest levels of cholesterol. [85]

Ravnskov also takes up issue with The American Heart Association and the National Heart, Lung and Blood Institute when, in their review *The Cholesterol Facts* they make the following observation: *"The results of the Framingham study indicate that a 1% reduction....of cholesterol [corresponds to a] 2% reduction in CHD (coronary heart disease) risk".* [86] Yet—according to the original report—mortality increased by 11 percent for each 1 mg/dl reduction in blood cholesterol. They also state *"The most important overall finding is the emergence of the total cholesterol concentration as a risk factor for CHD in the elderly".* As we have already stated, after the age of forty seven the levels became an irrelevance.

Further evidence that undermines the view of cholesterol being bad for us, and that we need to take statins, can be found in the books already mentioned. I will however draw your attention to a press release from the British Heart Foundation (BHF) about the Heart Protection Study published in 2004, one of the last really big statin trials:

HPS lead investigator Professor Rory Collins said:

'HPS shows unequivocally that statins can produce substantial benefit in a much wider range of high-risk people than had been thought. These new findings are relevant to the treatment of some hundreds of millions of people worldwide. If now as a result, an extra 10 million high-risk people were to go onto statin treatment, this would save about 50,000 lives per year – that's a thousand each week. In addition, this would prevent similar numbers of people from suffering non-fatal heart attacks or strokes.

The HPS team estimates that implementing these new findings fully would more than triple the numbers of people benefiting from statins. In the UK, the numbers treated with statins would increase from a current figure of less than 1 in 20 of the population aged over 40 (or about one million people) to about 1 in 8 (about 3 million people). This would save an extra 10,000 lives each year.' [87]

Dr Kendrick takes issue with most of the claims made in this trial. He says that raised cholesterol protects against heart disease in the over 70s especially in women for whom it isn't a risk for heart disease *at any age* as previously reported by Ravnskov. He adds that a raised cholesterol level is not only not a risk factor for stroke—it could in fact be beneficial. His biggest complaint is the most common complaint; that the HPS team decided not to release the total mortality data on women, the most important end point in any clinical trial of this nature, and also the easiest to measure. He re-affirms what Ravnskov and others have found, that statins do not save lives in women. He also reviews the terrible consequences of taking statins whilst pregnant, and the serious birth defects that have been noted, including severe defects of the nervous system, unilateral limb deficiencies, complex lower-limb abnormalities and much more. [88]

The ridiculous thing about the whole statin nightmare is that it is so totally unnecessary. As Kaufman pointed out, omega-3 supplements are far more beneficial without any side effects such as the rhabdomyolysis, brain problems, amnesia, depression, suicidal tendencies, intestinal problems etc. The following statistics may give you food for thought: Pfizer's income from atorvastatin was $9 billion in the USA alone in 2002 and, according to Marcia Angell, the combined profit for the ten drug companies on the Fortune 500 list of the world's most profitable companies was higher than the profit of all the other 490 companies put together. [89]

Alternative Theories for Heart Disease

With such mainstream commitment to the cholesterol/statin mantra, little attention has been paid to other areas of research into heart disease. One researcher, who had tried to resist the anti–cholesterol hypothesis, discovered that homocysteine was a much more significant player in the role of heart disease. Homocysteine is an amino acid that is created in the body and was found by Kilmer McCully M.D. to be linked to many disease conditions, including heart disease, stroke, blood clots and gangrene. He made his discovery back in 1969 but was ignored until, many years later, further research showed the link was justified. Today, the link of homocysteine to heart disease and a number of other degenerative conditions is widely accepted. McCully linked the elevated homocysteine levels to a lack of essential nutrients such as vitamin B6, B12 and folic acid. He discovered that high homocysteine levels predicted atherosclerosis, that many diets were deficient of these vitamins, and that foods such as over-processed carbohydrates and sugar aggravated the problem.

He found that simple measures such as taking supplements, removing over-refined carbohydrates, and simple exercise reversed the degeneration. He looked into the chemistry of homocysteine and discovered that vitamin C played a crucial role in the control of it; it enabled the body to convert homocysteine into harmless sulphate, and prevented the build-up of it to unhealthy levels. Vitamin C loss accompanies consumption of over-processed carbohydrates, and the consequential dramatic rise in blood sugar levels. [90]

His later work reviews the chemical pathology of homocysteine in atherogenesis, oxidative metabolism and carcinogenesis. Homocysteine is found to be a potent excitatory neurotransmitter which binds to the N-methyl-D-aspartate receptor and causes oxidative stress, cytoplasmic calcium influx, cellular apoptosis (cell death), and endothelial dysfunction(the endothelium is the thin layer of cells that line the interior of blood vessels).—McCully realised that homocysteine was a catalyst in the destruction of cholesterol, whereby it is damaged by oxidation and can become a component of arterial plaque. He believes the process is an inflammatory condition that can involve a number of factors:

> The creation of vulnerable plaques in advanced atherosclerosis is suggested to be related to formation of aggregates of homocysteinylated lipoprotein complexed with microbes, leading to trapping in vasa vasorum narrowed by endothelial dysfunction. The resulting obstruction of vasa vasorum causes ischemia of arterial wall, cell death, foam cell formation, rupture of capillaries with hemorrhage, and deposition of lipid in the intima, all of which are constituents of vulnerable plaques. This chain of events explains how risk factors for hyperhomocysteinemia, atherosclerosis, and endothelial dysfunction contribute to the pathogenesis of atherosclerotic plaques.[91]

A significant number of cardiologists recognise that more important indicators of heart disease can be missed if you are caught up in the cholesterol theory—such as the levels of Lipoprotein (a) and C-Reactive Protein (CRP). The late Linus Pauling discovered that Lp(a) could become an exceptionally potent risk factor, especially if there was a deficiency of vitamin C. Pauling was a two time Nobel Prize winner. He was aware that vitamin C was essential for the manufacture of collagen in the body—the structural protein which is a primary constituent of arterial walls. He suggested that Lp(a) levels could be reduced by ascorbate (vitamin C).

> There is epidemiological evidence that dietary ascorbate supplementation is equally effective in reducing the mortality rate for heart disease, cancer, diabetes, and other diseases in the elderly.[92]

After Pauling's death, his associate Mattias Rath M.D. continued using vitamin C and other nutritional support such as B vitamins, magnesium, Co-enzyme Q10 etc. He claimed he was able to reverse the progression of heart disease and, in many cases, enable some of his patients to avoid the stress and complications of surgery. He cites numerous examples in his book, *Why Animals Don't Get Heart Attacks – But People Do.* [93]

There have been important advances in our understanding of how nutritional deficiencies lay ourselves open to heart disease, and of how vitamin and mineral supplements can aid in the recovery of not just atherosclerosis but of all forms of heart disease, and even post-operative recovery from bypasses etc. Dr Stephen Sinatra and James C. Roberts M.D. take a multi-factorial approach in their practices, combining both conventional drugs and surgery techniques with modern nutritional supplementation. They are able to reduce a dependence on drugs (which can have adverse consequences) and even help some people avoid surgery. They also regard homocysteine, Lipoprotein (a) and C-Reactive Protein (CRP) as risk factors for heart disease. These are three of their listed "Dirty Dozen" risk factors for heart disease. The others include too much insulin, excess fibrinogen, excess levels of Ferritin (iron), trans fatty acids, toxic metals, oxidative stress, infection and emotional stress.

They published a joint book *Reverse Heart Disease Now,* in which they document their success with both nutritional support and conventional medicine. Due to the incredible success that they have had with their patients for a number of years, they lament the poor understanding of the value of this approach by many mainstream doctors. Any doctor, cardiologist or concerned citizen could learn a lot from their success. They regard Co-enzyme Q10 (Q10) as a miracle nutrient, and they use it liberally in their respective practices. It is easy to see why when you look at the reams of research (in excess of four thousand studies) documenting the effectiveness of Q10. It has been documented to slow the aging process and prevent disease. It has been shown to help all forms of heart disease, reduce hypertension and counteract some of the adverse effects of statins. It further protects against gum disease, and improves the nervous system and brain disorders. It is also helps generate strength and vitality in older people, and protects against cancer.

I will caution against rushing out and purchasing some Co-enzyme Q10 by saying there is a problem with it—in that not all supplements of it are biologically available, and therefore effective to the same degree. You will find instances where a supplement of Q10 has been studied and shown to be ineffectual. All Q10 studies of any repute should measure the levels of Q10 in the blood of all patients to validate the effectiveness of the absorption of Q10, and therefore the effectiveness of the supplement for treating the condition studied.

There are numerous vitamins and supplements that can aid in the prevention and treatment of heart disease and related conditions. What you will discover by reading this book is that many of the conditions are linked, both by common symptoms, and by related causes. Some are multi-factorial in that there is not one cause or solution. The treatment for two patients can vary, even with the same presenting conditions. I will give the main nutrients that help prevent the ravages of heart disease however, and some explanation of their benefit.

We already are informed on the benefits of B3 (niacin), Folic Acid and B12 (Colbalamin) by the research of McCully and others. McCully, like Linus Pauling and Rath, also recognised the importance of vitamin C in the synergistic relationship with homocysteine, and the protection of our arteries. Vitamin C is involved in the metabolism of fats for every fat molecule metabolised by the liver, a molecule of vitamin C is used up—which further increases blood glucose and insulin resistance. Glucose blocks the entry of vitamin C, to cells, so depressing the immune system for up to 5 hours after ingesting the sugary food. Vitamin C is also dumped when glucose levels become high. So it's not hard to see how a diet with highly processed carbohydrates—which we know produces high levels of triglycerides—would deplete vitamin C levels quickly.

Drs. Sinatra and Roberts, in their respective practices utilize what they refer to as the "awesome foursome" nutrients: CoQ10, L-Carnitine, D-ribose and magnesium.

L-carnitine is an amino acid that can be manufactured in the body by the combination of two amino acids, methionine and lysine—but only when there are adequate supplies of vitamin C, niacin, B6, and iron available, and the enzymes necessary for the conversion. IL-carnitine can also be obtained in the diet from meat, the best source being mutton. So there are significant deficiencies of L-carnitine in vegetarians as well as patients with heart disease. There are also deficiencies caused by medications—particularly anticonvulsants. L-carnitine is vitally important as a transport mechanism for fatty acids in and out of the cellular membrane—it is the only carrier than can do this. As such, it is crucial to the provision of energy metabolism in the ATP cycle, in the mitochondria. Increasing levels of L-carnitine increase energy production, whereas low levels reduce it.

L-carnitine has a number of other important uses. It removes waste products, such as acyl groups, the products of beta-oxidation; it helps remove lactic acid from the blood and tissues; and it helps break down ammonia into urea.

Roberts heard a talk at a cardiologist meeting advocating the use of D-ribose (or simply ribose) in cases of ischemia—and found that added to L-carnitine, it significantly increased the levels of energy available to the heart and muscles. D-ribose is a five carbon sugar molecule, and the only compound used by the human body to replace diminished ATP energy stores. It is well known that ischemia may cause hearts to use up fifty percent of the energy reserves of the heart from the ATP pool and that even when oxygen and blood flow are restored, that it can take up to ten days to replenish cellular energy levels and restore normal diastolic heart function. Sinatra and Roberts found by using ribose that this could be reduced to just a couple of days. After more than thirty years practice in cardiology, Sinatra had this to say about the "awesome four":

Over the years, I came to the conclusion that I could no longer practice effective cardiovascular healing without incorporating L-carnitine, coenzyme Q_{10}, magnesium and D-ribose in my patient care.[94]

Sinatra and Roberts noticed that by putting patients waiting for heart transplants on these supplements, many did not need a transplant by the time a heart became available, and they could be removed from the register. Every year in the US, approximately 2,300 people receive a heart transplant, many having to wait seven months, and up to 25% not surviving to receive it. He laments that, currently, coronary bypass surgeries (CABS) are still performed on the basis of clogged arteries alone, with no regard to the quality of life of the patient. Rates of complications from CABS, such as heart attack, infection, strokes and central nervous system dysfunction, he finds disturbing. He expresses his views:

Heart transplants may be necessary for some patients, but clearly supplements also have a major (and preferred) role to play. To rule out one of these options is just plain foolish.

With regards to the use of Coenzyme Q_{10} and L-carnitine which in he found provided a huge quality of life boost for many people, he had this to say:

Frankly, when I look back I don't know how I ever practiced cardiovascular medicine without them. Now it's unthinkable not to recommend them to my patients with coronary artery disease, heart failure, arrhythmia, angina and hypertension. Knowing what I know now withholding information about these nutraceuticals would be tantamount to malpractice for me! [95]

Dr Roberts his own observation on the use of supplements:
Now, twelve years out from being the number one cardiology emergency room admitter in my primary hospital, I don't have a single patient in the hospital the majority of the time. My heart failure readmission rate is nearly zero (and I haven't had to get out of bed in the middle of the night

to see a sick patient in over a year). I believe it's the coenzyme Q_{10} , L-carnitine and D-ribose that have kept my patients out of the hospital. Getting to the metabolic cause and effect of heart disease has helped their hearts get better and improved their quality of life.[96]

Aspirin is in commonly used by physicians for a number of disorders, and is commonly prescribed for heart attack, stroke patients, arthritis-sufferers, and even as a preventative measure for heart disease. The NIH sponsored the Women's Health Study 2005, the largest and longest trial ever of women using aspirin to prevent heart disease. Half of 40,000 healthy women 45 years old or more were given 100mg of aspirin every other day, while the control group was given a placebo. The trial lasted 10 years. Kaufman reports on the results, and is not impressed. He cites several types of side effects from the supposed benefits: More than 10 percent reported easy bruising, 2.4 percent reported nosebleeds, 0.8 percent reported blood in urine, 0.65 percent reported peptic ulcers, 0.8 percent reported gastrointestinal bleeding. Of these, 36 more on aspirin required transfusions. He complains that neither the press release, nor the abstract, mentioned that there was no difference in all-cause mortality. Nor did they mention what, in his view, was one of the more serious side effects of long term aspirin use—the doubling of cataracts. He also complains about the use of buffered aspirin (which is buffered with magnesium), used in some trials. These cannot remove the effect of the magnesium, which is known to have significant health benefits, particularly in heart disease. [97]

It has been known for a long time that magnesium reduces the level of coronary artery spasm, and reduces the incidence of serious abnormal rhythms of the heart. [98] Even without the addition of other supplements, magnesium has been shown to reduce death in acute heart disease patients. [99]

Users of un-buffered aspirin for the relief of arthritis pain over long periods have suffered so badly from the side effects that a large number of alternate drugs, such as Ibuprofen (Moxtrin ™), rofecoxib (Vioxx ™) etc. haven been developed. However, it was found that Vioxx caused nearly double the rate of congestive heart failure as aspirin. It was taken off the market by Merck before it could be recalled by the FDA. [100] Also, both aspirin and acetaminophen (Tylenol ™) can cause kidney and liver failure. [101]

Aspirin is further known to cause excretion of calcium, and to deplete levels of vitamin C and B5, and further deplete levels of sodium, potassium and folic acid. [102]

Another common nutrient that is used instead of aspirin by a number of cardiologists and doctors is vitamin E because it causes no known side effects when taken in normal circumstances.

In the Nurses' Health Study, over 87,000 female nurses were given vitamin E supplements containing 200 IU for more than two years. The result was they were found to have had 41 percent fewer instances of coronary disease of several types, and overall mortality was 13 percent lower. [103]

Kauffman refers to a meta-analysis (this is a large review of a number of trials) of vitamin E trials that appeared in 2004. [104] Kauffman found selection bias. Some of the successful trials were not included, and little attention was paid to the dose or type of vitamin E. Most of the trials used the inferior synthetic form of vitamin E—which is the d-alpha-tocopherol isomer alone. Vitamin E occurs naturally as a number of different isomers, alpha, beta, gamma and delta with the related tocotrienols. [105]

Chelation Therapy

To complete this brief look at heart disease mention must be made of Chelation Therapy. This used to involve intravenous administration of a synthetic compound called ethylenediaminetetraacetic acid (EDTA) which was originally used as an effective antidote to lead poisoning. When infused into the blood stream, this compound attaches (chelates) itself to minute particles of lead, and enables them to be removed from the body. Doctors began to report improvements in circulatory status with patients who had both chronic lead poisoning and arterial plaque deposits. It is estimated more than a thousand doctors in the US use this therapy to remove other harmful metals such as cadmium and aluminium, and to treat various symptoms of CHD. However, there is resistance against this form of therapy; it is opposed by the AHA, and Medicare will not cover the cost of it. Nevertheless, it has been practiced for more than 40 years, and many people swear by its use. There is now an oral version of the therapy, one using a formula called DetoxMaxPlus that is combined with phosphatidylcholine. Dr Roberts has used it successfully, and believes it a useful therapy for removing heavy metals. [106]

Kaufman does an extensive review of the evidence for the benefit of EDTA chelation therapy, and finds significant bias in some of the research condemning it. I do not intend to get into this debate in any great depth, and would simply refer you to his book *Malignant Medical Myths*, that gives a broad and balanced picture of the debate. He points out that the therapy helps diabetic ulcers to heal and either delays or eliminates the need for drastic mainstream treatments such as bypass operations, angioplasty or amputation of limbs. Cranton estimated that by the year 2000 more than a million patients would have received EDTA intravenous therapy without ill effects, provided the therapy was carried out correctly—and with approximately 80 percent of the patients significantly improving. He also reports a study of a 10-year follow-up of 59 patients who received chelation therapy, and who showed a 90 percent reduction in the incidence of cancer, compared to 172 control patients.[107]

To summarise what we have discussed in this chapter so far, and to clarify what can seem to be a lot of conflicting information, it has to be said that the cholesterol theory of heart disease does not mount up. The recommendations to eat a low fat diet clearly do not promote health. So what does cause heart disease? Drs Sinatra and Roberts, and many others, believe the problem is due to inflammation, perhaps a system-wide inflammatory process. Dr Ravnskov suspects that infection may play a significant role. What is clear is that there are more significant factors than cholesterol levels that should be associated with coronary artery disease, heart disease, stroke etc., such as homocysteine levels, lipoprotein (a), C-reactive protein, fibrinogen levels, gum disease, toxic metals etc. On top of this, a significant body of evidence implicates deficiencies of such nutrients as magnesium, folic acid, vitamin B_{12}, vitamin B_6, Vitamin E and vitamin C. The successes achieved by Dr Sinatra and others indicate that the supplements Q_{10}, L-carnitine and ribose must also be taken into account.

I will now endeavour to give some idea of the scale of the problem, and try to show the link between the various disease conditions of the body that arise from nutritional deficiencies. Although it is my endeavour to communicate to you information from verifiable sources at all times, I will add that it is my personal opinion, after a number of years of research, that the majority of people on western style diets who rely on supermarkets and industrialised agriculture for their food, are likely to suffer deficiencies that will affect their health, their energy levels and the speed at which their cells age. It is not so much whether people are deficient in vital minerals, vitamins and essential fatty acids etc., its more which particular nutrients are most significantly missing, and what is the impact of that on their health and wellbeing.

As previously reported, Sinatra, Rath and others found that just by giving inexpensive (compared to drug treatment and surgery) supplements and surgery) which have no side effects— (even when taken with conventional drugs), surgery and even transplants can be avoided—simply because the body is able restore itself to health. For example; 30 percent of angina sufferers do not have blocked arteries, but could be suffering from the electrical disturbance due to a lack of minerals such as magnesium. A significant proportion of sudden deaths from heart attack occur in the absence of clot formation or arterial blockage or previously diagnosed arrhythmia; the consensus suggests magnesium deficiency could be one of the main causes. [108]

A review of seven major clinical studies found that intravenous magnesium reduced the risk of death by 55 percent after an acute heart attack, as reported in such reputable journals such as *The British Medical Journal and others*. [109]   It is not my intention to get into any great depth as to all the causes for magnesium deficiency, but a significant one has to be the lack of sensible levels of magnesium and other nutrients in over refined food products such as white flour, sugar etc. and the lack of magnesium in industrialised agriculture. For a more detailed discussion of magnesium I would refer you to *The Magnesium Miracle,* by Carolyn Dean, M.D., N.D.

It is my intention to address nutritional deficiency in a future work to a greater depth. There is however considerable expertise already in the public domain which addresses any of the subjects raised. However, there is one unseen problem which contributes to the cause of Ischemic heart disease in ways that were not previously understood. This is the insidious effect of ionizing radiation.

Radiation and Heart Disease

Dr John Gofman, mentioned in the previous chapter on cancer, was a specialist in the field of nuclear physics and the health effects of various nuclear activities. In his 1999 book *Radiation from Medical Procedures in the Pathogenesis of Cancer and Ischemic Heart Disease,* he proposes the hypothesis that low-level radiation, primarily medical X-rays, fluoroscopy and CT scans are a significant cause of death from Ischemic heart disease. In his book, he suggests the mechanism may due to radiation-induction of mutations in the coronary arteries, resulting in dysfunctional clones—which he refers to as mini-tumours of smooth muscle cells. I don't have space to go into this topic to any great depth. Following the revelations of significant levels of heart disease in victims of the Chernobyl disaster, this discovery becomes even more pertinent.

One of the problems facing researchers looking into the whole aetiology of plaque formation is the variation in plaque consistency, even in the same individual. Gofman poses his 'unified theory', postulating that radiation damage, even of a low amount, can affect cells in the smooth muscle walls of arteries—but not in any unified way. In fact the opposite in some respects— due to the nature of the damage. This, he surmises, could explain such a divergence of plaque formation. For a cell to form a mutation, it needs to be damaged so that normal growth is curtailed—but not so much that growth is prevented resulting in apoptosis (cell death).

X-rays are part of the electromagnetic spectrum, like gamma rays, but with a different wavelength. As such they emit photons, which can act both as particles and in wave effects—such as in light diffraction. The biological damage does not come directly from X-ray photons but from the way the X-ray photons "kick" out electrons from their normal atomic orbit within human tissue. The electrons that have been "kicked" out have huge biological energy, and can simply smash through neighbouring cells until they run out of energy. The damage they create depends on the amount of energy they release, and the molecules they come into contact with. Their molecular victims could be chromosomal DNA or the structural proteins of DNA. It has to be emphasized that these energy changes can far exceed normal biological energy transfers, and can seem more like grenades and small bombs.

Gofman estimates that more than 60 percent of Ischemic Heart Disease (IHD) is strongly linked with low-level radiation due to medical X-rays. It has to be said that Gofman is not against X-rays, where there is a real value in their use, but he is against the uncontrolled use particularly by people who are not only unaware of their danger but who are also unaware of how their power can be effectively reduced. He gives suggestions for reducing exposure rates and cites examples of how this can be successfully achieved. Whilst there has been some improvement over the years, he still feels there is a long way to go. Although these books are written for professionals they are highly readable for the layman too. [110]

Many people are not aware that Gofman was renowned for his pioneering work with fat molecules, the lipids and lipoproteins we have already discussed. Gofman was the very man who separated out all the components of blood plasma, defined the different classes of cholesterol, and linked them with the risk of heart disease as long ago as 1955. Earlier in 2007, the *Journal of Clinical Lipidology* reprinted Gofman's seminal 1955 study, and the journal's editor in chief, W. Virgil Brown referred to Gofman as the "father of clinical Lipidology."[111]The story of low-level radiation is discussed more fully in Chapter 17.

Chapter 3
Making Connections

That Modern man is declining in physical fitness has been emphasized by many eminent sociologists and other scientists. That the rate of degeneration is progressively accelerating constitutes a cause for great alarm, particularly since this is taking place in spite of the advance that is being made in modern science along many lines of investigation.

Weston A Price, MS., D.D.S., F.A.G.D. [112]

Early studies of indigenous populations in rural Africa, -and in many of the populations met by missionaries and doctors in the less developed areas of the world, found an almost complete lack of many of the diseases that we regard as common in the West. Ailments such as diabetes, obesity, heart disease, cancer, appendicitis, peptic ulcers, haemorrhoids, constipation, etc. were rare.

However the advent of western influence on the diets of indigenous peoples has had an adverse effect—as has been well documented. In the early days, the main foods accompanying western exploration were the foods that could travel well such as sugar, molasses, refined flour and white rice—and these began to be adopted by the indigenous people. As a result the diseases mentioned above have become more common.

Numerous investigators subsequently felt there must be a link between these diseases and diet, particularly refined carbohydrate and refined sugars. However, that link could not be reconciled with Keys' hypothesis for heart disease in the 1970s.

There were differing opinions on how refined carbohydrates could be the cause. The physician Thomas Allinson, head of the Bread and Food Reform League noted that ingestion of white bread caused constipation, which led to accompanying problems such as piles, varicose veins, headaches, dullness, etc. There were those who believed that, as with refined white flour, refined white sugar and white rice—which are also almost totally denuded of nutrients—could be responsible, because of consequent vitamin and mineral deficiencies. This had already been found to be the case in diseases such as beriberi, scurvy, pellagra, and rickets.

A German by the name of Engelberg developed a machine for milling rice, for 'refining' it; this process removed the outside husk which we now know is a nutritionally important part of the rice. When outbreaks of beriberi occurred in Japan after the introduction of white rice, the common people realised what the problem was and reverted to using the traditional brown rice. The symptoms of beriberi subsequently disappeared. The more 'refined' classes, however, continued to eat white rice.

Beriberi

In Java in the 1890s there was an epidemic of beriberi. Top German-trained physicians and scientists were dispatched there to deal with the outbreak. Many 'treatments' were tried, but met with failure—and most of the physicians either died or were shipped back home on stretchers. One physician, Dr Christian Eijkman, survived and decided to return for one last attempt to get to grips with the plague. He worked next to a small hospital, and was experimenting with injecting chickens with the blood of beriberi victims. Eventually one of the chickens started staggering around, and exhibiting symptoms of the disease. It did, however, recover without any 'treatment'. Notwithstanding, other chickens who had not been injected began staggering around—and it was only then that Eijkman discovered the normal brown rice diet for the chickens had been swapped for white rice—and the significance became apparent to him. The hospital next door stopped feeding their patients with refined rice, refined sugar, and bread made with refined flour—and all recovered. Eijkman published his findings in 1893, but was ignored at the time. It fell to a colleague, Dr C Grinjs who in 1901 re-published the findings that they believed there was a substance in rice bran that must be essential to health. It was something many of the less sophisticated native population had already realised refusing to eat the refined foods.[113]

In 1911 a Polish biochemist from the Lister Institute in London, Dr Casimir Funk, decided to study Eijkman's findings. He ground rice and produced enough bran to distil out a liquid that he used to treat a pigeon sick with beriberi. The pigeon recovered within a few hours. He called the new substance a "Vitamine" based on the Latin root *vita* meaning 'life' and *amine* from amino acids, the components of protoplasm.

MAKING CONNECTIONS

Pellagra

There was another disease called Pellagra that was a considerable problem. For years it was considered an infectious disease. It baffled the best medical minds for over two hundred years. By 1914 it had reached epidemic proportions in the American South. A bacteriologist by the name of Joe Goldberger from New York, a specialist in tropical medicine, was dispatched to deal with the problem. He first went to the hospitals and discovered none of the medical staff were affected—which convinced him it was not a contagious infection. It also affected the poor more than the wealthier classes. He wondered whether there could be a diet relationship with this problem, being assured by hospital staff that this could not be the case. So he went to the local orphanages for to see for himself what was being consumed: he found the children were being fed hominy grits (ground maize), biscuits and molasses. Any meat and milk that was available was given to infants and teenagers, and Goldberger found that the in-between group, the six to twelve year olds, were the ones succumbing to pellagra.

He applied to do a study using the local prison population to test his evolving theory. The diet he gave included; biscuits, cornmeal mush, polished rice, cane syrup, coffee and sugar for breakfast; cornbread, collard greens, sweet potatoes, cane syrup and hominy grits at noon; and biscuits, mush gravy, cane syrup, coffee and sugar for the evening. A little meat was added occasionally. Within a few weeks the prisoners were complaining of backaches, stomach aches and dizziness—the early signs of pellagra. Eventually pellagra was believed established when the red rash that was associated with it showed up. Eventually Goldberger published his findings that pellagra was a deficiency disease based on a diet of refined cereals and sugar. A few accepted his theory but the majority created uproar at his findings and derided him. It was eventually discovered that maize lacked the vitamin Niacin (vitamin B_3).

Eventually, it was discovered that other important vitamins aside from niacin were lost in the grain refining process. Dr Robert R Williams, in 1936, succeeded in isolating five grams of pure crystals from a whole ton of rice polishings and unravelled its molecular structure. This was subsequently announced as the discovery of vitamin B_1 commonly referred to as thiamine in the New York Times August 23rd 1936.[114]

UNHEALTHY BETRAYAL

Diabetes Link

Hindu physicians had been condemning sugar for over two thousand years. They blamed it for diabetes, but there was no real understanding of the science of how diabetes came about. But, by the end of the nineteenth century it had been discovered that problems with the pancreas were responsible for the condition. Sugar consumption was already blamed for a host of illnesses, including tuberculosis—which had been prevalent in the UK in the 1700s—particularly amongst the sugar workers in the refineries and sugar factories. When Japan acquired a cheap source of sugar in Formosa, the incidence of tuberculosis rose dramatically. In India, the Hindus, who were vegetarian, had one of the highest incidences of diabetes. Sir Charles Havelock, surgeon general and president of the Medical Board of India, had noticed how under British rule, the number of diabetic cases had increased enormously, and that amongst the wealthy Bengalis it had reached 10% of the male population. Their diet was chiefly rice, flour, pulses and sugar.

According to Haven Emerson, director of the Institute of Public Health at Columbia University, death from diabetes increased up to almost 400% in American cities between 1900 and 1920. The incidence had increased in the UK proportionately, and he attributed the rise to both sugar consumption and a sedentary lifestyle. His belief was rejected by Elliot Joslin, one of the pioneers of insulin use as a treatment, and a significant figure in the diabetic medical fraternity. He wrote the book *The Treatment of Diabetes Mellitus* and the *Diabetic Manual* which were to become the bibles of diabetology. Joslin argued that increased sugar consumption had been offset by a reduction in apple consumption. [115] We now know that there is a major difference between refined sugar and natural fruit sugars, but this was not recognised at the time.

In 1923 a Canadian physician Frederick Banting was one of the main two discoverers of Insulin. He received the Noble Prize for medicine and a knighthood from King George V. However it wasn't until 1960 that the ability to measure its concentration in blood, along with other peptide hormones was discovered by Rosalyn Yalow and Soloman Berson. Yalow was awarded the Nobel Prize for her discovery in 1977 (Berson died in 1972).They were able to show that people who developed diabetes as adults had significantly higher levels of insulin in their blood than healthy individuals, not lower levels as was previously believed. This was also noticed in obese people in their studies.

Unfortunately, back in 1924, the science was not well known and there was considerable divergence of opinion. In 1924 Dr Seale Harris, professor of medicine from Alabama University, discovered that sugar consumption could cause *hyperinsulinism*. If people were given too much insulin they developed symptoms that came to be called insulin shock. He noticed that people who were not on insulin, or were diabetic, exhibited low glucose levels in the blood. He declared this to be a symptom of hyperinsulinism which is excessive insulin in the blood. He was ridiculed by the medical profession for reporting this discovery at the time. However he was awarded a medal by the AMA for his work 25 years later once drugs had been established to treat low blood sugar levels but the advice to remove refined sugar from the diet was still ignored.[116]

Joslin based much of his work on the research of Harold Himsworth from University College Hospital, London, who proposed the theory that diabetes was caused by an excess of fats and a lack of carbohydrates. Himsworth rejected the refined sugar hypothesis, citing a 1930 study that showed that Norway, Australia and elsewhere sugar consumption rose from 1922 to the end of that decade but diabetes mortality in these countries did not. He failed to take into account the rise of the use of insulin which prevented deaths from diabetes in this decade and failed to make the observation that of the thirteen countries with the highest sugar consumption figures, eleven of these were the countries with the highest diabetes mortality rates.

Himsworth was one of the first researchers to distinguish between type one and type two diabetes. Type one is associated with juvenile onset caused by the inability of the pancreas to produce sufficient insulin and is known also as insulin-dependent. Type two is associated with a late onset disease in adults who are often overweight.

According to Gary Taubes:

It was Himworth's research and Joslin's faith in it that led to a half century of diabetologists to believe unconditionally that diabetes is not caused by the consumption of sugar and refined carbohydrates.[117]

Despite the fact that in the US diabetologists accepted Joslin's and Himsworth's theory, research in other countries challenged their position. In 1961 an Israeli diabetologist from Hadassah University by the name of Aharon Cohen studied the differences between immigrant populations and established Jewish populations for incidences of diabetes. He noted that there was almost a 50% difference between the two groups. There was also a much higher incidence of heart disease, hypertension and high cholesterol levels. He looked at all the factors and the striking difference was the consumption of sugar.

UNHEALTHY BETRAYAL

Sugar, Over-Processed Carbohydrates and Disease

In the early 1950s Dr Stephen Gyland from Tampa Florida fell ill with a number of symptoms: he was suffering from weakness and dizziness, memory loss, lack of the ability to concentrate, rapid heartbeats, tremors and anxieties. He consulted fourteen physicians including three from the most reputable clinics in the US. He was given numerous diagnoses for his condition that included, diabetes, brain tumour, cerebral arteriosclerosis and neurosis, none of which helped—he was still unable to work and function satisfactorily. He eventually came across the work of a doctor Seale Harris—which prompted him to take a glucose tolerance test (GTT). It was shown that he had hypoglycaemia (low blood glucose). Following Dr Harris's advice, he went on a simple diet that removed all the refined sugar and white flour from his food intake. He quickly recovered and all his symptoms disappeared.

He was so affected by this affair that he wrote to the AMA (July 1953, vol 152) complaining about the treatment of Dr Seale Harris and revealing what he had learned. He went on to successfully treat more than six hundred patients with the same symptoms—with a complete restriction on refined carbohydrates (mostly white flour and sugar). He wrote an exhaustive report to the AMA but it was never published, in English.[118]

In 1956 a South African doctor called George Campbell, spent a year in Philadelphia working at the Hospital of the University of Pennsylvania. He noticed how the black population that he was seeing here had the same diseases as the white population in Durban: diabetes, coronary thrombosis, hypertension, appendicitis and others. Such conditions were almost completely absent in the rural Zulu population in South Africa. Eventually, he returned to Natal and began to notice that the urban black population was exhibiting a similar spectrum of disease to the white population, particularly amongst the Indian community. Campbell's clinic treated over 6,200 diabetics from an Indian population of 250,000. He suspected sugar as a culprit since a significant number of these people worked in and around the sugar plantations. The consumption of sugar in India at that time was in the order of twelve pounds per person yearly, but the Indians consumed nearer eighty pounds. At the same time, they did not consume high levels of either fat or carbohydrates. Campbell found a similar trend among the urban Zulu population.

One of the anomalies cited as a way of refuting the sugar hypothesis for diabetes was the lack of the disease amongst some of the sugar cane cutters. However, it is now known that this is because raw sugar cane is not the same as denatured highly concentrated refined sugar in its effect on our metabolism. The sugar cane workers also worked extremely hard and for long hours.

MAKING CONNECTIONS

Campbell was also one of the first diabetologists to suggest that diabetes has a long incubation period, probably between 18 -22 years. Joslin, however, expressed the view that if sugar consumption was the cause, it should show up in 24 hours.

In the early 1960s Campbell started collaboration with a retired Royal Navy physician, Surgeon-Captain Thomas L. Cleave and Professor N. S. Painter of the Royal College of Surgeons. In 1966 they published *Diabetes, Coronary Thrombosis and the Saccharine Disease.* They argued that most of the common diseases of mankind in Western populations were due to a single source and disorder that they referred to as "Refined Carbohydrate disease". This work was supported by Sir Richard Doll, director of the Statistical Research Unit of the Medical research Council in the UK, who wrote the introduction to the book.[119]

They argued that of all the foods processed by man, refined carbohydrates such as white flour and sugar are altered the most. Ninety percent of the cane or beet is removed, and thirty percent of the wheat. This represented the most dramatic change in human nutrition since the introduction of agriculture. They believed that refining affects us in a number of ways, first through over consumption. On average in the UK 5 oz of sugar is consumed per day. To eat the same amount of sugar in a natural food would take a lot of apples—which no-one would want to do. They also proposed that the refined sugar and flour would flood the body with sugar so quickly (since little digestion is needed), that the pancreas would not be able to keep up.

They further suggested one of the reasons the whole carbohydrate/disease theory had been obscured was due researchers had failed to distinguish between unrefined carbohydrates, i.e. foods in their natural state and the very refined carbohydrates. Future researchers would fail to discriminate between one carbohydrate and another; wholemeal flour would be in the same classification as refined flour. This inability to discriminate meant that the whole topic would be misunderstood for many years. A similar story also crops up with fat research also—where most researchers do not discriminate between unrefined oils and over-refined oils—which has a major bearing on our health.

Bruce Armstrong and Sir Richard Doll published an analysis of cancer and diet in 1975. They studied both the incidence of it, and mortality from it in different countries—and found that the higher the sugar consumption the higher both of the incidence and the mortality of cancer of the breast, colon, rectum, ovary, uterus, kidney, testicles and prostate. [120]

With regards to the influence of sugar alone they found support from John Yudkin who founded the Department of Nutrition at Queen Elizabeth College in London in 1953. He effectively blamed sugar as the cause of diabetes, heart disease and other chronic conditions. He advocated a low carbohydrate diet for weight loss in a book called *This Sliming Business*. He believed that sugar has no nutritional benefit and simply adds empty calories to the diet. He undertook a number of experiments with sugar and starch—which he fed to numerous animals, including people, and found it raised levels of cholesterol, insulin and triglycerides. Many people were beginning to feel that triglycerides were a more reliable indicator for heart disease—and found diabetics also had elevated levels. Yudkin retired in 1971, and his theory seemed to disappear with him.

However, it was impossible to bury all this research regarding processed carbohydrate and its connection with so many western diseases. Keys and his followers had to reconcile this information. It fell to Denis Burkitt to keep it alive. Burlitt proposed it was not refined flour itself that caused disease, so much as the lack of fibre and roughage in the diet. It was known that processed carbohydrates, particularly white flour, caused constipation. Burkitt argued that this was due to a lack of fibre—which slowed the transit times of food through the digestive process and so caused many other problems such as diverticulitis, appendicitis, polyps, colon cancer etc. He found an ally in Alec Walker from the South African Institute of Medical research. They both got into studying stool samples of different groups of people, hoping to deliver a scientific rationale for their theory that a lack of roughage was the problem, not refined sugar or refined carbohydrate per se. They published an article in The Lancet in 1972 after studying twelve hundred people in both rural and urban areas.[121]

This article was given considerable media coverage and came to be accepted as a significant contribution to the understanding of disease.

In the 1930s a pioneering Dental Surgeon, Weston Price, had decided to look into the question of diet and health. He wanted to see if the more traditional diets of peoples not exposed to white flour and refined sugar might explain the alarming incidence of dental disease that he was faced with in the USA at that time. Accordingly, he travelled to the more remote areas in the world where populations were isolated enough not to be exposed to the trade of white sugar and refined flour. And he found that they were remarkably healthy and lacking in tooth decay. He took notes and photographs of all the people he studied. He compared his findings with a subsequent study of members of the same population groups who had had contact with white travellers and traders. What he found astonished him. Within a generation there had been a significant change in the health of the second group. Tooth decay rates jumped from 0.1 percent of the population to 20 percent— and in some groups to more than 40 percent. In all cases, the introduction of white flour and refined sugar and in some cases canned foods, were a common factor. He also discovered that young children born in these populations suffered abnormalities such as crowded teeth, caused by abnormal dental arches and numerous other changes. In some cases the changes to the face structure was so severe that the nose was too narrow to allow normal breathing—and he called these the "mouth breathers". [122]

Price was so affected by what he saw that he made it his business to document everything he saw, and to travel to as many places as he could to check his findings in as many varied populations, climates and habitats as he could. He studied both isolated and modernised groups of people, including, Swiss, and Gaelic people, Eskimos, Africans, Peruvians, Aborigines, Melanesians, Polynesians, Maoris and other people. In every case he found that those on traditional diets were virtually free of the incidence of tooth decay (the average was about 0.2 percent) and all exhibited fine examples of dental arches with no teeth crowding. When he studied members of the same populations that were introduced to white flour and sugar, he found the incidence of tooth decay and other complications was far higher. The photographs he took of tooth decay, crowded teeth and the abnormal dental arches, and facial changes were exactly the kind of thing he saw back in his native USA. The full story of Price's findings can be found in his book, *Nutrition and Physical Degeneration.*[123]

Aside from the obvious abnormalities Price found in the facial characteristics of the individuals he studied, he observed more extensive changes. Whilst he noted the complete lack of crime, prostitution, drunkenness or depression that could be attributed to factors other than the diet changes of the time, there were a number of other significant changes that drew his attention including problems in childbirth. In the traditional cultures the women would go off on their own to give birth, unassisted and in many instances alone. There was complete lack of fear in giving birth. Price documented the case of an Eskimo woman who had remarried and had successfully given birth to 26 healthy children, mostly without any assistance. In many instances she had not even woken her husband until the following morning to present him with a new child.

In the case of the more modernised populations, the situation was considerably different; where there were modern facilities and the women were given free prenatal and postnatal care, the death rate of new-borns was rising; difficulties with labour and stillborn death rates were also increasing. There were higher incidences of cleft palate, club feet—and women had narrower pelvises which added to the problems with labour.

However, there was a significant lack of other disease conditions such as arthritis, heart disease cancer and gastro-intestinal problems. He consulted physicians in all the localities he visited, and noted the same problems occurred wherever trade in white flour and sugar goods had sprung up. He noted that there was virtually no incidence of conditions such as tuberculosis in the populations that still adhered to the traditional diets. His studies have influenced a number of researchers and spawned a number of organisations to promote his work and promulgate a greater understanding of the implications of his discoveries.[124]

Of course there is considerable resistance to accepting the effects of over-processed carbohydrates and sugar in our diets and the relationship to our health. There is a vast industry making enormous profits in the food industry, as well as the vast profits made by the pharmaceutical industry treating the diseases that follow.

But after the industrialisation of both agriculture and the food system, a further set of factors has been introduced that will also be found to significantly challenge our health, and that of future generations

Chapter 4
Fattening Up

Diabetes is the fourth main cause of death in most developed countries. Research demonstrates the association between excessive weight gain, central adiposity (fat around the waist) and the development of Type 2 diabetes. Diabetics are two to four times more likely to develop cardiovascular diseases than others, and a stroke is twice as common in people with diabetes and high blood pressure as it is for those with high blood pressure alone.

Professor Tim Lang [125]

The rates for both obesity and being overweight have increased dramatically in the last decade. In the UK in 2009, almost a quarter of the population (age 16 or over), 22% of men and 24% of women, were considered obese (BMI 30kg/m2 or over). Figures for being overweight are 44% for men and 33% for women (BMI 25 to 30kg/m2).

The rates for children (2-10 years) have also seen a dramatic rise. Statistics for 1995 showed that 16.9 % of boys and 16.8 % girls in England were obese. It is believed that without intervention, that one in five children — almost 1 million — will be obese by 2010.

In the USA the figures are even worse. But what is significant is how they relate to ethnic background and income. According to the CDC, 27 percent of blacks and approximately 21 percent of Hispanics of all ages are accepted as being obese, or at least 31 percent overweight. This compares with a figure of 17 percent for the white population. In numbers, this means approximately 26 million blacks and Hispanics are obese and at risk of serious health problems. Figures for lower income groups are even worse, and suggest that 66% of adults are considered seriously overweight, one in five young people are obese, and one in three is overweight. Since 1980, among children and adolescents, obesity prevalence has more than tripled. [126] All this happened despite the fact that consumption of fat has decreased.

Research on obesity has improved to some degree to enable us to predict future figures. For example, in a study at the University of Houston and Baylor College it was discovered that children with a high Body Mass Index (BMI) had a much higher chance of becoming obese at fifth grade (age ten to eleven) than a child with a low BMI. For example a child with a low BMI of 16.5 would have a 21 percent chance of becoming obese compared to a 70 percent chance with a BMI of 20.9, or a 91 percent chance with a BMI of 23.7.[127]

It has been recorded that, among the adult group of overweight and obese men and women, high blood pressure was observed in 48% of men and 46% of women who were obese, and in 32% of overweight men and women—compared to 17% in the normal range weight group.[128]

Obesity increases the risk of diabetes, heart disease, cancer and arthritic disability, as well as of high blood pressure. Type II diabetes is no longer referred to as 'adult onset' in the USA due to the numbers of children being diagnosed with it.

A study by Harvard School of Public Health discovered a link with the consumption of sodas and fruit drinks. They found that for every increase in the number of sodas drunk, the chance of becoming overweight increased 1.6 times per serving.[129]

A further study based on data from 350,000 people in eight countries led by Dr Dora Romaguera at Imperial College London with researchers from the InterAct consortium, looked at consumption of juices, sugar-sweetened soft drinks and artificially sweetened soft drinks, collected in the European Prospective Investigation into Cancer and Nutrition (EPIC study).

They found that approximately one can of fizzy drinks consumed per day increased the risk of type 2 diabetes by 22 percent. [130]

Metabolic Disorders and Over-Processed Carbohydrates

In this chapter it is my intention to review some of the background to the research into carbohydrate and fat metabolism as it has a significant effect on health.

In 1980 Gerald Reaven a Stanford diabetologist proposed the name syndrome X to describe the common metabolic conditions that link heart disease, obesity and diabetes. These include elevated levels of triglycerides, low levels of LDL cholesterol, hypertension, hyper-insulinemia (chronically high levels of insulin and low blood glucose), insulin resistance (insensitivity to insulin) and glucose intolerance (the inability to metabolise glucose correctly).

A number of other researchers have come across the same syndrome, but have given it different names including, Metabolic Syndrome, Insulin Resistance etc. It is regarded as a metabolic problem related to refined flour and sugar (refined carbohydrates). It's only in recent times that the significance of Metabolic Syndrome in other disease conditions—such as heart disease and other chronic illness—has been appreciated.

Scott Grundy is a nutritionist at the University of Texas Southwestern Medical Center, specialising in Lipid research and primary author of the 2003 Cholesterol Guidelines by the National Cholesterol Education Program; he was a supporter of metabolic syndrome and believed the incidence of metabolic syndrome in the Tokelauans was directly attributable to the increase in sugar and flour in their diets, which eventually developed into heart disease and diabetes. Although fat consumption by these people has decreased, obesity has risen. Metabolic syndrome seems to imply a breakdown of homeostasis in the body.

Homeostasis is regulated by the hypothalamus, a small organ at the base of the brain. It controls and regulates the autonomic nervous system and the endocrine system through a system of hormones. These control and regulate growth, reproduction, energy utilisation, and they maintain the body's fluid levels and other functions. Insulin is the most important hormone for the regulation of energy production, utilisation and storage. It regulates fat, and protein metabolism as well as carbohydrate metabolism. It regulates the synthesis of glycogen and fat deposits and the synthesis of proteins involved in the repair and growth of cells.

Insulin is the hormone that regulates and co-ordinates everything to do with the storage and use of nutrients in the body, and particularly the control of fat metabolism, carbohydrate metabolism and liver and kidney functions.

In the case of digestion of refined sugar and flour, the levels of blood glucose rise dramatically. The levels of insulin then rise in response and become chronically elevated (hyperinsulinemia). The outcome is that, over time, the tissues become resistant to insulin. Refined sugar is referred to as *sucrose,* it is composed of one molecule of glucose and one molecule of fructose (fructose is the natural sugar found in fruits). There is no equivalent way in nature being exposed to such high levels of fructose in the body as we get from ingesting refined sugar or drinks with highly refined corn syrup. Fructose is found in fruits and some root vegetables, but exists in very small quantities in these natural foods. The diseases associated with metabolic syndrome and the chronic diseases of mankind can be seen as a symptom of the dysregulation of homeostasis caused by excessive fructose, induced changes and the problems created by the insulin response.

Hypertension (defined as high blood pressure) has been known of since the 1920s and has been linked with obesity and diabetes and heart disease. Insulin levels are abnormally elevated in hypertensives and it is commonly referred to as the 'insulin resistant' state. Such is the link with obesity that the higher the blood pressure, the higher the triglyceride and cholesterol levels, the greater the weight and the greater the risk of diabetes and heart disease.

Whilst there are a number of researchers who believed that salt intake may be a factor in hypertension, there has been significant research which highlights the role of carbohydrate metabolism in the body levels of water—and its contribution to high blood pressure. This discovery was attributed to a German chemist Carl Von Voit in 1860. More recently in 1919 the director of the Nutrition Laboratory of the Carnegie Institute of Washington, Francis Benedict, observed that, with predominately carbohydrate diets, the body retains water but that with predominately fat diets the body expels water. The physiology was explained in the 1960s by Walter Bloom, director of research at Atlanta's Piedmont Hospital. He was studying fasting as an obesity treatment, and observed that eating carbohydrates caused the kidneys to hold onto salt—which, in turn, caused the body to retain water to maintain a constant sodium level. By the early seventies it had been demonstrated that this water retaining effect was, was in fact, caused by insulin secretion—which induced the kidneys to reabsorb sodium. By the 1990s Joslin had accepted the likelihood that insulin levels initiated hypertension in type two diabetics. A Harvard endocrinologist by the name of Lewis Landsberg suggested that insulin also increases heart rate and constricts blood vessels—which also raises blood pressure.[131]

In the 1950s John Gofman at the University of California Berkley, who was a chemist and a physician, used an ultracentrifuge to fractionate lipoproteins into different classes, depending upon density. Gofman possessed the only ultracentrifuge in the US at this time which was essential for this work. He discovered that both LDL and VLDL (the very low density lipoproteins) were good predictors of heart disease, particularly if counted together as an atherogenic index—the greater the index, the greater the chance of heart disease and atherosclerosis. He also noted that VLDL levels were increased with increased carbohydrate consumption.

By 1955 this view was further supported by Pete Ahrens from Rockefeller University—a lipid researcher specialising in the study of triglycerides. He noticed how triglycerides would shoot up in some low fat diets and fall in high fat diets. This was due to increasing carbohydrate in the diet; he termed the condition *carbohydrate induced lipemia* (excessive fat in the blood plasma). He took blood samples from the same patients and noticed that on the high carbohydrate diet the blood would be all milky coloured—yet on the high fat diet it would be clear. The percentage of fat in the blood rose with the levels of carbohydrate consumed.

FATTENING UP

Research proving the link with high triglycerides to heart disease when compared with cholesterol levels, increased with the work of Albrink, Man and Meigs from Yale, in 1960—and in the early 1970s by Peter Kuo from the University of Pensylvania, Lars Carlson of the Karolinska Institute in Stockholmand, later, with that of Joseph Goldstein and colleagues from the University of Washington. However with so few institutions having the equipment to measure triglyceride levels at this time, progress remained slow. In 1967, the NIH instituted a study by Donald Frederickson, future director of NIH, with Robert Levy, future director of NHLBI, and Robert Lees of Rockefeller University. They confirmed the relationship of elevated VLDL and increased levels of triglycerides to heart disease—and also confirmed their belief that a low fat diet would be counter-productive for treating heart disease where increased carbohydrate consumption raised the levels of triglycerides. They also demonstrated an inexpensive method for measuring cholesterol levels and triglyceride levels in various lipoproteins and came up with a simplified way of classifying lipoproteins.[132]

The NIH funded five further studies to measure LDL Cholesterol, VLDL and triglyceride levels in populations in San Francisco, Puerto Rico, Framingham, Honolulu and Albany, to discover the risk factors and relevance for heart disease. The results were released as two reports in 1977 after taking almost ten years to complete. The reports were unanimous in establishing that total cholesterol levels had no significance to heart disease, that LDL was a marginal risk factor, but that triglyceride levels were the most significant link with heart disease. Tavia Gordon the NIH biostatistician and his collaborators suggested that physical activity, weight loss and a low carbohydrate diet may be beneficial.

Prior to this report, two researchers, David Barr and Howard Eder of New York Hospital-Cornell Medical Centre (1951), had proposed links between HDL and lower heart disease. Gofman had also confirmed that when HDL was low, triglycerides were high, and when HDL was high, triglycerides were low—which indicated a relationship of some kind.

Interest in the Mediterranean diet, and its link with low heart disease, prompted two studies in the early 1990s, the Lion Diet Heart trial and GISSI-Prevenzione, an Italian study. These both observed that monounsaturated fat lowered LDL cholesterol and increased HDL levels—and so challenged the evidence that saturated fat would raise LDL levels, since saturated fat is 51% monounsaturated fat and 90% of it is oleic acid the same fatty acid as in olive oil.

Ronald Krauss, using Gofman's centrifuge back in 1980, undertook research into the different sub-classes of low density lipoproteins and their differing atherogenic properties, and their links with fat and carbohydrate metabolism. He chaired the American Heart Association, and was the primary author of the AHA nutrition guidelines for 1996 and 2000. He also suggested after twelve years of research, that he believed a high carbohydrate diet would cause heart disease for the majority of the population . He eventually identified seven discreet sub classes of LDL, the smallest and densest being the one that was most elevated in patients with heart disease. He also discovered that this had a strong negative correlation with HDL. He maintained that some people had large 'fluffy' LDL with a lot of cholesterol, lipids and triglycerides, whilst others had smaller denser LDL with less cholesterol, lipids and triglycerides. [133]

In 1980 Peter Kwiterovich, a lipid specialist from John Hopkins University, and Allan Sniderman, a cardiologist from McGill University, confirmed that a way to measure the lipoprotein levels in the body was by measuring the levels of the protein apo B—which is found in both VLDL and LDL particles—and found that the levels are raised in heart-disease patients. They collaborated with Kraus in three of his papers, and further discovered that elevated apo B protein levels were directly related to the volume of the smallest and densest LDL particles.[134]

Kraus observed that the total level of LDL cholesterol did not predict whether heart disease or atherosclerosis would exist in a patient. He did, however, discover that this depended on whether the LDL was the larger fluffy one or the smaller denser one. The smaller denser one stayed in the blood stream longer, and needed to be oxidised before it would cause atherosclerosis. He believed that the smaller size of the lower density LDL particle enabled it to lodge in places that the larger particle would be unable to. He called the large fluffy LDL particles Pattern A and (small denser particles of LDL Pattern B. In 1988 Kraus and his collaborators reported in JAMA that Pattern B was three times more likely to be observed in heart disease patients than Pattern A—so he called pattern B the atherogenic profile. He also noted that diabetics have the same profile.

Krauss undertook a number of further trials in the late 1980s to further understand the implications of the two patterns. He discovered that a low fat, high carbohydrate diet produced more of the low density LDL particles which was the atherogenic Pattern B. This basically confirmed that a high carbohydrate low fat diet creates a greater risk of heart disease. He further discovered that the more saturated fat in the diet, the more fluffy LDL would be observed—which was considered beneficial.[135]

When we eat a carbohydrate-rich meal, the body converts the starch into glucose, and the liver converts the glucose into fat for storage (triglycerides). The triglycerides are oil droplets, and are fused to the apo B protein—and cholesterol and become the VLDL lipoprotein. VLDL is then secreted into the blood and distributes the triglycerides for storage—a process that is called the *delipidation cascade*. The triglycerides get distributed, the particle becomes smaller and eventually becomes an LDL particle. In Krauss's mechanism, the rate at which fats accumulate in the liver affects the oil droplet size—which in turn affects which of the two pathways the body then takes. In a low-calorie low-carbohydrate diet, the oil droplets would be smaller and the carrier would be the intermediate lipoprotein IDL, denser than VLDL but less dense than LDL. Eventually it will end its life as the fluffy LDL particle.

Insulin Resistance

Gerald Reaven, the Stanford University diabetologist, began working with John Farquhar to further understand the relationship between insulin resistance and its role in disease. He had already reported heart attack survivors had both high triglycerides and glucose intolerance. He believed the more carbohydrates that were consumed, the more insulin would be needed to transport the glucose created into cells, but that the insulin also prompted the liver to synthesize triglycerides for fat storage. In the case of someone who is already insulin resistant, he showed that higher levels of insulin would have to be secreted, and that this would also increase the levels of triglycerides. By 1967 it had been discovered that insulin levels raise and lower in healthy individuals in a similar way, and that raising the amount of carbohydrate in the diet raised the insulin levels. It also became apparent that the higher the levels of insulin, the higher the apparent insulin resistance, and the higher the triglyceride levels. Eventually, a decade later, Ralph DeFronzo and Eleuterio Ferrannini, convinced diabetologists that resistance to insulin was a fundamental defect of Type 2 diabetes.

In 1987, in the Banting lecture for the American Diabetic Association (ADA), Reaven outlined his case for the implications of syndrome X (metabolic syndrome) which include the symptoms: insulin resistance, Hyperinsulinemia, high blood pressure, high triglycerides and low HDL cholesterol. All these conditions are found not just in Type 2 diabetes and obesity, but also play a significant role in heart disease, whether or not there is diabetes present. He later proved that the higher the levels of insulin present the higher the prevalence of heart disease. [136]

Measuring insulin resistance is a difficult process requiring accurate testing of blood sugar levels at different times while insulin levels are kept at a constant level and precise measurements of glucose are introduced into the system. This is beyond the scope of most physicians, so is limited to research projects. In 1996, Reaven published an article on syndrome X in the ASHA's journal

Circulation, in which he stated that a high carbohydrate diet would not be beneficial for a Type 2 diabetic.

In 1993 Reaven, working with Ron Krauss, reported that small dense LDL was another significant component of syndrome X, and that it was also related to insulin resistance, Hyperinsulinemia, high blood sugar, low HDL and hypertension. They also noticed that the higher the triglyceride levels, the lower the HDL, and the more likely it was that small dense LDL particles, and insulin resistance, would be present.

In the late 1960s, a researcher from Queens University Belfast, Robert Stout, published some studies demonstrating how insulin assists the transportation of fats and cholesterol into cells of the arterial wall, and facilitates the synthesis of them into the arterial lining. He reasoned that, as one of insulin's primary functions was to promote the storage of fat in fat tissue, that it could easily do the same in the linings of blood vessels. In 1969 with the British diabetologist John Vallance-Owen, he proposed that ingestion of large amounts of carbohydrate would lead to insulinemia, and then insulin resistance and finally atherosclerosis and heart disease. In 1975 he teamed up with a pathologist from the University of Washington, Russell Ross, and discovered that insulin promotes the proliferation of smooth muscle cells that line the inside of the arteries. This would lead to a thickening of the artery and could be considered a step further towards atherosclerosis and hypertension.

Reactive Oxygen Species and Glycation End Products

The majority of diabetologists understand that diabetic complications are caused by high blood sugar levels creating toxic products—such as *advanced glycation end products* (AGEs) and *reactive oxygen species* (ROS). The creation of AGEs occur during glycation and involve the attachment of a glucose molecule to a protein molecule without the normal benefit of an enzyme control. When enzymes attach sugars to proteins they fix them to particular sites—it is not a haphazard process. However in an AGE product it is haphazard and therefore can have unseen consequences. [137]

ROS products, on the other hand, can be produced by the burning of glucose in the cells, and can result in peroxides and *free radicals* which are unbalanced molecules of, in this case, oxygen with a missing electrical charge. They are highly reactive and cause what is termed oxidative stress. This has been compared with rust on metal because it is oxidised iron. It is linked with aging, both natural aging and premature aging. These products can be responsible for the oxidation of the LDL that is linked with atherosclerosis and heart disease. In the body's case, it protects against this threat to damage by the production and use of *antioxidants* such as *superoxide dismutase, glutathione peroxidase* and the main vitamin antioxidants such as *vitamins A C & E.*

AGEs are a heterogeneous group of molecules formed from the non-enzymatic reaction of reducing sugars with free amino groups of proteins, lipids, and nucleic acids. AGEs can *cross-link,* which means they can bind together. The sugars bind to each other's protein which can lead to further problems. They can also be produced by cooking at high temperatures—and the body can absorb them this way. They can accumulate in the lens, cornea or retina of the eye, and cause cataracts, or accumulate in the linings of the arteries, in the kidneys, and even nerve endings. Collagen which is an important component of bones, cartilage, skin tendons arteries etc. has been found to be very susceptible to glycation and cross-linking. An important constituent of collagen is vitamin C.

I bring up vitamin C at this point as it has a crucial bearing. The transport mechanism for moving vitamin C around the body is the same insulin dependent system used by glucose. So when you consume refined carbohydrates, one of the first things that happens is the body dumps the vitamin C to deal with the massive rise of blood glucose—which is a priority for the body to deal with, since the blood glucose level is critical. Daily consumption of carbohydrates, depending upon frequency and amount, can compromise the level of vitamin C in the body. In the long term, this can lead to less elasticity of the veins and arteries which, amongst other things can contribute to high blood pressure. It can also compromise the body's ability to fight free radical damage from various sources—such as ingesting damaged oil which has been over-refined, or oxygen free-radicals from the burning of glucose.

The accumulation and cross-linking of collagen formed AGEs cause the loss of elasticity in the skin, joints, lungs and heart, as well as the veins and arteries. Simple sugars like fructose (a component of sucrose) and galactose undergo glycation at about 10 times a higher rate than glucose. AGEs can also cause the oxidation of LDL particles, which are particularly susceptible, with the accompanying cholesterol leading to particles that can attach to arteries and cause atherosclerosis.

LDL particles seem to be particularly susceptible to both oxidation by ROS and to glycation. All parts of the lipoprotein are susceptible, the protein part, the lipid part, and the cholesterol part. These oxidised LDL particles seem to be significantly elevated in both diabetics and non-diabetics with atherosclerosis, and are found in the atherosclerotic lesions themselves.

The consumption of refined carbohydrates therefore raises blood sugar unnaturally—which increases the production of free radicals, oxidising agents and AGEs that will lead to vascular disorders such as atherosclerosis and heart disease, and accelerated degeneration of the body in humans, whether diabetic or not.

Glycaemic Index

One of the problems with identifying the reason why refined carbohydrates were not previously realised to be a significant problem was partly due to researchers not separating refined and unrefined products. There is a significant difference in the way each is metabolized in the body. It was generally understood that unrefined products took longer to digest, since the carbohydrate is bound up with fibre and indigestible cellulose and hemi-cellulose. The idea of a *glycaemic index* that measured the rate of digestion of various carbohydrates, and therefore the accompanying rate of rise of blood sugar levels, was developed and used to explain the difference between various foods in our systems. Below is what Diabetes UK has to say about it:

> The Glycaemic Index (GI) is a ranking of foods based on their overall effect on blood glucose levels. Slowly absorbed foods have a low GI rating, whilst foods that are more quickly absorbed will have a higher rating. This is important because choosing slowly absorbed carbohydrates can help even out blood glucose levels when you have diabetes....
>
> They continue:

> Slow acting carbohydrates will also reduce the peaks in blood glucose that often follow a meal, and this may have a role in helping to prevent or reduce the risk of getting Type 2 diabetes in those at risk. There are also benefits for weight loss. Low GI foods can help you to control your appetite by making you feel fuller for longer, with the result that you eat less. Research has shown that people who have an overall low GI diet have a lower incidence of heart disease.[138]

The idea of the glycaemic index was not initially well received, but has since gained widespread acceptance. The fact that it is referred to by organisations such as Diabetes UK is testament to the belief in its usefulness. There are however a number of problems with using the index. For example, the simple addition of fat and protein to a meal slows down the absorption of carbohydrate—which will affect blood sugar release. This would of course be more beneficial, than would have been the case with consuming, say, wheat by itself.

I went on the University of Sydney's web site for the *Home of the Glycemic Index* where you can search their database to discover the GI rating for over 400 foods, mostly the Australian versions. The problem is the figures vary wildly. For example if you search potatoes it will give a range of 56 to 94 for the same species of potato (baked without fat) another 111 (baked without fat) and another at 49 (boiled); white bread varied from 59 to 75, wholemeal varied from 68 (Hovis UK) to 85, brown rice varied from 48 to 87 and ice cream varied from 27 to 57. Sugar was given as 58 to 84. They list 70 and above as high, 56 to 69 as medium, and 55 and below as low GI.[139]

The 'wholemeal bread' index gives no indication of the flour content of different breads. Unless a bread is listed as 100% whole wheat, it is invariably mixed with considerable amounts of other refined flours, including white flour (the most commonly added flour) no doubt to make it more acceptable or palatable to all the people who have been bought up on refined white bread. The most serious deficiency of using the index at all, though, is its assertion that refined sugar has an index of 58 to 84. What is not shown by this figure is the fact that sucrose (refined white sugar) contains fructose and glucose in its structure (one molecule of fructose to one molecule of glucose) and the *fructose portion does not affect blood sugar,* as it is metabolised in the liver.

The Dangers of High Fructose Ingestion

Products like high-fructose corn syrup (HFCS-$_{55}$) which has been on the market since 1978 and had captured 50% of the sweetener market in the US by 1985, also contains high levels of fructose. It is 55% fructose and 45% glucose, which gives it a lower GI index than sucrose (refined sugar). However, this GI index totally ignores the effect of fructose. The problem is that fructose has traditionally been associated with natural plant sugars—which are not associated with causing harm to our systems. However highly processed plant products such as refined sucrose and corn syrup are not the same things. They do significantly increase blood sugar levels, but they also cause a massive input of fructose that would be impossible to replicate in nature.

This causes a huge load on the liver at the same time as the onslaught of glucose into the system is raising blood sugar levels. The liver has to convert the fructose into triglycerides and ship it out in lipoproteins for storage throughout the body. This is referred to as *fructose-induced lipogenesis.* Research into this area of study was carried out by Sheldon Reiser and his colleagues at the USDA Carbohydrate Nutrition Laboratory in Maryland, with Eleazar Shafrir from Hadassah Medical School, Jerusalem, and Peter Mayes a biochemist at Kings College Medical School in London.

Mayes suggested that the body will adapt to long-term changes in diet, such as a high fructose component, and that the pattern of metabolism can change over time. However he and his colleagues observed that the level of fructose is reflected in the levels of triglycerides secreted by the liver. They also noticed that fructose blocks glucose metabolism in the liver, and its conversion into glycogen, which forces the pancreas to increase secretion of insulin to deal with the elevated levels of glucose that are not being processed by the liver. This, according to Mayes, causes the muscles to become insulin resistant over time. Due to the fact that fructose is more reactive than glucose, it is much more likely to increase AGEs products (fructose is approximately ten times more effective at making the cross-linking necessary for this to happen). It also increases the oxidation of LDL markedly—which is part of the regression towards atherosclerosis.[140]

Unfortunately, this area of research of fructose metabolism has been neglected.

Recent studies by the Harvard School of Public Health have noted that the risk of type II diabetes is strongly related to the GI of food in the general diet, while other studies have shown a lower incidence of heart disease occurring with a lower GI diet. In 1999, WHO and the Food and Agriculture Organisation (FAO) made the recommendation that people base their diets on low GI food to avoid coronary heart disease and obesity.

Without a deeper breakdown of the information on how GI is determined, it is difficult to be confident about precisely what is being measured. We would expect improvements to be brought about by a move away from processed carbohydrates to unrefined carbohydrates and an increase in quality fats in the diet. There are, however, other factors that might affect overall health and these relate to insulin levels and carbohydrate consumption.

Insulin and Cancer

Howard Temin, who won a Nobel Prize for his cancer research, discovered that tumours in laboratory animals would cease to proliferate unless insulin was added to the growth medium. This was confirmed by Kent Osborne of the NCI and his colleagues. They reported that they had found breast-cancer cells "exquisitely sensitive to insulin"—that these have more receptors (two to three times as many) for insulin as they do for normal cells. They also respond to Insulin-like growth factor (IGF). Renato Basserga of Thomas Jefferson University discovered that by shutting down the IGF receptor in mice there was a "strong inhibition if not total suppression of tumour growth"

Most IGF is bound to small proteins that transport them throughout the body to where they may be required. Insulin appears to disrupt the level of binding proteins and this, it is suggested, may cause free IGF to bind to sites such as malignant cells which would then promote growth of the malignancy. David Cheresh a cancer researcher from the Scripps Institute in La Jolla, California found that both IGF and insulin will promote growth in benign tumours and promote the tumour to metastasize and spread through the blood serum to other sites. There is an increased risk of prostate, breast, colorectal and endometrial cancer with hyperinsulinism and elevated levels of IGF according to a number of epidemiological studies.[141]

Time for a Re-Assessment of the Cholesterol Theory

Currently there is a movement afoot in the USA supporting the idea that carbohydrates are more of a problem in diets and a more significant factor in disease than many people had previously recognised.

Dr David Perlmutter, a neurologist, and a Fellow of the American College of Nutrition, believes that low fat diets and the over-consumption of carbohydrates is also having a serious impact on our neurological health—particularly our over-indulgence with wheat. He refers to a number of studies in his book, *Grain Brain,* linking Alzheimer's disease with excessive carbohydrate consumption—which refer to Alzheimer's as a third type of diabetes. He further suggests that cholesterol is essential to good brain health, and that low levels are now being linked to cognitive impairment, ADHD, dementia, and depression. He further suggests, that low fat diets and high grain diets, create significant problems that we were previously unaware of. Gluten for example, initiates an inflammatory response in many individuals, leading to a release of harmful cytokines that can accumulate and attack the brain.

Dr Perlmutter suggests that historically as hunter gatherers our diets would have been approximately 5 percent carbohydrate and 75 percent fat—whereas currently, western diets are much nearer 60 percent carbohydrate and only 20 percent fats. This he believes is causing serious deterioration in our neurological health. [142]

Finally, if I haven't overdosed you on studies, I leave you with critical report by Dr. Sylvan Lee Weinberg, Director of Medical Education, The Dayton Heart Hospital, Dayton, Ohio, in 2003 in which he reviews the diet–heart hypothesis. It is a review that covers a long period of time and reviews a considerable body of work:

The low-fat "diet–heart hypothesis" has been controversial for nearly 100 years. The low-fat–high-carbohydrate diet, promulgated vigorously by the National Cholesterol Education Program, National Institutes of Health, and American Heart Association since the Lipid Research Clinics-Primary Prevention Program in 1984, and earlier by the U.S. Department of Agriculture food pyramid, may well have played an unintended role in the current epidemics of obesity, lipid abnormalities, type II diabetes, and metabolic syndromes. *This diet can no longer be defended by appeal to the authority of prestigious medical organizations or by rejecting clinical experience and a growing medical literature suggesting that the much-maligned low-carbohydrate–high-protein diet may have a salutary effect on the epidemics in question* (my emphasis).

He further concludes:

A balanced appraisal of the diet–heart hypothesis must recognize the unintended and unanticipated role that the LF-HCarb diet may well have played in the current epidemic of obesity, abnormal lipid patterns, type II diabetes, and the metabolic syndrome.

He further states that he believes the current rejection of the low carbohydrate high protein diet having a favourable impact on obesity, lipid patterns, type II diabetes and metabolic syndrome *is also no longer tenable.*[143]

It is now obvious that there is a link between heart disease, cancer, diabetes and the many metabolic disorders affecting Western society—and the effects of a modern diet. It has been argued by many people that the introduction of processed carbohydrates into the diet, particularly sugar and white flour has been the biggest radical change in our eating habits since the industrial revolution. There is a considerable body of research attesting to the negative aspect of this that has previously been ignored—for various reasons. Some cite the margarine and vegetable oil industry trying to shift the blame onto saturated fats in the 1960s as the cause. What needs to be taken now is a radical look at how we approach future research.

Any future studies looking at fat metabolism has to identify the quality of fat. To simply state that a fat is polyunsaturated does not tell us how refined it is or how damaged it is. It is now certain that damaged fats such as *trans fats* or over-processed oils which produce high levels of *free radicals* or any other damaged fat will not be metabolised in the same way as undamaged fats in human cells. We also have to differentiate between refined flour and unrefined flour, 'wholemeal' must mean '100% whole meal' and not just an arbitrary volume of refined to un-refined flour.

FATTENING UP

How we fund this research will also have a significant impact on what research is undertaken, and how it will impact on the future of medicine.

In these previous chapters we have reviewed some of the divergent opinions regarding heart disease, diabetes, and cancer and, in some small degree, the nutritional influences on these diseases. Some people believe that looking at single nutrient deficiencies are a reductionist approach to reviewing health, and that we need to look at the bigger picture. Professor Colin T Campbell in his ground-breaking book *The China Study,* which he refers to as 'the most comprehensive study of nutrition ever conducted' is exactly the person who has already done this. His book reviews his research over a number of years that included a monumental study of the relationship between the diet and health of 880 million Chinese people. What this revealed was that the rural populations had virtually no cancer or heart disease, and that they thrived on a diet of plant-based whole foods. His studies have led him to the opinion that most disease can be prevented by adopting such a diet, and cites considerable evidence to support this view.[144]

One of the problems with much of the research cited—to support the view that a carbohydrate-based diet is problematic for health—is that there is no differentiation between the *highly over-processed carbohydrates* and wholefood based carbohydrates. The processed carbohydrates in the typical western diet don't just come with denatured nutrients, they are also frequently loaded with over-processed fats, sugars and salt as well.

Campbell takes up this issue in *The Low-Carb Fraud:*

> Because fruits, vegetables, and whole grains are all high in carbohydrates, lumping all carbs together as unhealthy means demonizing plant-based foods as well as simple sugars. A diet low in carbohydrates is unavoidably a diet high in fat, especially saturated fat, because eliminating carbohydrates means relying on large quantities of animal-based products for energy and other nutritional benefits. Virtually by definition, therefore, a low-carb diet emphasizes the consumption of animal-based foods, while a low-fat diet emphasizes the consumption of plant-based foods.[145]

He also takes issue with the many studies comparing 'low-fat' diets with high-fat diets, by suggesting that—compared with the levels of fat in a whole food plant-based diet—many of these diets are still based on high consumption of dairy products and other fats that are still, in his view, comparatively high in fat. So he believes that all that is really being compared is a high fat diet with an *even higher fat diet*.

He has significant support from a number of other sources. Doctor John McDougall in his book *The Starch Solution*, argues that a starch-based diet based on whole foods is the best way to lose weight and create health. He provides numerous examples of patients being restored to health, having successfully treated more than 5,000 people with his program.[146]

Two other doctors, Caldwell Esselstyn and Dean Ornish are also promoters of a whole food plant-based diet to form the basis of a health-care strategy for their patients. They both specialise in the field of cardiovascular disease and have both, independently from each other, (one is based on the east coast, the other on the west coast) come to the conclusion that a plant-based wholefood diet works more quickly and more efficiently at restoring health to patients with all forms of heart disease. Both of them have undertaken peer-reviewed studies and have successfully proved the efficacy of these diets. They both claim more than a 95% success rate with this approach.[147]

Campbell accepts that some people may initially get some benefit from reducing the carbohydrate content of their diet, particularly if it has been based on over-processed products, but he is concerned about the long-term effect of this type of diet. The trouble is that many people have become intolerant to gluten, due to over-reliance on refined wheat products, so for them moving to a diet based on whole grain wheat will not necessarily help. However, there are a considerable number of other sources of starch to form the basis of whole food based diet, such as potatoes, brown rice and quinoa. Wheat and dairy intolerances are the most common food allergies.

No doubt the debate regarding cholesterol will continue to run, and even more conflicting studies will appear. There will also, no doubt, be a continuing debate over carbohydrates that will continue to confuse the general public.

I will leave this chapter with this observation: Three-quarters of the people living on this planet—live on a plant-based wholefood diet. They also have the lowest incidence of heart disease and cancer compared with people living on a typical Western diet—based on modern meat rearing practices, high in dairy products, over-processed fats, carbohydrates, sugars and salt.

Chapter 5
Food For Thought

An extraordinary strength of medical and scientific opinion throughout the world states that the food typically eaten today in Britain is the main single cause of the diseases we mostly suffer and die from, whether these be deadly, such as heart disease, stroke or cancers; disabling, such as diabetes, ulcers or gallstones; or debilitating, such as tooth decay, constipation or overweight.

Professor Jerry Morris, chairman of NACNE Committee. [148]

The industrialisation of agriculture and the food system has had a huge impact on world resources and the way they are managed. Currently 20% of the population consume more than 80% of the world's resources. Most of our food production is in the hands of big corporations. Maximising profits has led to much of our food production being greatly based on monocultures (the planting of single repetitive crops) which need ever increasing inputs of fertiliser, herbicides, pesticides etc. This leads to further degradation of the soil which in turn leads to falling yields and, consequently, even greater inputs of petrochemical fertilisers. Such continuing degradation of the soil has serious long term consequences.

It is estimated that 75 billion tons of topsoil are lost annually, leaving more than 80 percent of faming land "moderately or severely eroded"—according to a report at the Carbon Farming conference in 2010 hosted by the University of Sydney. China is losing topsoil 57 times faster than it can be replaced. In Australia the figure is 5 times, in the USA 10 times and in Europe 17 times. Scientists warn that British farming soil could run out within sixty years—which would lead, to a catastrophic food crisis. [149]

Traditional farming practices used a mixed agricultural system which entailed the rotation of crops and the addition of animal manures, calcified seaweeds, fish meal etc., to be added to the soil to replenish nutrients and leave the soil in a good condition for future generations. Farmers were caretakers of the land and were rewarded for their trouble.

UNHEALTHY BETRAYAL

Our current system of agriculture has been developed through artificial subsidies that have had unforeseen consequences for the land, the environment, and the health and wealth not just of farmers but of all of us.

Most of our food now comes from just a few large supermarkets chains. In some towns in the UK there is little competition for the large food giants such as Tesco and Sainsbury's because independent shops can't compete on price.

There are a number of reasons we are in a position where health and disease are so rampant in Western society today. These include: the way food is produced and marketed, social factors, political influence, the industrialisation of the agricultural system, the influence of our education system, the way science is funded and the way medicine is practiced in our society.

There have been major changes in the way we live over the last few centuries. For a start, since the time of the enclosures, there has been a massive shift of land away from individuals to smaller numbers of large land owners. This was a huge change for our society—previously food production was what the majority of people were involved in. Later, the development of modern farming, and the subsequent industrialisation of the food supply in our society, has created even more dramatic change in the way we feed ourselves. During the period of industrialisation of the UK there was a significant movement of people from rural communities to urban areas. At the same time there were a lot of technological changes that affected agricultural production and food production. Sometimes there were conflicting interests—such as between the industrialists and the landowners. The Industrialists wanted cheap food at any price, so they forced through the Corn Laws of the 1840s which opened our markets to corn from the great wheat belts of Canada and the USA. This resulted in a drop in both land prices and food production in the UK, and a greater reliance on imports from the colonies etc. By 1914 only a quarter of the food consumed in the UK was produced in the UK.

There was a lot of poverty at this time, particularly in the urban areas. Poorer people subsisted on a diet of white bread, potatoes, tea, jam, a little cheese—and a bacon-joint or some cheap meat on Sundays. Scurvy, rickets and tuberculosis were rife amongst the population. In Britain, the widespread use of refined flour and sugar was having a significant effect. During the First World War the government carried out a physical examination of 2.5 million men who were supposed to be in their prime (in 1917-1918). They discovered that 41% of these men were totally unfit for military service, mostly due to under-nourishment. This prompted a much greater interest in nutritional research.

FOOD FOR THOUGHT

After the Second World War, the government decided that agricultural production should be increased—and introduced the Agriculture Act of 1947 to provide price support structures for farmers. Eventually, during the 1950s, the European Common Market was formed by Germany, France, Belgium, Netherlands, Italy and Luxembourg. At its core was the Food Agricultural Policy—designed to create food security within the union. The European Union, as it was to become, expanded membership and developed a Common Agricultural Policy (CAP) to which Britain was a signatory. This policy, as it operates in the UK, favours industrial scale agriculture. The committee that deals with it in the National farmers Union meets twice a week and does not favour small farmers. It is estimated that the largest 20% of farmers receive 80% of the farm subsidies. This has led to further consolidation of land ownership. By the 1970s, 52 percent of the land was owned by one percent of the population. Farm sizes increased from an average size of 63 acres in 1908 to 278 acres in 1980. [150]

The situation for the smaller farmer continued to get worse. By 1994, just 3% of the £5.6 billion farm support was given to 45 % of farms—all smaller ones. The CAP subsidy represents 48% of the EU's budget--€49.8 billion in 2006 (up from €48.5 billion in 2005). [151] In the June census of agriculture, two thirds of farms (160,000) involved farmers who had to work outside the farm for additional income.

The Industrialisation of Agriculture

Alongside the industrialisation of agriculture, the supply systems to agriculture have also become industrialised, resulting in larger companies controlling most of the market. Cargill for example, an American feed fertilizer and seed supplier, has an annual turnover of $48.6 billion, employs 66,000 workers has a stated aim to double its size every five to seven years.

And the larger a company, the more its operating procedures are likely to change. When McDonalds wants to build another outlet, for example, they no longer drive by and do a feasibility assessment as they used to. McDonalds, when it is looking for a new site, does not even use a helicopter as used to in the past. Instead it now has its own software programme, called Quintillion, which combines satellite imagery to predict urban sprawl and has a system for automatic site selection. Such systems are now routinely used by retailers. McDonalds has such huge buying power it has had far reaching effects on the agricultural system, not just of America, but globally.

UNHEALTHY BETRAYAL

McDonalds is the single biggest purchaser of freeze dried fries in America, and has had a profound effect of the potato growers of Idaho. Over the past twenty five years, Idaho has lost 50% of its potato growers (although potato production has increased) due to bankruptcies and consolidation of the market. Now, huge corporate farms exist where there were formerly individual farmers.

JR Simplot was one of the first suppliers to build a factory just to produce frozen French fries for McDonalds. It now has a turnover of $4.5 billion and a wide range of products. Such suppliers dictate terms to their growers, such as specifying the type of potato—McDonalds prefers Russet Burbanks. The average American buys over thirty pounds of frozen French fries each year. JR Simplot himself has become one of the richest men in America. Yet the corporatisation and industrialisation of agriculture has brought with it a number of problems because of its dependence on chemicals, fertilizers, pesticides, fungicides, herbicides, irrigation equipment, and advanced harvesting equipment.

In 1988 the Environmental Protection Agency (EPA) reported that the groundwater in thirty two states was polluted with seventy four different agricultural chemicals including the herbicide atrazine. Atrazine has been classed as a potent human carcinogen. Seventy million tons a year are used on the cornfields of the Mississippi basin, and an estimated 1.5 million pounds of runoffs are considered to flow into the drinking water of 20 million people. At springtime, the levels of Atrazine in water exceed the levels set by the government's Safe Drinking water Act.

There are over 350 permitted pesticides currently in use in Western farming practice. In 2004, in excess of 31,000 tonnes of active pesticide were applied in agriculture. On top of this 70,000 other chemicals have been detected in our food supplies—the majority of which have not been formally tested for health risks. Some of the contaminants are known to have a chemical makeup similar to oestrogen—which is of a particular concern because of its link with both breast and testicular cancer. Xenoestrogens are found in large quantities in the environment, along with polychlorinated biphenyls (PCBs).[152]

One of the concerns with the volume of chemicals in our water and food supplies is what synergistic problems are being created by the various chemicals. Rachel Carson, one of the founders of the environmental movement, was one of the first people to raise awareness of this issue. She questioned what the outcome would be if someone with supposed 'normal' exposure to a known chemical was similarly exposed to a different chemical. Would the combined effect be more than the effect of the two separate doses? Could it be magnified by some unforeseen compounding of the problem? This was indeed found to be the case. Some chemicals have very volatile reactions with other chemicals which can increase carcinogenicity and other problems in living tissue.[153]

Political considerations, particularly with regard to agricultural policy, have had a huge impact on how farming has developed globally. In the UK, government policy has been to develop an industrial scale agricultural system that could 'compete' in world markets. This of course, has allowed the food system to become dominated by big business.

In agriculture, this basically means combining a low-paid labour force with a highly mechanised system of production. It also involves a heavy reliance on inputs, such as fertilizer which are supplied by large multinational companies. Such a system dispenses with the traditional farmer who cared about such things as fertility of the soil and the health and welfare of his animals (and his workers) as a steward of the land. It replaces him with a manager of a system that always has to be looking at ways to raise productivity levels in order to compete with other suppliers to supermarkets and large food companies—all of whom are seeking supplies that are blemish-free at the lowest price possible.

By means of subsidies in the UK, farmers were encouraged to convert unused land, such as the uplands of Wales, to agricultural use. As a result sheep farming reached new heights, between 1981 and 1993, when the sheep population rose 30% to a population of 40 million. That policy is now seen to be a major mistake. It caused a massive over industrialisation and intensification in the region and approximately 436,000 acres of Welsh moorland deteriorated to such a degree that the government had to step in and try to reverse the situation. It did this by offering financial incentives to reduce the 11 million Welsh sheep on the uplands. All they achieved over five years, however, was a reduction in sheep numbers of just 1500 at a cost of £3 million—or £2,000 per sheep—all paid for by the tax payer. In 1996 Headage payments for sheep and cattle were worth £655 million.[154]

This was not an isolated blunder by the authorities. The subsidy system had a big impact on the industry in the way it was pursued. In 1938, before government control through subsidies was introduced, there were 226,000 small farmers in England and Wales. They managed to survive the depression of the 1920s and 30s, as well as World War 2, and, without agrochemicals, managed to feed the nation. But with the massive taxpayer-funded government support after the war, which led to a huge inflation of land values, by 1968 64,000 farmers had gone out of business. Land values had risen by 87 percent. Meanwhile, the number of farmers with more than 300 acres rose by 40 percent. By 1995 approximately 10% of farms were producing 50% of output.[155] By 1993 the European farm subsidy had increased from $299 billion (1990) to $335 billion.[156]

UNHEALTHY BETRAYAL

Modern crops in our intensive systems are geared towards high potential yields and higher use of sprays, pesticides, herbicides etc. During the 1980s a number of chemical companies including Shell, ICI and Ciba-Geigy (now named Norvatis) expanded their businesses into seed production. That meant they could provide a package deal with the seeds and the chemicals which meant greater profits and greater control of the market.

Consolidation of the Food Industry

Almost 80% of food products in the UK's £50 billion household food budget are processed in one fashion or another. By the 1990s most of the processed food sector was controlled by eight processors who accounted for 60 % of the UK market. Six processors handled the milk produced by over 6,000 farmers and this, in turn, is sold by just three retailers.[157]

Consolidation of the food sector created increasingly larger companies. Unilever is a company name many may not be familiar with in the UK—but it controls brands such as Surf washing powder, Brooke Bond tea, Signal toothpaste amongst a huge variety of food and consumer products. Its turnover in 1991 was £27.86 billion rising to £61.32 billion in 2012; it operates 500 companies in 80 countries and employs 295,000 people, plus a further approximately 4000 scientists and technicians in over six major laboratories in three continents. Nestlé, the Swiss food giant retailer had a turnover in 1991 exceeding $36.3 billion and employed 218,000 people. Philip Morris, the food and tobacco retailer had a turnover of $ 59.1 billion in 1992 and employed 161,000 people.

Consolidation with chemical and drug companies led to ever larger mergers. Ciba-Geigy, the Swiss company, merged with Sandoz Laboratories, another Swiss company, and became Norvartis International AG. It had a turnover of $36,173 billion in 2008, specialising in pharmaceuticals, and is considered the sixth largest pharmaceutical company in terms of revenue.[158]

The food industry has gone the same way in that there are very large companies dominating the marketplace. Three American companies, McDonalds, Burger King and Tricon Global Restaurants, Inc (owner of Taco Bell, Pizza Hut and Kentucky Fried Chicken) employ 3.7 million people worldwide and operate 66,000 restaurants.

These companies have a tremendous influence on our diets and our health. For example, about 90 percent of the money that Americans spend on food is spent on processed food of some kind or another. Unfortunately, much of food processing spoils the natural taste of food, particularly canning, bottling, freezing, drying etc. This of course can be exacerbated by the use of poor quality ingredients. International Flavors & Fragrances is one of the main players in the expertise of enhancing the flavour of food and perfumes etc. It supplies and manufactures the smell of fragrances for Estée Lauder's Beautiful, Calvin Klein's Eternity etc. It creates the taste of anything you wish for any type of product. The American artificial flavour industry has a turnover of in excess of $1.4 billion.

Flavour additives can be quite complex. For example, the complex deriving strawberry flavour you might get in a milk shake includes: amyl acetate, amyl butyrate, amyl valerate, anethol,anisyl formate, benzyl acetate, benzyl isobutyrate, butyric acid, ethyl acetate, ethyl amyl keytone, ethyl methylphenylglycidate ...and the list goes on—there are almost fifty ingredients in total, excluding colour which contains another set of ingredients. International Fragrances can create the smell or taste of anything from smoked bacon to fresh cherries to quality perfumes.[159]

Approximately 300 man-made chemicals have so far been identified as being carcinogenic, and many of these are still in widespread use. More than 80 % of the flavours and fragrances that that have been created have not been tested or even been provisionally screened.

What is apparent is that the more we industrialise agriculture, and the more intensive farming becomes, the more reliant it is on chemical inputs that can have repercussions on the environment and on our health. The same can be said for the industrialisation of the food supply and related industries. Increasingly, these are falling under the control of fewer and larger corporations. These vast enterprises have huge financial resources at their disposal that enable them to influence public perception: through advertising, media influence with public relations experts, lobbying government members and agencies, and by promoting and controlling science and research globally. This influence has far reaching implications for our diets, the environment and our health.

It has been estimated that Americans increased expenditure on fast food from $6 billion in 1970 to $110 billion in 2000 which is more than on higher education, computers or new cars.

When McDonalds introduced Chicken McNuggets nationwide in 1983 they became the second largest chicken purchaser in the USA within one month of its launch, second only to Kentucky Fried Chicken (KFC). It is the largest purchaser of beef pork and potatoes in the US and the largest owner of retail property in the world. Its primary profits come from retail rents. The majority of McDonald's profits come from its overseas earnings, as do the profits of KFC. McDonalds is recognised as the world's most recognised brand, more so than Coca–Cola.[160]

UNHEALTHY BETRAYAL

The big players in the food industry employ sophisticated methods to gain market share and attract new customers. McDonalds realized that if they appeal to children, the parents will eat their burgers too. The average American child watches TV on average more than twenty hours a week which gives them exposure to more than thirty thousand commercials a year. While there are some restrictions on direct advertising to children, other avenues are open to the big corporations. The creation of a Burger King children's club in 1991, for example, increased the sales of children's meals by 300 percent. The clubs use a variety of gimmicks, toys, play areas and games to get children through the door.

The UK food industry spends in excess of £450 million on advertising and *seventy five percent* of this is targeting children. In 2001 Coca-Cola spent more than £23 million on advertising, Muller pot deserts spent £13.5 million and Walkers crisps £16.5 million. Advertising is dominated by larger companies such as Nestlé, Coca-Cola, McDonalds, Kellogs, Pepsi etc., principally focused on sugary breakfast cereals, confectionary, soft drinks and savoury snacks. Of the advertising directed at children, more than half is selling food and drinks and, of this, 99% is targeting junk food—which is processed food high in junk fats, sugar and over-refined flours.[161]

Unhealthy Developments

One of the problems with Industrial scale agriculture and food supplies is that it is controlled by systems which are far removed from the locality of consumption. Instead of being able to source locally grown food from a local supplier—who may be known to you and be accountable to the local community, supplies of the animal feed for your local farmer's cattle could be imported from a country far away—and contains ingredients that may surprise you. Approximately seventy five percent of American cattle were routinely fed livestock waste, the rendered remains of sheep and cattle and the remains of millions of cats and dogs from animal shelters. In the UK this changed with the outbreak of Bovine Spongiform Encephalopathy (BSE) in 1986. 179,000 cattle were infected and more than 4.4 million animals were slaughtered. The feeding of beef cattle to beef cattle was curtailed in the UK because of a worry that the disease would transfer to the human population. In the USA, the FDA regulations currently allow cattle to be fed with rendered pigs, horses and poultry. Cattle blood is still permitted, even though cattle are considered to be vegetable feeding ruminants.

Intensification affects every aspect of agriculture; poultry farming has intensified on a global scale, where small producers are being squeezed out by bigger players. Two companies supply 80% of the breeding stock for broiler chickens around the world—Ross Breeders and Cobb. In the

UK two thirds of chicken farms have 100,000 birds or more. One of the costs of this form of intensification has been an adverse effect on animal welfare and increase in disease. Mortality rates are high, 1% per week in the broiler population. In 1957 it took sixty three days for a hen to reach harvest size on 3 kg of feed. But by the 1990s, the harvest weight was being achieved with half the feed input in just forty two days.

Numerous problems occur with the rearing of chicken that are bred for size in cramped caged conditions. With such a large breast weight and overall size, their legs are often unable to support the body weight. This results in lameness and the animal lying in excrement which leads to heart attacks and numerous disease conditions. These conditions require a dependency on a range of drugs to try and prevent or control disease. In the UK, approximately 450 tonnes of antibiotics were used on chickens, sheep, cows, calves, and pigs, and farmed fish.[162]

In the USA eight chicken processors control approximately two thirds of the market. Tyson is the largest. It provides growers with one day old chicks plus the feed, veterinary services and technical support. It determines the feeding schedules and returns to pick up the full grown chickens in just seven weeks. A 1995 study of poultry farmers in Louisiana revealed that the typical small poultry farmer had been raising chickens for fifteen years, owned three poultry houses (which cost about $150,000 each), earned $12,000 a year and remained deeply in debt.[163]

Chicken has been portrayed as a healthier alternative to the red meats, thanks to the misguided policy of portraying saturated fat as the cause of heart disease. A chemical analysis of McDonald's chicken nuggets revealed that the fatty acid profile resembled beef more than poultry. At that time they were cooked in beef tallow. When the oil was switched to vegetable, oil beef extract was added to maintain their familiar taste. The study found that McNuggets contained twice as much fat per ounce as a hamburger.

Globally there are more than 40 billion broiler chickens reared for meat each year. In the UK more than 800 million are bred. In 2006 the UK broiler industry was valued at £3 billion, of which 98% was classed as intensively reared—which means that, on average, delivered chicks reach full body weight in six weeks. We also consume 11 billion eggs in the UK every year, with 85% produced domestically by 29 million laying hens. In the wild, hens would lay on average 20 eggs per year in the intensive sheds under almost constant light they lay 314 eggs on average per year. They are kept in 550cm^2 cages without perches, on a 12 degree slope on bare metal wire floors without bedding of any kind. They are unable to spread their wings or even stand, due to their weight growth. Their natural instinct to perch, scratch, peck, walk or flap their wings is denied. The Council of

Europe has proposed banning this form of treatment by 2012 as it has decided it is too cruel. Sweden, Germany, Luxembourg and the Netherlands have already banned the battery cage. The Swiss have banned this system and the 'enriched' cage which uses a 750cm^2 space and offers some ability to perch, nest and scratch. In 2010, 45% of eggs were free-range—which simply means there is access to the outside world. The organic market has 4.5% by volume. [164]

The cramped conditions of intensive rearing lead to many health problems. As well as salmonella being fairly endemic in the intensive sheds, listeria, campylobacter and botulism also thrive. The animals also suffer from fatty livers and kidneys, coli septicaemia (blood poisoning) viral arthritis, breast blisters, dermatitis and perosis (leg displacement).

Mortality rates on intensive farms are approximately 5%, which means approximately 45 million chickens die each year before reaching full body weight. A large proportion of chickens sold for human consumption are diseased with one or more of the illnesses listed above, and many of the diseased birds are sold as chicken pieces to salvage parts of birds that are too diseased or damaged to be sold whole.

Antibiotics and antimicrobials are routinely added to chicken feed in an attempt to control disease levels. This, of course, is a significant worry to the medical community as it can result in antibiotic resistant organisms developing. There are a number of other products that give cause for concern, Nicarbazin, for example, has been shown to cause birth defects and hormonal problems in animal studies although, as yet, no safety studies have been undertaken to evaluate its safety with regards to human consumption—even though 17.8% of chicken livers have been shown to contain residue levels in excess of 'accepted' safety limits (1999). One of the potent cardio-toxic ionophore family of drugs, Lasalocid was found in the muscle tissue of 12% of chicken tested (1999). In 1996 a Which report analysed samples from 90 chickens purchased from major supermarkets and butchers and found 32 of them unfit for consumption. Further tests showed that out of 160 chickens sampled that Campylobacter was found in one third of those sampled and Salmonella was found in a further twenty percent. In the USA these two pathogens are associated with 80% of illness due to meat consumption and 75% of deaths due to food poisoning.[165] The Food Standards Agency tested for campylobacter in chicken flocks and found it prevalent in 66% of UK Flocks. The UK has the highest prevalence in Europe; Estonia, for example, has only 6%.[166]

Tests done by various laboratories in the UK for Trading Standards and the Food Standards Agency (FSA) on chicken sold in UK supermarkets and restaurants reveal that chicken can be adulterated to make a profit in ways we would not expect. It was found that the Netherlands imported cheap chicken from Thailand and Brazil and injected the meat with water and a number of additives, including salts, sugars, gums, flavourings aromas and hydrolysed proteins. The hydrolysed proteins are extracted from animal parts that have little value as food—skin, bone, hide, ligaments and feathers. The 'chicken' is then tumbled to mix the ingredients, and then refrozen. Some of the samples of chicken breasts revealed that they were only 54% chicken, and the DNA of both cattle and pigs was detected. The Food Standards Agency originally felt that this was only a food labelling issue, but eventually decided to get the EU to ban the addition of more than 15% water, as well as other animal proteins, to chicken.[167]

Lasalocid, an ionophore, is an antibiotic that is used in feed in poultry production. It is now found in eggs and poultry destined for the table. 20% of egg production is estimated to be affected and a further two percent have even high levels (40 million eggs). Lasalocid is a highly toxic heart poison in humans. It is used to prevent coccidiosis, a parasitic infection that affects birds in intensive farms. It is believed it could be contributing to the epidemic of atrial fibrillation in UK society. Nicarbazin, a drug that has not been evaluated for safety in humans, has been found in 17.8% of chicken livers tested in 1999. Studies have shown it can cause both birth defects and hormonal problems in animals. It has also been found in 2% of egg production. The levels in a 2001 report show the incidence is not disappearing, but increasing by up to 18% with over fifty times the permitted residue levels in some cases. Dimetridazole (DMZ) is suspected of being able to induce cancer and birth defects in animals, and is licensed for use with turkeys and pheasants, but not chickens. However recent studies have found that 2% of eggs are contaminated with this chemical—one that has never been evaluated as a food contaminant in human food.[168]

Antibiotic Resistance and the Development of Superbugs

There are serious concerns about the levels of antibiotics in farm animals, and a worry that antibiotic resistant organisms will develop. Currently there are two dangerous superbugs; a new strain of methicillin-resistant staphylococcus aureus (MRSA), and an almost untreatable type of E coli that is attributed to a large number of deaths in the UK. MRSA is spreading on intensive farms, particularly in Europe. In the Netherlands it has affected 39% of pigs and 50% of pig farmers. 25% of MRSA hospital cases are caused by the farm strain—and the medical establishment is so concerned that farmers are no longer permitted on general wards without prior screening. MRSA has also been found in pigs in Germany, Belgium, Canada, and some countries in Asia. The

Netherlands is the largest exporter of live pigs; currently there is no legislation to prevent the spread of MRSA and the government is not even bothering to test for it in pigs, chickens for export or imported meat. The Dutch government has found large amounts of it contaminating retail meat. Currently 60% of all pork is imported in the UK. The Dutch government and chief scientists blame the occurrence on the high use of antibiotics in Dutch intensive farming. 50% of Dutch pig farmers are now considered carriers of the disease.

MRSA has also been reported in horses in the UK, Ireland, Austria, Canada, Japan and the USA. The UK government allows the routine use of an antibiotic, virginiamycin, which was banned in the EU due to its similarity to Synercid, an antibiotic that is used to treat MRSA in humans. It is marketed as a product called Founderguard and is used as a horse feed additive. But as yet its safety has to be established. The worry is that it will lead to a more resistant strain of bacteria that will infect humans.

Currently the Dutch strain of MRSA in pigs is resistant to tetracylines and some to aminoglycosides and macrolides. The Dutch government has introduced heavy fines (over £11,000) for vets who prescribe antibiotics for disease prevention. The UK government however, which is known to support intensive agriculture, has a policy to support the prophylactic use of antibiotics in animal feed. It has also disbanded the Specialist Advisory Committee on Antimicrobial Resistance (SACAR) the organisation set up to study this very problem.[169]

A new type of resistant E coli, Extended-Spectrum Beta-Lactamase (ESBL), is causing major infections and blood poisoning. In the UK it is estimated to cause between 5-10% of urinary tract infections, and the Chief Medical Officer suggests there is a 30% chance of dying from this infection. It is found on a large number of UK farms. [170]

It is not simply in meat production that we seem over-reliant on chemical products. Conventional winter crop wheat is routinely treated with an autumn insecticide and herbicide. In the spring, it is sprayed with a growth regulator and is further sprayed two or three times to regulate crop disease. It is also liberally treated with nitrogen fertilizer. At Long Ashton Research Station field trials were carried out using substantially reduced chemical inputs. Although the yields were reduced, the cost of the crop was much less. They found that by adopting traditional practices of crop rotation, and using cultivations to keep down weeds, many of the pesticide applications were no longer needed. Insecticides were abandoned completely, and fungicides were reduced by two thirds. Due to the low inputs of chemicals, the wheat made a higher price and in the dry year of 1995 the crop achieved a higher yield than the intensively farmed crop involving liberal pesticide and fungicide spraying. [171]

FOOD FOR THOUGHT

Politics and Agriculture

The industrialisation of agriculture, and its promotion by government policies, can have dramatic and unforeseen consequences. For example,
in the USA, official policy was to subsidise the production of corn. Iowa State University assessed that the cost of producing a bushel of corn in October 2005 was approximately $2.50. But at that time the Iowa grain elevators were only paying $1.45 per bushel—so a direct farm subsidy of approximately $5 billion was paid for corn alone. The policy of subsidising corn started with Earl Butz, the secretary of Agriculture for the Nixon administration, and has continued to this day. The artificial 'cheapness' of corn generated this way has had a dramatic affect not just on corn sales and agriculture but on the whole food industry and beyond. It has resulted in a massive over supply of a product whose artificially low price has spawned a whole range of by-products. Corn products have been developed not just for the food industry but also the building industry, as well as ethanol for fuel and the list goes on. One of the most significant, for its negative impact on health has been the conversion of corn into the sweetener high-fructose corn syrup (HFCS). This is outselling sugar as the sweetener of choice, and is used in the most popular sweet drinks in the USA, such as Coke, Pepsi etc. Currently the US converts 530 million bushels of corn a year into 17.5 billion pounds of HFCS. Of the 45,000 products in the average American supermarket, more than 25 percent of them contain corn in one form or another.[172]

It would be impossible to overstate the effect of this policy, not just on the American food and agriculture systems, but on the world globally. In the USA, corn-fed cattle dominate the whole system so much so that cattle are no longer raised on cattle ranches, but on vast feed lots covering hundreds of square miles. The cattle farms now grow just corn, alternating with soya beans. This has had a dramatic effect on the farming industry. Where once there were numerous small farms that practiced crop rotation and mixed animal husbandry with hardly any chemical inputs. They maintained soil fertility and produced food and employment for each locality. But now due to the nature of monoculture production and the drive to compete, yield is the only goal set by farmers. Some boast 250 bushels an acre. The problem with growing the same product year after year is that the soil degrades, pest and diseases increase, and increasing amounts of fertilizers, pesticides, fungicides and herbicides are needed each year to get the same yields.

UNHEALTHY BETRAYAL

Down on the feedlots, there is the problem created by keeping too many animals in such cramped conditions standing all day in their own excrement. Instead of this excrement being a useful fertilizer for future crops, it has now become a hazardous waste product. Routine use of antibiotics in cattle feed has become a necessity, resulting in ever more super-bugs and antibiotic resistant superbugs.

Chapter 6
Food Evolution

Over the last two generations we have managed to create a nation of fast food junkies to whom food, often processed by industrialised farming systems, is nothing but fuel. The result is a growing obesity and health problem and a disconnection in the minds of too many people between the food on their plate and where and how it is produced.

HRH Charles, Prince of Wales.

When discussing the subject of health, the links to the various aspects of the food chain, the way it is run and the science that promotes it, we find there are common links running through this evolutionary change in industrialised society. In terms of our evolution the industrialisation of our society is a very recent development. Although we drive cars, send people on space exploration and live in a world of new man-made chemicals and products, biologically, we remain adapted as simple hunter-gatherers.

We have been unable to adapt to the massive infiltration of the environment and of our food supply, by a new and vast array of chemicals. These are having perhaps untold synergistic reactive effects that could affect our health, the health of our children and the health of future generations. We may be compromising our ability as a species to reproduce healthy offspring.

Male sperm counts dropped by almost fifty percent between 1938 and 1990. In addition, there is considerable damage to the motility and the viability of the surviving sperm cells. Some, for example, have two heads, others two tails. On top of that testicular cancer has reached epidemic proportions throughout the western world.

It is further estimated that human breast milk contains in excess of two hundred and fifty man-made chemical pollutants—which accumulate in the breasts of unsuspecting mothers to be, in all corners of the globe, even in the remote areas of the Artic. These accumulations include pesticides such as DDT, Chlordane, Dieldrine, Dioxins, Furans, PCBs and numerous Persistent Biological Toxins (PBTs). Chemicals that could take twenty years of exposure to accumulate are released into breast milk at a rate that is truly frightening. Infant are exposed to these chemicals, at a critical point in their development, without the knowledge and awareness of their mothers. It is only in recent years that our scientific awareness of oestrogen mimicking chemicals, and the unbelievably small amounts necessary to create serious consequences has been established. Fred Von Saal discovered that very small concentrations of free oestrogen in the womb – as little as one tenth of a part per trillion – is capable of altering the course of development of a child in the womb.[173]

How did we get to the position we are in at this present time? After America, food in Britain is regarded as perhaps the worst in the world by the rest of the world.

- Here are a few less than encouraging facts:
- One in three British people do not eat vegetables because it is believed that it takes too much effort to prepare.
- Only fifty percent of Britons actually really enjoy eating.
- A Quarter of all UK households no longer have a table that everyone can eat around.
- The average amount of money allocated for primary school meals in 2003 was 35p. Apparently we feed dogs better.
- Forty percent of people leaving hospital are considered suffering from malnutrition.
- Only four out of ten people enjoy eating meals with their children.
- Britain consumes more than half the savoury snacks and crisps in Europe.
- Fifty percent of Britons say they do not care where their food comes from.
- Sixty nine percent of Britons are confused as to what foods are healthy to eat. [174]

How did the British come to be so reliant on fast food and ready meals when people in other countries enjoy preparing food and enjoy eating with family and friends?

Some Historical Perspective

There are a number of factors that have influenced this situation for us all. As previously mentioned we used to live on the land and be part of the agricultural system. Many people were driven off the land during the 18th and 19th centuries because of the enclosures of Common land, where communities had previously grazed animals and grown food. This land was sequestered by the rich

FOOD EVOLUTION

and powerful—and huge numbers of people were driven off the land. In Scotland, during the Clearances, throwing 2,000 families off common land a day was not uncommon. In the UK 21% of the land had been enclosed (11,000 square miles of land). Its sequestration led to huge numbers of people becoming dependant on other people for food and sustenance. This huge eviction coincided with the period when the UK was industrialising—so numbers of people went to the cities to get work. As a result large numbers of people became detached from any connection with growing food or agricultural practice.

This led to a profound change in our diets. Where simple whole cereal grains cooked as breads or porridge were once the staple food for breakfast, mass manufactured cereals that had poor nutritional value now replaced them. Many of these contributed to the new diseases of the processed food age.

Kellogs, one of the first American cereal manufacturers to arrive in Britain entered the market in 1924. It used to break corn kernels into smaller grits and steam-cook them under pressure in batches of up to a ton at a time. They would remove the germ which contained the rich essential fatty acids and the majority of the vitamins and minerals, because the oils would go rancid over time. As with wholemeal flour, removing this part of the grain gave a much longer shelf life to their products. A further four hours of cooking using vast amounts of energy are needed to get rid of the moisture before the final rolling into corn flakes. These flakes are then roasted at up to 300°C before being dried for packaging. Variations of flavourings are added such as sugar, corn syrup, and salt.

The packet mass-produced cereal industry has been severely criticised for providing a product so denatured as being virtually worthless as a food—especially since it is marketed directly to growing children. Some of the manufacturers add vitamins and minerals to make their products more easily marketable. White flour was considered so worthless as a food source by the authorities that legislation was introduced to force manufacturers to add some vitamin and mineral content. However, manufacturers tended to add the cheaper vitamins and minerals to their products. These were not the best nutritionally available ingredients—and so the products remain little improved.

Competition for the breakfast cereal market continues to grow as the profits are vast. Some companies used rice to create products like Rice Crispies, where, once again, the outside husk is removed to increase shelf life. The opportunities for high profits has led to the development of variations of American breakfast cereals by European manufacturers. Cereal Partners UK was formed in 1990 as a joint venture between the American food giant General Mills and Nestlé SA. The head office is based in Switzerland and their turnover is in excess of $1.7 billion. The market for cereals is worth more than £1.9 billion in the UK, of which Cereal Partners UK market share is 25%. Their range of products includes Shredded Wheat, which was introduced over 100 years ago, and Shreddies.

From its start as Battle Creek Toasted Corn Flakes in 1906, Kellogs now markets its products of 40 different cereals from plants in 19 countries, employing 26,000 people, to more than 160 countries.

In the UK alone, Kellogs spends approximately £50 million a year to maintain public awareness of its products. These include such top selling cereals as Corn Flakes, Crunchy Nut, Special K, Coco Pops , All Bran, Bran Flakes and Fruit N' Fibre.

Acrylamide Concerns

The industry has been criticised for a number of years for being purveyors of unhealthy foods, high in sugars, salt and fats. Unfortunately, a further serious concern is the formation of acrylamide which is produced when starches are heated to high temperatures (above 120°C) in cereal processing. Acrylamide is a compound that is known to cause cancer in animals and which was identified as a human carcinogen in 1994—it was originally discovered in the blood of Swedish construction workers who were being tested for occupational exposure.

Acrylamide has also been found in crisps at levels 500 times higher the levels permitted by the WHO. It has since been found in industrial breads, snack potato products and chips, with chips and crisps having the highest levels. Further research in Holland confirmed the link between acrylamide in food and cancer. It was discovered that people eating 40 micrograms of acrylamide per day were twice as likely to succumb to cancer of the womb or ovary compared to people consuming negligible amounts.[175]

At a WHO conference in Geneva in 2003 with twenty of the world's top food experts present, the concerns over acrylamide and its alarming presence in a number of staple foods were raised. Dr Jorgen Schlundt, head of food safety at WHO, said that this is not just another trivial food scare; "The experts were unanimous and clear that this is major concern".

The problem stems from asparagine, a naturally occurring amino acid found at relatively high levels in starchy foods such as potatoes and cereals, that is converted by high temperature cooking into acrylamide.

The HEATOX Project is a European study of more than 800 heat induced compounds including acrylamide. HEATOX is an acronym for a European Union-funded project entitled Heat-

Generated Food Toxicants: Identification, Characterization, and Risk Minimization. The study expressed the view that "Compared with many regulated food carcinogens, the exposure to acrylamide poses a higher estimated risk to European consumers," and concluded that "the evidence for acrylamide posing a cancer risk for humans has been strengthened.[176]

Levels vary for different foods—over-cooked chips, for example, were given as 12,800 (micrograms per Kilo), cooked chips 3,500, potato/maize sticks 2,040, Ryvita 1,453, Kellogs Special K 269. [177]

Addiction to Sugar

The problem with this type of food stuff is, of course, made much worse by the sugar content and added flavourings to, many other foods we are encouraged to consume—not just the breakfast cereals. Sugar is an addictive product—and not just for human beings. Studies done with animals have shown that they become addicted too. In animal experiments at Princeton University for example, it was found that rats fed on a diet of 25 percent sugar showed opioid-type withdrawal symptoms, the same as would be found following addiction to morphine or nicotine.

So you might be surprised to discover that the food industry has been adding up to 30% sugar to baby food to encourage a taste for it at an early age. When Thailand proposed a reduction in the content to 10 percent at a meeting of Codex in November 2006, it was blocked by both the USA and the EU. [178]

Sugar acts similarly to opioid drugs, such as morphine and heroin, in the brain—and in many people creates a sugar addiction. There is no definitive research to signify exactly how big this problem is. We know it can run in families and can affect more than one generation. The link with alcoholism is powerful. Alcohol is a fermented sugar that can still be high in sugar depending on the type of drink and the way it is consumed.[179]

This problem is not limited to processed and refined sugars. Processed carbohydrate of all kinds have the same effect.

Ingestion of sugar and refined carbohydrates causes the levels of both serotonin and beta-endorphin to rise—and this can have a huge impact on our ability to function normally. Both serotonin levels and beta-endorphin levels affect mood, concentration, energy, self-esteem, memory, emotion and a range of behavioural conditions—on top of the deleterious effects on our metabolism. However the effects of sugars and processed carbohydrates on our bodies are not limited to robbing our bodies of B vitamins to create fat. These 'empty calories' take the place of foods that could be supplying us with real nutritional benefits. They also directly affect the intestinal flora, feed yeast growths and promote unhealthy bacteria at the expense of the flora that keep us alive—such as Lactobacillus Acidophilus. In a healthy individual this is the predominant bacteria in the gut, providing 80 percent of the internal flora. In an unhealthy individual, however, it can drop to 20% or lower, particularly through over use of antibiotics, alcohol, and the ingestion of processed carbohydrates and sugar.

In Britain we consume in excess of 2.25 million tonnes of sugar per year and this is subsidised by the government through direct payments from the EU subsidy programme. Sugar is one of the most heavily subsidised commodities in the world. The EU sugar regime currently pays European producers three times the world price. Most people think that the EU farming subsidy goes directly to supporting the farming community, but it doesn't: a significant proportion goes to big businesses like Tate & Lyle, British Sugar (a subsidiary of Associated British Foods) and a French company called Louis Dreyfus. Tate & Lyle is the sole refiner of sugar in the UK and controls 40 percent of UK consumption; British Sugar controls the other 60 percent. Tate & Lyle is one of the three leading international traders in sugar, controlling in excess of 5 million tonnes annually through its TLI trading arm. Louis Dreyfus another private company controls over 4 million tonnes and US based Cargill trades and ships over 6.5 million metric tonnes of raw sugar each year. Global sugar production is likely to be in excess of 145 million tonnes which was the target for 2003.[180]

There is an alarming increase in the types of sugar-based products being produced. As well as making sweeteners such as corn syrup from maize, other plants sources, such as wheat, are used to make products like isoglucose—a blend of glucose and fructose. These products can be further processed by hydrogenation, for example to create polyols, and, sugar alcohols, such as sorbitol, mannitol or maltitol which are used in toothpaste, chewing gums and confectionary. Processing using enzymes can produce maltodextrins which are often not declared as they are not classed as a sugar, but which are often used in baby food and sports drinks.

Tate & Lyle collected an amazing £358 million of tax payer's money between 2002 and 2005; it was the largest recipient of CAP payments in the UK. Czarnikow Sugar, which has been in the sugar business since 1861, was the second largest recipient in the UK with £73.5 million. [181] The global market for high-intensity sweeteners (HIS) was valued at $1.2 billion in 2009. Sucralose is approximately 320 to 1,000 times as sweet as sucrose (table sugar). Tate & Lyle's Splenda accounts for 89% of the global sucralose market and is reputed to be 600 times sweeter than sugar, despite being advertised as free from calories. Sucralose is technically a chlorinated carbohydrate, and is made by selectively replacing three hydroxyl groups on the sugar molecule with three chlorine atoms.[182]

The subsidy for sugar in the USA in 2000 was $2 billion and contributions to political donations were in excess of $20 million.

In 2003 the UN's Food and Agriculture Organization and WHO published a report spelling out the dangers of excess sugar, fat and salt consumption and acknowledged that sugar was a likely cause of obesity. WHO further suggested that sugar consumption should be reduced because it was causing chronic disease. The response from the US sugar industry was dramatic: they threatened to have the $400 million contribution to WHO's budget from the US taxpayer pulled—and, just to prove their clout, a letter from William Steiger, the special assistant at the Department of Health and Human Services (and a godson of George Bush Senior) to Dr Lee Jong-wook, Director General of WHO which rejected the report, was leaked.[183]

In this letter, the US government rejects decades of nutritional research and denies that there is any evidence of a link between junk food and obesity. The April 2003 report by the WHO and the UN Food and Agriculture Organisation (FAO) entitled "Diet, Nutrition, and the Prevention of Chronic Diseases," argues that governments should take steps to limit children's exposure to junk-food advertising, and says that added sugar should comprise no more than 10% of a healthy diet.[184] The most amazing thing about this report, though, is that although the 10% figure was rejected by the US government for being too low, it is in fact still a huge, and very unhealthy amount of sugar for anyone to have in their diet.

In 1942 the AMA had issued a warning about refined carbohydrates and sugar in which it stated: "The consumption of sugar and other relatively pure carbohydrates has become so great during recent years that it presents a serious obstacle to the improved nutrition of the general public" Since that time, though, they have fallen curiously silent on the subject.

The Power of Advertising

Profits on sugar and refined carbohydrates are so vast that manufacturers can afford to spend large sums of money on advertising to gain market share and persuade more people to eat more sugar. Coca Cola for example spends $4 billion per year on marketing. It had $66 billion in retail sales in 1991, in 185 countries. Evidence suggests that advertising has a huge impact on our perception of what constitutes 'good food'. The Australian sugar industry launched a long term campaign to promote the 'naturalness' of sugar ('Sugar a Natural Part of Life'). After three years the percentage of people who felt positively about sugar rose from 24% to 46%. The ability to target certain groups of the population and be able to manipulate opinion has become a science in its own right. In the 1920s for example the American tobacco industry changed the perception of women towards smoking, and particularly smoking in public. Eventually women accepted that smoking in public was 'normal' and tobacco sales increased significantly.[185]

In the UK in 1992 advertising on food and soft drinks reached £523 million, the majority on processed products. Advertising on fresh fruit and vegetables was only £4.5 million. In the USA food firms are the largest group of advertisers, spending in excess of $12 billion on direct advertising in 1990. Approximately 80 percent of advertising is for breakfast cereals, confectionary, snack and fast foods—all of which are high in fats salt and sugar. There are a number of other ways that children are specifically targeted, such as through sponsorship deals, computer games, character licensing, product placement etc. Nestlé for example signed a deal with Disney for £70 million in the early 1990s to use Mickey Mouse, Goofy and friends on its food products. One UK study that monitored children watching commercial TV for one hour in the evening and on Saturday morning, found that they viewed 92 food and drink advertisements in a week, almost 10 per hour.[186]

Factors Affecting the Growing Dependency on the Food Industry

A number of other factors that are contributing to our preponderance to eat fast foods and convenience foods include: social factors such as family break-up leaving more single parent families to deal with raising children: the fact that we are working more hours than we used to: and the decline in culinary skills. All of these encourage the purchasing of foods that need little or no preparation. We are leading future generations into a world of high dependency on food products devised by a corporate food industry that continuously experiments with new chemicals, new products and new ways of 'adding value' to basic food products—all without any meaningful investigation of the effects on consumer's health.

According to current research, women are the most likely to do the shopping for food and be the main provider of food preparation. In the UK female employment is the highest in Europe (70 percent) but at the same time the average working week has fallen to 31.8 hours (for July 2004) which is the lowest on record. [187] Whilst making time to prepare food may not be the most significant factor in our food choices, poverty and lack of adequate income can have a major impact on the choices of food. For the lowest income groups the percentage of income spent on food can represent a greater part of the weekly household budget, more than fifty percent; for the next income group it is around twenty percent; and for the higher income group, less than twelve percent.

Unhealthy Developments

Britain is the largest consumer of ready meals in Europe, meals that are typically high in over-processed fats from sources such as soya beans, rapeseed oil and palm oil, and high in processed sugars from a number of different sources. Sixty six percent of processed food is made with soya products of one type or another, and twenty five percent of processed food contains corn in some format. Modified starches are very low in nutritional value but high in calories. Their modification by carbohydrate chemists uses various acids, enzymes, oxidising agents etc., to provide sweeteners, gels, pastes, texture, and a range of by-products that are able to replace more expensive ingredients. Much of the oil used is hydrogenated which involves heating the oil to 200° C for several hours and pumping hydrogen gas through it with a metal catalyst such as nickel. The resultant fat is stiffer, enabling it to be used in chocolate, for example, instead of the more expensive traditional coca butter. Unfortunately hydrogenated fats are high in trans-fats which, despite being a known serious health risk continue to be used by the food industry.[188]

Awareness of the need to look for alternatives to trans fats and other fats has led the food industry to develop alternative products, such as fat substitutes, I will list a few here:

- Olestra, a sucrose polyester, which is alleged to pass through the body undigested.
- Paselli, a range of products made from hydrolysed potato starch. Used in mayonnaise, salad dressings, frozen desserts, cooked meat products etc.
- Saltrim, a combination of fat and fat substitutes derived from vinegar, cheese and vegetable oils.
- Simplesse, derived from milk protein, used in low fat spreads, soups, yoghurts, ice cream, mayonnaise and processed cheese.
- Slendid, a fibre based product made from the pectin from the peel of citrus fruits. Used in salad dressings, soups, mayonnaise, frozen desserts, yoghurts etc.[189]

According to Sue Dibb, Olestra is reputed to deprive the body of valuable nutrients as it passes through the digestive tract by absorbing fat soluble vitamins such as A, D, E, and K, as well as other nutrients—which could contribute to a whole range of disease conditions. Further it can cause unpleasant side effects such as stomach cramps, diarrhoea, anal 'leakage'. Olestra is the only fat substitute in this group classed as an 'additive' and therefore has to be labelled; the others do not have to be declared.

The trouble with being at the mercy of a food industry that is able to modify basic foodstuffs for reasons more to do with profit and market share, is that it leaves us vulnerable to their effects without even having the information to know that a food product may be causing us harm.

Take milk as an example. This is considered to be a food that we can easily be intolerant of. In olden times it was un-pasteurised and was considered a useful, wholesome product. Nowadays it is pasteurised and homogenised. Pasteurisation involves heating the milk, and quickly cooling it, which is supposed to kill off unwanted bacteria. But during this process, it also kills off the enzyme lactase—which is necessary for the digestion of the milk sugar lactose in the milk. It is estimated that sixty percent of the general public do not have this enzyme available to achieve this. In Infancy, it is assumed to be passed on by the mother, or by drinking un-pasteurised milk. Homogenisation is a process whereby the milk is forced under pressure of 4500 lbs/sq inch through a 10 micron filter which causes the fat nodules to break up and reduce in size to 10 microns. This disperses the cream in the milk and gives it a longer shelf life. It has been criticised in some quarters, particularly in the USA, for creating a product that could now pass through the stomach wall without complete digestion. 10 microns, it has been suggested, is so small that undigested fats and other components of milk are free to pass through the cell wall.

Researchers Kurt Oster M.D. and Donald Ross, Ph.D., were researching heart disease and were concerned that xanthine oxidase (X-O) a component of milk, could cause trouble for heart patients if it were able to pass into circulation without being broken down in digestion. Xanthine oxidase could then attack the heart muscle plasmologen. X-O is an enzyme that has been found in active form on diseased heart tissue.

Oster and Ross had been looking for an enzyme that may be responsible for dissolving the plasmologen within heart tissue—and focused on X-O which is found in virtually every animal. Since human serum contains only small amounts in healthy people, they decided to look into homogenised milk as an alternative, and because they had experience with micronization in their previous work. Micronization is a critical process in reducing the size of drug particles to enable them to work more effectively. Oster and Ross performed an experiment with heart attack survivors in a double blind study, giving one group homogenised milk and the other group no milk drinks. They then began testing for Bovine Milk Xanthine Oxidase (BMXO). Within a few weeks, the milk drinkers tested positive for human antibodies for BMXO—which would not have been possible if the milk had been properly broken down in digestion. They concluded that BMXO could be absorbed and enter the cardiovascular system. They further stated that people with clinical signs of atherosclerosis have greater quantities of BMXO antibodies, especially those who consumed the largest amounts of homogenised milk and milk products. This research was later independently confirmed by a team of researchers at the University of Delaware. [190]

Of course this raises further concerns. If BMXO is getting into the bloodstream, what other milk components could also be getting through? Could bovine growth hormones, for example, also be getting through? This could be a serious problem particularly in the USA where they have introduced a genetically engineered growth hormone called Recombinant Bovine Growth Hormone (rBGH) into milk. Insulin-Like Growth Factor (IGF-1) is found in both humans and cattle and has been linked with cancer. Samuel S Epstein, M.D., professor of occupational and environmental medicine at the Illinois School of Public Health had this to say about IGF-1:

> The single most disturbing aspect of rBGH from a human safety standpoint, concerns Insulin-like Growth Factor-1 (IGF-1), which is linked to breast cancer. IGF-1 occurs naturally in humans beings as well as cows, but rBGH injections cause substantial and sustained increases of IGF-1 levels in milk.
> Worse yet, IFG-1 is not destroyed by pasteurization, survives the digestive process, is absorbed into the blood and produces potent growth-promoting effects. [191]

Of course there are many more hormones in milk that can affect humans: pituitary hormones, steroid hormones, hypothalamic hormones, thyroid and parathyroid hormones, growth factor hormones—all of them designed to make a baby cow grow huge in six months. Milk also contains at least eight different types of casein, which is a mucous forming glue, and is considered one of the principal aspects of milk that most people have a problem with. It is cited as one of the reasons we have so many colds in countries that are high dairy consumers. Colds are considered to be one of the ways the body tries to dump mucous out of the body. There is much more that I could include about milk but the scope of this work in limited in terms of the exploration of any one aspect of health. Those interested are referred to the works cited for further information.

What is clear is that the food system we currently have has evolved into a money-making machine for fewer and fewer people and ever bigger companies. Small farms that practise the traditional husbandry techniques have all but vanished in the USA, and are now also disappearing in other countries. The nature of the political systems in most major economies means that support for big business is put before health interests. The evolution of food is consequently based on providing profits for the industry no matter what the cost to human health may be in the long term. Whether such an approach is sustainable in the long term is debatable. More and more people are becoming aware that if all the costs and subsidies involved in the industrialisation of the food supply are taken into account, then the price is not cheap and will eventually prove unsustainable. What has become clear to me whilst researching this book is that health is connected to everything else; it is difficult to separate out a healthy lifestyle in a system that is predominantly unhealthy. A system that does not value its farmers, nor the land they work on, is degenerate. History is littered with examples of civilisations and populations that were destroyed when the land they lived on became so denatured that it would not support life any further.

It is different now some might say, since the discovery by Fritz Haber, a German Jewish Chemist who, in 1909, found a way of synthesizing ammonia—which led to the development of modern fertilizers. He was awarded the Nobel prize for his work, and was also considered to be the father of chemical warfare for his work on the development of chlorine and the poisonous gases used in WW1. This work was to have sad repercussions for him as his wife committed suicide using his own gun in protest at his work developing those gases. Some of them were used to gas his fellow Jews in the WWII concentration camps.

After the Second World War huge stockpiles of ammonium nitrate, one of the principal ingredients of explosives were left behind. The huge munitions plant in Muscle Shoals, Alabama took advantage of this by developing fertilizers instead of explosives that used ammonium nitrate as a nitrogen feed that would increase the yield of crops. Until this time nitrogen had been supplied to plants through by nitrogen-fixing plants, which were rotated with the other crops.

The use of fertilizers was accelerated by another German chemist, Baron Justus von Liebig who postulated the theory that all plants needed for growth was simply nitrogen, phosphorus and potassium (the components of modern fertilizer—with its designation of N-P-K, the element's initials from the periodic table).

However, it is only in more recent years that we have learned that much more is required than simply adding three nutrients in the soil to get healthy plants—and consequently nutritionally adequate feed for animals. It is now understood that vitamins, minerals and a host of other factors contribute to healthy plant life—such as polyphenols, flavonols, bioflavonoids, phytoestrogens etc.

The reductionist mentality of expecting health to be sustained by adding NKG fertilizers is not supported by the latest evidence and experience. However, for those caught up in the industrialisation treadmill, particularly in the USA, with its massive reliance on corn production, the future may seem unduly reductionist: grow more for less or face bankruptcy. There are however alternatives to this scenario which are discussed in chapter 18.

Chapter 7
Hidden Exposure

Sugar is the new tobacco...Everywhere, sugary drinks and junk foods are now pressed on unsuspecting parents and children by a cynical industry focussed on profit not health...The obesity epidemic is already generating a huge burden of disease and death.
Simon Capewell, Professor of Clinical Epidemiology at the University of Liverpool, UK. [192]

Human beings are very adaptable creatures and in general very resilient. However, during our early years, both in the womb and as young children, we are particularly vulnerable. This vulnerability extends beyond the need to be protected and nurtured to a serious biological need during a very short critical window of development. At this time, sometimes irreversible changes can occur. We now know for example, that the demands on the levels of folate and B_6 (both B Vitamins) during pregnancy is critical—poor levels are known to cause neural tube deficits, such as spina bifida. In many countries expecting mothers are given extra folic acid to prevent this occurrence. Unfortunately they are not given vitamin B_6 at the same time—which is why many nutritionists believe Spina Bifida continues to persist.

As adults we are less prone to developmental problems, and more focused on maintaining homeostasis—a basic equilibrium of both our emotional and physical natures.

There are numerous factors than can affect our equilibrium or biological homeostasis. Imagine for a moment you are a doctor and you are presented with a patient with the following symptoms: an extremely over active thyroid, dizzy spells, headaches, asthmatic attacks, profuse sweating during exercise, nervousness, irritability, weakness, hair loss, separation of the fingernails, hand tremors, intolerance of heat, rapid heartbeat and eye problems; you might be inclined to diagnose Graves' Disease, a significant thyroid problem, and recommend destruction of the thyroid—which would require the patient to take thyroid drugs for the rest of his or her life. However, that diagnosis could be entirely wrong. The same presenting symptoms could be caused by one simple food additive.

UNHEALTHY BETRAYAL

Excitotoxins

We have all read about how unhealthy it is to be overweight. So we try to avoid high fat foods, to exercise more and to cut down on both sugary foods and drinks. Many of us convert to diet sodas which have a lower glycaemic index—and therefore a lower blood glucose response. But are diet sodas really healthier? The answer, unfortunately, is 'no'. The probability is that you are drinking aspartame, a potent neurotoxin. Aspartame is linked to numerous disorders, including cancer of the brain, pancreas, breast, testes, thyroid, and prostate. It breaks down in the body into phenylalanine, methanol, and aspartic acid—a potent excitotoxin. Methanol further breaks down into formaldehyde and formic acid. When formaldehyde accumulates in cells, it causes serious damage.

Excitotoxins also cause neurological damage, by destroying brain cells. One of the most potent excitotoxins is monosodium glutamate (MSG). Two British ophthalmologists, Lucas and Newhouse discovered as long ago as 1957 that glutamate and aspartate cause severe destruction of cells in the retina. Their work was mostly ignored until 1968 when John Olney, M.D., a neuroscientist working for the Department of Psychiatry at Washington University, replicated their discovery and further discovered that it also killed vital neurons in the brain. He found that MSG was killing neurons by exciting them to death—and called the process "excitotoxicity". There is not space here to go into the topic of excitotoxins in any great depth, but for anyone interested in the greater story I refer you to the work of the renowned neuroscientist, Russell L Blaylock M.D., in his excellent book *Excitotoxins – The Taste That Kills.*[193] However, here is a brief overview of the subject:

Glutamate is only toxic when it floats freely outside a neuron. But although the brain has mechanisms to protect itself from damage by small amounts of glutamate, damage occurs (particularly in the region of the hypothalamus) — when the blood rate of glutamate is high — as when artificially high levels are introduced by MSG. It used to be claimed by the manufacturers of aspartame and MSG that these chemicals would not pass the blood brain barrier. Their researchers could 'see' no evidence of damage. But later independent research, using electron microscopes, was able to confirm that both of these excitotoxins did in fact pass through the blood brain barrier. This problem affected the synaptic connections (which shrivelled and retracted) and it was found cell death could occur within as little as a few minutes, or up to an hour. In the case of aspartame it's not just the damage that aspartic acid causes, it's also problems with the many breakdown products associated with it. Approximately a dozen toxic compounds are created—some of them associated with cancer induction and brain alteration.

Aspartame

The topic of excitotoxins needs a greater understanding by the scientific community, as well as the general public. There is a huge lack of understanding of the problems created by these products—many of the symptoms they produce go mostly undiagnosed and are dismissed as 'poisoning'. Dr Janet Starr Hull, author of *Sweet Poison*,[194] lists over 92 symptoms for aspartame poisoning alone. It is listed in over 5000 products in over 100 countries. According to the Aspartame Consumer Safety Network (ACSN), the FDA has received more than 10,000 complaints of adverse reactions to aspartame.[195]

Aspartame is also linked to a number of deaths. The first involved a study by Doctor Harry Waisman, who fed laboratory monkeys aspartame. One died after three hundred days, and five others had grand mal seizures. These studies were never shown to the FDA. By 1987 four deaths associated with NutraSweet had been reported to the FDA, all involving seizures. [196]

In 1987 Linda Tollefson of the Office of Nutrition & Food Services for Safety and Applied Nutrition (CFSAN) of the US FDA had received more than 3700 complaints about aspartame adverse reactions from various food sources. The most common complaint was headaches (1000), followed by dizziness and balance problems (461), mood swings (399), vomiting and nausea (364), abdominal pain and cramps (268), seizures and convulsions (211), and changes in vision.[197]

As a nutritionist I came across lots of cases of people suffering with aspartame and MSG poisoning problems. A few of the more common symptoms are: pain in the eyes, decreasing loss of vision at night, tunnel vision, tinnitus, numbness in arms, tingling sensations, confusion, anxiety, insomnia, depression, nausea, weight loss, hyperactivity, headaches etc. As you can see from such a variety of symptoms, it would be easy to miss-diagnose aspartame poisoning. If you do not ask the question "Are you taking aspartame or MSG?" how would you find out? This is part of the problem—doctors are not told to look out for problems deriving from aspartame or MSG, and nutrition is not a subject that they are encouraged to study in any depth. Doctors on average spend approximately five minutes with each client. By contrast nutritionists normally spend between 45 and 90 minutes with each client. It can take a considerable amount of time to ascertain the dietary link between any specific product and a specific symptom.

Excitotoxins (continued)

This leaves a big gap in understanding between those who research this topic and the rest of the community. Dr Blaylock believes there is a significant link between the ingestion of these excitotoxins and Alzheimer's dementia, Parkinson's disease, Lou Gehrig's disease (ALS), cancer and the increase in free radical damage to the brain and body in general.

Of particular concern is the health of growing children. We already know that nutritional status during pregnancy and in the early months after giving birth is critical. Numerous studies have demonstrated that the nutritional status affects both motor skills and intelligence. [198] According to Dr Blaylock, just one single exposure of sufficient concentration of an excitotoxin could create an irreversible brain lesion in a child. This exposure could occur through breast milk or by direct feeding of the child. In experimental animals 'MSG babies' were found to be short in stature, obese, to experience difficulty in reproducing, and have several disorders involving hormones of the hypothalamus — one of the main sites of attack by excitotoxins.[199]

The amount of MSG alone, added to food, has doubled in every decade since the 1940s, by 1972, 262 metric tonnes of MSG was produced. Similarly, by 2002 over 200,000 tons of artificial sweeteners were used around the world.

A long-term study into the effect of Aspartame on 1800 rats by Scientists at the independent European Ramazzini Foundation for cancer research, in Bologna, who undertook a large-scale and long-term study into the effect of Aspartame on 1800 rats, found that it caused cancer of the kidney and of peripheral nerves, mainly in the head. The study also linked aspartame to an increased risk of leukaemias and lymphomas in female lab rats "at doses very close to the acceptable daily intake for humans." [200]

However, it's not just the excitotoxicity problem that makes aspartame so worrying. Dr Blaylock found that when a radioactive tracer was used to follow the course of the formaldehyde breakdown, it was clear that the formaldehyde accumulated near the DNA in cells, resulting in numerous deletions and strand breaks in the nuclear material. He states:

> *Even more frightening is the finding that the damage is accumulative, so that even drinking one diet cola a day can produce significant genetic damage.* [201]

HIDDEN EXPOSURE

You may ask well ask how such a product has been allowed to enter the food chain. Surely we have organisations, such as the FDA to review these new products and test them for their safety. Unfortunately, I do not have the space to go into the whole sorry saga, but I can give you sources where you can get the information. Professor Erik Millstone of the Science Policy Research Unit, Sussex University, Brighton, published a report on the matter. Here is a sample of what he says:

> Several of the tests carried out to assess possible adverse health effects of the artificial sweetener, Aspartame, were investigated by the US Food and Drug Administration in the 1970s because questions had been raised about the conduct and reporting of the tests. In particular, there were doubts as to whether the tests could provide an adequate basis on which to assess the chemical's safety. As three pivotal tests have never been repeated, the public cannot be confident that Aspartame is safe. The way in which the decision was reached to allow this food additive on the market has worrying implications for both public safety and confidence.
>
> It is possible that, after further research, Aspartame may be found to be safe beyond reasonable doubt, at least in respect of its putative embryotoxicity and carcinogenicity. But the shortcomings in the conduct of the regulatory authorities over such a long period remain to be fully investigated and explained, and steps must be taken to try to ensure that such shortcomings are not repeated. Until these matters are subjected to rigorous and open inquiry, food and chemical companies may assume that they can get away with poor research and incomplete disclosure. There is a danger that, as a result, seriously toxic chemicals or environmentally-destructive materials, will reach the market, with potentially disastrous consequences. [202]

This may have put you off your diet cola for a while. So, as a nutritionist, one of the suggestions I always give is to drink water. Water is what we are mostly made up of, yet it is the one product that no-one seems to drink a lot of anymore. There really is nothing better than a drink of water when you are thirsty. I have always maintained that if I could find a politician who could supply water fit to drink he would certainly have my vote. However we can take a look at some areas where improvements could be made.

Water and the Fluoride Controversy

There is a lot more complexity to water than many people imagine. In the electronics industry, for example, specifically the production of silicon chips, water is used to clean the chips—but not just any water. The water is 'purified' by removing the free hydrogen and free oxygen from it. Water may be classified as H_2O, but it also contains free oxygen and hydrogen, various minerals and impurities and, depending upon the source, various contaminants and microorganisms. The water 'purified' by removing the free hydrogen (after filtering out all the contaminants) is so caustic that it has to be piped in special pipes. If you were to drink it, it would cause you severe damage and could even kill you, even though it's classified as 'pure'. However there is one man-made contaminant that is actually added to the drinking water in many parts of the world—fluoride.

Fluoride

Fluoride is so reactive that it can eat through steel, glass, aluminum and iron. As a byproduct of the aluminum, steel and fertilizer industries, it is classed as one of the most poisonous substances on earth. Yet it is commonly used not only in pesticides and pharmaceutical products but is also added to drinking water, and toothpaste. You would be right to question the wisdom of this, especially when the evidence that it reduces cavities in teeth is so poor. In fact it has been demonstrated in a number of studies that cavities are actually higher in fluoridated areas.

The Historical Context of Fluoride

One of the original proponents of water fluoridation was Gerald Cox, a member of staff at the Mellon Institute—the Mellon family being the owners of the Aluminum Company of America (Alcoa). One of the main waste products of the aluminum industry is, of course, fluoride — and due to its extreme toxicity and corrosiveness, its disposal had been an expensive and controversial problem. Fortunately for Alcoa, Andrew Mellon its founder, was also the US Treasury Secretary and, as such, had direct control of the US Public Health Service. His idea of fluoridation of the water supply did not go unchallenged, however. There were a number of doctors who protested their concerns—such as Dr John Yiamouiannis who warned that fluoride, being a powerful protoplasmic poison, could accumulate in human tissues. The American Dental Association (ADA), in its journal in 1944, warned that in concentrations as low as 1.2 -3.0 ppm, fluoride was associated with developmental disturbances of bones—such as osteosclerosis, osteoporosis, spondylosis and goiter.[203]

Finding ways of disposing of large quantities of fluoride had been a problem since WWII when its use was essential for the manufacture of bomb grade plutonium and uranium. It was essential for the enrichment of uranium and had been used throughout the cold war period in the manufacture of nuclear weapons. This might be news to many researchers since, it was considered a sensitive enough piece of information to keep under wraps for as long as possible. During the cold war period thousands of workers were involved in various aspects of the enrichment process and the eventual production of weapons grade material—and so were exposed to the deleterious effects of fluoride.

During this time there were also significant numbers of workers exposed to fluoride fumes from the steel and aluminum industry and from coal-fired power plants which also released fluoride. Monitoring the effects of the exposure was done in secret—it was considered more important to advance the weapons program than allow concerns for human health to be allowed to interfere with production. However, fluoride pollution became a serious concern to the atomic bomb program — during the cold war there were more damage claims for fluoride damage than for all other major air pollutants combined. Many people are not aware that Dr Harold Hodge, the leading fluoride researcher in the USA—who trained an entire generation of dental school deans in the 1950s and 1960s—was also the leading wartime toxicologist for the Manhattan Project—the name given to the US atomic bomb program. He was the same person who monitored the notorious experiments on people who were injected with plutonium and uranium, without their consent in order to study the toxicity in humans. He was also given the job of studying the toxicity of fluoride. [204]

Early Health Links

European scientists had already linked fluoride to a number of illnesses, such as central nervous system disorders, musculoskeletal problems, arthritic-like conditions and breathing problems. In the Danish colony of Greenland, which had one of the largest supplies of cryolite, a fluoride containing mineral that was used in the manufacture of aluminum, the workers there suffered from a number of crippling skeletal ailments, and other conditions. Professor P. Flemming Møller suspected that fluoride was responsible as cryolite was more than fifty percent fluoride. He charged Kaj Roholm, a young doctoral candidate to study the problem. Rohlom interviewed the workers, took x-rays and undertook lab tests on animal subjects. He fed pigs, dogs and rats fluoride in order to study the biological effects. He discovered that the poison accumulated in the teeth and bones, and seriously affected the lungs and kidneys. The spinal column was particularly affected, and caused serious mobility problems. Roholm further discovered malformation of the knees and hips, and thickening of men's skulls. Half the men suffered from pulmonary fibrosis, and many suffered from an emphysema-like condition. He also noticed that their ligaments grew hard, and sprouted boney spines — some of their bones became lumpy and irregular in shape. There was a large increase in rheumatic and arthritic ailments, and a significant number of workers suffered from chronic skin conditions, with rashes and sores that were pussy. Roholm also became aware of fluoride's ability to poison enzymes, and cause them to fail in their role as chemical messengers that control so many of the body's systems. He labeled the disease "fluorine intoxication" [205]

There were a number of other cases where the toxicity of fluoride was demonstrated. Dr. John Yiamouyiannis reported an article in the German Magazine Stern, in 1978, which revealed the discovery of a village in Turkey called Klizilcaoren—that suffered from a mysterious illness:

> The children, the young girls and the only horse in the village have brown teeth. Thirty-year-old men with hunched up shoulders painfully drag themselves around, leaning on sticks. Women produce dead babies after pregnancies of only four months. Forty-year-olds look like old men and women.
>
> A suspicion that all the villagers could be the victims of a creeping poisoning was first voiced...by a dentist. During a mass examination of the children, he discovered a dental disease unknown to him in all children aged over 7; brown pigmentation on the incisors of the younger children, completely brown teeth in the older. Adults in the village hardly had any teeth at all. The dentist alerted medical staff at the University Clinic of Eskisehir. Their investigations brought to light even worse news: every single inhabitant suffers from a bone disease- thickening of the ankles, stiffened joints, increased growth of bone substance. The people who live at Kizilcaoern have more bone fractures in arms and legs than other Turks.
>
> Both men and women suffer from this premature aging. Between 30 and 40, their facial skin becomes wrinkled, muscle tone weakens markedly and they develop walking difficulties.
>
> Again and again almost every family has premature births, with babies stillborn after 4 or 5 months of gestation. Though only 30 years old, one of the men admits he has lost interest in women, Many of the men suffer from severe depression because of their early impotence. Most of them do not even enjoy food.
>
> Not even the cattle are in good health. A white bearded peasant wearing a black pompom hat tells of sheep whose diseased livers after slaughter looked white and watery.
>
> Dr Yusuf C. Ozkan as well as his colleagues at the medical faculty of the University of Eskisehir suspected that the cause of all this suffering was the high content of fluorides..... in the drinking water of the village. Because in the neighboring villages which invariably receive their water from different springs or wells, the state of health was normal. The medical people say that the fluoride content of the water is 5.4 parts per million" [206]

HIDDEN EXPOSURE

Reports like this surfaced and were reported in numerous places. In Bartlett, Texas, in 1943 and 1953, researchers from the United States Public Health Service examined the inhabitants of Bartlett to see what effect having a fluoride content of 8 parts per million in their drinking water would have on their health. The mortality rate there was three times as high as neighboring Cameron which only had a fluoride content of 0.4 parts per million. It was found that at levels even as low as 1 part per million of fluoride in the drinking water collagen synthesis was disrupted. Collagen is one of the most important building blocks of the body; so the disruption of collagen formation has serious consequences.[207]

Fluoride's Ability to Disrupt Normal Enzyme action and Collagen Formation

Fluoride had been used for years by biochemists to inhibit the action of enzymes—particularly since the 1950s. Some of these scientists raised concerns about the toxicity of fluoride. Dr James Sumner, winner of the Nobel Prize for his work in enzyme chemistry, is quoted as saying:

> We ought to go slowly. Everybody knows that fluorine and fluorides are very poisonous substances and we use them to poison enzymes, those vital agents in the body. That is the reason things are poisoned, because the enzymes are poisoned and that is why animals and plants die. [208]

Fluorides interfere with enzymes in a number of ways. In the body, the fluoride ions (with a negative charge) combine with other positively charged ions, often metal ions such as magnesium and particularly calcium. They can combine with aluminum and form an ion AlF_4^-, the same size and shape as a phosphate ion PO_4^{3-}, which has huge potential to cause problems in biological systems. One well documented problem created by fluoride is its ability to disrupt transmission of important messages across cell membranes, and switch on G proteins (enzymes are large protein molecules). [209]

G proteins are located in the outer cell membranes, and form part of the transmission process of messages across cells. Hormones and growth factors are water soluble and cannot cross through cell walls and interact with G proteins to initiate the correct response in the cell. AlF_4^- is able to fool the G protein into being switched on, so preventing a critical messenger, such as a hormone, being able to do its job correctly. A G protein switched on is understood to interfere with hormone signals, growth-factor signals and some neurochemical signals. And thyroid-stimulating hormone is one of the hormones that aluminum fluoride is known to mimic.[210]

Enzymes are large molecules of proteins composed of between 100 to 1000 small molecular building blocks of amino acids having catalytic activity. These accelerate the rates of chemical reactions in biological systems typically by a factor of 10^6. The special feature of enzymes is their specificity of action. Some enzymes act on one single substrate and are considered absolutely specific. In many instances they rely on co-factors such as free ions of metals including magnesium, sodium or potassium. But, as has been shown, malfunctioning enzyme in any bodily system has the potential to cause a myriad of complications, which will inevitably harm the the body.[211]

The amino acids can be viewed as chain links, with each type of amino acid possessing its own unique structure. When they are assembled as a chain protein, amides are formed as the links in the chain molecule. The differing arrangements of the amino acids in their size and structure, and various combinations, are what differentiate their unique capabilities and their own particular susceptibilities to damage by fluoride—or indeed other poisons or chemicals. One of the discoveries of how fluoride can cause damage to biological systems was made in 1981, by Dr. John Emsley, from Kings College in London. He discovered that fluoride formed very strong hydrogen bonds with the group of atoms, the amides, that connect the protein chains together. It caused the hydrogen bonds of the protein chains to break apart and form bonds with the fluoride instead. It can even break apart DNA chains that are held together with hydrogen bonds. In fact, it can so distort protein molecules that the body no longer recognizes the protein as part of the body—and the immune system destroys it as it would any other foreign body. [212]

One of the proteins produced by the body that is of great significance to our health is collagen. Collagen is produced inside cells and transported to the outside of the cell to be further thickened into fibers. It is produced in five different cells in the body, depending upon the type of collagen needed. Osteoblasts, for example produce collagen for the structural support of the body which, with the addition of calcium and phosphate and further minerals, will eventually form bone. Fibroblasts produce collagen for the structural support of the skin, tendons, ligaments and muscle. Chondroblasts produce collagen for the support of cartilage. Ameloblasts help create tooth enamel, and odontoblasts create collagen that helps produce the inner part of teeth called dentin. Collagen contains two additional amino acids not found in any other proteins—hydroxyproline (HP) and hydroxylysine (HL). This is important because, when collagen synthesis breaks down or is interfered with, the levels of these two amino acids increase in the urine and blood.[213]

Researchers from NIH and Harvard University have known since the 1960s that collagen synthesis is disrupted by fluoride from studies published.[214]

Later studies done in the 1980s onwards have confirmed these original findings. [215] It appears that, when normal collagen synthesis breaks down, the body tries to compensate by producing bigger quantities of imperfectly formed collagen. In some instances where, in normal circumstances collagen is only mineralized, such as tendons, that should not be mineralized. If this happens, movement is restricted, and other complications can occur. It can also result in both faster aging and fluoride damage.

Currently there are more than 180 million Americans and a further 200 million people worldwide drinking artificially fluoridated water. Yet there is no official body in the USA that will accept liability or responsibility for the decision to fluoridate the water supply. In the UK the authorities have passed legislation absolving water companies from any claims for compensation for health damage caused by adding fluoride to the water. Yet many of us do not realize that the fluoride used is not a pharmaceutical grade product, but a waste product from the fertilizer industry and aluminum industries that also contains other contaminants such as arsenic. For an up to date idea of the situation with fluoride *The Case Against Fluoride,* written by Paul Connet PhD, James Beck, MD, PhD, and H.S.Micklem, DPhil, is a book I can heartily recommend. It is a well-balanced book giving both sides of the story, written by some excellent researchers. Professor Connet for example was originally a pro-fluoride scientist who, after reviewing all the research, realized that he would have to change his view, despite all the orthodox official bodies such as the AMA, the ADA, the American Public Health Association (APHA), the British Dental Association (BDA), and the British Medical Association, continuing to support fluoridation.[216]

Fluoride Science—More Politics than Science

The full story of the fluoridation issue will be found in his book, *The Case Against Fluoride,* as well as in Christopher Bryson's book, *The Fluoride Deception.* However, I will cover some of the main points over the next few pages, and explain why there is more politics than science involved.

The science behind it is, of course controversial and not widely disseminated because there is very little evidence in support of the idea of adding such a poison to the water supply or toothpaste. One of the biggest studies by the National Institute of Dental Research (NIDR) involving more than 39,000 children, found little difference in the amount of tooth decay in children in fluoridated areas, compared to non-fluoridated areas—i.e., fluoridation does not help prevent tooth decay.[217]

A significant number of other studies also attest to the fact that dental caries do not increase when water fluoridation stops.[218] On the contrary, a large number of them show that the incidence of cavities is actually higher in fluoridated areas.

At the turn of the 20th century, it was observed that there were significant areas of the USA where children had a high incidence of damaged teeth, with a mottling of the tooth enamel (later identified as dental fluorosis)—where there were naturally higher levels of fluoride in the water. This discovery led to the American Dental Society and the US Public Health Department to call for the removal of fluoride from the water in these areas. Teeth were found to be white spotted, yellowed and brown stained or pitted. In the USA 25 percent of school children are thought to be affected with fluorosis. [219] The lowest incidence of fluorosis exists where the water is not fluoridated. [220]

There had been considerable opposition to fluoridation when it was initially introduced in Michigan in January 1945. Nevertheless Mellon and his fluoridation team convinced the council of Grand Rapids to institute a fluoridation trial. But *before* the trial results were even published, the AMA and ADA completely reversed their stance on fluoride and started promoting its use. The study eventually showed that tooth decay rates were not improved by the addition of fluoride, but that they were falling across the whole of the country probably because of better nutrition at that time.

That the ADA had done an about-face on the toxicity of fluoride in just a few months aroused the suspicions of the US representative for Nebraska, Dr A L Miller, who also happened to be Chairman of the Special Committee on Chemicals in Foods. He could find no studies to support the massive about-face by the AMA and ADA, but was keenly aware of the connection to Alcoa of Oscar Ewing the Federal Security Administrator, who had previously been hired as a lawyer for $750,000 by Alcoa. He was also aware that if this fluoridation went ahead, that Alcoa would not only get rid of its toxic waste, but that they would also get paid to do it. To Miller, it looked like an unprecedented scam. There were a number of other scientists who shared Miller's views but, because of the huge sums of money at stake, no expense was spared to silence them. Take for example the treatment of Dr Yiamouyiannis, a former editor of the Chemical Abstracts Service, the world's largest chemical information service. When the fluoride lobby discovered that Dr Yiamouyiannis was writing a critical report on fluoridation his superior was contacted and told that $1.1 million of

Federal funding would be in jeopardy if he did not stop his criticism of fluoridation. He was given a number of warnings, but was unwilling to suppress the truth—and was eventually forced to resign. Those wishing to get a more complete picture of this would do well to read his excellent book, *Fluoride, The Aging Factor*.

Dr Yiamouyiannis was not the only casualty in the name of fluoride. Dr Phyllis Mullenix a neurotoxicologist was at the cutting edge of studying the effects of chemicals affecting the brain and central nervous system—and had developed bold new technology that involved cameras monitoring behaviour, and computer modelling to ascertain behaviour changes following exposure to various chemicals. She was considered the best in her field and was given a job with the prestigious Forsyth Dental Center in Boston. Here she went on to and set up what was to be the first dental toxicology centre in the country. It was associated with Harvard Medical School and was known as one of the finest dental research centres in the world. Mullenix received large donations for her work from a number of industry sources including Monsanto, the American Petroleum Institute, Amoco, and Mobil Oil. Digital Equipment Corporation donated much of the powerful computer equipment she used there. She had a sound reputation within industry, appeared in a number of court cases in their defence, and was considered an 'industry' scientist. [221]

The Director of Forsyth, Jack Hein was keen to establish the sensitivity of the system that Mullenix had developed, and her computers were connected to huge data processing machines via phone connections to Iowa State. It was Hein who suggested that she carry out a study on fluoride. He himself was a supporter of fluoridation and with Mullenix's reputation as an 'industry' scientist together with her state of the art equipment, he believed they would be able to bury the controversy about fluoride once and for all. But by 1989, after two years studying the behaviour of rats exposed to fluoride, her team had enough data to establish that, far from burying the issue, there was indeed a problem. The rats displayed not only cognitive defects, but also retarded behaviour and sexual differences.

At the time Mullenix was often visited by Harold Hodge (the senior toxicologist with the Manhattan project — and one of the people who had studied fluoride and given it a clean bill of health). Mullenix was not only unaware of this, but also of the fact that it was Hodge's testimony to Congress that was most often cited in support of the use of fluoride.

Initially, Jack Hein had been excited about Mullenix's discoveries, and suggested they inform NIH and give a talk about her findings. Ironically she arrived to reveal her discoveries on the fortieth anniversary of the Public Health Service's endorsement of community water fluoridation (1990).

However, she got a completely hostile reception after her talk and left later that day. Instead of getting support to do further work on fluoride, and to inspire other scientists to look at the problems, she found herself effectively stonewalled. Her principal supporter, Jack Hein, retired from Forsyth in June 1991 but, although Mullenix had been warned that publishing her report would jeopardise funding for Forsyth, she felt obliged to publish what she considered was serious concerns about fluoride's effects on the brain and central nervous system. Her report was finally accepted for publication on May 18th 1994. And just four days later she was fired by Forsyth. For more detail on Mullenix's discoveries, refer to Bryson. [222]

However, Mullenix's paper did arouse interest elsewhere, and a number of studies were undertaken (23) on fluoride that reported a lower IQ in children in a number of different countries around the world. There were also more than eighty studies done demonstrating that fluoride accumulates in animal brains, causing damage in areas of the brain associated with memory and learning. Behavioural changes were also noted. All of these studies are reviewed in *The Case Against Fluoride*. Other work discovered that fluoride increased the uptake of aluminium into the brain, which caused morphological changes in the kidney as well as the brain. These triggered the formation of beta-amyloid deposits that are associated with Alzheimer's disease. [223]

In 2006 the National Research Council (NRC) reviewed the literature on fluoride. This was the first government appointed review body to look at the available research in animal and human studies. The panel reviewed the available information and had this to say:

> On the basis of information largely derived from histological, chemical and molecular studies, it is apparent that fluorides have the ability to interfere with the functions of the brain and body by direct and indirect means....
> Fluorides also increase the production of free radicals in the brain through several different biological pathways. These changes have a bearing on the possibility that fluorides act to increase the risk of developing Alzheimer's disease. [224]

Fluoride Disrupts Normal Glandular Function

The review also expressed concerns about the ability of fluorides to affect the endocrine system— which consists of a number of glands including the thyroid, parathyroid and adrenal glands, which secrete various hormones into the blood system and regulate a number of bodily functions. Hormones, being water soluble, are not able to cross the cell membrane—so utilise receptors located on the cell wall to initiate their various actions. The receptors are uniquely designed to fit each hormone like a specific piece of a jigsaw puzzle. They are generally different proteins.

A number of studies link fluoride with problems with the thyroid function via various mechanisms—which include mimicking the switch of the receptor sites—and also with the pineal gland. Dr Jennifer Luke, a UK dentist, discovered that the pineal gland, which has the highest blood flow per unit volume of any tissue except the kidney, had high levels of fluorides in subjects analysed—ranging from 9,000 ppm to 21,000 ppm. The pineal gland is responsible for the level of melatonin in the body. So anything that will affect its ability to produce and regulate melatonin can have very serious consequences. Those interested in a more in depth understanding of the mechanisms involved in the thyroid disruption mechanisms of fluoride will find this information in Paul Connet's book.[225] There is also an extensive history of the fluoride/thyroid problem that is too extensive to discuss here, on the web site for Parents of Fluoride Poisoned Children (PFPC).[226] Dean Murphy, a dentist, in his book *The Devil's Poison—How fluoride is killing you*, reviews much of the science behind fluoride's toxic nature and is another good source of information.[227]

It has long been known from early studies that fluoride causes bone defects. In comparisons of Newburg and Kingston, both cities in New York State, one with fluoridated water, the other without it, it was found that double the number of cortical bone defects occurred in the fluoridated city.[228] There have also been a number of studies where higher incidence of bone fractures occur in fluoridated areas in both children and adults—a recent one in Mexico in 2001.[229]

Further studies link fluoridation with arthritis. One in five Americans has some form of arthritis (in excess of 46 million and still rising). In places such as India and China, where there are high levels of naturally-occurring fluoride in the water, the symptoms of skeletal fluorosis mimic arthritis—which makes it very easy to misdiagnose, particularly where physicians are not trained in detecting fluorosis. There are also a significant number of studies linking hip fractures with high fluoride intake—approximately 300,000 Americans are hospitalised for hip fractures each year. For a review of the studies see Connet et al. [230]

Other studies link fluoride with a number of cancers, including osteosarcoma, liver and oral cancers and thyroid follicular cell tumours. Professor Connet reviews all this evidence and also assesses the risks of kidney damage and its significance to long-term health.[231]

UNHEALTHY BETRAYAL

The WHO Report on the Irish Experience of Fluoride

In 2013 a Public Health Investigation into the epidemiological data on disease and mortality in Ireland, resulting from water fluoridation and fluoride exposure, was published. The report was for the Government of Ireland, the European Commission, and the World Health Organisation. Its key findings were made sobering reading:

> This report demonstrates how overexposure of a population to fluorides through artificial fluoridation of public water supplies applied to almost the entire population of the Republic of Ireland (RoI) is perhaps the largest single overall contributor to the disease burdens present in Ireland today. Fluoridation of public water has significantly increased the total dietary exposure of the population to fluorides regardless of the individual's nutritional status or health in an uncontrolled manner impacting on every aspect of health.

The report is extensive and I only have space for the main findings of the 2006 US National Research Council part of it. I can, however recommend the full report as a good source of information:

> The NRC concluded that there was evidence to demonstrate that fluoride exposure contributed to causing cancers and well as promoting cancers, fluoride exposure impairs glucose metabolism, causes impaired glucose tolerance and decreases insulin production.

> Fluoride exposure increases the production of free radicals in the brain, impairs brain function, causes neurotoxic effects on the brain, affects the general nervous system and increases the risk of developing Alzheimer's. Cytogenetic effects of fluoride exposure may contribute to Down's syndrome.

> Fluoride exposure contributes to musculoskeletal disease with associated symptoms such as chronic joint pain, arthritic symptoms, calcification of ligaments, and osteosclerosis of cancellous bones as well as weakens bone and increases the risk of fractures.

> Fluoride exposure contributes to hyperparathyroidism, increased calcium deficiency, osteoporosis, and may be associated with hypertension, arteriosclerosis, degenerative neurological diseases, diabetes mellitus, some forms of muscular dystrophy and colorectal cancer.

Fluoride contributes to other adverse health effects including increased concentration of lead in critical organs and nutritional rickets. Fluoride is an endocrine disruptor contributing to hypothyroidism and hyperparathyroidism.

Fluoride exposure decreases melatonin production that may indirectly contribute to increased anxiety reactions, development of postmenopausal osteoporosis, anti-carcinogenic effects and psychiatric diseases.

Fluoride directly affects the immune system while silicofluorides inhibit cholinesterases, including acetylcholinesterase which is a contributory factor in Alzheimer disease. Human leukemic cells lines are also susceptible to the effects of silicofluorides and symptoms such as oral ulcers, colitis, urticaria, skin rashes, nasal congestion and epigastric distress may be due to sensitivity of some sufferers to silicofluorides or fluoride.

Fluoride also forms complexes with other elements including aluminium, sodium, iron, calcium, magnesium, copper and hydrogen that may have implications for neurotoxic effects. [232]

This makes it abundantly clear there is a significant amount of evidence that fluoride, far from being a chemical that is 'great for your teeth', is in fact linked with significant harm both at critical times in the growth of children, and over time as it builds up in our bones. It is not that there is just one health issue here: there are a multitude of conditions that are affected by fluoride. The question has to be asked is: that if fluoride is so great for us all, why is it that the countries who support and promote fluoride use refuse to do any studies to prove one way or the other whether fluoride is harmful or not? The above study is the first one I am aware of. Unfortunately there is no answer to this important question other than ones which involve political expediency and massive ignorance. There are, however a number of web sites devoted to increasing the information available on this topic.[233]

The Toxic Legacy of Agricultural Industrialisation.

There is no doubt that the massive industrialisation of the food supply has created many problems not just for we consumers but also for the people who directly work in the various fields associated with it. The promoters of the industrialisation of agriculture wish to have us believe that this type of system is necessary to feed the world—that due to the ever increasing population, traditional agriculture would not be able to meet the demand. They also claim that the industrialisation of agriculture results in cheaper food. This is part of the myth that they would have us believe—but the reality is somewhat different, as will become apparent from the information on the following pages.

We started this chapter looking at how a simple chemical can affect homeostasis (the body's ability to regulate its normal functions to keep us healthy). In the pages to come we will look a little deeper into the consequences of our over-reliance on industrial scale agriculture and the industrialisation of our food system. Numerous chemical compounds found in today's food, air and water are now found in every person. Depending upon locality, exposure, and a number of other factors, these can lead to disease—and even death. They can affect our neurological and endocrine systems which, in turn, can cause brain dysfunction, depression, autoimmunity problems, reproductive dysfunction, cancer and a host of others.

Since 1976, the U.S. Environmental Protection Agency (EPA) has been conducting a survey into human chemical exposure by analysing human adipose tissue from specimens of autopsied cadavers. In 1982 they expanded their search to look for 54 different environmental toxins—and the results were astounding. Five of these toxins were found in every single sample tested—dioxin (OCDD), and the solvents xylene, ethylphenol, styrene and 1.4-dichlorobenzene. Not only that—they were also found at worrying levels. Nine more chemicals, including another three dioxins, benzene, toluene, chlorobenzene, ethybenzene and DDE (a breakdown toxic compound of DDT), were found in 91-98 percent of all samples. They also found PCBs (Polychlorinated biphenyls) in 83 percent of all samples, and beta-BHC in 87 percent. Seventy six percent of the people analysed had levels in excess of 25,000ng of total toxic compounds per gram of fat, and contained at least 20 toxic compounds. [234]

A study of four-year old children in Michigan in 1989 revealed that it was not just older people who were contaminated, DDT was found in seventy percent of these youngsters and PBB in twenty one percent. Nursing was considered the primary source for these children. [235]

Testing for contaminants in food is undertaken to various degrees throughout the world. One of the better surveys is the on-going study by the U.S. FDA, the Total Diet Survey. This reveals alarming levels of contamination with chlorinated pesticides. DDE was found in 100 percent of samples of beef, spinach and raisins, and ninety-three percent of samples of cheese, hamburger, chicken, turkey and others. What is worrying is that since 1972 both DDT and DDE have been banned in the USA. So it's assumed that much of this contamination must come from imported products. [236]

HIDDEN EXPOSURE

One of the problems with these sorts of chemicals, particularly the pesticides, is the fact that they can remain active for long periods of time. Lindane for example is still toxic after fourteen years, and herbicides such as parquet and simazine are still toxic after 5 years.

In the UK, evidence given to the Agricultural Committee of the House of Commons by the East Anglia Water Authority found atrazine, simazine, dimethoate, mecocrop, and lindane regularly in their monitoring sites.

One of the problems in dealing with the various contaminants that we are all exposed to is how the various toxins may react with one another. For example, it's well known that chlorine—which is used routinely as a water treatment agent—can react with herbicides such as 2.4.D and produce human carcinogens such as the chlorophenols. Aldicarb, a pesticide, can break down into aldicarb sulphoxide, which is recognised as being even more toxic than the original aldicarb.

When DDT was introduced in 1944, during WWII, when more soldiers were dying from insect-borne diseases, such as malaria and typhus, than from actual fighting, it was considered an improvement on the lead-arsenate insecticides that had been previously in use. It then took until 1972 for it to be eventually banned in the USA. It had become recognised as a possible carcinogen and was known to have led to the near-extinction of the Bald eagle. Rachel Carson's book *Silent Spring* was credited with galvanising opinion against DDT, and launching the environmental movement. In 1967 a group of scientists and lawyers had launched the Environmental Defense Fund, and made it one of their goals to have DDT banned. Now it is known to be a persistent organic pollutant with a half-life in excess of thirty years. It is considered a genotoxic compound and an endocrine disrupter. It affects a number of enzymes and, to date, we still do not know all the harm that it is capable of. Yet as a result of its persistence, it is now found in the blood of just about every human being on the planet, including the Eskimos in the far north (they actually have high levels of it due to the fact that it builds up in whale and seal blubber).

The same company that invented DDT, Geigy of Switzerland, developed a new product to replace DDT called Atrazine. Atrazine became hugely popular with farmers, and was the best-selling herbicide on the market, earning substantial profits for Norvartis (Norvartis was formed when Ciba ltd which had already merged with Geigy to form Ciba-Geigy in 1970, merged again with Sandoz Corporation in 1997).

Since the 1970s, Geigy had been aware of studies which showed that Atrazine caused cancer in laboratory rats. In 1987, more than twenty five years after its introduction, a new study undertaken for Ciba-Geigy noted that rats fed Atrazine contracted mammary tumours—and this could not be ignored by the US Environmental Agency (EPA).[237] Later that same year, an Italian researcher discovered that women who were exposed to Atrazine were much more likely to contract ovarian cancer. He did a follow-up study and confirmed his original findings when he discovered that women exposed to atrazine developed tumours 2.7 times more frequently than women who were not exposed to it. [238]

Atrazine has also been shown to induce gene mutations. Animals fed high doses of Atrazine have suffered liver, heart and kidney damage. Recent studies have further linked it with hormonal changes. Out of ten hormone-disrupting pesticides (including several known carcinogens) tested, it was found that only DDT had as damaging an effect as Atrazine on the metabolism of oestrogen. [239]

Widespread Water Contamination

As cattle are routinely fed corn, 98 percent of which is treated with Atrazine, it soon showed up in the human food chain in corn, beef and milk. It was also found to be one of the leading contaminants in drinking water.[240]

Out of 589 samples of water from the Missouri River, 441 were found contaminated with Atrazine and, of these, 165 exceeded the EPA's safety standard of three parts per billion. The situation was similar in other parts of the country: of 580 samples from Illinois, 448 tested positive for Atrazine—in some cases by as much as 39 parts per billion, which is 13 times the EPA's safety standard. [241]

The US Geological Survey did an extensive evaluation of more than 1600 water samples drawn from Midwestern streams, rivers, reservoirs and aquifers from 1989 to 1994. They found Atrazine in 990 of them. It was even found in the rainwater — and could be detected in rainwater 15 states away from the original source in northern Maine on the East Coast of the USA. [242]

It is of course, not just pesticides and herbicides that contaminate our water supplies. In Maine, New Hampshire and Massachusetts, the main polluter to cause concern, is arsenic, in California its boron, in Nebraska uranium and in Texas, lithium. Manganese and arsenic contamination are both widespread. In the first national effort to monitor wells for 24 trace elements, thirteen percent contained at least one contaminant at levels exceeding federal health regulations.[243]

HIDDEN EXPOSURE

Of course contamination of the water supplies and food supplies is not limited to the USA — this is now a global problem—much of the US grain is exported and is found in the food products of many countries, a lot of which do not have to be labelled.

Pesticide Contamination a Global Problem

In the UK, we have the same problems of pesticide contamination. In the late 1980s the Ministry of Agriculture's specialist working party found pesticide residues in one third of dietary staples, such as milk bread and potatoes, and in twenty percent of fruit and vegetables. Six percent of fresh samples of produce contained contaminants in excess of the Maximum Residue Level (MRL). Some of the lettuce sampled for residues of dithiocarbamate fungicides was found to be contaminated in excess of 44 times the MRL. [244] A change in the way samples were analysed in 1995 revealed that a significant proportion of carrots tested exceeded permitted organophosphate contamination levels by twenty five times. [245]

Organophosphates are neurotoxic compounds that were developed during WWII to be used as nerve gas. As with the ammonium nitrate stock piles left over from bomb-making, it was decided that these chemicals could be used in agriculture. The problem with many of them though, is that they are able to penetrate the flesh of plants, to such an extent that peeling fruit or vegetables would not prevent exposure. This was highlighted by a Ministry of Agriculture committee in 1993. It raised the concern that doing an analysis of only the skin or peel of fruit and vegetables could seriously understate the amount of pesticide consumed by individuals. [246]

In Canada, Dr Margaret Sanborn and others undertook a systematic review of studies published since 1992 on the major health effects of pesticides, including nine types of solid tumours, non-Hodgkins lymphoma, leukemia, genotoxic effects [causes genetic damage], skin diseases, neurological diseases, and reproductive effects. The report expresses concern for children and the unborn:

> Children are ubiquitously exposed to low levels of pesticides in their food and environment, yet there has been a paucity of studies on the long-term health effects of these exposures. Many pesticides persist in the environment, are often transferred long distances from their original area of application, are routinely detected in human tissue, and are transferred across the placenta and via breast milk.
> Relative to adults, children eat more in proportion to their bodyweight, resulting in more concentrated exposures...

UNHEALTHY BETRAYAL

Children present a number of unique characteristics with regard to risks from exposure to pesticides and other environmental pollutants. The most vulnerable time is during fetal development when the brain is known to be subject to environmental influences at all phases of development, with critical windows at different points. Since in the female, ova are formed in the fetal stage, and environmental contaminants have been found in follicular fluid, *the next generation of children born may be affected by their grandmother's exposures* [my emphasis]. The newborn child has low levels of the enzyme paraoxanase-1, which detoxifies organophosphate pesticides.

Environmental contaminants may pose a greater risk to children than adults for another reason: children have a longer life expectancy in which to develop diseases with long latency periods.

Their review found four studies associating pesticides with brain cancer, several implicating hematologic tumours in children, several more linking elevated childhood leukemia rates—one of which associated maternal pesticide exposure with childhood leukemia. While not wishing to downplay concerns regarding the serious implications of the links with cancer (I have only reported a few examples from this report), these researchers also expressed concern for the neurodevelopmental effects:

> Studies in children have so far demonstrated subtle neurotoxic effects of low level, intrauterine, or early childhood exposures to a variety of environmental agents including lead, methyl mercury, and PCBs. While studies of pesticide health effects in children are still lacking, it is possible that a parallel model may emerge for low-level exposures to pesticides, some of which are by design neurotoxic. A range of developmental disabilities including learning disabilities, attention deficit hyperactivity disorder, developmental delays, autism, and behavioural disorders are of great importance due to possibly increasing incidence, and personal and public health costs. [247]

Our pesticide exposure is not limited to what we eat. In 1999, the *New Scientist,* reported on research by Swiss researchers which showed contamination of rain by such high levels of pesticides that it would be illegal to supply it as drinking water. The researchers found rain over Europe laced with atrazine, alochlor and other common agricultural poisons. Stephan Muller at the Swiss federal Institute for Environmental Science and Technology in Dubendorf, reported finding one sample of rain containing 4000 nanograms/litre of 2,4-dinitrophenol, a common pesticide, and atrazine at levels exceeding 100 nanograms/litre (in 9 samples). This was at a time when the EU had set a limit of 100 nanograms/litre for any individual pesticide).[248] Another study by Greek researchers found one or more pesticides in 90% of 205 samples on rainfall in Greece. Atrazine was found in 30% of samples.[249]

In 2010, the Annual Report by the (US) President's Cancer Panel, reported:

Pesticides (insecticides, herbicides, and fungicides) approved for use by the U.S. Environmental Protection Agency (EPA) contain nearly 900 active ingredients, many of which are toxic. Of the numerous solvents, fillers, and other chemicals listed as inert ingredients on pesticide labels many are toxic—but are not required to be tested for their potential to cause chronic diseases such as cancer. Agricultural fertilizers and veterinary pharmaceuticals are major contributors to water pollution—both directly and as a result of chemical processes that form toxic by-products when these substances enter the water supply.[250]

Industrial Chemicals Add to the Cocktail of our Exposure

In 2009 the CDC released a report that undertook to monitor chemical pollutants in the blood and urine of the US population. It assessed exposure to 212 chemicals from data collected between 1999 and 2004. They found that exposure to some commonly used industrial chemicals was widespread.

- Polybrominated diphenyl ethers are fire retardants used in a number of manufactured items. It was found that they can accumulate in the environment and also in human fat tissue. One particular type of polybrominated diphenyl ether, BD-47, was discovered in the serum of nearly all the NHANES participants (a random sample of participants from the National Health and Nutrition Survey).

- Bisphenol A, a component of epoxy resins and polycarbonates was found in more than ninety percent of urine samples. It is considered it may have the ability to affect reproduction in humans. It is believed that this may be attributed to contact with food in some way.

- Several perfluorinated chemicals were found—one perfluorooctanoic acid (PFOA)—is a by-product of the synthesis of other perfluorinated chemicals. It is commonly used in the manufacture of a polymer that is found in non-stick coatings in cookware. Most participants had measurable levels of this environmental contaminant.

- Acrylamide is formed when carbohydrates such as corn or potato (as in French fries) are cooked at high temperatures, as mentioned in earlier chapters. As it is a reactive chemical, acrylamide can bind to proteins—and the reaction products are referred to as adducts. The CDC developed a new method to measure acrylamide and its metabolite, glycidamide and their data in the Fourth Report found that exposure is extremely high in the U.S. population.

- The Fourth Report looked at mercury exposure for people aged one year and older. Levels increased for all age groups until the age of 50 and then decreased. The blood levels were primarily composed of methyl mercury which is believed to enter the body through the ingestion of seafood. Levels were found to be higher in the black population.

- Seven forms of arsenic were found in most people.

- The report also showed that all NHANES participants had detectable levels of perchlorate in their urine. This is a naturally occurring chemical in the environment, but is also man-made, and used in the manufacture of fireworks, flares, explosives and rocket propellants. It is known that it can affect thyroid function.

- There are a number of volatile chemicals that exist in the air we breathe, such as the hydrocarbons and halohydrocarbons, 33 of which are monitored in the report. One such example is the gasoline additive methyl *tert*-butyl ether (MTBE). This can come from contaminated water courses as well as in the air we breathe. A high percentage of NHANES participants exhibited detectable levels of MTBE

- The report revealed that five percent of the population aged 20 years or older had high levels of cadmium. Recent research has revealed that urinary cadmium levels as low as 1 microgram per gram of creatinine could affect the kidneys, and lead to an increased risk of bone mineral density. It is thought that cigarette smoke is the most likely source for these higher cadmium levels.

- The report, however is not all bad news. Blood levels of cotinine are related to exposure to tobacco smoke—and this has reduced significantly (approximately 70%) following public health interventions. Levels of lead in children have also significantly reduced from the high levels of the 1970s. [251]

The problem with all these pollutants in our food, water and environment is that we are mostly unaware of their existence—and also have little idea about their effect on our health particularly with regard to the synergistic relationship of one chemical to another. This is the situation where the combination of one or more chemicals produces a more pronounced effect when they are combined than they do separately. Here we are in unknown territory since the human race, and all the creatures and plant life we depend on, are now subjected to a chemical cocktail that did not exist before the current era.

Chapter 8
Blind Faith

Silent Spring was an eloquent and urgent warning about the dangers posed by manmade pesticides. Carson not only described how persistent chemicals were contaminating the natural world, she documented how those chemicals were accumulating in our bodies. Since then, studies of human breast milk and body fat have confirmed the extent of our exposure. Human beings in such remote locations as Canada's far northern Baffin Island now carry traces of persistent synthetic chemicals in their bodies, including such notorious compounds as PCBs, DDT, and dioxin. Even worse, in the womb and through breast milk, mothers pass this chemical legacy on to the next generation.

– Vice President Al Gore Jan 22 1996 [252]

Technology is advancing at a blistering place. There is a seemingly unquenchable thirst for new products, the latest gadget, and the next miracle of science. However, in biological terms, we are still basically the same human beings we were two thousand years ago—except that we are exposed to a very different environment now. The industrialisation of agriculture, our food system and our health care systems has been dramatic over the last few decades. But this unfortunately has brought with it significant new challenges. We have only recently come to realise that all the advances made have come at some cost and may have far reaching implications for our future health and the health of our children.

It is sometimes only when things go wrong that we begin to question whether what we are doing is, in fact in our best interests—or even whether we should be doing it at all. We put great reliance on the political structures we voted for to look after our best interests. We also came to regard the people who work in science, and develop it, with a kind of mythical trust—taking it for granted that they would be truthful and considerate of their actions. We somehow expected them to have the ability to look into the future and see the long term consequences of all the new discoveries they were making. Only in recent years we have come to realise this confidence is misplaced.

UNHEALTHY BETRAYAL

There is no doubt that both world wars led to a huge development of new chemicals, and were a catalyst for the development of new industries. During this period, particularly the Second World War, there was a significant shift into products developed from oil, and away from coal, and plant sources. Instead of cotton, linen, celluloid glues etc., being the basis for new developments, oil enabled the development of polyesters, plastics, nylon and formaldehyde resins etc.

Creating these new chemicals became big business. But at the same time, regulation of the industries responsible for the various chemicals was either lacking or non-existent. Rachel Carson's book *The Silent Spring*, released in 1962, was one of the first to make people aware of the problems with many of the chemicals in our environment, particularly DDT. But it wasn't until December 1970 that the Environmental Protection Agency (EPA) was finally set up (in the USA) to look into the better regulation of these chemicals. Yet to this day only a few chemicals have ever been tested. Unless a chemical has already been shown to cause significant harm, it is generally ignored. And proving significant harm can be a long and arduous process. Unfortunately, it seems that the wheels of industry are governed more by the profit motive than by the safety of the environment. So this has encouraged them to exert influence on the politicians and the very organisations set up to control them. Such is the nature of profit motives that, in the drug industry for example, pharmaceutical companies spend more money on lobbying, advertising, legal posturing, and science posturing than on the actual development and production of the very drugs they sell.

Most people assume that the organisations, such as the EPA in America, are set up to monitor chemicals such as pesticides in order to safeguard our interests, our health and our children's health. Unfortunately past experience shows that this is not the case. If you study examples of any number of the chemicals that are considered harmful to humans and animals, you will find there has been a massive reluctance to take measures to protect our long-term health. This reluctance to investigate harmful chemicals has spawned a number of citizen groups, organisations and individuals to fight for greater clarity and openness.

Personal Experience

Carol Van Strum is an individual who was spurred into action after her children and her property were sprayed with herbicides when she was living in Oregon. She writes, in her book, *A Bitter Fog*,[253] about her experiences and the experiences of her neighbours of having their properties and children sprayed by planes and helicopters—and even truck sprayings of the local roadsides bordering their land. She published a book documenting the struggle of the entire community to get the spraying stopped and get some recognition for the terrible effects experienced, such as miss-carriages, deformed births, increase in cancer incidence, and a host of neurological and other problems. One thing you do not get working in a laboratory studying data, is the kind of direct experience they had. They did not need a forestry official or a government employee to tell them the herbicide they were sprayed with had been given a clean bill of health, and could not be causing the problems they complained of. They were only too aware that when people miscarried all at the same time of year, just after the spraying, there had to be a connection.

Carol Van Strum's book was a collaboration, in that it documents what occurred from a number of individual's viewpoints. It tells of their struggle for recognition and justice, and the complete failure of the government and industry to recognise what the fallout from their spraying program was in human cost. She documents the research they uncover, the litigation they had to resort to, and the eventual recognition that what they were claiming was proven to be true when further research proved their story true. Until that time, virtually the entire community had been activists to varying degrees from confrontations, and threats to the destruction of a spray helicopter. What was obvious was the strength of feeling in the community. After the helicopter was torched, far more people claimed responsibility than could possibly have done it. Many were overheard offering to help out with the next one!

What is touching is the intimate nature of Van Strum's story. Here's an example from, Larry, a neighbour who was attending the birth of his daughter:

"We went in the hospital together. When Kaleen (his first daughter)was born, you know, I was there the whole time, watching. And maybe this sounds corny, but that was the most beautiful moment of my entire life-just being there....

"So I was there this time too, but it was another thing altogether. The baby—it was a girl. She was perfect from her toes up to her eyebrows. I mean her face was perfect, too—kind of like Kaleen's almost. But that was it. It ended at the eyebrows. That was all there was—just this kind of bowl, with a kind of film of tissue over it. She couldn't breathe. There wasn't any brain to tell her to breathe. So they give her oxygen, and she lived for about an hour. An hour and twelve minutes. I don't know how Laura (his wife)stood it. I would've broken up then but she didn't.

"These people who say herbicides are so safe—I could give them something to think about. I'd like to put everyone of 'em in a delivery room to see a baby born like that, like 'em to have to watch their **own** kid born like that. To them, to everyone, our baby was just a statistic, a number. I want 'em to see the real thing. They just want numbers. They want to blame it all on anything but what it could be. And they sure as shit don't want to find out.

"I made the doctor take samples—tissue samples—from her, from the baby. He was supposed to get them tested—at O.S.U., he said and another one at Colorado. That was a whole year ago (1979), and we never heard nothin' about it. I went in there once to ask him about it, and he wouldn't even come out and see me. He was there, and he wouldn't even come out and talk to me. That's how much he cares, how much he wants to know.

"I knew, see. I knew how much of that stuff I got on me all the time I was growing up, my brother and me-we used to spend all our time in the woods around our place—I mean all the time. That's where we went when there was nothing else to do. And we used to find little deer embryos-about the size of a cat they were, all in their little sac—whole—just dropped where they fell out of the mother. Three of 'em we found one year. We thought they were babies-human babies—at first. It was real spooky, till we looked close at one and could see it was a deer. We never thought nothin' about 'em then, except they were so spooky, just findin' 'em laying on the ground like that.

"So when our baby was born, I knew. I asked the doctor could it be me—could it be that stuff in me? And he said I could go up to Portland and have my blood tested and all, but it would cost—oh six hundred dollars a test or something. Fat chance of that. I work in the gas station, and we have this trailer, and we pay the rent for space, and I am still paying the hospital bill and funeral bill for our baby.....[254]

Van Strum's Book is a heart-felt rendition of a community looking for answers, mostly with regard to the phenoxy herbicides such as 2,4-D and 2,4,5-T (more about these later). It is well researched and documented by an able author and, in my view, needs a wider audience. It should be required reading for all epidemiologists, scientists and bureaucrats researching toxins, pesticides etc. Too often, the human reality, the consequences the real human cost is not appreciated by some policymakers. In Larry's case, he would have had a difficult time trying to prove the cause of his misfortune. The trouble with exposure to chemicals such as herbicides and pesticides is that the damage could have affected him long ago, and only have manifested itself in the birth of his child. How do you prove the cause? Fortunately, aside from people like Van Strum, organisations have sprung up to help people find the answers.

One such organisation, The Center for Public Integrity, reviewed just four chemicals: Formaldehyde, Atrazine, Alachlor and Perchloroethylene in their book *Toxic Deception*. This book will be of particular interest to those looking into the ways science can be manipulated for profit over health—and the politics involved. *Toxic Deception* addresses the problem as it manifests in the USA, and the institutions there. But the reality is the same in most countries, as we shall see.

BLIND FAITH

Formaldehyde

Let's start with Formaldehyde. Most of us know of it from our time at school as a chemical that preserves frogs, or as an embalming fluid for funeral homes. But by far its biggest application is as a glue, in wood products such as particle boards, plywoods and veneered boards of different kinds. It was found that when it was mixed with urea it formed a resin-glue. When it was further mixed with sawdust, wood chips or wood waste, it became a vital component of saleable sheets and boards. One of the problems with formaldehyde is the smell — the gases given off cause significant problems with some people's health and have led to numerous lawsuits. This problem was not limited to the workplace though. There have been numerous cases of people becoming ill when buying new homes with significant amounts of formaldehyde laden materials installed. Tens of thousands of families have become ill with flu-like symptoms, rashes and neurological illnesses. Many buyers of mobile homes also suffered because many urea-formaldehyde products are used in their construction. One such family, the Pinkertons of Clay County received $140,000 for medical expenses and $63,000 for property losses. The outraged jury also awarded them $16 million in punitive damages (it was the longest trial in Clay County history at that time). Mary Pinkerton, diagnosed with multiple chemical sensitivity, would become ill with asthmatic symptoms caused by formaldehyde and other chemicals. [255]

Urea formaldehyde insulation was discontinued after a flurry of successful lawsuits. Since the 1970s it had been known to cause cancer in rats, and the International Agency for Research in Cancer labelled it a probable human carcinogen. By the late 1980s the National Cancer Institute had discovered a heightened incidence of brain cancers in embalmers and anatomists and a rare nasal-pharyngeal cancer in industrial workers who had been breathing high levels of formaldehyde gas.[256]

Perchloroethylene

Perchloroethylene the dry cleaning chemical of choice, particularly in the USA, was another hazardous chemical studied by the Center for Public Integrity. Scientists had known since the early 1970s that Perchloroethylene caused liver cancer in mice. The EPA classified it as a known carcinogen in high doses. However little was known about the exposure and prevalence of 'perc' at that time. It was eventually found that there were high levels of it in butter and other fatty items in grocery stores that were situated next to dry cleaners. Levels of perc fumes in apartments twelve stories up, were found to exceed the levels set to protect the workers below. Levels in closets where dry cleaned clothes were put were found to be exceedingly high. As a result of used perc being dumped down drains or poured onto the land to avoid costly waste disposal fees, it also became a contaminant of the land.[257]

A study published in 1994 by the National Institute of Occupational Safety and Health discovered the rates of esophageal cancer in workers at dry cleaning businesses were seven times the national rate, and that they had twice the national average rate for bladder cancer.[258] Studies undertaken in Massachusetts on people who had drunk water contaminated with perc were found to have between five and eight times more leukaemia than their neighbours who had not drunk contaminated water.[259]

It is estimated that there are approximately 30,000 dry cleaning establishments in the USA, of which approximately 85 percent use Perchloroethylene. There is however a non-toxic alternative, using 'professional wet cleaning' that is a modern computer controlled system that enables accurate cleaning of the finest fabrics. However, as yet, these are not used in any significant numbers.

Atrazine

Another chemical assessed by the Center for Public Integrity was Atrazine, a herbicide developed by Geigy in Switzerland. Atrazine was able to kill plants quickly by preventing photosynthesis, and worked effectively against grasses and broadleaf weeds but was found to have little effect on sorghum, sugar cane and corn (maize). Nevertheless, it rose to become one of Geigy's most successful products. Farmers liked it because it did not dissolve in the rain, it was relatively cheap, and it was long lasting—they only had to treat their crops once or twice in the growing season. Before the introduction of Atrazine, about one fifth of the yearly corn crop had been treated with herbicide, and this had risen to 96 percent by 1998. But by 1995 Atrazine considered the best-selling pesticide in the US, with sales in excess of 70 million pounds. Ciba-Geigy is now part of Norvartis, and Atrazine is still considered one of its most successful products.[260]

Ever since the 1970s, studies had shown that Atrazine caused cancer in laboratory rats. But it wasn't until 1984 that the EPA finally accepted its carcinogenicity, following the results of a new study showing that female rats fed Atrazine developed mammary tumours.[261] In the same year, an Italian researcher found women exposed to Atrazine, and other closely related herbicides, had a significantly increased risk of developing ovarian cancer than other women. In a larger follow-up study, involving a larger group of women, he discovered that women exposed to Atrazine developed tumours 2.7 times more frequently than women who hadn't been exposed to it. [262] Atrazine has also been shown to damage DNA and induce gene mutations (Ciba-Geigy disputes this). Animals that have been fed high doses of Atrazine suffered heart, liver, and kidney damage and, more disturbingly, has been linked to signs of hormonal changes. Some research suggests that Atrazine can change the way the body metabolizes oestrogen—which could further lead to an increased risk of cancer. [263]

The Atrazine problem came home to roost in that it began to show up in supermarket products, including corn, beef and milk in the USA, cattle are fed corn, which is routinely treated with Atrazine. [264] Even more alarming was the discovery that Atrazine was one of the leading contaminants in drinking water. Since 1976 levels of Atrazine as high as 17 parts per billion had been detected in the Mississippi River and was particularly heavy after the peak of the spraying season. Further studies in the 1980s found that Atrazine showed up in rivers, lakes, aquifers and rain in Iowa, Ohio and throughout the Midwest. [265]

Atrazine is water-soluble so, in disrupting photosynthesis of plants, it migrates into both their roots and leaves. This makes it able to migrate into water courses, evaporate and travel through air currents and find its way into rain droplets, thus creating havoc in unintended places. It has been shown to poison plankton, aquatic plants, algae and a number of chloroblast-bearing organisms that form the basis of our freshwater food chain.[266]

Another human victim of the chemical war on humanity is Sandra Steingraber PhD, a biologist who contracted cancer. She decided to research cancer toxicology and wrote an exhaustively researched book on the subject: *Living Downstream*. It is very readable, and you do not have to be a scientist to understand it, because it is written from a very human perspective, as she is dealing directly with her cancer throughout the writing of the book. I introduce her here because she sheds new light on the subject. For example, she details a suspected pathway by which Atrazine is believed to cause the estrogenic effect—i.e. by increasing the production of the enzyme aromatase. This is the enzyme that is believed to convert the male hormone androgen into estrogen (the US spelling for oestrogen is used here but I use both spellings interchangeably) which then binds to estrogen receptors which provoke the estrogenic effect seen by others. She also cites a 2008 study that found Atrazine was able to make ovarian cancer cells proliferate by binding to a different receptor called GPR30. She further refers to research in 2009 on rats which investigated whether Atrazine could affect the metabolic rate, and possibly influence obesity. It was discovered that

Atrazine did indeed damage mitochondrial function (this is the energy powerhouse inside each cell), and also damaged insulin signalling and so induced insulin resistance in the rats, which became fat.[267]

The EPA took a tougher stance on Atrazine in 1991 when it set a standard limit of three parts per billion for drinking water. Water suppliers reacted slowly to this because it involved costly filtration equipment. The cost was considered to be up to $465 million per year according to the American Water Works Association. Ciba-Geigy sued the EPA to raise the safety standard to 20 parts per billion. The EPA initiated a special review of Atrazine, and two closely related herbicides, Simizine and Cyanazine in 1999. Dupont, the maker of Cyanazine agreed to phase out their product, but Ciba-Geigy decided to fight, and reputedly spent more than $25 million defending their product. One of the methods developed by the industry to undermine effective regulatory control was to get famers and as many other people as they could to flood the EPA with letters which would tie up their time and delay their capacity to respond. This became an effective tool that reached its peak with Atrazine. The EPA received more than 87,000 letters about it, the highest total ever for a pesticide.[268]

In 2006 the EPA released the Finalization of Interim Reregistration Eligibility Decision (FIRED) and their Completion of Tolerance Reassessment and Reregistration Eligibility Process for Atrazine, and came to the following position:

> The Agency recently completed its cumulative risk assessment for the chlorinated triazine class of pesticides and has concluded that, with the mitigation measures in the 2006 simazine Reregistration Eligibility Decision and the 2003 atrazine IREDs, the cumulative risks associated with these pesticides are below the Agency's level of concern.

> They further clarified: In other words, the Agency has found that there is a reasonable certainty that no harm will result to the general U.S. population, infants, children, or other major identifiable subgroups of consumers from aggregate exposure (from food, drinking water, and non-occupational sources) to cumulative residues of atrazine and the other chlorinated triazine pesticides. [269]

In their review of cancer data, they stated that they were aware of the incidence of prostate cancer in the plant workers at the St Gabriel plant in Louisiana (where Atrazine is manufactured) and accepted that it was significantly high. But they decided that *proximity to atrazine manufacturing did not appear to be correlated with risk.* However, they also stated that they did not rule out an association.

The Estrogen Link

In 1993 a number of researchers were working on the on-going puzzle of the increasing rates of breast cancer and deaths in older women that were linked to higher levels of estrogen. These researchers were from various institutions in the US, and they hypothesized that synthetic chemicals may be acting as estrogen mimics — or may alter the way the body metabolises estrogen. H. Leon Bradlow and his colleagues from Cornell Cancer Research Laboratory discovered evidence that linked synthetic chemicals with increasing cancer risk by the way the body processed a form of estrogen called estradiol in two different ways. One way produced a weak form of estrogen, and the other produced a more potent form of estrogen that could increase the risk of cancer.

They found that a substance in broccoli, cauliflower, brussel sprouts and other members of the cabbage family reduced cancer risk by channelling estrogen into the healthy pathway. However they also found that hormonally active chemicals channelled estrogen metabolism into the harmful route, and so increased cancer risk. In their experiments they exposed breast cells to a range of chemicals which included DDT, PCBs, kepone, endosulfan and atrazine. They discovered that all these had a profound effect and greatly increased the levels of the harmful estrogen. [270]

In July 2000, the National Cancer Institute released a study looking into breast cancer that that cost over $8.7 million, and was called the Northeast and Mid-Atlantic Breast Cancer Study (NEMA). They made the following statement with regards to their study: *"There was concurrence among projects in observing no association between breast cancer risk and blood levels of the organochlorine compounds, DDT pesticide and its metabolite, dichloro-2, 2-bis (p-chlorophenyl) ethylene (DDE) and polychlorinated biphenyls (PCBs)".* They did, however, acknowledge that there was a significant relationship with breast cancer and serum levels of vitamin B-12 that they felt was worthy of further research.[271]

This research flies in the face of previous research that had looked at the incidence of breast cancer in particular with organochlorine compounds and PCBs published in their own journal. Mary S. Wolff, Ph.D., from the Division of Environmental and Occupational Medicine, Mount Sinai School of Medicine, looked into the link with these chemicals and had this to say:

Organochlorines such as DDT [2,2-bis(*p*-chlorophenyl)-1,1,1-trichloroethane] and PCBs (polychlorinated biphenyls), which have been used extensively as insecticides and as fluid insulators of electrical components, respectively, are known to be persistent environmental contaminants and animal carcinogens. These agents have been found in human tissue due to their inefficient metabolism and their solubility in lipids, which lead to lifelong sequestration in adipose tissue.

Wolff studied blood specimens of 14,290 New York women enrolled between 1985 and 1991 in the New York University Women's Health Study. She found a fourfold increase in relative risk of breast cancer for an elevation of serum DDE concentrations from 2.0 ng/mL (10th percentile) to 19.1 ng/mL (90th percentile). DDE is the breakdown product of DDT. She concluded;

"These findings suggest that environmental chemical contamination with organochlorine residues may be an important etiologic factor in breast cancer. Given the widespread dissemination of organochlorine insecticides in the environment and the food chain, the implications are far-reaching for public health intervention worldwide". [272]

Further studies undertaken by Dr C Charlier, of Belgium, from the Laboratoire de Toxicologie Clinique of Liege, also looked into breast cancer and the link with DDT and also hexachlorobenzene (HCB). Blood levels of HCB and total DDT (which included all DDT and DDE isomers) were compared with 159 women with breast cancer, and 250 presumed healthy controls, and found that mean levels of total DDT and HCB were significantly higher for breast cancer patients than for the controls. [273]

Later studies looking into the rise of the incidence of non-Hodgkin's lymphoma (NHL), unrelated to HIV infection, has noticed a steady increase over the past several decades. Limited evidence suggests that increased concentrations of polychlorinated biphenyls (PCBs), measured in blood or fat tissue, are associated with increased risk of NHL. Lawrence Engel, of Memorial Sloan-Kettering Cancer Center, reviewed a three-cohort study. A cohort study is a study where people are classified as exposed or unexposed, and are followed through time until disease or death occurs. He concluded: *The results from these three cohorts suggest that concentrations of certain PCBs in blood are associated with increased risk of NHL.* [274]

BLIND FAITH

The Revolving Door of Science

I put these studies in for a number of reasons. These chemicals are considered persistent; they exist in the adipose tissue of most of us in varying concentrations, depending upon exposure, and are found to some degree in our blood. Yet, as I have just demonstrated you can have one study that shows a positive correlation between breast cancer and organochlorines, and yet another showing no correlation. The problem we face is that the majority of research undertaken is undertaken by the very industrial concerns that need to prove their chemicals are harmless or, in the case of drugs, that they are without serious side effects. The very institutions that are set up to monitor and safeguard us are manned by people from the industry they are supposed to be monitoring. Numerous authors have referred to the revolving door that exists between industry and government oversight departments.

The Center for Public Integrity, for example, looked into the lobbyists and lawyers who worked for the chemical companies and trade associations that their book *Toxic Deception,* reviews in depth. Of 344 lobbyists and lawyers that they identified as having worked for the industry from 1990 to 1995, at least 136 had passed through the revolving door and had previously worked for federal departments or agencies, or in congressional offices. They found that half of the EPA officials who left top-level jobs in toxics and pesticides within the previous fifteen years went to work for chemical companies, their affiliated trade associations, or their lobbying firms. They further investigated the funding of more than three thousand trips that EPA employees took that had been paid for by corporations, trade associations etc. Having someone from the inside, with intimate knowledge of the way the EPA or the FDA works, would give considerable advantage to any pesticide manufacturer or drug company manufacturer wishing to tie up time or evade legislative problems. The door, of course, swings both ways. Some examples are cited here: John Byington, former chairman of the consumer product Safety Commission, advised the formaldehyde industry on how to deal with his ex-employer. Linda Fisher joined Monsanto in 1995 as its vice president for government affairs, after previously working for the EPA as an assistant administrator for prevention, pesticides and toxic substances. Peter Voyek, the very scientist who oversaw the initial assessment of Perchloroethylene in the early 1980s, working in the EPA, became the director of the Halogenated Solvents Industry Alliance, the industry's chief lobbying organisation. Georgia Pacific's director of environmental policy, training and regulatory affairs, Susan Vogt, was previously with the EPA as one of Linda Fisher's top deputies. The revolving door is not just limited to the EPA and

FDA. It includes members of Congress, special assistants to the President, a White House chief of staff and a White, House chief counsel. [275]

Costly Business to Whom?

There are many factors stacked against a straight forward understanding of whether a chemical is a significant problem or not. The industry argues against studies showing carcinogenicity in animal studies, arguing that the high levels given to the animals in the study would never be ingested or absorbed at the same levels in humans—and further, that just because a particular animal responded the way it did, does not mean that humans necessarily would. The same companies, of course, would argue vociferously for their own studies of their products showing no adverse effects on animals. So, to get acceptance to market new products, in this case, the animal studies would be expected to be accepted as highly relevant.

There is no doubt that it is a costly business bringing new products to the market, something that big business complains about often. Another view, however, is that due to the high cost, very small companies are put off bringing new products to market, giving larger companies the exclusive position of being able to do this.

There is of course a significant cost to the tax payer. In the USA for example there is a so called indemnification provision of federal pesticide law that discourages enforcement by the EPA by requiring the government to buy banned products—so allowing manufacturers to profit from products considered dangerous. This has led to situations where the federal government has spent more money buying banned pesticides than it has on regulating pesticides and herbicides. In 1988, for example, the government spent $53 million on the storage and disposal of banned products, but only $45 million on the control and testing of pesticides. When the weed killer Silvex was banned in 1979, Chevron Corporation was paid $12.8 million by the government—and a further $7 million was paid out to other Silvex manufacturers and wholesalers. [276]

The whole issue of compensation is very significant. For example: in the U.S., whenever there is a settlement for a claim against a manufacturer for causing a significant health problem or even death, the tendency is to settle out of court. And frequently included in the settlement is generally a binding agreement of confidentiality and non-disclosure of all material pertaining to the suit. This generally means that any other person wishing to sue a company for a harmful product has to go through the long and arduous process without the benefit of reference to previous cases— even when it may be exactly the same product. The onus remains on the litigant to prove harm.

BLIND FAITH

Oestrogen Mimics from Plastics

The secrecy of non-disclosure also works against researchers who are trying to make sense of problems they are faced with. There are, for example, a number of ingredients in pesticides that are classified as inert, as we have previously discussed. That is to say, they are not the active part of the pesticide and so are not disclosed, despite the fact they may be harmful in some other respect.

In 1985 two researchers, Dr Ana Soto and Carlos Sonnenschein of Tufts Medical School in Boston, were looking for a way of inhibiting the proliferation of cancer cells having already found a way of filtering out oestrogen from blood serum—a known multiplier of the particular strain of cancer they were studying. They had been working together since 1973, and by 1985 they believed they had discovered an inhibitor. They left serum samples in the presence of this inhibitor for four days, but −after this period- found the exact opposite of what they expected: massively increased growth. The results completely stumped them. They re-tried the experiment with meticulous care numerous times, but each time with the same outcome. It took four months before they eventually used a different brand of lab tube, one made by Falcon instead of the previous tube made by Corning—and this produced the result they had anticipated. Instead of the plastic tube being inert, it was biologically active.

Upon meeting with Corning representatives in July 1988, they learnt that the company had recently changed the plastic resin used to manufacture the tubes. When Dr Soto requested information on what may be the chemical responsible for the change, Corning refused to give them any information, saying the plastic was considered a "trade secret". Both Soto and Sonnenschien were outraged by this response, since in their view it had far-reaching implications for human health. It set them on a course of investigation and eventually at the end of 1989 they had a positive identification of the chemical involved. This was p-nonylphenol, one of the family of synthetic chemicals called alkylphenols. It was added to polystyrene and polyvinyl chloride (PVC) to make them less breakable.

Soto and Sonnenschien looked into the chemical further. They found that it had been added to numerous products: detergents, pesticides, personal care products and other PVC products. Vast quantities of alkylphenol polyethoxylates were being used—600 million pounds globally, in 1990 over 450 million pounds in the US. Some European countries had already banned it from household cleaners.[277]

On the opposite side of the USA, a Stanford University team of researchers had discovered yet another oestrogen mimic—bisphenol-A. This was leaching from a different kind of plastic, a polycarbonate used in the manufacture of lab flasks, and a number of consumer products. The team discovered that bisphenol-A could generate an estrogenic response in solutions with as little as 2 parts per billion. Clearly, this area of research would be of vital interest to people such as Soto and Sonnenschien but, sadly, neither received further funding to investigate biologically active plastics and other synthetic hormone disrupting chemicals. [278] Oestrogen mimics are considered a significant threat to our health—even to our survival as a species since they affect our ability to reproduce, and have vast implications for new born children, as I will discuss a little later. However, the treatment of Soto and Sonnenschien is another way that industry can disrupt the flow of information; they control the purse strings of so much research. Universities rely on corporate funding for much of their budget and consequently most research is not as impartial as we would like—the majority of it is dictated by the company supplying the funding.

Our Chemical Load

Most of us are subjected to a multiple chemical load; many of the chemicals we are exposed to are ubiquitous in the environment—even according to the EPA. The number of chemicals the EPA's TEAM study found in the air included: benzene, p-zylene, o-zylene, Tetrachloroethylene, ethylbenzene and 1,1,1-trichloroethane. They also found that carbon tetrachloride, styrene, dichlorobenzene, and chloroform were often present, but not always. Their study also showed that exposure levels increased when people visited a service station or dry cleaners, smoked, or drove a vehicle. They also noted higher exposure levels in various occupations, such as painters, and people working in the plastics or chemical industries. [279]

Monitoring of contaminants in our food is undertaken to varying degrees in most countries. The FDA in the USA reviews and publishes data on pesticide contamination which is available to all. In other countries such as in the UK, this information is difficult to obtain. The FDA Total Diet Survey looks at a number of different chemicals in our food, and their research reveals a number of contaminants that are cause for alarm. They discovered that DDE (the breakdown product of DDT) was found in 100 percent of samples of spinach, chili con carne, raisins and all beef. It was also found in 93% of American processed cheese, chicken and turkey, hot dogs, hamburger, bologna and collard greens. The figure for lamb chops, salami and butter was 87%. It must be assumed that since DDT and DDE have been banned in the USA since 1972, a significant part of this contamination must be attributed to imports from countries where it remains in use. [280]

Volatile chemicals also evaporate in warmer climates and are borne by the wind to colder countries where they are likely to condense in the cooler air. This helps to explain the high levels of contaminants found amongst the indigenous animals and people in the Artic.

Organochlorines (OCCs) are known to have significant detrimental effects on us, affecting our immune systems, decreasing our ability to fight infection and tumours, increasing our sensitivity and susceptibility to allergies, and creating autoimmune problems. DDT, itself an organochlorine, has been noted to affect the immune system by reducing the killing capacity of polymorphs, decreasing phagocytic activity (all which affect the effectiveness of our immune systems), reducing the number of plasma responder cells, increasing degranulation of mast cells—and further cause leukopenia and affect changes to the spleen, thymus and lymph glands. Organophosphate pesticides, whilst not as biologically persistent as OCCs, are also toxic to the immune system, and lead to high rates of autoimmunity—as is also found with heavy metal exposure.[281]

Phenoxy Herbicide Development

At this point, it is worth giving a little background to the development of phenoxy herbicides to help explain why there was such reluctance on the part of the American authorities to acknowledge that such products could have serious consequences. In the 1940s, researchers had isolated the plant hormone auxin, a 3-indole acetic acid, which is the hormone that regulates plant growth. This led to scientists creating synthetic hormones that could manipulate plant growth. In certain combinations and doses they were also found to kill various plants—which gave rise to the Phenoxy herbicides.

Investigations into the military uses of herbicides began around 1941 when the then Secretary of war, Henry Stimson, was urged to look into the dangers of biological warfare. He consulted the National Academy of Sciences and National Research Council who advised setting up a committee to investigate the topic. Two scientists on what became the ABC committee, Dr E. J. Kraus, head of the Botany Department of Chicago University, and one of his doctoral students, John Mitchell, working at the U.S. Department of Agriculture's Plant Industry Station in Beltsville, Maryland, played a significant role in the development of phenoxy herbicides. Kraus was interested in two particular products, 2,4-dichlorophenoxy acetic acid (2,4-D) and 2,4,5-trichlorophenoxy acetic acid (2,4,5-T) which he believed might be used for destroying enemy crops. Both products were found to be very effective, whether used in combination or singly, but were not actually used in WWII. They were, however, used in the Vietnam War. A number of preparations were developed, some water-based, and others oil-based. To avoid cross contamination or clogging of the fine nozzles used in the aerial spraying, the products were coded with colour bands on the side of the drums. Six colours were used, blue, white, green, pink, purple and orange. The blue and white ones were the two water-based systems and the others were the oil-based mixtures which all contained 2,4,5-T. The agents green, pink and purple were eventually dropped in 1964 in favour of the mixture orange agent which was a combination of 2,4-D and 2,4,5-T — which was considered more effective. It has been estimated that in excess of 11 million gallons of agent orange were used up until its curtailment in 1972.[282]

My main reason for relating the story of agent orange, though, is that it set the agenda for repeated failures to regulate and control industrial chemicals – not only in the USA, but in many countries around the world.

Many of the US servicemen who had served in Vietnam, and came into contact with agent orange, subsequently succumbed to a number of serious disabilities that have been linked to the use of 2,4-D and 2,4,5-T. Obviously, had it become public knowledge that the government had been complicit in the poisoning of its own soldiers—let alone the poisoning of the civilian Vietnamese population and its own civilian population—that would have created unimaginable difficulties for it. So the outcome was that this natural reluctance to come clean set the scene for the whole problem of regulating and controlling industrial chemicals in the environment ever since.

At this point I would like to indulge in a little of the science behind the manufacture of phenoxy herbicides, not to bore you to death but hopefully to demystify the subject to some degree. If you are not interested in the science, please skip to the next section: Opposition to the use of 2,4,5-T grows.

Dioxin Creation

The principal method for producing phenoxy herbicides is by chlorinating various phenols such as 2,4-dichloro, 2,4,5-trichloro, 2,3,4,6-tetrachloro and pentachlorophenol. In the case of the last three phenols there is unfortunately a chemical by-product that is considerably toxic called, variously, polychlorinated dibenzo-p-dioxin (PCDDs) or more commonly simply dioxin. One of them for example is 2,3,7,8-tetrachlorodibenzo-p-dioxin (TCDD). The terminology for TCDD is relatively simple, tetrachloro refers to four chlorine atoms attached to the two benzene rings (dibenzo) —

dioxin refers to the two oxygen bridges holding the two benzene rings together. The numbers simply refer to the location of the chlorine atoms in the phenol molecule which designates which phenol is which, by the various positions. For now, simply understand that of the total number of dioxin isomers which number 75, we shall concern ourselves with one that is the most toxic—the TCDD referred to above. This dioxin is produced in the manufacture of the herbicide 2,4,5-T, and the amount produced varies, depending upon the production process. It is known to increase with the levels of heat generated, and its levels of contamination can be predicted to some degree by the final temperature. [283]

Dioxin is considered one of the most toxic chemicals we know of. There is no safe limit of exposure—it is toxic at levels not of parts per million, or even parts per billion, but is toxic at levels of parts per trillion! It is expensive to measure at these minute levels of contamination. There are two other chemicals that are closely related to dioxin, namely the polychlorinated dibenzofurans (PCDFs) of which there are 135 in number and polychlorinated biphenyls (PCBs) of which there are 209, though only 13 of these are considered to be dioxin-like in their biological activity. These compounds often co-exist and can transmute from one to another. PCBs, when heated, can form much more harmful furans and dioxins. However it is the fact that dioxin is so indestructible that in part makes it so dangerous—our bodies cannot break it down, and it is very persistent in the environment with a half-life of seven years.[284]

Because dioxin is so widespread it is next to impossible to find any population that is not exposed to it. Indeed, due to its ability to persist, it can build up in biological systems. According to Colborn, Dumanoski and Petersen Myers in their thought provoking book, *Our Stolen Future*, [285] humans carry in excess of 250 chemical contaminants in our body fat regardless of where we live or in how remote a location. They confirm the irony that populations in the remote Artic have some of the highest concentrations in their body fat, and further that, unwittingly, *all* mothers that breast-feed their babies will pass on high doses of these chemicals to their babies. Due to the levels of these chemicals in breast milk, in just six months of breast-feeding a baby in Europe or the U.S.A. is exposed to a lifetime dose of dioxin, and five times the daily allowable dose of PCBs for a 150-pound adult, as set by international health standards. The authors also discuss the revelation that just one single hit of dioxin, at a critical time, is enough to make permanent catastrophic changes to the development of an embryo; in their example—damage to the male reproductive system of a rat.

However, we get ahead of ourselves. It is worth giving some background to the dioxin story. One of the symptoms of dioxin contamination is a skin condition called chloracne which in mild forms takes the form of blackheads, mostly around the eyes and ears, and in more serious cases there are also large pustules and cysts. It has a fairly rapid onset and is considered a classic symptom of dioxin and related compounds. It can, however, affect the neck, shoulders, genitals, chest and lower trunk, and in the worst cases, the hands legs and feet. There can be permanent scarring, and the condition has been known to persist for in excess of eighteen years. A German dermatologist from the University of Hamburg, Dr Karl Shultz was the first person to associate this condition with dioxin poisoning. That was as a result of an explosion at a trichlorophenol plant owned by the German company Boeringer. Shultz subsequently tried to contaminate a lab mouse with pure trichlorophenol, although to no avail. But when he used the commercial grade product, it worked. So he concluded correctly that the condition was caused by a contaminant. It was only later, when a colleague came down with chloracne after opening a container of dioxin in the lab, that Shultz made the connection that dioxin was in fact the contaminant. He worked with George Sorge, the Boehringer chemist, and they established that this was the case and that too much heat had caused the explosion and the build-up of the levels of dioxin. The plant where the explosion had been was old and too contaminated to be used again, so was dismantled and disposed of. To their credit Schultz and Sorge notified other manufacturers of trichlorophenyl of the inherent risks of letting their reactors heat up too highly. Unfortunately, this fell on deaf ears and there were numerous other explosions that caused widespread damage and contamination. An Amsterdam-based company, Philips-Duphar, manufacturing trichlorophenol, had their reactor blow up on 6th March 1963. Following extensive decontamination and reconstruction, it was found that the building was still too contaminated and poisonous following animal toxicity testing, and was subsequently closed and totally demolished. It was so toxic that the all the contaminated buildings were loaded into barges, sealed and towed out to sea and sunk. It was only subsequently that it was uncovered that they had routinely disposed of much of their waste during manufacture at a tip called Volgermeerpolder, five miles from the centre of Amsterdam. Significant levels of dioxin were found in the topsoil at this site.[286]

In 1968 another trichlorophenol reactor blew up, this time in the UK—at the Fine Chemicals Unit of Coalite and Chemical Products Limited in Bolsover. After the explosion, Coalite re-opened the plant, but kept the trichlorophenol section sealed off. However many workers came down with chloracne and conjunctivitis — and there were 79 cases of skin disease. The conditions persisted, and eventually this plant, too, was closed down and dumped down a disused mine shaft. In 1969 a new plant was built, but in the course of construction some of the workers came down with chloracne which was eventually traced to a large metal container that had been in use on the original site that had been presumed thoroughly decontaminated. One of the workers wives, and one of their children, were also affected, presumably due to contact with the employee. Whilst both recovered, the child was still pockmarked five years later.

By far the single biggest event to raise awareness of the dangers of trichlorophenol production, and the dangers of dioxin, was the explosion of the plant at Seveso in Italy in the summer of 1976. Seveso was important because it was close to a large residential population. The reactor was owned by a Swiss company, Givaudan, itself owned by the parent company Hoffman-La Roche. The reactor exploded on Saturday night (10th July) but it took many days before any action was taken to safeguard the health of the local population — apart from being told not to eat their garden produce. People came down with sickness, vomiting, diarrhoea, skin rashes etc. Emergency meetings were held on Friday morning of 23rd July with the Provincial Health Council, leading scientists, doctors and academics from Milan and Rome, where it was agreed what measures should be taken. However Roche's clinical director Guiseppi Reggiani recommended immediate evacuation of the area — but it was some time before this was actually done. Children were the most badly affected and all pregnant women were offered abortions where feasible. Four women suffered mis-carriages. By June 1977 eight women in the contaminated area had given birth to malformed children. This did not include 89 additional anomalies that were not officially notified. [287]

Virtually all of Seveso's entire domestic stock of animals was wiped out. More than 80,000 animals were killed; horses, cattle, pigs, sheep, goats, poultry and rabbits. The first human death was a young 35 year old woman, but her death was not listed as dioxide poisoning. Chloracne was identified in 193 people mostly children under the age of 15 (170 of them) and some brain damage was found but was considered 'non-acute'. [288] All this devastation means that Seveso prompted one of the largest studies into the effect of dioxin contamination. The epidemiologist Pier Alberto Bertazzi and his colleagues have been monitoring some of the forty five thousand people, men women and children who have received some of the highest dioxin exposure levels recorded. Residents of the most contaminated area, labelled zone A, had significantly elevated levels of mortality for non-Hodgkin's lymphoma, multiple Myeloma, and leukaemia. By 2008, they also had lower levels of immunoglobulin G (circulating antibodies) relative to their exposure levels and their dioxin blood levels. The immune system is one of the significant targets for dioxin contamination, and those affected by it are open to parasites and infection. Residents in zone B, the second most contaminated area, were assessed and found to have increased rates of leukaemia, multiple myelomas, soft tissue sarcomas and three times the rate of liver cancer. Later studies showed that, for women who were less than 40 years old at the time of the explosion, high dioxin exposure doubled the risk of breast cancer 25 years later. [289]

One positive effect of the Seveso disaster was that it concentrated the minds of some of the scientists and authorities. In the UK, the Health and Safety Executive (HSE) ordered Coalite, in no uncertain terms, to monitor the health of its workers. A study was run by George May, the company general practitioner, with two doctors from Sheffield University, Eric Blank and Anthony Ward, and with Dr Jenny Martin, consultant chemical pathologist from Chesterfield Royal Hospital. Dr Ward who was asked to look at the immune systems of the people monitored found that the exposed workers suffered short-term immunological memory. Dr Martin discovered liver function damage, and elevated levels of cholesterol and fat proteins. Dr Martin claimed that her data was manipulated and the report did not reflect the true picture—so undertook a further study. However, her house was broken into and material used for the study was removed—so rendering her unable to publish the results. Nothing else was taken, and future monitoring of the health of these workers came to a halt. However the Ministry of Agriculture found high levels of dioxin in milk in the surrounding farms and in June the following year, the British Government banned the sale of milk from these farms, suspecting contamination from Coalite's incinerator.[290]

Large scale contamination was not limited to exploding reactors or to workers employed in industries that manufactured products such as trichlorophenol. In May 1971, in Missouri, the Bliss Waste Oil Company disposed of waste from a trichlorophenol reactor by spraying it onto un-paved dusty roads and land — which included some horse arenas. Within days of the spraying, Cats, dogs, horses and birds started dying. The contaminated soil was removed and replaced in October 1971, and again in April 1972. But still, horses died and mares miscarried—or their foals died soon after birth.[291]

Following dramatic flooding in December 1982, the contamination spread to the 2,242 inhabitants of Times Beach. When the EPA visited the area, and took samples of soil, they found that levels of dioxin were hundreds of times above safe levels. The decision was eventually taken to evacuate the town at a cost of $32 million. Among the evacuees there was a two to three-fold increase in nervous system defects and children were found with undescended testicles. However, due to the relatively small number of people in the study, it was not considered 'statistically significant'.[292] Other reporters, though, found women suffered miscarriages; children were born with other defects such spina bifida, and there were many cases of leukaemia in both adults and children. Children suffered various seizures, succumbed to liver problems, allergies, severe acne, kidney and bladder problems, thyroid disorders and bone tumours. Approximately 1500 residents were compensated with $45 million in settlements. However, I doubt many will ever feel really compensated when the true cost to their health finally becomes apparent.[293]

The company that manufactured the trichlorophenol ceased production in 1971 because of the collapse of the market for the bactericide, hexachlorophene. Originally, hexachlorophene was used as a bacteriostatic preparation for acne, impetigo, skin burns etc., it was also used for scrubbing-up routines in hospitals—and even used as a routine wash for new-born babies. In the late 1950s, hexachlorophene had also been used in common consumer products. It was widely promoted on television as a new wonder product in soaps, deodorants, even vaginal sprays. It was found to control Staphylococcus infections particularly Staphylococcus aurens — this made it particularly popular in nurseries. However subsequent reports, one commissioned by the EPA, had shown hexachlorophene to cause cerebral edema, brain lesions and hind-limb paralysis in rats; another reported the neurological damage and subsequent death of 36 infants in France who had been given talc with 6% hexachlorophene (considered a manufacturer's error). By the time the deaths had been traced to the talc powder, 36 children had died, 8 had been permanently maimed and 145 had serious nerve damage. It was also next to impossible to find any waste disposal company that would remove the waste products from the manufacture of hexachlorophene. [294]

Opposition to the Use of 2,4,5-T Grows

Over a period of time, opposition to the use of the herbicide 2,4,5-T grew. The U.S. Forest Service engaged in extensive spraying in different areas of the U.S., supposedly to control broad-leafed trees and encourage the growth of the more profitable softwood trees. 2,4,5-T was also being heavily used on rice crops in Arkansas. But people were so worried about the effect on their health of the use on rice crops that they took out a lawsuit against the Forest Service, claiming that it violated the National Environmental Policy without proper authorisation. They succeeded in stopping the spraying until a proper environmental impact statement was approved. Injunctions were also taken out in Michigan and Wisconsin (as well as the case in Oregon previously mentioned). 2,4,5-T was also sprayed on rangelands where cattle grazed—due to EPA secrecy, no-one knew to what extent this was occurring. Many scientists however, struggled to believe the industry hype that dioxin simply degraded in the soil due to bacterial action and sunlight.

In 1970 the U.S. government introduced restrictions on the use of 2,4,5-T around homes and around lakes, ponds, and irrigation ditches; the Department of Agriculture also introduced restrictions on non-liquid formulations for household products and on food crops. Dow Chemical appealed the restriction that affected rice crops, and was joined by Hercules Inc., and Amchen Products Inc., a vendor of 2,4,5-T. It was revealed that some one hundred thousand acres were being routinely sprayed in Mississippi and Arkansas. The appeal process is a lengthy one during which the spraying does not have to stop. By this time other environmental groups were becoming concerned about the use of 2,4,5-T on food crops—and the effect on people's health. Harrison Wellford, an associate of Ralph Nader, formally demanded that the Department of Agriculture (DOA) place a full suspension order on the use of 2,4,5-T on all food crops — and restrict other uses of the herbicide. He was joined by the Consumer Union. They were refused their demand, and so decided to appeal, asking that the government be ordered to protect the public health. The Court of Appeal held that the DOA had not given sufficient importance to the possible hazards to human health in the permitted uses of the herbicide—in particular that farm workers might be affected by it. At this this time, the Environmental Protection Agency (EPA) was taking over the regulation of pesticides and herbicides from the DOA — so in March 1971 the Appeals Court ordered the EPA to reconsider the DOA's refusal to place a firmer restriction on the use of 2,4,5-T.[295]

The EPA responded by announcing that they would impose restriction, but that they would set up an advisory panel to evaluate the safety of 2,4,5-T. The safety panel reported back two months later, saying they could not find any significant health hazard, but recommending that further research was needed on the potential of dioxin to accumulate in food chains. The report was badly received by a number of prominent biologists, such as Mathew S Meselson, Barry Commoner, and Samuel S Epstein. Eventually Ruckelshaus, the administrator of the EPA, allowed the EPA to sidestep the regulatory machinery. He issued a review of the report citing the known facts about the teratogenicity of dioxin—which is a contaminant of 2,4,5-T. He would have been aware of the study by Bionetics Research Laboratories, of Bethesda Maryland, in which they discovered that 2,4,5-T was teratogenic in mice and rats. Teratogenic means it affects foetal development—and in this case deformed offspring and foetal death had occurred. Whilst this study was undertaken in 1966 -1968, the report was not published and its contents were hard to obtain. Copies were, however, leaked. The government was criticised at the time for underplaying the significance of the research.[296]

Dow went to court again to get an injunction against the EPA's action. Ruckelshaus continued the cancellation orders, declaring it was abundantly clear that Dow had not met the burden of proof that 2,4,5-T was harmless. EPA appealed Dow's injunction which was obtained in the Arkansas District Court—and the Court Of Appeals in St Louis upheld the EPA's appeal.

Whilst the legal wrangling caused delay after delay, research from other sources was coming to light. Dr Ruth Shearer, a molecular geneticist and consultant in genetic toxicology from Issaquah, Washington, was concerned about the potential harm of herbicides like 2,4,5-T and 2,4-D, and was particularly interested in the possible carcinogenicity of herbicides like 2,4-D. A Russian study had found that pre-malignant cells exposed to 2,4-D would turn into fully malignant cancer cells. Shearer found that 2,4-D contained another chemical, 2,4-dichlorophenol as an impurity, and that as the original 2,4-D (2,4-dichlorophenoxyacetic acid) broke down by microbial action in the environment, it formed more of this impurity. She found that it was an even stronger promoter than 2,4-D, as well as being a cancer initiator (a carcinogen). She revealed that 2,4-D induced mutations in both animal and human cells in cultures and damaged DNA in a similar manner to ionizing radiation. It also caused developmental toxicity in offspring when given to pregnant female animals, and foetal hemoraging at a low dose in rats. In the presence of the breakdown product, 2,4-dichlorophenol, increased synergistically.[297]

In 1976, Lennart Hardell from the University Hospital of Umeå came across a number of workers suffering from soft tissue sarcomas that were known to have been exposed to phenoxy herbicides. This was a rare condition, but there were too many sufferers for it to be a simple coincidence. He undertook further research and eventually published his results in 1977. He had found that exposure to phenoxy herbicides increased the risk of soft tissue sarcoma six fold. The response from the Swedish EPA was not encouraging—nor was it from the unions. He undertook another study, this time with fellow researcher from Umeå, Mikael Eriksson, and came to the same results.[298]

Dioxin's Link with Cancer and Numerous Health Issues

As time passed, more and more information accumulated about phenoxy herbicides and dioxin. Dioxin researcher James Huff observed "In every species so far exposed to TCDD... and by every route of exposure, clear carcinogenic responses have been found"

Cancers include cancer of the lung, nose, mouth, adrenal glands, thyroid, lymphatic system and skin. Dioxin is now also known to affect the hormone system in a number of different ways, by altering the metabolism of hormones, their transport through the blood stream, and increases the number of hormone receptors responses, which makes any organism more sensitive to its own hormones, and upsets the normal hormone mechanism. It can affect the levels of vitamin

A and calcium in the body and affect serum triglyceride levels. It can also affect growth factors such as interferon and interleukon. Exposure of rats to dioxin in the laboratory revealed exposures in early life can permanently affect the mammary gland, and pre-birth, and it predisposes rats to breast cancer.[299]

Dioxin has certainly proved a challenge to researchers, and findings have not been easily reproducible. It was found that different dioxins produced different cancers, particularly when exposure involved such a variety of sources. It is only in recent years that we have had the technology to measure compounds in the parts per trillion that is needed when dealing with dioxin. There are only 40 WHO-recognised labs in the world capable of this. One of the problems with studying the effects of a toxin like dioxin is that it has a number of guises—the furans and PCBs can have different effects, and how they react synergistically is anybody's guess. PCBs can contain both furans and dioxins—as PCB degrades it adds an oxygen molecule and becomes a furan, add two molecules and it becomes a dioxin.

The same chemical can produce different symptoms in different people with the same exposure at the same time. What of course we don't know is what level of toxic burden is experienced by the various people exposed, up until the moment of this new exposure. When a chemical like dioxin can seriously affect the immune system so much so that you get a chest infection which develops into pneumonia and you die from it, what do you think they will write on your death certificate? You can be sure it won't be dioxin poisoning. They didn't do that for the first death in Seveso.

In this chapter I have discussed some aspects of the problems with some of the 'magic chemicals' of the 20th century, and hinted at the background of some of them. It might seem that I have indulged the dioxin/furan/PCB area more than others—and I have. This is for a number of reasons. Firstly since it is a persistent poison, it bio-accumulates in fatty tissue in living organisms and has a long half-life. Even though it was banned in the USA, Europe, and many other countries it still has an effect on our lives today. I could discuss many other toxins, out of the many thousand un-tested chemicals that we are exposed to, but that is not the purpose of this book. It would take many volumes to do that. I am hoping that by concentrating on the true impact of current and past policies I will give a broader picture of what we are facing, both as a legacy and as a future. There are quite a number of excellent sources of information given for those who wish to delve further into any topic raised, not just the in references I cite, but also in the resource section at the end of the book. The book, *Dying From Dioxin—A Citizen's Guide to Reclaiming Our Health and Rebuilding*

Democracy, by Lois Marie Gibbs and the Citizens Clearinghouse for Hazardous Waste, is an excellent book on dioxin, its history, politics etc. Lois introduces her book with the following:

> The Dioxin story includes coverups, lies, and deception; data manipulation by corporations and government as well as fraudulent claims and faked studies. For the public, it's a story of pain, suffering, anger, betrayal, and rage; of birth defects, cancer, and many other health problems. It's a story of money and power; of how corporations influence government actions and how this collusion affects the public.[300]

It would be easy to state that the majority of pollution that has occurred in the past was in large part due to a lack of care or interest in the environmental consequences of the industries where it was produced. There are many instances where the profit motive has been the overriding consideration in how products were developed, and still are developed. Numerous writers have documented instances where workers have been denied compensation for illnesses suffered due to workplace exposures where manufacturers have denied responsibility. A few are documented here. Most of us have read about the pollution caused by developments carried out by some western companies in southern Countries (I use this terminology in place of 'third world'). Petroleum producer's laxity of concern for environmental consequences has been notorious—away from the glare of western media. Unfortunately, much of our attitudes and responses to our current problems are rooted in this unhappy past.

The Development of Chlorine Chemistry

In the late 19th century German chemists were at the forefront of industrial science. They had synthesized dioxin in the late 1800s. Chlorine was discovered soon afterwards by passing electricity through water with a high salt content. This was the chlor-alkali process; it produced sodium hydroxide, hydrogen and chlorine. The sodium hydroxide, commonly known as caustic soda, was by far the more desirable discovery—the demand for it by industry has been a priority since its discovery, and has increased virtually every year since. Chlorine, on the other hand was more like a poisoned chalice. Chlorine is highly reactive and extremely dangerous because of the products it creates and their effects on biological systems.

The discovery of chlorine led to a number of developments. Fritz Haber, a German chemist received a Nobel prize in chemistry 1918 for the synthesizing of ammonia and its by-products that were vital for explosives during the war — after the war, they were used as fertilizer. He was also credited for the development of gas warfare, where chlorine and phosgene gases were used as chemical weapons. As previously mentioned, his wife, also a chemist, killed herself due to his work on the development of biological weapons which culminated in the gassing of people in the trenches and concentration camps. A short time later, his son followed suit.[301] Herbert Dow, The founder of the US chemical corporation, Dow Chemical, developed a whole range of new chemicals by combining chlorine with organic chemicals to produce chlorinated hydrocarbon compounds—the organochlorines (these are also called halogenated aromatic hydrocarbons). Organic in the chemical sense simply means carbon based.[302]

The first significant production of polychlorinated biphenyls (PCBs) was undertaken for the army by Anniston Ordinance Company in 1914, making shells for the army. The company was taken over by Monsanto in 1935,[303] and Monsanto went to become the major producer of PCBs in the USA. As you might imagine, during the war there was a lot of interest in being at the forefront of all pertinent developments in chemistry. But new technologies created new problems. When new illnesses surfaced because of these new technologies, worker safety was not always at the top of the agenda. As with the cover-up of fluoride poisoning during the Manhattan project there was a tendency to bulldoze away such concerns like worker health or environmental contamination. However, when peacetime returned the tendency to hide the true facts about chemical exposures persisted—and the collusion between industry and government continued and still continues, except when public pressure is intense enough to galvanise action to the contrary.

PCBs were used in a large variety of ways, as insulating oils in transformers, as hydraulic liquids, heat transfer fluids in such things as deep fat fryers, lubricating oils, plastics, inks, paper and paints etc. Awareness of the danger of PCBs was aroused when a serious contamination occurred in upstate New York: A collision with an electricity utility pole caused a problem in the electric transformers that connected the University campus of New Paltz two miles distant. The electrical system went haywire, one of the transformers exploded and caught fire, smoke contaminated with PCBs, furans and dioxin poured through a hall of residence. Within minutes, a chain reaction had occurred, further transformers exploded and more residence halls and college buildings were covered in toxic smoke. Fortunately for the students, they were away on their winter break, so casualties were limited to fire-fighters and people in the area. Three years later, and after spending $35 million on the clean-up, decontamination is still not complete—and lawsuits have been filed.[304]

One of the fallouts from this 'accident' was the information that came to light from the vast collection of papers made available during the subsequent hearings and court proceedings.

BLIND FAITH

Large numbers of lawsuits came from utility workers and consumers who suffered from the actions of those who were perceived to have profited from the sale or use of PCBs—but had failed to warn the public of their dangers. Documents revealed that three of the biggest corporations in America, Monsanto, General Electric (GE) and Westinghouse had known since the 1930s of many of the harmful effects associated with PCBs, but had deliberately chosen to keep this information to themselves. Whilst the accident had been a major surprise to the general public, it had not apparently been to those in the know. One internal memo dated 1974, produced by GE, revealed their awareness (both GE and Westinghouse) of the likelihood of transformer explosions. This was a decade before the EPA had raised warnings about the possibility. It was also news to many that some grades of PCB create an explosive gas when there is a serious transformer malfunction—and, further, that during combustion dioxins and dibenzofurans, (considered by many researchers to be even more toxic than PCBs), are released. This information had been concealed from their customers.

PCBs Restricted

Much of this similar information was released after the explosion and the subsequent hearings. Monsanto was the only source of PCB manufacture in the USA for four decades. It was found that it had falsified data on cancer, and fudged the results to delay implementation of federal regulations restricting PCB use — and these were not introduced until 1976. Monsanto was accused of allowing significant exposure to the population and contamination of the environment throughout this period, resulting in increased incidences of cancer and related illnesses. It was revealed that Monsanto was more concerned for their corporate image than the public's health.[305]

When the US Congress finally introduced legislation on PCBs, banned any future production in the US they restricted the use of them to enclosed systems, such as transformers that were already in existence. By this time, however, it has been estimated that in excess of 3 billion pounds (excluding Russian production) had been produced and let loose on the planet, beyond recall. According to one lawsuit, new PCB oil could be contaminated with dibenzofurans in concentrations of up to 10 parts per million which considerably increases as the product ages. A 1938 study of PCB oil-mixtures manufactured by GE and Westinghouse demonstrated that liver damage could be caused by skin contact alone—and recommended the "greatest personal hygiene "to minimise risk. It was also revealed that Monsanto had in its files a 1947 report recommending a requirement to give warning about the toxicity of PCBs. They had also known since 1965 that dioxin could be a "potent carcinogen" [306]

Even after the US had banned the production of PCBs, world production continued at 33 million pounds a year (1980-84) and decreased somewhat to 22 million pounds (1984-89). However they are still in production today. Estimates vary widely as to how much is currently in use' and how much is in the environment—in lakes, soil and sediments, and landfills etc. However, it is estimated that only one percent has so far reached the oceans. PCBs tend to flourish in the food chain: bigger fish eat smaller fish, toxins accumulate, people eat fish—and the higher up the chain, the more the toxin is concentrated. Many large marine mammals, such as dolphins, whales, sea lions, seals etc. lack the necessary enzymes to detoxify PCBs efficiently, as do some large birds. Those toxins further build up and are passed on to offspring through their eggs and milk. One of the most worrying aspects of the contamination is the ability of PCBs to mimic hormones. It has been established that marine mammals are already experiencing difficulties with reproducing, miscarriages, premature births etc. Introducing hormone mimics is a recipe for disaster in any organism. Some researchers believe there is a distinct possibility that all large marine mammals could become extinct when more PCBs reach the oceans. Although the dioxins and furans are considered more toxic than PCBs, it is the PCBs that are considered more of a threat to reproduction. PCBs are present in human breast milk in varying quantities, depending upon where you live, but can approximate out one part per million (ppm) in the milk fat — which can mean for an infant that they are exposed to five times the "allowable daily intake" as recommended by WHO. Infants exposed to what is referred to as "background levels" have loss of muscle tone, weakened reflexes at birth, delays in psychomotor development, and diminished visual recognition at 7 months. [307]

PCBs found to Be Even More Dangerous

Knowledge about the dangers of PCBs was known as early as 1936 when workers at New York City's Halowax Corporation became exposed to chlorinated diphenyls (as they were referred to then) and chlorinated napthalines, and subsequently suffered debilitating conditions such as chloracne (chloracne I have previously described). Three workers died, and their autopsies revealed severe liver damage. Cecil Drinker from Harvard University was asked to investigate. Drinker had a meeting with Halowax, US Public Health Service officials, State health officials from Massachusetts and Connecticut, as well as Monsanto and General Electric. Drinker undertook experiments on rats, which he exposed to the diphenyls and napthalines and found they suffered severe liver damage. He concluded that the chemicals caused systemic effects. Sanford Brown, the President of Halowax, was recorded as stressing the "necessity of not creating mob hysteria on the part of workmen in the plants" where safety inspections were been undertaken. He suggested that the problems would probably continue for years.[308]

According to a report in the Washington Post, [309] Monsanto had a PCB manufacturing plant in Aniston, Alabama, that allegedly routinely discharged toxic waste into the nearby West Anniston creek, and dumped millions of pounds of PCBs into open pit landfills. Documents later acquired showed Monsanto had concealed information for decades; some of the documents were titled "CONFIDENTIAL: Read and Destroy".

In 1966, Monsanto executives were shown how polluted West Anistion creek was when fish in the creek turned belly up, started spewing blood—and began shedding skin as if being par-boiled. In one creek, levels 7,500 times the accepted legal limits for PCBs were found. Monsanto apparently decided there was little point in going to the extreme expensive of limiting the discharge. Instead they enjoyed a very lucrative monopoly of PCB production for forty years. The EPA, by contrast, ordered General Electric to spend $460 million to dredge out the PCBs that it had dumped in the Hudson River. Monsanto were much luckier at Anniston, according to Grunwald. They only had to spend $40 million on clean-up operations (reputedly, they had to spend more than that on legal settlements; at the time of the Washington Post article, it was a mere $80 million—but I understand there was further lawsuit involving 3,600 plaintiffs that was due to be heard.[310]

The same article goes on to state that the levels of pollution (according to Professor David Carpenter, a leading environmental health researcher with Albany University of New York), are much higher in Anniston compared to the Hudson river where GE had to do the dredging. Professor Carpenter found that the PCB levels in the Anniston population were the highest of any populations he had so far seen; ten times that of the Hudson River.

The undertaker, Sylvester Harris—he lived across the road from the plant—always believed there must be something wrong with the place because he was burying too many young children. Monsanto eventually purchased and demolished approximately 100 homes that were contaminated by its PCB operations there.

Anniston lawsuits have uncovered a large number of documents which detail the behind-the-scenes manoeuvring dating right back to the 1930s — many of these documents were obtained by the Washington Post. One of the company memos that originated from the time when Monsanto acquired the 70 acre plant in 1935 stated "cannot be considered non-toxic". In a 1937 Harvard study, it was found to cause liver damage and produce the severe rash called chloracne—and Monsanto had hired the scientist who led the study. Subsequent memos referred to the "systemic toxic effects" of Aroclors which was the name of their PCB product. Monsanto began warning its industrial customers to protect their workforces from Aroclor by insisting on showers after every shift, supplying all of them with clean work clothes each working day, and keeping fumes off the factory floor.[311]

Professor Jack Matson, an environmental engineer from Pennsylvania State University, who had previously undertaken consultative work for Monsanto, supplied a report for some of the Anniston plaintiffs. This reported that the company had failed to observe even basic industry practice at the plant. It had no catch basins, settling ponds or carbon filtration systems to clean its wastewater—it simply washed spills into the sewers.[312]

Widespread contamination of the food chain in the US was reported by Dr Robert Riseborough, for the University of California, Berkeley, during his work on Peregrine falcons. This was first reported in the San Francisco Chronicle by David Perlman under the title of "A Menacing New Pollutant" (Feb 24th 1969) and subsequently received much wider coverage. Monsanto quickly launched a counter-offensive public relations exercise, firstly claiming that the chemicals found were not PCBs, and secondly dismissing the allegation that polychlorinated biphenyls are 'highly toxic' by saying simply: "This simply was not true." They further commented "The source of marine-life residue identified as PCB is not yet known. It will take extensive research, on a worldwide basis, to confirm or deny the initial scientific conclusions." [313]

Eric Francis, writing for *Sierra Magazine* reports that Monsanto already had the information necessary to either confirm or deny the claim. A Swedish chemist by the name of Soren Jensen, whilst working on DDT in 1966, came across some PCBs in blood samples — but at that time did not know what they were. It took him two years of investigations to find out during which time he discovered that all of Sweden and its adjacent seas were contaminated. He even found traces of it in hair samples taken from his wife and three children. More ominously, the highest levels were found in his nursing infant daughter. According to Francis:

> Jensen's discovery, first reported in 1966 in the English journal New Scientist, set in motion the chain of events that Monsanto, GE, and Westinghouse had hoped to avoid. The European press took notice immediately, and other scientists soon began investigating PCBs.[314]

In 1968 further worries about PCBs had surfaced in Japan after PCB fluid leaked into rice-bran oil (called yusho), and caused a mass food-poisoning outbreak — more than 1600 people were initially exposed. People suffered from severe chloracne, respiratory ailments and failing vision. Later, other problems surfaced—low birth weights, birth defects, a three-fold increase in liver cancer in women and six-fold increase in men, all within nine years. Despite the international exposure of this incident, Monsanto's corporate development committee embarked on a four year goal of increasing its sales of therminol heat transfer fluid (its name for the PCB fluid in therminol) by twenty times — just two months after this pollution incident in Japan.

While Monsanto was denying that there were problems linked with PCBs in 1969, their internal documents revealed another story. In its "Pollution Abatement Plan" in which it acknowledges that "the problem involves the entire United States, Canada and sections of Europe, especially the United Kingdom and Sweden.... [O]ther areas of Europe, Asia and Latin America will surely become involved. Evidence of contamination [has] been shown in some of the very remote parts of the world."

The Pollution Abatement Plan proposed three options (shown with charts documenting potential profits and liabilities:

1. Do Nothing. This they noted would watch their profits decline and their liabilities extend into the future. "If we took no action we would likely face numerous suits."
2. Discontinue Manufacture of PCB. This would have the effect that profits would cease and their liabilities would soar because "we would be admitting guilt by our actions."
3. Responsible approach. This would involve acknowledging certain aspects of the problem, tightening restrictions but continuing to manufacture and sell PCBs. Profits would increase while liabilities would decrease and eventually vanish by the mid-1970s.

Monsanto chose the third option and decided to go into battle with regulatory forces to keep PCBs on the market — despite growing evidence that they posed a public health disaster and an environmental nightmare. From this point on, Monsanto made all its customers sign agreements indemnifying it against any future liabilities. In 1970, Emmett Kelly, a Monsanto physician, revealed that cattle feed from several grain silos were being contaminated by paint flaking and leaching into grain which affected milk from at least three known herds of animals. It was known that there were up to 50 similar silos in the state with the same formulation of PCB paint, and Kelly warned that there could be "legal and publicity overtones," He further warned "This brings us to a very serious point. When are we going to tell our customers not to use any Aroclor in any paint formulation that contacts food, feed, or water for animals or humans? I think it is very important that this be done.... I think we should make a blanket recommendation against these uses." Francis goes on to mention that despite the years of lawsuits, manufacturers have never been able to produce any evidence that these warnings were given. [315]

Industry Cover-ups Exposed

For years, industry scientists claimed that there was no evidence to support the view that dioxins cause cancer in humans. Two studies that supported this view have been revealed to be fraudulent, one produced by Monsanto and one by BASF. A scientist who worked for the EPA, Dr Cate Jenkins, accused Monsanto publicly of falsifying data to support its claim that dioxin does not cause cancer in humans. She worked as a chemist in the EPA's Office of Solid Waste and Emergency Response— and maintained that the EPA relied on Monsanto's fraudulent data in setting standards for dioxin. She asked that the EPA's Science Advisory Board re-open the question of dioxin standards and review the evidence.[316] The EPA were not happy with Jenkin's whistle-blowing antics, and they grounded her. She complained to the Department of Labour who agreed that this was a case of illegal harassment. The EPA appealed to the courts, but the judge found in her favour. The even appealed to the Secretary of Labour, but he too found in her favour. The EPA was forced to investigate Monsanto but then with no reason given they dropped their investigation in August 1992.[317]

In 1989, Stephanie Wanchinksi published an article in the *New Scientist*, a British technical Journal, titled a "New analysis links dioxin to cancer." In it she reported the work of a West German epidemiologist who she believed may have established the first clear evidence of a link between cancer in humans and dioxins. Friedemann Rohleder, an independent researcher, produced a report on workers who were exposed to dioxins during an industrial accident in 1953 and, who had a high incidence of cancer. The plant was operated by BASF and manufactured trichlorophenol. Rohleder claims the company "presented the data in a way that disguised the cancers."[318]

Both cases involved industrial accidents in which workers were exposed to dioxins. The follow-up medical studies were published in mainstream scientific journals and claimed that that no excess cancers occurred in the exposed workers. However, it turned out that this was not the case. Excess cancers had occurred but it was alleged that the data had been manipulated to hide this.[319]

BLIND FAITH

In 1971, Monsanto engaged Industrial Bio-test Laboratories (IBT) of Northbrook Illinois, to do safety studies on Aroclor, its PCB product, to help establish their position that they believed that PCBs were not highly toxic. One of Monsanto's toxicologists, Dr Paul Wright took a job at IBT labs in part to help supervise the study. After its conclusion, he returned to work for Monsanto and was given $1,000 award for "forestalling EPA's promulgation of unrealistic regulations to limit discharges of polychlorinated biphenyls." Seven years later (IBT) would be at the centre of a massive scandal, probably one of the most far-reaching scandals to affect the scientific world. Hundreds of its studies were revealed, through FDA and EPA investigations, to be fraudulent or grossly inadequate. Paul Wright was eventually convicted of multiple counts of fraud in what was one of the longest criminal trials in American history. His legal fees were paid by Monsanto. In 1977, IBT president Joseph Calandra, Wright and others were brought to trial on Federal fraud charges.[320]

A number of memos came to light during the trial that revealed the way Monsanto executives had influenced the outcome of the study. Monsanto's Elmer Wheeler had written, in March 1970 to the IBT president Calandra, . "I think we are surprised (and disappointed?) at the apparent toxicity at the levels studied, I doubt that there is any explanation for this but I do think that we might exchange some new thoughts." Two months later he commented on a set of new test results, "We would hope that we might find a higher 'no effect' level with this sample as compared to the previous work." A few years later Monsanto was quoted even more directly "In two instances, the previous conclusion of 'slightly tumorigenic' was changed to 'non-carcinogenic,'" Monsanto later wrote in July 1975: "The latter phrase is preferable. May we request that the Aroclor 1254 report be amended to say 'does not appear to be carcinogenic'." A couple of weeks later Calandra replied : "We will amend our statement in the last paragraph on page 2 of the Aroclor 1254 report to read, 'does not appear to be carcinogenic' in place of 'slightly tumorigenic' as requested." Testimony in the hearings against Monsanto revealed that IBT was well aware that PCBs caused extremely high incidences of tumours in test rats, with in excess of 80 percent developing tumours when fed Aroclor 1254 at 10 parts per million and 100 percent at 100 parts per million. Yet IBT certified PCBs as a non-carcinogen.[321]

It's hard to overestimate the problems created by the whole saga of IBT labs. The Centre for Public Integrity's view is that "The U.S. regulatory system is tailor made for fraud. The subjects are arcane, the results subjective, the regulators overmatched, and the real work conducted by—or for—the manufacturers themselves." IBT was the nation's largest toxicological laboratory, and conducted 35-45 percent of all toxicological testing in the U.S.A. this was not just for industrial chemicals but also for drugs, tests that both the EPA and the FDA came to rely on. This had bigger implications because much of the rest of the world relied on this data and the official American position for their own regulatory procedures.

The IBT lab was initially exposed when an FDA pathologist, Adrian Gross, questioned a rat study, dealing with the arthritis drug Naprosyn, that seemed a little too good to be true. Federal regulators then discovered other evidence that dozens of studies had been faked. Some were found to be total fabrications, based on no data at all—and eventually hundreds of studies were declared invalid. When a team of investigators descended on IBT in January 1978, for a top-to-bottom inspection they found many documents shredded. But by interviewing employees and sifting through pages of other documents, they discovered that some chemical companies actually knew what was going on. They also found evidence that Monsanto may have known about the fakery. 322

Dowell Davis, a research pharmacologist from the FDA, who was part of the investigative team, had this to say, "IBT is the worst anyone's ever seen. They were hell-bent on providing their clients with favourable reports. They did not care about good science. It was about money. They really had what was almost an assembly line for acceptable studies." Paul Wright, the research chemist from Monsanto, whilst only at the lab for eighteen months, was believed by the investigators to have colluded in a series of studies that benefitted Monsanto. According to internal memos, Monsanto knew studies were faked and sent them to the EPA and FDA anyway. Monsanto executives vehemently deny that before the cheating was exposed in 1976, anyone at the company, other than Wright, knew that the IBT studies were faulty. But the investigators found numerous other cases, one involving Machete, a rice and sugarcane herbicide, where extra lab mice were added to bias the result; another involving monosodium cyanurate, a swimming pool chlorinator, showed that animal deaths had been concealed and raw data replaced. The final report included claims about procedures and observations that never happened. 323

That this scandal was a major revelation at the time was in no doubt. The EPA and FDA were forced to question their oversight of product testing. Yet this was not an isolated example. Craven Laboratories Inc., of Austin, Texas, was also caught faking pesticide studies. These studies were intended to make sure that the general public was not ingesting unsafe levels of pesticides in fruits, grains and vegetables. Craven, at the time, was considered one of the top testing laboratories for pesticide manufacturers such as DuPont and Monsanto. But this time, after an employee had informed the authorities of various frauds perpetrated, things changed. When the investigators visited the laboratory, however, they could find nothing wrong—the labs had been tipped off and covered up what was going on in a very sophisticated way. However, following further help from an employee, the investigators uncovered how Craven had faked the studies of 20 pesticides used on more than fifty crops. Dona Allen Craven, the lab owner, and fifteen employees, eventually pleaded guilty to fraud charges. [324]

It wasn't just how reports were produced in laboratories that achieved the aim of distorting science—many other tactics were used. An example from *Toxic Deception* concerns contamination of water supplies in Fayette County, Iowa. An official by the name of Richard Kelly, from the Iowa Department of Water, Air and Waste Management, was doing a study of contaminants in the State's water supplies—and decided to include weed killers in his survey. A previous researcher from the Iowa Geological Survey, George Hallberg, had previously found high levels in a small 1983 study, so Kelly decided to check how the situation was now (1985). He found them in almost every water source he tested. The industry response is best illustrated by Kelly's own report of it. "When we got hits on alachlor and atrazine, the pesticide industry came down on us like a bunch of storm troopers... They came out and publically criticised our study, and it was routine to get phone calls from their local reps telling me what an idiot I was." [325]

In the summer of 1985 Monsanto, under instructions from the EPA was conducting a nationwide monitoring survey. The EPA at this time was in the middle of its own special review of Alachlor—and Lyle Jackson, the chief public health official of Fayette County, was responsible for seeing that the wells were safe. He was well aware of the major spraying of the State's soya beans and corn with atrazine, alachlor and other weed killers. But neither Kelly nor Jackson was happy when they discovered which wells, rivers and lakes Monsanto was sampling for their study. In Jackson's recollections "It was not really an objective type of study". Instead of sampling shallow wells in sandy terrain where pesticides were easily found, they had chosen to sample deep wells in clay-bound areas where it was unlikely to find contamination — clay soils don't drain like sand does. Jackson and Kelly both agreed: "The study was systematic—it was systematically designed not to find the product." They both complained independently to the EPA, but Monsanto claimed they were both wrong. Their research manager, Andrew Klein, who helped to design the 1985 surveys, had this to say, "Nobody's criticised the scientific validity of either of those studies." He maintained, "We did not do a survey of Fayette County, we did a survey of alcholor use, and we looked at vulnerable and less vulnerable areas." [326]

One of the problems currently faced by our society is the massive number of different chemicals in the environment—estimated at approximately 80,000, the majority of which are untested. In December, it had been in 1970 during the presidency of Richard Nixon, that the Environmental Protection Agency (EPA) had been set up, following rising concerns of the general public about problems with pesticides such as DDT, after the publication of Rachel Carson's book *Silent Spring*.

Following on from the set-up of the EPA, The Toxic Substances Control Act came into force, in 1976. However, the problem with the way this law was set up was that it allowed chemicals to stay on the market until they were proven to be a risk, and, further, that the EPA would rely on research submitted by the manufacturers, rather than carry out its own tests. This method had a huge impact globally because it quickly became the norm internationally. This situation effectively means that industry can make vast profits polluting the world unless the taxpayer or very wealthy individual is prepared to invest the money to prove that a chemical is harmful. The problem here is that absolute proof harm is very difficult to achieve. How do you prove that your personal cancer was caused by exposure to pesticides or some other chemical?

In the report *Reducing Cancer Risk: What We Can Do Now*, by the US Department of Health and Human Services in conjunction with the NIH and ACI, this approach was criticised as follows:

In the United States, about 42 billion pounds of chemicals are produced or imported daily. Many of these chemicals are used in massive quantities exceeding one million tons per year... A number of environmental health scientists and advocates believe that some exposure levels deemed safe by regulators are in fact too high. They maintain that exposures far below the reference dose are causing harm and in some cases, inducing cancer development. Moreover, they believe that some agents cause harm at very low doses and that regulatory prudence is indicated until potential effects such as these are better understood.

However, the prevailing regulatory approach in the United States is reactionary in that it:

- Requires incontrovertible evidence of harm before preventative action is taken.
- Places the burden on the public to show that a given chemical is harmful.
- Does not consider potential health and environmental impacts when designing new technologies.
- Discourages public participation in decision making about the control of hazards and the introduction of new technologies, chemicals, or other exposures.

They further add the comment:

Industry has exploited regulatory weaknesses, such as the government's reactionary (rather than precautionary) approach to regulation.[327]

That industry has exploited this weakness in regulation will be explored in the next chapter (and is a concurrent theme in this book).

Chapter 9
Choking On Science

For decades tobacco companies have killed more Americans than all the armies, terrorists, and criminals combined...this morally revolting story...exposes the biggest public-health scandal of the past century.

Ronald L. Numbers, Hilldale Professor of the History of Science and Medicine, University of Wisconsin. [328]

History has a way of repeating itself, especially if we refuse to learn its lessons. Looking into the historical record can give us insight about where we are now, how we got here—and perhaps enable us to avoid some of the pitfalls we previously made. Decisions made in ignorance of all the available facts have disastrous consequences for our own health, and the future health of our children. The lessons from the whole saga of tobacco, or our love affair with lead, can be very instructive. Human beings are decidedly easy to manipulate, and much of our perception of danger is orchestrated by sophisticated media manipulation. The way the tobacco industry has used, and still uses, its vast resources to orchestrate its PR machine makes sobering reading. We'll now look at that story and how it affects us today.

The Cancer Link with Tobacco

Cancer was first linked with tobacco in 1761 by John Hill of London, who recorded cancer of the nose from the use of snuff (powdered tobacco). Nearly a century later, in 1858, by Percival Pott identified cancer of the lip of the mouth from the same source. By the end of the 19th century, tobacco cancers had been found in the lips, tongue, jaw, mouth, and nasal cavities. Medical students wrote doctoral theses on the subject; they were referred to by physicians as "smokers' cancers." In those days tobacco was rarely inhaled, because it was considered too harsh on the lungs. Most of the nicotine was absorbed through nose and mouth. It was not until a new process of curing tobacco (flue curing) rendered the tobacco milder, so much milder that it was able to be inhaled deeply into the lungs without coughing. Tobacco consumption grew dramatically in the late nineteenth century and the early twentieth century. In the early periods of the 20th Century people seemed to turn a blind eye to the health hazards of tobacco, a blasé attitude permeated the U.S. particularly; cigarettes were freely included with K rations for US troops—which resulted in a significant rise in tobacco smokers returning from the Great War of 1914-1918.[329]

In the 1930s Germany had some of the highest incidences of cancer in the world. Lung cancer in particular had risen fivefold by 1933, and claimed one in eight cancer victims. This prompted a significant movement that sought to improve the health of the German people, the *Gesundheit Über Alles*—healthfulness over all. In 1939 the *Gesundheitsführer*, Leonardo Conti, set up the Bureau Against the Dangers of Alcohol and Tobacco. Its research showed that men who smoked suffered ten times more lung cancer than non-smokers. Restrictions on the use of tobacco were subsequently introduced: Pregnant women were barred from purchasing cigarettes, and smoking was banned on trains and in public places. Steps were taken to limit the use of white flour and sugar, and to reduce exposure to aniline dyes and other known industrial toxins. Hitler himself was very supportive of the measures to ensure the health of all Germans—he may have had a particular aversion to cancer, having watched his mother Klara die of it when she was forty seven and he was just eighteen. That had been a particularly painful episode, she had already had a breast, and much of the tissue behind it, removed—and the wound had never healed; Hitler alone had had to help her, his abusive father having died three years previously. [330]

Germany prized itself on its scientific research. It's not surprising that some of the first evidence for linking the smoking of tobacco with cancer came from Dr Fritz Lickint from Dresden in 1929, the second worst city for cancer in Germany, after Chemnitz. Lickint showed that cancer patients were particularly likely to be heavy smokers, and went on to publish *Tabak und Organismus* in1939, a monumental work of 1200 pages reviewing 8,000 publications worldwide. He documented cancer of the lip, tongue, mouth, oesophagus, windpipe and lungs, all that he attributed to tobacco. He also linked tobacco to arteriosclerosis, infant mortality, ulcers and numerous other maladies. He identified tobacco as a powerfully addictive drug, and he compared tobacco addicts to morphine addicts. He also introduced the belief that passive smoking (*passivrauchen*) posed a serious threat to non-smokers. He postulated that that tobacco contributed to 7,000 male deaths in Germany per year. He became labelled as the physician most hated by the tobacco industry.[331]

CHOKING ON SCIENCE

Tobacco was thought to limit the prowess of German soldiers and hamper the abilities of Luftwaffe pilots to function—at least in part because of the carbon monoxide in the blood from smoking. Tobacco was linked to gastritis by other German researchers as well as to gastric malignancies and stomach cancer—which was the leading cause of death among both European and American men in the 1920s and 1930s. Other German doctors linked tobacco with heart disease, and Dr Franz Bücher, a pathologist from Freiburg, labelled tobacco "a coronary poison of the first order." Martin Stämmler was a physician who argued that tobacco use by pregnant women was responsible for the increasing incidences of still-births and miss-carriages. [332]

In the early thirties a researcher from Buenos Aires, A. H. Rofo, director of the new Cancer Institute, undertook a study of the toxicity of tobacco. He distilled the tarry residue from tobacco smoke, and applied it to the ear linings of rabbits—who subsequently developed tumours. In the later thirties, Franz Hermann Müller, from the University of Cologne's Pathological Institute, observed that cancer prevalence was six times more prevalent among men than women. He postulated that this could be due to the fact that many fewer women smoked than men, and looked into possible mechanisms that caused their deaths. He believed that one could be a breakdown of the physiological defence mechanism of the lung, particularly the action of the ciliated epithelium (the little hairs lining the bronchiole tubes are called cilia). When the cilia malfunction, they fail to remove debris from the lungs efficiently, so allowing hazardous materials including carcinogens to enter the body. His study was also published in the Journal of The American Medical Association (Sept 30 1939) a year after the German publication.[333]

As a survey-based retrospective case control study, using questionnaires and medical histories, Muller's work was considered one of the first epidemiological investigations. Its results were dramatic: the lung cancer victims were more than six times as likely to be "extremely heavy smokers." He concluded that "the extraordinary rise in tobacco use" was "the single most important cause of the rising incidence of lung cancer".

It must be remembered that the climate for growing tobacco in Germany was very difficult. Nicotine had been identified as the active ingredient in it in the early nineteenth century. By the mid-twentieth century attempts to remove it were available and in use; by 1940, five percent of the German harvest, 30,000 hundredweight was nicotine-free. There was also a lot of concern about the health implications — people referred to cigarettes as 'coffin nails', and those who missed work for more than four weeks due to "cigarette stomach" were required to attend hospital evaluations; those who failed to quit and kept missing work could be sent to nicotine withdrawal clinics. Hitler himself denounced tobacco as "one of man's most dangerous poisons". For a more in depth review of the German period, Robert Proctor, in his report, *Tobacco and Health,* does an excellent analysis.[334]

In 1950 there were five studies that implicated tobacco and the link with lung cancer. One was *Smoking and Carcinoma of the Lung,* from Bradford Hill and Richard Doll of the UK, published in the British Medical Journal. They observed that heavy smokers were fifty times more likely to contract cancer than non-smokers.[335]

Public Relations and the Tobacco Industry

In December 1953, after a seemingly endless amount of bad publicity about tobacco, Dr Alton Ochsner declared in a speech in New York that "The male population of the United States would be decimated unless some steps are taken to remove the cancer-producing factor from cigarettes." Apparently tobacco stocks dropped four points the next day. The tobacco industry responded by consulting Hill and Knowlton, the PR Company who had waged successful campaigns for industry in the past (and would figure significantly in the future). [336]

Meanwhile, legal actions, have led to the release of documents (and others by whistle-blowers) that give an interesting insight into the machinations of the tobacco industry. (There are a large number of sites on the internet where many of these documents can be found, and a considerable body of written work detailing the historical background).

One document from Hill and Knowlton, addressed to the Planning Committee, reveals a comment made by one of the industry's "Research Directors," Walter Winchell:

The burden of proof has shifted. It is no longer up to the scientist to prove that smoking causes lung cancer. It's the duty of all concerned to prove they do not.

The author of the document, reputedly Edwin F Dakin, follows up with the observation—

And this, of course, is exactly what no individual in the whole world can prove at this juncture- and until that proof comes in some form, arguments over the logic of some scientist, and criticism of his particular ideas of cause-and-effect, can satisfy neither scientists nor public; or get anywhere...

He continues with his evaluation of the problem facing the industry as he saw it:

CHOKING ON SCIENCE

There is only one problem, confidence, and how to establish it; public assurance and how to create it—in perhaps a long interim, when scientific doubts must remain. And, most important, how to free millions of Americans from the guilty fear that is going to arise deep in their biological depths regardless of any pooh-poohing-logic- every time they light a cigarette... and that gentlemen, is the nature of the unexampled challenge to this office.

He continues with a number of problems that they need to address: problem four is of special interest:

Problem 4. We must early decide our own attitude towards the findings of men like Wynder, Roads, Ochsner et al. We have a choice as previously indicated, of: (a) Smearing and belittling them; (b) Trying to overcome them with mass publication of the opposed viewpoints of other specialists; (c) Debating them in the public arena; or (d) We can determine to raise the issue far above them, so that they are hardly even mentioned; and then we can make our real case. [337]

In further documents, John Hill himself (of Hill & Knowlton) suggests setting up an organisation to deal with the problems facing the tobacco industry. He suggests they use the word *"research"* in the title of the organisation they set up... and further *not engage in a merely defensive campaign.. They should sponsor a public relations campaign that is entirely positive in nature and is entirely "Pro cigarette."* [338]

Further documents reveal how they suggest setting up an organisation to defend the interests of the industry. They eventually call it the Tobacco Industry Research Committee (TIRC) later to become the Council for Tobacco Research (CTR). They propose setting up the committee using reputable scientists, and also suggest making a statement to the general public proposing a format that would *seem* to address public concerns. They enclosed a draft copy for an advertisement.[339]

The actual statement was released on January 4th 1954, and was referred to as the Frank Statement, part of which I will reproduce here:

RECENT REPORTS on experiments with mice have given wide publicity to a theory that cigarette smoking is in some way linked with lung cancer in human beings.

Although conducted by doctors of professional standing, these experiments are not regarded as conclusive in the field of cancer research. However, we do not believe that any serious medical research, even though its results are inconclusive should be disregarded or lightly dismissed.

UNHEALTHY BETRAYAL

At the same time, we feel it is in the public interest to call attention to the fact that eminent doctors and research scientists have publicly questioned the claimed significance of these experiments. Distinguished authorities point out:

1. That medical research of recent years Indicates many possible causes of lung cancer.

2. That there is no agreement among the authorities regarding what the cause is.

3. That there is no proof that cigarette smoking is one of the causes.

4. That statistics purporting to link cigarette smoking with the disease could apply with equal force to any one of many other aspects of modern life. Indeed the validity of the statistics themselves is questioned by numerous scientists.

They continue with:

We believe the products we make are not injurious to health.
They further suggest what their intentions are:

Regardless of the record of the past, the fact that cigarette smoking today should even be suspected as a cause of a serious disease is a matter of deep concern to us.

Many people have asked us what we are doing to meet the public's concern aroused by the recent reports. Here is the answer:

1. We are pledging aid and assistance to the research effort into all phases of tobacco use and health. The joint financial aid will of course be in addition to what is already   being contributed by Individual companies.

2. For this purpose we are establishing a joint industry group consisting initially of the undersigned. The group will be known as TOBACCO INDUSTRY RESEARCH COMMITTEE.

3. In charge of the research activities of the Committee will be a scientist of unimpeachable Integrity and national repute. In addition there will be an Advisory Board of scientists disinterested in the cigarette Industry. A group of distinguished men from medicine, science, and education will be invited to serve on the Board. These scientists will advise the Committee on its research activities.

This statement is being issued because we believe the people are entitled to know where we stand on this matter and what we intend to do about it.

CHOKING ON SCIENCE

What is especially interesting is to see the original draft document, and the markings written over the typed sentences giving suggestions for amendments by an un-known hand:

Crossed out of the original draft was the sentence: "We will never produce and market a product shown to be the cause of any serious human ailment." The following statement was also crossed out, but with cross-hatching with a vengeance: "The committee will undertake to keep the public informed of such facts as may be developed relating to cigarette smoking and health and other pertinent matters".

This crossing-out is highly significant in the light of what is eventually revealed in various court documents. I have attached some memos detailing the setting up of TRIC to help make sense of the approach of the tobacco industry—and its response to future revelations from the scientific and medical research community and the general public at large. A number of researchers have gone into the topic a lot deeper, and there are numerous books on the topic that I will refer to. Suffice it to say that there are many people who hold the view that the industry organisation, Tobacco Industry Research Committee (TIRC), was merely a PR vehicle and not a serious research organisation at all. There are numerous documents detailing how the TIRC was significantly controlled by lawyers, and not motivated to be involved in studying the adverse effect of tobacco on our health. To quote one source:

> The tobacco industry has used three primary arguments to prevent government regulation of its products and to defend itself in products liability lawsuits. First, tobacco companies have consistently claimed that there is no conclusive proof that smoking causes diseases such as cancer and heart disease. Second, tobacco companies have claimed that smoking is not addictive and that anyone who smokes makes a free choice to do so. And, finally, tobacco companies have claimed that they are committed to determining the scientific truth about the health effects of tobacco, both by conducting internal research and by funding external research. [340]

This statement was published in *The Cigarette Papers,* By Professor Stanton Glantz of the University of California, San Francisco and his associates. He was a recipient of a vast amount of documentation that was dumped on his doorstep by a whistle-blower who worked for Brown and Williamson, the tobacco company. The book is about the revelations of these documents and others acquired. The book documents both the official views given out by the industry and the behind the scenes shenanigans of a completely different viewpoint. The papers are now all posted online.

UNHEALTHY BETRAYAL

One further quote from the book is of interest here, that of C Everet Koop, M.D., Sc.D. Surgeon General USPHS 1981-1989:

It was my privilege to serve as surgeon general of the United States Public health service from 1981-1989. The issue of smoking was on my desk when I arrived; it was on my desk when I left. As I learned more and more about smoking during my tenure as surgeon general, I was increasingly disturbed by the way the tobacco industry treated the American and world public. The analysis of the previously secret papers from a major tobacco company presented in this book demonstrates that the tobacco industry was even more cynical that I had previously dared believe.

The surgeon general is perhaps best known for the Surgeon General's reports on smoking and health. During my tenure, eight reports on smoking and health were submitted to Congress and the American public, including the 1988 report, Nicotine Addiction, *which concluded that nicotine is an addictive drug similar to heroin and cocaine. At the time - as it does today - the tobacco industry vigorously attacked the report (and me) for going beyond the scientific evidence. But now this book confirms that scientists and executives from Brown and Williamson and British American Tobacco routinely appreciated the addictive nature of nicotine a quarter of a century earlier in the 1960s.*

I'll leave you with his closing remarks about *the Cigarette Papers*:

This book is a vital weapon in the battle against tobacco. I do not believe that anyone who reads it can remain passive in the struggle against tobacco. We all need to raise our voices to clear the air for a healthier America. [341]

The Sowing of Doubt

There are a number of writers and researchers who have tried to draw attention to the way industry in general, not just the tobacco industry, tries to sow doubt in the minds of not only the general public, but in the minds of the Federal authorities, the scientific community and the world at large., They manufacture uncertainty, and demand proof where it can never be obtained, all to divert people away from the realisation that their product causes harm to human beings, or to the environment as a whole. David Michaels, an epidemiologist and director of the Project on Scientific Knowledge and Public Policy at the George Washington University School of Public Health, is one researcher who has written extensively about this topic, specifically in his highly recommended book, *Doubt is Their*

CHOKING ON SCIENCE

Product- How industry's assault on science threatens your health.[342] He cites one example that I will repeat here — a memo from the tobacco company Brown and Williamson:

"Doubt is our product since it is the best means of competing with the "body of fact" that exists in the minds of the general public. It is also the means of establishing a controversy."[343]

On January 2nd 1964 in the State Department auditorium, Luther L. Terry, M.D., Surgeon General of the U.S. Public Health Service, released the first report of the Surgeon General's Advisory Committee on Smoking and Health. The 1500-page Surgeon General's report was expected to be somewhat muted, due to the fact that it had to have unanimous approval from all the participants— and there were people associated with the tobacco industry on the committee. However, the report detailed that on the basis of more than 7,000 articles relating to smoking and disease, already available at that time in the biomedical literature, that cigarette smoking is:

- A cause of lung cancer and laryngeal cancer in men
- A probable cause of lung cancer in women
- The most important cause of chronic bronchitis
- It further went on to refer to the discovery of seven cancer-causing compounds that were in heavy enough concentrations to arouse concern.
- They mentioned that these compounds were so volatile they were difficult to quantify and were probably in larger concentrations than they could measure.

They also raised the question of whether there is a threshold for effective dosage of a carcinogenic agent, and acknowledged that this point was considered controversial at that juncture in time. [344]

It is fair to say from reactions inside the industry that this report was far more damning than they were expecting. The backlash from it had considerable repercussions. Yet, following on from it, another that caused the industry even greater concern. The Federal Trade Commission (FTC) decided to intervene. Paul Randall Dixon, chairman of the FTC had been appointed by President Kennedy, and it was anticipated he might re-vitalise the renowned lack-lustre Commission. He was a trial lawyer and became chief counsel of Senator Estes Kefauver's subcommittee investigation into corrupt business and labour practices. According to Richard Kluger the author of *Ashes to Ashes*, an excellent book on the whole tobacco story, the Surgeon General, Luther Terry's General Advisory Committee on Smoking and Health (SGAC), issued their report calling for "appropriate remedial action," regarding the tobacco industry. It was subsequently decided to introduce a draft resolution in which it was to be mandatory to have a warning label on every cigarette pack and advertisement. They issued a sample warning:

CAUTION-CIGARETTE SMOKING IS A HEALTH HAZARD. The Surgeon General's Advisory Committee has found that cigarette smoking contributes to mortality from specific diseases and to the overall death rate.

Apparently Dixon was put off taking action during a visit to the White House (the new incumbent was now Lyndon B Johnson). However he decided to go ahead against the wishes of the White House. The tobacco industry marshalled their forces behind Abe Fortas, a high power lawyer who was known to have the President's ear, and what was referred to as the "secret six" panel of general counsellors. These lawyers tried to argue that such an important move should not be left to a mere administrative industry—that, instead, it should be decided by Congress. They further argued that the industry was engaged in a legal business that played an important role in the development of the US economy generally, and that it was especially important economically for the southern tobacco states. They finally ended with a "where-will-all-of-this-end" defence, citing a previous statement made by Governor Sanford from North Carolina, "The automobile is the most dangerous machine invented, but we don't require a warning on the steering wheel. Nor do we require airlines to put a warning on their tickets that accidents sometimes happen. It makes no more sense to require a skull and crossbones on a cigarette package."

However, these arguments failed to deter the FTC from making a formal proposal in June 1964. But this was not the end to the endeavour. The Arkansas Democrat Representative put in a formal request to the FTC to delay the implementation of the proposal so that Congress would have the opportunity to debate the matter. Dixon buckled and withdrew the regulation.[345]

Tobacco Industry Delay Tactics

Delay became the name of the game. Anything that delayed action against the industry just simply meant, business-as-usual. Tying things up with regulations or proposed regulations was a very time consuming process in the wheels of government. David Kessler, former Commissioner of the U.S. Food and Drug Administration (FDA), documents his struggle with trying to get nicotine classed as a drug so that the FDA could impose controls over the tobacco industry—as they did over other drugs. He documents his struggle with the tobacco industry in his book, *A Question of Intent, A great American battle with a deadly industry.*[346] He discusses many of the delaying tactics that were used to prevent the FDA from moving against the industry.

Early on, when Kessler had joined the FDA, he had come across an informant who told him that all tobacco company executives in the public eye had to learn the industry script written by lawyers: "backwards and forwards, no deviation allowed. The basic premise was simply that smoking had not been proven to cause cancer. Not Proven, not Proven, not Proven—this would be stated insistently and repeatedly. Inject a thin wedge of doubt, create controversy, never deviate from the prepared lines. It was a simple plan, and it worked."

Even though the Surgeon General's report of 1988 declared nicotine in cigarettes to be addictive, the tobacco industry lawyers disputed the claim. One of Kessler's associates gave him some facts which illustrated how addictive nicotine is: "There are forty-nine million smokers in the United States. Three quarters of them say they are addicted, and two thirds say they want to quit. Seventeen million smokers try to quit every year, but more than ninety percent fail... After surgery for lung cancer, nearly 50 percent of those who survive resume smoking. Even when a smoker's larynx is removed, 40 percent start smoking again."

Kessler goes on to recount how The FDA was controlled by other factors over which he had no influence. He had to appear before Henry Waxman's Sub-committee on Health and the Environment, to request additional powers. But tobacco industry executives were terrified by the idea that the FDA could regulate their industry, so they set about preventing the FDA from claiming those powers. One of the members of the committee, Thomas J Bliley, a Republican representing Richmond, Virginia, sent the FDA a two page letter asking for a huge amount of information to support their claim that nicotine was an addictive drug, a taste of which I offer:

"Specifically, he wanted written summaries of all our conversations and copies of all documents we had received in connection with this 'allegation,' along with the names, addresses, and titles of anyone

who had provided us such information. The letter also asked for documentation supporting other statements......All other information or 'evidence' brought to the FDA's attention."

He goes on to state that this was one of numerous requests that he would receive from members of Congress with strong ties to the tobacco industry. He was of course legally obliged to reply as far as he was able, but it tied up vast numbers of his staff in time consuming-work. Even worse, it saved the tobacco industry having to do their own research to enable them to plan their counter-attack.

Kessler discusses how the industry was able to use its enormous wealth to stifle the argument that tobacco smoking causes cancer. For example, Philip Morris donated $200,000 to Memorial Sloan-Kettering, the renowned cancer research institute, in the sixties when Ernst Wynder was working there. Wynder had been a thorn in the industry's side throughout his career due to his tobacco research. Yet now, he was subjected to muzzling or, as better described by a memo, "more rigorous screening procedures before letting him speak in the name of the institute. This has had a proper and pleasing effect....The deductible contribution to Sloan-Kettering is probably the most effective of all health insurance contributions"—as it was described in one official Sloan-Kettering memo.

Kessler goes on to refer to the acceptance of $10 million by the AMA from six tobacco companies to refund research (on February 12, 1964). This was one month after the release of the Surgeon General's report, and followed the FTC decision on warning labels. It was also around this time that the Medicare proposals were due to be voted on by Congress. The AMA viewed Medicare as a form of socialised medicine and a menace to their livelihoods. Kessler quotes a tobacco executive, Sir Philip Rogers, head of British Tobacco Association, on a visit to the United States:

"The AMA appears more concerned with safeguarding the financial interests of doctors through political lobbying than with the doctors patients."

Kessler goes on to document some of the methods used by the industry to circumvent the threat to its profits. In December 1976, executives from seven tobacco companies got together in secret at Shoderwick House in Bath, England to address their worry that they *"would be picked off one by one and that the domino theory would impact on all of us."* They decided a united front would benefit them all and they agreed to pool resources into a new organisation, the International Council on Smoking Issues (ICOSI).

Kessler records information given to him by an insider who talked about a "company within a company" that controlled Philip Morris's most sensitive research. INBIFO was set up by Philip Morris in Cologne, Germany and was used not just for research but also as a refuge for material that was too dangerous to keep in the USA. He refers to a document written by Thomas Osdene, the director of science and technology at Philip Morris giving instructions for handling sensitive documents, *"Ship all documents to Cologne...keep in Cologne...OK to phone and telex (these will be destroyed)....If important letters or documents have to be sent please send to home- I will act on them and destroy."* [347]

Kessler tried throughout his term in office to find incriminating evidence to classify tobacco as a drug and nicotine as being addictive. In the end, there was enough political will to make this happen. Whilst in public the industry maintained the position that nicotine was not a drug, nor was it addictive, it is well documented they had known for years they were both these things. Below is an often cited statement by Sir Charles Ellis, a scientific advisor for the Research and Development arm of British American Tobacco Company (BAT). In a discussion with Dr Haselbach, in November 1961, Sir Charles Ellis made the following comments about nicotine addiction: "It differs in important features from addiction to other alkaloid drugs, but yet there are sufficient similarities to justify stating that smokers are nicotine addicts." He goes on to express concern for the tobacco industry's ability to withstand competition from the pharmaceutical industry: "...the rapid increase in the use of 'tranquilisers' and 'pep' pills which may become very serious competitors to smoking...if the competition is to be met successfully it must be important to know how tranquilising and stimulating effects of nicotine are produced, and the relation of addiction to the daily nicotine intake."[348]

BAT is the second-largest private cigarette manufacturer in the world. It operates forty five factories in thirty nine countries. It has a turnover of £43,855 million and sells in excess of 708 billion cigarettes worldwide out of the estimated 5,400 billion cigarettes manufactured. [349] Brown and Williamson used to be a wholly owned subsidiary of BAT but they signed an agreement on Oct 27, 2003 to merge the Brown and Williams operations with R.J. Reynolds, forming Reynolds American Inc. [350]

The Surgeon General's report of 1988 was the first report in which nicotine was officially referred to as addictive. The surgeon general had this to say:

> "Cigarette smoking is the leading preventable cause of disease and death in the United States. We have an enormous opportunity to reduce heart disease, cancer, stroke, and respiratory disease among members of racial and ethnic minority groups, who make up a rapidly growing segment of the U.S. population."

> —David Satcher, MD, PhD, Surgeon General [351]

A further document, one of many available — quotes Adison Yeaman, the general counsel at Brown and Williamson (B&W):

> "Moreover, nicotine is addictive....We are then in the business of selling nicotine, an addictive drug effective in the release of stress mechanisms" [352]

California's Clean Indoor Air Act gets tripped up.

I do not intend to go into the shenanigans of the tobacco industry further, I am using their story to illustrate the way information is manipulated, giving you hopefully just enough of a taste to get the general picture. I could just as easily have chosen the lead industry—some information about which I will give below. For those of you who would like a more, blow-by-blow account, I refer you to the sources quoted and *The Cigarette Century* [353] by Allan Brandt. I will however provide a brief review of California's Proposition 5 (1978), and the industry's response to it.

As time progressed, the issue of tobacco smoking shifted to the effects of 'passive smoking' or environmental pollution. Proposition 5, the Californian Clean Indoor Air Act of 1978, was the first attempt in the USA to pass a state-wide clean indoor air law. It would have mandated smoking and non-smoking sections in restaurants, workplaces and public places. The tobacco industry, wishing to ward off this assault, and realizing that it had little credibility with the general public, decided to act through a nominally independent campaign committee, the Californians for Common Sense (CCS). Suffice it to say that this strategy succeeded in defeating the proposition through a very clever PR campaign. Ernest Pepples a lawyer for B & W, details some of the strategy in a memo after the successful defeat:

CHOKING ON SCIENCE

Two decisions made in 1977 account for the victory that was achieved on November 7, 1978:

(1)   The commitment by five major cigarette manufacturers to participate in a program of early planning and research.

(2)   The commitment by those companies to provide early and adequate financing for the project.

   He describes the strategy further:

The first step was to form a California-based campaign organisation, Californians for Common Sense.

The concept: A broad based citizen membership, operating under the bi-partisan co-chairmanship of prominent and respected Californians who have no past or present connection with the tobacco industry...

   He records how they acquired the services of a polling organisation, Tarrance Data, to discover what the general electorate felt before their campaign started. He records:

It showed that more than 82% of the electorate approved the idea of a new state law requiring smoking and nonsmoking sections in public places... The same survey showed that the California voters' perception of the tobacco industry's credibility was very low. It removed all doubts that this campaign had to be California-grounded, with the tobacco Institute as far in the background as possible and with tobacco industry involvement limited to financial contributions to a California citizens committee.[354]

   Pepples gives details of the campaign strategy:

(1)   *The first phase program was to redefine the enemy. The enemy CCS selected is the foe of every voter. He passes stupid laws, wastes billions of taxpayer dollars, contributes nothing useful, dreams up useless initiatives. He is ubiquitous and he is obnoxious. Who is he? To take a small liberty with the imperishable wisdom of Pogo "We has met the enemy, and they is They" Phase one: "They're at it again!"*

(2)   *Phase two sharpened the picture of the enemy, defined him more narrowly, crowded him into a small territory. It introduced the thought that this kind of regulation is dangerously precedent setting. Voters were reminded that freedom dies a bit at a time. If they regulate smoking now, what will they regulate next? Freedom of assembly? Freedom of speech? Phase two: What will they regulate next?*

(3) Third phase asked for the order. Voters had moved onto our side in gratifying numbers but there were still many who hadn't taken the last step. They were no longer sure that Proposition 5 was right; but still hadn't decided to vote against it. Question, yes; conviction, no. Objective was to convert the doubt to a no vote. It is of course, better to show than tell-better to demonstrate than argue. CCS showed its conviction and confidence by offering to send voters a copy of the initiative. CCs made the voter a part of the progress, suggested they read it for themselves-read the fine print then decide. This not only made our point, it suggested inferentially that the other side had something to hide and CCS didn't. Phase three: <u>Read the fine print</u>."[355]

When the poll information results were undertaken they indicated that a majority of voters would not agree the measure if it was going to cost the taxpayer too much money. Specifically, it was found that if the costs were to exceed $60 million, the majority would vote against it. The tobacco industry hired a consulting firm to produce figures for the cost of the venture. And guess what figure the consulting firm came up with? Yep, you got it—$63 million. Supporters of the motion later found that those calculations were fatally flawed, and that the true figure could be counted in the thousands, not millions. There is more to the story, but I mention it here to give an indication of the tactics industry uses — and, not just the tobacco industry. Apart from *The Cigarette Papers* [356] a wealth of detail on this topic is available from a whole host of websites, many of which are listed in the Resource Section.

I will give the tobacco industry a break now, but feel inclined to finish with the immortal words of Brown and Williamson's lawyer, Ernest Pepples discussing the conundrum facing the industry:

> "If we admit that smoking is harmful to heavy smokers, do we not admit that BAT has killed a lot of people each year for a very long time? ...Moreover, if the evidence we have today is not significantly different from the evidence we had five years ago, might it not be argued that we have been 'wilfully' killing our customers for this long period? Aside from the catastrophic civil damage and governmental regulation which would flow from such admission, I foresee serious criminal liability problems."[357]

That the tobacco industry has used deceit and denial of the health risks of cigarettes can no longer be disputed. The tobacco's industry's fantastic PR machine and its public face differed widely from what it discussed and understood in private. The knowledge that tobacco was addictive and caused serious harm to human health, such as heart disease and cancer, was known and withheld from both governments and the general public for years.

Lead's harmful legacy

Unfortunately it's not just the tobacco industry which uses such tactics. The asbestos and lead industries adopted similar tactics, despite both products having been considered hazardous centuries before the industrial revolution.

The discovery of lead was inextricably linked to the discovery of silver, as far back as 2000 years ago. Lead was considered a by-product of silver production and, in time, uses were found for lead. The Romans used significant quantities for piping water, conduits, all manner of things, paint, additives to wine etc. There is a serious suggestion that the reason for the decline of Rome and the neurotic development of the Caesars was linked to neurological damage caused by lead poisoning. For years people used to put white lead on their faces as a cosmetic. In the 1920s physicians discovered that thousands of Japanese and Chinese infants had been killed or poisoned by ingesting white lead powder from their mother's faces and breasts—a practice that was also common in Europe. White lead was even added to paints from early times—and it has been suggested that Van Gogh's 'madness' may have been caused by him being poisoned by it—it was quite common for some artists to suck their brushes because of its sweetness. This also played some part in the problem with children chewing and ingesting it.[358]

Alice Hamilton was an occupational physician who studied lead for a number of years. She noted the toxicity of lead in 1908 and stated: "lead is a most potent producer of abortion". She also made the observation that it was a rare occurrence for a female lead worker to bear a healthy child at full term. She found that workers involved in lead-intensive industries such as battery production, lead-glazed ceramics, painting etc., had a high risk of disease and death.[359] She reviewed a number of factories involved in white lead production and made recommendations for improvements in their production processes to protect workers. She was instrumental in educating people in these industries to the fact that lead entered the body through inhalation and swallowing—not just through the skin. She co-authored with Harriet Hardy, one of America's preeminent occupational health physicians, a widely used textbook on occupational medicine, in which they condemned the proposed concept of a safe threshold limit of exposure to lead. Both of them argued throughout their careers that they believed growing children were most at risk of lead poisoning. [360]

However, as we have seen, official policy is often dictated by scientists who subsequently are often proved wrong. Robert Kehoe was assistant professor at the University of Cincinnati where he studied the effects of toxins including lead on proteins. In 1923 he was approached by Thomas Midgley, Jr. and Charles Kettering from General Motors (GM), following a string of deaths and poisonings in their tetraethyl lead plants. Tetraethyl lead was developed as an additive to petrol as an anti-knock compound. They hired Kehoe to investigate the cause of the poisonings. In 1925 he was named medical director of the Ethyl Gasoline Corporation and special consultant of Dupont. Kehoe established the Kettering Laboratory of Applied Physiology at the University of Cincinnati. He was responsible for establishing a threshold limit for lead exposure of 80 µg/dL as a guide for lead poisoning in blood samples. He maintained for decades that below this level there were no clinical symptoms and therefore no need for concern about lead exposure that did not breach this level. He maintained that humans were successfully able to metabolise lead and excrete it sufficiently well for it not to be a problem.[361]

Meanwhile, problems with lead poisoning came from numerous sources; the *Times* uncovered more than three hundred cases of it at Dupont's Deepwater Chemical plant in New Jersey in two years. The Deepwater plant was nicknamed "the House of the Butterflies" due to the hallucinations experienced by the poisoned lead workers who hallucinated flying insects. [362]

One of the first cases of lead poisoning in children from paint was reported in 1914 by two physicians, Henry Thomas and Kenneth Blackfan from Harriet Lane Home in Baltimore. A child who had chewed the paint off his crib was admitted to hospital, after complaining of pains in his face and head, restlessness at night. He deteriorated, and started vomiting, later suffered convulsions, went into a coma and eventually died. In the 1920s numerous reports of children succumbing to lead poisoning were reported—yet many felt there was significant under-reporting. The *Journal of the American Medical Association* published an article by John Ruddock in 1924, in which he expressed the view that lead poisoning was understated because many mild cases of it had the symptoms as spasms and colic which were missed by many doctors. A Harvard physician, Charles F. McKhann detailed seventeen cases of lead poisoning in 1926, and expressed the view that it was a relatively frequent occurrence in children. [363]

It is only in retrospect that we know there was significant underreporting for decades of lead poisoning — as our understanding of the condition slowly improved. One of the symptoms of severe lead poisoning is encephalopathy of the brain which was often miss-diagnosed as tubercular meningitis. In 1949, post mortem examination of three Cincinnati children who were recorded as having died from polio were found to have died from lead poisoning. One of the first areas in the

US to recognise the extent of lead poisoning was Baltimore in the 1930s. Huntington Williams, commissioner of health there, developed ties with John Hopkins University and the University of Maryland — where paediatricians were interested in understanding and eliminating lead poisoning. They were the first to introduce comprehensive screening for lead poisoning, as well as abatement programs to eliminate lead from housing. In 1942, Baltimore reported nearly one quarter of America's lead-poisoning fatalities—and was labelled a black spot—but this turned out to be because the Baltimore Health Department had been actively looking for lead poisoning. When other areas eventually did the same, it was found that these levels were reflected throughout the whole of the USA. [364]

In 1928, The Lead Industries Association (LIA) was set up by the National Lead Company, St Joseph Lead Company, and a number of smaller rivals. It served for many years as the industry spokesman, and served the trade by promoting the use of lead and expanding lead markets. As such, it did everything in its power to downplay and obscure the dangers associated with lead. Felix Wormser, the LIA's secretary, was the man who led the industry's battle against any negative publicity from 1928 to 1947. He contracted with Harvard University's lead researcher, Dr Joseph Aub (who had previously worked for the National Lead Company) to support his research into lead poisoning and metabolism in *adults*. He never addressed the lead effects in children. For the next three decades Aub's research at Harvard, and Kehoe's research at Kettering, dominated toxicological information on lead.[365]

In the summer of 1930 a concerned statistician from the Metropolitan Life Insurance Company, Louis Dublin, was trying to come to terms with a sudden increase in childhood lead poisoning amongst his policyholders. He decided to send a survey to seventy-five pediatricians around the country to get their views on lead poisoning. A number of them wrote back, detailing the source of poisoning as lead paint on cribs, toys, furniture and woodwork, as well as breast ointments and lead nipple shields. He published the results of his investigations in the Metropolitan's "Statistical Bulletin". It resulted in considerable publicity and "strong remonstrance by the Lead Industries Association." However, in the 1930s, the realisation of the differences between childhood lead poisoning and adult poisoning was starting to dawn. It was found that children were far more prone to central nervous system problems, and those who recovered were far more likely than adults to suffer from permanent brain damage.[366]

In many countries white lead was already banned, or severely restricted, for use as an interior paint in many places: France, Belgium and Austria in 1909; Tunisia and Greece in 1922;

Czechoslovakia in 1924; Great Britain and Sweden in 1926; Poland in 1927; Spain and Yugoslavia in 1931; and Cuba in 1934. This was during the period of intense marketing in the USA. Markowitz and Rosner expressed the situation succinctly:

> The most cynical response of the lead industry to reports of danger was a fifty-year advertising campaign to convince people that lead was safe, and most insidiously, to target its marketing campaign specifically to children.[367]

Beginning in 1918, the National Lead Company adopted the Dutch Boy logo and began an enduring advertising campaign targeting children and advertising how lead "helps guard your health." They ran posters and ads showing children painting with their lead-based paints; they produced painting books for children; they showed babies with their hands smudging their fingers on walls that were painted with lead paints—as if to show there was absolutely no need to be concerned for the health of children. In 1949 one of their trade journals made the following points:

> The appeal [of its advertising] was particularly strong to children and the company has never overlooked the opportunity to plant the trademark image in young and receptive minds. One of the most successful promotions for many years was a children's paint book containing paper chips of paint from which the pictures (including of course several Dutch boys) could be colored....The company will still loan a Dutch Boy costume-cap, wig, shirt, overalls and wooden shoes-to any person who writes in and asks for it for any reasonable purpose, and the little painter has graced thousands of parades and masquerades. [368]

In 1931, McKhann delivered a paper before the American Neurological Association in Boston, in which he explained his discovery that the most common means of lead ingestion by small children was by chewing paint from toys, cribs and other woodwork in the home.[369] This was confirmed in the same year by Edward Vogt in the Journal of the American Medical Association.[370] Both McKhann and Vogt were involved in developing the understanding that lead affected children differently from adults. Adults usually expressed lead poisoning by colic and constipation initially, followed by 'wrist drop' or 'foot drop' which involved the central nervous system. Children, on the other hand, were found to be far more likely to suffer from central nervous system problems. Many were found to suffer permanent brain damage after they 'recovered' from the early stages [371]

However, while there was at least some publicity on the dangers of lead in paints, there was none at all on the dangers of Tetraethyl lead in petrol (gasoline). Tetraethyl lead was known to be a dangerous compound—it was fat soluble, easily absorbed through the skin or lungs, and was seriously damaging to the nervous system. It was so toxic that the United States War Department had tested it as a nerve gas, but decided mustard gas was better for combat purposes. [372]

Very few people were aware that the deaths of seven workers from GM's Dayton plant in Ohio in September 1923, and DuPont's New Jersey factory in the fall of 1924 were caused by tetraethyl lead. Yet Standard Oil opened a new and even more hazardous plant in New Jersey — where five workers died in one week from what was subsequently realized to be lead poisoning. On October 27, 1924, a mysterious gas began poisoning workers at the new section of Standard Oil's refinery near Elizabeth, New Jersey. Several workers had to be subdued and confined to straightjackets, and were found to be black and blue from all the uncontrolled muscle spasms they were experiencing. They also were suffering from paranoia, delusions and hallucinations; many were found cringing from phantoms and grabbing at imaginary flying insects. They became suddenly violent and suicidal. When the first worker died in hospital writhing in agony, the horrified medical staff called in the District Attorney to investigate. [373]

Yale professor Yandell Henderson identified the mystery gas as Tetraethyl lead and labelled it "one of the most dangerous things in the country today." Henderson was well aware of Tetraethyl lead (TEL)—he was an expert on the effects of gas warfare and automobile exhaust. He had previously turned down an offer to study it for GM, citing his reason: "I should want a greater degree of freedom of investigation and funding—in view of the immense public, sanitary and industrial questions involved—than the subordinate relations which you suggest would allow." [374]

The response to the deaths in some quarters was swift; New York City Department of Health, the city of Philadelphia and a number of municipalities of New Jersey banned the sale of leaded gasoline. The day after the fifth victim died, the U.S. Bureau of Mines released the preliminary findings of a report it had been preparing that was funded by General Motors and was subjected to serious control by the Ethyl Gasoline Corporation; it did little to allay fears regarding Tetraethyl Lead. The report tried to allay fears and stated the view which; "indicates the danger of sufficient lead accumulation in the streets through the discharging of scale from automobile motors to be seemingly remote." The report was met with scepticism in most quarters; Cecil K. Drinker, professor of public health at Harvard University and editor of the *Journal of Industrial Hygiene* called the report "inadequate." Dr David Edsall of Harvard Medical School was also critical.[375]

UNHEALTHY BETRAYAL

Yandell Henderson, the Yale physiologist, expressed many people's worries at the time. He warned: "There will be vast numbers of people in all our cities who throughout their lives will have a continual low grade of lead poisoning." He also expressed the accurate view that the long range health effects would "not appear tomorrow or next year. The important effects will appear ten or even twenty-five years from now."

The Surgeon General, facing mounting concerns, appointed a committee of seven scientists to review the evidence for or against leaded gasoline, with the proviso that they announce their findings in January 1926. The committee subsequently analysed data from the employees of 252 gas stations. Their report revealed that there were elevated levels of lead in the employees, whether they pumped gas or not. This was deemed not strong enough evidence to warrant a prohibition of tetraethyl lead production or distribution. Dr Alice Hamilton, one of the foremost authorities on lead—addressed the conference and expressed the view that she believed the environmental issues with lead were far more important than the occupational health and safety issues, "You may control conditions within a factory, but how are you going to control the whole country?" After the conference she went further, "I am not one of those who believe that the use of this leaded gasoline can ever be made safe. No lead industry has ever, under the strictest control lost all its dangers. Where there is lead some case of lead poisoning sooner or later develops, even under the strictest supervision." Yandell Henderson also addressed the conference and expressed horror at the idea that hundreds of thousands of pounds of lead would be deposited on the streets of American cities. He argued that: "conditions would grow worse so gradually and the development of lead poisoning will come on so insidiously...before the public and the government awaken to the situation." [376]

The question of environmental exposure was based on an Ethyl lab test finding which estimated that 70% of the lead from the fuel stayed in the engine because it could not be measured in the exhaust gases. It was further estimated that, of the remaining 30%, half would be accounted for in the crankcase oil. Committee member Reed Hunt made a "very tentative" estimate that daily exposure to lead from auto traffic would be less than 0.5 to 1mg of lead per cubic meter (0.02 micrograms) which was the occupational threshold for lead poisoning. His calculations were shown to be woefully inadequate in the 1960s by orders of magnitude in excess of a hundred times right across the USA. It seems farcical now that most people once accepted that 85% of the lead would not be expelled into the atmosphere. WE have a lot to thank Henderson and Hamilton for.[377]

To be fair to the committee when they released their final report, did say it had limitations because of the short timescale it covered, and they did say that further study was essential:

In view of such possibilities the committee feels that the investigation begun under their direction must not be allowed to lapse... It should be possible to follow closely the outcome of a more extended use of this fuel and to determine whether or not it may constitute a menace to health of the general public after prolonged use....The vast increase in the number of automobiles throughout the country makes the study of all such questions a matter of real importance from the standpoint of public health and the committee urges strongly that a suitable appropriation be requested from Congress for the continuance of these investigations under the supervision of the Surgeon General of the Public Health Service. [378]

However, those statements were ignored, and no further tests or monitoring were undertaken.

It is a little known fact that Joseph G Leslie, one of the workers who was thought to have died at Standard Oil's Bayway plant accident in New Jersey was, in fact, was not killed, but isolated in a psychiatric hospital for 40 years. When he died in 1964, his family were shocked to learn he had been put away. And it was not until 2005 that they learned the whole story of the refinery accident, the severe lead poisoning, and resulting violent insanity amongst the workers. [379]

In 1965 Clair Patterson, a geochemist, published a report dispelling the myth promoted by the lead industry that pollution levels of lead in the environment were insignificant, and no more than two times above natural levels. BY contrast, he estimated the levels of lead in blood samples to be in the order of one hundred times above natural levels. Yet he was criticised by Kehoe as being more of a zealot instead of a scientist for the raising these warnings. Another labelled his conclusions "rabble rousing". Patterson wrote to Governor Brown of California emphasizing the high levels of lead in the air in Los Angeles two years running. At the end of the second one, Governor Brown signed a bill directing the State Department of Public Health to hold hearings and establish air standards for California by February 1997.Patterson also wrote to Senator Muskie, chairman of the subcommittee on water and air pollution offering to appear before their committee. He complained that most officials did not understand the difference between 'natural' and 'normal' levels of lead in humans. 'Natural' referred to the incorrect data of the levels in pre-industrial man, whereas 'normal' referred to the high levels found in industrial society. He was able to show that levels of lead in ice in Greenland were indeed a hundred times higher than they had been in pre-industrial times. [380]

When laws were passed in the 1970s, lead was gradually phased out from gasoline. What was soon discovered that the levels of lead in children's blood dropped accordingly — by 55%

between 1976 and 1980. These facts motivated the EPA to speed up the timetable for the removal of lead in gasoline.[381]

For years the industry had argued that removing lead from fuel would have little impact on human blood levels. They also argued that there was no alternative to tetraethyl lead, and that it was critical to the American economy. William Kovarik PhD, Professor of Communication at Radford University in Virginia, disputed this fact and offered a number of alternatives that were available at the time. He suggested that the profit motive may have played a more significant part than had been recognised to date. He cites a statement made by Thomas Midgley, the chemist from GM who was instrumental in the development of tetraethyl lead as an additive, at an American Chemical Society meeting:

> So far as science knows at the present time, tetraethyl lead is the only material available which can bring about these [anti-knock] results, which are of vital importance to the continued economical use by the general public of all automotive equipment [382]

Kehoe was another voice for the industry and he always argued on the basis of four principals:

1. Firstly that lead absorption is natural, that every human body contains lead.
2. Secondly that the human body can deal with these 'Natural levels.'
3. That there is a threshold level of lead in blood that if not exceeded will cause no ill effects.
4. The general population's exposure to lead is so far below this level that there is absolutely no reason to be concerned about lead exposure.

Kehoe quoted a safe threshold level of 80 µg/dL for decades until it was shown to be woefully inadequate.[383] One of the people to challenge this level was Dr Herbert Needleman, pediatrician at the University of Pittsburgh. He found that there were significant problems with children's brains at levels below 40µg/dL—and a demonstrable deficit in their IQ levels.[384] Since that time there have been a number of studies that show adverse effects on children with levels of even less than 10 µg/dL. [385]

Needleman testified at the hearings in 1984 when Senator Dave Durenberger from Minnesota sponsored a bill to ban the use of lead in gasoline — and presented his figures for the

10µg/dL threshold level. This level was subsequently adopted by the CDC in 1991 — although on their site they state: *No blood lead threshold has been identified in children.* OSHA has adopted a workplace standard of 50µg/m³ averaged over an eight hour day for adults. However, workers reaching levels of 60 µg/dL or more are required to be removed from exposure until their levels are reduced to 40µg/dL (with pay and seniority maintained). [386]

A number of reports that reveal that, even below the 10µg/dL level, there is still significant damage in a number of areas that cause concern for childhood development. Canfield et al., for example, found an inverse relationship with blood levels of lead affecting children's IQ scores at three and five years of age and had this to say:

> Blood lead concentrations, even those below 10 microg per deciliter, are inversely associated with children's IQ scores at three and five years of age, and associated declines in IQ *are greater at these concentrations* than at higher concentrations. These findings suggest that more U.S. children may be adversely affected by environmental lead than previously estimated. (my emphasis) [387]

A further study assessed the relationship on 4,853 children aged between 6-16 years, using data from the Third National Health and Nutrition Examination Survey (NHANES III, conducted from 1988 to 1984).This was to assess the relationship between blood lead levels and a number of performance related abilities—such as arithmetic skills, reading skills, short-term memory and nonverbal reasoning skills. They discovered: for every 1 microg/dL increase in blood lead concentration, there was a 0.7-point decrease in mean arithmetic scores, an approximately 1-point decrement in mean reading scores, a 0.1-point decrement in mean scores on a measure of nonverbal reasoning, and a 0.5-point decrement in mean scores on a measure of short-term memory. An inverse relationship between blood lead concentration and arithmetic and reading scores was observed for children with blood lead concentrations lower than 5.0 microg/dL. They concluded that the deficits in cognitive and academic skills occurred in children with blood levels even lower than *5µg/d.* [388] This confirmed Needleman's initial worries, and also agreed with Alice Hamilton's previously stated concerns.

Some people might question whether we are worrying too much about such a level of exposure (I am referring to the people in the industry as opposed to parents with children), who may feel the cost to society is too much of a burden to be concerned about. This subject will be discussed further in a later chapter, but even ignoring the social consequences just for a moment (I intend to discuss the social consequences later also), the costs are manifold and understood by too few.

According to the World Bank, countries are able to save five to ten times the cost of converting to unleaded gasoline in both health and economic benefits. It computed that the USA saved more than 10 dollars for every one it invested in the conversion, thanks to reduced health costs, *savings on engine maintenance and improved fuel efficiency* (my emphasis).[389] Savings on fuel efficiency and engine maintenance had been one of the reasons people in the industry argued for *adding* the lead in the first place. Frank Howard of the Ethyl Gasoline Corporation had this to say about the health issues raised: " You have but one problem, is this a public health hazard?...Unfortunately our problem is not that simple" He suggested that automobiles and oil were essential to industrial progress, "Our continued development of motor fuels is essential in our civilisation," he proclaimed. He related that over a decade of research had gone into the effort to develop tetraethyl lead, and called its discovery an "apparent gift of god." According to Rosner and Markowitz, this put the opposition spokespeople on the defensive, making them appear to be reactionaries with a limited vision of the country's future—people who would retard progress and harm future generations.[390] It is only in retrospect, that we now know who was really harming who.

Is this the end of the lead story? Personally I don't believe there ever will be an end. For example an article in the Financial Times, March 2010, reported that Lord Justice Thomas warned Richard Alderman, Serious Fraud Office Director, not to repeat a judgement that led to Cheshire based Innospec, of the UK, being fined $12.7 million (£8.5m) for bribing Indonesian officials to win contracts for tetraethyl lead. The Lord Justice said that Innospec had used approximately $8million in bribes in "systematic and large-scale corruption" of senior Indonesian officials to prevent Indonesia from ceasing production of Innospec's fuel additive, tetraethyl lead, in line with what was happening in the industrialised world simply for the safety of its own population. The Lord Justice praised Mr Alderman's "vigorous prosecution", but said that he had exceeded his authority in striking a joint deal with the US authorities over the total fine of just $40 million. He regarded the fine as "wholly inadequate", he believed that the fine should have been in the tens of millions for such a "very serious" offence. [391]

You can take this story in a number of ways. It obviously reflects what is commonly known about the strategies of many industrial companies facing increasing restrictions, and in some cases litigation, over their products in their home markets; they are now seeking to sell their goods in markets where the restrictions are much more lax, or even non-existent. This strategy will be discussed further a little later. It will obviously have a huge impact on global health, and that is extremely worrying. You can also take this as a victory for common sense. Even though the fine was a pittance, as judged by Lord Justice Thomas, they were caught—and it could be taken as a warning for future companies seeking to bribe their way into vulnerable markets. Personally I take it as a positive sign. I am an optimist at heart!

What I do feel is worth emphasizing here is how the legal system impacts on every level of the problems we are facing, in every country with regards to corporate responsibility. Its judgements will have a critical impact on the success of any measures introduced—and the implications cannot be overstated.

I will end this chapter with the view of Philippe Grandjean, adjunct Professor of Environmental Health at Harvard School of Public Health where he refers to chemicals that destroy brain development as 'brain drainers':

'We now recognise lead as brain drainer number one. It has damaged brain cells in an entire generation of children, at least worldwide. This metal has inflicted more deficits to human intelligence than any other pollutant.'

Chapter 10
Pandora's Box

About a century ago, we opened a Pandora's Box of poison. Now we see its contents and their terrible consequences. We cannot turn back the hands of time, but we can learn from our experience. Having endangered everything we know and love by opening the box, it is time we choose now to reach out and shut it.

Professor Joe Thornton, University of Oregon [392]

Our technologies have advanced, our knowledge has increased—and with this progress has come an awareness that many decisions made in the past have burdened not just us but future generations for decades to come. No-one anticipated the health problems that have arisen, and no-one even imagined that the very nature of life as we know it would be threatened.

In previous chapters I gave some background to the development of chlorine and the problem with production of some organochlorine products such as trichlorophenol—and its hazardous by-products such as dioxin, the furans, and the PCBs that are so toxic. These problem chemicals have been known about for some time, but what is not so well known is how pervasive they are, how they are affecting our daily lives now, and the threat they continue to pose to our future.

At this stage, I need to give a little more of the basic chemistry behind the problem. I previously mentioned, chlorine is a highly reactive chemical. It is a large atom with two electrons in its inner shell, eight in its middle shell and seven in its outer shell—which leaves it unbalanced and needing another electron to give it stability. Sodium, on the other hand, has a single electron in its outer shell, which it would love to lose. So, when confronted with chlorine, it readily combines, violently, and produces sodium chloride—which then becomes a more stable compound, and valued to us for common table salt, or sea salt if you prefer. One of the other characteristics of chlorine due to its large size, is its affinity for fat and its insolubility in water. Chlorine's reactivity is particularly strong with organic matter, that is, to carbon-based molecular compounds. This gives rise to the huge range of organochlorines that now exist in our world today. It is due to its ability to attack all living things that makes it so dangerous and enables it to be used, as previously stated, as a war gas weapon.

Today we have vast numbers of man-made organochlorines in our environment that never existed in nature before. There are over 11,000 organochlorines that have been identified, and thousands more that remain unidentified. No-one really knows what these are capable of—the only thing we know for sure is that we have created a cocktail of man-made chemicals that continue to react and create new organochlorines that dramatically affect biological systems. To say we have opened a Pandora's Box may be no exaggeration. Chlorines reactivity with organic matter makes it a very useful product for use as a disinfectant or bleach. But the very toxic nature of the organochlorines, and their ability to persist and accumulate in biological systems, makes them one of the most dangerous chemicals known to man.

Organochlorines tend to accumulate in biological systems (commonly referred to as bioaccumulation), due to their affinity to fat and oil. Generally the more molecules of chlorine in an organochlorine compound, the less soluble in water it is, and the more soluble in fat—in considerable orders of magnitude. Thus hexachlorobenzene is approximately fifteen hundred times more oil soluble than mono-chlorinated compounds such as the benzenes and the phenols. Pentachlorophenol is over 4,500 times more soluble than phenol. Because we would never have been exposed to these man-made compounds historically, we have never developed the enzymes to break them down in our bodies. So these products have the ability to persist for a long time. Polynuclear aromatic hydrocarbons (PAHs) such as dioxin, have a half-life of 7 – 11 years. Even worse an octachlorodibenzofuran has an estimated half-life listed as "infinite" by the EPA. The infamous 2,3,7,8-tetrachlorodibenzo-p-dioxin (TCDD) is not just a problem because it is extremely toxic, but also because it does not appreciably break down in the environment. That means that once released into the environment it will most likely exist indefinitely. [393]

The ability of organochlorines to bioaccumulate becomes more serious as you move up the food chain. If you are a simple phytoplankton and you ingest a small amount of PCBs for example, it's not such a problem—even in the zooplankton it's not amplified greatly. But when you go up the chain from forage fish to predator fish it changes dramatically—to the point where dolphins, for example, can carry levels of PCBs in their bodies 13 million times higher than the levels in the surrounding water. In the case of DDT, levels have been measured 37 million times higher than water concentrations. [394] With humans at the top of the food chain it is not hard to see why Eskimos have such high levels in their blood. The problem affects all of humanity now.

Organochlorines of course do not just affect sea creatures and their predators. Some of them are highly volatile and evaporate into the air where they exist in various concentrations, depending upon their atmospheric half-life. Many of them are serious ozone depleting chemicals such as trichloroethane, carbon tetrachloride, and the chlorofluorocarbons. Chloropentafluoroethane, for example, has a half-life of more than 380 years, (The half-life if you remember is the time taken to degrade to half its original concentration.) One of the further problems with such chemicals is that the product that they degrade into can be much more toxic than the initial product. Tetrachloroethylene (Perchloroethylene) breaks down into a number of products, transforming it from a toxic product that is not a persistent compound per se, but can break down into carbon tetrachloride, which has a half-life of twenty-four years making it much more persistent and even more problematic than the original Perchlorethylene. [395]

Polyvinyl Chloride Production

One of the biggest users of chlorine is the vinyl chloride industry: polyvinylchloride (PVC) utilises approximately 40% of US chlorine production. Worldwide production of PVC totals more than 30 million tons per year, the majority destined for building products, electronics and furnishings. PVC is the only major material employed in the building trade that is an organochlorine. One of the problems with the production of chlorine products such as PVC is that large quantities of hazardous organochlorine by-products are produced throughout its production process. This process begins with the chlor-alkali process and the production of the initial chlorine; the next stage is the production of ethylene dichloride (EDC), followed by the production of vinyl chloride monomer (VCM), the feed stocks for PVC. Over a million tons a year of hazardous organochlorine by-products are created in this way each year. A further sting in the tail of PVC is what to do with the end product after its useful lifespan is over—it remains extremely durable, so it will not break down easily. So the options are primarily landfill or incineration. Incineration is fraught with problems because heat causes the release of the more toxic compounds such as dioxin. The same problem occurs with the incineration of the waste products from VCM and EDC production, where dioxins, PCBs, dibenzofurans, hexachlorobenzene (HBC) and octachlorostyrene are produced. These are the known toxins that are produced; there are in addition a large number of as yet unidentified chemicals that are also produced in the whole production process. In fact if you consider the entire lifecycle of PVC it is associated with more dioxin formation that any other single product. [396]

UNHEALTHY BETRAYAL

In addition to the hazards of PVC, there are additives that are included in the products that use it—such as stiffeners and, in some cases, plasticisers. The dominant plasticisers in vinyl are phthalates which introduce further health and environmental hazards. They constitute a major health hazard as they are in plastic wraps and beverage containers; they even line metal food containers. They are similar to the organochlorines in that they also accumulate in fat tissue, and are easily absorbed through the skin. They are in varying degrees estrogenic and toxic to the testis. Phthalates are also carcinogenic in animals. [397] The EU has voted to ban many phthalates and restrict the use of others in children's articles.

Lead is one of the most common stabilizers added to PVC, but cadmium and organotins are also used. Organotins are able to supress the immune system, and also disrupt the endocrine system. Lead toxicity we have already discussed. Do you get the feeling we haven't learnt anything from history?

Due to the hazardous nature of PVC production, there are a number of health risks to workers in the industry. Both EDC and PVM are known carcinogens. There is no threshold level below which VCM does not increase the risk of cancer. Both compounds are also toxic to the nervous system and cause a number of other health problems. Severe contamination has been detected around the production plants of VCM—in waterways, in land and in humans. Action to deal with the problems of PVC varies. Most European countries have some restriction on uses of PVC because of concerns over dioxin and phthalates. Sweden voted to eliminate soft and rigid PVC in 1995, and called for a voluntary phase-out of these products by industry, and fro safer substitutes to be developed. Sweden's program has reduced PVC use by 39 percent.[398]

In the USA in the 1970s, ten companies supplied vinyl monomer from fourteen plants, employing more than fifteen hundred workers. Another twenty-three companies using thirty-seven plants produced PVC employing a further five thousand production workers. [399] By 2002, global PVC production reached 27 million metric tons valued at approximately US$19 billion. The USA and Canada between them manufacture approximately 7 million metric tons, the majority for domestic use. [400]

One of the first people to bring the carcinogenic effects of vinyl chloride to our attention was Dr Pierluigi Viola, from the Regina Elena Institute for Cancer Research in Rome. He presented a paper in 1970 to the International Cancer Congress in the USA in Houston. He reported that rats exposed to 30,000 ppm of vinyl chloride monomer gas developed tumours of the skin, bones and lungs. He published this paper in the following year in *Cancer Research. [401]*

His work was confirmed by Cesare Maltoni, director of the Bologna Centre for the Prevention and Detection of Tumours and Oncological Research. Maltoni was hired by European vinyl manufacturers to see whether Viola's findings were accurate. He did not just confirm Viola's findings; he found cancers induced in even lower levels than Viola had found. [402] This was of concern to many people working in the industry. Eventually the news provoked the US Occupational Safety and Health Administration (OSHA) to set levels limiting exposure of workers to vinyl chloride monomer gas from 500ppm to 1ppm. [403]

It was not just in manufacturing that people were exposed to VC gas; a number of consumer products included VC gas as a propellant in hair spray—levels in hair salons were widely equal to or even greater than the levels in polyvinyl chloride plants (until sometime in 1974). The problems were not limited to air exposure either; concerns about its use in food packaging also became widespread. Prior to Maltoni's revelations, the FDA had received others from the Bureau of Alcohol, Tobacco and Firearms—who had been testing bottles manufactured with PVC. They discovered that these plastic bottles were leaching vinyl chloride monomer and creating an unpleasant taste in alcohol products—and the FDA quickly responded by banning the use of these bottles for alcohol. [404] In January 1973, NIOSH issued a "Request for Information" on the potential hazards of vinyl chloride. [405] This put pressure on one of the industry's front organisations, the Manufacturing Chemists Association (MCA), to provide all the information they had on the health effects of polyvinyl chloride exposure. I don't propose to elaborate on the way the industry people handled this affair, suffice it to say there was a cover-up and a withholding of information revealed by Markowitz and Rosner, who give a fairly detailed analysis of the whole vinyl chloride story. [406] The industry response was pretty much typical of an industry that puts profit before health or safety. When OSHA proposed to introduce the 1ppm limit for worker exposure, the industry issued dire predictions of job losses and plant closures, just as they did with the restrictions on tetraethyl lead. However, within two years the major proportion of US manufacturing was able to meet the new targets set, whilst at the same time achieving rapid growth in production and sales volumes. [407]

In January 1974 B.F.Goodrich revealed the deaths of four workers (at its plant in Louisville, Kentucky), from an extremely rare cancer, angiosarcoma of the liver. Dr John Creech had been undertaking a review of the plant following his discovery of acroosteolysis in a number of workers at the plant. This was a degenerating bone condition that had already been found in a number of VCM plants. In response to the revelations, OSHA immediately called a hearing to enable them to set a new emergency exposure level. At the hearing, a number of eminent scientists posed questions and passed comments that raised serious unanswered questions. Dr Irving Selikoff, a leading occupational physician, and director of the Environmental Sciences Laboratory at New York's Mount Sinai School of Medicine, had previously worked on asbestos related disease. He wanted to know why it was only now that the dangers of vinyl chloride were beginning to be recognised, it was not in his opinion a new problem. He argued that there has been evidence for potentially serious illnesses in both vinyl chloride and polyvinyl chloride manufacture for twenty five years. Why was it, he asked, that this problem had been completely unappreciated and inadequately approached by scientists and government? His comments were recorded for posterity:

"In other words, this is not a new problem. What is new is the vigor and the extent of our attention to it. As far back as 1949, 25 years ago liver damage was found in 15 of 48 workers in Russia and disease of the liver, skin, and other organs was reported in the next 17 years, not only from Russia but from France and Romania as well. In 1966 and 1967 attention was drawn to still another lesion, acroosteolysis, an affection of the skin and bones of the hands and feet, and further reports of hypertension, vascular lesions, nervous system and kidney damage and scleroderma later appeared.

Therefore, we have had ample warning that cells, tissues, and organs could be badly damaged during VC-PVC production. Despite this, our approach to the problem, as I said, seems to have been leisurely."

He continued to express concerns about cancer incidence, and its latency period before manifestation being 14 to 27 years—and further that the cancers were invariably fatal. He reiterates information from Marsteller who in Germany ten weeks previously, had studied twenty workers there who had worked between 1½ and 21 years; after careful examination nineteen had been found to have liver damage. Only four exhibited any sign of acroosteolysis—and liver enlargement was only diagnosed by physical examination in six. However gross changes of the liver and spleen were discovered by direct inspection at laproscopy in fourteen. He adds, "it is evident that these gross clinical tests may seriously under-read the extent of liver damage."

He makes a further comment regarding the meeting itself, "it marks a failure on our part to protect workers who have every right to expect that scientists, industry, and governmental agencies would protect them against known or suspect hazards. This we failed to do." He gives one final comment, " 'invisible pollution'... is now becoming visible in terms of disease and death. Our task here today is to address this and to ensure that it go no further. No effort should be spared and no control considered too rigorous."[408]

PANDORA'S BOX

I have quoted Selikoff's comments as he, like many of the previous academics I have quoted, tried to warn us about the peril of ignoring the effects of chemical pollution on our lives.

Dr Thomas F Mancuso, professor of Pittsburgh Graduate School of Public Health, addressed the response to health concerns faced by occupational health professionals. "Invariably, whenever a new occupational cancer is discovered, it is played down for fear of alarming the workers and the general public. The motivation may be one of not really knowing the facts. Nevertheless, from past experience, what happens is that further work is undertaken and information obtained, the problem gets broader and broader with more implications." He refers to the level of ignorance of what we are dealing with, "This situation, the chance recognition of an occupational cancer by a unique combination of circumstances, clearly demonstrates what is not known about the carcinogenic potential of thousands of industrial chemicals that have been in use for decades and further focuses attention on the total absence of a national concerted study of occupational cancer in this country."

He continues and makes a point that may come back and haunt us. "The serious national question that is raised and not resolved, because it is either too shocking to contemplate or because the agencies responsible for the protection of the public are reluctant to open this complex Pandora's Box." He goes on to refer to the vast number of chemicals already released into the environment and the fact that few of them have been studied for carcinogenic potential, "the real carcinogenic potential of these chemicals acting alone or in combination with each other has never been established."[409]

A review by the International Agency for Research on Cancer (IARC) classed vinyl chloride as a human carcinogen and gave the sites most commonly attacked as the liver, brain, lung and the haemo-lymphopoietic system. They go on to state, "there is no evidence that there is an exposure level below which no increased risk of cancer would occur in humans." They further reviewed the data in 1987, when they cited more recent research and further evidence for brain tumors, lung tumors, hepatocellular carcinoma and malignancies of the lymphatic and hematopoietic system. [410]

Whilst the war of words between the industry PR machine, government bureaucracies and the scientific community rage on, the industrial machine continues pumping out serious amounts of toxic chemicals. At the stage of the production process from the chlor-alkali to ethylene dichloride (EDC), huge quantities of dioxins and persistent organo-chlorines are released directly into the environment. Globally, the PVC industry releases each year, in excess of 100,000 tons each of EDC and VCM into the air; and in excess of 200 tons of EDC and 20 tons of VCM into surface water.

Whilst these compounds are not particularly persistent, they are both highly toxic. VCM is a known carcinogen and EDC is a probable human carcinogen. Both cause a range of serious biological problems, including liver damage, immune suppression, testicular damage and neurological toxicity. On top of this problem is the range of by-products that are produced, many of which cannot be re-processed. These are estimated to be responsible for 3% of the 570,000 tons of VCM produced each year—resulting in an excess of a billion pounds of waste by-products. Many of the by-products are not yet identified, but those that are include hexachloroethane, hexachlorobutadiene and PCBs. It has been estimated that the worldwide amount of PCBs produced by the oxychlorination of EDC is an incredible 20,000 pounds per year. This is of a chemical so dangerous it has been banned since the late 1970s internationally. EDC is also estimated to being one of the largest sources of dioxin. Levels of release into the environment from the various plants vary, but limited studies have been undertaken to monitor this problem. [411]

I don't intend to discuss the vinyl chloride story any further. Those who wish to pursue this story, and the way the health implications have been covered up, should read Markowitz and Rosner.[412] Those who would like a brief summary of the science controversy could try Jennifer Beth Sass, Barry Castleman, and David Wallinga, *Vinyl Chloride: A Case Study of Data Suppression and Misrepresentation.*[413] For now, I will leave this topic with some comments by Thornton:

> *When its entire lifecycle is considered, this seemingly innocuous plastic is one of the most environmentally hazardous consumer materials produced, creating large quantities of persistent, toxic organochlorines and releasing them into the indoor and outdoor environments. PVC has contributed significantly to the world's burden of POPs and endocrine disrupting chemicals— including dioxins and phthalates— that are now in the environment and the bodies of the human population. Beyond doubt, vinyl has caused considerable occupational disease and contamination of local environments as well.* [414]

Water Contamination by Chlorine and its By-products

Let's now turn to a different area of concern, but still another source of organochlorines. In excess of 100 million tons of wood pulp is bleached to produce white paper, utilising chlorine and chlorine-based bleaches each year. When chlorine combines with lignin and the other organic materials in wood pulp, more than 1000 organochlorine by-products are produced. The majority have not even been identified—although, approximately 300 have so far. The paper mill industry is responsible for the largest source of organochlorine releases into waterways, in excess of 4 million tons annually.[415] Softwood pulping creates more undesirable organophosphate compounds than hardwoods.

The Baltic countries have a significant paper pulp industry using predominantly softwoods—and they suffer from high pollution levels. A Swedish EPA conference in 1991 revealed the extent of the problem in the Baltic Sea, by estimating the toxic load of absorbable organic halogens (AOX) into the marine ecosystem. They estimated the area around Sweden to be in the order of 38,600-48,300 tons/year, excluding sources from the Soviet Union, Poland and Germany. They estimated the atmospheric precipitation to be 4,600 tons - 6,000 tons of AOX in a sea volume quantity of 150,000-325.000 tons, which corresponds to an AOX concentration of 7-15µg/litre.[416] Other studies have assessed the levels of extractable chlorinated hydrocarbons (EOCIs) in both the water and sediment in the Baltic Sea, and have concluded that large amounts of chlorinated organic matter have accumulated since chlorine bleaching was introduced in the early 1940s. They concluded that, in spite of the recent reductions, the Baltic Sea will remain polluted with large amounts of chlorinated organic matter for many decades. The long-term toxic effects remain largely unknown. [417]

Chlorination of drinking water was considered a triumph of the twentieth century because it was effective at killing most pathogens that became associated with our water supplies. However, the first contaminants that were found to accompany this process were products such as chloroform and other trihalomethanes. Later it was found that the chlorine was reacting with numerous organic products in the water, creating thousands of organochlorine by-products. A large number of these are carcinogenic or mutagenic in laboratory animals. Whilst chloroform is already a known carcinogen, the now-ubiquitous by-product 3-Chloro-4-(dichloromethyl)-5-hydroxy-2(5H)-furanone, more commonly known as MX, is of greater concern. It is very toxic and considered responsible for one third to one half of all mutagenic activity in chlorinated drinking water. It has been found to cause cancer of the liver, lungs, thyroid, adrenal glands mammary glands and leukemia, even at extremely low doses.[418] Fortunately, there are now a significant number of water treatment plants using ultraviolet light instead of chlorine. Although this not suitable for all situations, it is less problematic than another alternative, ozone treatment, which has a number of by-products that are a cause for concern.

There is not enough space in this volume to do justice to the whole problem that has developed for humanity due to mankind's development of chlorine chemistry. The subject deserves a much larger exposure and a more thorough explanation than I can offer here. Joseph W. Thornton

PhD, assistant professor at the Center for Ecology and Evolutionary Biology at the University of Oregon has published numerous articles of the subject and in his book, *Pandora's Poison,*[419] he makes the case for the total phasing out of chlorine from industrial use as the only sensible option against the mounting onslaught of the most persistent toxic chemicals known to man. He is certainly not alone in this view—significant numbers of researchers, scientists, doctors, etc. have written papers that support him.[420]

Part of his reasoning for a complete reduction of the use and dependence on chlorine stems from the fact that, of the known 11,000 organochlorines in the environment, let alone the thousands of unknown ones, little toxicity testing has been done on any significant number of them. This is because a thorough toxic analysis of each individual chemical would take hundreds of years. Testing for the synergistic reaction of different chemical combinations would take a vastly longer time—and the cost would be enormous. However, as this view is perceived as a serious potential threat to profits for members of the chlorine industry, in the short term at least, we can expect a concerted effort by industry and its massive PR machine to counter this evidence in every way it can.

For a more comprehensive review of the organochlorine problem, I would refer you to Thornton's excellent book, *Pandora's Poison.*

The Principal of Using Caution

One of the problems with the health issues we face is the difficulty of linking a particular biological effect with a specific chemical exposure. We have already discussed, for example, how the tobacco industry argued that smoking did not cause cancer, that there was no scientific *proof* that it did. It took many years before the sheer weight of evidence to convince government agencies to act. The tobacco industry had known all along that *absolute* proof of the link between tobacco and cancer would be extremely difficult to provide. And the same can be said of virtually any other harmful product. The mechanism by which vinyl chloride caused workers to get angiosarcoma was not fully understood at the time it was discovered. Due to its extreme rarity, it was understood to be the cause *by association*, and precautionary measures were undertaken to reduce exposure levels. A whole science has now evolved around the principal of controlling chemicals, to reduce risk, and risk assessments are undertaken to set safe levels of exposure for individuals working in industries using various chemicals. The EPA in the US, for example, sets levels for some known pollutants. Industry of course argues that the limits are too low, and will cause financial burden. They demand 'proof' from the EPA of the science behind their decision, and this can take the EPA years to come up with. As a result, industry often wins by default. This, of course, is not just an American issue.

In 1998 a group of international scientists, lawyers, government officials and other concerned groups and individuals held a meeting in January over a few days (23rd - 25th) at Wingspread in Racine, Wisconsin. They came from Canada, the US, Germany, Britain and Sweden in response to the growing environmental problems we are facing to discuss a more precautionary approach. After meeting for two days they issued the following consensus statement on the precautionary principal:

Wingspread Statement on the Precautionary Principle

"The release and use of toxic substances, the exploitation of resources, and physical alterations of the environment have had substantial unintended consequences affecting human health and the environment. Some of these concerns are high rates of learning deficiencies, asthma, cancer, birth defects and species extinctions, along with global climate change, stratospheric ozone depletion and worldwide contamination with toxic substances and nuclear materials.

"We believe existing environmental regulations and other decisions, particularly those based on risk assessment, have failed to protect adequately human health and the environment the larger system of which humans are but a part.

"We believe there is compelling evidence that damage to humans and the worldwide environment is of such magnitude and seriousness that new principles for conducting human activities are necessary.

"While we realize that human activities may involve hazards, people must proceed more carefully than has been the case in recent history. Corporations, government entities, organizations, communities, scientists and other individuals must adopt a precautionary approach to all human endeavors.

"Therefore, it is necessary to implement the Precautionary

Principle: When an activity raises threats of harm to human health or the environment, precautionary measures should be taken even if some cause and effect relationships are not fully established scientifically. In this context the proponent of an activity, rather than the public, should bear the burden of proof.

"The process of applying the Precautionary Principle must be open, informed and democratic and must include potentially affected parties. It must also involve an examination of the full range of alternatives, including no action." [End of statement.] [421]

In the Annual Report of the (US) President's Cancer Panel they suggested that the prevailing regulatory approach in the United States is reactionary rather than precautionary. It requires incontrovertible evidence of harm before preventative action is taken. It also places the burden on the public to show that a given chemical is harmful. It does not consider potential health and environmental impacts when designing new technologies. They further comment:

> Industry has exploited regulatory weaknesses, such as the government's reactionary (rather than precautionary) approach to regulation. Likewise, industry has exploited government's use of an outdated methodology for assessing "attributable fractions" of the cancer burden due to specific environmental exposures. This methodology has been used effectively by industry to justify introducing untested chemicals into the environment.[422]

The principal of using caution of course is not new. The phrase "Look before you leap!" is an example of it. What is significant about the Wingspread Statement, though, is the point that the burden of proof should lie with the proponent, not the public. At present, Industry dumps whatever toxic burden it likes on us, leaving the general tax payer, us, with the costs of waste disposal, toxic dump clean-ups, health costs, illness and even deaths—while they just make the bigger and often massive profits. This creates a major imbalance in the way resources are distributed that has significant implications for us, and for future generations and will be developed further in later chapters.

Public Relations, the Weapon of Choice for Industry

Unfortunately it is not science that dictates public policy on chemical releases. In numerous documented cases, it is the public relations arm of industry that calls the tune. The problem is that government policies set up to control the chemical industry are open to influence in a number of ways. In some countries this can be straight forward bribery, both overt and covert, often referred to as 'inducements'. But there is a whole industry involved in the manipulation of government policy, involving such tactics as campaign contributions, party donations and lobbying. Whilst this topic in itself could fill a number of volumes, I will cite just a few examples to illustrate how both public perception and government policy can be influenced—in a way that corporate profit benefits and public health suffers.

One of the largest PR companies in the world is Ketchum. This agency operates in more than 65 Countries and employs more than 11,000 people. [423]

In the early 1990s a document was faxed to Greenpeace US's Seattle office by a Ketchum whistle-blower. It was titled "Debt Crisis Management Plan for the Clorox Company." This had been prepared by Ketchum in response to Greenpeace announcing an initiative to phase out the use of chlorine globally, and the company's concern that Clorox household bleach would suffer large drops in sales.

Under the heading of STRATEGIC SUMMARY they made the following observations:

A number of current environmental issues hold potential for presenting a public relations crisis for the Clorox Company. The following are issues we consider significant offering high potential for causing the most damage.

- The negative stream of news articles about chlorine, resulting about health questions arising from such uses as pulp paper bleaching and water purification.
- The toxicity of chlorinated organic by-products, which are produced during normal home use of liquid chlorine bleach, fuelled by the labelling of all chlorinated organics as equally hazardous by environmental activists.
- The association between chlorine use and formation of dioxins.

There were then a number of crisis scenarios referred to.

The first followed the twentieth anniversary of Earth Day where it was suggested there could be a backlash against Clorox, and it gave a number of crisis scenarios:

CRISIS SCENARIO # 1

To date, Greenpeace's anti-chlorine campaign has garnered a moderate amount of press attention in the United States....In Europe, however, the message has been hitting home more directly, and public response has begun to show up in lower use of household chlorine bleach in some areas.

Worse Case Event: Greenpeace activists arrive at Clorox headquarters with signs, banners, bull horns and several local television crews and proceed to launch a rally. They release the results of a new "study" linking chlorine exposure to cancer. AP Radio and the San Francisco Chronicle are on the scene and interviews three unsuspecting employees on their way to lunch, who agree that the safety of chlorine may be in question. Corporate communications receive several calls from local and national press who want comments.

One of the "Strategies" listed under "Recommended Response" is quoted:

Announce that the company will seek an independent third-party review of the Greenpeace study and promise to report back to the media. [While this last strategy may seem to be counter to the objective, the independent report will gain little media attention if it supports the company position; its primary value will be to cause reporters to question Greenpeace's integrity and scientific capabilities.]

That was just a glimpse of their strategy. In a 62 page report, they give a second scenario:

CRISIS SCENARIO # 2

The Issue:... As a result a whole new round of simplistic and misguided ways to "save the Earth" are likely to be espoused...Liquid chlorine bleach could very well become a target for these "save the Earth" activists.

Worse Case Event: A prominent columnist targets the hazards of liquid chlorine bleach in an article, which is critical, which is syndicated to newspapers across the country. The columnist calls for consumers to boycott Clorox products since Clorox is guilty of widespread contamination of the environment. Local chapters of Greenpeace take up the cause by spearheading the "anti-Clorox" picketing campaigns outside supermarkets in 10 major cities across the country. The picketing campaign is receiving widespread media coverage in those cities, resulting in a dramatic drop in sales of Clorox products, in response to these concerns, Congress schedules hearings on the environmental safety of liquid chlorine bleach products.

Again here is a sample of their suggested responses:

- Teams of scientists are dispatched to the 10 cities to conduct media tours.
- Fact sheets and brochures are distributed to all the affected supermarkets to provide relief.
- Enlist the support of the union and the national union leadership since jobs are at stake.

- Conduct research to determine if and how a slander lawsuit against the columnist and/or Greenpeace could be effective.

- Industry association advertising campaign; "Stop Environmental Terrorism," calling on Greenpeace and the columnist to be more responsible and less irrational in their approach.

CRISIS SCENARIO # 3

Worse Case Event: This is in reference to the release of the National Toxicological Program (NTP) study-

The final NTP study analysis concludes chlorine is indeed an animal carcinogen.... Greenpeace holds a satellite news conference—to launch a concerted campaign to eliminate all uses of chlorine in the United States. Greenpeace targets the following uses of chlorine: pulp and paper manufacturing, water purification and liquid chlorine bleach-based products.

Their "Recommended Response:"

- Objective: Work with other manufacturers and the chlorine Institute to forestall any legislative or regulatory action pending further review of the NTP report and subsequent human and animal studies.

They go on to make suggestions for a more complete strategy: Identify potential industrial allies from industry trade associations, professional groups and individual companies who have a vested interest in similar environmental issues to solicit their support....Identify key federal and state government officials who will need to be reached....enlist scientific community support....solicit the involvement of a number of scientists to demonstrate broad agreement—establish a broad network of medical and academic organisations that may be called upon by the media to comment,

These groups are to include the American Medical association, the American Academy of Pediatrics, the American Academy of Family Physicians, the National Academy of Sciences as well as chapters of the American Public Health Association.[424]

It is useful to include those extracts to illustrate the way industry uses public relations companies to promote their agendas. If you look into the tactics of any other industry, you will find the same ethos exists, the same methods employed. In some ways they are quite predictable, but their predictability does not help us—they are effective anyway. I do not wish to condemn their activities: they are simply an expression of the state of social and economic conditions today.

Yet these kinds of activities are only the tip of the iceberg. Mongoven, Biscoe and Duchin, for example, a public relations company based in Washington D.C., specialises in providing intelligence to its clients on the activities of activist organisations that can affect their businesses. The following documents were leaked to the Center for Media and Democracy, and published in their 1996 issue of *PR Watch*. Both reports are addressed to the Chlorine Chemistry Council.

The first one refers to a number of groups that are actively joining the anti-chlorine movement—the Clean Water Network (CWN), the National Resources Defense Council (NRDC), Greenpeace, and the US Public Interest Research Group (PIRG):

Greenpeace had called the EPA draft Dioxin Reassessment Study justification for a global chlorine ban. It said the study clearly indicated a national public health emergency. . . .

That dioxin reassessment began in 1991, and, Greenpeace began its U.S. anti-chlorine campaign, based on potential birth defects, in late 1992. They said action was needed to ban chlorine in incinerators, paper and plastic because levels of dioxin currently found in the bodies of the general human population, in the food chain, and in the environment were "already in the range at which severe effects on reproduction, development, and the immune system occur."

Greenpeace said the U.S. EPA study, a draft summary of a three-year scientific reassessment of the toxicity of dioxin, "confirms that fetal developmental and immune system damage are among the most serious health threats from dioxin exposure." Having obtained a draft of the report before its scheduled release in June, they called for immediate action to restrict major industrial uses of chlorine and chlorinated chemicals—which create dioxin when produced, heated, processed, or burned. They also reported that there is no safe level of dioxin exposure and that any dose, no matter how low, can result in health damage. New findings on the mechanism of dioxin toxicity showed that tiny doses of it disrupt the action of the body's natural hormones and other biochemicals, leading to complex and severe effects including cancer, feminization of males and reduced sperm counts, endometriosis and reproductive impairment in females, birth defects, impaired intellectual development in children, and impaired immune defense against infectious disease.

Currently, many industrialized nations allow industries to release dioxin within "acceptable discharge limits." But since any dose of dioxin is hazardous, no discharge can now be considered "acceptable." Further, dioxin is so persistent that even small releases build up over time, both in the environment and in the human body.

Revelations in a further report leaked, which I detail below—give recommendations on how to counter the wave of negative publicity regarding chlorine and its by-products. Its main recommendation is to mobilise science against the precautionary principal:

Attached is a brief report on anti-chlorine groups' activities in August along with our characterization of those activities. Recommendations regarding the individual activists were forwarded with the original detailed reports.

Also attached is a list of all the recommendations we provided [the Chlorine Chemistry Council] in August as to how best to counter the activists. ***The main recommendation--to mobilize science against the precautionary principle--still applies*** and dovetails with the long range objectives regarding sound risk assessment.

It is obvious that the battleground for chlorine will be women's issues—reproductive health and children—and organizations with important constituencies of women opinion leaders should have priority (my emphasis).

This recommendation to mobilise science against the precautionary principal is more than ominous. Following are a number of their recommendations:

- Take advantage of the schisms [within] the Administration, i.e. within EPA and among EPA, USDA and FDA on the risk assessment section of the Dioxin Reassessment. CCC should quietly work with the industry coalitions to ensure that USDA and FDA are perceived to have the support of strong constituencies. .

- Engage [Ketchum Public Relations] to reach out to editorial boards to highlight flaws in the risk assessment portion of the dioxin reassessment.

- Take advantage of the opportunity . . . to highlight the need for some established criteria on risk assessment which will be widely accepted by scientists, industry, the people and governments.

- Move quickly to take advantage of the visibility of the shortcomings of the current system by having scientists and Congressmen ready to call for the process on risk assessment CCC and [Chemical Manufacturers Association] would like to see put in place.

- Schedule, through [Ketchum Public Relations], editorial board meetings in Dayton prior to Department of Health and Human Services Devra Lee Davis speech to a forum on breast cancer sponsored by Greenpeace and [the Women's Economic and Development Organization] to be held in Dayton, Ohio, in October.

- Continue existing CCC public relations and communications programs to counter activists' claims of the evils associated with dioxin as a weapon against chlorine chemistry.

- Also, use the grassroots extremist's charges against the role of science in shaping public policy as a call to arms within the professions whose credibility and relevancy are at stake.

- Urge the Vinyl Institute to begin immediately to build alliances on the PVC issue, beginning with those with an obvious economic stake, e.g., home builders, realtors, product manufacturers, hospitals and others who are immediately targeted.

- Form an alliance on PVC issues with the Mid-States Oil and Gas Association which is concerned about expansion of the activist anti-PVC program in the Gulf of Mexico and is seeking allies in the chemical industry. . . .

- Bring the state governors in on the issue of risk assessment by communicating the benefits to them from being able to rely on a national standard.

- Establish third-party entities devoted to developing these standards in the near future.

- Take steps to discredit the precautionary principle within the more moderate environmental groups as well as within the scientific and medical communities. .

- It is especially important to begin a program directed to pediatric groups throughout the country and to counter activist claims of chlorine-related health problems in children.

Following are further set of recommendations under the sub heading "Prevent Medical Associations from Joining Anti-Chlorine Movement"

- Create panel of eminent physicians and invite them to review data regarding chlorine as a health risk and as a key chemical in pharmaceuticals and medical devices.

- Publish panel's findings and distribute them widely to medical associations and publications.

- Stimulate peer-reviewed articles for publication in the [Journal of the American Medical Association] on the role of chlorine chemistry in treating disease. . . .

- Convince through carefully crafted meetings of industry representatives (in pharmaceuticals) with organizations devoted to specific illnesses, e.g., arthritis, cystic fibrosis, etc., that the cure for their specific disease may well come through chlorine chemistry and ask them to pass resolutions endorsing chlorine chemistry and communicate their resolutions to medical societies.

They go on to cover the organisation, the National Wildlife Federation (NWF):

The NWF is highly respected by mainstream environmentalists, conservationists, industry and government. That respect combined with the vast resources NWF controls, provide the NWF substantial influence on national policy decisions related to environmental and consservation matters (miss-spelling in the original).

The NWF printed 1,000 copies of *Fertility on the Brink*, which is almost depleted and a second printing is expected. . . . The publication of and demand for *Fertility on the Brink* may signal that the claims of destructive health problems attributable to toxic exposure has become more widely accepted by the public and will probably become a larger issue. . . .[425]

Risk Assessment Based on the Needs of Children

Anti-chlorine activists are also using children and their need for protection to compel stricter regulation of toxic substances. This tactic is very effective because children-based appeals touch the public's protective nature for a vulnerable group and that makes it difficult to refute appeals based on its needs. The tactic also is effective in appealing to an additional segment of the public which has yet to be activated in the debate, particularly parents....

The tone of the debate will focus on the needs of children and insist that *all* safeguards be taken to ensure their safety in development. For most substances, the tolerances of babies and children, which includes fetal development, are obviously much lower than in the general adult population. Thus, "environmental policies based on health standards that address the special needs of children" would reduce all exposure standards to the lowest possible levels. . . .

Dioxin and Risk Assessment . . .

Anti-chlorine groups will probably devise tactics which promote the adoption of the "precautionary principle." The principle, which shifts the burden of establishing a chemical's safety to industry, is unlikely to be adopted. The debate over the "precautionary principle" will elevate the dioxin issue to a more conspicuous level. . . .

The final part of the report under "Breast Cancer, Fertility and Reproductive Problems Caused by Pesticides" attacks the distinguished scientist, Devra Lee Davis PhD:

Devra Lee Davis is expected to direct the Clinton Administration's policy governing breast cancer and we expect her to try to convert the breast cancer issue into a debate over the use of chlorine. As a member of the administration, Davis has unlimited access to the media while her position at the Health and Human Services (HHS) helps validate her "junk science." Davis is scheduled to be a keynote speaker at each of the upcoming . . . breast cancer conferences . . . sponsored by Women's Economic and Development Organization (WEDO). . . . Each conference is expected to emphasize a regional interest. . . . Topics include "Environment and Breast Cancer," "Organochlorines, Pesticides and Breast Cancer" and "Environmental Justice."[426]

I have included these reports to illustrate the way PR companies operate and how industry mobilises against a perceived threat to their profits, in this case in regards to the coming confrontation about chlorine and its implications for our health. As with the basic format of this volume I will try to restrict my involvement in getting involved too deeply in the topic of PR and how industry utilises it to promote its own agenda, hopefully giving you enough information to get the general picture. Again for those who would like further information I would recommend Sheldon Rampton and John Stauber's book, *Trust Us We're Experts—How Industry Manipulates Science and Gambles With Your Future.* [427] I cannot recommend this book too highly. John Stauber is the founder of the *Center for Media and Democracy,* they both write and edit the quarterly *PR Watch,* their web site is a great resource, the articles above are available on their site.[428] I also refer to other works on PR, Lobbying etc. including other works by Stauber and Rampton later in this chapter.

They also refer to the above articles (my original source) and refer to the Chlorine Chemistry Council having amassed a "war chest" for public relations and lobbying in 1993 that amounted to $12 million. I have no figures for their current "war chest;" but ask you to imagine what it would be if you add all the other groups such as the Chlorine Institute, the Vinyl Institute, the Chemical Manufacturers Association, the National Association of Manufacturers as well as the above quoted groups referred to by the MBD article, what the "war chest" would be valued at today? I imagine there is a vast amount of money sloshing around, available for a PR and lobbying campaign to support the profitable production of chlorine and all its products.

One of the tactics use to attack science that is inconvenient or even threatening to industry's interests is simply to disparage the source with name calling. Label their work as "junk science," label them as "wacko environmentalists," suggest they are suffering from "technophobia" or "chemophobia," are all basically good old fashioned mud-slinging techniques; as the old adage goes if you throw enough some of it will stick. The attack mentioned above on the work of Devra Davis PhD., MPH, is an example. She is the director of the Center for Environment Oncology at the University of Pittsburgh Cancer Institute, and professor at the Department of Epidemiology, Graduate School of Public Health. She has authored over 190 publications in books and journals,

PANDORA'S BOX

The Secret History of The War on Cancer, being one of her books that I have already referred to. Any reference to her work as "junk science" is as ludicrous as it is insulting. However, anyone working in environmental science and not for industry is likely to be a target. I assume by writing this work that even I could be a likely target for attack. If you dare stand up and speak against ruling interests, threaten the status quo, someone is sure to throw something at you.

Dr Turner Banks believes we are already in the Third World War—and that this one is an information war. [429] There is no doubt that we are in a war of words, certainly if the PR machine is anything to go by.

Gilbert Rapaille, considered a marketing specialist with a background in psychology believes that the words we use have a huge impact on our decision making. He believes there are trigger words that influence us, that we should use positive trigger words and avoid the negative ones. In a talk to the International Food Information Council, he gave advice with regards to biotechnology. Words he advised to avoid included: biotechnology, chemical, DNA, experiments, industry, laboratory, machines, money, pesticides, profit, radiation, safety, scientists etc. He also gave a list of positive words to use: beauty, bounty, children, choices, cross-breeding, diversity, earth, farmer, flowers, fruits, future generations, hard work, heritage, improved, organic, purity, quality, soil, tradition and wholesome. He composed a sentence to illustrate the effect:

New genetic discoveries allow us to be successful gardeners of the 21st century and to accomplish cross-breeding at a highly sophisticated level, fulfilling a vision of the gardeners of the 19thcentury. [430]

What was the sentence being replaced? How about: "Scientists predict Genetically modified food is set to expand markets, producing increasing global profits into the next century by manipulating DNA and developing pesticide resistance." Sounds quite different doesn't it?

Science for Sale

Basically, what this means is that we are facing a challenge on a number of fronts. There is an extremely sophisticated public relations industry out there, as well as powerful lobbying interests working with various corporations to promote their interests. As consumers, we are in a difficult position. How do we know what is true anymore? Who do we trust? It is no longer simply about science. Science is for sale, and the amount of independently-funded science is shrinking year by year. As the financial repercussions of the last few years start to come home to roost, it is going to be even harder to be an independent scientist. The way funding is set up has direct consequences on the quality of the research undertaken. It is fairly obvious when you read the literature that many researchers are forced to work for industry, under their direct control, because that's where the money is.

Sheldon Krimsky of Tufts University undertook a study of 1,105 researchers who published 789 papers in leading life science and medical journals to assess financial disclosures and industry connections. He found that in one third of the papers he looked into, at least one of the chief authors had a financial interest connected to the research. [431] Another method employed by industry to influence the content of medical journals is to sponsor scientific symposiums. The *New England Journal of Medicine* published a survey of 625 symposiums. They found that an increasing proportion of the marketing expenses of the pharmaceutical industry had gone to funding symposiums—rising from $6 million in 1975 (adjusted for inflation to 1988 dollars) to $86 million in 1988. Of the 625 symposiums studied, 42% were sponsored by just one pharmaceutical company. The reviewers made the following observations:

> Our data suggest that industry-sponsored symposiums are promotional in nature and that journals often abandon the peer-review process when they publish symposiums. The featuring of unapproved and noninnovative drugs suggests that manufacturers of these drugs are seeking preapproval promotion to allow them to get a jump on the market, increase product recognition, or enhance investor interest.[432]

There are numerous ways that industry seeks to influence opinion. Frequently, they like to use a third party source, a medical expert with no apparent ties to the industry. This not only gives respectability, but also the appearance of independence. Would you believe, for example, the information coming from a drug company promoting some new drug? Many of us may initially be a little sceptical, but that scepticism is likely to be quickly abandoned if the recommendations come from a professor with no apparent ties to the company. This same third party policy is employed in numerous other ways. Such as the following one used to great effect by the tobacco industry:

> A few years ago, for example, documents came to light regarding an industry-funded campaign in the 1990s to plant sympathetic letters and articles in influential medical journals. Tobacco companies had

secretly paid 13 scientists a total of $156,000 simply to sign their names to these letters and articles. One biostatistician received $10,000 for writing a single, 8-page letter that was published in the Journal of the American Medical Association. Another received $20,000 for writing four letters and an opinion piece to the Lancet, the Journal of the National Cancer Institute and the Wall Street Journal. These scientists did not even have to write the letters themselves. The tobacco industry's law firms did the actual drafting and editing. So in essence they were being paid for their autographs. [433]

If you imagine such tactics might be a rare occurrence, you would be wrong. Check out Michaels, Rampton and Stauber or Markowitzt and Rosner for more of the ingenious ways that industry subverts science. [434]

Caution under Attack

Another group under attack by industry front groups and even the Wall Street Journal, was that of Theo Colborn, Dianne Dumanoski and John Peterson Myers who wrote a book called *Our Stolen Future*. The Wall Street Journal labelled this an environmental "hype machine." The industry-funded Washington think tank, the Competitive Enterprise Institute, attacked it, and so did the industry-funded Advancement of Sound Science Coalition. Another organisation called Consumer Alert, labelled it a "scaremongering tract." The Advancement of Sound Science Coalition called a press conference and introduced 10 scientific sceptics who described the book as "fiction." The American Council on Science and Health (ACSH), another industry group well known for being a defender of both dioxin and DDT, obtained a copy of the book before it was released and issued an eleven-page attack on it.

Here is an extractfrom it, written by Elizabeth Whelan to help you come to your own conclusions:

I don't buy into the Precautionary Principle, for several reasons. First, it always assumes worst-case scenarios. Second, it distracts consumers and policymakers alike from the known and proven threats to human health. And third, it assumes no health detriment from the proposed regulations and restrictions. By that I mean that the Precautionary Principle overlooks the possibility that real public health risks can actually be associated with eliminating minuscule, hypothetical risks. As an ancient philosopher said, "It is a serious disease to worry over what has not occurred."

UNHEALTHY BETRAYAL

We seem to be a nation fixated on hypothetical risks. My former colleague, the late Aaron Wildavsky noted that the Precautionary Principle plays well to the crowd, by placing the environmental advocacy on the side of the citizenry: "I care about your health, and I propose an intervention that will protect you." And it allows environmentalists to portray those disagreeing with them as indifferent or even hostile to the public health and perhaps motivated by a desire to profit from whatever product or process is held to be risky.

But in reality, the Precautionary Principle itself can be hazardous to our health. It's well known that the health of citizens is consistently correlated with their countries' standard of living. Dismantling our industrially based high standard of living, as the authors of *Our Stolen Future* would like to see happen, will diminish our standard of living and lead to poorer, not better, overall health. [435]

I wonder how many people would still consider our 'industrially based high standard of living' quite so easy to accept after the recent 2008/2009 fallout from the bank collapses and financial turmoil. If you think this is unconnected, and a separate issue, please read on—and hopefully clarity on this point will prevail. Whelan says she doesn't "buy into the Precautionary Principle", she reveals an interesting flaw in her approach. She does not relate it to a specific product, chemical, class of chemicals or drug product. Instead, she is against the very principal alone. Well— we are at risk every moment of our lives to one degree or another. We embrace the Precautionary Principal throughout our lives—by looking both ways before we cross the road, for example. It is no different with regards to chemical exposure, drug exposure, or any other potential for harm. Caution is, after all, a basic human instinct that keeps us from falling off cliffs, jumping without a parachute or accepting sweets (candy) from strangers.

So to see what all the fuss is about, let me give you a sample of the information in *Our Stolen Future*. Of the authors, Dr Theo Colborn, is a Professor Emeritus at the University of Florida, Gainesville. She was formerly a senior scientist with the World Wildlife Fund, and is a recognised expert on endocrine-disrupting chemicals. Dr John Peterson Myers is founder, CEO and Chief Scientist at Environmental Health Sciences, and Dianne Dumanoski is a science journalist. Their book documents the problems uncovered by wildlife biologists from the early days, such as the decrease in animal populations due to man-made chemicals. They discuss alligators in Florida with tiny penises, the massive seal die off in Northern Europe—that was eventually linked to PCB levels, the fertility drop in human populations etc. And they explain how difficult it was for scientists to uncover the cause of these problems.

They also describe the disaster that was caused by the synthetic estrogen, diethylstilbestrol, more commonly known as DES. It was given to huge numbers of women in the USA, Canada, the UK, Australia, and other countries. Yet it turned out to be a massive human experiment that wreaked havoc on the lives of more than five million pregnant women. They report how in 1957 the *Journal of Obstetrics and Gynecology* enthused how it produced "bigger and stronger babies," and recommended DES for "ALL pregnancies".[436] Thankfully this advice was not taken up by all. The fallout was massive, but it did not become apparent until 1970 when a rare form of vaginal cancer turned up in the daughters of the mothers who had taken DES. Studies eventually revealed that the daughters had abnormalities of their reproductive organs, reduced fertility, miscarriages, premature births and immune problems. The sons suffered from small and undescended testicles, abnormal semen and hypospadias (a condition where the opening to the penis is located other than at the tip). The mothers themselves were found to have significantly elevated levels of breast cancer. [437]

As a point of interest, it's worth noting at this point that Robert Kehoe, the great defender of the lead industry was quite familiar with DES. The Germans had used it in animal feed to fatten cows, pigs and chickens. But when they discovered that the male workers at the factory had developed painful swollen breasts, Kehoe's solution was to suggest that women do the work because they, after all, already had breasts. [438]

What added to the tragedy of DES is that it did not even do the job that it was supposed to do in the first place. In 1952 at least four studies demonstrated that it was ineffective at reducing morning sickness or miscarriages. Later studies showed that, worse than being ineffective, it actually *increased* miscarriages. Yet, despite the warnings of these studies, the FDA continued to sanction its use. Later studies found that DES exposed women to autoimmune diseases such as Hashimoto's thyroiditis, Graves' disease, rheumatoid arthritis, and other immune-related problems. Researchers also discovered that the immune problems actually got worse as they aged.

The Thalidomide Tragedy

Professor Colborn also mentions the thalidomide disaster, where women were given a drug to counteract morning sickness. This caused appalling birth defects, children born without arms or legs, hands sprouting from their shoulders and even worse deformations, in eight thousand children in forty-six countries. Some children were born with lesser symptoms such as heart and lung defects, deafness, autism, epilepsy and blindness. What was eventually realised was that this was simply to do with the *timing* of the exposure. What does bear a mention—is the fact that Americans did not suffer as badly as many other countries—due to the caution exercised by a physician at the FDA by the name of Frances Kelsey. She was sceptical about the use of this drug and its possible effect on the as-yet-un-born foetus and demanded more data from the manufacturers. Colborn does not go into this aspect in much detail, but I feel Dr Kelsey's action is worth more credit as it is had a huge impact on the degree of damage to US children.

Kelsey, as well as being a physician, was also a pharmacologist, and the thalidomide issue was her first major assignment since joining the FDA. The company applying for the drug application was Richardson-Merrell for their version of the drug, called Kevadon. Their application was submitted to the FDA on September 12 1961. Kelsey was unhappy about a number of things in the application, some of which I list here:

1. The animal studies were not reported in sufficient detail, and the study on the absorption of the drug in rats was not supported by evidence.
2. The company had failed to report the clinical studies in full detail. In addition, an insufficient number of cases had been studied. Kelsey also observed that many of the 3,156 cases cited were in foreign literature reports and in many instances the reports did not represent detailed studies to determine the safety of the drug.
3. Chronic toxicity data was incomplete, leading to the obvious conclusion that 'no evaluation can be made for the safety of the drug when used for a prolonged period of time.'
4. The application contained rather limited information about the drug's stability.
5. Side effects were passed over lightly. 'The impression is left that the "hangover" frequently observed by Lasagna was due to overdosage, yet in double blind studies this investigator was unable to elicit a therapeutic response with lower doses.

According to files at the FDA, Kelsey had learned from a report in the *British Medical Journal,* by a Dr Florence, that thalidomide caused peripheral neuritis, but that this was not disclosed by Richardson-Merrell. She revealed the information of the neuritis and demanded further evidence from the manufacturers. She met with Richardson-Merrell representatives who told her that the condition was reversible after discontinuance of the drug (which was not true in many cases). She then made the obvious point: "The field of usefulness of the drug is such that untoward reactions would be highly inexcusable." She also was not convinced that the effects of neuritis were reversible, and demanded studies proving this to be the case.

The end result of this saga was that Richardson-Merrell did not come up with satisfactory answers to convince Kelsey to approve thalidomide. Ironically, her actions saved Richardson-Merrell a fortune because of the lawsuits that would have rained down on them. Kelsey, for her part, was regarded as a heroine—and was awarded a gold medal by President Kennedy himself, for single-handedly saving many American children from disaster. [439]

Her handling of the thalidomide tragedy is a fine example of the merits of the Precautionary Principal.

Synthetic Hormones and Immune problems

Colborn, Dumanoski and Myers' book reviews a lot of evidence that caused them concern, particularly regarding organochlorines such as the PCBs, furans and dioxins. Many of the man-made chemicals now in our world have been found to react in biological systems in ways previously unheard of. Their effects have often been hard to detect and researchers all over the world have spent an enormous amount of time detecting them. Take hormone disruption, for example, which can upset hormonal development in a huge number of ways. Hormones have specific sites in the body where, when engaged, they fit like a key in a lock, and do the job they are supposed to do. Synthetic hormones can copy their effect by acting like the key, but they can also block the effect by taking up residence in the receptor site in error—so preventing normal hormonal functioning or even promoting entirely different reactions. Other actions of man-made chemicals can also affect enzymes that metabolise hormones, so disrupting normal hormonal signalling. Whereas many people express concern about the ability of the organochlorines to induce cancers, Colborn, Myers and Dumanoski are equally concerned about the effects on the immune system, the endocrine system, the effect on our ability to reproduce, and neurological impairment. These effects can be very subtle and hard to detect but are also insidious.

But here's a problem—If you are exposed to a chemical that causes your immune system to break down so that you develop a chest condition which eventually kills you through pneumonia, how can anyone ascertain what actually happened to you? This is one of the major challenges with immune-related problems. Science, by its very methodology, finds it very difficult to *prove* anything, it can often only link things together. Nobody *proved* with direct evidence that thalidomide caused birth defects; it was established by its causal connection. When the tobacco companies said there was no proof that tobacco caused cancer (which they still maintain to this day), it became accepted as fact only because of the sheer weight of evidence that there was a direct causal relationship—in this case by the body count.

Linda Birmbaum, who at the time was head of the environmental toxicology division at the EPA had this to say about synthetic chemicals:

> Estrogen is just one component in the complicated integrated endocrine system,...synthetic chemicals target other parts of the system more commonly than they disrupt processes involving estrogen. The adrenal glands, which produce stress hormones, get hit more than any other organ by man-made compounds, followed by the thyroid gland. Insults in any part of one system tend to quickly ripple through other systems of the body as well. So while breast cancer could be linked to estrogenic pesticides, it could also be linked to other kinds of hormone disruption...depressed thyroid levels have been linked to breast cancer just as increased estrogen exposure has.

The authors also refer to the work of Earl Gray, senior reproductive biologist and toxicologist at the EPA for his work on vinclozolin, a synthetic chemical widely used to kill fungus on fruit—and one which is frequently detected on the foods children commonly eat in the USA. Grey was discussing the way vinclozolin created hormonal havoc in rats. He showed male rats with breasts and explained how vinclozolin targeted the androgen receptor and blocked it so that the normal testosterone messages simply did not get through. Without testosterone signals, male development gets derailed and boys don't become boys. Instead they become stranded in an ambiguous state, where they cannot function as either males or females, so called "intersex" individuals. [440]

Generations at Risk is another book in a similar vein, written by Ted Schettler, M.D., M.P.H. Gina Solomon, M.D., Maria Valenti and Annette Huddle. Its sub-title is *Reproductive Health and the Environment,* which is exactly what it is about. The authors discuss the difficulty faced by researchers in the field of toxicology and reproduction. Despite the dramatic defects of thalidomide, it took six years to establish a causal relationship between the drug and over 6,000 deformed babies. They suggest that today it would still be difficult to detect a new hazard that would cause birth defects for a number of reasons. For example, there are few effective registries able to monitor birth defects, and studies undertaken in small population groups would not show up as "statistically significant,"— not until the levels became considerable.

They review heavy metals, organic solvents, pesticides, endocrine disrupters, etc., and come to similar conclusions to those in *Our Stolen Future*. Here's what they had to say about the regulatory state of affairs regarding our right to know when we are exposed to harmful substances, either at work or personal use of inadequately labelled products:

"As we have documented, people are regularly exposed to hazardous and inadequately tested substances, without being informed and without their consent. Their right to refuse has been denied. Environmental justice is not even close to being recognised as a fundamental human right." [441]

Generations At Risk also reviews a number of estrogenic compounds, such as Bisphenol-A and the phthalates. Bisphenol-A is a major component of epoxy resins, polycarbonate plastics and flame retardants. It can be used to coat the insides of food cans and is used in the manufacture of polycarbonate containers neither of which should be used with food, as it leaches out into the food, particularly when heated in the containers. Bisphenol-A is also known to exert estrogenic effects and stimulate the growth of estrogen-responsive breast cancer cells. Phthalates are testicular and ovarian toxicants and have estrogen-like activity. The authors are also concerned about the neurological problems and immune problems that are so hard to diagnose and link with individual exposures.

Our Chemical Body Burden

The US EPA monitored human exposure to toxic substances annually from 1970 till 1989 through its National Human Adipose Tissue Survey (NHATS), which collected human adipose tissue from various cadavers and other sources. The survey studied three different age groups, 0-14, 15-44 and 45+. In 1982 they expanded from their normal range of chemicals to look for the presence of 54 environmental toxins—and their results astounded everybody. Five of the chemicals, OCDD (a dioxin) and four solvents: xylene, ethylphenol, styrene and 1,4-dichlorobenzene were found in every sample that they studied. The levels in samples varied and some were alarming; OCDD varied from 19-700 ng per gram of fat (ng/g), styrene from 8-350 ng/g, dichlorobenzene 12-500 ng/g. Another nine chemicals were found in 91-98 percent of samples, and included benzene, chlorobenzene, ethylbenzene, toluene, one furan and three dioxins. DDE, the breakdown product for DDT was also found and so were PCBs (in 83 percent of samples).[442]

This provoked a lot of concern and induced other organisations to look into the body burden of our toxic load resulting from environmental contamination. The Environmental Working

Group, for example, undertook a small study led by Mount Sinai School of Medicine, studying people who were not working with chemicals in industry to see what levels of contaminants they were effected by, they found 167 chemicals. Of these 76 cause cancer in humans or animals, 94 are considered toxic to the brain and nervous system, and 79 cause birth defects or abnormal development. None of the participants lived near an industrial facility.[443]

The Environmental Working Group undertook another study that they published in 2005, looking into chemical contamination of new-born babies' blood. They found an average of 200 industrial chemicals and pollutants in umbilical cord blood from 10 babies born in August and September of 2004 in U.S. hospitals. Tests revealed a total of 287 chemicals in the group.

The chemicals they found ranged from organochloride pesticides (DDT and dieldrin, for example), chemicals from consumer products (brominated fire retardants and PCBs, for example), and chemical pollutants from waste incineration and fossil fuel combustion (such as polychlorinated and polybrominated dioxins and furans, polychlorinated napthalenes and mercury). They made the following observations:

> Of the 287 chemicals we detected in umbilical cord blood, we know that 180 cause cancer in humans or animals, 217 are toxic to the brain and nervous system, and 208 cause birth defects or abnormal development in animal tests. The dangers of pre- or post-natal exposure to this complex mixture of carcinogens, developmental toxins and neurotoxins have never been studied.[444]

In 2003, the World Wildlife Fund undertook a study in the UK of 155 volunteers from 13 different locations in England, Northern Ireland, Scotland and Wales. They took blood samples which were analysed for 78 chemicals by Lancaster University. All the 155 people tested were found to be contaminated with a cocktail of highly toxic chemicals that had been banned from use in the UK during the 1970s because they posed unknown health risks. Here are some of their results:

- They found 70 of the chemicals that they had set out to find.
- The highest number of the chemicals they were testing for in any one person was 49.
- Every person was contaminated with each group of chemical, Organochlorine pesticides, PCBs and flame retardants (PBDEs).
- The highest level contaminant was for DDE, the breakdown product for DDT which had been banned in the UK for more than 20 years.

- Levels varied depending upon area. Volunteers tested in Nottingham had the highest levels of PCBs, organochlorine pesticides and DDE. They also had the highest overall chemical contamination levels generally.

- Older people had higher PCB levels.

- Women had lower levels of PCBs, depending on the number of babies they carried and breast-fed. As with previous research, it was assumed this was due to them passing on some of their toxic burden to their children.

Here's the conclusion they drew from this and previous studies:

In WWF's view, the only way to stop this contamination, and the threat to future generations, is to prevent the marketing of chemicals that are found in elevated concentrations in biological fluids such as breast milk. This is also one of the primary recommendations of *Chemicals in Products,* the Royal Commission on Environmental Pollution report published in June 2003.

Bioaccumulative chemicals in use now should be urgently phased out, using existing legislation. The proposed new EU chemicals regulation known as REACH, the Registration, Evaluation and Authorisation of Chemicals provides a once in a generation opportunity to secure adequate controls for these substances. Hazardous chemicals, such as the very persistent and very bioaccumulative chemicals (vPvBs) and the endocrine disrupting chemicals (EDCs), should be subject to prior authorisation under the REACH proposals. This would mean that in the first place, there would be a presumption against the use of such chemicals. To secure the phase-out of these chemicals, however, the current draft of the REACH legislation needs to be improved. Authorisation to use hazardous chemicals should only be granted when there is no safer alternative *and* an overwhelming societal need for them. [445]

A further small study was undertaken as a collaborative report looking at the contamination in umbilical cord blood (27) and maternal blood (42) of a group of volunteers. This was a joint venture between WWF-UK and Greenpeace. They decided to look for evidence of contamination of eight chemical groups; Alkylphenols, artificial musk, Bisphenol-A, bromated flame retardants, organochlorine pesticides, perfluorinated compounds, phthalates and triclosan. The samples were taken at the University Hospital Groningen.

Phthalates were detected in 29 maternal and 24 cord blood samples; they are known to be toxic to reproduction. Musk ambrette, the chemical which had been banned for use in cosmetics in the EU since 1995, was still found in 15 maternal samples and 12 cord samples. Nonylphenol ethoxylates, one of the alkylphenol compounds that used to be extensively used as an industrial cleaning agent that has also been banned in the EU, was found in 12 of the 17 cord samples. The authors of the report state this is of particular concern since it has been banned. The antibacterial agent triclosan was found in 50 percent of the samples. DDT, the notorious pesticide had been banned in Norway and Sweden in 1970, banned in the US and Germany in 1972, and much later in the UK, 1984. Yet it was still found in virtually all samples. The organochlorine hexachlorobenzene, also subject of a global ban, was detected. Perfluorinated compounds such as PFOS and PFOA (used to make non-stick pans and water repelling agents) were present in all but one blood sample. PFOS was detected in all cord samples, and PFOA in approximately 50%. The authors come to the following conclusion:

> The research concludes that hazardous chemicals are common contaminants in both maternal and umbilical cord blood, indicating that these chemicals can pass from the mother to the baby across the placenta. How then can we better protect our children from exposure to such potentially harmful chemicals? The only answer is for governments to put in place mechanisms that will drive industry to replace those substances with safer alternatives.[446]

Furthermore, the *UK Royal Commission on Environmental Pollution* had this to say about chemicals found in breast milk: "Where chemicals are found in elevated concentrations in biological fluids such as breast milk, they should be removed from the market immediately." [447]

Stavros Dimas, the European Commissioner for the Environment (2005), had this to say about the growing awareness of chemical pollution, and the more recent findings on the health implications:

"There is a worrying increase in health problems that can be partially explained by our use of chemicals, such as growing numbers of hyperactive children, dramatically dropping sperm counts; increases in testicular cancer, breast cancer and other types of cancer." [448]

In truth, no-one knows what the long term effect of our chemical exposure is likely to be. Even though there have been attempts to limit dioxin exposure, for example, it is still ubiquitous in the environment. The Environmental Working Group reviewed data on breast feeding and made this observation:

> EWG analysis of data from peer-reviewed scientific reports has found that a breast-fed infant three to six months old, with an average weight of 16 pounds, consumes up to 77

times more dioxin and dioxin-like compounds than the EPA's suggested safe daily dose (RfD).

So it is virtually impossible to predict what the effects of this one exposure are going to mean for the development of our children—let alone a cocktail of numerous chemicals. The German government's Council of Environmental Advisors concluded in 1991: "The dynamic growth of chlorine chemistry during the 50s and 60s represents a decisive mistake in twentieth century industrial development, which would not have occurred had our present knowledge as to environmental damage, and health risks due to chlorine chemistry, then been available." [449]

One thing is for sure—there is increasing evidence globally that chemical pollution of our environment is having an untold effect on humanity; new information is coming to light on the mechanisms virtually week by week. It is not just chlorine chemistry that is of concern, of course. Thousands of other chemicals directly linked to the development of oil-based products are proving just as hazardous.

However, not all the news is negative: the European Union has voted to reconfigure its chemical policy, introducing REACH-Registration, Evaluation, Authorisation and Restriction of Chemicals. This now requires producers and importers of old and new chemicals, disclose toxicity data before their products can enter or remain on the market. These restrictions also cover the sixty-two thousand chemicals that have been exempted under US law. The responsibility for proving that a chemical is safe is consequently being shifted to industry.

The Stockholm Convention on Persistent Organic Pollutant's Treaty became international law in 2004. This treaty aims to eliminate the worldwide production of chemicals that are inherently harmful and which persist in the environment. The original treaty involved just twelve chemicals and since that time another eight have been added. It's not a lot, but it is a start and is a move in the right direction.

Media Manipulation and Public Relations

How industry responds will no doubt vary. There are sectors of industry that are embracing the idea of 'green chemistry' and are actively developing new products that do not impose such a toxic legacy. But there will no doubt be a significant reaction by other sectors, seeking to defend their profits at all costs. There are of course further sectors of industry that will wish to portray themselves as 'green' without being green—and have a very effective PR machine portraying them that way. Some of these companies are the ones who are spending an estimated $1billion plus on the services of anti-environmental PR professionals to undermine all efforts save our environment. US corporations pump $100 billion into advertising in the USA alone, and their influence is enormous.

The PR industry has significantly increased in size virtually every year in the last decade. The media, generally, has become more consolidated and controlled by a small number of large companies. In the US, for example, five companies dominate the industry: Time Warner, Disney, Murdoch's News Corporation, Bertelsmann of Germany and Viacom. The result has had a significant effect on journalism and the way media is controlled. For a start, there are a lot fewer journalists now pumping out the 'news', as big business seeks to reduce staffing costs. So a larger proportion of 'news' is reduced to news wired across the country. In the UK, the wiring service is dominated by the Press Association (PA), while in the USA it is the Associated Press (AP)—which is also an international wire agency along with Reuters.

This concentration of news sources has had a major impact on the flow and control of information—and, PR industry has taken up much of the slack. Nick Davies of *Flat Earth News* has undertaken to study just this effect—and has uncovered a very disturbing picture of what is going on. Basically, he commissioned some research from Cardiff University in the UK to establish to what degree the PR industry impacts on our media. They discovered that 60% of quality print newspaper stories consisted of no more than wire copy and/or PR material. A further 20% contained similar elements of wire copy and/or PR with other material added. This left simply 12% attributed to reporters themselves. There were, of course, variations from paper to paper: the London *Times'* percentage of wire/PR was 69% and the *Guardian*'s was just over 50%.[450]

In the USA, just as in the UK and most other countries, PR people now outnumber journalists. PR Newswire, for example, is a company that is headquartered in New York in the USA, but has offices in 16 countries and sends news direct to newsrooms in 135 countries. It is a subsidiary of United Business Media of London. PR Newswire claims to reach 27,000 media outlets and 6,000 websites for more than 15,000 clients.[451] This does not include the direct access that is exercised by all the PR companies themselves. WPP plc. is a global advertising agency that controls a number of major PR companies such as Burson Marsteller and, Hill and Knowlton, two of the larger ones, as well as Young and Rubicam, one of the world's largest advertising agencies.

What Davies discovered in his research, not just in the UK, but in the USA and most of the other countries, is that because of the pressure on journalists to produce material to fill newspapers (as well as radio and TV programmes), the opportunity to resort to the wire services and PR services is irresistible (he terms this 'churnalising'). In most cases, the journalists don't have the time to verify the information in any meaningful way. The result of all these changes—the consolidation of the media, the reduction of journalists, the reliance on wire/PR that is not checked or verified and the continuing trend for people not to read books (a decrease of 7% from 1992 -2002, [452] means we are left open to increasing degrees of manipulation.

The use of PR by government has also increased dramatically. In the UK, for example the use of it under Margaret Thatcher increased more than 500% in ten years. In 1988, expenditure on the Central Office of Information reached £150 million—which did not include outside public relations services or advertising. Under the following Blair government, expenditure on PR continued to rise, and a further 310 press officers were hired. Expenditure on election campaigns had increased almost five-fold by 1997, to £54.3 million, most of which was spent on PR and marketing. Government 'spin' and global 'spin' is handled by the same people that control corporate PR and 'spin.' In the USA the situation is the same, just the figures are higher.

Here is a quote from someone in the industry:

A Grey and Company executive (senior vice president) was speaking about the successful airing of an advertisement, for one of its clients, not sold as 'advertising' to NBC in the US, that was not disclosed by NBC as PR material or its source revealed:

"Most of what you see on TV is, in effect, a canned PR product. Most of what you read in the paper and see on TV is not news.... Of course it's labelled, it has our name all over it. They are free to use it. Not to use it. Use it for B-role. Write their own scripts. Most of them take it straight off the air and broadcast it. Rip and read. Rip and read." [453]

When you read 'New cure for cancer discovered' where do you think the article came from? Or 'New arthritis drug shows tremendous promise'. We are, of course, expected to believe that this is serious journalism and not simply pharmaceutical industry propaganda, but that's often what it is. When articles about diet quote reports from organisations such as the Social Issues Research Centre, the British Nutrition Foundation or the International Life Sciences Foundation, you wouldn't expect them to be funded by Kraft, the Sugar Bureau, Nestlé, Kellogs, the Dairy Council or Cadbury Schweppes. But *Flat Earth News* reports all those organiosations have received significant funding from them.

We'll leave this chapter with one more quote, this time from Edward Bernays, considered by some to be the founding father of PR who put it this way:

UNHEALTHY BETRAYAL

The conscious and intelligent manipulation of the organised habits and opinions of the masses is an important element in a democratic society. Those who manipulate this unseen mechanism of society constitute an invisible government which is the true ruling power of our country. In almost every act of our daily lives, whether in the sphere of politics or business, in our social conduct or our ethical thinking, we are dominated by the relatively small number of persons...who pull the wires which control the public mind. [454]

Chapter 11
Unhealthy Medicine

Mathematics may be compared to a mill of exquisite workmanship, which grinds you stuff of any degree of fineness; but, nevertheless, what you get out depends upon what you put in; and as the grandest mill in the world will not extract wheat-flour from peascod, so pages of formulae will not get a definite result out of loose data.

Thomas Huxley [455]

Spending on healthcare in the US hit $2.5 trillion in 2009, representing 17.6% of gross domestic product; this was despite the slowest annual growth increase in health spending following the recession of 2007/2008. Nevertheless, as a result of declining Federal revenues, this represented an increase in spending share of Federal revenues from 37.6% in 2008 to 54.2% in 2009.[456] This is an amazing figure. Healthcare in 2009 took up more than 50% of total Federal revenues.

With such fantastic sums of money being spent on it, Americans must have been receiving the best healthcare in the world, right? Unfortunately, that was not the case. Why it wasn't, we will now look into.

The attitude to health in America epitomises the Western approach to what we commonly refer to as 'modern medicine' or allopathic medicine. No doubt when we're asked what makes a good doctor we would come up with all sorts of answers—but I doubt that many of us would give the answer from an oriental point of view, "No patients!" Of course, this is the best answer because; "no patients" means everyone is so healthy that they don't need a doctor. But obviously this would mean creating an environment where our children had access to the fundamentals for achieving good health, a nurturing environment supplying quality nutrition, health-giving fresh nutrient-rich food, clean vibrant energising unpolluted water, clean air to breath and adequate exercise—all as a basic starting point.

Is this what we provide? Well, personally, I've had some real water once. When travelling through Norway, we stopped at a mountain stream for a drink; the water was rushing down the side of the mountain as clear as you will ever see. I never realised water could have such an effect on me—truly vibrant, wonderful and energising. Yet, today we consider ourselves lucky just to have a water supply, even if it is chlorinated. At least we have fresh water.

But if we could prevent disease from occurring by creating a healthier environment in the first place, this would be much cheaper in the long run than to spend vast sums of money on treating the healthcare problems that a less healthy environment engenders. There seems to be something fundamentally wrong with our current approach—yet despite all the evidence, we are doing very little about it.

Modern (or allopathic) medicine is based on drugs, surgery or radiation to treat virtually any form of 'illness'. There are many who feel this approach has many serious drawbacks. The Institute of Medicine reviewed healthcare in 1999, and came to the following conclusion:

> Health care in the United States is not as safe as it should be—and can be. At least 44,000 people, and perhaps as many as 98,000 people, die in hospitals each year as a result of medical errors that could have been prevented, according to estimates from two major studies.
>
> Among the problems that commonly occur during the course of providing health care are adverse drug events and improper transfusions, surgical injuries and wrong-site surgery, suicides, restraint-related injuries or death, falls, burns, pressure ulcers, and mistaken patient identities. High error rates with serious consequences are most likely to occur in intensive care units, operating rooms, and emergency departments.
>
> Beyond their cost in human lives, preventable medical errors exact other significant tolls...loss of trust in the health care system by patients. [457]

There are many people who believe that the way allopathic medicine is practiced and controlled has a much bigger impact on our society than most of us are led to believe. Gary Null PhD and his associates, Martin Feldman MD, Debora Rasio MD, and Carolyn Dean, MD, ND, undertook to review significant recent evidence and concluded that conventional medicine is killing nearly 800,000 people a year. They have written an entire book about it and give some sobering figures:

- Deaths due to Adverse Drug Reactions – 106,000+
- Deaths due to hospital medical errors – 98,000.

- Deaths due to bedsores -115,000.

- Deaths due to hospital infections – 99,000

- Deaths due to nursing homes and malnutrition – 108,000

- Deaths due to outpatient drug reactions – 109,000

- Deaths due to unnecessary surgical procedures

- Deaths due to surgery – 32,000.

This adds up to a total figure of 794,936+ deaths; the researchers also give a cost, of in excess of $282 billion to the taxpayer. [458] The emotional and financial losses to the families of the victims add to this burden. In their book *Death By Medicine, Hull and associates* give an up-to-date breakdown of how they arrive at their figures—and also provide a DVD with the book. However, other research suggests that even their figures may be conservative. Under-reporting of medical errors and drug problems is endemic in medicine—and figures of people who have survived, but who have not been healed, are hard to come by. Doctors often do not know that the medication they are giving may often cause harm.

There is a wealth of literature in the public domain documenting drugs that were released and found to be harmful, some that I have already documented such as thalidomide and DES to name but two. So let's look at some more—there is something to be learned from them.

Heart Treatments That Increased the Chance of Dying

In the early 1980s, pharmaceutical companies were experimenting with creating new chemicals that they believed would be profitable and break into new markets, one of which was for drugs that could affect the heart rate. Scientists postulated the theory that perhaps death from heart attacks could be prevented by influencing the heart rate where there was a problem with patients with electrically unstable hearts. Bernard Lown had postulated this theory back in 1978. Scientists developed what were known as antiarrhythmic drugs such as Tambocor and Enkaid. Tambocor was developed by 3M, and Enkaid by Bristol-Myers Squibb. Although Tambocor was approved by the FDA in 1985, there had been no serious study undertaken to test its true effectiveness.

Robert Temple, the FDA official who approved Tambocor, originally had misgivings about approving it. There had, for a start, been unexplained deaths, in some cases, where it had been unusually difficult to resuscitate the patients. There was enough concern about this amongst cardiologists at the time that 3M commissioned a further study of 39 patients who had other severe heart problems, Tambocor was found to improve some heart irregularities, but failed to affect extended bursts of premature beats. In this study 18 percent of the patients died—all but one from cardiac arrests.

Enkaid, meanwhile, was faring no better. In the Compassionate Use trial 18 percent also died. A Stanford cardiologist, Roger Winkle, had already published a warning about Enkaid in the *American Heart Journal*. AS a result, Robert Temple sent a letter to 3M imposing a number of restrictions on Tambocor use which would have reduced its profitability and market share. 3M came back to see Temple three weeks later with another report containing more positive evidence about Tambocor—and succeeded in persuading him to back down and only impose some very minor modifications to the original approval. [459]

Consequently, two years after Tambocor's launch pharmacists were fulfilling 57,000 prescriptions for it a month. Enkaid, on the other hand, was a full year behind Tambocor. So Bristol-Myers decided to try winning doctors over with a post-approval trial in which they would pay the doctors to switch their patients to Enkaid. They recruited 191 cardiologists and 1277 patients. Yet after only six weeks of the trial, 39 had died, mostly from cardiac arrests.

Meanwhile, the FDAs Monitored Adverse Reaction system (MAR) had been discontinued, for Tambocor. As it had been set up, it had only been monitoring heart attacks, not sudden deaths or cardiac arrests—so no adverse information had accrued under it. The National Heart, Lung, and Blood Institute decided to sponsor a trial called the Cardiac Arrhythmia Suppression Trial (CAST). Up until this nobody had undertaken a serious evaluation of antiarrhythmic drugs—but this was a serious trial. It would involve 300 researchers, cost more than $40 million, and study 27 sites for five years. However, the trial had to be prematurely stopped because it revealed that, far from saving lives, both Tambocor and Enkaid were, in fact causing more deaths. Thomas Moore, documents the story of the estimated 24,000 -70,000 unnecessary deaths attributed to this tragedy in his book *Deadly Medicine - Why tens of thousands of heart patients died in America's worst drug disaster.* [460]

But the disaster was not limited to just these two drugs. The authors of the original CAST trial were still convinced there had to be a use for antiarrhythmic drug—so they continued trialling the other antiarrhythmic drug Ethmozine, in their CAST II trial. But unfortunately, the same thing happened, 102 people died in the treated group, compared to 86 in the placebo group. [461]

I chose this particular story about class 1 antiarrhythmic drugs to illustrate what is now a significant problem—drugs being released without adequate testing. The testing that is undertaken is simply to meet the minimal requirements of the FDA to prove that a drug is 'effective.' This work is financed by the drug companies and is generally undertaken by them. They do not have to prove that a new drug is more effective than existing comparable drugs or even *equally* effective. Most of the time they deliberately choose not to compare their new drug with another existing drug because, it may not look so 'effective.' Generally, they play safe and compare it with a placebo (a non-reactive sugar pill). And its true effectiveness remains unproven.

The drug industry has access to massive amounts of money that enable it to influence the entire political system, and so continue to make vast profits, irrespective on the effect on our health. It's well known that it spends more on its public relations and lobbying than it does on reliable drug research. It goes to great lengths to attack those who challenge the safety or efficacy of its products. The FDA in the USA is the organisation that reviews all drug applications and licenses. It has been a political football throughout its existence, and has been accused of immense bias towards the pharmaceutical industry. Frequently, it supports industry profits over health, and relentlessly attacks competing therapies, including nutritional therapists and homeopaths etc.[462] However, there are a number of individuals who have worked within the FDA, and who believe they have stood by their principals (some of whose work I have already discussed). They have tried to warn us of the dangers of giving approval to drugs that have not been properly evaluated. I feel it would be instructive to look at some of these scientists' views.

Non-Steroidal Anti-Inflammatory Drugs (NSAIDS)

In the UK, anti-inflammatory drugs account for the highest proportion of adverse reactions of any class of drug—a finding corroborated by the French experience. [463] Accurate calculations of the adverse effects are difficult to gather, and are considered greatly underreported. However Singh Gurkirpal, MD assessed:

"Conservative calculations estimate that approximately 107,000 patients are hospitalized annually for nonsteroidal anti-inflammatory drug (NSAID)-related gastrointestinal (GI) complications and at least 16,500 NSAID-related deaths occur each year among arthritis patients alone. The figures of all NSAID users would be overwhelming, yet the scope of this problem is generally under-appreciated." [464] A further report in 1999 addressed the problem further:

It has been estimated conservatively that 16,500 NSAID-related deaths occur among patients with rheumatoid arthritis or osteoarthritis every year in the United States..... If deaths from gastrointestinal toxic effects from NSAIDs were tabulated separately in the National Vital Statistics reports, these effects would constitute the 15th most common cause of death in the United States. Yet these toxic effects remain mainly a "silent epidemic," with many physicians and most patients unaware of the magnitude of the problem. Furthermore the mortality statistics do not include deaths ascribed to the use of over-the-counter NSAIDS. [465]

Drug Testing Troubles

In November 2004, one of the FDA's leading scientists, David Graham, gave testimony to US Senate Committee regarding his concerns about another NSAID, called Vioxx:

'My name is David Graham, and I am pleased to come before you today to speak about Vioxx, heart attacks and the FDA. By way of introduction, I graduated from the Johns Hopkins University School of Medicine, and trained in Internal Medicine at Yale and in adult Neurology at the University of Pennsylvania. After this, I completed a three-year fellowship in pharmacoepidemiology and a Masters in Public Health at Johns Hopkins, with a concentration in epidemiology and biostatistics. Over my 20 year career in the field, all of it at FDA, I have served in a variety of capacities. I am currently the Associate Director for Science and Medicine in FDA's Office of Drug Safety. During my career, I believe I have made a real difference for the cause of patient safety. My research and efforts within FDA led to the withdrawal from the US market of Omniflox, an antibiotic that caused hemolytic anemia; Rezulin, a diabetes drug that caused acute liver failure; Fen-Phen and Redux, weight loss drugs that caused heart valve injury; and PPA (phenylpropanolamine), an over-the-counter decongestant and weight loss product that caused hemorrhagic stroke in young women. My research also led to the withdrawal from outpatient use of Trovan, an antibiotic that caused acute liver failure and death. I also contributed to the team effort that led to the withdrawal of Lotronex, a drug for irritable bowel syndrome that causes ischemic colitis; Baycol, a cholesterol-lowering drug that caused severe muscle injury, kidney failure and death; Seldane, an antihistamine that caused heart arrhythmias and death; and Propulsid, a drug for night-time heartburn that caused heart arrythmias and death. I have done extensive work concerning the issue of pregnancy exposure to Accutane, a drug that is used to treat acne but can cause birth defects in some children who are exposed in-utero if their mothers take the drug during the first trimester. During my career, I have recommended the market withdrawal of 12 drugs. Only 2 of these remain on the market today-Accutane and Arava, a drug for the treatment of rheumatoid arthritis that I and a co-worker believe causes an unacceptably high risk of acute liver failure and death.

Let me begin by describing what we found in our study, what others have found, and what this means for the American people. Prior to approval of Vioxx, a study was performed by Merck named 090. This study found nearly a 7-fold increase in heart attack risk with low dose Vioxx. The labeling at approval said nothing about heart attack risks. In November 2000, another Merck clinical trial named VIGOR found a 5-fold increase in heart attack risk with high-dose Vioxx. The company said the drug was safe and that the comparison drug naproxen, was protective. In 2002, a large epidemiologic study reported a 2-fold increase in heart attack risk with high-dose Vioxx and another study reported that naproxen did not affect heart attack risk. About 18 months after the VIGOR results were published, FDA made a labeling change about heart attack risk with high-dose Vioxx, but did not place this in the "Warnings" section. Also, it did not ban the high-dose formulation and its use. I believe such a ban should have been implemented. Of note, FDA's label change had absolutely no effect on how often high-dose Vioxx was prescribed, so what good did it achieve?'

He goes on to discuss the magnitude of the problem, suggesting figures that he believes are still conservative, estimating from '88,000 to 139,000 Americans affected. Of these, 30-40% probably died. For the survivors, their lives were changed forever.'

He goes on to express his concern over Vioxx:
'To begin, after publication of the VIGOR study in November 2000, I became concerned about the potential public health risk that might exist with Vioxx. VIGOR suggested that the risk of heart attack was increased 5-fold in patients who used the high-dose strength of this drug. Why was the Vioxx safety question important? 1) Vioxx would undoubtedly be used by millions of patients. That's a very large number to expose to a serious drug risk. 2) heart attack is a fairly common event, and 3) given the above, even a relatively small increase in heart attack risk due to Vioxx could mean that tens of thousands of Americans might be seriously harmed or killed by use of this drug.

Vioxx is a terrible tragedy and a profound regulatory failure. I would argue that the FDA, as currently configured, is incapable of protecting America against another Vioxx. We are virtually defenseless.

It is important that this Committee and the American people understand that what has happened with Vioxx is really a symptom of something far more dangerous to the safety of the American people. Simply put, FDA and its Center for Drug Evaluation and Research are broken.'[466]

That is a pretty serious statement to be made by a respected FDA scientist such as Dr Graham. Vioxx (rofecoxib) was eventually withdrawn on 29th September 2001. At the time, it was Merck & Company's biggest selling painkiller, and its Chief Executive Raymond Gilmartin was quoted as saying that the study findings that tied Vioxx to risk of heart attack and stroke were "unexpected." But emails and interviews with outside scientists (as well as marketing materials) indicated that Merck aggressively fought for years to keep safety concerns from undermining Vioxx's commercial potential. More of the controversy surrounding Merck's behaviour is revealed in the *Wall Street Journal* article by Anna Wilde Mathews and Barbara Martinez—for those who would like more of the story. [467]

Vioxx was what is referred to as a Cyclooxygenase-2 (Cox-2) inhibitor, one of the newer generation of drugs that were not supposed to be as problematic as aspirin. Aspirin affected the COX-1 molecules that protect the lining of the stomach, as well as the joints, and is known to cause intestinal bleeding and, in extreme cases, death. As with Celebrex, Vioxx is a fluoridated drug, in theory designed to be more effective. Currently it is estimated that 30% of all pharmaceuticals contain fluoride. There are many scientists who worry at the extensive use of fluoride in pharmaceuticals, due to its ability to accumulate in the body, resist being broken down and excreted, and further to create more toxic breakdown products.[468]

Merck chose to do a study comparing its product to naproxen (Aleve). When the trial results came back in 2000, participants who took their drug for an average of nine months were found to have four times the risk of having a heart attack as the patients taking naproxen. This meant that Vioxx increased the risk by 400 percent. Merck apparently was not put off: they argued with the FDA that it was not the case that Vioxx increased the risk of heart disease by 400 percent, more that the naproxen *reduced* heart disease by 80 percent! It spent around four years arguing this point.[469] Eventually, as the injury toll rose and the claims mounted, Merck decided to settle the 27,000 lawsuits filed against it—three years after the withdrawal of Vioxx. The whole saga was reviewed by Amisha Patel from the viewpoint of a public relations exercise. [470]

A further interesting review was undertaken by John Abramson MD, in his excellent book, *Overdosed America*. This is a review of the problems he came across while working as a physician in America and the inherent faults in the system. He is a very perceptive doctor, very capable of finding any faults in scientific papers—as he does with the Vioxx studies. In his book, he is critical of the FDA and the *New England Journal of Medicine* for failing to bring to the attention of the medical community the extent of the 'serious adverse events,'—complications that usually led to hospitalisation or death in the VIGOR study. He put these at 21 percent more than the naproxen users. His main criticism of the problems with Vioxx, though, was that it raised serious issues about both the regulatory process and drug approval process. In his view, it is impossible to understand the long-term effects of a drug that is only tested for the six to eight weeks that most drugs are tested for. He is certainly not the only doctor with this view. [471]

There are many people in the world of medicine who feel unable to criticise the pharmaceutical industry. The medical journals, for example, receive much of their funding from advertising by the various pharmaceutical companies and have been known to terminate advertising when given negative press. Marcia Angell, M.D, former editor-in-chief of the *New England Journal of Medicine,* spent twenty years on the front line dealing with every aspect of the world of medicine. She noted the increasing influence of the pharmaceutical industry and the effect this had on research: "As I saw industry influence grow, I became increasingly troubled by the possibility that much published research is seriously flawed, leading doctors to believe new drugs are generally more effective and safer than they actually are." She goes further: "Drug companies have the largest lobby in Washington, and they give copiously to political campaigns. Legislators are now so beholden to the pharmaceutical industry that it will be exceedingly difficult to break its lock on them."

She refers to the fact that Americans spend a staggering $200 billion on prescription drugs per year, and that this figure is still growing at 12% a year. She relates how the pharmaceutical industry seems able to raise its prices willy-nilly. She cites Schering-Plough's top selling allergy drug, Claritin, which went up thirteen times over a period of five years—at over four times the rate of inflation. She worries about the cost of drugs on consumers, particularly the elderly many whom are taking around six drugs daily, full time. With the average cost of a drug at $1500 per year this adds up to an annual bill of $9,000. Without supplementary insurance, this is a huge financial burden on the frail and elderly. The pharmaceutical industry has for years ranked as the most profitable industry in the USA. They have always argued that their high profits are essential to cover the cost of research and drug development. But Angell reviews the evidence and finds this is patently not the case. She does not mince her words when she says: "Contrary to the industry's public relations, you don't get what you pay for. The fact is that this industry is taking us for a ride, there will be no real reform without an aroused and determined public to make it happen." [472]

The majority of new drugs are not really new. They are simply variations of existing drugs, what are commonly referred to in the US as 'me-too' drugs. It is a very simple process to copy a highly profitable drug and make minor changes to it. Similarly, there is an incentive for a drug company with a successful product on which the patent is due to expire, to simply reconfigure its molecular structure slightly, and obtain further patent rights on the 'new' drug for another twenty years. Many of the really innovative drugs are actually developed using taxpayer funded research at academic institutions, small biotech, companies or large publically-funded bodies such as the National Institute of Health (NIH). [473]

In 1992, the US Congress passed the Prescription Drug User Fee Act (PDUFA) which permitted drug companies to pay user fees to the FDA. This was to enable the FDA hire more staff and speed up the review process for new drugs. It was re-visited in 1997 and re-authorised, and the Food and Drug Administration Modernization Act (FDAMA) was added to it. This increased the use of the "accelerated approval" and 'surrogate endpoints' in clinical trials. Surrogate endpoints are parameters or markers that may be looked for such as the raising or lowering of blood pressure, or changes in cholesterol levels etc. These are a convenient substitute for more clinically meaningful end points such as curing a particular disease, reduction of symptoms or a lower death rate. FDAMA also changed the legal standard for drug approvals from two clinical trials to just one.

In 1998 two doctors, Sidney Wolfe, and Peter Lurie released a report on the FDA to analyse what effect, if any, the changes had had on the review process. This followed a year when three drugs had had to be removed from the market due to serious safety issues: dexfenfluramine (Redux), mibefradil (Posicor) and bromfenac (Duract). In each case, significant concerns about these drugs had been revealed in the data prior to approval. In September 1998 Wolfe and Laurie sent letters to 172 FDA Medical Reviewing Officers with a seven page questionnaire. All respondents were guaranteed anonymity. Fifty-three people responded—and revealed a troubling testimony:

- Nineteen Medical Officers identified a total of 27 new drugs in the past three years that they had reviewed and thought should not be approved but which were approved.

- One Medical Officer stated: "My feeling after more than 20 years at FDA is that, unless drugs cannot be shown to 'kill patients' outright, then they will be approved with revised labeling and a box warning."

- One Medical Officer reported: "In the last 2 years, I recommended that two drugs not be approved. They were both approved without consulting me. This never happened before. In one case, the drug did not meet the standards set up by the division, so they nullified the standards."

- Eight Medical Officers reported 14 instances in the previous three years in which they had been instructed, usually by the Office Director, not to present their own opinion or data to an FDA Advisory Committee when to do so might have reduced the likelihood that a drug would be approved.

Here are some of the comments made by the FDA officers:

"We are shifting the burden of proof of safety onto ourselves. Instead of asking the drug companies to prove the drug safe, we are trying to prove the drug dangerous. If we cannot show that the drug is dangerous, then it is assumed safe."

"The standards are good if it comes to simply identifying a problem or determining how well a drug works. However, implementation is a problem. So often, we identify a problem pre-approval, and it is simply inserted into the label with everything else the practitioner has no time to read."

"Rapid approval often means insufficient time to examine carefully original data, accepting 'on faith' validity of randomization, screening, use and misuses of inclusion and exclusion criteria. There is insufficient time to discuss outlying observations."

"The official times allowed for the review process keep getting shorter and shorter. The recently passed 'FDA Modernization Act' is making things a lot worse."

"The agency forfeits its most powerful weapon—withholding approval. Essentially all Phase IV studies which are required are for safety reasons. If a problem is identified, the agency negotiates with the company for labeling changes. Withdrawal is extremely unlikely even if its problem is very serious."[474]

These are sobering comments from people in the FDA who review new drugs. Were any lessons learned from this experience? One or two people may have noticed, but don't expect to see anything radical that could slow the pharmaceutical industry's ability to carry on making vast profits without any real concern for the health consequences. In the previous chapters, I discussed diabetes and its obvious link with diet. Instead of educating people about the true cause of diabetes, and showing them how to change their dietary patterns to a healthier alternative—dumping fast food, high fats, and an over-reliance on over-processed carbohydrates there is money to be made from keeping people ignorant and suggesting there is a simpler way to lose weight. Yep just swallow a few of these pills...

UNHEALTHY BETRAYAL

Weight-loss Drugs —A Health Disaster

Fenfluramine (3-trifluoromethyl-N-ethylamphetamine), a weight-loss drug was introduced into the market in the USA in 1973 as Pondimin. It was not a popular drug—it caused the release of serotonin which regulates mood and appetite amongst other things. It also made people feel drowsy. Phentermine on the other hand, is a phenethylamine stimulant, similar to an amphetamine. It was used as an appetite suppressant for weight-loss. Unfortunately it also caused problems—in this case palpitations and insomnia. So Mike Weintraub had the idea of combining these drugs in the hope they would neutralise each other and so assist weight-loss without side effects. He convinced A H Robbins, the then owner of Pondimin, the NIH and Lou Lasagna to support a study to see if his idea was correct. This study was completed in 1987 but was not published until 1992. After a bout of publicity in 1995 sales took off. Wyeth, the owner of A H Robbins, controlled the license for pondimin and supported Weintraub's work. The combination drug would become known as Fen-Phen (a fluoridated drug). Meanwhile the parent company of Wyeth, American Home Products, merged with American Cyanimid that at that time controlled Interneuron Pharmaceuticals, a company started by Dick Wurtman, who by coincidence was in the process of getting approval for a drug called Redux (dexfenfluramine—another fluoridated drug). Redux was also an appetite suppressant, that released serotonin into the brain; it was the d-enantiomer of fenfluramine.

The concept of the d-enantiomer is worth closer examination. It is simply a mirror-opposite isomer. If you look in the mirror you see an image of yourself, but if you were to step out of the mirror and be confronted with the real you, you would look different to an observer. The same is the case with the mirror opposite isomers; they are not identical in their behaviour. These mirror opposite isomers are useful to drug companies. If there is a successful drug on the market, other companies will try and come up with a d-enantiomer of the drug, and hopefully market it with its own patent. This can be a cheap way of coming up with a 'new' drug.

Dr Leo Lutwak, a former professor of biochemistry and nutrition from Cornell University (who died in 2006), worked for the FDA reviewing drugs dealing with obesity and bone disorders. He had expressed a number of concerns with Redux, a drug for use in diabetes. Maenwhile, Dr John Lehmann, a neurologist at Hahnemann Hospital in Philadelphia, when working for a previous employer, Servier Laboratories (1988-1990), had observed 'degeneration' of brain cells over time in his studies of animals using both Pondimin and Redux. This implied that these drugs were neurotoxic—and he had communicated this to the FDA. Yet, although he was later fired for doing this, it was enough to raise concerns about the long-term effects of their use. On top of this, Leo Lutwak had learned of reports from Europe of pulmonary hypertension (PH) and primary pulmonary hypertension (PPH) from Servier—the company that was marketing dexfenfluramine in Europe under the trade name Isomeride. Leo had studied the reports, and expressed his concerns about Redux to his associate Solomon Sobel "This drug is going to blow up, and I want there to be a paper trail." [475]

At the first FDA examination of Redux, it failed to be passed. Both Wyeth and Interneuron were sent a letter expressing the FDA's concern over its neurotoxicity. Within weeks they proposed to undertake further research on its neurotoxicity as part of a phase 4 study, but not until *after* the approval of Redux. The FDA then agreed to revive the New Drug Application (NDA). In what some might consider a rather controversial appointment, Mike Weintraub, the developer of the Fen-Phen drug combination, was appointed to the FDA by Carl Peck. Whilst working for the FDA he would turn up on TV talking about the success of the combination drug use for weight loss, which in a legal respect for the FDA was what was known as an 'off-label use.' This promotion by an FDA official would certainly make it harder for them to complain about the industry's own marketing of the same combination, even though it was 'off label'.

Information from Europe was going to give them cause for much more concern, thanks to a study funded by the French Government, called the International Primary Pulmonary Hypertension Study (IPPHS). A prominent epidemiologist, Dr. Lucien Abenhaim, gathered ten of the world's foremost epidemiologists, cardiologists and pulmonologists, which included Stuart Rich from Chicago, to help with the study. They presented a preliminary report in March 1995 to Servier, and then to Interneuron and Wyeth. Whilst primary pulmonary hypertension usually affects only one or two people per million, the study showed that with the use of Redux or Pondimin the numbers rose tenfold. With longer use, more than three months, the numbers increased significantly. As a result, the European Health Commissioners imposed severe restrictions on the use of both drugs.

The study did not impress some people in the FDA however, and was dismissed outright by Bruce Stadel. Subsequently, Dr Abenhaim went to the US to address the FDA Advisory committee, on September 28, 1995 to inform them of an impending epidemic of what was invariably a fatal lung disease. His concerns were derided by American Home Products' (AHP) consultant Gerry Faitch, as well as Bruce Stadel. Abenhaim explained that his figures were very conservative, and that the deaths were rapidly increasing—as a result of which the committee voted 5-3 against Redux. However, Jim Bilstad, a director of the FDA, took the highly unusual step of convening a meeting to review Redux again. This took place at a time when the two neurotoxicologists, Mark Molliver and Lewis Seiden, who both had concerns about the neurotoxicity of the drug, would not be able to attend. At the next meeting the industry representatives were even better prepared: they came with eleven advisors, compared to the eight at the original meeting, including two strong Redux supporters. This time Redux was passed by a vote of 6-5. [476]

Stuart Rich is a professor of medicine and director of the Rush Heart Institute Center for Pulmonary Heart Disease in Chicago. He attended the first meeting as a consultant and voiced concern at the way the whole thing was handled. Little surprise then, that neither he nor any of the other consultants nor any of the consultants was invited back to the second meeting. Further, he didn't see the point in getting involved with drugs that were patently ineffective at best:

"If you looked at the efficacy studies, you found out that its efficacy was minimal, at best. Three percent weight loss after one year. If you weighed 300 pounds, I could say, "End of the year, I'll get you down to 291, with a risk of dying of pulmonary hypertension."

"So when I saw all of that, then I really couldn't believe that the FDA would ever give serious consideration to this."

When he was asked what he thought about the whole affair his response reflected how intimately he was involved with the illness the drugs caused:

"Do you want the truth? It was despair. My reaction was despair. Why despair? My specialty is I treat patients with pulmonary hypertension. These are the sickest cardiovascular patients that exist. They're young people. They're tragic stories.

We have some treatments—they are very difficult treatments. It's a death sentence, and it's a slow death, like drowning over months to years, if you can envision what that's like. My heart breaks with every new patient that's referred to me." [477]

Little known to many people is how a lady called Pam Ruff, an echocardiogram sonographer at the Merit Care Clinic in Fargo USA, discovered the link between taking Fen-Phen and heart valve problems. She kept getting patients for echocardiograms who were suffering from shortness of breath and constant fatigue, and this shocked her. The mitral valves of the heart looked 'weird,' they contracted more than normal, were sticking, and not operating normally. Such a condition would not have shocked her in a seventy year old—but she was finding it in thirty year olds! It was not long before she discovered that each of these younger patients had been taking Fen-Phen to lose weight. She recorded each case she came across over a period of two years, after which she took her discovery to MeritCare's Administrator, Dr. Bruce Pitts, who convened a committee of doctors. Following her revelations, one of the doctors, Jack Crary, was spurred into action by yet another patient, also on Fen-Phen, who was so damaged she was going to need heart surgery. He called an associate at the Mayo Clinic and discovered that one of their cardiologists, Dr. Heidi Connelly, had been working on the same problem. After sharing all their information, it was agreed that Connelly would draft a preliminary report and send it to *The New England Journal of Medicine (19th February 1997)*. Meanwhile, Dr. Crary sent reports of the first thirteen cases of valvulopathy to the distributors of Phentermine and Wyeth's offices. What Wyeth did with that information became the subject of numerous lawsuits and entered the realm of legend. Dr. Pitts, meanwhile, ordered all MeritCare doctors to stop prescribing Fen-Phen or Redux. In late April, Connelly got a rejection letter from *The New England Journal of Medicine (NEJM)*, citing the fact that she only had five cases to report—and suggesting she send her report, as a letter to the editor. When he received this, the *NEJM* editor was taken aback—she had included nineteen more cases. He urged her to call the FDA, which she did on 27th June—and apparently what they read was news to them.[478]

By the time the *New England Journal of Medicine* article was published on 28th August, the FDA had become aware of fifty-eight cases of valvulopathy from both The Mayo Institute and Fargo's hospitals. Reports now showed that people who took fenfluramine and phentermine for as little as 23 days succumbed to pulmonary hypertension. This was, as mentioned before, a serious condition—one woman died within eight months. [479]

In August the previous year, the full IPPHS report had been reported in the *NEJM*, at the same time as a promotional campaign by Interneuron and Wyeth was under way and Wall Street was predicting sales for Redux could hit $1 billion a year. Stuart Rich, co-author of the study, appeared on the *Today* show, trying to warn people that these drugs were, in fact killers. After returning from the show he took a call from Marc Deitch, Wyeth's Medical Affairs Director who warned him off speaking any further in public. In an interview with Frontline Rich had this to say about this unexpected call:

"When I got back to my office at the Medical Center that morning, he called me directly. He told me he saw my interview on the *Today* show, and warned me that it was very dangerous for me to talk to the press about that; that if I had any issues regarding their product that I wanted to publish in a scientific journal, so be it. But if I spoke to the media about their drug, bad things would happen.

What did you understand that to mean, "Bad things would happen?" I mean, those are actually the words he used?

"Bad things would happen" was the exact phrase he used. ... I took the threat very, very seriously. I decided, OK, it's a little unpredictable when you talk to the press anyway — sometimes you want to say a story, and it comes out a little differently — so maybe I wouldn't talk to the media. I never did, from that point on, and I was approached by all of the major news stations—CBS, ABC, NBC....

I never talked to the press again, because I didn't know what they had in mind. They are a very big, a very powerful company." [480]

AHP and Wyeth had hired a number of PR companies to help them deal with the flack that they were getting. In July they had acceded to a black box warning on valvular heart disease, but they termed it "evidence of a causal relationship". Meanwhile, pressure was building on the FDA to act—and when they eventually summoned Wyeth and Interneuron executives (on September 12), they told them to voluntarily remove these drugs from the market or face official recall proceedings that would inevitably generate numerous lawsuits.

By the end of 2000 there were approximately 300,000 people, mostly women, joining a mass settlement claim for possible valve damage. This was based on FDA had reports linking Redux as a suspect with 123 deaths. In January 2001, American Home Products (AHP) had increased its liability reserve fund by $7.5 billion to $12.5 billion, to cover the lawsuits; this was more than its net income had been for the previous decade. [481]

With more than a hint of irony, the day after the drug withdrawal was the day that Congress passed the new FDA reform law. This would force the FDA to approve drugs even more quickly—and barred it from using the extra money it received from industry to study the safety aspects of drugs once they had been approved.

Ghost Writing

Following the lawsuits against Fen-Phen revelations were made about ghost writers being used to tout the efficiency of the drug. Excerpta Medica, a medical communications company based in New

Jersey, is part of Reed Elsevier, a Dutch conglomerate that publishes over a hundred scientific Journals throughout Europe and America. Excerpta Medica controls *Clinical Therapeutics* and *Current Therapeutic Research*. Excerpta/Elsevier publishes *The American Journal of Medicine,* which is sent out to doctor's offices. *The Journal of the American College of Cardiology* is also part of the Elsevier empire.

Apparently Wyeth hired Excerpta to write several papers on obesity. The articles would have an important "opinion leader" as author, and would be tailored to the company's requirements. They would downplay side-effects, and even remove some descriptions of them entirely. One of the Authors, Dr Albert J Stunkard of the University of Pennsylvania, whose article was published in the *American Journal of Medicine* in February 1996, claimed to have no knowledge that the article was funded by Wyeth. He complained "It's really deceptive,... It sort of makes you uneasy." Excerpta Medical allegedly received $20,000 for each article. But when questioned about this practice, it turned out not to be an isolated incident. Wyeth spokesman Doug Petkus commented, "This is common practice in the industry. It's not particular to us." [482]

The Former FDA commissioner, David Kessler was known to have complained about Excerpta for a number of years because they were stuffing doctor's offices with "so—called" medical papers as a way of circumventing the FDA ban on advertising. He complained "Doctors are getting inaccurate information about the safety and efficacy of drugs, because it's coming to them in medical publications that they think are independent." [483]

Research published in the *Journal of the American Medical Association* in 1998 reviewed 809 published articles written by "ghost authors", and another 19% by "honorary authors" who had not contributed enough to warrant being listed as authors.[484]

Concerns for the future of scientific research have increased following serious investment by three of the largest advertising companies, Omnicom, Interpublic and WPP that have invested tens of millions of dollars into companies that conduct clinical trials of experimental drugs. One former editor of the *NEJM,* Dr. Arnold S. Relman, professor emeritus at Harvard Medical School, made the observation: "Ad agencies are not in the business of doing science." Professor Thomas Bodenheimer expressed concern over the way drug companies manipulate results of clinical trials by controlling a study's design or by selective publication of the data. He believed that where ad agencies are involved, things can only deteriorate. "It introduces another bias into the whole clinical drug trial picture." He continued, "The American public and the physicians in the United States are not going to know, really, the true facts about the drugs." [485]

UNHEALTHY BETRAYAL

Federal law prohibits drugs being promoted before they have been approved but published research and "medical education" are not constrained by these rules. Doctors, of course, are free to prescribe drugs however they see fit. So the pharmaceutical companies employ vast resources to promote their products directly to doctors. They fund seminars, fund doctors' continuing "education", and send doctors on expense-paid trips to conferences promoting their products— amongst numerous other tactics. Critics complain that the industry exploits these and other techniques to promote their products prior to approval.

Following the removal of Fen-Phen and Redux, there were a number of other attempts made to promote drugs to 'treat' obesity:

- In 2007 the FDA rejected approval of Acomplia a drug marketed by Sanofi-Aventis after it was linked to depression and suicidal thinking.
- In 2008 Merck had to withdraw Tarabant, their anti-obesity drug, because of side effects which included psychiatric events.
- In 2010 Abbott Laboratories removed Meridia after it had been linked with heart attacks and strokes.
- The FDA also rejected Qnexa, marketed by Vivus, due to concerns about cardiovascular problems. It further rejected Lorcaserin, from Arena Pharmaceuticals, because of worries about tumour growth revealed in rat studies.
- In 2011 the FDA rejected Contrave from Orexigen Therapeutics and Takeda Pharmaceuticals asking for a further clinical trial to investigate long-term heart risk. [486]
- The consumer watchdog, *Public Citizen,* petitioned the FDA in April 2011 to remove the weight loss drugs Alli and Xenical due to the growing risk of side effects which included liver damage, pancreatitis, kidney stones, stool leakage and diarrhoea.

Dr Sidney Wolfe, the director of Public Citizen's Health Research Group, explained their concerns. 'These drugs have the potential to cause significant damage to multiple critical organs, yet they provide meagre benefits in reducing weight loss in obese and overweight patients.' An estimated 40 million people worldwide have taken either Xenical or Alli. Sales for Alli were $145 million in 2000, the year it was approved as an over-the-counter drug. The drugs supposedly worked by blocking absorption of a number of protein enzymes that enter the body—which was supposed to reduce fat absorption. Instead, the fat is supposed to pass through the gastrointestinal tract until it is excreted. Unfortunately these medications also block fat-soluble vitamins including vitamins A, B, and K. [487]

Qnexa was a controlled release formulation that contained phentermine (from Fen-Phen fame) added to topiramate which is supposed to increase the feeling of fullness. Topiramate is aslo sold under the brand name Topomax, marketed by Johnson and Johnson, to treat migraines and seizures. Further studies of the Topiramate component have been linked with increased birth-defect risk. [488] Just in case you think these are isolated examples of drug problems, there are a significant number of diabetes and weight-loss drugs that are associated with cancer; bladder cancer and pancreatic cancer, reviewed currently in the national media. [489]

No doubt there will be further attempts to throw even more drugs at the obesity epidemic instead of dealing with the root cause.

Academic Medicine for Sale

For a number of years now there has been a significant encroachment by pharmaceutical companies into the field of higher education. They have not only exerted influence over doctor training, but also funded medical research in universities and other academic institutions. Since 1980, after Congress passed the Bayh-Dole Act—which made it legal for universities to own and license patents in the USA—there has been a significant shift in emphasis of what drives research. By the year 2000, universities were earning more than a billion dollars a year in royalties and license fees. And some twelve thousand academic scientists were engaged in collaborative ventures with industry. Faculty members found they were able to supplement their incomes considerably as consultants for industry, but also to advising law firms and PR companies. According to Derek Bok, former president of Harvard University and Dean of the Harvard Law School, this has led to conflicts of interest that had barely existed before. He also expresses concern that there is now a new code of secrecy that did not previously exist. Academic institutions no longer exchange information as freely as they used to. A study published in 2000 that found that only 3 of 250 medical schools and research institutions required their investigators to disclose their financial to patients before enrolling them in drug trials or clinical experiments. Further, only 7% of these institutions required their researchers to disclose conflicts of interest when publishing their research.[490]

Marcia Angell, M.D., former editor-in-chief of the *New England Journal of Medicine,* is so concerned about these conflicts of interest that she has written a book about it. A typical example she cites is that of the head of Brown University's Department of Psychiatry making over $500,000 a year as a consultant for anti-depressant manufacturers. When a study was published by this gentleman and his colleagues, there was not enough room to print all of the authors' conflict-of-interest disclosures. The full list had to be put on the website. Angell wrote an accompanying editorial titled "Is Academic Medicine for Sale?" expressing of her concerns about these conflicts of interest. A reader sent in a letter offering the following reply; "Is academic medicine for sale? No the current owner is very happy with it."[491]

Angell is not alone in her views. A colleague of hers, fellow *NEJM* editor, Jerome P Kassirer M.D., Distinguished Professor at Tufts University School of Medicine and Adjunct Professor of Medicine at Yale University School of Medicine, has also written about the problem. He mentions that during the 1990s it became harder to maintain the policy of restricting conflicts of interest—and that when he retired from the editorship of the journal in 2002, the new incoming editor, Dr Jeffrey Drazen, changed the policy complaining that he had found it extremely difficult to find authors who were free of conflicts. [492]

This conflict of interest is of course not confined to the U.S.—it is a universal problem. In 2002 the editor of the *British Medical Journal,* Dr Richard Smith, also published an editorial on this issue. He quoted numerous sources and gave many examples including that of a study into calcium channel antagonists. Here, it was found that scientist who had financial relationships with manufacturers of calcium channel antagonists were much more likely to be supportive of the drugs— yet they rarely declared any conflict of interest. In findings as to whether passive smoking was harmful or not the major determining factor was whether the authors had financial ties to tobacco manufacturers, or not. With regard to the link between third generation contraceptive pills and the increase observed in thromboembolic disease, studies funded by the pharmaceutical industry found that that there was no link whereas studies funded by public money found there was. The article also raised the problem of the amount of funding:

> It seems likely that different degrees of conflict are probably raised by being bought a cheese sandwich by a company or by being flown on Concorde to New York to give a lecture and spend five days in the Ritz-Carlton Hotel. But at the moment we don't ask for amounts, partly because we British are even more embarrassed to talk about money than about our sex lives. But should we change? [493]

Kassirer, in his book *On The Take,* goes into the myriad ways the pharmaceutical industry is able to promote their drugs, including funding symposia, doctor's further 'education,' and 'consultancies'. He illustrates the problem of conflict of interest with the following example of another diabetes drug, Rezulin—and this story deserves a wider hearing. Rezulin was one of the first drugs selected for the $150 million National Diabetes Prevention Study by the National Institutes of Health (NIH)—with which there was controversy from the start. Dr Jerrold Olefsky, a highly regarded diabetes researcher, initially chaired the committee that selected Rezulin. Yet it was later revealed that Dr Olefsky held three separate patents as the sole or first inventor of the drug, and was also co-chair of a group called the National Diabetes Initiative which happened to be sponsored and created by Warner-Lambert, the company that was marketing Rezulin. Dr Olefsky spoke on behalf of Rezulin as a paid consultant by Warner-Lambert. He was eventually replaced as chair of the committee after the revelation of the conflict of interest, but was allowed to remain on the study's steering committee. Another doctor with a substantial conflict of interest was Dr Richard Eastman, who at that time was the NIH's top diabetes researcher with direct responsibility for the National Diabetes Prevention Study. He was a paid advisor to Warner-Lambert, and had received $74,455 from them. He was also a speaker for the company-sponsored group that recommended doctors use Rezulin for their patients. He apparently had several other ties with other companies.[494]

Failure of the Regulatory Regime

Troglitazone, is an anti-diabetic and anti-inflammatory drug, that was marketed under the different brand names, Rezulin, Resulin and Romozin. It was developed from a previous compound, ciglitazone, that had been found to lower blood sugars. But ciglitazone lowered blood sugars too severely—and was also was found to be toxic to the liver. So scientists decided to investigate if a similar product would prove more useful. Troglitazone marketed as Rezulin was one of the first drugs granted fast-track review by the FDA. [495]

The task of assessing Rezulin was assigned to Dr. John L. Gueriguian, a veteran medical officer of the FDA. He concluded that Rezulin "offered very little significant therapeutic advantage" over existing diabetes drugs at a staff meeting in August 1996. By the fall of 1996 he concluded that Rezulin was not fit for approval due to its toxicity to the heart and liver. Warner-Lambert objected to the way Gueriguian was dealing with the application and complained about his "intemperate" language. They complained to his superior, Dr Murray Lumpkin, deputy director of the FDA's drug evaluation center. Lumpkin responded by removing Gueriguian from the evaluation process and removed his medical review from the agency files on November 4th 1996. [496]

Troglitazone, marketed as Romozin was launched in the UK in October 1997, by early November news of 40 cases of serious hepatic reactions had been reported worldwide with the use of Troglitazone, none originating in the UK. One of the patients died and another required liver transplantation. GlaxoWellcome and Sankyo Pharma the companies that were marketing Troglitazone in the UK, wrote to doctors and pharmacists warning about these problems and gave advice about monitoring patients with liver function tests. By December after becoming aware of 130 cases of serious hepatic reactions which included six fatalities it was decided that the benefits were too few to justify continuing use. It was withdrawn in the UK December 1st 1997. [497]

Rezulin was officially approved in the USA in January 1997 and after a successful marketing strategy sales in the US sored. By the fall/autumn, dozens of patients had been hospitalised and a handful of liver cases had been reported to the FDA. The FDA's response was to make a series of label changes which included recommending monitoring patients liver functions. Not everyone at the FDA was happy with the situation with Rezulin. Dr David Graham expressed the view that he believed that Rezulin was the most dangerous drug on the market and that patient monitoring would not protect them from liver failure. Three people who were supposedly being monitored had already died including one from the NIH study. [498]

The death in the NIH study was a tragedy that should have never happened. This trial, sponsored by the government, was not even studying diabetics who were already seriously ill—it was merely a study using Rezulin to prevent individuals considered 'at risk' of getting diabetes from succumbing to the disease. The NIH was in fact administering a potentially fatal drug to patients who didn't even have the disease it was designed to treat. Dr Eastman of the NIH apparently regarded the decision of Glaxo to withdraw their version of the drug in the UK as "a marketing decision, rather than a regulatory decision,"—which was sent by way of a letter of reassurance to physicians. Within six months of that letter, a previously healthy Illinois teacher, who had been taking Rezulin in the NIH prevention study, developed fulminant liver toxicity. Although she was being monitored, her health seriously deteriorated and she died. Parke-Davis insisted that the death had nothing to do with their drug. But within a month of it, the NIH dropped Rezulin from the trial. Nevertheless, the drug remained in widespread use in the USA for almost two more years. [499]

Sales of Rezulin had reached $2.1 billion before it was eventually withdrawn on March 21st 2000. Up until its removal, senior government officials had played down the drug's ability to cause liver failure, and had expressed their confidence that its ability to reduce blood sugar levels outweighed the serious risks. Lumpkin of the FDA apparently had no regrets that he aided the drug to stay on the market in the U.S. for such a long period after it was withdrawn in the UK.

The newly appointed commissioner of the FDA, Jane E. Henney, ordered a re-evaluation of Rezulin following revelations by the investigative reporter of the *Los Angeles Times,* David Willman. Willman did a series of reports (for which he was awarded the Pulitzer Prize) on a number of drugs that included Rezulin. In my view it is investigative journalism at its best. [500]

David Graham was the FDA's leading specialist in evaluating and preventing deaths caused by prescription drugs, and he was given the task of re-evaluating Rezulin. Within two months Graham had delivered his report to the advisory committee—the same that had unanimously endorsed Rezulin previously. Among his findings were:

- He estimated that more than 430 patients had suffered liver failure.
- That 1 in 1800 patients on Rezulin could be expected to have liver failure, not 1 in 100,000 as suggested by Warner-Lambert.
- Regular monitoring of patients would offer no safety guarantee. He cited the death of Audrey Jones and Rosa Valenzuela who died despite being monitored in a clinical trial.

However the committee was un-persuaded and voted 11 to 1 to keep Rezulin on the market. Three of the advisory committee were granted conflict-of-interest waivers by the FDA after receiving compensations from Warner-Lambert and some affiliates. [501]

Dr Sidney Wolfe, of the Public Citizen's Health Research Group, wrote to the FDA on 14th March 2000 requesting an investigation into the charge that the liver toxicity data available to Wyeth-Lambert in February 1997 had not been submitted until October 21st. According to federal law, it should have been sent within fifteen days of their application, not six months. He stated that this omission caused significant harm that could have been avoided. He further petitioned the FDA, with the assistance of Larry Sasich of Public Citizen's Health Research Group, to initiate a ban on troglitazione, and asked "how many more Americans will have to die or require liver transplants?" [502]

Not everyone who had approved Rezulin at the FDA was as happy with their actions as Lumpkin, Dr Robert L. Misbin, a diabetes specialist, who worked at Ceiba-Geigy after graduating from Boston University medical School in 1976, had had to defend another diabetes drug, phenformin, that had proved lethal. He was not at all happy to be experiencing feelings of déjà vu with another diabetes drug. So he wrote to Rep. Henry A. Waxman (D-Los Angeles) and seven other lawmakers, and turned over e-mails and other correspondence involving the US Congress in the affair. This gave him the status of a whistleblower. He included damning reports by people such as Dr Janet McGill who alleged that the company had "deliberately omitted reports of liver toxicity and misrepresented serious adverse events experienced by [Rezulin] patients in their clinical studies." [503]

He was reprimanded by his boss: "You need to understand that the pharmaceutical industry is our client." His response was "That's odd, I always thought our clients were the people of the United States."[504]

The FDA's handling of Rezulin was not without other critics; Dr Alistair J.J. Wood, a drug therapy editor for the *New England Journal of Medicine* at a conference sponsored by Georgetown University Medical Center, equated the FDA's label-change approach to Rezulin as to managing a risk similar to that of falling off a cliff:

"The point was, you don't keep putting up more and more signs if people continue falling off the cliff," Wood said. "You try to do something more definitive, like try to prevent them from falling off. You put up a fence." [505]

The Therapeutic Goods Administration (TGA) of Australia, the equivalent of America's FDA, refused to approve Rezulin for use in Australia—a concern for irreversible liver damage was enough to refuse it. New Zealand's drug review body, the New Zealand Medicines and Medical Devices Safety Authority (Medsafe), also refused to license it a few months later. This was before New Zealand's and Australia's bodies decided to merge into one effective agency for both countries, which they agreed to do in December 2003. [506]

There is far, far more to the story of troglitazone, than even I have given here. Discussions about the financial conflicts of interest will no doubt rage on. Dennis Cauchon reviewed the FDA and came to a number of conclusions in an article in *USA TODAY*:

- More than half of all experts hired to advise the government on the safety and effectiveness of medicines have financial relationships with the very pharmaceutical companies that would stand to benefit from their decisions.
- The Federal law is supposed to prohibit the FDA from using experts with financial conflict of interests. The FDA simply waives the restriction something it has done more than 800 times since 1998.

- The FDA has kept secret the financial details of conflicts of interest that it has declared since 1992 so it is impossible to understand just how much money is involved.

- Financial conflicts of interest are even more common when regulatory policy is discussed. Cauchon found at 57 regulatory meetings that committee members had conflicts 91 percent of the time.

- At the 102 meetings involving specific drugs, it was discovered that 33 percent of committee members had a direct financial stake in the outcome.

- Since 1997, following a new law that was passed the FDA now officially includes representatives from industry in advisory committees. They are supposed to participate in the deliberations, but not be allowed to vote. [507]

To conclude the story of troglitazone (Rezulin in the USA) I will leave you with comments of UK Professor Edwin Gale, Diabetologist at Bristol University who has devoted a complete website to the story of troglitazone. Following is an extract from his editorial:

This Editorial is about the voices that were not raised when troglitazone was on the market, and the curious collective amnesia that has afflicted the diabetes community ever since. Hundreds of people died or underwent liver transplantation because of troglitazone, and thousands more experienced liver damage as a consequence. This was the most dangerous diabetes therapy since phenformin. And yet the story outlined here, long familiar to readers of the Los Angeles Times, has never to my knowledge been considered at any length in the medical literature, which contains more than 800 papers about troglitazone. Why? On-going litigation is estimated to have cost the companies involved some US$750 million in legal fees and compensation, but the drug still generated a healthy profit and—more importantly—helped maintain share values until the company was taken over. No inquiry has been held, no one has apologised, no one's career has suffered (with the exception of Richard Eastman), and a lot of people are wealthier in consequence. Clinicians and researchers working with diabetes did well out of troglitazone, and some still talk with nostalgic regret of its wasted potential. The most striking thing about the story is that the medical community remained resolutely silent on the subject of patient safety. No prominent physician, anywhere in the world, ever stood up to say that a pill for diabetes is not worth dying for. [508]

It would be a mistake to view the Rezulin story as an isolated or freak incident. It is just one more example of something that is basically wrong with the way medicine is currently practiced today. There are many who hold that it is simply one more symptom of a bigger tragedy that goes far beyond the regulatory approach of just one country, such as the USA.

Profits before Health

It is true that the way a country regulates its medical and pharmaceutical industry will have numerous consequences, not just on personal health, but on the cost of health care generally—and even on the environment. In the USA, for example, there is little control over the prices set for drugs and little or nothing charged to companies for monitoring the safety of most drugs. This is part of the reason that drug companies can make such vast profits, and consequently spend so much on the promotion of their products. In 2001, drug companies in the US spent $4.6 billion on "detailing." This is the industry term for drug rep's sales calls to doctors. The number of sales reps has tripled in the last ten years to the extent that there is almost one rep for every five doctors. This leaves the industry able to spend $10,000 on every one of the 490,000 office-based doctors in the US every year. That figure does not include the cost of free samples left by the sales reps.[509]

Vast profits allow undesirable consequences in different ways. Take another drug, Neurotin, for example, a drug marketed by Pfizer that achieved sales of over $2 billion per year. Pfizer were fined $430 million by the US government for promoting "off label" use of it. They estimated that 94% of its sales revenue had been off-label. Many would consider the fine to be pocket change in relation to the income. [510]

In April 2003 Bayer Corporation, a German company, was fined $257 million to settle allegations that it had engaged in a scheme by which it sold re-labelled products to a Health Maintenance Organisation (HMO) at deeply discounted prices. It then proceeded to conceal this deception, and to avoid their obligation to pay the millions of dollars it owed in additional rebates to the US Medicaid program. They were fined a further $5.5 million for a count of Medicare fraud.[511]

Whenever the topic of excessive profits comes up the pharmaceutical industry plays out the mantra of needing to make large profits to enable it to do the research that is needed to develop new drugs. They never seem, however, to show any interest in developing the drugs that people could actually benefit from. They seem to prefer to gravitate towards the areas where they will find large markets over the long-term. As regards the need to make profits for research, I leave that to Peter Rost MD, a former drug company executive, to put it in perspective. These were comments he gave to a press conference and panel discussion at Capitol Hill:

UNHEALTHY MEDICINE

Big Pharma's arguments that lower prices would hurt R&D simply didn't hold water and I used Merck as an example. "In 2003, Merck recorded revenue of $22.5 billion. Of this they spent $3.2 billion or R&D. That is not quite as much as they paid out in dividends--$3.3 billion, and much, much less than their 'marketing, sales and administrative' costs —$4.6 billion. After other charges and taxes, the company still recorded a profit of $6.8 billion."[512]

On top of being able to smother its largesse on doctors, it is reputed to have 1,274 lobbyists that enable it to lobby every member of Congress with at least two people. Senator Chuck Grassley, (R-Iowa), chairman of the Senate Finance Committee, expressed the situation in his down-to-earth fashion: "They are powerful. You can hardly swing a cat by the tail in that town without hitting a pharmaceutical lobbyist." [513]

Another symptom of the largesse is executive remuneration. Whilst the pay of the average worker remained flat in the USA at $27,000 from 1990 to 2004, average chief executive pay has risen from $2.8 million to $11.8 million—which works out to a ratio of more than 400 to 1, as revealed by the institute for policy studies.[514]

There probably would not be so much criticism of the medical industry if it didn't cost the taxpayer the earth, or if it could be considered truly effective and value for money—without the human cost of its failures. In 1999, the US Institute of Medicine, part of the National Academy of Sciences, reported that medical errors are responsible for the deaths of between 44,000 and 98,000 people every year. They believe that most of the deaths could have been avoided by safety improvements and by identifying and rectifying flaws in the way hospitals and clinics operate. The report goes on to list a number of instances of failures: since 1996 surgeons in American hospitals have operated on the wrong arm, leg, eye or other body part more than 150 times. The report cites some specific examples, such as how a prestigious hospital could have transplanted a heart and two lungs of the wrong blood type into Jésica Santillán, 17, who died after receiving a second heart-lung transplant. In 1994 at the Dana-Farber Cancer Center in Boston, a Harvard teaching institution, a 39 year-old woman was given an overdose of chemotherapy for breast cancer, which caused her death. In 1995 Sloan Kettering's chief neurosurgeon operated on the wrong side of a patient's brain, said to be partly due to a mix-up of X-rays. [515]

In July 2001, Piero Impicciatore and others undertook a meta-analysis of paediatric in/outpatients prospective studies of adverse drug reactions (ADRs). The incidence varied between 4.37% to 16.78%. The average number of drugs given to the children studied ranged from 1.5 to 7.6. They estimated that 50% of the variability in the ADRs could be explained by the different prescription rates. In their first study, 30% of the ADRs involved the use of drugs outside their product license—with regard to dose or the age of the patient. In their more recent, study 6% of the ADRs were associated with unlicensed or "off-label" use. They discovered that in 74% of the ADRs classed as 'severe' drugs had been used in an unlicensed or "off-label" manner. [516]

In July 2000, Dr Barbara Starfield, of the Johns Hopkins School of Hygiene and Public Health, published an article in the *Journal of the American Medical Association,* asking the question "Is US health really the best in the world?" The answer she came to was that it was not, and that, conversely, it contributed to poor health. She gives some stark statistics of unnecessary deaths per year:

- 12,000—due to surgery
- 7,000—due to medication errors in hospital
- 80,000—due to hospital infections
- 106,000—non-error negative effects of drugs
- 20,000—other errors in hospitals

This represents 250,000 deaths due to iatrogenic causes, that is due to a "physician's activity manner or therapy." She goes on to suggest that these figures are conservative, and may be much higher. [517]

Aside from the problems with necessary surgery and drugs there's a body of research that feels that we are over-medicalised. It is difficult to come up with accurate figures, but attempts have been made, for example, to determine how much unnecessary surgery is undertaken. Dr Lucian L Leape undertook a study in 1989 into this very topic, and these are his findings:

> Unnecessary surgery is a problem of unknown dimension but undeniable significance. While it is impossible to estimate the extent of unnecessary surgery in the United States with any precision, we have seen that for some controversial procedures 30 percent or more may be performed for inappropriate reasons. Elimination of these operations would result in significant savings of lives and resources. [518]

There are many people, including many doctors, who are unhappy with the direction in which modern medicine is headed. The cost of it in all the major economies is increasing at an unsustainable rate. What is the cause of this, and where will it lead us? How will it affect our own health, and that of our children? Those are the questions, and the implications of them, that I will discuss in the next chapter.

Chapter 12
Alternative Thinking—Threat to Profits!

Who does not know the truth, is simply a fool...
Yet who knows the truth and calls it a lie,
is a criminal.

B.Brecht: *Galileo Galilei*

In a time of universal deceit, telling the truth becomes a revolutionary act. George Orwell

How is it we have got ourselves in the position we have today, where obesity is increasing at an alarming rate, cancer and heart disease are affecting large swathes of industrial society, and we seem unable to reverse the trend? There are many people who believe that modern medicine is failing us, that it is allowing society's health to deteriorate by simply throwing intense medical interventions at us, such as powerful drugs, surgery and radiation. While this can have some successes in slowing down the epidemic, it misses the point.

To understand how we have arrived at this situation, it can be helpful to understand the development of modern medicine and how it has evolved into what it is today. There has always been competition amongst health care providers—even from before the time that it began to be referred to as 'health care'. There are a number of practitioners, more commonly referred to as 'alternative' practitioners, who have been criticised for offering an alternative view of what real health is and how we can achieve it as a society.

Some Historical Background to Modern Medicine

There is a historical precedent for this throughout history. In the reign of Henry VIII of England, the medical profession even tried to introduce laws to prevent anyone except physicians being able to prescribe herbs or herbal remedies, salves, compresses and ointments. Fortunately Henry VIII, no matter what else he was reputed to be, had a keen interest in herbal medicine, was known to have administered herbal treatments to himself, as well as to have concocted herbal remedies, some of which have survived to this day. His response to the attack by the medical profession was to produce a Charter for the protection of the herbalists—which became law in 1512, the third year of his reign. This effectively guaranteed the ability of herbalists to survive the attack in perpetuity. I have copied the final paragraph of the Charter, referred to as the Herbalist's Charter, below:

> In consideration whereof, and for the Ease, Comfort, Succour, Help, Relief, and Health of the King's poor Subjects, Inhabitants of this Realm, now pained or diseased: Be it ordained, established, and enacted by Authority of this present Parliament, That at all Time from henceforth it shall be lawful to every Person being the King's subject. Having Knowledge and Experience of the Nature of Herbs, Roots, and Waters, or of the Operation of the same, by Speculation or Practice, within any part of the Realm of England, or within any other of the King's Dominions, to practice, use, and minister in and to any outward Sore, Uncome Wound, Apostemations, outward Swelling or Disease, any Herb or Herbs, Ointments, Baths, Pultess, and Emplaisters, according to their Cunning, Experience, and Knowledge in any of the Diseases, Sores, and Maladies beforesaid, and all other like to the same, or Drinks for the Stone, Strangury, or Agues, without suit, vexation, trouble, penalty, or loss of their goods; the foresaid Statute in the foresaid Third Year of the King's most gracious Reign, or any other Act, Ordinance, or Statutes to the contrary heretofore made in anywise, notwithstanding. [519]

Nevertheless, attacks resurfaced against the herbalists, although often in a more sinister manner. In the 1600s, in Europe, there was a widespread persecution of herbalists that resulted in a considerable number being tried and put to death for the practice of 'witchcraft.' During this time, particularly in the rural communities where the majority of the population lived, healthcare was provided by the local 'wisewoman' and in some cases 'wiseman.' The wisewoman was generally the local midwife who was also a herbalist, proficient in the use of potions and remedies, the use and application of which had evolved from time immemorial. She was supported by the local community as a valuable member of the village.

Wisewomen were resented by doctors—who mostly practiced in the urban areas, and purged them at the witch trials, during which the practice of 'swimming' was most commonly used to determine guilt: if you floated you were guilty, and then burnt: if you were innocent you sank, which meant you drowned. So this was the 17th century's version of "Catch 22." There were many people who met their demise in this way, mostly those who had no protector; women with wealthy male protectors were rarely persecuted.

ALTERNATIVE THINKING—THREAT TO PROFITS

In the countryside the herbalist traditions survived much longer than in the towns and cities, but gradually the majority of wisewomen were eradicated—and with them the vital role of healer. The information on herbs and remedies that had served from time immemorial was lost to future generations. [520]

In the 1700s, the social structure of medicine reflected the social stratification of society in general. Physicians considered themselves as members of a learned professional elite: below them were surgeons and apothecaries—and, each group had its own Guild. In those days physicians did not actually touch their patients, they merely observed, speculated and prescribed a remedy. Surgeons belonged to the same Guild as barbers—although they also prescribed medicines. Beneath these layers were lay healers and midwives. At this time physicians retained the classical view of the four humours; that of blood, phlegm, yellow bile and black bile. Treatment still included blood-letting, and the emptying out of the stomach contents with powerful emetics, and cathartics. The wisewoman was all but extinct. A few survived, such as a Mrs Hughes, who advertised in 1773 that, as well as practicing midwifery, she also cured ringworms, piles and 'scald heads' as well as making ladies dresses and bonnets—a poor imitation of her predecessors.[521]

During the 1800s, as science progressed and the industrial revolution created a more mobile population, the role of the physician changed. Increasingly, surgeons practiced as physicians, and the line between apothecaries, surgeons and physicians muddied until the term "general practitioner" became common. In 1858, the UK Parliament created a single register for all medical practitioners.

In the USA there was less cohesion amongst medical practitioners. There existed the lay practitioners, midwives, 'botanic practitioners,' bone setters, abortionists, cancer doctors and sellers of 'nostrums.' The first medical school was chartered in Philadelphia in 1765, and the American Medical Association was formed in 1846. However, training for the medical profession varied substantially from place to place. Competition for students in medical schools was fierce—and this gave rise to often serious conflicts. In 1855, the Eclectic Medical Institute of Cincinnati split into two opposing factions over both the new "concentrated" medications and the use of the school finances. This resulted in "the declaration of war," which, according to the school's historian, involved the use of "Knives, pistols, chisels, bludgeons, blunderbusses, etc." which were all freely displayed. Apparently, order was only restored when one of the sides produced a six-pound cannon![522]

Against such a backdrop, two of the richest and most powerful men in America, representing the vast industrial wealth of the sprawling empire of IG Farben, entered the fray. I G Farben is so vast and was so clever at concealing its identity, that even today there are few who know the true extent of its business empire. According to General Eisenhower, after the War the spread of IG Farben was so pervasive, with interlocking cartel arrangements of which there were over two thousand, that it would take over an hour just to say their names. A list of the companies that it controlled outright would fill many pages of a book. It dominated large chemical companies such as Imperial Chemical Industries in the UK (ICI), Kuhlman in France, Allied Chemical in Belgium etc. It also had ties with numerous companies in the USA such as General Electric, General Motors, Eastman Kodak, Atlantic Oil, Dow chemical, Gulf Oil, Monsanto, Standard oil, Ciba-Geigy, Parke-Davis, Remington Arms, Abbott Laboratories—and hundreds more. Rockefeller and Carnegie were behind it all and those who would like a more detailed picture of their story should refer to Edward Griffin's book *World Without Cancer*. [523]

John D Rockefeller and Andrew Carnegie arguably had the biggest single effect on the development on modern medicine, not just in the USA but globally. They combined forces through the clever use of foundations to both gain tax advantages and make maximum use of their wealth. They employed two people to further their objectives, Fred Gates and Abraham Flexner. Fred Gates was a minister of the church, but was more a businessman than a minister. He caught the attention of John D Rockefeller by the way he had helped the flour magnate, George A Pillsbury. Gates had advised Rockefeller how he could invest a portion of his estate in such a way that he would receive maximum public approval, and at the same time capture control of money from other sources. So Rockefeller, following Gate's advice and formula, entered philanthropy with a $600,000 donation to the Baptist University of Chicago—on the condition that the dry-goods merchants and the meat packers of the city also contributed $400,000. His praises were sung from the pulpits of most Baptist churches, and one commentator wrote "No benefaction has ever flowed from a purer Christian source." What was not realised at the time was how Rockefeller was eventually able to effectively take control of the university and purged it of all the staff who were not happy with his influence—the anti-Rockefeller dissidents. [524]

Rockefeller had set out to consciously and methodically capture the control of American education, and specifically medical education. He started the process with the creation of the Institute for Medical Research in 1901. Included on its board was Simon Flexner, the brother of Abraham Flexner who was on the teaching staff of the Carnegie Foundation for the Advancement of Teaching.

The American Medical association (AMA) had already created the Council on Medical Education with the purpose of trying to improve the poor professional status of the medical profession at the time. A time when medical degrees could be obtained by post with little, or even no training, and where medical schools were continuously undercutting each other to get students. The AMA, however, was itself seriously underfunded, and was making very little progress. And here's where Simon Flexner comes in. When Henry S Pritchett, the president of the Carnegie Foundation, approached the AMA and offered to take over the entire project of their investigation of all the medical schools, Abraham Flexner was the man given the task of investigator. Yet, despite its shortage of funds, much of the work had already been undertaken by the AMA, and the cost to the Carnegie Foundation of Flexner's work, was only $10,000. Nevertheless, when the report was eventually published in 1910, the Carnegie Foundation took all the credit.[525]

At the time of Flexner's report, there were 131 medical schools and over half of them had an income of less than $10,000. Flexner noted that laboratories were few and far between, libraries had few books, many faculty members were in private practice, and that conditions were generally quite poor. He recommended reducing the number of schools to 31, even though it would have left twenty states without medical schools, which many considered politically unacceptable.

Funding of schools was not uniform, Rockefeller's General Education Board had, by 1936, invested $91 million in such a way that two thirds of the funds went to just seven institutions. What soon became apparent, however, was that this was creating a medical educational model much more closely tied to medical research than to medical practice. Paul Starr's research into the transformation of American medicine is extensive, and he expressed the situation well with regards to Rockefeller's and Carnegie's policies: "These policies determined not so much which institutions would survive as which would dominate, how they would be run, and what ideals would prevail." [526]

By 1927 the number of medical schools had dropped to 80. Of those that were left, the common theme was that they followed the mould of Flexner's initial report—which strengthened courses in *pharmacology,* and insisted on *research* departments in all "qualified" medical schools. What dominated was the role of a curriculum based on drug use, and research.

Following the Gates formula, not all the money funding this revolution was supplied from the Carnegie Foundation and Rockefeller's General Education Board alone. A number of other foundations also contributed—such as the Ford Foundation, the Kellogg Foundation, and the Commonwealth Fund to name just three, but none compared with the input of Carnegie and Rockefeller in terms of sheer financial input, especially over such a long period of time.

The net result of this development meant that the new schools started attracting the kind of student who were more interested in research and pharmacology than those who wanted to practice medicine and work as doctors in the community. The high cost of the training program impacted the social composition of the profession as did the more stringent application requirements—fewer students from lower income groups applied. Deliberate discrimination also reduced the numbers of Jews, women and blacks—which further homogenised the medical profession. [527]

These developments had a major effect on the American Medical Association (AMA). Fewer medical schools had reduced the number of doctors who were trained each year—and that had resulted in a significant rise in doctor's incomes. The AMA set about persuading the government to introduce legislation that gave it effective control of education in medicine. This meant that students could now only obtain an M.D. degree that had been accredited by the AMA. The AMA provides continuing information through its publications to newly qualified doctors and to those already qualified with scientific articles, research, essays, editorials, letters, symposia and conventions. The main source of revenue to the AMA is its journal, the *Journal of the American Medical Association (JAMA),* which is funded mostly through carrying advertising by drug companies.

The AMA also has significant influence over government, through the FDA. It has a major influence over the appointment of the commissioner of the FDA, and has the biggest lobbying influence over government of any organisation other than the rifle association. However, the AMA's structure gives it the allusion of being democratic with its House of Delegates which meets twice a year, but in reality it is an autocratic institution. Not all physicians are happy with the AMA, or the way it was set up, and many of its policies have been controversial. The *Illinois Medical Journal,* in 1922, accused the AMA of becoming an autocracy, that ignored the will of the membership—and that its policies seemed more concerned with building a financial empire to benefit the people who controlled it, rather than with serving the doctors who support it. [528]

American Medical Association Ruthlessly Attacks Competition

The AMA has consistently tried to prevent competition from alternative practitioners. Its fight against homeopathy has been a particularly enduring one. Since its inception in the USA in1825, homeopathy has been offering an alternative approach to ill health that many physicians have embraced. But the AMA engaged in a constant campaign against it, labelling it as "unscientific" and trying to get doctors to stop using it. The battle became polarised to such a degree that the New York's State Medical Society was expelled from the AMA because it refused to give up homeopathy; it was replaced by the New York Medical Association.[529]

ALTERNATIVE THINKING—THREAT TO PROFITS

The AMA's attacks on the chiropractic profession became even more divisive. A number of measures were used against them, such as covertly attending their meetings, restricting their access to X-rays, lobbying health insurance companies not to cover their treatments etc. They even formed two special committees, the Department of Investigation and the Committee on Quackery to fight chiropractors and all others who they perceived as legitimate targets. The attack on chiropractors took an interesting turn when Dr Jerome McAndrews, executive vice president of the International Chiropractors Association was sent a book, *In the Public Interest.*[530] This documented how the AMA was intent on completely wiping out the chiropractic profession. It contained memos from the Committee on Quackery to its board of trustees that had not been intended for external scrutiny. The memos discussed how the committee was well on the way to achieving its primary goal of containing the chiropractic profession, and was moving towards its ultimate goal of eliminating it completely.

Further revelations came in 1975 when various AMA documents were sent to numerous newspapers including the *New York Times,* the *Washington Post,* the *New York Daily News,* and other—as well as to Congressional committees. The revelations gave further evidence of how the role of the Committee on Quackery was to destroy chiropractic therapy—and any other therapy that competed with it.

The AMA responded by closing down the committee, and the fight then inevitably moved into the courts. For the full story of that battle, please refer to Wolinsky and Brune's book, *The Serpent on the Staff—The Unhealthy Politics of the American Medical Association.* Meanwhile, I will relate some of the better known ways that the AMA appears to put industrial interests before patient health. It is well known, for example, that the AMA received considerable advertising revenue from the tobacco industry, that it had shares in the industry, and that it refused to acknowledge the harm that tobacco was having on the health of Americans.[531]

It is estimated that more than 14 million Americans have died from lung cancer, heart disease and other tobacco-caused diseases. Conservative estimates put the health costs at over $68 billion. Yet, throughout all this, the AMA actively promoted tobacco. It opened its journal to any advertisements of a non-medical medical nature, so allowing tobacco adds to become a regular feature—and even allowed ads showing physicians giving approval to cigarettes. Dr Morris Fishbein, the editor of the AMA's journal, worked also to help promote tobacco for Philip Morris. When eventually the AMA did decide to stop the tobacco advertising in 1953, the decision was to cost it more than $100,000 a year in lost income. Around the same time, they also agreed to stop advertising alcohol. However, they continued investing in tobacco stocks until a concerted attack on their tobacco policy in 1980 forced them to sell their shares. Whilst there were many organisations lobbying Congress to curtail tobacco, the AMA never added their voice significantly to this call.[532]

FDA's Role in the Suppression of Alternative Therapies

Although many people are aware of the role the FDA plays in evaluating new drugs, many are unaware of the way it has taken on the role of attack dog against all forms of alternative health treatment. If you think I may be exaggerating, the following are a few examples of their activities:

Dr Jonathan Wright, an expert in nutritional biochemistry based in Tacoma, Washington, caught the FDA in full flight in 1991 when he filed suit for the return of some dispensary stock of L-tryptophan. Almost immediately he found he was under investigation and, on 6th May, twelve FDA agents in flak vests, together with ten King County policemen, broke down the doors of his Tacoma clinic and burst in with guns drawn from three directions. They pointed guns at staff (one straight into the face of the female receptionist), and ordered them to raise their hands. When one of the staff tried to call an attorney, a police officer ripped the phone off the wall and threw him into a chair. Dr Wright arrived a short while later and promptly made a call to his attorney.

What followed was a fourteen-hour 'search and seize' operation, where documents, patient records, hard discs etc., were seized. Some vitamin B_{12} that Dr Wright used to treat patients with allergies was impounded; this had come from Germany and was the only B_{12} available that did not contain preservatives or additives. The FDA removed approximately $100,000 worth of medicines, office supplies and equipment. The raid incensed huge numbers of former patients and other people, who wrote letters of complaint from far and wide. A few days after the raid, the FDA Commissioner David Kessler, defended it and described the FDA's actions as "standard operating procedure." [533]

Many people feel there is a concerted campaign against competing forms of therapy that challenge the approach of modern medicine, allopathic medicine, with its focus on drug use, surgery and radiation to treat illnesses. Dr James Carter, author of *Racketeering in Medicine – The Suppression of Alternatives,* cites numerous examples alternative therapies being supressed, and makes the following comment on the Flexner report:

> Flexner is responsible for the heavy emphasis in American medical education on scientific research and high technology. The Flexner model of learning has all but destroyed the holistic approach of the

clinically-effective physician to his patients. It has valued scientific research at the expense of teaching. It has helped ensure an exclusive and extremely expensive brand of medicine.

What has emerged in medical education and clinical practice in the seventy-eight years since the Flexner Report in some ways is a tribute to the growth of medical technology. In other ways it is a travesty of the humanistic, compassionate approach to caring for the sick. [534]

Dr Carter's expertise and knowledge is widely—based. He completed his doctorate in medicine in 1966, is a nutritionist and a particular supporter of chelation therapy. Chelation (pronounced key-lay-shun) for example is a therapy that was originally developed for detoxifying people with lead poisoning. During its development, however, it was found that it also appeared to remove plaques from arteries and to improve blood flow. There are numerous cases of people who were facing coronary bypass operations or foot or leg amputations who were helped by chelation therapy to such an extent that they no longer needed their operations. Why would this therapy be ignored or suppressed you may ask? The general consensus believes that its low cost, $3,000 compared to a bypass operation of $30,000 - $50,000 is too much of a threat to the medical industry. A further bee in the industry's bonnet is the fact that many people who use and benefit from alternative treatments also use and benefit from nutritional supplements. [535]

Many in the industry believe that nutritional therapy, and the knowledge of how diet improve health, is the single biggest threat to pharmaceutical interests. The fact is that the metabolic consequences of diet, and our exposure to the chemical cocktail of modern industrialised society, could threaten more than just pharmaceutical and medical interests.

Global Assault on Alternatives

Of course this situation is not restricted to the USA—it is a global phenomenon. In Canada, for a start, Health Canada, the Canadian equivalent to the FDA in the USA, has been accused of trying to push through legislation that would classify nutritional supplements and herbs as drugs—which would effectively kill off their use in any meaningful way. On January 1, 2004 the Canadian government introduced the Natural Health Products Directorate which is estimated to cost small businesses with a turnover of less than $2 million, $100,000 in the first year, and $50,000 per year every year afterwards. It is expected as a result that between 15-20,000 dietary supplement products will disappear permanently from the Canadian market, and that 80% of the small to medium-sized companies will go out of business. [536]

Dr Dean, in her book *Death by Modern Medicine—Seeking Safe Solutions,* also cites numerous instances of suppression of alternative therapies. She believes she was the victim of a concerted campaign to remove people, like her, who practice nutritional therapy in Canada. Following an interview with her on *The Dini Petty Show* on CTV, during which she physically spooned out ten teaspoons of sugar to represent the amount in a can of soda, and twenty-seven teaspoons for a milkshake, she was contacted by the College of Physicians and Surgeons of Ontario (CPSO). A little while later, they descended on her surgery and without warning, raided her office, and removed a number of files and patient charts. Initially they did nothing more, but in mid-July 2005 when she was out of the country, they took away her license without any prior warning. She hired a lawyer who reported back that if she gave a commitment not to practice natural medicine she could have her license back.

Dr Dean cites numerous other practitioners who were attacked by the CPSO, such as Dr Josef Krop who endured a fourteen-year inquisition which cost him more than a million dollars to hold onto his licence. He had dared to recommend that some of his patients eat organic foods and drink spring water — the CPSO accused him of not conforming to the "standard practice of medicine." She also cites Dr Michael Smith, a medical doctor, psychotherapist and hands-on bioenergetics therapist, who had a complaint of sexual impropriety levelled at him by an unstable patient. When the patient became aware of the venom of the attack by the CPSO against Dr Smith and his family, supposedly on her behalf, she withdrew all charges. This had little effect on the CPSO who pursued Dr Smith relentlessly until they revoked his license in 1992, a few days before Christmas. Sadly, two weeks later, Dr Smith apparently went to his home office and shot himself.[537]

Yet another example mentioned by Carter, who we have mentioned above, cites the case of Dr Joseph Lister who proposed that deadly infections from surgery could be reduced if aseptic techniques could be universally implemented. His ideas were ridiculed and ignored for decades— which we now know resulted in thousands of needless deaths and suffering. Evan way back in 1859, the Austrian physician, Dr Ignaz Semmelwies was persecuted for urging doctors to wash their hands before delivering babies to prevent maternal death from childbirth fever. For this, he was persecuted into a nervous breakdown and an early death. Yet again we now know he was right and that mothers needlessly died and suffered throughout Europe due to the failure to even look at his proposal. Carter cites numerous examples of physicians and alternative practitioners who have been targeted by the medical establishment. This is his experience:

ALTERNATIVE THINKING—THREAT TO PROFITS

Investigations against alternative practitioners follow a pattern of arrogance, dogmatism, depravation of constitutional rights and a might-makes-right attitude. To suppress alternative medicine, organised Med resorts to bad behaviours: disinformation, smear campaigns of libel and slander, harassment, unwarranted IRS audits, enticement of patients and family members to sue doctors when there is no reason (even offering financial payment to do so), entrapment by undercover agents posing as sick patients who may persistently beg for alternative treatments, illegal wiretaps, and break-ins and records theft.[538]

Carter discusses how dietitians in the USA sought to establish their own monopoly by trying to introduce state legislation that would control who could undertake nutritional counselling. In Ohio, for example, new restrictive laws have been introduced that restrict nutritional counselling so that only dietitians certified by the state's Board of Dietetics are allowed to practice—and no other degree, training or education is adequate. Dietitians were until recently restricted in their use of nutritional supplements although there seems to be some relaxation of this more recently. Dr George Kindness PhD, a biochemist of international renown and a writer in the field of nutrition and food technology, found himself restricted by the new regulations, being that since he was not registered with the state's Diatetics Board—even though he had already been practicing nutrition before the Diatetics board even existed.

Dr Dean reports the harassment of Strauss Herb Company by Health Canada—who filed 219 charges against them after they brought out a food-based product called Heartdrops® which had been used effectively to treat heart disease, and which they had tried to promote during the Strauss-sponsored Canada Cup of Curling. Thankfully on September 20, 2004 they were cleared of all charges, the case being dismissed by the judge due to lack of any evidence to support the charges. However, the case and its effect on sales cost Strauss millions of dollars. The company, however, is still in business—and has now supplied clinical evidence to support its products. [539]

The Canadian government introduced Bill C-51, as an amendment to the Food and Drugs Act in April 2008, to have natural health products renamed "therapeutic products"—which would make them subject to toxicity testing and trials just like synthetic drugs. Furthermore, Health Canada inspectors would have powers of enforcement exceeding those of the police, enabling them to enter premises without a warrant, remove anything they liked, make the owner pay for the cost of removal, freeze bank accounts so it wouldn't be possible to take legal action and fine you up to $5 million for disobeying them. It also meant that any university or institution proposing research involving nutrition in the treatment of disease would have to be approved by the minister first. [540]

The effect of this on natural food suppliers would be to force most of them into bankruptcy. The larger ones would simply be controlled by shareholder interests—which would result in far poorer quality foods and supplements being supplied instead. It is well known in the field of nutrition that the best high quality supplements, those that are more biologically active and effective, are made by the smaller companies. According to Helke Ferrie, health writer and publisher, the end result would be much like what happened in Australia. Big Pharma persuaded the Australian government to pass a similar law to the Canadian proposal C-51 some years ago—and, as predicted, all the small and mid-sized natural health product companies that produced the high quality supplements have closed down. Australia now has one large neutraceutical company producing high-priced, poor quality supplements—and innovation in the industry has all but died. [541]

These moves to eliminate or severely reduce the effectiveness of nutritionists, nutritional supplementation and the use of natural remedies—is being orchestrated globally. The FDA in the USA is unrelenting in its attack on organic vitamins and food supplements. It has tried to regulate the vitamin industry on a number of occasions between 1966 and 1973. It tried to limit the amount of a vitamin that could be supplied to no more than 150 percent of the RDA (recommended daily allowance). Anything over that limit would be classed as an over-the-counter drug and combinations of vitamins and minerals would have been prohibited. This would attack all practitioners who routinely use higher levels than the RDA's, which are known to be inadequate. Fortunately, there was a huge backlash against these proposals by the American public which prompted Congress to enact the Proxmire Amendment in 1976. This prohibited the FDA from regulating vitamins as prescription drugs—yet it had little effect on them. It continued to descend on natural food companies and health food stores and to confiscate products such as Vitamin C, herbal teas, aloe vera gels etc. On one occasion they raided twelve health food markets all at once and removed 250 products valued at $25,000 because they bore health claims or labels with the words "immune" or "diet." None of the products was removed because of safety concerns. When you contrast this behaviour with its almost complete acceptance of the synthetic drugs that have contributed to modern medicine now being regarded as the number one killer, overtaking cancer and heart disease, words begin to fail. The words of former FDA Commissioner, Dr Herbert Lee give an interesting perspective:

"The thing that bugs me is that people think the FDA is protecting them. It isn't. What the FDA is doing and what the public thinks it is doing are as different as night and day." [542]

ALTERNATIVE THINKING—THREAT TO PROFITS

But as we have said, the assault on alternative products is a global phenomenon. In the EU, there is the European Traditional Herbal Medicinal Products Directive (THMPD)—this originated in the EU, but became part of UK law, where it came into force in April 2011. It is set to take the place of Section 12(2) of the 1968 Medicines Act. This meant that all "over the counter" herbal medicines sold in shops had to have a Traditional Medicines License by 2011—which significantly added to their cost. It is expected that many herbal medicines will be removed from public access as a result, leaving mostly the products of large pharmaceutical companies to dominate. There has been a significant move by the pharmaceutical industry to buy up some of the smaller supplement and herb suppliers in the last few years.

The Human Nutrition Report

Elaine Feuer in her book *Innocent Casualties – The FDA's War Against Humanity,* documents a number of cases where the FDA victimised alternative practitioners. She also heard of a report on nutrition, produced by the Department of Agriculture, that no-one seemed to have a copy of. Eventually, after a lot of effort and freedom of information requests, and after having received official denials of its existence, she found that the report actually did exist. She obtained a copy of the report from a Canadian source. The full story of her struggle to get hold of a copy is documented in her book.[543] I am indebted to her for bringing the report she eventually got hold of to my attention. Titled *Human Nutrition Report No.2—it* was published in August 1971, but was never released. It was a study that cost more than $30 million which, in the 1970s was no small sum. So why was it never published and released? Apparently it was too hot to handle even for the National Enquirer. It is very difficult to get hold of. So I will not only document some of the more pertinent points below, but I will also publish a copy on my website www.FundamentalHealth.org. You will then be able to come to your own conclusions as to why this amazing document has been hidden for more than 40 years. Following below are excerpts from the report with two accompanying tables. The first table is an edited version—the full version is on my site. I have included quite a bit of the text:

> Better health, a longer active lifespan, and greater satisfaction from work, family and leisure time are among the benefits to be obtained from improved diets and nutrition. Advances in nutrition knowledge and its application during recent decades have played a major role in reducing the number of infant and maternal deaths, deaths from infectious diseases, particularly among children, and in extending the productive lifespan and life expectancy. Significant benefits are possible both from new

knowledge of nutrient and food needs and from more complete application of existing knowledge. The nature and magnitude of these benefits is estimated in Table 1.Potential benefits may accrue from alleviating nutrition-related health problems, from increased individual performance and satisfactions and increased efficiency in food services. A vast reservoir of health and economical benefits can be made available by research yet to be done on human nutrition.

Major health problems are diet related. Most all of the health problems underlying the leading causes of death in the United States (Fig.1) could be modified by improvements in diet. The relationship of diet to these health problems and others is discussed in greater detail later in this report. Death rates for many of these conditions are higher in the U.S. than in other countries of comparable economic development. Expenditures for health care in the U.S. are sky-rocketing, accounting for 67.2 billion dollars in 1970--or 7.0 percent of the entire U.S. gross national product.

As a contrast to this figure for 1970, in 2004 the US bill for prescription drugs alone was more than $200 billion! Total healthcare in 2008 reached a staggering $2.4 trillion on healthcare which represents 17% of the US gross national product (GDP) and 2012 it is expected to reach $3.1 trillion! [544]

The real potential from improved diet is preventive. Existing evidence is inadequate for estimating potential benefits from improved diets in terms of health. Most nutritionists and clinicians feel that the real potential from improved diet is preventative in that it may defer or modify the development of a disease state so that a clinical condition does not develop. The major research thrust, nationwide, has been on the role of diet in treating health problems *after they have developed* (my emphasis).This approach has had limited success. USDA research emphasis has been placed on food needs of normal, healthy persons and findings from this work have contributed much of the existing knowledge on their dietary requirements.

Benefits would be shared by all. Benefits from better nutrition, made possible by improved diets, would be available to the entire population. Each age, sex, ethnic, economic, and geographic segment would be benefited. The lower economic and nonwhite population groups would benefit most from effective application of current knowledge.

These savings are only a small part of what might be accomplished for the entire population from research yet to be done. Some of the improvements can be expressed as dollar benefits to individuals or to the nation. The social and personal benefits are harder to quantify and describe. It is difficult to place a dollar figure on the avoidance of pain or the loss of a family member; satisfactions from healthy, emotionally adjusted families; career achievement; and the opportunity to enjoy leisure time.

Major health benefits are long range. Predictions of the extent to which diet may be involved in the development of various health problems have been based on current knowledge of metabolic pathways of nutrients, but primarily of abnormal metabolic pathways developed by persons in advanced stages of disease... Early adjustment of diet could prevent the development of undesirable long-range effects. Minor changes in diet and food habits instituted at an early age might well avoid the need for major changes, difficult to adapt to later in life.

Regional differences in diet related problems. The existence of regional differences in the incidence of health problems has been generally recognized and a wide variation in death rates still exists among geographic areas (Figs. 2, 3). These differences in death rate may reflect the cumulative effect of chronic low intake levels of some nutrients throughout the lifespan and by successive generations. A number of examples of regional health problems attributable to differences in the nutrient content of food or to dietary pattern could be given. Perhaps the best known is "the goiter belt" where soils and plants were low in iodine and the high incidence and death rate of goiter was reduced when the diet was supplemented with iodine. Another situation existed in some of the southern states where pellagra was a scourge a few decades ago. Corn was the major food protein source for low income families in these areas. The resulting niacin deficiency raised the incidence of pellagra to epidemic proportions.

The highest death rate areas generally correspond to those where agriculturists have recognized the soil as being depleted for several years. This suggests a possible relationship between sub marginal diets and health of succeeding generations. [545]

There are a number of interesting points raised in the foregoing report. The Pellagra story and the deficiency of iodine, I have already discussed. The final paragraph is welcomed; nutritionists for years have known that nutrient soil depletion was a significant contributory factor in dietary insufficiency. You cannot extract from foods nutrients that are not there in the first place.

Following are two tables that review the potential savings of improved diets, not just of the economic benefit and health benefits but of the social benefit too.

Table 1

Magnitude of benefits from nutrition research

PART A. Nutrition related health problems

Health Problem	Magnitude of Loss	Potential savings from improved diet
Heart and vasculatory	Over 1,000,000 deaths in 1967 Over 5 million people with definite or suspect heart	

	disease in 1960-62 25% reduction $31.6 billion in 1962	25% reduction $31.6 billion in 1962 20% reduction
Respiratory and infectious	82,000 deaths per year 246 million incidents in 1967 141 million work days lost in 1965-66 166 million school days lost $5 million in medical and hospital costs $1 billion in cold remedies and tissues	20% fewer incidents 15-20% fewer days lost 15-20% fewer days lost $1 million $20 million
Mental Health	Infant deaths in 1967--79,000 Infant death rate 22.4 per 1,000 Fetal death rate 15.6 per 1,000 Maternal death rate 28.0 per 100,000 live births Child death rate (1-4 yrs) 96.1 per 100,000 in 1964 15 million with congenital birth defect	50% fewer deaths 50% fewer deaths 50% fewer deaths 50% fewer deaths Reduce rate to 10 per 100,000 3 million fewer children with birth defects
Early aging and lifespan	49.1% of population, about 102 million people have one or more chronic impairments People surviving to age 65 White males -- 66% Negro males -- 50% White females – 81% Negro females -- 64% Life expectancy in years: White males -- 67.8 Negro males -- 61.1 White females -- 75.1 Negro females -- 68.2	10 million people without impairments 1% improvement per year to 90% surviving Bring Negro expectancy up to white
Arthritis	16 million people afflicted 27 million work days lost	8 million people without afflictions 13.5 million work days

	500,000 people unemployed 125,000 people employed Annual cost $3.6 billion	125,000 people employed $900 million per year
Diabetes and carbohydrate disorders	3.9 million overt diabetic 35,000 deaths in 1967 79% of people over 55 with impaired glucose tolerance	50% of cases avoided or improved
Osteoporosis	4 million severe cases 25% women over 40	75% reduction
Obesity	3 million adolescents 30 to 40% of adults 60 to 70% over 40 years	80% reduction in incidence
Eyesight	48.1%, or 86 million people over 3 years wore corrective lenses in 1966 81,000 become blind every year $103 million in welfare	20% fewer people blind or with corrective lenses
Digestive	8,495 thousand work days lost 5,013 thousand school days lost About 20 million incidents of acute condition annually $4.2 billion annual cost 14 million persons with duodenal ulcers $5 million annual cost 4,000 new cases each day	25% fewer acute conditions Over $1 billion in costs
Cancer	600,000 persons developed cancer in 1968 320,000 persons died of cancer in 1968	20% reduction in incidence and deaths

TABLE 1

PART B. Individual satisfactions increased

Satisfactions	Magnitude of loss	Potential savings from improved diet

Improved work efficiency		0.5% increase in on the job productivity
Improved growth and development	113,000 deaths from accident 324.5 million work days lost 51.8 million people needing medical attention and/or restricted education	25% fewer deaths and work days lost

Here is another extract of the report that goes into a little more depth:

RESPIRATORY AND INFECTIOUS DISEASE

Despite great advances in the control of infectious diseases in the past decades, acute respiratory infections remain the most frequent cause of illness and the most important cause of loss of time from work and school in the U. S. Pneumonia and influenza ranked fifth and other bronchopulmonic diseases tenth as causes of death in the U. S. in 1967; together they accounted for over 85,000 deaths. Acute respiratory infections are the most important single cause of illness. One-third to one-half of industrial absenteeism from sickness is caused by acute respiratory infections. In addition, mild infections may reduce efficiency without occasioning absenteeism. Young adults and children suffer the highest incidence of these infections, while the long lasting morbidity associated with chronic diseases is more frequent in older adults. The economic importance of morbidity from acute respiratory infections is impossible to determine precisely, but it has been estimated to be well over five million dollars per year. In addition, one billion dollars alone are spent for cold remedies and facial tissues.

Diet and the nutritional State of the individual involved are clearly associated with the incidence, duration, and severity of respiratory and infectious diseases. Nutrition is most likely to be a factor when the lower respiratory tract is involved, when bacteria are involved, or a chronic condition exists. Individuals in good nutritional state are less likely to succumb to the disease and those with high levels of nutrient reserves are more likely to recover quickly. These reserves are of special importance when the disease state results in loss of appetite due to coughing and vomiting, and increased caloric expenditure due to added difficulty in breathing.

There are many reports that malnutrition lowers resistance to infection and that nutritional deficiencies may be precipitated by an acute infection in subjects with borderline nutrient inadequacies. Few statistics are available to show a direct relationship between nutrition and infection. One of the best studies was carried out in Guatemala at INCAP. Three matched villages were studied. In two, health measures were introduced, the third remaining as a control. The health measures in one village involved adding supplementary food to the diet of children during and after weaning; in the other village, preventive and curative medical care was offered. Overall death rates declined in all three villages beyond what was expected from trends prior to the study. Reductions in mortality were as follows: in the medical care village 31 percent (50 percent beyond that expected), in the feeding village 56 percent, and in the control village 38 percent. Fully half of the deaths occurred during the second year of life.

A reduction in mortality by 56% in children, with half the mortality occurring up to the age of two, is significantly good when compared with current mortality rates generally.

Further evidence of the relationship between nutrition and infection rate has been observed. Virus infections hit harder among the undernourished, and the severity of the infection is directly proportional to the degree of malnutrition—these data are from studies with mice. Acute diarrhea in young infants results from a synergism between poor nutritional state and infection.

In children, acute infections such as pneumonia, rheumatoid arthritis, acute tonsillitis, and rheumatic fever reduce the levels of vitamin A in the blood as does vaccination against small pox and measles. Xerophthalmia, night blindness, frequently follows these infections indicating the depletion of body reserves of vitamin A. Vitamins B_1, B_6, and C, and protein also are implicated. Unfortunately, there are no satisfactory ways to determine the extent of body stores for most nutrients or to identify the level of nutrient intake needed to maintain adequate stores for resistance to infection.

MENTAL AND EMOTIONAL HEALTH

Mental illness is difficult to define and even specialists in the field are dissatisfied with present classifications... The National Association for Mental Health estimates that 19 million people in the United States (about 1 in 10) are afflicted with some form of mental or emotional illness requiring mental care. Moreover, mental disorders are a significant factor in many physical illnesses. Estimates, based on a study by the Commission of Chronic Illness in Baltimore in 1952-55, and other data indicate that at any point in time 12 percent of the population are suffering from psychiatric disorder and that 2.5 percent (over 52 million persons) are severely or totally disabled by it. Only 19 percent were considered entirely free of psychiatric symptoms. Prevalence of mental illness increases with age and is higher in the lowest socioeconomic groups.

A direct relationship can be drawn between nutrition and much of the mental illness resulting from organic brain disorders. Dietary improvement results in increased resistance to infection, better management of alcoholics, fewer circulatory disturbances and cardiovascular conditions, control of metabolic disturbances due to diabetes, hyperthyroidism, and nutrient deficiencies. The relationship of nutrition and mental disorders not associated with organic brain damage is less clear... it is clearly established that good nutrition is necessary for proper development and function of the central nervous system. Recovery from mental disability can be delayed if the condition is complicated by nutritional inadequacy.

Conceivably as much as 80 percent of the U.S. population could benefit from improved mental health with 12 percent having a major benefit. Benefits would be economic, through reduced hospital and psychiatric costs, improved ability and opportunities on the job, and fewer work days lost (Table 8). Social benefits would be of even greater importance; less family stress, fewer broken homes, and greater social acceptance of the individuals and their families.

INFANT MORTALITY AND REPRODUCTION

The first evidence that a change in maternal nutrition could disrupt the normal development of mammals appeared in 1935. The relationship was established between diets deficient in vitamin A and a variety of birth defects including missing eyes in pigs. Since that time, a number of abnormalities have been deliberately induced by nutritional deficiencies. Among the nutrients studied were riboflavin and folic acid. Significantly, folic acid and vitamin A are two of the vitamins most likely to be deficient in the U.S. diet.

One of the earliest deficiencies to be recognized for its effect on prenatal development was a deficiency of iodine. This results in the birth of a somewhat overweight, but seemingly normal, infant. However, by the sixth 'month, the clinical picture of cretinism is clearly defined. This is of particular economic significance in the U. S. at the present time because of the increasing prevalence of goiter in several parts of the U.S. among girls of childbearing age. This increased incidence may be due to the increasing consumption of prepared foods made with salt which has no iodine added.

The tragedy of nutritional deficiencies is not just the deformities and handicaps—there are huge financial and social costs too. And these are so much more galling when you know they can be prevented, particularly when they are due to political inaction, extreme ignorance, or the serving of vested corporate interests. Approximately 12 billion people worldwide live in iodine-deficient areas, and in China millions of people are mentally handicapped due to iodine deficiency. In India, the problem was so bad that they introduced a law in 1986 to make the addition of iodine to table salt mandatory by law. This led to a drastic reduction in mentally handicapped new-borns—from 9.8 percent to 1.4 percent. The WHO estimates that 400 billion people worldwide are affected by iodine deficiency. In Switzerland iodised salt has been the only available salt—and this has led to a reduction in thyroid disease of 90 percent. In Germany, one in seven people is affected by iodine deficiency, and in Bavaria it is eight times higher than in northern Germany. East Germany, on the other hand, used to use iodised salt and had the same status as Switzerland as regards incidence of goitre and thyroid disease; however following re-unification with Western Germany, the health status of Eastern Germany was eroded within five years. Dr Wenzel terms this interference and strict control of iodised salt in Germany as "unwarranted bureaucratic restriction." [546]

Since 1910 the percentage of infant deaths due to birth defects has steadily increased. Many millions of children have handicaps (Fig. 17) In fact, the 1964 Vital Statistics Survey in the U. S. showed that congenital defects, including genetic metabolic disorders, was the leading cause of death in the first year. At least 62,000 deaths each year in all age groups in this country may be attributed to birth defects. Actually, as a cause of death, birth defects are outranked only by heart disease. The National Foundation has estimated that today in the U.S. there are 15 million persons with one or more congenital defects that affect their daily lives. There is considerable evidence relating to the relevance of birth defects to poor nutrition. The Health Insurance Program of New York and others have found that babies who weighed less than 5.5 pounds at birth are twice as likely to have birth defects. Some of these relationships have been discussed elsewhere (EYESIGHT). The incidence of blindness is two to three times as high in infants of low birth weight. The long-range effects of malnutrition on brain development are discussed in IMPROVED LEARNING ABILITY.

Malnourishment in the mother usually results in the birth of a baby who is underweight. These babies are more likely to have birth defects. This has particular significance in the U.S. where there are probably more child pregnancies than in any other nation in the world (Table 11). In 1965 in the U. S., there were more than 196,000 live births to girls 17 years of age or younger. Statistics are not available to show the relation of the age of the mother to the incidence of birth defects. However, young mothers are in the sex-age group most likely to have nutritional deficiencies as indicated by the National Nutrition Survey and the data for individuals obtained during the Nationwide Food Consumption Survey of 1965. In the Nationwide Nutrition Survey of 1968 in Louisiana, 40 percent of 7- to 17-year-olds had unacceptable plasma vitamin A values. This vitamin has been implicated in birth defects.

Complications during pregnancy resulting in maternal death may also be related to the nutritional state of the mother. In 1967, the maternal death rate was 28.0 per 100,000 live births. The rate for white mothers was 19.5 and for nonwhite mothers 69.5 (Table 10). While hygiene and other factors are also causative agents, the role of nutrition may be very important particularly with the nonwhite mothers, many of whom are from low economic groups. There are a number of ways in which nutrition influences maternal death. The frequency of misshapen pelvic bones, a cause of difficult labor and frequently of adverse effects on the infant, has been much reduced by the prevention of childhood rickets. Because the principal cause of rickets is an inadequate intake of vitamins A and D and is more often present among economically deprived populations, we have an example of the influence of economic status and malnutrition in early life on the outcome of pregnancies many years later.[547]

275

UNHEALTHY BETRAYAL

In previous chapters I have mentioned that in the UK we have two areas where there is now an epidemic of rickets, Southampton and Dundee in Scotland. Here the number of cases has not been seen since the 1920s—and is most likely due to vitamin D deficiency.

This US Department of Agriculture report is, as you would expect fully referenced with each topic discussed in detail. What is remarkable is the depth of research and the understanding that was available in 1971, which was then withheld almost as soon as it was published. This anomaly poses the question: 'What would the American health situation be like today if this report had not been withheld?' Numerous doctors are documented as having regretted that their training had too little information on nutrition. Some doctors even state that the idea of nutrition was ridiculed when they studied medicine; people interested in nutrition were labelled "health faddists."

So we have to ask the question: 'Who could have benefited from withholding such a publication?' It certainly wasn't the American people, and certainly not the American tax payers who funded the $30 million study. Today there are few people who even know of its existence.

So let's imagine where we might be today if the report had not been withheld and its recommendations had been followed up with further research and education involving the American public. How great would public awareness be of the true role of nutrition today? How would things have been different in financial terms, in social problems and in the chronic poor health that is widespread today?

The answer, as we shall see, is quite a lot. But first, let's take a look at the situation we find ourselves in today:

The Demise of Health

The CDC in the USA admitted a significant problem in a report on chronic disease and health promotion:

- 7 out of 10 deaths among Americans each year are from chronic diseases.
- In 2005, 133 million Americans, practically 50 percent of the adult population, suffer from chronic illness of one sort or another.
- Obesity has become a major concern, as 1 in 3 adults are considered obese and 1 in 5 youths between the ages of 6 and 19 are obese.

ALTERNATIVE THINKING—THREAT TO PROFITS

- Diabetes is the leading cause of kidney failure, nontraumatic lower-extremity limb amputations, and blindness among adults aged 20 -74.

- More than 43 million American adults (approximately 1 in 5) smoke. In 2007, 20% of high school students in the United States were cigarette smokers.

- Nearly 45% of high school students report consuming alcohol in the past 30 days, and over 60% of those who drink report binge drinking (consuming 5 or more drinks on one occasion) within the past 30 days. There are a significant number of studies which provide strong evidence that drinking alcohol is a risk factor for primary liver cancer, and more than 100 studies have found a higher risk of breast cancer with increasing alcohol intake. The link between alcohol consumption and colorectal (colon) cancer has been reported in more than 50 studies.

- In 2007, fewer than 22% of high school students and only 24% of adults reported eating 5 or more servings of fruits and vegetables per day.[548]

The former editor-in-chief of the *New England Journal of Medicine,* Marcia Angell, M.D., believes there is too much reliance on drugs at the cost of much simpler solutions:

> I find it hard to imagine that a system this corrupt can be a good thing, or that it is worth the vast amounts of money spent on it. But in addition, we have to ask whether it really is a net benefit to the public to be taking so many drugs. In my view we have become an overmedicated society. Doctors have been taught only too well by the pharmaceutical industry, and what they have been taught is to reach for a prescription pad...Patients have also been well taught that if they don't leave the doctor's office with a prescription, the doctor is not doing a good job. The result is too many people end up taking drugs when there may be better ways to deal with their problems.

She cites a large trial sponsored by the National Institutes of Health (NIH), on strategies to prevent high-risk patients from getting adult onset diabetes. The study was divided into three groups, the first was given a placebo and in that group 29% developed diabetes within three years. The second group was given the drug metformin which was the generic form of the Bristol-Myers Squibb's blockbuster Glucophage. In this group 22% developed diabetes. The third group were placed on a moderate diet and exercise program and only 14% developed diabetes. [549]

Our belief in modern medicine and the high technology solution to our health woes is being seriously challenged by some other senior authorities. Dr John Gofman has a PhD in nuclear and physical chemistry as well as being a medical doctor. He discovered uranium 233, worked on the Manhattan project and was the first person to isolate plutonium. He has been studying the effects of radiation on human health for years. And he's concerned that some modern technology, including X-rays, angiography, CT scans, mammography, and fluoroscopy are a contributing factor to 75 percent of new cancers. He believes we will be facing 100 million premature deaths over the next decade as a direct result of the use of ionizing radiation. The radiation levels that patients are exposed to for a full-body CT (computerised tomography) scan is equivalent to the same level of radiation exposure as experienced by the victims of Nagasaki and Hiroshima. Yet very few doctors that are aware of this information. As a result few patients are made aware of the risk they take when having X-rays and other ionizing radiation practices. [550]

Nutrition and Schizophrenia

We tend to think that modern medicine is progressive, that we are moving forward with up-to-date science, at the cutting edge so to speak, that this is the best we can offer. Sadly that is not the case. There is no doubt that in some areas of medicine there have been great advances, particularly in traumatic injury, but in other areas we often seem to be going backwards. Abram Hoffer, M.D., PhD., a psychiatrist for most of his life, with a PhD in biochemistry obtained in 1944, is Master of Science in Agricultural Chemistry and obtained his medical degree in 1949. He was one of the founders of Orthomolecular Nutrition which is used to overcome debilitating mental conditions such as schizophrenia. Hoffer practiced psychiatry right up to his retirement in 2005. He wrote extensively on the role of nutrition in psychiatry in a number of books and numerous scientific papers. His book *Psychiatry—Yesterday (1950) and Today (2007), From Despair to Hope with Orthomolecular Psychiatry,* is a comprehensive review of the profession over that period.

He starts by mentioning that the English Doctor, John Conolly, reported a recovery rate of fifty% amongst his patients way back in 1850. Conolly defined recovery as patients free of symptoms and signs, getting on well both in the community and with their families, working in productive roles and paying income tax.

Hoffer notes that apart from a few dedicated psychiatrists and the Quakers, the general consensus is that schizophrenia is not considered curable; he mentions that the word "cure" has never occurred in any psychiatric dictionary. He relates how, at a hearing in King County, Washington in 2000, a psychiatrist testified that of the ten thousand patients he had treated, none had recovered.

ALTERNATIVE THINKING—THREAT TO PROFITS

With this background, he discusses how his research led him to look more closely at the use of vitamin B_3—or niacin as it is more commonly referred to. In the early part of the 1900s, what is now referred to as schizophrenia used to be called dementia praecox—and it included the disease pellagra, scurvy and syphilis of the brain. One quarter of admissions used to be pellagra sufferers and the pellagrologists who treated them would give them vitamin B_3. Those patients who did not respond were considered schizophrenics. [551]

In 1930, 30,000 Americans died from pellagra in the southeast United States. Pellagra was characterised by the four D's, dermatitis, diarrhoea, dementia and death. As mentioned in earlier chapters, Dr Joseph Goldberger was instrumental in the discovery that pellagra was a result of chronic malnutrition, particularly a lack of B_3 (niacin). The dementia or psychosis associated with pellagra could not be distinguished on clinical grounds alone. However, once niacin had been identified as the treatment for this condition, patients who did not recover after a few weeks of receiving up to 1,000 mg of niacin daily were regarded as having their dementia caused by schizophrenia. When the United States government introduced mandatory fortification of white flour with niacinamide (a form of niacin) in 1942, pellagra seemed to disappear and became forgotten. No-one thought to increase the dose of niacin for patients who did not respond to the initial niacin treatment, nor to pursue the treatment for a longer period of time.[552]

In the early 1950s, Hoffer suspected that schizophrenia was characterized by excessive oxidation and had identified a new compound in the urine of the majority of schizophrenics (which was later identified as kryptopyrrole). Further research revealed schizophrenics also had several oxidised catecholamines such as adrenochrome (oxidised adrenaline), dopachrome (oxidised dopamine) and noradrenochrome (oxidised noradrenaline). Niacin, however, protects against excessive oxidative stress related to adrenaline. So Hoffer began studies into the use of niacin to treat schizophrenics—and these culminated in six double blind controlled studies by around 1960. Other nutritional factors were also found to be effective including pyridoxine, vitamin C and zinc. Hoffer was able to restore health to up to 90% of his patients, depending on how long they had had their condition. Late chronic cases (patients who had had the condition for more than two years) had success rates of 75% according to his criteria. It has to be said that Hoffer maintained that orthomolecular therapy by itself was insufficient to achieve successful resolution of a patient's condition. His ideal treatment protocol included three other factors, (1) Shelter, (2) Optimum nutrition and (3) Civility.[553]

For years, schizophrenics had been virtually incarcerated and kept on drugs that kept their symptoms sufficiently in check for them not considered problematic. In some places, this remains the treatment method today. Hoffer believed that patients needed to be involved in their own therapy and to be treated with respect and civility in an environment that nurtured their recovery. This required a diet that was not totally impoverished of nutrients, such as over-processed foods, sweet foods or foods de-natured of their nutrient value.

Other people, such as Carl Pfeiffer, PhD., M.D. in the USA, had come to similar conclusions about treating schizophrenia with niacin—and other nutritional or orthomolecular approaches. Pfeiffer founded the Brain Bio Center in Skillman, New Jersey, a non-profit making clinic and research center that specialised in the treatment of schizophrenia and other mental disturbances. His center employed thirty-five other people, of which seven were research scientists. Pfeiffer discovered that, aside from the marker of the mauve factor (the evidence of pyrroles in their patient's urine), histamine levels and copper and zinc levels also played a critical part. Whilst he, too, achieved great results with niacin, some of his patients did not respond as well as he would have liked. In these cases, further tests revealed hypoglycaemia (low blood sugar), high copper levels, zinc deficiencies, high histamine levels (histadelia), low histamine (histapenia) and brain allergies. Further details of his response to these findings can be found in his book *Nutrition and Mental Illness, An Orthomolecular Approach to balancing Body Chemistry.*[554] Pfeiffer also published numerous papers on the subject.

Meanwhile, Hoffer had been finding that the response to his work varied from simple denial to various degrees of hostility. He complained that the more modern drugs made it much more difficult to treat patients than many of the older drugs. The side effects were more severe; they were more addictive, they caused obesity and a number of other serious problems, and they were much more expensive. Long-term use of the modern drugs was introducing effects on the brain that were irreversible. He believed that tranquilizers should be used sparingly, and, not as a crutch. Long-term use produced what he termed as "tranquilizer psychosis." He found there was a direct correlation between cerebral cortex atrophy and the amount of tranquilizers taken over years (in grams) which decreased the ability of patients to make a full recovery. He believed that xenobiotic (unnatural chemicals to the body) psychiatrists provided their schizophrenic patients with two choices: remain psychotic without drugs or become psychotic with drugs. He found that some patients had to be legally forced into taking many of the modern drugs because of their aversion to tranquilizer psychosis. He also laments the fact that the majority of the research with orthomolecular medicine that is published in journals such as the *Journal of Orthomolecular*

Medicine, is not available on Medline which, by default, amounts to censorship by the US government. As a result, most physicians are unaware of this research, which is a tragedy.

On my website www.fundamentalhealth.org, links to the archive of the above journal as well as its website address. [555]

Medicalizing Emotion

In the early part of the 20th century depression was considered a rare disorder. Nevertheless, by the early 1960's benzodiazepine drugs such as Librium and Valium had been developed. These tranquilizers were designed and marketed for numerous complaints, such as 'anxieties', hypertension, and 'stress-problems' which were all due to the new urban lifestyles, and the faster pace of modern society. Sales of Valium soared until it became the best-selling drug on the market—in the UK benzodiazepine use reached 30 million prescriptions a year. [556] However, this love affair with tranquilizers lost its charm when it was turned out that users became dependent on them—and suffered very unpleasant withdrawal symptoms if they stopped taking them. Nevertheless, the pharmaceutical industry had had got a taste for the profits to be made from tranquilizers, and set about developing new ones. There were indeed a lot of people who needed tranquilizers, but what made Librium and Valium exceptional was astute marketing. A former medical director of Squibb pharmaceutical gave a significant comment on this:

> *'The incidence of disease cannot be manipulated and so increased sales volumes must depend at least in part on the use of drugs unrelated to their utility or need'.* [557]

Benzodiazepines are a family of tranquillizers that include Halcion (triazolam), Valium (diazepam), Librium (chlordiazepoxide), Ativan (lorazepam) Mogadon (nitrazepam), Xanax (alprazolam), Restoril (temazepam), and Dalmane (flurazepam).Tranquillizers were prescribed for numerous non-medical reasons as well as medical ones, ranging from divorce, shyness, cystitis, lack of confidence, bereavement, socialising, asthma, retirement and infertility, to business problems. In the early 1990s 10% of the population in Europe and America were prescribed benzodiazepines. Of these people, approximately one third were long-term users. There were many who believed there was an excess of overprescribing. Professor Malcolm Lader, a psychopharmacologist from the Institute of Psychiatry in London expressed his concern:

UNHEALTHY BETRAYAL

"The indications for these drugs are being insidiously widened and the boundary between normality and illness increasingly blurred."[558]

In 1990, the US National Institute of Mental Health reported that eight percent of the population suffered from anxiety of one type or another; three million people suffered panic disorders or recurrent attacks of anxiety, eleven million people suffered obsessions, phobias and chronic levels of apprehension. There was also a prevalence of chronic insomnia in the American public affecting 10% of the adult population—which was estimated to be costing the US more than $90 billion. [559]

A huge industry grew up around the treatment of depression and anxiety, involving the pharmaceutical industry, the psychiatric profession and medicine generally. This development had a lot to do with changing perceptions of how people coped with 'modern living'. That there were people who suffered from anxiety and depression was not in doubt. Doubt did exist though, as to the cause of these problems. In the early 1950s key neurotransmitters such as serotonin, norepinephrine, and dopamine had been discovered, and that had led to considerable debate as to whether mental disturbances could be caused by imbalances of these chemicals. Drugs like the tricyclic antidepressants blocked the operation of norepinephrine, and a whole new range of chemicals were developed called Selective Serotonin Reuptake Inhibitors (SSRIs). These were to treat the numerous conditions that affected the levels of serotonin. So by this time the psychiatric profession had quite an arsenal of chemicals with which to mould and influence behaviour.

There are many who feel that simply throwing drugs at the various mental and emotional conditions in our society has created a self-perpetuating system that can only result in increasing problems. There's no doubt that drugs are able to subdue manic people and give some element of control that was not there before—and this is considered very useful. When you are faced with people who are seriously disturbed and distraught, it is very useful to be able to treat them with something. However, some people are now asking: 'Is this the right treatment for less seriously ill people, or is it driven by the profit motive of the pharmaceutical industry?'

In 1952, the American Psychiatric Association published its own manual, the *Diagnostic and Statistical Manual for Mental Disorders* (DSM). In this book they classified 112 mental disorders, including neuroses of various types, personality disorders, such as alcoholism, drug addictions, sexual deviations such as homosexuality, and a whole host of 'conditions.'

In each subsequent edition of the DSM manual, the number of psychiatric 'disorders' increased. Some conditions were re-classified, others such as anxiety neurosis, were broken down into a number of different conditions, such as generalised anxiety disorder, panic disorder, post-traumatic stress disorder, obsessive compulsive disorder and social phobia. The current DSM manual, DSM IV, lists *more than 800 conditions*. Here for example are a few listings under personality disorder:

- 301.0 Paranoid personality disorder
- 301.20 Schizoid personality disorder
- 301.22 Schizotypal personality disorder
- 301.7 Antisocial personality disorder
- 301.83 Borderline personality disorder
- 301.50 Histrionic personality disorder
- 301.81 Narcissistic personality disorder
- 301.82 Avoidant personality disorder
- 301.6 Dependent personality disorder
- 301.4 Obsessive-compulsive personality disorder

The DSM manual has become a defining document that is recognised in a court of law. So what has come to be accepted is that most conditions can be treated by a specific drug of some kind—at least, that is the view promoted by the pharmaceutical industry. What is actually happening here? Are we effectively providing real solutions to what seem a myriad of problems? I believe there are few people who would argue that we are. Just take the way drug therapy and intervention has mushroomed, throughout the population, from young children to old people. The problem with this is that there is no such thing as a drug without a side effect. Drugs, by their very nature are synthetic chemicals that have been developed by drug companies to make money; they are created in such a way that they can be patented to protect future profits. And they are marketed to maximise returns. By far the best illnesses to treat for making money are long-term, chronic conditions that large number of the population are likely to need.

The words "anxiety" and "depression" can mean different things to different people. There are many situations that people may consider stressful, or disturbing. Losing your livelihood after 45 years, divorce, or a death in the family are all examples of events we can associate with emotional turmoil. Loss of sleep, trouble at work, harassment by neighbours, and isolation can also contribute to our emotional instability. In these situations, most people turn to their doctors.

The Dangers of Halcion, Used to Treat Insomnia

What is clear is that there is now a vast industry dealing with this issue. In 2008, the anti-depressant market was worth over $11 billion.[560] But how many people are aware that there are associated risks with just about all the drugs currently in use? Take Halcion as an example used to treat insomnia. Numerous studies were done on this drug, giving varying reports as to how effective it was. Those funded by the industry tended to show it in a good light but many others showed it to be not just ineffective but hazardous. The book, *The Therapeutic Nightmare – The Battle over the World's Most Controversial Sleeping Pill.* It was written by Professor John Abraham, Co-director of the Centre for Research in Health and Medicine at the University of Sussex, and Julie Sheppard, Head of Communications at University College London Hospitals, tells the full story behind the nightmare it created for very many people.[561]

There are numerous adverse reactions (ADRs) reported with Halcion, more than would normally be expected even from benzodiazepines. Theresa Woo of the FDA became very concerned about Halcion, she had seen many more ADRs with this drug, 339 central nervous system (CNS) ADRs compared to 83 for Dalmane or 56 for Restoril. On top of this other countries had unfavourably reviewed Halcion. But it wasn't just in the US that problems occurred. They showed up all over the world. In March 1979 a Dutch psychiatrist, Dr Kees van der Kroef wrote to the *Lancet* expressing his dismay at the number side effects (45) he had observed in twenty-five of his patients. The adverse reactions included amnesia, paranoia and aggression. His article was very critical:

> During the past nine months I have been confronted in psychiatric practice with a syndrome which is almost certainly induced by the benzodiazepine triazolam ('Halcion'). I have made a close study of 25 patients. Triazolam can produce the following symptoms: severe malaise; depersonalization and derealisation; paranoid reactions; acute and chronic anxiety; continuous fear of going insane; depression and deterioration of existing depressions; nightmares; restlessness; inability to concentrate; verbal and physical aggression; severe suicidal tendencies; hallucinations; impulse actions; amnesia; dysphagia [difficulty in swallowing] accompanied by a nasty taste... muscular cramps and paralyses, catatonically impaired motor functioning....[562]

In July 1979 Van der Kroef published his full report in the *Dutch Medical Journal.* Following his revelations, the Dutch Ministry of Health (DMOH) saw an enormous increase in the numbers of doctors' reports of adverse reactions—by August they had received in excess of 1000. The DMOH suspended Halcion on the grounds of safety on 6th August 1979. Upjohn, the manufacturer of Halcion, had filed its New Drug Application with the FDA in 1976—and were no doubt concerned that this kind of adverse publicity would affect their application. Even worse, Dr Theresa Woo, the FDA's chief medical reviewing officer, was concerned about reports linking Halcion with amnesia. Then in March 1977 the FDA convened a meeting to review Halcion with the Psychopharmacological Drugs Advisory Committee (PDAC), and Woo had a chance to express her concerns:

> The other thing I am very concerned about is the chemically induced amnesia.... I had to really search carefully 147 volumes of the NDA to collect 50 cases and I am sure this is underreported and it is not the kind of thing you would find unless you looked for it. [563]

Dr Paul Leber, Woo's superior at the FDA was more upbeat about Halcion, and the later negative reports from the Netherlands, believing that the Dutch had approved too high a dose—in the UK Halcion had been approved on smaller dose of just 1mg dose. Halcion was eventually approved in the USA, on 15 November 1982, at a daily approved dose of just 0.5mg except for geriatrics who were advised to take 0.125 – 0.25 mg. By 1987 Halcion had become the world's top-selling sleeping pill, had created sales of around $220 million for Upjohn. [564]

However reports continued to come in about problems with it, including early morning insomnia associated with its ability to be metabolised quite quickly, and which was followed by daytime anxiety. [565] In 1986, two researchers in the FDA,s Division of Epidemiology and Surveillance (DES), Dr Diane Wyskowski and Dr David Barash, produced a report on Halcion's ADR. This contrasted Halcion, Dalmane and Restoril from 1980 -1985 as registered by the spontaneous reporting system. They found that Halcion had between 8 and 30 times more ADR reports than the other two combined. The five most reported events for Halcion were 133 cases of confusion, 109 cases of amnesia, 59 cases of bizarre or abnormal behaviour, 58 cases of agitation and 40 cases of hallucination. The report was not cleared by Wyskowski's superiors for two years prior to publication in a medical journal, and just sat collecting dust. [566]

Another FDA researcher, Bob Wise, had written an in-house executive summary concerning Halcion and Xanax's ability to cause hostility, including expressions of rage, anger, assaults and even murders. Peter Breggin, an American Psychiatrist and author of numerous books and papers, commented:

More such reports of this type have been received by the FDA for triazolam [Halcion] and alprazolam [Xanax] than any other drug product regulated by the Agency. Reporting rates, which adjust for differences in the extent of each drug's utilization, reveal much higher ratios of hostility reports to drug sales for both triazolam, and alprazolam than for other benzodiazepines with similar indications.

The public health importance of these reactions lies in their severity, with occasionally lethal behaviour unleashed, in the context of large population exposures as the popularity of both drugs continues to rise.[567]

Wise found 113 reports of suspected Halcion-induced hostility, followed by Xanax with 79. Apparently, among 318 other medications, three-quarters had only one or two reports of hostility. Breggin added the figures for Versed (46) and Valium (34) which he concluded gave "benzodiazepines an across-the-board victory, finishing in first, second, third, and fourth place."

In the UK, the Committee on the Safety of Medicines introduced a ban on the use of Halcion in December 1991.

When mania arises in an individual it is diagnosed as a manic episode. If it is accompanied by depression, it is diagnosed as a bipolar (manic-depressive) disorder. When it is caused by a medication such as an antidepressant, it is diagnosed as substance-induced mood disorder. This distinction can have far reaching consequences. Breggin gives numerous examples of people who were victims of substance-induced mood disorders—which go into the consequences in detail. I'll recount part of a story of Dr Vernon Kirklander, a successful surgeon, who developed anxiety and was given a tranquiliser, Klonopin (2mg) each day. He apparently took this for a number of years—while at the same time taking steroid medications. One day, he decided to remove a 150lb compressor from his hospital, and hauled it down a flight of stairs, past security cameras to his car. At which point he realised he was doing something foolish so, having failed to return it, hid it behind a dumpster. He went and confessed to the hospital administrator what he had done, and agreed to seek psychiatric evaluation. When he received this, he was diagnosed as having attention-deficit hyperactivity disorder (ADHD) and was on Adderall. A few months later he reduced the Adderall by half to 30mg (considered the usual maximum dose) and added 80mg of Strattera a day.

Then, one evening, he rode his eighteen-speed bicycle fifteen miles to a construction site. He apparently started a piece of machinery and drove it around various obstacles for entertainment. After that, he left his valuable, and potentially identifiable, bike at the site and decided to drive home in a fuel tanker—which he parked in his driveway. His wife asked him what it was doing there, but got no reply. By morning he had moved it.

On another occasion he returned a backhoe (in the UK we might refer to this as a digger or JCB) to a friend, and borrowed a cherry picker (this is a truck with a hoist, the type used by phone linesmen). He drove this vehicle to a construction site where he stole a trailer with a backhoe and drove through his village with it in broad daylight, noticed by all. He carried on to his friend's house and parked it in his barn. When his friend noticed it there he called the police who came and removed it.

His escapades increased and he collected two more backhoes, two tractors, three industrial trailers and a pile of lumber. He was eventually caught when he tried to tow away yet another backhoe on a triple-axel trailer with his car, a luxury Lexus sedan. This was on a Sunday less than one block from the police station. The twenty-five ton load had been too much for his car, the trailer and its cargo came adrift and fell onto his vehicle and caused an obstruction to the traffic. Kirklander was found a short distance away, with his battered vehicle, trying to pump up a tire. The police decided to search his house and found all the other equipment parked outside in broad daylight. Dr Kirklander was jailed for his actions, but given a fairly lenient sentence. When he was released, he was advised by to get proper psychological and psychiatric treatment. The judge told him "I don't believe your offenses were economic in nature, I think there are other forces that drove you and you need to sort all that out". Kirklander stopped all his medications while in jail, and although he suffered psychotic withdrawal symptoms, was able to understand and come to terms with what the drugs had done to him about a year later. But he never got his medical license back. [568]

The Dangers of Benzodiazepines

A number of researchers report that many of the effects of benzodiazepines pass un-noticed. Peter Breggin M.D. who I have already cited, published a serious critique of the over-use of drugs by psychiatrists in a number of books: *Toxic Psychiatry*, *Talking Back to Prozac* and *Talking Back to Ritalin*, amongst others. Here are some of his views:

> The benzodiazepines can produce a wide variety of abnormal mental responses and hazardous behavioural abnormalities, including rebound anxiety and insomnia, mania and other forms of psychosis, paranoia, violence, antisocial acts, depression, and suicide. These drugs can impair cognition, especially memory, and can result in confusion. They can induce dependence and addiction.

Severe withdrawal syndromes with psychosis, seizures, and death can develop. The short-acting benzodiazepines, alprazolam (Xanax) and triazolam (Halcion), are especially prone to cause psychological and behavioural abnormalities. [569]

As previously stated many of the problems associated with drug treatment and withdrawal pass un-noticed:

The severity of the psychological, occupational, and social consequences of benzodiazepine toxicity and withdrawal problems are rarely if ever adequately addressed in the psychiatric literature (discussed in Jacobs, 1995). In my clinical and forensic medical experience, individuals under the influence of benzodiazepines can commit crimes involving fraud and violence that are wholly out of character for them. Family assets and family life may be sacrificed to drug abuse and addiction. David Jacobs (1995) points out that many psychiatrists seem too indifferent toward adverse drug effects. He notes that in medical and scientific papers, adverse drug reactions are usually reported as isolated events that do not impinge upon other people and upon the individual's overall life. Jacobs (1997) maintains:

"Many people tacitly assume that when a person experiences an adverse drug reaction, he or she can and will simply stop taking the medication, thus terminating the adverse drug reaction. The picture when it comes to the benzodiazepines is commonly very different." (p. 1)

As Jacobs observes, the consequences of continuous benzodiazepine use - such as lethargy, emotional flatness, disinhibition, depression, and a worsening of anxiety - are not likely to be understood as drug-related by patients, their families, or their physicians. When patients try to reduce or stop the medication, they do not realize that their increased insomnia or anxiety are a result of rebound. The patient's personal and work relationships may deteriorate due to physical, cognitive and emotional problems induced by the drug. Withdrawal can be experienced as torture, and the effects of withdrawal can disrupt social and occupational life. Rage, mania and other drug-induced reactions that reach psychotic proportions can ruin lives and wreak havoc among loved ones and innocent bystanders.[570]

Dr Breggin introduces the concept of 'medical spellbinding' to explain why so many people take psychiatric drugs that do more harm than good—and describes spellbinding as an extension of the brain-disabling principal:

The brain-disabling principal states that all the physical treatments in psychiatry—medication, electroshock and lobotomy—have their primary or "therapeutic" effect by causing malfunctions in the brain that are misidentified as "improvements." Spellbinding more specifically builds on a brain-disabling corollary, which states that patients receiving medications and other mind-altering treatments "often display poor judgement about the positive and negative effect of the treatment on their functioning."

As illustrations of the overall brain-disabling principal, the apathy or euphoria created by antidepressants is misinterpreted as an improvement in depression—the blunting of all emotions and self-awareness caused by antipsychotic drugs is seen as an improvement in the psychosis; and the generalised sedation and suppression of brain function caused by antianxiety drugs is viewed as a treatment for anxiety. In reality, no specific improvements have occurred in the underlying depression, psychosis, or anxiety. Instead the brain has been partially disabled, artificially changing the individual's mood and rendering the patient less able to feel, to perceive, or to express their underlying mental condition or outlook. [571]

To expand on that point, I'll give an example from a different writer that involved a physician. After taking Halcion on just one occasion this physician reported that he had suffered amnesia, confusion, loss of coordination, bizarre behaviour, hallucinations and paranoid schizophrenia. He had been due to perform surgery the following morning but, because of his bizarre behaviour, he was locked in his house by his girlfriend. Nevertheless he managed to find some keys and went to work as normal. None of his colleagues noticed anything strange at first, but when his behaviour became more and more strange, he had to be physically removed from surgery and be replaced by another surgeon. Subsequently he reported that he continued to have further episodes of bizarre behaviour, even though he had stopped taking the drug. [572]

Yet Another story deserves re-telling. A Utah woman, Llo Grundberg, sued Upjohn Company for $21 million claiming that after taking Halcion, she killed her mother, shooting her in June 1988. The murder charge against her was dropped by the judge after two psychiatrists testified that the killing was a result of the drug. And an out-of-court settlement was agreed with the Upjohn Company. [573]

The Dangers of Selective Serotonin Reuptake Inhibitors

Many doctors and psychiatrists are concerned that many of the newer drugs are causing even more damage than earlier ones. Selective Serotonin Reuptake Inhibitors (SSRI's) for example are linked with increased suicides, violent behaviour and homicides. Dr David Healy, a distinguished and conventional psychiatrist for many years, eventually found himself questioning the relationship with the pharmaceutical industry, the nature of depression and the treatment of it. He wrote extensively, published numerous papers, and found many failings in the current system. His book, *Let Them Eat Prozac, The Unhealthy Relationship between the Pharmaceutical Industry and Depression*, describes his findings in detail. He discovered that there is little good science behind serotonin chemistry and the SSRI phenomenon—and; that drugs like Prozac are seriously problematic. He found that drugs like Prozac significantly increase violence and the suicide rate. He himself eventually agreed to appear in court to defend individuals who had found themselves trapped in the side effects.

Back in 1993, he helped recruit sixty volunteers from the medical and nursing staff of the psychiatric unit he was working in, as well as psychology students, and some clinical psychologists, to take part in a trial. This was to be a randomised single blind trial to study the effects of certain drugs on healthy subjects. They were given a one-off dose of 5mg of droperidol, an antipsychotic; 1 mg of lorazepam, a benzodiazepine tranquilizer; or a placebo. The drugs were chosen so that they could be concealed in orange juice. Each participant was subjected to tests both at the beginning of the trial and after three hours on the drug. The results astounded him. One senior university colleague became irritable and belligerent. Another woman, a consultant psychiatrist, became very restless and unsettled over an extended period of time and at times was suicidal. One person was reduced to tears within an hour, whilst others said they felt dysphoric, unsettled and disturbed. Many said that for whatever reason they were motivated to think about the worst moments of their lives, of unhappy times, broken relationships etc.

Dr Healy has specifically undertaken the study because he wanted to know what the effects were on healthy subjects. The industry had previously argued that the suicide rates on their drugs could simply be attributed to the fact that people taking them were suicidal *before* doing so—or that they were naturally at risk. However, an earlier study by Gregory Simon and Michael Von Korff around 1990 had shown this was not the case. Working with depressed patients in the Puget Sound, some treated with drugs and some without, they found that whilst the suicide rate was zero among those not taking the drugs, suicides among those that were on drugs were forty-three per hundred thousand.[574]

Healy undertook more research and discovered further studies confirming his suspicions. Of the forty million people who had taken Prozac, he estimated that this would have produced between twenty thousand and forty thousand extra suicides depending upon which studies you used to estimate the problem. He further discovered that if you looked at all the available data, the older drugs were easily as effective as the newer ones. They also did not have such worrisome side effects— and were far less expensive. He noted that German regulators were wary of introducing SSRIs. Plans for introducing fluoxetine in Germany in 1984 were resisted by the regulators for six years.[575] Fluoxetine is a fluoridated drug and Prozac is one of its many trade names.

At this point you might be wondering 'what is going on here?' What is the problem? Surely these drugs are tried and tested and are safe effective treatments right? Well you would be wrong on every point. Even the basis for their supposed beneficial effect is completely flawed, that is if you are under the impression that Selective Serotonin Reuptake Inhibitors (SSRIs) are effective because they address a chemical imbalance of the brain, i.e., insufficient levels of serotonin. At this point I feel it would be worth a little of your indulgence in the SSRI story. As previously mentioned, serotonin and norepinephrine are two neurotransmitters that belong to the group of monoamines. They enable impulses to transmit from one neuron to another in the synaptic junctions of the brain. Some of the neurotransmitter molecules are broken down by enzymes and some are recycled, referred to as reuptake.

Alec Coppen, a physician from West Park Hospital in Surrey was one of the first people to advance the theory that serotonin lack was the cause of depression. In a study in 1967 he concluded: "There is good evidence that drugs such as imipramine and the monoamine oxidase inhibitors, which increase the effective activity of brain monoamines, alleviate depression."[576] The drugs that countered this effect were termed monoamine oxidase inhibitors or MAOI type antidepressants. This work was also confirmed by other researchers such as Julius Axelrod and Joseph K Inscoe. [577] What was overlooked was that Axelrod had also discovered that reserpine also inhibited the reuptake of these neurotransmitters, but this was a drug that was supposed to *induce* depression. In a later autobiography he explains:

> After labeling adrenergic neurons in the brain (Glowinski and Axelrod,1964), we examined the effect of psychoactive drugs on brain biogenic amines. We found that only the clinically effective antidepressant drugs block the reuptake of 3H-norepinephrine in adrenergic nerve terminals. This finding, together with the observation that monoamine oxidase inhibitors have antidepressant actions and that reserpine, a depleter of biogenic amines, sometimes causes depression, led to the formulation of the catecholamine hypothesis of depression. [578]

Numerous recent studies have been undertaken since these earlier studies but a research team at the University of Amsterdam conducted a comprehensive review of the literature in 2007 and came to the conclusion that there was no basis for the theory that lowered levels of monoamine transmitters were responsible for causing depression. They found that in healthy volunteers there was no effect on mood levels. [579]

Placebos and Sugar Pills Work as Well as SSRIs

So where does this leave us? According to Irving Kirsch, Professor of Psychology at the University of Hull, there was very little evidence to support the use of SSRIs in the first place. He undertook a study of thirty-eight clinical trials while researching the placebo effect, involving more than 3000 patients suffering from depression. He looked at the differences between drug treatment, psychotherapy, placebo treatment and no treatment, and discovered that the difference between placebo and drug treatments was so small it raised more questions than answers. How could such a negligible difference prompt billions of pounds to be spent on a drug that was not only expensive, but had numerous side-effects? He published his study in 1998, and it immediately proved controversial. [580]

So a colleague of Kirsch's, Thomas J. Moore, senior fellow in health policy at the George Washington University School of Public Health, suggested he replicate the study with more in-depth data, using the US Freedom of Information Act to obtain all the original data from the FDA that had been submitted by the drug companies. He and Kirsch subsequently requested data on the six most widely used 'new-generation' antidepressant drugs: Prozac, Seroxat (Paxil in the US), Effexor, Dutonin (Serzone), Lustral (Zoloft) and Cipramil (Celexa). They obtained the data not just from published studies, but also a number of un-published studies that the industry had chosen not to expose to public scrutiny. Their analysis showed that 82 percent of the response to medication *had also been produced by a simple inert placebo* which suggested that less than 20 percent of the response to antidepressant medication could be attributed to the drug effect. Kirsch observed: "In fact, most of the clinical trials submitted by the drug companies failed to show any significant benefit from their drugs at all." This was not due to too low a dosage—SSRIs are just as effective at low doses as high doses (conversely the side effects *are* dose-dependent). [581]

Kirsch and Moore were not the only people who found little evidence for the efficacy of these modern drugs. Healey discusses this issue at length and relates how, when Leber became a pivotal figure in the FDA he promptly caused extreme consternation in the industry. He raised the issue that trials of a new drug rarely showed that they worked as well as the old ones did—although adding it could be the case that neither drugs worked. When he suggested that new drugs should be compared to placebos, there was uproar from the industry. However the trials went ahead—and many new drugs could not be shown to work any better than a placebo. Two of the biggest failures were two of the biggest sellers—Prozac and Mianserin, a European anti-depressant.[582]

It is common practice for drug companies not to publish studies if the findings will not be conducive to successful product marketing. During the 1990s, for example, GlaxoSmithKline conducted three clinical trials on the efficacy of Paxil (Seroxat in the UK), for the treatment of major depression in children and adolescents. One study showed mixed results, another found little difference between the drug and a placebo and the third showed the placebo in a better light, more effective than Seroxat for children aged seven to eleven. Those studies were not published.

Increased Risk of Suicide

Paroxetine (Paxil) is 1 of 6 SSRIs that Britain and the US have since banned for pediatric use because of increased risk of suicide.

This action was prompted by (or maybe in spite of) a document produced by the Central Medical Affairs team, a division of SmithKline Beecham—now part of GlaxoSmithKline following its merger with Glaxo Wellcome. Following the revelation that the trials showed virtually no benefit, the document recommended that the company "effectively manage the dissemination of these data in order to minimize any potential negative commercial impact."

This information was included in an a report by Wayne Kondo and Barbara Sibbald titled: *Drug company experts advised staff to withhold data about SSRI use in children,* published in the Canadian Medical Association Journal.

The result was that only one of the studies was published, the largest trial to date on using an SSRI in a pediatric population in the US, from 1993-1996. This was, of course, the best of the lot, even though it concluded paroxetine to be no better than a placebo. When it was published in 2001, the authors concluded that paroxetine is "generally well tolerated and effective for major depression in adolescents." What they did not publish was that amongst the 93 adolescents taking the drug there were five serious cases of "emotional lability" which indicates suicidal ideation and gestures.

Medicalizing Our Children

The report estimated that as many as 3 million Canadian children and 11 million Americans are taking antidepressants and sales of Seroxat amounted to $4.7 billion worldwide in 2003.[583]

UNHEALTHY BETRAYAL

In addition to simply publishing the trials that favour their drugs, drug companies practice what is referred to as 'salami slicing'. This involves repackaging positive trials under different authors' names (or even the same author as a new trial, but using the same data). In some cases, any mildly negative data in the first paper was dumped so that the new paper will seem much more positive about the drug in question.[584]

The problem with such manipulation of data (and of the truth) is that doctors are unable to make truly informed decisions about which drugs are safe to prescribe for individual patients. As a result, we may often not get what's best for us. Increasingly, children are diagnosed with Attention Deficit Hyperactivity Disorder (ADHD) and given stimulants and other drugs for treatment. Following is a list of stimulant drugs that may be prescribed:

Ritalin, Methylin (methylphenidate).
Focalin (d-methylphenidate).
Dexedrine, Dextrostat (d-amphetamine).
Adderall (amphetamine mixture).
Desoxyn (methamphetamine).
Cylert (pemoline).

Also there are longer acting stimulants:

Concerta, Metadate ER, Ritalin SR, Ritalin LA, Methylin ER (methylphenidate) and Adderall XR (amphetamine mixture).

It is not my intention to give a comprehensive review of drug treatment of children for ADHD but I cannot ignore reporting some of the catalogue of effects that afflict children unfortunate enough to be so burdened. According to Breggin the first thing to point out is that "All psychoactive drugs disrupt normal brain function". He goes on to explain: "The pharmacological action of any psychoactive drug is demonstrated by how it disrupts the normal function of an animal's brain. That disruption is the basis of the psychoactive effect." [585]

Dr Breggin was so concerned about this issue he wrote extensively about it in a number of his books (a useful source of information should you wish to explore this topic in greater depth). In the process of his research, he found much to worry him. When researching Ritalin, for example, he found hundreds of cases of Ritalin-induced psychiatric reactions from FDA reports. Following, are some of the more commonly reported reactions listed in order of most reported: agitation, hostility, depression and psychotic depression, abnormal thinking, hallucinations, psychosis, and emotional instability. On top of this were many reports of overdose, intentional overdose and suicide attempts. He also found that experts from the US Department of Education in 1992 found that cognitive toxicity of stimulants occurred at commonly prescribed clinical doses. "Cognitive toxicity" refers to a deterioration of mental function such as thinking, learning attention and memory. They found cognitive toxicity from Ritalin in excess of 40% of the typically treated cases. They also found that this was represented by affecting the high-order cognitive functions such as flexible problem-solving and divergent thinking.[586]

The trouble with using medications such as Ritalin is that the short-term effect of blunting the brain of a child can be perceived as a positive effect—and the longer term effects are missed or misinterpreted. The *Harvard Review of Psychiatry* noted in 2009 that the primary diagnosis of ADHD occurs as a result of teacher complaints. The 'disorder' is seldom experienced in a doctor's surgery. [587] Whilst the reviews note that there is *initially* a better response in the classroom after a drug has been prescribed, there are more worrying reasons to be concerned in the longer term. Critics of the therapy cite how children are more zombie-like, are passive, submissive, socially withdrawn, humourless, apathetic, lacking in spontaneity etc. Noted psychologist James Swanson, director of the ADHD Center at the University of California, Irvine, was not the first person to use the term "zombie-like" or the first to realise that the long-term prospects were poor, both educationally and for emotional health. [588]

Russell Barkley and Charles Cunningham at the Medical College of Wisconsin reviewed the literature back in 1978 which was before "attention deficit disorder" was even officially included in the *Diagnostic and Statistical Manual* (this occurred in 1980 in the third edition, DSMIII), and prior to the subsequent massive rise in ADHD diagnoses. They made the following observations:

> Stimulant drug studies based primarily on measures of teacher opinion have frequently concluded that these drugs improve the achievement of hyperkinetic children. However, a review of those studies using more objective measures of academic performance revealed few positive short-term or long-term drug effects on these measures. What few improvements have been noted can be readily attributed to better attention during testing. *The major effect of the stimulants appears to be an improvement in classroom manageability rather than academic performance* (my emphasis).

It would seem that the stimulants are not able to influence those etiologic factors, other than overactivity and inattentiveness, which predispose hyperkinetic children toward school difficulties. Hence, since the goal of pediatric intervention with these children should be to enhance school performance as well as reducing hyperactive behavior, the two should be independently and objectively monitored. Since stimulant medications fail to improve the academic performance of most of these children, additional educational assistance must be provided. [589]

In 1999 the *Canadian Journal of Psychiatry* published a five-year review on the psychotic effects of stimulants on children diagnosed with ADHD. Of the 192 children in the study 98 received treatment with stimulants, and were followed for an average period of a year and nine months. Nine children developed psychotic symptoms that included: Visual hallucinations, Bizarre behaviour, Paranoia, Visual hallucinations, Auditory hallucinations; Aggressive, agitated behaviour, Unrealistic fear of being harmed by other children, Depression, Suicidal behaviour, Decreased sleep, Increased energy, and Severe depression. *Most* of the children and adolescents improved upon removal of the MPH (methylphenidate –Ritalin).[590]

Breggin, in reviewing the above study, made the comment that the children who did not recover were probably driven into chronic psychosis by the medications. Breggin claims that much of the information you will find in his work will not be found in many other places due to the selective reporting of research. His views on this selective reporting are shared by numerous others. In April 2004 the *Lancet,* published an editorial on this topic and had this to say:

> It is hard to imagine the anguish experienced by the parents, relatives, and friends of a child who has taken his or her own life. That such an event could be precipitated by a supposedly beneficial drug is a catastrophe. The idea of that drug's use being based on the selective reporting of favourable research should be unimaginable. In this week's issue of *The Lancet* (p 1341), however, a meta-analysis by Craig Whittington and colleagues suggests that this is what has been happening for research into the use of antidepressants in childhood. Their results illustrate an abuse of the trust patients place in their physicians. They also represent an abuse of the trust placed by trial volunteers in the medical and pharmaceutical establishments. [591]

The article ends with the following comments that address the very real issues that we are facing:

ALTERNATIVE THINKING—THREAT TO PROFITS

People around the world understand the desire to achieve success and to work in a profitable environment. They will not, however, tolerate the notion that in biomedical research this could be at the expense of their children's lives.

Breggin gives his views on the problem with the action of stimulants on the brain:

Stimulant drugs "rev up," or overactivate, at least three neurotransmitters or chemical messengers—dopamine, norepinephrine, and serotonin. These neurotransmitter networks reach into every nook and cranny of the brain, affecting most of its functions. Disrupting any of these large, complex pathways would be sufficient to endanger the proper function, growth, and development of a child's brain; disrupting all three at once is a prescription for disaster.

When stimulants cause neurotransmitter systems to become overactive, the systems try to compensate by shutting down. The brain tries to reduce the impact of the overactivity in its neurotransmitter system. When the drugs are removed, these compensatory mechanisms cause rebound and withdrawal problems, and can lead to abuse in children.

The brain is injured directly by the toxic effects of the drugs and indirectly by the brain's own attempts to compensate for the toxicity. Animal experiments indicate that both the direct and indirect effects can become persistent and even permanent.[592]

He goes on to relate how commonly used stimulants have been found to cause structural abnormalities in the brains of animals—stimulants taken for only five days a week for five weeks. He goes on to cite a study where the frontal lobes became irreversibly deformed with amphetamine. [593] These studies have not just been repeated, and confirmed; more recent studies from the Research Institute of Neurosciences *Vrije* Universiteit, Department of Pharmacology, Medical Faculty, Free University, Amsterdam, have revealed that *a single dose* of an amphetamine was sufficient to induce long-term behavioural, neuroendocrine and neurochemical sensitization in rats. [594] Breggin found that some of the brain changes lasted from a few months to two years, depending on the level of exposure. In some of the more severe cases, damage was permanent. He also cites animal research that documents severe brain damage, from the use of methamphetamine. Damage to the dopaminergic cells in the substantia nigra after 5-8 days treatment with methamphetamine caused 40-50 percent cell death. [595]

On top of the damage that was found, there is also disturbing evidence of brain atrophy in children, as well as stunted growth due to the drug treatment. An experienced researcher from Duke University Medical Center, Dr Everett Ellingwood, professor of psychiatry and pharmacology, expressed concern over the levels of drugs given to children that have been shown to cause persistent damage in animals: "Drug levels in children on a mg/kg basis are sometimes as high as those reported to produce chronic CNS [central nervous system] changes in animal studies."[596]

According to the Centers for Disease Control (CDC), one in every twenty-three American school children were taking stimulants for ADHD in 2007. This phenomenal situation in the USA means that American children *are being prescribed three times the amount of the rest of the world's children combined.* In the UK, the Medicines and Healthcare Regulatory Agency (MHRA) essentially banned the use of SSRIs, with the exception of fluoxetine, for use in people under the age of eighteen. [597] Australian scientists reviewed all the available data on SSRIs and concluded:

The trials consistently found large improvements in placebo groups, with statistically significant additional benefits for active drug on some measures only. These results make a major benefit from newer antidepressants unlikely...Randomised controlled trials usually underestimate the serious adverse effects of drugs. The fact that serious adverse effects with newer antidepressants are common enough to be detected in randomised controlled trials raises serious concerns about their potential for harm. The magnitude of benefit is unlikely to be sufficient to justify risking those harms, so confidently recommending these drugs as a treatment option, let alone as first line treatment, would be inappropriate.

We are concerned that biased reporting and overconfident recommendations in treatment guidelines may mislead doctors, patients, and families. Many will undervalue non-drug treatments that are probably both safer and more effective. Accurate trial reports are a foundation of good medical care. It is vital that authors, reviewers, and editors ensure that published interpretations of data are more reasonable and balanced than is the case in the industry dominated literature on childhood antidepressants. This is particularly true in the light of the increasing reliance on online abstracts by doctors who lack the time or the skills for detailed analysis of complete trial reports. [598]

A disturbing further development that is occurring in North America is the rise in the numbers of children diagnosed with Bipolar disorder. Between 1996 and 2004, the number of bipolar children discharged from hospitals rose five-fold. The numbers of children with ADHD that go on to develop psychotic symptoms, as found by Canadian psychiatrists in 1999, was almost 10%, a substantial number whom were less than ten years old. [599] These symptoms are often diagnosed as bipolar disorder—which is worrying when Harvard University researchers found that 25% of children treated for depression convert to bipolar within four years.[600] A Washington study found that 50% of their control group of prepubertal children treated for depression (with drugs), converted to bipolar disorder within ten years.[601] Robert Whitaker the author of *Anatomy of an Epidemic—Magic Bullets, Psychiatric Drugs, and the Astonishing Rise of Mental Illness in America*, does an excellent appraisal of the epidemic of mental illness in the USA. He estimates that if 2 million children are treated with SSRIs for depression, this would create between 500,000 and a million new cases of bipolar disorder. He further estimates that treating 3.5 million children with stimulants for ADHD would create approximately 400,000 additional cases of bipolar disorder! [602]

That these figures are appalling is not in question; they do however reflect what is being experienced, predominantly in the USA. It could be argued that this is due to the way drugs are marketed in the US, and the way ADHD is 'sold' in the USA. This is however a direct reflection on how the use of drugs rather than basic nutrition or other therapeutic or social interventions has produced unseen consequences that will no doubt have implications for decades to come.

B_{12} the Hidden Epidemic

Following is a list of symptoms that are frequently presented to physicians:

Predominantly mental ones, such as irritability, apathy, sleepiness, depression, memory loss, dementia, hallucinations, violent behaviour, autistic behaviour, developmental delay in children.

Neurological ones such as; diminished sense of touch temperature or pain, weakness (of legs and arms), tingling and numbness of legs and arms, tremors, spasticity of muscles, incontinence, paralysis, impotence, vision changes (decreased vision), atrophy of the optic nerve, and neuritis.

Vascular ones, such as strokes, congestive heart failure, palpitations, pulmonary embolism, coronary artery disease, myocardial infarction (heart attack), deep vein thrombosis (blood clot to the arm or legs), transient ischemic attacks (TIAs or "mini strokes").

And other symptoms, such as shortness of breath, generalized weakness, chronic fatigue, diarrhoea, constipation, loss of appetite, increased susceptibility to infection, balance problems and in new born children—failure to thrive.

This is a huge variety of symptoms and many may be presented together. What they all do indicate, however, is a deficiency of vitamin B_{12}. Unfortunately, although the above list is by no means exhaustive, not all physicians that are aware that vitamin B_{12} deficiency can be what's behind them. Adequate levels of B_{12} are essential to our health. Its lack causes homocysteine levels to rise and accelerate not only the problems already mentioned, but also progress of heart disease and strokes. The Hcy test, for homocysteine levels in our blood serum, is one of the ways to help diagnose B_{12} deficiency. One of the more serious effects of deficiency is nerve damage, due to demyelination. This is where the soft fatty tissue protecting the nerve is destroyed, much as with Multiple Sclerosis (MS). In fact there is a considerable body of opinion amongst doctors who believe that as many as 10% of MS sufferers are not in fact suffering from MS at all, but simply B_{12} deficiency. This is good news for those who are lucky enough to have a doctor who will check for it, if caught early and treated properly, can remove all the symptoms. However, for those unlucky enough to have a doctor who is unaware that B_{12} deficiency can appear with the same symptoms as MS the damage can be irreparable.

In this chapter we have reviewed the creation of the medical industry, and how the way it was set up has led to its emphasis on a pharmacological approach to illness. We have documented what can only be seen as a deliberate policy by the pharmaceutical industry to ignore or downplay the importance of good nutrition basis to all of us, as well as the beneficial effects of good nutrition in preventing certain mental illnesses—in people of all ages.

We have also touched on the subject of the drug treatment of children for ADHD and depression, and for people who would like more detail on this, I would recommend *The ADHD Fraud: How Psychiatry Makes "Patients" of Normal Children* by DR Fred Baughman Jr., a child neurologist, and a fellow of the academy of Neurology. [603]

As regards the profession of psychiatry, numerous books explore this subject. I would particularly recommend *Unhinged- The Trouble with Psychiatry—A Doctor's Revelations about a Profession in Crisis. By D*r Carlat M.D., a Harvard trained psychiatrist.[604]

Many people would argue that it is greed, self-interest and the profit motive that created this situation we currently find ourselves in. This is particularly exhibited in the American experience with regards to ADHD and subsequent Bipolar epidemic in children and adults. The consequences of this are far-reaching, and will affect generations to come.

According to Philippe Granjean, Adjunct Professor of Environmental Health at Harvard School of Public Health, and Philip Landrigan, Professor of the Children's

ALTERNATIVE THINKING—THREAT TO PROFITS

Environmental Health Center, Mount Sinai School of Medicine, disorders of neurobehavioural development affect 10 -15% of all births. And this is only part of what they refer to as 'The global, silent pandemic of neurodevelopmental toxicity'. They note that there are 201 chemicals have been reported to cause injury to the nervous system in adults, and more than 1000 chemicals have been reported to be neurotoxic in animals. They are concerned about the levels of chemicals that are found in both umbilical cord samples and mother's milk.

One of their concerns is that, in many cases, exposure to certain toxic chemicals can be hard to identify—and the effects may not become apparent until a long time after exposure. They cite the example of lead toxicity causing decreases in brain volume, reduced school performance, reduced IQ, and delinquent behaviour later in life. We now know that there is no safe level of exposure to lead. They point out that the murder rate in the USA fell sharply after the removal of lead from petrol. Children are particularly vulnerable, because their systems are smaller and immature, and are still developing. Foetal exposure can be even more problematic. They say that maternal alcohol consumption during pregnancy, even in very small quantities, has been linked to a range of neurobehavioural problems, such as reduced IQ, sensory problems, seizures, impaired executive function, social judgement and other neurological signs.

Professor Grandjean refers to a number of chemicals, including: pesticides, phthalates, Bisphenol A, methylmercury, and others that have been found to neurotoxic. He cautions:

> Our very great concern is that children worldwide are being exposed to unrecognised toxic chemicals that are silently eroding intelligence, disrupting behaviours, truncating future achievements, and damaging societies, perhaps most seriously in developing countries. A new framework of action is needed.

So—are we simply medicating children who are simply unable to function adequately because they have been damaged by toxins in the environment and food supply? And then later in life when underlying problems surface and affect their behaviour in more serious ways, medicate further?

The costs to society of environmental pollution are significant. As well as the human cost in terms of suffering, we propose to discuss the financial implications of government policy on health, and the machinations of the pharmaceutical and chemical industries. But for now let's now take a look at the financial implications of it all, from a larger perspective.

Chapter 13
The Road to Bankruptcy

Although it is the money system which is to be accused of dishonesty, those who use and depend upon a dishonest system, knowing that system to be dishonest, cannot themselves be regarded as honest men.

Vincent C. Vickers, Director of the Bank of England (1910-1919)

I see in the near future a crisis approaching that unnerves me and cause me to tremble for safety of my country; corporations have been enthroned, an era of corruption in High Places will follow, and the Money Power of the country will endeavor to prolong its reign by working upon the prejudices of the People, until the wealth is aggregated in a few hands, and the Republic destroyed.

Abraham Lincoln, letter to Col. William F. Elkins, Nov. 21, 1864.

The more you look at the circumstances that are affecting the health of people, the closer you get to the reasons that unite much of the problem. In the next chapters I hope to reveal what I believe to be the underlying causes behind many of the problems affecting us at this juncture in time.

One of the biggest pressures faced by many people throughout the world is their inability to purchase adequate nourishing food. Quite simply, this is because they don't have enough money. And why is that? It's because in every country in the world we are saddled with debt—at a national level, a business level, and a personal level—on an unprecedented scale.

UNHEALTHY BETRAYAL

The economic circumstances we find ourselves in have a huge impact at every level of society. Our current economic system is based on continuing debt creation to increase the levels of lending—and this, clearly, is unsustainable.

Debt levels in the USA have risen astronomically; in 2004 the debt of the US government passed $7.6 trillion, which is more than three times the level of all the Third World countries combined. By April 2005, the ratio of US debt, both public and private, had risen to more than 300 percent of gross domestic product (GDP). [605] Currently as I write this the European Union is in turmoil over the collapse of the Greek economy and the Spanish banking system's insolvency.

So how did we get ourselves into this position, and what can we do about it? Our current financial difficulties began with decisions made long ago—so let's take a look at it all. Money is simply a means of exchange. In earlier times it took different formats. In England, for centuries, we used the tally system which originated under King Henry I, son of William the Conqueror. Tallies were pieces of wood that were marked in particular ways to record transactions, such as paying dues to the crown. Taxes were collected as goods produced on the land; once collected, all goods were 'tallied' up and elaborate marks were recorded on a piece of wood which was then broken into two halves, one half kept by the crown and the other by the payee. They were impossible to forge as no two pieces of wood had the same markings, and two tallies from the same transaction would fit perfectly together, as no two pieces of wood break the same way. Henry VIII insisted that all his people should use them, and they became a credible money exchange unit. They made up the bulk of the money supply in the Middle Ages, and by the end of the seventeenth century 14 million pounds worth were in circulation. They were used for more than five centuries before the use of gold and silver coins took over. [606]

The use of precious metals, though, had many disadvantages; it was relatively scarce, it was heavy to carry in large quantities, and there was a greater risk of being robbed. So the goldsmiths saw an opportunity, and perhaps without realizing it-gave birth to the banking system. They stored gold on their shelves, for which each customer was given a receipt—and this is where the problems began. The people who had deposited gold quickly found it was easier to pay others with promissory notes than with physical gold—and the notes effectively traded as currency. These promissory notes were traded as money as we do today with our paper money and bank checks. The goldsmith also practiced usury, which meant that they charged interest on their loans. The problems with this system developed when they realised that very few people actually redeemed their gold, so successful and convenient were the notes. They found that they only needed to keep a fraction of the gold as a reserve for each client so they lent out gold that did not actually exist as promissory notes which were effectively traded as currency. So since not many depositors were redeeming their physical gold, it wasn't long before the goldsmiths realized they could issue more promissory notes, as loans, without them being backed by physical gold. The benefit to them was that they could charge interest on these 'loans'. Inevitably, some of them became reckless, and lent out many times their holdings (there being no regulations to restrain them). So, eventually, the ensuing blatant exhibitionism of their wealth became their undoing. When people went to withdraw their gold, most of them found that the cupboards were bare. Goldsmiths found themselves saddled with a horrific reputation for charging high levels of interest on gold that did not actually exist!

Nevertheless, the goldsmiths laid the foundations of our modern fractional reserve banking system—the fraction kept as a reserve, being in theory, mandated by government regulation. A system whereby bankers only had to hold around 7% of the amount they were lending in reserves of gold was already underway—and this effectively created money out of nothing. Before the UK currency ceased to be backed by gold, the fraction of it considered necessary to be backed by gold, to maintain confidence in the currency, was 10%. What many of us do not realise is that current banking practice still creates money out of nothing—and charges interest for the privilege.

Debt Creation and Banking

It is important to understand this point, so I'll quote from Rothbard's, *The Mystery of Banking:*

> *The deposit banker has become a loan banker;* the difference is he is not taking his own savings or borrowing in order to lend to consumers or investors. Instead he is taking someone else's money and lending it out *at the same time* that the depositor thinks his money is still available to him to redeem....At the same time, the original depositor thinks his receipts are represented by money available at any time he wishes to cash them in. [607]

If you go to a bank and ask for a loan and they agree to it, you sign a piece of paper, they punch away at a keyboard and, hey presto, you have £10,000. This money was created out of nothing other than your agreement to pay back the amount you borrowed, plus interest. You could now take this 'money' and pay for your new kitchen. The kitchen supplier could deposit this check in his own bank, where it would be registered as a deposit. That bank now has money to create further loans against. Assuming they keep a 10% fractional reserve (nowadays it's nearer 3%), they can then lend £9,000 to a new client. Suppose this new client spends it on home improvements, his or her builder will then deposit this £9,000 into their own bank—which can then lend out a further £8,100 and so on, each bank keeping just 10% as a reserve. This will allow further loans amounting to around £90,000. So your initial £10,000 loan has enabled the banks to create a further £100,000, all out of nothing. Most people find this hard to believe, but the most important thing to understand is that for each loan there is interest charged—and that is for the whole £100,000. This model is commonly referred to as the 'multiplier model' and is considered outdated and inappropriate for modern banking. The more modern approach is called the 'endogenous money theory' and the fundamental difference is due to the fact that in modern banking, it is through the process of lending that banks create deposits and increase the money supply—they are not tied to cash supplied by the general public or deposits, if there is a shortfall between the money they lend out they can seek funds from other banks or the central bank in the short-term.[608]

Some economists argue that banks actually don't actually create money, but create credit. This is very apparent when a bank fails, and its creditors find that the bank actually has no 'money'—only accounts and liabilities. If you deposit cash with a bank it becomes the property of the bank, it is entered as an asset on the bank's balance sheet the same as loans are listed as assets. In return you acquire a liability on the bank; that obliges the bank to make transfer payments on your behalf up to the amount of the deposit. Due to the fact that money is only created by bank lending—when loans are paid off, the money supply shrinks accordingly. So in a downturn, people shedding their debt to more prudent levels actually exacerbate the problem, by effectively shrinking the money supply which inevitably leads to a recession. [609]

However, let's return to the time of the goldsmiths to try and make things a little clearer. Having been widely discredited and having been evicted from most European cities the money lenders found haven in Holland. Henry VIII relaxed the usury laws somewhat after the break with the Catholic Church which was still against usury. Usury in this context refers to the principal of charging interest for a loan *without any liability*. For example if a farmer wished to borrow money to buy seed, which he does, and his subsequent harvest fails leaving him unable to repay the debt, the debt would have to be written off, this is accepting the shared risk. In the practice of usury, there is no shared liability, no shared risk; the land could be taken from the farmer for failure to pay the debt. The Jewish faith was less critical of usury which led to a significant number of Jewish people becoming bankers and a consequential anti-Semitism followed as the result.

As regards to usury, in Athens around 600 BC the class of small farmers was disappearing, and land was being concentrated into the hands of the oligarchy. Following the introduction of money, small farmers had found things were quite satisfactory when money was cheap, even though commodities dear. But, when the time came to repay the loan, they were shocked to find that commodities were cheap and money was dear. Usurious rates of interest, poor weather and smaller than expected harvests could be enough to bring foreclosure on small farms—and even put some farmers into slavery. Solon, the great Greek reformer, increased the monetary supply, and gave land seized back to the farmers. He forbade export of agricultural products, other than olive oil, and introduced measures to support farmers. Many of his reforms achieved international recognition. The point of this story is simply to show that in Greece at least there was awareness of both the effect of usury, and a lack of money supply, and their harmful effect on the populace. Wealth became concentrated into the hands of the few, and investment in agriculture would decline. Money lenders much preferred to lend for dubious enterprises, where there was no risk to themselves, than they would to help farming or even general commerce. Does this experience ring bells today? It seems we are unable to learn from history. Zarlenga, in his book argues that the real story of money and banking has been deliberately hidden and obscured to hide the preposterous reality of modern banking.[610]

Ancient Knowledge Lost

It is worth backtracking even further into antiquity to discover how money evolved into what it is today. In Greece, in the time of Aristotle, they had already an advanced system of money, called Nomisma. Far from being a simple commodity-based money system, like using gold or silver by weight, Nomisma involved numbers (values) established by law. Since it was one of the easiest materials to mine, the Greeks used copper for coinage. Its value, however, was not linked to the value of the commodity on the open market, it was set much higher, given a legal value, and its supply restricted. This system worked very well and enabled Greek traders to exchange goods and to develop an economy which enabled Greece to flourish.

The Greeks were well aware of Sparta however, a country that had thrived for three centuries using coinage of iron, that also had a legal value and a restricted supply—and where gold and silver were both outlawed. The Greeks had witnessed the fall of Sparta, which abandoned its numisma system, about 415 BC, following campaigns of foreign conquest—which resulted in capturing large amounts of gold and silver. It became apparent that once they began to undertake naval expeditions outside their borders, that neither their iron currency nor the exchange of their crops for commodities which they lacked, would suffice their needs. This led to a degeneration of the use of their iron currency and gold and silver crept into use, mostly as a commodity form of money. Countries that were able to understand the fundamental differences between Nomisma and commodity-based monies were not restricted to the supply of the precious metals for their money supply; this problem was to plague the Europeans in later years. As with the lack of precious metal, over-supply would also cause grave problems to economic conditions, the currency would become debased and lose value, which would undermine trade. The Nomisma system was much more stable, was restricted by law and was under the direct control of the government, and not private individuals. Under this system Greece—and others thrived. [611]

The Romans for example had their 'Numus' system, based on the Greek model, using copper coinage set at a higher value than the commodity value. Only as the Roman Empire degenerated did their currency become reduced to commodity money-no more than a crude form of barter. During this period the currency was continually debased, there were also wild fluctuations in the value and in prices generally, causing great financial instability. The study of money is instructive and gives a much better understanding of current monetary practice. For those who would like a fuller picture of such declines, I would recommend Steven Zarlenga's book, *The Lost Science of Money—The Mythology of Money—The Story of Power.* [612]

The European Experience

When Queen Mary (a Catholic) took to the throne of England, she tightened the laws on usury that had been relaxed by Henry VIII. This caused a serious contraction of the money supply which led to severe strife amongst the population. When Elizabeth 1 subsequently took to the throne, she determined neither to fall into the usury trap, nor to create the problems that Mary did. So she issued her own debt-free coinage, and issued a proclamation that it would be treason for anyone else to create any other coinage. This move was detested by the goldsmiths, and they worked incessantly to undermine it. Nevertheless the country thrived under the system, in combination with the tallies, neither of which created debt.

Things were to change however with the arrival of Puritanism and its champion, Oliver Cromwell, a key figure in the Civil War against Charles 1, a Catholic, supported by both the nobility and the Catholic Church. Into this conflict the moneylenders saw their opportunity and quickly offered to provide funds to Parliament to fund the Civil War on condition they be allowed back into the country and that they would have their loans guaranteed. This meant that the King would have to be permanently removed and his capture and execution was necessary to secure the loans.[613]

THE ROAD TO BANKRUPTCY

The money lenders consolidated their financial power and plunged Britain into a series of costly wars. War was a very profitable enterprise for them: they could fund both sides, obtain high interest rates and leave each country in debt for years to come. They took over a square mile in the centre of London which became known as the City, and became their financial base for further expansion. To this day it is not under the jurisdiction of the crown, and even has its own police force. Among other enterprises they conspired with their Dutch counterparts to fund the invasion of England by William of Orange who overthrew the Stuart king, James II.[614]

After he became king, William married James's daughter Mary, and they reigned together as William and Mary from 1689. It was not long before William was persuaded to enter into the conflict with Louis XIV of France. To finance this war, he borrowed 1.2 million pounds of gold from the money lenders, whose names were to be kept secret. The loan came with a number of important conditions that were to have repercussions that would affect not just England, but the global economy for centuries to come. The conditions included:

- A permanent loan would be issued on which interest was payable but the principal portion of the loan would not be repaid.
- The lenders were to be granted a charter to establish a Bank of England, which would issue bank notes that would circulate as the national paper currency.
- The Bank would create banknotes out of nothing, with only a fraction backed by gold.
- Bank notes created and lent to the government would be backed by government I.O.U.s, which would act as 'reserves' for additional loans to private businesses or individuals.
- Interest would be payable on the loan at 8 percent.
- The interest would be paid from direct taxes raised from the general population.

The Beginning of the National Debt and Income Tax

The charter further forbade private goldsmiths from storing gold or issuing receipts. They had to store their gold in the Bank of England vaults. This effectively gave the Bank a complete monopoly over the creation of money and the raising of income tax for the first time ever. The working public have never stopped paying income tax to this day. This was the beginning of the National Debt that has grown almost continuously to the mammoth levels it's at today. [615] Income tax was introduced from the same date. Within four years the debt had increased to 16 million pounds in 1698. By 1815 it had reached 885 million pounds. By 1963 it had ceased to be measured in millions it had reached the dizzy heights of £9 *billion!* By 1997 it had reached £ 780 billion. Today in the UK it stands at a staggering £1.65 Trillion! [616]

This problem with escalating debt is now a huge global problem, but we need to backtrack a little to understand why. However, the information we need is not so freely available. The banking industry, right from its inception, has involved secrecy, probably more than any other industry. It has been accused of being the main power behind governments, war and the impoverishment of humanity. But by the banking industry, what we really mean are the International Bankers, the Merchant bankers, the big players such as the Rothschilds, the banking dynasty founded by Mayer Amschel Rothschild and his five sons (Mullins omits the "c" and spells it Amshel, I use both spellings). I don't intend to get into this story in any big way; it has been well documented by others such as Eustace Mullins in his book *The Secrets of the Federal Reserve*. Some of this background, however, is worth repeating. Originally, his surname was Bauer but he changed it to Rothschild which was a translation of "Red Shield" an adaptation of the coat of arms of Frankfurt in Germany where Amschel set up a money lending business in his goldsmith's shop. He sent his five sons to the major cities of Europe, Jacob to Paris, Solomon to Vienna, and Nathan Mayer to London, whilst the eldest, Anselm Maier remained in the German headquarters. [617]

Knuth documents how the great financial crash in the USA in 1929 was instigated in part by a massive movement of money reserves (gold) out of America by the international bankers—and made this observation about the House of Rothschild:

> The fact that the House of Rothschild made its money in the great crashes of history and the great wars of history, the very periods when others lost their money, IS beyond question. [618]

Nathan Rothschild had previously visited the battlefield of Waterloo and decided that Napoleon would lose any battle there. So, although he was still in Germany at the time, when Napoleon embarked on his campaign, he made his way as fast as he could, bribing a sailor to take him to England for 2000 francs. The following morning he started selling stock and large amounts of securities (Consols) and so convinced everyone that England had lost to Napoleon. This resulted in massive selling by everyone else. As soon as the prices dropped sufficiently, his agents bought up the rock bottom securities in secret, and he gained nearly a million in sterling in a single day. By these actions he effectively won control of the Bank of England. It was said that the true winners of the war were not the allies but really Nathan Rothschild. [619] He is reputed to have built up a fortune of over £50 million, which at the time was vastly in excess of the entire money stock of Britain. The national debt at this time was £850 million (around 1810).

Nathan's father, Mayer Amschel, is reputed to have invited twelve other wealthy and influential men to combine their resources to create of a movement that would be able to control the world. He put forth a plan of action that has been documented by Carr. [620] As regards to the power of gold in influencing political outcomes, or creating financial disaster, he is reputed to have explained that it mattered not whether established governments were destroyed by external or internal foes—because the victor had, of necessity to ask the aid of capital which 'Is entirely in our hands'. He added that wars should be directed so that nations on both sides would be further in their debt. It has been documented by a number of authorities that the House of Rothschild became the primary force behind the Bank of England. It is also suggested that the merchant bankers who set up and controlled Europe, also by secret machinations, were instrumental in setting up the Federal Reserve in the USA. Again I am not going into this story in any depth, those who would like to know the story should refer to Mullins work *The Secrets of the Federal Reserve*. I will however give some background to how America got landed with the same debt-based system as Great Britain, and has ended up with unsustainable debts. Amshel Mayer Rothschild was not reticent about his influence; he is reputed to have said in 1838: "I care not what puppet is placed upon the throne of England to rule the Empire on which the sun never sets. The man who controls Britain's money supply controls the British Empire, and I control the British money supply."

The American Experience

There is no doubt that the merchant bankers could inflict serious consequences on any economy, either through the serious increase of debt obligations, by restricting the money supply, by refusing to lend, or by hoarding gold. There were times when the lack of gold alone caused massive problems. In America, for example, there were few natural gold reserves, and when the European Bankers restricted supplies to America, they caused deep unrest and hardship. Some colonies responded by issuing their own money, paper money. Massachusetts was the first local government to do this in 1691. This was debt-free money that did not require large debts to the central government. Other colonies followed suit, and this allowed a rapid increase in the development of the colonies, enabling businesses to grow and prosper. Benjamin Franklin was a real enthusiast for the new money independent of debt, and wrote a pamphlet called *A Modest Enquiry into the Nature and Necessity of a Paper-Currency* in 1729—which became a popular book. He advocated the use of a paper currency that was neither backed by gold, nor involved debt to private banks. As a printer himself, he helped by printing notes for use by the colonies. The provincial government offered loans at 5% and was able to survive without the raising of income tax until the French and Indian Wars in 1750. Not all the colonial currencies were so successful. Some could not be used for the payment of debt, and some could be used for public debts but not for private transactions. Generally, though, the currencies were well accepted. The merchant bankers, in contrast, were disturbed by their use and their independence from their own control.

In 1751, King George II enacted a ban on the issue of new paper money, while allowing existing issues to still be renewed. Benjamin Franklin went to London in 1764 to petition the King (now George III) to lift the ban. He described how the colonies had set up versatile paper currencies, fully supported by the local government that was very beneficial to the whole economy. But his appeal was vigorously opposed by the London bankers. Instead of easing the ban, Parliament responded by banning even the re-issue of existing currencies. They further demanded that the colonialists pay all future taxes to Britain in silver, gold, or notes drawn on the Bank of England. The result of going along with this was that the money supply became severely restricted, causing wide-spread poverty, unemployment, hunger and interest bearing debts.[621]

The colonialists put up with this situation for a while, but eventually resorted to issuing their own paper money. This was considered an act of rebellion by the European bankers and by Parliament. A historian of the time expresses how this provoked a Revolution, and led to the War of Independence:

> The creation and circulation of bills of credit by revolutionary assemblies,. coming as they did on the heels of the strenuous efforts made by the Crown to suppress paper money in America [were] acts of defiance so contemptuous and insulting to the Crown that forgiveness was thereafter impossible...There was but one course for the Crown to pursue and that was to suppress and punish these acts of rebellion...Thus the bills of credit of this era which ignorance and prejudice have attempted to belittle into mere instruments of a reckless financial policy were *really the standards of the Revolution. They were more than this: they were the Revolution itself!* [622]

The thirteen Colonies formed a governing body called the Continental Congress to coordinate the Revolution. Its first act was to issue a new currency, called the Continental. They succeeded in financing the war without raising taxes, and issued $200 million in script. Nevertheless, the new currency was undermined by significant forgeries, estimated by Thomas Jefferson at $200 million. It was generally believed that the majority of this was printed by the English Government, trying to undermine the Continental Congress.

By the end of the war there was much disillusionment with the currency, as it had fallen greatly in value. There was also the matter of debt, some $42 million, due to the fact that some of the financing of the war had been issued as promissory notes, which had fallen due. Treasury Secretary Hamilton proposed a new national bank that could issue new money, and further argued that it would more likely survive if the wealthy were allowed to invest in it. [623]

Not everyone was convinced by the idea of their currency being in private hands, Thomas Jefferson was not a supporter, and expressed his views, leaving no doubt where he stood:

> If the American people ever allow the banks to control the issuance of their currency, first by inflation and then by deflation, the banks and the corporations that will grow up around them will deprive the people of all property until their children will wake up homeless on the continent their fathers occupied. The issuing power of money should be taken from the banks and restored to Congress and the people to whom it belongs. I sincerely believe the banking institutions having the issuing power of money are more dangerous to liberty than standing armies. [624]

His warning is one of the many that came from people who were closest to the corridors of power. Within five years the government was in debt to the bank to the tune of $8.2 million—a sum that the bank had created out thin air, and which they were now receiving interest on. The government had sold its shares in the Bank, largely to British financiers—which resulted in the bank falling under foreign control.

The European bankers funded opposition to the War of Independence, the war of 1812, and the Civil War, for which they funded both sides. In all, this led to increased government debt, inflation, and the creation of a new bank to fund the debt. Jefferson was instrumental in the refusal of Congress to renew the charter of the first US Bank in 1811. When the bank was eventually liquidated, the extent of foreign ownership became clear, with 18,000 of the 25,000 shares owned mostly by English and Dutch bankers.[625]

The second bank fared little better. When its charter was due for renewal in 1832, Andrew Jackson, the seventh President of the United States (1829-1837), vetoed its charter renewal. He referred to the bank as a "hydra-headed monster, eating the flesh of the common man." In a speech recorded for posterity he expressed his revulsion for the bank in no uncertain terms:

> I have had men watching you for a long time and am convinced that you have used the funds of the bank to speculate in the breadstuffs of the country. When you won, you divided the profits amongst you, and when you lost, you charged it to the Bank. You tell me that if I take the deposits from the bank and annul its charter I shall ruin ten thousand families. That may be true, gentlemen, but that is your sin! Should I let you go on, you will ruin fifty-thousand families, and that would be my sin! You are a den of vipers and thieves, I have determined to rout you out and by the eternal, I will rout you out. [626]

John Adams one of the Founding Fathers, expressed his view how ignorant most people are about money:

> "All the perplexities, confusion and distress in America arises, not from the defects of the constitution or confederation, not from want of honour or virtue, so much as from downright ignorance of the nature of coin, credit and circulation."[627]

Probably one of the most important figures in America's history in relation to money, must be Abraham Lincoln, the 16th President of the United States, serving from March 1861 until his assassination in April 1865. He had to deal with treason, insurrection and national bankruptcy in the first week of his presidency. He had as an advisor, Henry Carey, viewed by some as one of the first American economists. Carey viewed England's "free trade" and "gold standard" policies as a form of economic warfare, twin financial weapons for its own purpose. Lincoln's Government produced their own currency, popularly called "Greenbacks". These were basically receipts acknowledging work done or goods delivered; they were backed by the value of labour rather than borrowed gold. The impetus for the creation of this money supply was initiated following the outbreak of hostilities leading to the Civil War and the need for funds to fight it. The Eastern banks had offered a loan of $150 million at extortionate interest rates of between 24-36%, which, Lincoln realised, would be impossible to pay off and would result in debt-slavery. According to Treasury figures, Lincoln's decision to use the Greenback route saved more than $4 billion in interest payments alone. [628]

THE ROAD TO BANKRUPTCY

Lincoln was against the idea of allowing private banking interests to control the country's money supply right up to his assassination in April 1865. His views, too neglected today, are nevertheless preserved for posterity:

> The Government should create, issue and circulate all the currency and credits needed to satisfy the spending power of the government and the buying power of consumers. By the adoption of these principals the taxpayers will be saved immense sums of interest.
> The privilege of creating and issuing money is not only the supreme prerogative of government, it is the government's greatest creative opportunity. – Abraham Lincoln[629]

The trouble, though, was that Lincoln's management of the American economy was seriously upsetting the plans of the European Merchant bankers. The views of Otto Von Bismarck, Chancellor of Germany express the situation very clearly:

> I know with absolute certainty, that the division of the United States into federations of equal force was decided long before the Civil War by the high financial powers of Europe. These bankers were afraid that the United States, if they remained in one block and as one nation, would attain economic and financial independence, which would upset their financial domination over Europe and the world. Of course, in the "inner circle" of finance, the voice of the Rothschilds prevailed. They saw an opportunity for prodigious booty if they could substitute two feeble democracies, burdened with debt to the financiers,...in place of a vigorous Republic sufficient unto herself. Therefore they sent emissaries into the field to exploit the question of slavery and to drive a wedge between the two parts of the Union.... The rupture between the North and South became inevitable; the masters of European finance employed all of their forces to bring it about and to turn it to their advantage. -Otto Von Bismarck.[630]

Lincoln's issuance of the Greenbacks, had not just been provoked by the enormous interest that the US government were being asked to pay. The government had already had to introduce the first ever tax on income in American history, to pay off the considerable debts accrued during the Civil War. When it was introduced again in 1894, it was challenged in the Supreme Court and declared unconstitutional. However, following the financial panic of 1907, the ever increasing debt burden and high interest payments, the right of Congress to collect income taxes was introduced by the Sixteenth Amendment in 1913. Earnings above $3,000 were taxed from 1-7%. By 1916 this had more than doubled to 15%, by 1917 it was hiked to a staggering 67% and in 1918 raised even higher to 77%. No wonder bankers love war—there is no faster way to raise a country's debt![631]

UNHEALTHY BETRAYAL

One wonderful quote that I believe speaks volumes about the threat of Lincoln's debt-free Greenbacks is captured by a circular attributed to the London Times (1865):

"If this mischievous financial policy, which has its origin in North America, shall become indurated down to a fixture, then that Government will furnish its own money without cost. It will pay off its debts and be without debt. It will have all the money necessary to carry on its commerce. It will become prosperous beyond precedent in the history of the civilized governments world. The brains and wealth of all countries will go to North America. That government must be destroyed or it will destroy every monarchy on the globe."

Just before the assassination of Lincoln, the National Banking Acts were passed in 1863 and 1864, and laid the foundation for much of the banking industry we have today. A lot of the detail of these Acts, however, was missed by a great number of people. Treasury Secretary Chase, who recommended the Acts to Congress, believes he was coerced into allowing their passage by powerful banking interests. When the realisation of the full implications hit home, he lamented his action:

My agency in procuring the passage of the National Bank Act was the greatest financial mistake of my life. It has built up a monopoly that affects every interest in the country. It should be repealed. But before this can be accomplished, the people will be arrayed on one side and the banks on the other in a contest such as we have never seen in this country. [632]

Eventually the bankers prevailed and by the turn of the century the use of the greenback had faded into oblivion. The bankers next major coup was to get the legislation for their new Central Bank passed which they achieved just before Christmas, December 23, 1913, when many Congressmen had already left to spend time with their families.

The foundation for the set-up of the Federal Reserve was concocted in secret by a group of bankers, including Frank Vanderlip, president of the National City Bank of New York, Benjamin Strong from J P Morgan, and Paul Warburg from Kuhn, Loeb and Company. They were led by Senator Nelson Aldrich, head of the National Monetary Commission. They met in November, 1910 on Jekyll Island, and for over nine days formulated a plan for a new Central Bank. They decided the name was crucial, and came up with: the Federal Reserve. This name functioned in many ways; it gave the impression that it was truly Federal, instead of being seen as just a private bank, people would see it as a government owned institution. To this day most people do not know that the Federal Reserve is a privately owned bank whose profits benefit its shareholders. The name also suggests that the bank has reserves, which lends a sense of confidence to it. [633]

That confidence is misplaced. Congressman Wright Patman, chairman of the United States House Committee on Banking and Currency (1965–75), describes in his book, *The Primer of Money,* what happened when his visited the Federal Reserve and asked to see the 'reserves.' He was shown some bonds and when asked to see the cash reserves, was simply shown a ledger and some blank checks. He commented "The cash in truth does not exist and has never existed. What we call 'cash reserves' are simply bookkeeping credits entered upon ledgers of the Federal Reserve Bank. The credits are created by the Federal Reserve and then passed along through the banking system."[634]

For an excellent introduction to the story of the Federal Reserve I recommend Eustace Mullins' book *The Secrets of the Federal Reserve,* in it, Mullins attempts to dispel many of the myths around its existence, and makes the following comment regarding its ability to create vast sums of money out of nowhere for the government or for business and also to charge interest on the money it has created—and lent:

> This is the most incredible part of the Federal Reserve operation and one which is difficult for anyone to understand. How can any American citizen grasp the concept that there are people in this country who have the power to make an entry in a ledger that the government of the United States now owes them one billion dollars, and to collect the principal and interest on this "loan"?

Modern Banking Practice and the Growth of Debt

Most people are unaware of the nature of the banking industry and the role of Central Banks. No doubt what has been said in this chapter will come as a surprise to many. So let's just look into it all a little more deeply. As I mentioned previously you don't need a degree in economics to understand the basic mechanism of the banking industry, or Central Banks. Nor do you need a degree in economics to realise that you are being taken for a ride. Part of the problem is the secrecy involved, and the intentional obfuscation of the truth. Here's how a world-famous economist, Kenneth Galbraith puts it; "The study of money, above all other fields in economics, is one in which complexity is used to disguise or to evade truth, not to reveal it."

It is impossible to overemphasize how important it is for the general population of every country to understand the basics of the banking system, how the bankers create money out of nothing—and charge interest for the privilege. Debt is the basis of the banking system. The only way the banking system can increase lending is to increase debt. Currently, estimates put total American debt, as of 2008 at $53 trillion. One thing that's absolutely certain is that it's much more today and will be much more tomorrow. That it has created an unstable and uncertain future is beyond question. There have been many people in the past trying to draw attention to this issue, but most criticisms have had little exposure. Here are the views of an inside man, Robert H Hemphill, Credit Manager of the Federal Reserve Bank of Atlanta, Georgia, in 1935:

"We are absolutely without a permanent money system... It is the most important subject intelligent persons can reflect upon. It is so important that our present civilisation may collapse unless it becomes widely understood and the defects remedied very soon."

Most of us have been kept in the dark for a long time, but it is no longer possible to keep us in ignorance forever. Many people may find some of this information hard to believe—a view aptly expressed by Reginald McKenna, past Chairman of the Board, Midland Bank, UK Home Secretary and Chancellor of the Exchequer (up until 1916):

"I am afraid that the ordinary citizen will not like to be told that banks can and do create money... and they who control the credit of the nation direct the policy of governments and hold in the hollow of their hands the destiny of their people." [635]

We are not alone in our ignorance. There are few politicians who truly understand that banks create money out of nothing. On September 30, 1941 Congressman Wright Patman, at a hearing before the House Committee on Banking and Currency, interviewed the Chairman and Governor of the Federal Reserve, Marriner Eccles to get a better understanding of the Federal Reserve. He asked the following:

"How did you get the money to buy those two billion dollars worth of Government securities in 1933?
ECCLES: We created it.
MR PATMAN: Out of What?
ECCLES: Out of the right to issue credit money.
MR PATMAN: And there is nothing behind it, is there, except our Government's Credit?
ECCLES: That is what our money system is. If there were no debts in our money system, there wouldn't be any money."

Governor Eccles was further interviewed on June 17, 1942 by Mr Dewey:

THE ROAD TO BANKRUPTCY

ECCLES: "I mean the Federal Reserve, when it carries out an open market operation, that is, if it purchases Government securities in open market, it puts new money into the hands of the banks which creates idle deposits.

DEWEY: There are no excess reserves to use for this purpose?

ECCLES: Whenever the Federal Reserve System buys Government securities in the open market, or buys them direct from the treasury, either one that is what it does.

DEWEY: What are you going to use to buy them with? You are going to create credit?

ECCLES: That is all we have ever done. That is the way the Federal Reserve System creates money. It is a bank of "issue." [636]

So let us re-cap what we now understand about how the banks create money from debt, both the commercial banks and the Central banks. When the Government wants more money, it increases borrowing, the Central Bank, in this case the Federal Reserve, 'creates' the money simply by typing into a computer. This type of lending has grown exponentially. If you were to see it on a graph, it would show as an ever steeper curve. This situation cannot go on forever and ever, just like building up a credit card bill, you cannot increase it beyond your ability to pay it back. Here's how it was expressed by Kenneth Boulding, himself an economist:

"Anyone who believes that exponential growth can go on forever in a finite world is either a madman or an economist."

There are few economists who have the ability to clearly explain the true implications of our debt-based economy more clearly than Michael Rowbotham in his landmark book *The Grip of Death- A Study of Modern Money, Debt Slavery and Destructive Economics*. The title is a direct reference to the medieval word 'mortgage' which literally translated as 'death-pledge' or 'death-grip.' Few people realise to what extent our debt-based financial system, by its very nature, continuously transfers wealth to the richer people and increases the debt burden of the lower income earners. Current-day mortgages are a classic example of this. In the UK for example, approximately 3 million houses carried a mortgage in 1963. By 1996 the number had risen to 11 million, or 45% of the housing stock. All mortgaged properties are legally owned by the banks or building societies until the entire mortgage/loan is paid off. From 1960 to 1996 the number of homes that were owned outright, with no loan or mortgage in the UK dropped from 51% to 35%. In the UK in 1960, the average amount outstanding on a mortgaged house was £990 which represented 1.1 times the average annual wage. By 1996 the average amount outstanding had leapt to £38,000, which was equivalent to twice the average annual wage. So when they say that outstanding mortgages increased from £3.5 billion in 1963 to £411 billion in 1996, what this is expressing is how much more in debt we are as a society.[637]

Rowbotham quotes from a speech by Lord Josiah Stamp, former director of the Bank of England in a public address he made in Westminster near the end of his illustrious career in 1937. He warned about the consequences of the banking industry in no uncertain terms:

> "The modern banking system manufactures money out of nothing. The process is perhaps the most astounding piece of sleight of hand that was ever invented. Banking was conceived in iniquity and born in sin. Bankers own the earth; take it away from them, but leave them with the power to create credit, and with the stroke of a pen they will create enough money to buy it back again... If you want to be slaves of the bankers and pay the costs of your own slavery, then let the banks create money." [638]

Rowbotham comments that the word "slavery" is a big word and might be construed as simply being used for literary effect. But he goes on to defend its use and adds the further qualification that "it is a term that is both justified and penetratingly accurate."

One of the most significant effects of our debt-based financial system is the forced economic growth that results. There is a continual push for more growth, continuous expansion, higher profits and increased competition. This can be put down to three factors, according to Rowbotham, intense competition for money; lack of purchasing power; and near-total wage dependency. Whilst it may seem that there are vast sums of money in circulation at any one time, the fact that it is almost entirely debt-based means that the majority of it is actually being returned to banks as interest payments, debt payments etc. If all our debts were to be paid off, there would be nothing left as our debts are larger than the money supply. Most people are desperate to keep their jobs particularly as things deteriorate. Competition for jobs is fierce. Alongside this is our falling ability to purchase what we need, a chronic lack of purchasing power.

The more debt-based money released into circulation, the higher is inflation. Inflation robs the poorer sections of society and favours the rich. If you own property or capital in an inflationary spiral the values increase. However, as is the case with domestic property, the majority of us do not gain, unless you have a property with no loan attached or a small loan. However it also makes the possibility of younger people purchasing a house increasingly difficult.

Although the main purpose of this book is to discuss the effect that big business has on the kinds of food we eat, the effect these foods have on our health, and the way we treat our illnesses, I have gone into this history of banking because banking practices today influence all those things.

I would argue that everything I have written in the earlier chapters of this book has been heavily influenced by the way our economy came to be based on runaway debt and the consequences of it.

The fact that private corporate banking has been able to enjoy a monopoly of money creation has led to far-reaching changes in the world financial system and global business in general. The massive expansion of banks has been one consequence of this monopoly. In 1960, the assets of the top four banks in the UK were Barclays at £2.5 billion, Midland Bank £2.0 billion and Lloyds Bank £1.8 billion which represented respectively 10%, 8% and 7% of gross domestic product (GDP) of the UK. By 2010 the top four banks were represented by: Royal Bank of Scotland with assets at £1,696 billion, Barclay's Group at £1,526 billion, HSBC Holdings group £1,463 billion and Lloyds Bank £1,027 billion. These represented respectively; 122%, 110%, 105% and 74%. This basically means that the top four banks have combined assets in excess of four times the entire gross national product of the UK. In the USA, the consolidation of banks follows the same pattern of growth. For example, Bank of America in 1960 had assets of $11.2 billion which represented 2.1 % of US GDP, by 2010, Bank of America's assets had leapt to $2,363.9 billion and represented 16.7% of GDP. Morgan Guarantee Trust had assets of $4.1 billion in 1960; currently J P Morgan has assets of $2,014 billion, representing 14.3 % of GDP. In 2010 Citygroup was capitalised with assets of $1,937.7 billion and Wells Fargo with $1,225.9 billion—reflecting 13.7% GDP and 8.7% GDP respectively. The American banking sector's comparison with the UK bank's percentage relationship of GDP reflects the huge difference in size of the two country's GDP, but nevertheless reveals how colossal the banks have become.[639]

Sir Mervyn King, the Governor of the Bank of England drew attention to this phenomenal expansion in a speech in October 2010:

> For almost a century after Bagehot wrote *Lombard Street*, the size of the banking sector in the UK, relative to GDP, was broadly stable at around 50%. But, over the past fifty years, bank balance sheets have grown so fast that today they are over five times annual GDP. The size of the US banking industry has grown from around 20% in Bagehot's time to around 100% of GDP today.

He further states that, aside from this phenomenal growth the degree the banks were leveraged had drastically affected their capital ratios:

> While banks' balance sheets have exploded, so have the risks associated with those balance sheets. But capital ratios have declined and leverage has risen. Immediately prior to the crisis, leverage in the banking system of the industrialised world had increased to astronomical levels. [640]

It should be obvious by now that the banking industry has made vast amounts of money purely by creating money out of nothing and charging interest on it. On top of that, since bank deregulation, they have been free to 'invest' this money. Where banking is concerned 'investing' mostly simply means 'gambling.'

Andrew Jackson and Ben Dyson have written a brilliant book called *Modernising Money—Why our Monetary System is Broken and How it Can Be Fixed*, in which they review our current banking system, and its roots—and provide a clearly detailed way of changing it to a non-debt-based system. Fundamental to the new system is exactly what Lincoln, Jefferson and many others realised would be a much fairer and much more beneficial system: that is to take away the ability of banks to create money and return it to the government—effectively return it to the people. The book is written from the perspective of the UK banking system, but the principals are the same for any economy. To illustrate the point, they show that in the five years running up to the financial collapse of 2008, UK banks created £2.9 trillion in lending to households and individuals (excluding businesses)—while during the same period government spending was just £2.1 trillion. If the government had created that £2.9 trillion instead, it could have paid off a significant proportion of government debt. So let's imagine they had, in fact, done that, that we are five years down the road and the government debt has been paid off. The next tranche of £2 trillion or so could be used to either reduce taxes or improve the level of services. The idea of government creating of money instead of the banks seems radical, but in their book, Jackson and Dyson clearly explain how this can be achieved without a huge change to current banking practice. Their book is well written and easy to understand—you don't need a degree in economics to follow what they are proposing. I intend to discuss the ramifications of debt-free money more in the last chapter. [641]

One of the problems with having money creation in the hands of private corporations, which is what our banks are, is that since their de-regulation their focus has been almost entirely on chasing short-term profits. Currently less than 10% of bank lending actually goes to support businesses that contribute to the gross national product (GDP). The other 90% is invested in speculative investments.

THE ROAD TO BANKRUPTCY

Yet this has occurred despite history being littered with examples of such over-exuberant lending leading to financial bubbles that cause havoc for us all. The sub-prime lending crash of 2008 caused financial chaos around the world.

Along with many others, Jackson and Dyson suggest that money creation should be in the hands of the government rather than private corporations, and that the private banks should be split into two, one which lends to the real economy (and distributes the money created by the Central Bank, while the other invests in speculative ventures).

Unlike money creation by private banks, money creation by the Central Bank would be debt-free. This is a fundamental difference that could change everything.

Investment Banking and Derivatives

Billionaire investor Warren Buffet refers to derivatives as "financial weapons of mass destruction". Derivatives are funded by mostly "phantom" money borrowed into existence from foreign banks. To illustrate the absurdity of it, JP Morgan Chase Bank, one of most dominant players in the derivative market, has derivatives approaching four times the entire Gross Domestic Product of America. Bank of America comes next with $14.9 trillion, followed by Citibank with $14.4 trillion. The top seven derivative banks hold 96% of the entire US banking system's notional derivative holdings. Ellen Hodgson Brown made the following foreboding comment about derivative banks: "If these banks suffer serious impairment of their derivatives holdings, *kiss the banking system goodbye.*" [642]

Some explanation of what a derivative is may be useful. There are many types of them, but all are basically contracts specifying certain conditions, dates etc., made between various parties. There are 'futures' for example, where you can bet on the price movement of commodities, foreign exchange derivatives where you can bet on currency movements, interest rate derivatives and a whole host of others *that you can bet on.*

One form of trading derivative know as short-selling has been called a form of fraud, because it defrauds companies and so in the end, all of us. Short sellers buy and sell stock they do not actually own. They do this to speculate on the price movements of stock, usually securities, by, in theory, 'borrowing' the stock from a third party, usually a broker. The idea is that if you can sell a security at a high price now, and buy it back at a later date when its price falls, there is a profit to be made. It is a form of transaction that has existed for centuries; some say it was an old Dutch trick invented by the Dutch Merchant Bankers in the early 1600s.

However the activity has been variously described as a fraud or a form of counterfeiting. I'll quote from a financial analyst, David Knight:

> Short selling is a form of counterfeiting. When a company is founded, a certain number of shares are created. The entire value of that company is represented by that fixed number of shares. When an investor buys some of those shares and leaves them registered in his broker's street name, his broker makes those same shares available to someone else to sell short. Once sold short there are *two investors owning the same shares of stock.*
>
> The price of stock shares are set by market forces, i.e., supply and demand. When there is a fixed supply of something the price adjusts until demand is met. But when supply is not fixed, as when something is counterfeited, supply will exceed demand and the price will fall. Price will continue to fall as long as supply continues to expand beyond demand. Furthermore, price decline is not a linear function of supply expansion. At some point, if supply continues to expand beyond demand, the "bottom will fall out of the market," and prices will plunge.[643]

In 1772 the London banking house of Neal, James, Fordyce and Down collapsed, precipitating a major crisis—which included the collapse of many Scottish banks, and further caused a massive liquidity crisis in the two major banking centres of London and Amsterdam. At the time the bank had been speculating by selling East India Company stock short on a huge scale.

A more recent example would be when George Soros sold short more than $10 billion worth of British Pounds on what became known as 'Black Wednesday'—on 16 September 1992—breaking the Bank of England. It forced the British Government to withdraw the Pound Sterling from the European Exchange Rate Mechanism (ERM). George Soros reputedly made over US $1 billion profit for his one day's activity. Short sellers were also partly blamed for the Wall Street crash of 1929 (in addition to the removal of gold already mentioned), the Asian currency crisis of 1997, and the financial crisis of 2008. The Securities and Exchange Commission announced termination of short-selling of 799 financial stocks, as well as action against 'naked short selling', as a result of that crisis.[644]

'Naked short selling' is supposedly illegal; it is where a sale is executed without the stock even being borrowed. However, before elaborating on the problems with this and other ramifications of our financial system, I feel it would be worth reviewing a comment from George Soros himself, the billionaire financier. In 1997 he said of the Asian financial crisis: "We sold short the Thai baht and the Malaysian ringgit early in 1997 with maturities ranging from six months to a year." He added as a footnote: "We entered into contracts to deliver at future dates Thai baht and Malaysian ringgit *that we did not currently hold*," (my emphasis).

Soros was accused by the Prime Minister Mahathir of Malaysia, of causing the crisis but Soros responded with the following explanation: "We were not sellers of the currency during or several months before the crisis; on the contrary, we were buyers when the currencies began to decline—we were purchasing ringgits to realize the profits on our earlier speculation (much too soon as it turned out)."

He also made some observations on the South Korean collapse; the economy was dominated by *chaebol* (conglomerates) that were highly leveraged. The average debt to equity ratio of the thirty largest *chaebol* was 388% in 1996. These companies represented approximately 35% of Korea's industrial production. Some of the *chaebol* debt levels reached between 600 -700%! The interest coverage of the thirty largest *chaebol* was 1.3 times in 1996 and 0.94 times in 1997—which meant that the interest charges were not covered by earnings. As part of their industrial policy, Korean banks had extended easy credit to the *chaebol,* but when these loans became nonperforming, the banks borrowed even more money from abroad and invested it in 'high-risk instruments' in countries like Indonesia, Russia, Ukraine and Brazil. This, Soros believes, was an important factor in the Korean crisis. [645]

By now you can appreciate that the hazards of derivatives and short-selling have serious ramifications, not just on businesses but on countries also. 95% of short sales are undertaken by broker-dealers and market makers. Market makers are generally associated with banking investment operations, whereas the broker-dealer is the person who actually buys and sells stock for other people. If you buy some stock and leave it with a broker, he can use it for making 'shorts'. What is interesting is that when he uses the stock for making shorts, at this point the stock is owned by two people, both you and the broker, which is of course a ludicrous situation. It's effectively the same as the banks creating money out of nothing. When millions of shares are "sold", without ever being in the possession of the real owners, these 'phantom sales' can drive down the price of stock— in a way that bears no resemblance to the financial soundness of the company at all but the end result can be a collapse of the share price which has serious ramifications for the shareholders, and for the company itself.

What makes this situation even more problematic is that there are huge companies called Hedge Funds that are set up just to exploit this market. Whilst there have been movements to try and curb some of the worst excesses their activities cause in the market, more than 8,000 of the 9,800 operating worldwide have registered their operations in the Cayman Islands, where regulation is extremely lax. By 2006, the Bank for International Settlements (BIS) revealed that the volume of the "notional value" of derivative trades had reached $370 trillion, and by December 2007 had reached the unbelievable figure of $681 trillion. Just to give this some perspective, the entire GDP of the world was only $66 trillion.

Following the turmoil of the Asian crisis, and George Soros's attacks on both the UK currency and, later, the Italian currency, the Committee on Banking, Finance and Urban Affairs, of the U.S. House of Representatives held a series of meetings to see what action needed to be taken. The following testimony was submitted by Christopher White, contributing editor of Executive Intelligence Review [EIR] and Richard Freeman, of EIR's economics desk, in 1994:

> The derivatives market, in which there are $16 trillion in derivatives holdings held by commercial banks and financial institutions in the United States, with an annual turnover trading volume of $300 trillion, is the greatest bubble in history. It dwarfs the Mississippi Bubble in France and the South Sea Island bubble in England. This bubble, like a cancer, has penetrated and taken over the entirety of our banking and credit system; there is no major commercial bank, investment bank, mutual fund, etc. that is not dependent on derivatives for its existence. These derivatives suck the life's blood out of our economy. Our farms, our factories, our nation's infrastructure, our living standards are being sucked dry to pay off interest payments, dividend yields as well as other earnings on the bubble.
>
> It is time that Congress, through its appropriate committees, begins to discuss the question of how our national monetary and financial affairs might be reorganized such that national life can continue, after the collapse of the biggest financial bubble in human history has run its course.
>
> This committee is correct to highlight the activities of the hedge funds. They engage in the most wildly speculative behavior. Hedge funds are, for the most part, offshore, unregulated gambling casinos, relying on mountains of leverage..... Hedge funds work on anywhere from 5 to 1, up to 50 to 1 leverage. That means for every $1 billion of the hedge fund's own money which it has under management, it borrows from $5 to $50 billion. [646]

White and Freeman go on to explain how this 'leveraging' operation, by which they borrow vast sums of money from banks, to make their gambles, puts the whole banking system at risk. For example, the collapse of Long Term Capital Management (LTCM) which lost $4.6 billion in less than four months following the Russian financial crisis required financial intervention by the Federal Reserve Bank, before it was finally closed in early 2000.

In June 2006 The European Central Bank undertook a review of the world financial status and had this to say about the Hedge fund problem:

> The concern is that the pricing of CRT [credit risk transfers] products could prove vulnerable to an unexpected upturn in risk-free interest rates or an adverse turn of the credit cycle. Moreover, there has been growing unease about the relentless and exponential growth of CRT markets, coupled with the growing presence in these markets of hedge funds – institutions which tend to be rather opaque about their activities. These concerns have included uncertainties about the obscure way in which these markets have redistributed credit risks in the financial system and about the capability of these markets to function under stress, especially concerning the settlement of complex contractual arrangements. [647]

What is important to understand is that all this speculation, by banks, hedge funds, and most other financial funds, does not benefit ordinary people—because it is all based on debt. Rowbotham makes this clear by examining the money supply. For example, in 1997 the total money supply of the UK (M4) stood at £680 billion. This included all coins, notes and bank and building society deposits. M4 had been increasing steadily, from £14 billion in 1963, to £53 billion in 1975, reaching £205 billion in 1980, and £680 billion by 1997. However, of that £680 billion, only £25 billion had been created by the Treasury on behalf of the UK Government. So where had the other £655 billion come from? Well, if you have read this far, you won't be surprised to hear that it was 'created' by banks and building societies out of nothing. So this leaves just 3% of real money, with the rest created out of loans. Such figures, especially when added to those of the USA and other debt creation economies, can help us understand how banks like JP Morgan Chase can have derivatives that are close to four times the U.S. Gross Domestic Product.

Another insider, from the Bank of England, Vincent Vickers, Director of the Bank of England, and Deputy Lieutenant of the City of London, has had the fortune of seeing things from the inside. His views are worth taking a look at:

> The existing monetary standard is unworthy of our modern civilisation and a growing menace to the world.... I am qualified to tell the public that in my view, it is entirely mistaken if it believes that the monetary system of this country is normally managed by 'recognised monetary experts' working in accordance with the most scientific and up to date methods known to modern economists... The

Bank of England should no longer attempt to stifle the efforts of modern economists, nor persist in regarding all the 'Monetary Reformers' as impertinent busybodies trying to usurp her authority.....When we see great sections of the community clamouring for monetary reform then, surely, it is time for the government to seek advice elsewhere, and to encourage open discussion....It is not 'productive industry' with its new machinery which is the root cause of our unemployment and our uncertainty, but 'Finance', with its antiquated mechanism, which has failed to adapt itself to modern requirements. [648]

Rowbotham explains that *"bank-credit constitutes a dysfunctional form of money"* and that any economy based almost exclusively on bank-credit and debt will have an intense need for continuous growth—regardless of actual human need or demand. He further believes that it creates instability, dependence on financial systems, and growth distortions throughout the economy. He adds that reform of the debt-based financial system is clearly not a minor issue; it is not simply a matter of fiddling around with taxes and interest rates or any other financial mechanism. A much more radical change is required. He then goes on to put forward solutions that would enable an even-handed and non-confrontational approach to a new debt-free solution, using our existing banking system. [649] It is absolutely essential if we the taxpayers, are not to continue bailing out banks that have gambled and lost—through such measures as quantitative easing. All that does is give them more profits and burden the rest of us with even more debt that we already have.

Beware of all those politicians and economists who offer supposed 'solutions' that will only lead to further bank bailouts. Bailouts mean MORE DEBT!

Real and debt-free solutions, to the problems our financial system is currently saddled with, will follow throughout the rest of this book. In the next chapter, though let's first take a look at the consequences of the horrendous situation we currently find ourselves in, should nothing be done to change it.

Chapter 14
Global Impoverishment

Debt is a social and ideological construct, not a simple economic fact. Furthermore, as understood long ago, liberalisation of capital flow serves as a powerful weapon against social justice and democracy. Recent policy decisions are choices by the powerful, based on perceived self-interest, not mysterious "economic laws". Technical devices to alleviate their worst effects were proposed years ago, but have been dismissed by powerful interests that benefit. And the institutions that design the national and global systems are no more exempt from the need to demonstrate their legitimacy than predecessors that have thankfully been dismantled.

— Noam Chomsky [650]

Before delving into this topic I feel bound to mention that what I am recording here is a subject that has concerned me all of my life, that I have been researching for decades now. I have to say that initially I had difficulty understanding the nature of debt, the monetary system, and particularly being clear about the solutions. Works by the Austrian economists, Frederick Hayek, *The Road to Serfdom*, Henry Hazlitt, *Economics in One Lesson,* and people such as Ron Paul, who wrote *End the Fed* had persuasive arguments, and at the time, they were initially convincing in their approach. But as soon as you realize their solution to the problem is a return to the gold standard, without the eradication of debt-based money, you realise they don't quite 'get it'. Once you 'get it' there is no turning back, clarity prevails and you begin find that there are many many more supporters for debt-free money than you ever imagined.

There is one thing I would like you to consider at this stage. Wherever you live, just sit back and think about what kind of world you see out there. Is it one of gross inequalities, uncertainty, and fear of collapse? Or is it a planet that has an incredible industrial base, human beings with a multitude of talents, and a fantastic potential. I hope it is the latter, because all that's holding it back is the banking system that controls the monetary system for short-term profit at the expense of everything, and everyone else. Rowbotham puts it succinctly when refering to Alan Greenspan, the former Chairman of the Federal Reserve, and his control of interest rates:

"There could be no greater indictment of contemporary financial economics than this; that a fluctuating financial digit on a single computer system in a single street in a single country should have the ability to dominate the economics of an entire planet." [651]

There have been, it has to be said, attempts to follow some of the principals of Henry Carey and the American Populists in other parts of the world. Japan had observed the way the British imperialists had tried to subdue China by forcing opium onto their population, and followed that with a war when China tried to resist. The Japanese government decided to take care of what happened inside their own borders, they abolished ownership of land and returned it to the nation paying the feudal samurai nobles a financial recompense. They founded their own Central Bank, the first independent state bank in Asia, and issued their own fiat money, with which they paid the nobles. The country prospered, and the feudal dynasties became multinational Japanese corporations. Japan's economic model was quite a contrast to the western economies, but it prospered. Following the end of the Second World War, it had no military spending to drain its spending and it thrived, eventually creating large trade surpluses.

Japan's huge trade surplus was considered threatening to US economic interests and Washington put pressure on Japan to cut its interest rates. This resulted in large floods of money into Japan and its stock market producing an ever-expanding market bubble. The Japanese government tried raising their interest rates but, as they did this, Wall Street investment banks, led by Morgan Stanley, using new derivatives and by short-selling Tokyo stocks, created a melt down and panic selling. Within months, virtually $5 trillion had been wiped off the value of Japanese stocks. Following this success, each of the Asian Tiger economies were attacked, and each succumbed.[652]

The fall-out from the collapse of a major economy such as Japan's has huge implications for the rest of the world. Less obvious are the effects on all the Southern Countries, often referred to as the Third World. Most of us have some awareness of the indebtedness of these countries, but few of us are as aware of how that can have a big impact on developed countries too.

Debt—A Form of Control

Debt has a way of enslaving whoever it touches. Goldsmiths and bankers realised this long ago—and their successors certainly haven't forgotten it. It is still used to further the goals of banking interests in every aspect of our culture. Southern countries, for example, were specifically targeted as a matter of policy. John Perkins, a financial consultant for an American company, became what he referred to as an Economic Hit Man (EHM), whose sole task was to get countries into debt. He eventually became so disillusioned with this 'work' that he quit, and decided to write a book about his experiences—*Confessions of an Economic Hit Man, The Shocking Story of How America Really Took Over the World*. It's a well written book, documenting his experiences in numerous countries around the globe. Here's a glimpse of what he says:

> Economic hit men (EHMs) are highly paid professionals who cheat countries around the globe out of trillions of dollars. They funnel money from the World Bank, the U.S. Agency for International Development (USAID), and other foreign "aid" organisations into the coffers of huge corporations and the pockets of a few wealthy families who control the planet's natural resources. Their tools include fraudulent financial reports, rigged elections, payoffs, extortion, sex and murder. They play a game as old as empire, but one that has taken on new and terrifying dimensions during this time of globalization. I should know; I was an EHM. [653]

In his book Perkins describes how systematically all the Third World Countries were targeted, and, in his case not just them but Saudi Arabia too—engaging them in massive projects for bringing their country into the 21st century. However, it's the effect on the poorer countries that do not have reserves of oil wealth that I will again leave to Perkins to describe:

> There are two primary objectives of my work, First I was to justify huge international loans that would funnel money back to MAIN [the consulting firm who he worked for] and other U.S. companies (such as Bechtel, Halliburton, Stone & Webster, and Brown & Root) through massive engineering and construction projects. Second, I would work to bankrupt the countries that received those loans (after they had paid MAIN and other U.S. contractors of course) so that they would be forever beholden to their creditors and so they would present easy targets when we needed favors, including military bases, UN votes, or access to oil and other natural resources.

Perkins goes on to describe how, if the politicians he was dealing with didn't play ball, his bosses would as he explains, "send in the jackals". This involved much more serious measures, usually violence if not death—and if the 'jackals' failed then "young Americans are sent to kill and die". He describes his relationship with Jaime Roldós, a university professor and a lawyer, who became President of Ecuador. In 1981, Roldós proposed a new hydrocarbons law that would have meant reforms to the country's relationship with the oil companies who extracted Ecuador's oil. The oil companies responded with a series of media attacks against Roldós, to inflame the situation. Roldós responded by warning that foreign companies who did not go along with his plans to help Ecuadorian people may be forced to trade elsewhere. Soon afterwards his plane was blown up on a journey south, and, Perkins believes he was assassinated. To add credence to his belief, Omar Torrijos, the Panamanian President, who was not considered pliant to US corporate will either, met a similar fate two months after Roldós' death. Perkins said these events deeply affected him, he had known both men, and they were good people, educated men who only had the best interests of their respective peoples at heart. They had also had the balls to stand up to the Reagan administration. [654]

There are some people who will be horrified to learn that there could have been a deliberate policy by the US to get Third World countries into debt. But it is nothing new. Just read this piece by Mr Reginald McKenna, chairman of Midland Bank, who also served as Home Secretary and Chancellor of the Exchequer in the UK. What follows is part of his address to the American Bankers Association in New York, on October4, 1922:

> For over two centuries British capital has been lent to other countries. Year by year England has produced more than she consumed herself or could exchange for the products of other nations, and she could not obtain a market for the surplus unless she gave the purchaser a long credit. Foreign loans and foreign issues of all kinds were taken up in England and the proceeds were spent in paying for the surplus production. British factories and workshops were kept in good employment but it was a condition of their prosperity that a part of output should be disposed of in this way.... .....British creditors received a good return on their investments, but the ability of the debtors to pay has been dependent, speaking generally, on the development of their country being fostered by the receipt of further loans. If we take the whole field of British foreign investments, we shall find that every year England has returned more in loans than she has received in interest and the balance of the world's indebtedness to her has been steadily growing....Now if the payment of past debts depends necessarily upon the receipt of further loans, debts on balance are not paid at all. Though an individual investor may well gain out of foreign investments, it is *an arithmetical certainty that a nation must lose out of them in the long run* [my emphasis]."[655]

Norman Smith MP, put it very succinctly: "Repayment in full has no place in the economic scheme of things under a system of bank-created debt money. The whole idea of foreign business is to get the other man into your debt to an extent that he cannot repay, and then take the skin off him."[656]

The Rebound Effect of Third World Debt

Susan George, author and researcher, who wrote the book, *The Debt Boomerang, How Third World Debt Harms Us All,* [657] documents the effects of debt on Southern countries and details how this debt rebounds on us all—and in ways many of us may not have realised.

One of the most obvious problems facing us currently is the degradation of the planet, the massive acceleration of the destruction of the forests of the Amazon and of many other countries. How is this related to debt you may wonder? Most Third World countries are facing increasing debt. So to pay the interest on this they are having to increase exports of food (and others goods) to the western economies.

Of the major effects of this for the indigenous peoples is that the best quality land is prioritised for the export market—pushing them to more marginally productive land and even forests when they get desperate. Their standard of living drops and their incomes drop.

Land where food crops for local people used to be grown is now also used for cultivating crops for such things as ethanol production—to supply the US.

Much of the food production for export is carried out by large companies using modern pesticide and herbicide techniques, and modern fertilizers. Regulations for the use of these in most Third World countries is very lax, so food imports are liable to contain chemicals such as DDT and other pesticides that are banned in western economies.

The lax regulatory framework and cheap labour naturally attracts big businesses that see greater profits in this kind of environment. Unfortunately, the host countries have little choice but to allow them to come and pollute the local environment in ways that would be illegal in the West would be outlawed. They are desperate to attract business that can add to their exports. However, pollution of the environment has a way of coming back and stinging us in the tail in ways we have only recently come to understand. In earlier chapters, I have already documented how the pollution from pesticides can migrate, through evaporation, from warmer countries to colder areas and then disperse into the environment below, even into the pristine environment of the north and south poles. I have documented how all of us who walk this earth have levels of dioxin and PCBs in our bodies irrespective of where we live. The same could probably be said for radiation levels, particularly since the tsunami hit the Japanese nuclear power station in 2011.

You may feel you are insulated from much of these effects if you live in the West. Perhaps you are, but the effects of crippling Third World debt go far beyond their borders in so many ways. Susan George examines many of these effects and points out that the high volume of imports by the West has a negative effect on their own balance of payments. That is they often find themselves spending more on imports that they receive from selling exports. In this way, money is being sucked out of the Western economies.

High Profits—Displaced People

Often, reading another writer's work is very instructive. I never realised, for example, the extent to which the banks make money out of these deals. So I'd like to pass on some of the figures Susan George quotes from US direct investments abroad. Whereas returns from manufacturing in developing countries varied between 1.4% in 1983 and 14.9% in 1980, for banking the returns were much more lucrative. Returns varied from lows of 28.3% in 1984 to the fantastic returns of 42.8% in 1981, averaging out at a 36.75% return from 1979 to 1984. Not bad for just sitting behind a desk and watching the interest on your loans come rolling in—beats working for a living.

Many of the policies on host countries, by the IMF, and the World Bank cause large displacements of people. These migrants often head to the wealthier countries to find work. Whilst, in some cases, it can be said that they are welcomed by industry, mostly because they are regarded a cheap source of labour, the effect on the national economy is to depress wages and increase unemployment.

One very noticeable effect of the loss of productive farming land in South America, for example, has been the move into drug production. Desperate people will work in any sector they can to survive. Coca plants are cultivated to supply the cocaine industry, which for any country desperate for foreign earnings, becomes a valid source of income. If not 'officially sanctioned' the leaves or refined products still count as trade, as long as the money returns to the host country. In 1989, 64% of Americans cited drugs as being the number one problem of the United States. Susan George quotes Alan García, former President of Peru:

"The drug trade is Latin America's only successful multinational"

GLOBAL IMPOVERISHMENT

Back in 1982, Bolivia was paying an average $2 billion a year in debt servicing—yet its debt levels have steadily increased. It has the lowest life expectancy (some 50 years), the highest child mortality rates, it has chronic malnutrition and 85% of the rural population live below the poverty line. It is estimated that between one third and one quarter of Bolivian working people are working either directly or indirectly for the drug industry. Coca production increased from approximately 9,000 tons in 1972/4 to between 100,000 – 150,000 tons in the early 1990s. [658]

Banks Take the Profits—Tax Payers Carry the Can.

Another way that Third World debt affects us is brought about by the way the banks are allowed to conduct their loan business. Obviously, when they are receiving 40% interest, they are happy to just sit back and collect. But, when things get bad they can make 'provisions' or 'loan-loss reserves'. These are basically ways of accounting where the loan instead of showing on the balance sheet as an asset, is shown as a liability, which reduces its tax liability, even though it may still be able to collect the interest payments. The loan can also be repackaged and sold onto a secondary market, at a loss, but still be a viable performing loan. In both cases the tax liability is reduced. The debt can also be converted to government debt as opposed to commercial debt—and this has been proposed as a measure by the International Monetary Fund (IMF) as a condition for new loans. Yet this has been declared by some as a 'travesty of justice' and 'illegal' since it effectively guarantees the loan to the bank. There is no risk attached—except to the taxpayer who carries it all. [659]

Taxpayers frequently have no choice but to come to the rescue when bank loan turn sour. Banks are happy to take the profits, and even happier to pass on their losses to them. The banks also get tax breaks and are allowed tax credits with regards to loans to Third World countries. They are also the recipients when there is a flight of capital from those countries. These flights of capital, registered in foreign hands, are not subject to normal tax regulations.

There are many ways that loan costs are passed on to taxpayers in the West. Some are not well known some are not obvious, at least in the way they are connected to Third World debt problems. Many would not immediately associate farm bankruptcies in the West with this, for example. Farm exports in the US grew by 47% between 1978 and the peak in 1981, while worldwide sales rose from $29 billion to $43 billion. During that period farmers were encouraged to invest, but, when the debt crisis hit, global sales dropped by 15% and sales to Latin America fell by 30%. In the 1981-1982 crop year the US supplied 48% of world wheat, by 1984-1985 the US share was reduced to

35%. Meanwhile Argentina for example in the same period had doubled its exports. The same situation occurred with soya beans and other crops. In the same period, US soya bean exports fell by 36% while both Brazil and Argentina doubled their exports to control 27% of the world Soya market.[660]

In 1985, Cargill announced its intention to import 25,000 tons of wheat from Argentina at $30 per tonne less than US market prices. At that time, thanks to high levels of debt in the US farming community, the cost of wheat was $110 per tonne compared to $50 per tonne in Argentina. Cargill eventually backed down on its proposal. US farm bankruptcies rose by 900% between 1982 and 1985. Farm bank failures represented half of all bank failures at the same time. Also during this period, the rates for suicide, divorce, depression and breakdowns increased dramatically. It was estimated that approximately 860,000 jobs had been lost as a result of the decline of exports to Latin America alone. It was later estimated that exports to developing countries were $60 billion less than would have occurred in the absence of debt and recession, representing 1.8 million jobs.[661]

Despite experiencing an average increase in GDP of 4.6% from 1946 – 1985, Latin American countries went further into debt. Brazil, for example, increased its GDP fourfold between 1960 and 1980. But while 30% of its export revenues went on debt repayments in 1960, that level had risen to 78% by 1980. By 1990 Brazil's exports had reached $31.4 billion, whereas its imports were only $22.5 billion, giving it a trade surplus of $8.9 billion. This was nevertheless wiped out by debt repayments leaving a net deficit. By 1980 the eighteen major debtor countries of the developing world were exporting 25 percent of their GDP, but still going deeper into debt. [662]

In 1970, the total debts of developing nations were $68 billion which represented 13% of those countries' GDP. By 1989 this debt level had risen to $1,262 billion which, by then, represented 31% of GDP. By 1997 total debts had increased to a staggering $2,100 billion. [663]

In contrast with the experience in America, the UK farming industry UK farming has been the least profitable and most heavily indebted sector of the economy for the last fifty years. Aggregate income from the whole of the farming industry was three times higher in 1948, in real terms, than it was in 1990. Rowbotham offers the following condemnation:

"There could be no greater demonstration of the severity of the financial conditions under which farming has had to operate than a fall in net income by nearly 50% over 14 years, and a parallel increase in debt interest charges of 44%."[664]

GLOBAL IMPOVERISHMENT

This is a terrible indictment of the inability of our economy to supply what is arguably one of the most fundamentally important needs of a society, that of food for its people and decent living for its farmers. I have already criticised some of the more industrial scale practices of farming, such as the chemical inputs that are hazardous to our health and the environment. But it also has to recognised that there are serious financial pressures on farmers. Farming bankruptcies are a disgrace. The loss of large numbers of small and medium-sized farmers is also a loss of considerable expertise developed over decades. You cannot easily replace a farmer who has intimate knowledge of a farm that he may have worked for more than forty years and absorbed knowledge from previous generations; this loss is arguably a loss of one of our country's most precious assets.

State Assets Sold Off to Pay Interest on National Debt

That all this is going on globally is, in my view, an expression of the degenerate nature of our financial system. The result of the world's huge indebtedness has, in most cases, been a transfer of wealth from the poorer and more indebted populations to the owners of capital. Third World countries with high levels of debt have been encouraged to swap some of their debt for equity. This basically means they have been encouraged to sell off state assets, usually at rock bottom prices. These deals seldom have much of an effect on reducing the debt burden, but it can have far reaching effects on the host country. Argentina, for example, sold off ENTel, its vast phone company; but in doing this it was only able to reduce its debt level by less than 10%.[665] These sales can, over time, prove to be more costly—in the longer term. Take as an example the sale of public transport services. From experience we know that, once privatised, this usually means cutting services. Instead of viewing the networks as a valuable service to the public (that reduces the number of cars on the road), the new objectives are to maximise profits and returns to shareholders, or the new private owners.

In the UK during the Thatcher years, there was a massive privatisation program, in which the majority of the state's assets were sold off. One of the other noticeable results of privatisation is the inexorable rise in prices, leaving the general population with even less purchasing power than before. Did this massive sell-off reduce our national debt? Well—not judging by the current debt levels of the UK.

UNHEALTHY BETRAYAL

Bretton Woods, the World Bank, & International Monetary Fund

Third World debt will not go away, nor will the issue of debt in countries in the West. That the two are inextricably linked is inescapable—although the IMF, the World Bank and their economic brethren would love us to believe otherwise. Both organisations were the result of the Bretton Woods Conference in New Hampshire in 1944. The conference itself was held after the earlier global depression which followed the series of competitive devaluations of the Pound Sterling and the Dollar after both currencies had been taken off the gold standard in the 1930s. Two of the principal architects of the Bretton Woods agreement were the British economist Maynard Keynes and US Assistant Treasury Secretary, Harry Dexter White. Keynes proposed the establishment of a clearing union that would promote multilateral trade between nations and would encourage a balance of trade. He proposed a range of fiscal mechanisms that could be used to support this balance. Finally he proposed a new international currency, the Bancor that would be used for all international transactions and would be held by a new institution, the International Clearing or Currency Union. The Americans rejected this proposal and suggested a stabilisation fund should be set up, for all nations to contribute to, and that could lend funds to debtor nations. This was the basis of the International Monetary Fund (IMF). They also proposed a second institution, to help some of the economies that had been shattered by the war. This was the International Bank for Reconstruction and Development (IBRD), which became known as the World Bank.

The UK Parliament was informed that the latest War Loan to Britain would be dependent on acceptance of the American conference proposal, so the proposal was ratified. White also proposed that gold was to be the international currency, and that it was to be valued in dollars. As America held 70% of the world's gold, this made the dollar, ipso facto, the international unit of account.[666]

According to Henry Norman Smith, Member of Parliament (1945-1955), a man with a greater understanding of finance than many, the whole Bretton Woods agreement was thrust onto Parliament by the then Prime Minister, Atlee, with one week's notice that it had to ratified promptly, if Britain was to get its War loan from America. Consequently, MPs didn't have time to analyse the agreement, and Smith himself wrote of his disgust at the way it was rushed through:

"The business was rushed shamefully and disgracefully through on the monstrous pretext that the United Nations financial experts had in 1944 fixed the end of 1954 as the date for ratification."

GLOBAL IMPOVERISHMENT

He complained that such an important agreement should have had extensive discussion, as the repercussions would be felt for decades.

He further wrote:

> The British public must be told plainly that any monetary system based directly or indirectly on gold, and having its main objective the maintenance of the exchange value of one currency in terms of other currencies, must necessarily subordinate home industrial prosperity to other considerations [667]

It must be said that he had been through the depression of the 1930s and two world wars and had observed how the Bank of England's policy of restricting credit, particularly after the First World War, had caused a major recession and resulted in widespread misery and poverty. He further commented:

> "It has always seemed to me a curious fact that money is forthcoming in any quantity for war, but that no nation has yet produced money on the same scale to fight the evils of peace—poverty, lack of education, unemployment, ill health."

In his book, *The Politics of Plenty,* he quotes Major General Fuller who shares some of his sympathies:

> "As wars cannot continue for ever, and as in peacetime more can be produced in an eight hour day than can be consumed, the logical solution would seem to be: first to provide the people with increased purchasing power; and secondly when consumption is saturated, to cut down the hours of work and so give the workers leisure wherein to enjoy their earnings. Never let it escape us that work is but the means to an end, namely, the enjoyment of leisure; and if both victor and vanquished can live joyous lives, what economic cause will there be left to fight about?"

As regards the Bretton Woods agreement, he was mistrustful of Lord Maynard Keynes who was at that time a director of the Bank of England. He felt Keynes' proposal could have led to a world governing body of unelected officials who could dictate policy that could be counterproductive to the world. He also believed that debt levels needed to be addressed. He felt most people voted simply in the hope that it would deliver everyone from the curse of war. He commented "But a lifebelt is one thing, a pair of handcuffs is quite another."

UNHEALTHY BETRAYAL

He further wrote:

"Each nation should have its own honest currency, related not to gold but to the nations own capacity for production. Once all countries—or even one or two of the most important producing nations—adopt debt-free currencies of the kind suggested in this book, the international exchanges will proceed to settle themselves on the principal that the exchange value of a currency, other things being equal, is proportionate to what it will buy in retail goods in the home market." [668]

As soon as it had been passed into law, there were reservations about the Bretton Woods agreement and the way it had been setup. This only increased concerns about the operation of the nascent International Monetary Fund and the nascent World Bank—which both came under increasing scrutiny. To date, there are few countries that can be said to have been effectively helped by them, except in the very short term. The original idea was that they would enable disadvantaged economies to grow to such a degree that they could maintain a healthy balance of trade. **Yet today, there is not one Third World country whose debt is not increasing**.

From 1982 to 1990 these countries paid an average of $6.5 billion to the wealthier nations every month—in interest payments alone. When you add all the efforts to start paying off the principal of the loan, the payments were $12.45 billion per month. [669]

What must be clarified though, is that, this money goes to the wealthier nations—to the banking industry, international bankers, the IMF and World Bank, yet not to their government's taxpayers. Cheryl Payer undertook a comprehensive review of the IMF and World Bank and did an in-depth analysis of these loans taken by Indonesia, the Philippines, Yugoslavia, Brazil, Korea and a number of other countries. She found that although there was a short-term improvement in their economies immediately after receiving their loan, their economies completely deteriorated following IMF protocols in every single case. She documents the gradual (in some cases, not so gradual) deterioration in such detail that, she came to the conclusion the IMF "would have to tear up its constitution and become a different animal altogether before it could conceivably play a positive role in the development of the Third World." [670]

Joseph Stiglitz, a leading economist who has dealt extensively with growth and development in the Third World, was chairman of the Council of Economic Advisers, a cabinet member of Bill Clinton's administration, senior vice-president and chief economist of the World Bank, and winner of the Nobel Prize in Economics (2001) was well-placed to observe the workings and policies of both the World Bank and the IMF. In his book *Globalization and its Discontents,* he documents how he observed IMF policies in action, and found them wanting. He referred to their policies as being based on "a curious blend of ideology and bad economics, dogma that sometimes seemed to be thinly veiling special interests." He found that open and frank discussion was discouraged, and that countries were expected to follow IMF guidelines without debate. He witnessed first-hand the devastating consequences of globalization on some countries and realised that "something has gone horribly wrong... globalization has become the most pressing issue of our time." Despite all the promises of poverty reduction because of global trade, the number of people living in poverty has actually increased by 100 million at a time when world income increased by an average of 2.5 percent annually. More than 1.2 billion people live on less than one dollar a day and more than 45% live on less than 2 dollars a day (2.8 billion people). [671]

Rowbotham also reviews the activities of the IMF and World Bank and comments: "The fact that no Third World nation has ever succeeded in restoring solvency once funds have been borrowed from the World Bank and IMF strongly argues that the theoretical model constitutes a flawed paradigm." He argues that, as total debts and annual interest payments continue to increase, they are "inherently un-repayable." He mentions that, since 1960, there has not been one year that the total of Third World debt decreased and that this debt requirement has become a larger proportion of GNP, increasing from 17% of GNP in 1970 to 33% of GNP in 1998 and, of course, it is significantly higher today. He goes further and accuses those who would suggest that this problem is caused by 'economic incompetence' or 'corruption' by Third World governments of "the most extraordinary arrogance!" He accuses the IMF and World Bank policies of being "an economic, financial, social, and cultural disaster—and debtor nations are left with the legacy of debt." [672]

Stiglitz reviews the effects of IMF policies with the knowledge of hindsight and his years of experience when he worked at the World Bank. He expressed some of the problems with globalization:

> The problem is not with globalization, but with how it has been managed. Part of the problem lies with the international institutions, with the IMF, World Bank and WTO [World Trade Organization], which help set the rules of the game. They have done so in ways that, all too often, have served the interests of the more advanced industrialized countries—and particular interests within those countries—rather than those of the developing world. [673]

UNHEALTHY BETRAYAL

The Destructive Nature of Growing Corporate Global Control

Vandana Shiva in her excellent book, *Stolen Harvest—The Hijacking of the Global Food Supply*, discusses how just ten corporations controlled 32% of the worldwide commercial seed market, valued at $23 billion (in 2000), and 100% of the market for transgenic or genetically engineered seed. These same corporations control the global agrochemical and pesticide market. Just five control the global trade in grain. Both Monsanto and Cargill were actively involved in shaping the Uruguay Round of the General Agreement on Trade and Tariffs, which led to the establishment of the World Trade Organisation (WTO). She explains why, in her experience, the WTO was simply set up to serve as a vehicle to serve the interests of the organisations that set it up:

> Over the past two decades every issue I have been engaged in as an ecological activist and organic intellectual has revealed that what the industrial economy calls "growth" is really a form of theft from nature and people.
>
> It is true that cutting down forests or converting natural forests into monocultures of pine or eucalyptus for industrial raw material generates revenues and growth. But this growth is based on robbing the forest of its biodiversity and its capacity to conserve soil and water. This growth is based on robbing forest communities of their sources of food, fodder, fuel fibre, medicine, and security from floods and drought.
>
> While most environmentalists can recognise that converting a natural forest into a monoculture is an impoverishment, many do not extend this insight to industrial agriculture. A corporate myth has been created, shared by most mainstream environmentalists and development organizations, that industrial agriculture is necessary to grow more food and reduce hunger. Many also assume that intensive, industrial agriculture saves resources and therefore, saves species. But in agriculture as much as in forestry, the growth illusion hides theft from nature and the poor, masking the creation of scarcity as growth.
>
> These thefts have only stepped up since the advent of the globalized economy. The completion of the Uruguay Round of the General Agreement on Tariffs and Trade (GATT) in 1994 and the establishment of the World Trade Organization (WTO) *have institutionalized and legalized corporate growth based on harvest stolen from nature and people* (my emphasis). [674]

In later chapters I relate how massive areas of forest, in South America, in Paraguay, Brazil and Argentina, have been destroyed and replaced by genetically modified crops of soya bean and maize. Large numbers of people who were previously self-sufficient have been forced off their lands, and given no choice but to migrate to rural areas in the hope of finding work. The majority are found in the urban slums surrounding the outskirts of the cities in makeshift shelters, with materials scrounged from tips etc. Whilst the South American governments are not unaware of the serious nature of these problems, they are influenced by the fact that the soya crop, for example, (which is mostly destined for animal feed in the industrialised nations) helps reduce their national debt repayments, if only in a small way. Such action is desperately short-sighted; the consequences on health and the long-term prosperity of the nation, both financially and ecologically, are dire. Some of these consequences I discuss in later chapters.

Few disagree that the level of desperation amongst the Third World countries is rising. This is effectively expressed by President Luiz Inacio Lula da Silva of Brazil:

> Without being radical or overly bold, I will tell you that the Third World War has already started - a silent war, not for that reason any the less sinister. This war is tearing down Brazil, Latin America and practically all the Third World. Instead of soldiers dying, there are children, instead of millions of wounded there are millions of unemployed; instead of destruction of bridges there is the tearing down of factories, schools, hospitals, and entire economies . . . It is a war by the United States against the Latin American continent and the Third World. It is a war over the foreign debt, one which has as its main weapon interest, a weapon more deadly than the atom bomb, more shattering than a laser beam." [675]

These Brazilian President's words are more pertinent when you compare the poverty levels between rich and poor countries. Compare, for example, Eastern Europe's debts with those of Brazil and Mexico. In 1990, interest payments were made up of 5.6% of exports from Poland and 10.1% from Hungary. Yet in the same year, interest payment from Mexico made up 27.3% of exports and 36.1% from Brazil. A World Bank survey found that the poorest fifth of the population of Hungary received 6.9% of total income, while the poorest fifth in Brazil received only 2%. At the same time, the richest fifth in Hungary took home 35.8% of total income, while the richest fifth in Brazil took home a massive 66%. [676]

The Fallacy of Free Trade

Rowbotham argues that there is no such thing as "free trade". The concept is very nice, but the reality without balanced trade (where trade between counties is roughly equal) is something else. When the Asian markets were 'liberated' by the free trade 'doctrine of convergence' the end result was a mass withdrawal of capital, massive falls in their currencies and stock markets, and a huge transfer of assets to foreign interests. His assessment was captured in the following quote "This was theft—an international commercial robbery carried out under the cover of 'free trade' and 'sound economics'…. It is a violation as serious as any military invasion."[677]

Stiglitz came to similar conclusions when he watched the effects of the IMF imposing high interest rates on many countries. It would often force them into further recession and any companies with borrowings into insolvency and bankruptcy. To make his point, he showed how Malaysia fared much better than Thailand and Indonesia, for example, because it's President refused to accept the IMF dogma and did the opposite. Instead of liberalizing its markets, he imposed financial controls which limited exchange rate volatility—and so enabled Malaysia to fare much better than others had anticipated. He limited the extent of his country's indebtedness and, contrary to expectations, was able to maintain lower interest rates, reduced bankruptcies, and prevent a deep recession. Foreign investment also increased. Both India and China had capital controls, and both countries weathered the international storm much better as a result. Stiglitz warned against some of the IMF's policy decisions provoking riots—and was proved right. He added:

> Riots do not restore business confidence. They drive capital out of the country; they do not attract capital into a country. And riots are predictable—like any social phenomenon, not with certainty, but with high probability. [678]

In the late 1980s there were worries about the collapse of the financial system as a result of Latin American countries defaulting on their debts. Irwin Stelzer noted that Bank of America had lost money in four of the last five quarters and had a loan loss reserve that covered less than half of its "non-performing assets" (loans on which not even interest is being paid). He further noted that American banks were in the process of lending Mexico and other borrowers additional billions to permit them to pay interest on the *loans that will never be repaid*. As long as interest payments are made, such loans need not be classified as "non-performing" and written off as bad debts. [679]

Debt Transfers Wealth to the Already Wealthy

In his book *Goodbye America! Globalisation Debt and the Dollar Empire*, [680] Rowbotham further argues that this debt is purely a reflection of artificially created debt, and that there is no longer any moral justification for it:

GLOBAL IMPOVERISHMENT

"In Third World debt, what we have is not real debt, in the sense of the genuine obligation between a lender and a borrower. Third World debt is a numerical phenomenon; a paper debt; an illegitimate debt with absolutely no economic meaning or validity, other than as a measure of money created in a global economy where all money is created as debt."

In his book, Rowbotham concludes that it would be in all our interests to have this debt cancelled—and it spells out how it could be achieved relatively painlessly, even for the banking industry. The benefits that would accrue be immense in the light of the difficulties faced by Third World countries that I have just outlined.

The views of corporate insider, John Perkins sum up succinctly the situation that we are faced with:

> The real story of modern empire—of corporatocracy that exploits desperate people and is executing history's most brutal, selfish, and ultimately self-destructive resource-grab—has little to do with what was exposed in the newspapers.... And everything to do with us. And that, of course, explains why we have such difficulty listening to the real story. We prefer to believe the myth that thousands of years of human social evolution has finally perfected the ideal economic system, rather than to face the fact we have merely bought into a false concept and accepted it as gospel. We have convinced ourselves that all economic growth benefits humankind, and the greater the growth, the more widespread the benefits.[681]

Well there are many people who will question the 'benefits' today. The financial system we are in currently generates massive inequalities. As the debt levels increase, transfers of wealth can only accelerate from poorer populations to the wealthier populations, which is a reflection of its degenerate nature.

According to the Congressional Budget Office, between 1979 and 2007 incomes of the top 1% of Americans grew by an average of 275%. From 1992-2007, the top 400 income earners in the U.S. saw their income increase 392% and their average tax rate reduced by 37%. In the year 2000, a study by the World Institute for Development Economics Research at United Nations University, reported that the richest 1% of adults owned 40% of total global assets, and that the richest 10% of adults accounted for 85% of the world total. The bottom 50% of the world adult population owned 1% of global wealth. Moreover, another study found that the richest 2% own more than half of global household assets.

UNHEALTHY BETRAYAL

The situation in the UK reflects more or less the global experience: The top 1% own 21% of total UK wealth, the top 5% own 40% of all UK wealth, and the top 50% own 93 % of all UK wealth.[682]

It is not always easy to see how accelerating debt levels can create accelerating wealth for the few. If you consider some of the anomalies of debt driven economics, and if you are a banker, you have by far the largest volume of money to play with; you are also in a more or less unregulated market, able to gamble however you wish. There are vast amounts of debt-created money sloshing around, so for the financial markets, global markets and top executives there is always higher pay and money to be made by playing the game. Stiglitz documents how during the Russian collapse of 1998, that Moscow was forced to pay 60% interest on its rouble loans—and within weeks the rates soared to 150%! He criticises the way Russia converted from a state controlled economy to a supposed 'free market' economy through IMF policies—which led to a further massive bailout of $22.6 billion in 1998. He further adds that whilst the banks can make massive returns on these loans, they also make money when state assets or companies are sold off. [683]

Corporate Growth and Debt

The ways in which economies operate have a huge influence over the make-up and the types of business that flourish in them. Global corporations have many advantages in our debt-based economic system. If you are a large corporation, you are profit-driven, and you get preferential treatment from the banks, most notably in lower interest rates than are ever available to smaller businesses and individuals. At the same time, you are far less likely to be refused loans. You have a far greater access to a multitude of tax avoidance schemes—so you often pay a lower rate of tax, relative to earnings than do ordinary individuals. On top of all that, you will have been enjoying access and influence over politicians for many decades.

On the other hand a small business operates by selling a useful product or service to make a profit—and if it does that well enough it might accrue sufficient capital to expand. Big corporations can simply borrow money to fund acquisitions and fund growth, which is one of their main methods of expanding. They are continually looking to expand yet reduce costs, particularly labour.

When big corporations court Third World countries, those countries' politicians fall over themselves to offer them persuasive deals, turning a blind eye to their pollution and poor working conditions, so desperate are they for more foreign investment. It is a highly competitive dog-eat-dog market, where wages are always trimmed to the bone. A further fall-out from the Third World's debt problems, and the resultant desperation, is that multinationals have been able to relocate much of their manufacturing base to these cheaper labour markets. This of course has resulted in a reduction in the manufacturing base of Industrialised nations, and a consequential rise in unemployment with few other job opportunities to take up the slack.

Rowbotham argues that the drive for globalisation, and the rise of the multinational corporations, is a direct response to our world of debt. Large corporations can be effective monopolies, can drive prices down through bulk discounts, use cheap labour sources and reduce costs in ways that smaller companies cannot. They can produce goods at much cheaper prices than smaller producers—although most of the time this means poorer quality and inferior goods. However, when consumers are faced with reduced purchasing power and rising levels of debt—in most countries these companies find their products will sell easily. Whilst most of us would prefer a better service or better quality product that lasts, most of our purchases are driven by price. In a debt-driven economy, choice is mostly an illusion, most of our decisions on what to buy are decided by what we feel we can afford.

Free Trade Zones

As the debt levels escalated in the 1960s and 1970s, Third World countries were advised to create special free trade zones (FTZs) or export processing zones (EPZs) within which multinational corporations were given tax breaks, sometimes for ten years or more. These zones were set up with special infrastructures that enabled costs to be cut and speedy access to be provided to main roads and airports to accelerate exports. Countries would compete with each other for business by offering sweeter deals. These zones were promoted by the IMF and World Bank, even though they were aware that setting up the infrastructure would involve the countries in more debt. Corporations were allowed full repatriation of profits, as well as exemption from duties on equipment, raw materials and components. By the 1980s there were more than 120 such zones worldwide, employing large numbers of people; in Malaysia, for example, its four free trade zones employed eighty thousand female workers.

Women were the preferred employees as they were paid less than their male counterparts and were more accepting of the atrocious conditions they often had to work under. Although their pay was only 60 cents an hour, $12 a week was deducted for their housing in dormitories measuring just 12 x 10 foot—for between 6 and 10 workers. In some cases, where there was 24-hour production, bunks would be used by all three shifts. When one shift ended the previous shift would have to give up their bunks to the next incomers. The zones would include a no-strike policy and have little or no union representation. In the Philippines, Hong Kong, South Korea and Taiwan, hundred hour weeks were the norm. The majority of workers were in either the garment industry or the electronics industry. Both groups suffered from numerous ailments due to the working conditions. Women in the garment factories suffered from respiratory ailments and brown-lung due to the high levels of textile dust and dampness. The electronic industry operated in cold working conditions to protect electronic parts and workers suffered from the additional hazard of breathing fumes from tin and lead solders. The work of wiring circuit boards often involved peering through microscopes for ten hours a day leading to severe eye strain. As a result, most women were unable to continue the work after three years. They would also be exposed to chemical vats of highly carcinogenic substances, and would develop liver and kidney damage, skin disorders, reproductive disorders and respiratory disorders. Critics of these 'free-trade' zones have estimated that more than six million women below the age of thirty were "used up" and abandoned by the multinationals in just fifteen years. [684]

You may possibly believe that there is little that can be done about these conditions in Third World countries and that most of us are insulated from the horrors their populations face by not having close contact with them. As I have already documented, this is not the case, companies simply move their production base away from countries where employees have more reasonable salaries and rights, to countries where these protections do not exist. William Greider documented how numerous corporations benefited from the tax breaks introduced by the Reagan administration. General Electric (GE) for example, benefitted from a tax rebate on corporate profits of $6.5 billion during 1981-1983 to the tune of $283 million. Its tax burden went from $330 million to minus $90 million. Greider estimated that this saved GE more than $1.3 billion over several years. However, instead of investing this windfall into American jobs, it shed more than 50,000 people from its payroll and used the money to finance an aggressive acquisition campaign. Most of the money that American companies saved was invested in foreign countries. As Greider observed; "American taxpayers, in other words were unwittingly subsidising the globalisation of their own industrial structure".[685] On top of that, taxpayers inherit the debt; whenever multinationals escape paying tax, or even get a rebate, tax revenues are reduced and the government has to cut public services or increase its debt. All the time multinationals reduce their tax burden through loopholes or offshore havens it *increases the debt burden on ordinary people.*

The textile industry used to be one of the largest employers in Northern Ireland, but in the late 1970s companies like ICI Fibres Ltd., Courtaulds Ltd., and Du Pont Company (UK) Ltd., closed their plants and moved offshore to the very free trade zones highlighted. During the 1970s, more than fifty UK companies established operations in the Philippines in eleven EPZs providing, as Nelson observed, "the basic zone free lunch". She further observes that if you include the fact that employees are discarded after about four years, unemployment in the host country actually increased.

To avoid the higher labour costs of western countries, the electronics industry has hopped from country to country, exporting the most labour-intensive and polluting operations. Nelson documents how EPZ and FTZ development parallels the industry's search for the ever more "favourable business climate". Mexico and Hong Kong were the favourites in the early sixties, Taiwan and South Korea in the mid-1960s, Singapore in 1969, Malaysia in 1972, and so on. [686]

Free trade zones, however, are not restricted to Third World countries. The Thatcher government introduced them into the UK in 1979, offering exemption from industrial and commercial property taxes, income tax concessions, customs relaxation, tax holidays and reduction in red tape, amongst others. The government also invested in infrastructure to further encourage multinationals to locate their businesses in the UK. Consequently, by 1982, Scotland was producing 40% of the microchips that were being produced in the whole of Western Europe, employing some 40,000 people. Unfortunately, once the tax-break holiday was over (often after about ten years), many of the companies simply moved their operations to the next haven. The US followed suit with its own version of FTZs, initially on a state-wide basis. This was followed country by country, so much so that variations of FTZs exist in virtually every country these days. According to the Department of Housing and Urban Development (HUD), President Bush had to accommodate $1 billion in lost revenues due to the introduction of these zones, on top of the estimated loss of more than $21 billion through tax loopholes that already existed.[687]

Corporate Growth at the Cost of Local Economies

This is not the only way corporations have been able to create a "favourable business climate" for themselves; George Monbiot in his book *Captive State, The Corporate Takeover of Britain*, documents numerous ways that corporations have moved into markets and into communities and taken them over. Take the food industry, for example, and the growth of the large supermarket, the so-called superstores. While there was significant awareness that these large superstores would have a negative impact on local economies, such as loss of jobs, loss of businesses, lower wages, reduction of the quality and variety of life, greater pressure on the transport system, and the displacement of local suppliers, the local governments and national government encouraged them. Monbiot reports that every time a large supermarket opened its doors, there was a net loss of 276 jobs (in a study of 93 stores). He also disclosed how, while one new job would be created for every £50,000 spent in small local shops, £250,000 needed to be spent to create one new job in a superstore.[688]

The supermarkets have consolidated their positions, put in numerous planning applications for expansion of existing stores and the creation of new stores. Wal-Mart, the world's largest retailer, made a successful bid for the UK's ASDA Stores in 1999 for £6.9 billion. In 2010, ASDA's share of the grocery market was 16.5 % in the UK, second only to Tesco's which is considered to be the third largest retailer in the world (measured by revenues), and the second largest measured by profits. It has a 30% market share of the UK grocery trade. [689]

You might say that these stores are more efficient and that they offer greater choice. However, the choice is mostly illusory. The reality is that the fruits you buy are all the same varieties in every supermarket, mostly shipped from faraway countries, whilst there are local producers with apples that they are unable to sell. This can be said for much of the food sold in supermarkets—and transportation is a significant part of their costs. The food that is shipped is often shipped green, no longer sun-ripened, often treated with chemicals to give the illusion of being ripe—and so often leaving consumers with tasteless nutrient deficient produce.

Rowbotham sums up the situation about the globalisation of food:

> Globalisation can almost be defined as the epitome of abuse, wastage and inefficient use of resources, and neglect of human priorities. What greater and more obvious misallocation of resources could there be than the monopolisation of land in poverty-stricken nations to produce food for the industrialised nations—food that loses its nutritional value during transport and storage—whilst the indigenous population go hungry, and acres of land suitable for growing quality foodstuffs lie neglected within the northern hemisphere? [690]

Depressing Volatility

Another aspect of our current financial system is its volatility, its boom and bust cycles and the ability of the banks to raise interest rates or reduce lending. Currently, interest rates are relatively low due to the Federal Reserve and Central banks maintaining a low prime rate. This wasn't always the case. In the early 1980s, when President Reagan was in office, the US prime rate reached 21.5%--which led to insolvencies, bankruptcies, layoffs etc. It produced a recession and more business collapses than at any time since the Great Depression. In the 1990s, corporate insolvencies were again on the rise—

they shot up by nearly one third to 2,156, while businesses going into receivership involving clearing bank creditors went up by more than 50%.[691]

Mullins puts the case that the Great Depression was caused on purpose by the Federal Reserve, and documents his reasons for this in his book, *The Secrets of The Federal Reserve.* [692] It was only in later years that officials of the Fed actually admitted that their actions had led directly to the Great Depression of the 1930s. One positive thing grew out of this, however—the desire to reform our financial system. Rowbotham reports that the Swedish economist, Brynjolf Bjorset, recorded over 2000 schemes for monetary reform being advanced before 1930. Whilst these all differed, they had a common theme of recognising that *this common industrial and government debt was fraudulent, and that a new source of debt-free money needed to be established.* Many people felt it was strange that there was no money for jobs, and people were going hungry, yet as soon as the idea of war entered the horizon, industrial production kicked into top gear and suddenly there was plenty of work. War put paid to any radical monetary reform and, afterwards, the Bretton Woods agreement sealed the fate of the world economy. [693]

Insider Views

It's not often that businessmen on the inside are quoted, but Warren Buffet, reputed to be the second richest man in the world, has always been known for his forthright views. In an interview with Ben Stein of the *New York Times*, he was recorded as saying that he only paid 19% of his income for 2006 ($48.1 million) in total federal taxes (thanks to them being from dividends & capital gains), while his employees paid 33% of their income, despite making much less money. "How can this be fair?" Buffett asked, "How can this be right?"

Stein agreed with him, but commented that if anyone tried to raise the issue, they would be accused of fomenting class war. Buffet retorted: "There's class warfare, al-right, but it's my class, the rich class, that's making war, and we're winning. [694]

Buffet also gave his views on the continuously expanding US trade deficit: he believed it would devalue the dollar and US assets, and result in a larger proportion of American assets becoming owned by foreign interests. He predicted that net ownership of the US in 2015 would amount to $11 trillion. The US trade deficit has being rising continuously for the last three decades, reaching $817.3 billion in 2006. [695] This is yet again a symptom of Third World trade that is changing trade balances driven by debt, affecting the US directly.

Another wealthy mogul, Sir James Goldsmith, the billionaire financier, the person who confessed he once called up the Rothschilds to tell them he was richer than they were, had the view that much of Western civilisation is built on false premises—such as throwing money at environmental problems instead of trying to understand where we have gone wrong. He cites the example of the widespread belief that large-scale mechanised agriculture is cheaper than more traditional farming methods. He observed, "This is true at the level of farm costs, but when you add the economic and social costs of chasing people off the land into towns where they cannot find jobs, and where they live in slums where we have to pay for keeping them, the food is infinitely more expensive. Furthermore, communities are destroyed, arable land is damaged and intensively-farmed food is often poisonous."

His understanding of the financial markets, and ability to predict their developments was legendary, and explains why he was able to amass such an immense fortune. His understanding of environmental issues was reputedly due to his vast library and his consummate interest in acquiring knowledge and reading. On being asked how long he felt it would be before an ecological meltdown, he was emphatic "I have absolutely no doubt that the bill will be paid during my children's lifetime."

He also believed that the economic crisis will kill environmental measures on cost grounds. "Already the oil crisis is an excuse for reviving the nuclear industry, with the additional fig-leaf of suggesting that nuclear plants are less damaging to the environment." [696] Sir James died aged 64, July 1997.

Dysfunctional Nature of a Debt-Based Money Economy

Sir James's views are revealing, and raise an interesting point, which is part of the reason for this and the previous chapter being based on money and debt-creation. It became obvious to me early on that writing a book detailing defects in our approach to health care may fall on deaf ears, particularly as the world economy deteriorates. So it quickly became clear that the far bigger issue was why our political institutions were failing to address many of the health issues raised in the previous chapters. For example, the bias of the FDA in looking after the interests of big business, particularly the pharmaceutical companies—and this was not just a US issue. The same could be said to be the case in *every* country that you look at, the problems in the UK, Canada, and Australia I have already described to some degree. The problem is global. The pollution problem is global. The corporatisation of agriculture and the food industry is global. The pharmaceutical and drug industrial complex is global. The promotion of the allopathic medical paradigm and the pseudo-science behind it is global.

GLOBAL IMPOVERISHMENT

Information is now global due to the internationalisation of the media and the internet. Whilst there are differences between countries, the move to globalisation by massive multinational companies has been the predominant feature of our economy for decades and, according to all the available evidence, is accelerating in just about every sector.

So it became obvious that the majority of the ills facing our society can be attributed to the imbalance in our financial system. Money is simply a medium of exchange, but it is what is behind the creation of it that is crucial. Because the answer is DEBT! Unless we come resolutely to terms with this issue, it seems that our society faces a precarious and uncertain future. What cannot be argued with is that we cannot increase debt forever, either personally or nationally. It's not hard to get our heads round, yet millions of us, including our leaders, still struggle to.

I have copied a graph of US National Debt below, illustrating the growth of debt from 1940 to 2013. This has now reached the staggering figure of over $17 trillion. When you look at a graph like this, it is not difficult to see how totally unsustainable it is. Currently 25% of the entire federal revenue is simply paying interest on this debt. According to Gregory Mannarino this is projected to double in just seven years. Yet this is not even the whole picture. If you want to know what the total debt of the USA is, including personal debt, it is somewhere in excess of $60 trillion.[697]

Our politicians seem unable to address either this debt problem or, its cause—the privately-owned banking system. Nor do they have any proposal to tackle the issue. Austerity measures are about as far as they can get. Meanwhile more than 47 million US citizens receive food stamps.

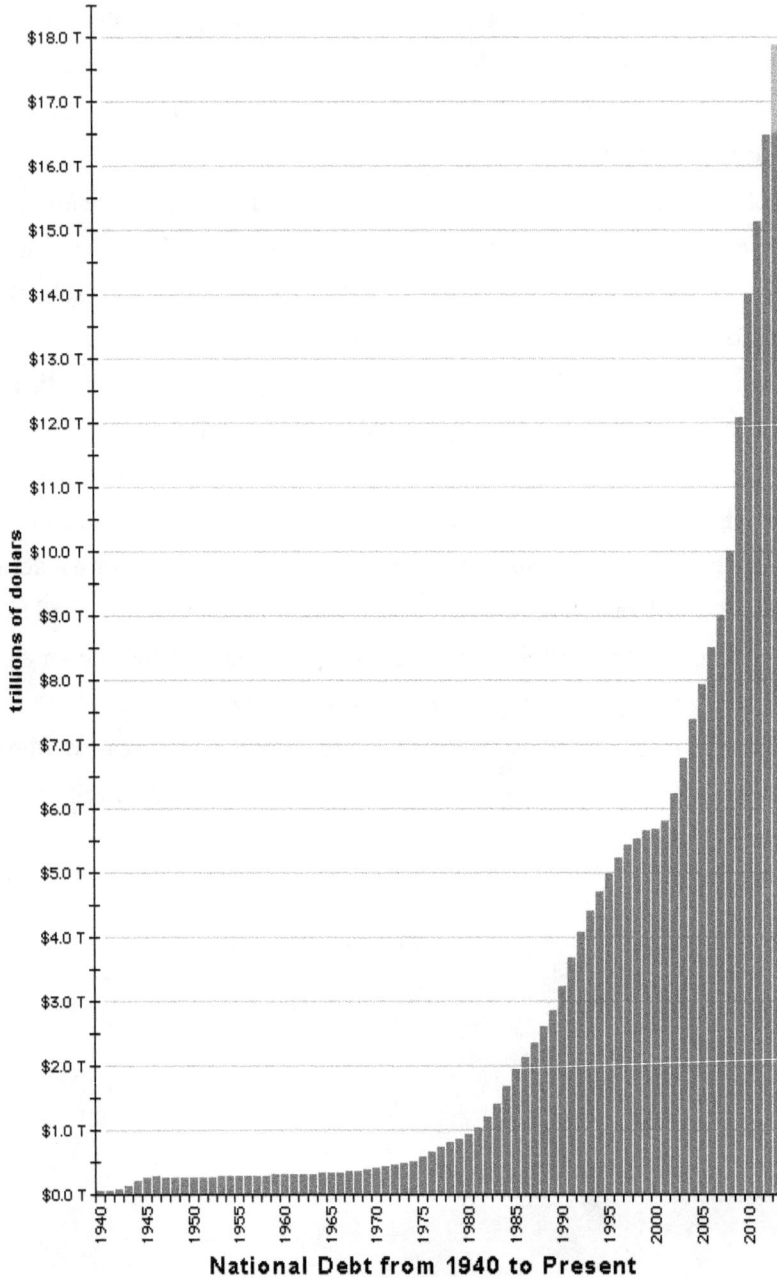

National Debt from 1940 to Present

Source: U.S. National Debt Clock
http://www.brillig.com/debt_clock/

To me, the debt problem is like a parasitic cancer that has invaded the body; except the body in this case is our society, our political system, our financial system, and our social system. It is so pervasive that it affects every aspect of our lives. Whilst I would accept that there are always actions we can take to make improvements in our lives on, every level, I also believe that to treat the cancer of debt as timidly as we currently are would be the same as trying to put out a raging inferno with a glass of water. As a nutritionist, I find it very difficult to give appropriate advice, when most of the people who really need help cannot afford to come and seek it, let alone afford the likely diet that would be recommended or the cost of supplements that may also be recommended.

Trying to defeat the effect of the food industry's massive PR and advertising capability with just the simple truth might be considered naïve and unrewarding, and most likely doomed to failure, as much of these first fourteen chapters has so far suggested.

For me, the clearest reason for the worsening ill-health of our society is the inability of ordinary people to get access to clean un-polluted air, adequate wholesome fresh food, water fit to drink, and the time to be able to relax and enjoy the preparation and consumption of their food. I would add that, given the knowledge to make *truly informed* decisions about their health, and their lives in general, would also be a profound benefit. That our decaying financial system and consequential debt burden will be the single biggest obstacle to achieving this, I have no doubt. But don't take my word for it—here is a true insider's view, that of Vincent C. Vickers, Director of the Bank of England (1910-1919):

> Although it is the money system which is to be accused of dishonesty, those who use and depend upon a dishonest system, knowing that system to be dishonest, cannot themselves be regarded as honest men. Moreover, it may be that the present system, which international finance has forced our democratic government to adopt, uphold, and protect by every possible means, has undermined the character of the people and forced them to alter their definition of the word honesty so that it may be made to comply more nearly with modern practice. [698]

Our economic system, or lack of it, pervades every aspect of our lives in ways that many of us struggle to come to terms with, so often do we hear that we are 'free' people and we live in a 'democracy'. Here's the view of an economist:

> "The dominant consideration in our economic system is not what people want, either as consumers or workers, but what people can afford or be persuaded to buy, and what they can be persuaded by force of circumstance to do for money, as a job. To put the matter another way, the modern economy is driven, not by the aggregate desires of what people want out of the economy, but by what the economy can get out of them. The only fitting word for this is slavery." [699]

UNHEALTHY BETRAYAL

The only true democracy is an 'economic democracy'. Being slaves to debt is not a democracy. Having economic and political policy dictated by huge corporations with turnovers larger than a lot of countries is not a democracy. Once again I give you the views of an insider, John Perkins:

"We must shake ourselves awake. We who live in the most powerful nation history has ever known must stop worrying so much about the outcome of soap operas, football games, quarterly balance sheets, and the daily Dow Jones averages, and must instead re-evaluate who we are and where we want our children to end up. The alternative to stopping to ask ourselves the important questions is simply too dangerous." [700]

There are many conspiracy theorists out there, many books purporting to have the inside information one way or another. I don't personally wish to get into that debate. To me it is simply irrelevant whether four old men or four hundred old men, created the mess we are in, nor do I feel it is critical to understand whether they arrived at this mess through design of just plain stupidity and ignorance. What is relevant to me, *is that we accept that we are in a mess and that we are grown up and capable enough to find our way out of it.*

Chapter 15
Corporatizing Life

We can have democracy in this country, or we can have great wealth concentrated in the hands of the few, but we can't have both.

Supreme Court Justice Louis D. Brandeis

I believe there are more instances of the abridgment of the freedom of the people by gradual and silent encroachments of those in power than by violent and sudden usurpations.
James Madison, speech, Virginia Convention, 1788

Unless you become more watchful in your states and check the spirit of monopoly and thirst for exclusive privileges you will in the end find that...the control over your dearest interests has passed into the hands of these corporations.
Andrew Jackson, 7th President of the United States, farewell address March 4th 1837

The rise and dominance of corporate interests has gone hand in hand with our debt-based monetary system. Corporate growth has been fuelled by debt in that most of corporate expansion has been through debt-financed takeovers, buyouts and mergers. For the banking system, corporate lending is highly remunerative and risk-free, as compared to lending to individuals and small companies.

Law Professor Joel Bakan discusses the rise and dominance of corporate control over our lives in his excellent book *The Corporation, The Pathological Pursuit of Profit and Power*. In it he discusses how corporations were set up—and given rights akin to individuals. When they were given limited liability status (in the UK the Limited Liability Act was introduced in 1855). This basically meant that individuals investing in their pursuits could not be sued for more than their investment—meaning any legal action against a limited company ceased to be a threat to them. Because a significant number of them were created, that subsequently collapsed and were associated with dubious ventures in the UK, they were effectively banned for fifty years. Critics of the limiting of liability believed it would turn out to be a grave mistake because it would remove moral responsibility from corporations. Bakan regards the limited liability corporation as a 'pathological institution' that becomes more problematic with increasing size, dominance and power. An example of that power increasing occurred when restraints on mergers and acquisitions were removed, and more than 1800 corporations were consolidated into just 157 large corporations between 1898 and 1904. Originally, such consolidations were considered to be no more than a method for the wealthy to exploit resources more powerfully as groups than as individuals. And very little has changed since. Currently 50% of the stock of corporations is owned by 1% of the population, while just 4% is owned by the bottom 80% of the population. [701]

The status and focus of corporations was heavily influenced by the landmark decision of the *Ford v Dodge* case, when the Judge ruled "a business corporation is organised and carried on primarily for the profit of stockholders" and that corporations duties were not "for the merely incidental benefit of shareholders and for the primary purpose of benefitting others." That decision, according to corporate lawyer Robert Hinkley, prevented corporations from benefitting the wider community by its very nature—as he himself found in his twenty-three years of practice; he expressed the view, "that the law in its current form, actually inhibits executives and corporations from being socially responsible." He added: "Corporate law casts ethical and social concerns as irrelevant, or as stumbling blocks to the corporation's fundamental mandate." [702] This does not mean they cannot spend money on promoting the *idea that they are socially responsible*—that is simply good public relations—actually *being socially responsible* is another matter entirely.

The manic quest for continuous corporate growth is a fatal flaw that has disastrous consequences, both environmentally and socially. The debt-based economy, by its very nature, encourages this unquenchable craving for growth at all costs. It also fuels speculative investment and financial manipulation on a massive scale. In a world of real money, it would not be possible for all this to take place.

KKR and Corporate Take-Over Frenzy

George Anders of the Wall Street Journal has written a book about the rise and dominance of a small company started by three men, Jerry Kohlberg, Henry Kravis, and George Roberts in 1976.

CORPORATIZING LIFE

Kohlberg Kravis Roberts & Co., (KKR as it was known) used debt, junk bonds, and anything but real money to take over companies such as RJR Nabisco. In total, they completed 38 buyouts costing a total of $60.3 billion before its fall. In each acquisition, the amount of KKR equity involved was very small. The company's borrowing of course, resulted in it taking on massive proportional debt. The RJR Nabisco deal, its largest acquisition cost $26.4 billion, of which KKR equity was originally just 5.6%. This does not mean that the KKR partners actually paid this amount out of their own pockets; it came from their equity fund. Anders named his book *Merchants of Debt,* and in it he tells the inside story of KKR's rise and fall.

The story is instructive in that it captures a period when corporate raiders stalked the land and corporate takeovers, buyouts and acquisitions reached a peak. KKR made unbelievable and unprecedented sums of money, both through their fees and through their 'restructuring' of the companies involved. Their rise coincided with the dramatic rise of Michael Milken of Drexel Lambert, the junk bond trader who eventually was indicted after a two-and-a-half-year government investigation on ninety-eight counts of racketeering and securities fraud. Junk bonds were bonds that carried a high risk of default, and which Milken and others packaged up and sold on. However it is the 'restructuring' and the resulting massive profit to be made that is of interest here. Before it all turned sour, when the US economy sank into recession, they were making returns of 50% a year and in some cases higher than 80% (they made 87% a year on Norris Industries Inc., over three years following their acquisition of it in 1981).

Their formula was consistent—they took over a company and either installed a new chief executive or promoted existing executives who were amenable to their approach. This enabled them to persuade the management to sell off assets to reduce some of the massive debt burden the company had acquired, cut staffing levels to reduce running costs, pare back product lines, reduce wages, and generally focus on paying off the debt as fast as practically possible. Another vital aspect of their formula was to get the new executives to invest their own money into the company. This was to incentivise the management to carry out the necessary drastic action to achieve a profit and, in many cases, to make the management rich in the process.

In 1986 they took over Safeway Stores Inc., for $4.2 billion, which at that time had 180,000 employees and a turnover of $20 billion a year. One of the first things they did was to remove bonuses that were un-related to performance, and to re-introduce them with performance targets and, ambitious profit targets—although, not necessarily sales growth. In this way managers who cut inventory levels, reduced perks, or sold off less productive stores were able to increase profits in the short term. In the first few months, more than 8,000 headquarters and regional staff lost their jobs. More than one hundred individual stores were closed, inventory levels were slashed, and 'operating costs' were cut. As a result, the stock climbed $14 within five and a half years and made at least thirty of the Safeway managers millionaires. The workers however faced pay restrictions for years and, in some cases, a pay cut of 10%. A policy of using lower-paid part-time workers for restocking shelves, bagging groceries and even meat-cutting, (which was the union's highest-paid job) was introduced. [703]

There were few people who actually approved of the deal, however. Four years after the takeover, the company still laboured under an interest bill of $400 million a year, and remained $3.1 billion in debt. Its net income was $2.5 million in 1989. KKR was able to sell 10% of the company back to the general public at a price that valued their own holding at more than $800 million—four times more than their original cash investment. Three investment banks made $65 million out of the original deal, the law and accountant firms made $25 million and KKR charged Safeway $60 million just to put the deal together. [704]

Susan Faludi, wrote an article (for which she won the Pulitzer Prize for Explanatory Journalism in 1991), showing some of the human cost of a lot of figures bandied around about leveraged buyouts (LBOs). She cites the comments of Vince Macias, a twenty-five year old trucker who complained of 16 hour shifts, being so overworked that he considered he was "dangerous" on the highway. Many employees said morale was so low they believed they were driving customers away. Another trucker, James White who had been employed by Safeway for almost 30 years in Dallas, marked the one year anniversary of being told he was redundant by telling his wife he loved her, then going into the bathroom and blowing his brains out with his hunting rifle.

He was not the only Safeway employee who was made redundant and subsequently tried committing suicide. Bill Mayfield, a mechanic in the Safeway dairy since it opened in 1973, slashed his wrists and shot himself in the stomach. He miraculously survived—the bullet just missed his vital organs.

A survey of other former Dallas employees found that almost 60% of them had still had not been able to find full time employment more than a year after being made redundant. Safeway's long-time motto "Safeway Offers Security" had been ruthlessly cast aside. [705]

Peter Magowan, the Safeway's chief executive may have been made $30 million richer by the deal, but eventually the tide turned against the wave of leveraged buyouts that had made it possible. The fact is that short-termism never works. It became obvious that companies were not really being improved. In this case, it became obvious—relatively quickly—that they were not making more money by providing a better product, increasing quality or, in fact adding to the gross national product. No, the increases in profits were more to do with accountancy rules. KKR, for example was able minimise its tax bill, both by setting its huge borrowings off against tax, and by boosting the value of its assets to be eligible for huge appreciation allowances. The wealth realised by their methods was fantastic; *Forbes* estimated Henry Travis's wealth at $330 million in 1988, rising by approximately $100 million a year. His income was only eclipsed by that of Michael Milken, the junk bond trader, who helped raise many of the fantastic sums that enabled KKR to make the grand takeovers they did; his earnings with Drexel in 1986 were $295 million, rising to $550 million in 1987. Eventually, though, the tide turned and the banks refused to lend for such ventures. Drexel Lambert paid its top dealmakers $250 million in bonuses in January 1990 and then ran out of money. The following month they filed for bankruptcy. [706]

Financial Rewards No Longer Linked to Real Growth

The legacy from this period is still with. us in many ways. Numerous companies noted what KKR and other corporate raiders had done, and themselves started trimming staff, reducing wages, and cutting overheads—all to increase the earnings of top executives, rather than improve working conditions for their staff and provide a better service to their customers. However, instead of requiring their executives to put their own money into the business as KKR had done, they were incentivised by stock options, bonuses, and other rewards. Nowadays the actual performance of senior executives is often not even related to their total remuneration. Take the Royal Bank of Scotland (RBS), for example. Following the financial upheavals of 2008, RBS had to be bailed out by the taxpayers. Nevertheless, it paid out bonuses to its staff worth nearly £1 billion in 2010—even though they reported losses of £1.1 billion for the same year. [707]

Fred Goodwin, the former boss of RBS who oversaw the disastrous multi-billion pound deal to take over its Dutch rival, ABN Amro, at the height of the financial crisis, also presided over the subsequent total collapse of RBS and its subsequent £45 billion rescue by UK taxpayers. For this collapse, he was rewarded with an annual pension of £650,000 which, following public outrage, was eventually reduced to £342,500 per annum. [708]

The fallout that affected KKR has also affected many other companies, even those like Levi Strauss who, in 1994, had won an award from the Council on Economic Priorities for its "unprecedented commitment to non-exploitive work practices in developing countries," and who, in 1984, had been named one of the hundred best companies to work for in the USA. Nevertheless, in the 1980s it still closed fifty-eight factories in the US, laid off 10,400 employees, and moved much of its production overseas. [709]

It's not simply a case of very high financial rewards being paid to top executives in the aftermath of the buyout boom; at the same time, the general labour force has been faced with reduced salaries, job uncertainty, insecurity, longer hours, harsher conditions, rising costs and larger debts.

There is much more to be said about the fallout from the debt-based economy. When we remind ourselves that the 'money' borrowed for these buyouts is money created out of nothing, as a result of the lending regulations, and that the banks nevertheless charge interest on it, many of us will shudder at the possible consequences.

Many large companies now mostly pay no tax where they used to pay substantial sums. In fact big business is allowed to escape paying tax with a whole host of avoidance measures. Many more of them are able to emulate Rupert Murdoch's News Corporation, for example, which has earned profits of £1.4 billion ($2.3 billion) in Britain since 1987, but paid no corporation tax in the UK (according to *The Economist* in 2007). The same journal made the following comment about the meeting in Davros of the World Economic Forum:

> Take the bosses of the world's 1,000 largest companies, accounting for four-fifths of world industrial output, and 33 national leaders, including the president of the United States. Assemble them in a secluded Swiss ski resort, and then surround them with gun-toting police. Is it any wonder that the annual meeting of the World Economic Forum in Davos this week has become, to some, a sign that there is a global economic conspiracy perpetrated by the white men in dark suits who run the world's multinational corporations? Many people—and not just the folk with ponytails and placards who disrupted last December's meeting of the World Trade Organisation in Seattle—now think of multinationals as more powerful than nation states, and see them as bent on destroying livelihoods, the environment, left-wing political opposition and anything else that stands in the way of their profits.

The article continued:

> None of this is new. Three decades ago, multinationals were already widely denounced as big, irresponsible, monopolistic monsters... Yet now the hostility has returned. One explanation is the sheer speed at which multinationals have recently expanded abroad. This has made them the most visible aspect of globalisation, buying some local firms and driving others out of business. Even to rich, well-run countries, their sheer size can seem threatening. Thus the Irish sometimes fret about the fact that

foreign firms account for almost half of their country's employment and two-thirds of its output; and Australians point nervously to the fact that the ten biggest industrial multinationals each has annual sales larger than their government's tax revenue. [710]

The Rise of Corporate Dominance

Corporations are now bigger than countries and governments. Revenue of corporations exceeds that of most countries. Of the top 200 financial entities, 161 are corporations—just over 80%. Only 57 national governments are considered to be even in the same ball park as the Fortune 500 companies—who each have a turnover of $9 billion or more. Yet even comparing the revenue of corporations with entire nations doesn't accurately reflect their power and influence. The GDP of countries is represented by the whole population of business and individuals, whereas the income of a large corporation is in the hands of one decision-making body. Only seven countries outrank the richest corporations. The revenue from the top 490 corporations in 1999 exceeded $11.5 trillion—approximately 35% of the entire worlds GDP.[711]

Wal-Mart, for example, has more than a quarter of a trillion dollars in annual sales and operates 4300 stores; it was founded by Samuel Moore Walton who, when he died in 1992, had accumulated the biggest family fortune in America. His surviving wife and four children control approximately 39% of Wal-Mart stock, worth some $90 billion, which makes them the richest family in the USA. When Sam Walton died, his family avoided large inheritance taxes because he had set up ownership of Wal-Mart stock in a family partnership. At the time of Sam's death, each of the four children held a 20% share of Walton Enterprises, while Sam and his wife each held a 10% share. His wife Helen inherited Sam's stake tax-free. As for the future, there seems no limit to the expansion plans for Wal-Mart. The company currently purchases more than $1 billion of international real estate *each* year. [712]

Vast as Wal-Mart is, it does not have the wealth capacity of the top 6 companies—Exxon-Mobil, General Motors, Ford, Mitsui, Daimler-Chrysler and Mitsubishi—together these have more annual revenues than any national government except the United States. Charles Grey compared corporate revenues with government budgets and found that 66 of the top 100 were corporations and only 57 national governments had budgets anywhere near the *Fortune 500* companies.[713]

Yet size in itself is not really the issue. The real issue is how large corporations, in their pathological pursuit of profit and domination of world markets, pay little regard to the welfare of ordinary citizens—or the environment we all live in. It is not just our physical health that's at stake, quality of life, diversity and cultural expression are also casualties of the bland plastic takeover of life that many complain of. However, it is the effect on personal and global health that is our main concern here. What is of concern is that, with the drive for ever increasing profits and markets, corporate globalisation, left unchecked in so called 'free-market economics' not only threatens our own health, but also that of the planet we live on.

Corporate Assault on Environmentalism

It is has been stated by numerous people in the corporate world that the environmental movement is the single biggest threat to corporate profits. Bob Williams, a consultant for the oil and gas industry expressed this clearly in his book *US Petroleum Strategies in the Decade of the Environment,* when he said that the industry needed "to put the environment lobby out of business", and added "There is no greater imperative.. If the petroleum industry is to survive it must render the environmental lobby superfluous, an anachronism." His views were echoed by another industry consultant, Ron Arnold, at a meeting of the Ontario Forest Industries Association. "You must turn the public against environmentalists or you will lose your environment battle as surely as the US timber industry has lost theirs." It was even more succinctly put by Frank Mankiewicz, a senior executive with the PR firm Hill and Knowlton:

"The big corporations are scared shitless of the environmental movement...they sense that there is a majority out there and that emotions are all on the other side—if they can be heard." [714]

These quotes can be found in Sharon Beder's book *Global Spin—The Corporate Assault on Environmentalism,* which sets the tone of the challenge undertaken by the corporate world to great effect. Beder's book deserves a much wider audience, it is the most authoritative account of how corporate resources have been marshalled over decades to hijack public sentiment and manipulate both science and the media. Their intention is to maintain high levels of profitability, while leaving the taxpayers with significant health problems, a destroyed environment and such a massive debt burden that repairing the damage becomes an impossible challenge. The industry's euphemism for this transference of the liability is "externalising costs."

The corporate business world spends vast sums of money lobbying politicians, influencing law-making and controlling public perceptions. By 1980 there were 12,000 lawyers representing business interests in Washington, with 9,000 lobbyists, 50,000 trade-association personnel, 8,000 PR specialists, 1,300 public affairs consultants and 12,000 specialized journalists reporting to particular industries on government developments. Since the 1980s these figures have continued to grow. In 2000, the top 25 public relations companies received more than $3,600,000,000 in revenues, representing yearly growth of 42% over the previous year. The PR industry in the UK is worth over a billion pounds, and employs more than 30,000 people. A 2000 survey found that one of the top six reasons for the growing importance of PR was environmental issues and regulations. [715]

In the USA, one of the mechanisms used by corporations to influence legislation that may affect them is through Political Action Committees (PACs). These committees enable them to support a particular political candidate or cause. PACs have been around since the 1930s in the US and were first associated with the labour unions. In 1972 there were fewer than 100 corporate PACs, but by 1980 there were over 1,100 and more than 1,800 by 1988. [716] In his book *Green Backlash-Global Subversion of the Environment Movement*, Andrew Rowell documents the massive rise corporate political donations via PACs in the 1980s—particularly by the oil industry. This turned out to be a significant factor in bringing the anti-environmental Reagan to power. Rowell quotes Harold Robbins, a Washington lobbyist for the Independent Petroleum Producers Association, as saying "We came to a decision some time ago that the only way we could change the political fortunes of the petroleum industry was to change Congress." The industry used its wealth not to support incumbents, but challengers who were more supportive of the industry. Those victories changed the face of Congress, not just at that time, but arguably from that time onwards. [717]

There is no doubt that the corporate attack on environmentalism has now become much more sophisticated. It is very fashionable to appear 'green' and seem to be responding to public concerns for the environment, without actually being so. Bruce Harrison runs a firm specialising in environmental PR, and cites how more than three quarters of Americans consider themselves environmentalists and do not trust big business to protect the environment. [718] At the same time, these corporations are portraying themselves as being more responsible and more environmentally friendly, while funding the very organisations that are undermining environmental standards and threatening our welfare. The very nature of corporate business is based on the "consumer society" where people are encouraged to 'consume', 'consume', 'consume', so there can be corporate 'growth'. This is obviously as totally unsustainable as the debt creation that generally accompanies it.

One of the ways corporations get around the public's mistrust of their intentions is to use support 'front' groups with eco-friendly sounding names and names that often include the words 'reasonable', 'sensible' and 'sound'. In this way, corporations can cut their costs by combining their resources to achieve their goals, while confusing the public at the same time. The Alliance for Sensible Environmental Reform, for example, represents the interests of polluting industries, such as the chemical companies. Another of the tactics used by industry is to polarise the debate around jobs versus the environment, as though you cannot have a safe environment *and* jobs. The cost to industry is always played to the hilt; costs to meet environmental regulations are portrayed as crippling industry, and leading to job cuts. One of the main advantages of using front groups is that you can both portray yourself as environmentally friendly and at the same time fund outright attacks on legislation designed to protect the environment. Merrill Rose, the Executive Vice-President of the public relations firm Porter/Novelli gave the following advice to industry:

> Put your words in someone else's mouth... there will be times when the position you advocate, no matter how well framed and supported will not be accepted by the public simply because you are who you are. Any institution with a vested commercial interest in the outcome of an issue has a natural credibility barrier to overcome with the public." [719]

Corporate Greenwashing

Another of the ways in which a corporation can re-brand its image is through what is referred to as "greenwashing" in the industry. British Petroleum, the world's second largest petroleum company for example reputedly spent $200 million on a PR and advertising campaign to greenwash its image. It shortened its name from British Petroleum to BP, coined the slogan "Beyond Petroleum" and initiated a huge rebranding exercise, with a new corporate insignia, replacing its old shield image with a green, yellow and white sunflower logo. It also partnered itself with the National Wildlife Federation (NWF) which allowed it to decorate its fuel stations with NWF toys and logos. BP's chief executive, Lord Browne also diverged from other petroleum companies with his acknowledgement of global warming at a speech at Stanford University in March 2001during which he said: "Climate change is an issue which raises fundamental questions about the relationship between companies and society as a whole, and between one generation and the next." He added, "Companies composed of highly skilled and trained people can't live in denial of mounting evidence gathered by hundreds of the most reputable scientists in the world." [720]

BP, of course,faces an uphill task promoting itself as environmentally friendly following the world's biggest oil spill disaster in the Gulf of Mexico that has affected thousands of miles of coastland along Texas, Louisiana, Mississippi, Alabama and Florida in 2010. Previously, in 1991, BP had been cited as the most polluting company in the USA, according to the EPA's toxic release data. In 1999 it was further charged with burning polluted gases at its refinery in Ohio, and subsequently agreed to pay a $1.7 million fine for this. Even that wasn't the end of things. It paid a further fine of $10 million to the EPA in 2000 and had to reduce pollution from its US refineries by tens of thousands of tons. Between January 1997 and March 1998 BP Amoco was responsible for more than 100 oil spills in America's Arctic. In 1999 after admitting illegally dumping hazardous waste at its 'environmentally friendly' oil field in Alaska, it was fined $500,000 for failing to report it, and had to pay a further $6.5 million in civil penalties associated with the waste's disposal. [721]

One of the more disturbing developments in the PR industry is the use of so called 'grassroots' organisations. These are typically funded by industry to promote their own causes, under a 'front' that is seemingly run by ordinary people. The illusion is designed to hijack public sentiment, and manipulate politicians and the media. Such artificially created grassroots coalitions are referred to as 'astroturf' (named after the synthetic grass). Jack Bonner of Bonner & Associates is one of the leading specialists providing these services for industry. He has a sophisticated computer system and three hundred phone lines. His staff call all over the country, looking for people who can be enlisted in support. Members of Congress are targeted apparently uncoordinated mail shots and phone calls that are not obviously from one source. They go out of their way to use different envelopes and stationery to create the impression that the communications are from genuine grassroots movements. [722]

The creation of such a mass movement is a manipulation of the population that is hard for the general public to see through. Ron Arnold was a man who saw the potential of mobilising grassroots organisations, and getting them to join forces and unify their strategy. With the help of Alan Gottlieb, a direct mail fundraising specialist and founder of the Center for the Defense of Free Enterprise, he managed to engineer a whole movement of a large number of groups in the USA with a similar right-wing agenda that was anti-environmental and pro unfettered development. It became known as the Wise Use Movement. In 1988, Arnold and Gottlieb organised a conference with more than 200 groups that would oppose the environmental movement in Reno, Nevada. In 1992 Arnold expressed his views on the environmental movement: "There is no compromising with the environmental movement, there is no redemption for it. It cannot be reformed. It must be dismantled entirely and replaced." [723]

Environmentalists were blamed for the demise of the timber industry following a decade of low timber demand and low prices—largely attributed to overcutting and log exportation. So the subsequent layoffs and closures provided an opportunity to blame environmentalists for the downturn. People were told that the environmental movement was out to close down their industry, take away their livelihoods and even their properties.

Burson-Marsteller (B-M) is a worldwide PR company that specialises in environmental issues and which has worked for a number of large corporations. In 1987 the timber giant Louisiana-Pacific, which had been a B-M client for more than a decade, was blaming the environmental movement for job losses that occurred soon after they had broken their workers' union. They bussed loyal workers to anti-environmental rallies to try and mobilise opinion. At the same time however, unbeknown to most people, the company was building a state-of-the-art plant in Mexico where it could pay its workers less than $2 per hour. By 1990, it was sending old growth timber by barge to its Mexican plant. As with so many situations, it was only with the passage of time that the true story of the company's attempts to blame environmentalists for the loss of jobs was revealed. [724]

The Rise of the Use of Think-Tanks

Another way that corporations have found useful to advance their cause is through the use of think-tanks. Think-tanks are generally private, tax-exempt research organisations that are supposedly non-political, yet have huge influence over governments and populations. The majority of them are extremely conservative. The Heritage Foundation, for example, is one of the wealthiest Washington-based think-tanks with a budget in 2000 of over $28 million. It has over 200 employees of which 50 are resident scholars. Heritage was one of the forces behind the Republicans' 'Contract with America' which included a number of measures designed to reduce environmental regulations and protections. America has more think-tanks than any other country, many financed by wealthy American families, as well as big business. The Heritage Foundation was founded in 1973 by a group of conservatives, and financially supported by Edward Noble, the petroleum tycoon and Joseph Coors the beer magnate. Joe Coors also went on to found the Coors Foundation which also attacked environmental regulation. [725]

The Cato Institute, established in 1977, is another Washington-based think-tank that has vigorously opposed environmental regulation. It was founded by Charles Koch, part owner of Koch Industries, one of the largest private run companies in the world, with annual revenues of $100,000,000,000. The company is also co-owned with his brother David, considered the richest resident of 740 Park Avenue, with an estimated personal fortune of $25,000,000,000 ($25 US billion). David is executive vice-president of the company and C.E.O. of its Chemical Technology

Group. David Koch actually ran for the US Presidency on a libertarian ticket in 1980, but failed to win more than 1% of the vote. It was assumed that this setback was what induced the brothers to utilise their vast fortunes to influence policy through campaign contributions, party donations and the use of think-tanks to advance their own agendas. Charles Koch was one of the founders of the ultra-conservative think-tank, the Cato Institute which was another organisation that has opposed environmental legislation. In 1995 the Federal Government sued Koch over a reported 300 oil spills at pipelines owned by the company—and which dumped an estimated 3 million gallons of oil into lakes and streams in 6 US states. In 2000 Koch Industries settled the case and agreed to pay $30 million for its role in those spills—and the largest fire in EPA's history.[726]

Forbes ranks Koch Industries as the second largest private company in the US after Cargill and says its consistent profitability has enabled the combined fortunes of the Koch brothers to be exceeded only by Bill Gates and Warren Buffett. Their influence in mainstream politics and environmentalism is vast. Greenpeace labelled Koch Industries as a "kingpin of climate science denial" and pointed out that the Kochs immensely outdid Exxon Mobil in donations to organisations fighting climate change legislation. They also opposed Obama's health-care reform, so-much-so that in political circles their network is referred to as the "Kochtopus". After the 1980 election, the brothers stepped back from public life and poured more than a hundred million dollars into dozens of supposedly independent organisations. Charles Lewis the founder of the non-partisan watchdog group, the Center for Public Integrity, said this of the vast wealth that the Koch brothers were able to throw around: "The Kochs are on a whole different level. There's no one else who has spent this much money. The sheer dimension of it is what sets them apart. They have a pattern of lawbreaking, political manipulation and obfuscation. I've been in Washington since Watergate, and I've never seen anything like it. They are the Standard Oil of our times." [727]

It is difficult to overstate the importance of think-tanks' influence over the political machine—as with other organisations there is a revolving door with their employees and government. When Ronald Reagan took office, at least twenty research fellows from the American Enterprise Institute (AEI) joined his administration. After leaving office, others of his appointees went to work at AEI. At the same time, the Heritage Foundation was able to place thirty-nine of its staff in Reagan's administration. What's more, most of the Heritage Foundation's policy recommendations were implemented by the Reagan administration. Sometimes it is not simply a matter of dictating policy, more a matter of sowing the seeds of doubt, simply to undermine concerted action as happened to the case for action on global warming. In the UK, the Environmental Unit of the Institute of Economic

Affairs (IEA) produced an article *Global Warming: Apocalypse or Hot Air* in 1994 to advance the case for the problem being overstated. The Australian Institute of Public Affairs (IPA) produced a paper in a similar vein called *Greenhouse Panic*. This was reprinted in *Engineering World* magazine and was quoted at conferences as being from an authoritative source, not from the far less authoritative IPA. Following a further report by the George C. Marshall Institute in the USA, George Bush used this report to justify his administration's more lenient approach to the whole problem of global warming. [728]

The Heritage Foundation played a significant role in the 1980s as a dominant public relations organisation, promoting the enterprise zone concept. Following Reagan's election, there was a concerted attack on the whole environmental movement, led by the Heritage Foundation— which found ways to blame environmentalists for just about every social problem affecting the country at that time. Considerable funds were made available by a lot of rich foundations to support these agendas. They all took their lead from the success of the Rockefellers and Carnegies, and their use of foundations to direct and control corporate strategies that were tax-free. Sharon Beder notes that as few as fifteen such foundations were able to finance hundreds of ultra-right and conservative organisations which, together with funding from corporate interests, gave the illusion that the far right is a rich and diverse group of a growing population of right-minded independent thinking people. [729]

Controlling Public Perception

"It is easier and less costly to change the way people think about reality than it is to change reality." [730] That quote from media critic Morris Wolfe sums up the approach of much of industry to people who get in their way. Put simply, it would cost them far more to take steps to save the environment than it would to pay public relations experts to manipulate public perceptions.[731]

It can be no surprise that corporations will continue to influence us and control the media as much as they can to support their own agendas.

The National Broadcasting Company (NBC), the first major American commercial broadcasting network was created by Radio Corporation of America (RCA) in 1926. It is headquartered in the General Electric building in New York's Rockefeller Center. In 1986, control of NBC passed to General Electric (GE) on the purchase of RCA for $6.4 billion. NBC owns and operates ten television stations, and a further 200 affiliates in the US and its territories.[732]

CORPORATIZING LIFE

General Electric, according to Forbes Global 2000 list, is rated as number three in the world with revenues of more than $147 billion, and assets in excess of $700 billion. It is one of the largest and most diverse conglomerates in the world, manufacturing light bulbs, home appliances, locomotives, jet engines, and nuclear power plants to name just a few. According to EPA documents, only the US government, Chevron Corporation and Honeywell are responsible for producing more Superfund toxic wastes sites. Based on data for the year 2000, the Political Economy Research Institute (PERI) listed GE as the fourth-largest corporate producer of air pollution in the US, with 2,000 tons of toxic chemicals released into the air. [733] In 2007, it was upgraded to third largest polluter by PERI.[734]

GE funds a number of conservative think tanks which include the Institute for International Economics, The American Enterprise Institute and the Center for Strategic and International Studies. These organisations supply 'independent' experts to bolster GE's position in a number of different ways. They are always available to appear on its NBC network to counter any negative publicity that may arise. GE employed Ronald Reagan himself in the 1950s and 60s, which was considered the beginning of his political career. When Reagan came to power he instituted tax cuts which resulted in, as previously stated companies like GE not having to pay a large tax bill on its earnings, and in GE's case actually getting a tax rebate of $283 million. Greider estimated that the 1981 tax legislation probably yielded GE as much as $1.3 billion over several years and probably even more in the long term.[735]

After the generous tax cuts of 1981 capital investment by American corporations accelerated, but not in the USA. Most of their investments were made in foreign countries to which many corporations were relocating to take advantage of lower labour costs and lax environmental laws. GE cut approximately 50,000 people from its payroll at this time—even while it was also pursuing numerous acquisitions such as RCA.[736]

A year after its acquisition by GE, NBC, broadcast a special documentary promoting nuclear power, using France as a model. Yet a short time after this airing, there were a number of accidents at French nuclear power stations. Approximately a third of French citizens were known to be against nuclear power but this was never aired by NBC. NBC was also accused of giving a one-sided account of the Three Mile Island disaster. The program apparently portrayed a local resident, Debbie Baker as not being as afraid of nuclear power as she used to be. She was shocked at this portrayal; her son was born with Down's syndrome nine months after the accident. She eventually received $1.1 million compensation for this. No mention was made of the other 200 families' settlements, covering injury, birth defects and death following the 1979 disaster. Instead a nuclear power industry expert was featured expressing the view that the plant's back-up safety systems had worked successfully. NBC was not alone in failing to report the true consequences of the disaster; the *New York Times* ran an article on the tenth anniversary of the accident with the headline *Three Mile Island: The Good News*, which argued that the accident was actually good news for the nuclear power industry because it provoked the management to improve their safety and management strategy. No mention was made of 2000 residents that had filed claims for cancer and other health problems resulting from the disaster, nor was there any mention of the 280 personal-injury settlements that had already paid out. No mention was made of the clusters of leukaemia, birth defects or hypothyroidism around the plant.[737]

There is more on the nuclear industry controversy in a later chapter, but for now I wish to stay with the role of PR and the way corporations are able to manipulate the public to their own ends. In 1991, the whole greening movement was in full swing, and the Seventh Annual Harlan Page Hubbard Lemon Awards for the *worst* advertisements in the USA took place. Two of the top ten 'awards' went to companies for deceptive green advertising, GE being one of them. The following year, one of the recipients was the US Council for Energy Awareness, for misrepresenting the environmental benefits of nuclear power, something they have been doing for decades. In the UK, Friends of the Earth had devised its own 'Green Con Award' which it awarded to British Nuclear Fuels Ltd (BNFL) in 1989 for misleading the public by trying to promote nuclear power as environmentally friendly, admitting that it produces little carbon dioxide, but neglecting to mention that it produces radioactive waste that lasts for thousands of years, together with deadly radiation.[738]

More serious than these awards for 'greenwashing' was the criticism by Ritt Bjerrgaard, the European Union Environment Commissioner, who condemned the Republican assault on environmental laws following both their refusal to back the EPA's enforcement of the clean air and water standards, and their lack of support for environmental protection. He said "The US has a responsibility to play its role in global leadership. And what is going on in the US Congress now is very discouraging... More and more often you hear claims that environmental legislation is bad for business or bad for competition. I do not agree with the thinking behind this and I do not think the public – in the US or Europe – agrees with this thinking."[739]

The acceptance by the public of products in the market place cannot currently be achieved without manipulation and control of the full information about them. This means the true impacts on our health are obscured from us—in such a way that in can become at least difficult, if not impossible to discover the causes of not only illnesses but also death.

CORPORATIZING LIFE

In the next chapter we move into even thornier territory where the full impact of information control, the PR machine, and damage limitation is revealed to an even greater degree.

Chapter 16
The Genie is Out of the Bottle

The gene genie is fast getting out of control. The practitioners of genetic engineering biotechnology, regulators and critics alike, have all underestimated the risks involved, which are inherent to genetic engineering biotechnology, particularly when it is misguided by an outmoded and erroneous world view that comes from bad science. The dreams may already be turning into nightmares.
Dr Mae-Wan Ho [740]

The dramatic changes in agriculture, and their effect on the food system, have already been partially discussed. But with the advance of genetic engineering, these developments have even more profound ramifications. It is well known that Nelson Rockefeller was a significant player in the development of agriculture in the USA and Latin America. He was Assistant Secretary of State for Latin America under Roosevelt, and he funded a new company called International Basic Economy Corporation (IBEC) to introduce mass–scale agriculture to the US and Latin America. Rockefeller's IBEC invited Cargill, the privately owned US agribusiness giant, to work with it in Brazil. They turned Brazil into the third largest corn producer in the world, and later developed its soya bean industry. Through the Foundation that bears his name, Rockefeller developed agriculture and promoted genetic research, and it was he and his team who coined the term 'agribusiness'. The Rockefeller Foundation, in conjunction with the Ford Foundation, created the International Rice Research Institute (IRRI) in the Philippines, and the International Maize and Wheat Improvement Center (CIMMYT) with the Mexican Government, and eventually combined their resources to form the global Consultative Group on International Agriculture (CGIAR). This put Rockefeller in the position to shape global agriculture policy. Engdahl, in his book, *Seeds of Destruction, The Hidden Agenda of Genetic Manipulation* explains how Rockefeller ensured his policies would prevail by the way he involved the United Nations and the World Bank:

To ensure maximum impact, CGIAR drew in the United Nations' Food and Agriculture Organization (FAO), the UN Development programme (UNDP) and the World Bank. Thus, through a carefully-planned leverage of its initial funds, Rockefeller by the beginning of the 1970s was in a position to shape global agriculture policy. [741]

Development of Genetically Modified Crops and the Agricultural Industrial Giants

Beginning in the 1990s Monsanto spent some $8 billion buying up seed companies to complement its agri-chemical business. Dupont completed its $7.7 billion takeover of Pioneer Hi-Bred, a company founded by Henry Wallace of Rockefeller fame, and which held the largest proprietary seed bank in the world. These companies were considered to be two of the four industrial giants promoting the use of genetically modified organisms (GMO) or transgenic crops. Dow AgroSciences, a $3.4 billion seed and agrochemical conglomerate, active in 66 countries, is the third. The fourth, Syngenta, based in Switzerland, claimed to be the largest agrochemical corporation in 2005, and the third largest seed company. It grew out of the merger of the agriculture divisions of Norvartis and AstraZenica into a $6.8 billion company. These companies can be considered to be at the forefront of the march to the global proliferation of genetically modified food.

Early Warnings and Flawed Science

Response to genetically modified food has not been uniformly enthusiastic. One of the first approved farmers to use genetically-engineered corn for growing in Germany was Gottfried Glöckner of North Hessen. He discovered that the Syngenta Bt-176 genetically engineered corn that he fed his cattle resulted in their deaths, destroyed his milk production, and poisoned his farmland. Syngenta's corn had been engineered to produce a toxin of bacillus thuringiensis which was claimed to be deadly to an insect—the European Corn Borer. For the first three years Glöckner had found little problem, but when he increased production and started to feed his cattle exclusively on the corn, they started getting violent diarrhoea, gluey-white faeces, and had blood in their milk. Some stopped producing milk; calves started dying and then the cows. He lost most of his heard of seventy cattle.[742]

Professor of Biochemistry at University of California, Berkeley, John Neilands, believes that GMO foods may bring about a disaster of epic proportions. Since genetically modified food is already in the food chain, and is un-labelled, he suggests we should all grow our own, if at all possible. He believes that labelling should be compulsory for all transgenically modified foods (in this text we use both "transgenically modified" and "genetically modified" as the same thing). He further mentions that the use of the Bt toxin by biotech companies will create resistant strains of the toxin and render it useless to organic farmers. This would be unfortunate, as it is one of the few non-chemical natural remedies that is popular with organic growers. The ramifications barely bear thinking about. [743]

There has been a sea change of opinion about genetically engineered food since the discovery that RNA is not just a simple carrier mechanism, as was previously thought. In 2007, *The Economist* published an article that captured the general sentiment at that time:

"It is beginning to dawn on biologists that they may have got it [genetics] wrong. Not completely wrong, but wrong enough to be embarrassing."

The article goes on:

RNA has been more or less neglected as a humble carrier of messages and fetcher of building materials. This account of the cell was so satisfying to biologists that few bothered to look beyond it. But they are looking now. For, suddenly, cells seem to be full of RNA doing who-knows-what. And the diversity is staggering.

Scientists have discovered that there are numerous types of RNA, and more are still being discovered. They found, for example, that piRNA are abundant in developing sex cells, and that all mammals, fish and flies can be infertile without them. [744]

Now that the science behind genetic engineering has been seriously challenged, this poses a problem for the governments that have promoted it without reservation. Don Lotter, Ph.D. reports on the controversy:

A major conflict over this issue has developed. On one side are scientists, universities and corporations who have invested nearly 25 years and tens of billions of dollars in the genetic engineering of crop plants. On the other side is a flood of evidence that the process of food plant transgenics (genetic engineering) is deeply and fatally flawed and has been resting on a theoretical foundation that has crumbled away as the science of genetics reinvents itself... The fatal blow to this one-gene one-protein model came in 2003 with the shocking results of the Human Genome Project which showed that humans have vastly fewer genes than previously believed. [745]

UNHEALTHY BETRAYAL

Barry Commoner the renowned cellular biologist made the following comment on the results of the Human Genome Project: "The fact that one gene can give rise to multiple proteins ... destroys the theoretical foundation of a multibillion dollar industry, the genetic engineering of food crops." [746]

This is not to say there had been a universal acceptance by the scientific community of genetically engineered food prior to the discovery that RNA is a lot more complex in its behaviour than previously understood.

Dr Pusztai Ridiculed

Dr Arpad Pusztai, a geneticist and a specialist in biotechnology for over 35 years, was undertaking research for the Rowett Research Institute in Scotland. Pusztai was considered the world's leading expert on lectins and the genetic modification of plants—and was considered an enthusiast in his field. Pusztai had undertaken a study whereby potatoes had been modified with a lectin that was supposed to act as a natural insecticide. He had been feeding rats on a diet of GM potatoes, and found that rats fed for more than 110 days on this diet showed marked developmental changes. He found that the GMO rats had remarkably smaller liver, heart, and even brain sizes and further that they demonstrated weaker immune systems. However, he made the mistake of airing his research and his views on the popular ITV program *World In Action* in August 1998. In this he referred to his research on the genetically modified potatoes and mentioned he had discovered "slight growth retardation, and an effect on the immune system." He further added: 'If I had the choice I would certainly not eat it". He demanded tighter rules over GM foods, and warned: "I find it's very unfair to use our fellow citizens as guinea pigs. We have to find guinea pigs in the laboratory." Initially he was congratulated for his work by his immediate boss. But, within 48 hours, this 68 year old researcher was effectively fired, along with his wife who had been a researcher with Rowett for more than 13 years. He was told that he was never to speak to the press again about his research, nor was his research team, under threat of legal action. His papers were seized and his research team disbanded. In the following weeks, his reputation was attacked and his work ridiculed. [747]

That began a controversy that put him in conflict with the biotech industry, the scientific establishment, and both the US and UK governments, as was revealed some years later by Andrew Rowell:

THE GENIE IS OUT OF THE BOTTLE

Now, five years on, there are disturbing claims that this distinguished scientist was the victim of behind-the-scenes manoeuvring at the highest political level. Some of the allegations are truly explosive. They raise profound questions about the extraordinary network of relationships between senior Labour figures and the biotech companies. They also throw new light on why the multi-billion-pound GM industry continues to press ahead in the face of huge public opposition. [748]

Pusztai is convinced that there was direct pressure by President Clinton to Prime Minister Blair, and thence to the Rowett Institute, on behalf of Monsanto, something that is denied by Pusztai's boss, professor Philip James. However, colleagues from the institute have confirmed to him that they believe it was in fact, the case. In February 1999, 30 leading scientists from 13 countries signed an open letter supporting Pusztai, which was published in the *Guardian*.

Worries Abound—the Inherent Danger of GMO Foods

Pusztai was not the only scientist who was victimised for expressing concerns about GMO foods. Dr Mae-Wan Ho, director of the Institute of Science in Society, senior academic scientist at the Open University in the UK, and previously Fellow of the National Genetics Foundation in the USA, spoke out at what she regarded as slipshod scientific claims about GMO safety. At an international Independent Science panel on GM plants, she warned that genetic modification was not like normal plant breeding:

"Contrary to what you are told by the pro-GM scientists, the process is not at all precise. It is uncontrollable and unreliable, and typically ends up damaging and scrambling the host genome, with entirely unpredictable consequences." She was forced into early retirement. The Blair government introduced new codes of conduct for all state-funded research, whereby anyone who spoke out about GMO findings could face court injunctions or be sued for breach of contract, as well as instant dismissal. [749]

Dr Mae-Wan Ho continued her work and published a number of books and papers on genetic engineering. She explained her belief that genetic modification of food is based on an obsolete theory, and hence was both ineffective and dangerous:

Genetic engineering of plants and animals began in the mid-1970s in the belief that the genome (the totality of all the genetic material of a species) is constant and static, and that the characteristics of organism are simply hardwired in their genome. But geneticists soon discovered that the genome is remarkably dynamic and 'fluid', and constantly in conversation with the environment. This determines which genes are turned on, when, where, by how much and for how long. Moreover, the genetic material itself could also be marked or changed according to experience, and the influence passed on to the next generation... These processes are precisely orchestrated and finely tuned by the organism as a whole, in a highly coordinated molecular 'dance of life' that's necessary for survival.

In contrast, genetic engineering in the laboratory is crude, imprecise and invasive. The rogue genes inserted into a genome to make a GMO could land anywhere; typically in a rearranged or defective form, scrambling and mutating the host genome, and have the tendency to move or rearrange further once inserted, basically because they do not know the dance of life. That's ultimately why genetic modification doesn't work and is also dangerous. [750]

Dr Ho is not alone in her belief that genetic modification is dangerous. Dr Robert Mann, a retired biologist and senior lecturer from the University of Auckland compares genetic modification with nuclear power—everyone was so gung-ho to start with, until it became clear it was dangerous and had unforeseen consequences. On the lack of scientific credibility, he had this to say:

One tawdry old argument we have heard since 1974 and can expect to hear again in all its flagrant deceit, is the claim that gene transfers occur naturally so GE is only hastening them. This line of talk is a smoke-screen designed to obscure the fact that GE usually performs artificial transfers which are not believed to occur in nature. If we change the rates, or even worse the specificities, with which genes can jump around, we may wreak biological havoc on a global scale.

He goes on to quote Professor Abigail Sayers, an expert on genetic transfers: "According to conventional wisdom, a plasmid used to introduce a gene into a genetically engineered microorganism can be rendered nontransmissible... [on the contrary] there is no such thing as a "safe" plasmid... conjugative transposons, as modern sphinxes, are challenging us with a riddle we may have to answer in order to survive: what can be done to slow or stop the transfer of antibiotic-resistant genes...?"

He further comments:

But the gene jockeys claim they can, godlike, foresee the evolutionary results of their artificial transposings of human genes into sheep, bovine genes into tomatoes, etc. This is extreme, deluded arrogance; for the theologically inclined.

He further expresses his concern at the total inadequacy of risk analysis for genetic manipulation:

Attempts at risk analysis for GE are, obviously, doomed to be even more misleading. The system of a living cell, even if no viruses or foreign plasmids (let alone prions) are tossed in, is incomparably more complex than a nuclear reactor. There is no prospect of imagining most of the ways it can go badly wrong after the abuse entailed in foreign genes inserted by glass needle, or by micro-shotgun, or by infective particle of whatever sort. Evidently, one cannot begin to estimate the risk of a mishap the qualitative form of which has not yet been imagined. We do not and cannot know how to put useful, justified numbers on the chances of severe GE mishaps.

He cites a number of genetic mishaps, which included the death of at least 27 people who were killed by taking a tryptophan supplement manufactured by a Japanese company, Showa Denko, using a genetically engineered microbial culture. Thousands of people remain crippled and Showa Denko reputedly paid out US $2 billion to avoid being taken to court.

Dr Mann further questions the sense of gambling with our future: "The prostitution of science is most complete and most dangerous in the selfish commercial gene. When will we muster the ethical power to wake up from this sleepwalking?" [751]

According to Steven Drucker in his book, *Altered Genes Twisted Truth* estimates for those affected are much higher, estimates vary from 5,000 -10,000, and the death toll was also much higher, at least 80 died according to the CDC. Drucker believes that there was a huge reluctance to acknowledge this disaster as being due to genetically modified organisms—due to the adverse effect this could have on the un-regulated nature of the industry. His book reveals how the proponents of genetic engineering were allowed to circumvent any real oversight of their work and unleash whatever genetic modifications they fancied—whilst government agencies such as the FDA and EPA did little to prevent them.[752]

If you have heard about the tryptophan disaster, you are probably thinking that it happened some time ago, and steps will have been taken to stop it happening again. Well you would be both right and wrong. Over-the-counter sales of tryptophan were banned in 1989, following the disaster. However, Henryk Behr was able to order some tryptophan from a British company, Biovea, in September 2010—and documents how, one hour after taking a second 500mg capsule as directed, in his words "the gates of hell opened and they have not closed to this day." This he documents in his book *A Momentary Lapse of Reason – Living with L-Tryptophan Induced EMS and the Hidden Dangers of Genetic Modification of our Foods*. He now suffers from Eosinophilia Myalgia Syndrome (EMS), a very rare condition that he has found to be an incurable, untreatable autoimmune disease. He relates how his life went from a happy and contented, busy family life to a life of sitting on a couch in severe pain every day, where he can no longer play with his children, or watch television. He complains he has been unable to sleep more than two hours a night in the last seven months and has been unable to perform sexually. At times he is unable to even walk. He suffers from severe depression and anxiety because of it.[753] Meanwhile, several other companies had been producing L-Tryptophan without using genetically engineered bacteria – and had no problems with it, in total contrast to the GE version.

Problems with genetically modified organisms were not new to the Japanese: research undertaken in Japan in 1995 had already identified problems with genetically engineered yeast when they discovered an accumulation of a highly toxic compound that did not exist in the non-engineered cells. Their comments make sober reading:

> The results presented here indicate that, in genetically engineered yeast cells, the metabolism is significantly disturbed by the introduced genes or their gene products and the disturbance brings about the accumulation of the unwanted toxic compound MG in cells. Such accumulation of highly reactive MG may cause a damage in DNA, thus suggesting that the scientific concept of `substantially equivalent' for the safety assessment of genetically engineered food is not always applied to genetically engineered microbes, at least in the case of recombinant yeast cells. In order to apply recombinant yeast cells to practical fermentation processes, the safety level of MG in cells should be established.
>
> Thus, the results presented may raise some questions regarding the safety and acceptability of genetically engineered food, and give some credence to the many consumers who are not yet prepared to accept food produced using gene engineering techniques. [754]

Reasons Cited for the Need for GMOS Are Fundamentally Flawed

One of the main reasons cited for the promotion of genetically modified crops is that it is necessary to feed the growing population. There is little evidence to support this. There is in fact a growing body of research demonstrating the opposite. A review put out by the Union of Concerned Scientists found the evidence for any benefit sorely lacking—and certainly not if you take into account the increased pesticide use that generally accompanies it. They concluded:

> Our analysis shows that despite tremendous effort and expense, genetic engineering has only succeeded in measurably increasing the yield of one major food or livestock feed crop—and this contribution has been small compared with other available methods.[755]

Doug Gurian-Sherman one of the authors of the report, added: "Despite 20 years of research and 13 years of commercialization, genetic engineering has failed to significantly increase U.S. crop yields".

What seems to be ignored by many people is that progress in agriculture does not rest on genetic engineering; great strides have been made and will continue to be made, using conventional breeding techniques. Another study by the University of Michigan analysed a data set of 293 examples in agriculture to compare yields of organic agriculture versus conventional agriculture—and this led them to some important conclusions:

> These results indicate that organic agriculture has the potential to contribute quite substantially to the global food supply, while reducing the detrimental environmental impacts of conventional agriculture. Evaluation and review of this paper have raised important issues about crop rotations under organic versus conventional agriculture.

> Model estimates indicate that organic methods could produce enough food on a global *per capita* basis to sustain the current human population, and potentially an even larger population, without increasing the agricultural land base. [756]

They found that organic farming can yield up to three times as much food on individual farms in developing countries as could be produced by high-intensive methods on the same land. This research refutes the long-standing claim that organic farming methods cannot produce enough food to feed the global population. [757]

According to André Leu, we are currently producing more than double the amount of food needed to feed the world, and as the FAO figures confirm, world hunger stems from the lack of the ability of the poor to afford to buy adequate food.[758]

Much of Our Food is Wasted

So let's be clear here, that food poverty is not due to lack of food production, but to a lack of the *ability to pay for it*. As previously stated, we are already producing vast food surpluses. On top of this must be added the extensive food waste that is generated by our disastrously inefficient food system.

Currently we produce approximately four billion metric tonnes of food per year but, due to poor harvesting practices, poor storage and transportation practices, consumer and retail wastage, it is estimated that as much as 50 percent (1.2 – 2 billion tonnes) of all food never reaches the human stomach. A report on those figures by the Institution of Mechanical Engineers stated: "This figure does not reflect the fact that large amounts of land, energy, fertilisers and water have also been lost in the production of foodstuffs which simply end up as waste. This level of waste is a tragedy that cannot continue if we are to succeed in the challenge of sustainably meeting our future food demands.

They go on to detail some of their findings:

Major supermarkets, in meeting consumer expectations, will often reject entire crops of perfectly edible fruit and vegetables at the farm because they do not meet exacting marketing standards for their physical characteristics, such as size and appearance. For example, up to 30% of the UK's vegetable crop is never harvested as a result of such practices. Globally, retailers generate 1.6 million tonnes of food waste annually in this way.

Of the produce that does appear in the supermarket, commonly used sales promotions frequently encourage customers to purchase excessive quantities which, in the case of perishable foodstuffs, inevitably generate wastage in the home. Overall between 30% and 50% of what has been bought in developed countries is thrown away by the purchaser. [759]

Their report also details land, water and energy usage during food production. Currently, for example the agricultural sector is responsible for approximately 70% of human water consumption. At the same time, one hectare of land can produce enough rice or potatoes to feed 19-22 people, whereas the same area of land can only produce enough lamb or beef to feed one or two people. Beef production also uses 50 times more water than vegetable production, and considerably more energy.

On a global scale 3-5% of the world's natural gas supply is used in agrochemical manufacturing, such as fertiliser and pesticides, while a further 3% of total global energy consumption is used by the agricultural sector. [760]

THE GENIE IS OUT OF THE BOTTLE

The Rise of Monsanto and its Reach into the Corridors of Power

However, it would obviously be unrealistic to expect companies like Monsanto to give up marketing genetically modified products after investing so much in them. By 2002 GM crops were grown on 58.6 million hectares of land in 16 countries, with 68% of this based in the USA, 22% in Argentina, 6% in Canada and 3% in China. Monsanto's seed technology accounted for 91% of the world total of GM crops in 2001.[761]

Monsanto is listed as being 197 in the *Fortune 500,* with global revenues of $11.74 billion in 2009. [762] In 2007 it acquired Delta & Pine Land, the largest owner of cotton seeds and the owner of the patent for Genetic Use Restriction Technology (GURT), colloquially known as terminator technology or suicide seeds. This technology meant farmers would have to buy seed each year from their supplier instead of saving their own seed as they have done for millennia. Delta was also the leader in the second generation T-GURT seeds, commonly referred to as Traitor technologies, whereby plant growth can be controlled by the application or with-holding of a chemical inducer. This technology proved cheaper to produce. [763]

Monsanto's influence reaches far into the corridors of power in the Obama administration; three of their executives hold high positions in it. Michael Taylor, a senior advisor to the U.S. Food and Drug Administration (FDA), used to be a vice-president of Monsanto. Islam Siddiqui, a former vice-president of the Monsanto funded lobbying group, CropLife, and is now a negotiator for the US Trade Representative on agriculture. Roger Beachy, the former director of a plant science center funded by Monsanto, is the director of the National Institute of Food and Agriculture. Obama's nomination of Elena Kagan to the US Supreme Court can also be considered to have been helpful to Monsanto—she was the lawyer who defended Monsanto's right to contaminate the environment with GM alfalfa. Michael Taylor used to be a partner of the law firm that represented Monsanto on bovine growth hormone issues. Yet, as the FDA's deputy commissioner for policy, he wrote the rBGH (recombinant bovine growth hormone) labelling guidelines that insisted there was no difference between rGBH and regular milk. When Monsanto got approval for the use of the artificial bovine growth hormone, the person in charge of receiving it, and evaluating it was Margaret Miller, deputy director of Human Safety and Consultative Services. Guess who at Monsanto who was in charge of preparing the report? Yep you got it—Margaret Miller in her previous incarnation. Taylor moved to the FDA in July 1991, to fill the newly created post of Deputy Commissioner for Policy. Following his oversight of the entrance of genetically modified food, starting with rbGH milk, he was given the post of Vice-President for Public Policy. On July 7, 2009, Taylor once again returned to government as Senior Advisor to the FDA Commissioner. That's what you call a well-greased revolving door! [764]

But what is the response of the GMO companies to all the negative science? Perhaps David Rowe of Dow Agro Sciences, (a branch of Dow Chemical Co) summed it up best when, at a food technology conference, he said "Perhaps the greatest challenge we face lies not in the area of technology, but in marketing" and called for more investment in 'education' (ie PR). The conference was also told by another delegate to lose the use of "GMO" or "genetically modified organism" and instead use the terms "food biotechnology" or "agricultural biotechnology". Seven companies in the biotechnology industry subsequently formed the Council for Biotechnology Information which was funded to the tune of $50 million to help build public support. [765]

Many people in the industry might feel they have an uphill task promoting genetically modified (GM) products, as there is now increasingly adverse information available about them. In 2003, The Alliance for Bio-Integrity produced a report quoting numerous studies showing that the yields from GM crops were lower than those from conventional crops, and that the latter created further problems, including pesticide resistant weeds, and insects resistant to the Bt toxin. They cite studies of Iowa farmers between 1998 and 2000, by economist, Dr Michael Duffy, who found that the seed companies and chemical companies reaped the primary benefits of biotechnology, while the farmers who planted genetically modified corn and soybeans fared no better financially than farmers who grew conventional crops.[766]

Serious Health Risks and GMOs

By the beginning of 2007 there were just over 20 peer-reviewed studies on GM crops for food. Of these, 19 studied animals and 1 humans. Yet all were industry-funded and all lacked true scientific integrity. They have been criticised as 'notorious for using creative ways to avoid finding problems', typically failing to investigate the impacts on gut function, liver function, kidney function, the endocrine system, immune system, allergy responses, cancer incidence, and the effect on the unborn. Jeffrey Smith, in his book *Genetic Roulette, The Documented Health Risks of Genetically Engineered Foods,* puts it quite succinctly by saying 'They've got "bad science" down to a science.'[767]

Proponents of GM food would like us to believe that genetic modification is a clever and exact science—no more of a concern than traditional breeding techniques. They say it is fundamental to progress, and that about any negative impact on health implications are totally unwarranted. However, according to the World Health Organization, Genetically Modified Organisms (GMOs) are

THE GENIE IS OUT OF THE BOTTLE

"organisms in which the genetic material (DNA) has been altered in such a way that does not occur naturally." The American Academy of Environmental Medicine expresses how uncertain this science is by explaining that "genetic engineering", "biotechnology" or "recombinant DNA technology" consists of *randomly* (my emphasis) inserting genetic fragments of DNA from one organism to another, usually from a different species. They cite the example of the development of the use of the pesticide Cry1Ab protein, more commonly referred to as Bt toxin, (its source originally the bacteria, Bacillus Thuringiensis). Due to the fact that it inserted into the DNA of corn randomly, both the location of the transgene sequence in corn DNA, and the consequences of the insertion, differ with each insertion. Following the insertion, these plant cells are then cultured in a lab that allows them to grow into plants. [768]

According to Jeffrey Smith, rats fed Monsanto's MON 863 Bt corn for 90 days developed numerous reactions, including increased blood sugar levels, kidney inflammation, and liver and kidney lesions amongst other symptoms. In another study of mice fed GM potatoes engineered with the Bt toxin, abnormal and excessive cell growth of the lower part of the small intestine was discovered. Some of the cells were damaged or broken off, while others were abnormally shaped, and even had multiple nuclei. These studies consequently expose the myth that the toxin wouldn't survive the digestive process. In India, more than 1800 sheep from different herds died, after being fed on Bt cotton plants. In one village, the death rate in 42 herds was 25%. Death followed in just five to seven days after ingestion. Visits to other villages revealed further cases, and farmers estimate the total number of casualties to have been as high as 10,000. Numerous workers in India also complained of allergies associated with Bt cotton, with eyes becoming red and swollen, excessive tears and nasal discharge, facial itching and other skin related problems. [769]

Some more recent studies suggest there may be many other serious health risks associated with GM foods, such as immune dysregulation, infertility, dysregulation of genes associated with cholesterol synthesis, insulin regulation, protein formation—as well as the previously mentioned changes to the liver, kidney and gastrointestinal systems. In some animal studies, the actual structure and function of the liver was affected, lipid and carbohydrate metabolism was altered, and cellular changes that could lead to accelerated aging were discovered.[770]

The American Academy of Environmental Medicine expressed its general concern about GMO food with the following caution:

> Because GM foods pose a serious health risk in the areas of toxicology, allergy and immune
> function, reproductive health, and metabolic, physiologic and genetic health and are without

benefit, the AAEM believes that it is imperative to adopt the precautionary principle, which is one of the main regulatory tools of the European Union environmental and health policy and serves as a foundation for several international agreements. [771]

Their urge for caution was echoed in a 2001 report by the Expert Panel of The Royal Society of Canada, which took the view that '(a) it is "scientifically unjustifiable" to presume that GE foods are safe and (b) the "default presumption" for every GE food should be that the genetic alteration has induced unintended and potentially hazardous side effects'. They further recommend that a national research program be established to monitor the long-term effects of GM organisms on the environment, and both human, and on animal health and welfare. [772]

As the evidence accumulated, revealing that there were few if any benefits with GMO food production to farmers, it became ever more clear that the only beneficiaries were the seed and pesticide suppliers. Here's a comment from one prestigious organisation (*The Lancet*):

Crops genetically modified to have reduced susceptibility to pests are promoted as a solution to low food yields in developing countries. The motive of these promoters is profit, not altruism. ..In view of this unbridled commercial approach to genetic modification, it is perhaps not surprising that companies have paid little evident attention to the potential hazards to health of genetically modified foods. But it is astounding that the US Food and Drug Administration has not changed their stance on genetically modified food adopted in 1992.

The issue of genetically modified foods has been badly mishandled by everyone involved. Governments should never have allowed these products into the food chain without insisting on rigorous testing for effects on health. [773]

There are numerous examples of failures with genetic modification. Take the rats that developed significant structural changes and serious health effects, after only ten days on GM food. They were still exhibiting the same symptoms after 110 days—the equivalent of approximately ten years in human terms. There are also worries that the Bt toxin will cause insect tolerance, and remove one of the most useful non-chemical tools used by the organic industry. Some scientists also worry about horizontal gene transfer where, for example, the property of Bt toxin could transfer to humans. Susan Bardocz a biochemist and nutritionist expressed the situation thus: "As shown in the human feeding experiment, a fully functional transgenic construct rendering Roundup Ready soya resistant to glyphosate can partially survive, be taken up by bacteria resident in the alimentary tract and convert us and our animals into pesticide factories." [774]

THE GENIE IS OUT OF THE BOTTLE

The Hazards of Gene Insertion

One of the great fallacies that biotechnology promoters would love us to believe is that this is a highly accurate and safe science. So let's start examining that belief by looking at how gene insertion is actually done. The procedure is commonly undertaken with a gene gun, which basically entails coating thousands of shards of gold or tungsten with a foreign gene and then blasting it into the DNA with a 22-calibre gene gun. As you can imagine, to say this is imprecise would be an understatement. There is a lot of structural damage caused by this process, and there is no way of knowing exactly what will result. However, attached to the inserted gene is an Antibiotic Resistance Marker (ARM), which will protect the gene when the whole mixture is doused with antibiotics. Only the cells that survive this process will have the gene inserted into their DNA. These surviving cells are then grown in a culture medium.[775]

The principal problems with this process are that the precise location of the gene in the DNA cannot be known, and that insertion damage can also be caused. This latter, often referred to as insertion mutagenesis or insertion mutation can have unknown consequences. It wasn't until 2003 that any large systematic study was undertaken to assess the risk—and later studies have confirmed how unpredictable the whole process is. Dr Jonathan Latham, Executive Director of The Bioscience Resource Project, with a team of researchers, reviewed much of the work since this period and came to the following conclusion: "Transgene insertion is infrequently, if ever, a precise event. Mutations found at transgene insertion sites include deletions and rearrangements of host chromosomal DNA and introduction of superfluous DNA... Insertion sites can be associated with extensive chromosomal rearrangements, while those of particle bombardment appear invariably to be associated with deletion, and extensive scrambling of inserted and chromosomal DNA." [776]

However, it is not just with the insertion procedure that problems arise, Dr Latham again: "Ancillary procedures associated with plant transformation, including tissue culture and infection with *A tumefaciens*, can also introduce mutations. These genome-wide mutations can number from hundreds to many thousands per diploid genome."

He continues: "Despite the fact that confidence in the safety and dependability of crop species rests significantly on their genetic integrity, the frequency of transformation-induced mutations and their importance as potential biosafety hazards are poorly understood."

The conclusions they reach in their wide review are sobering: "We conclude that much remains to be discovered about genome-wide and insertion-site mutations. In particular, lack of information, especially for crop plants and particle bombardment, means that plant transformation may be even more damaging than is apparent from this review." [777]

Jeffrey Smith raises the point that many geneticists rely on what is called the Southern Blot test for evaluating insertion effects. However, this is only capable of picking up major changes, whereas the more thorough method, DNA sequence analysis, is able to pick up mutations, fragmentations or additional insertions etc. Not surprisingly, this is a more expensive and time-consuming operation. But since very few people take the trouble to use the more expensive approach, he makes the point: "This means on the whole, biologists who create GM plants and the regulators that approve them, have no idea of the extent of DNA damage or the associated unintended effects."[778]

It is hard to understand what effect our actions have when the effects cannot be easily observed. For some time now, molecular biologists have used the Cauliflower Mosaic Virus (CaMV) to enhance a plant cell's defensive devices against foreign DNA from upsetting the cell's homeostasis and regulatory mechanisms. It acts like a light switch and activates the gene that has been added. The trouble with this approach though, unlike a normal cell in which operations are turned on and off as needed, is that CaMV has to be turned on all the time, there is no 'off' switch. This is obviously a matter for concern, and Professor Joe Cummins and his team who researched the CaMV promoter, had this to say: "The findings suggest that transgenic constructs with the CaMV 35S promoter may be structurally unstable and prone to horizontal gene transfer and recombination. The potential hazards are mutagenesis, carcinogenesis, reactivation of dormant viruses, and generation of new viruses."

There are those who argue that CaMV cannot be harmful because we have all probably eaten infected cauliflowers and cabbages and survived to tell the tale. But professor Cummins responds: "What we have been consuming is predominantly intact virus and not naked viral genomes. Naked viral genomes have been found to give full-blown infections in nonhost species that are not susceptible to the intact virus."

He further cautions: "It is not inconceivable that the 35S promoter in transgenic constructs can reactivate dormant viruses or generate new viruses by recombination." [779]

For many people who believed all the initial hype about genetically modified products, the reality may prove a disappointment. The first major shock came in May 2000, after Monsanto's Roundup Ready soybeans had been on the market for seven years. It was then found that there were two additional gene fragments in the soya DNA that were not supposed to be there. Andrew Pollack in the New York Times had this to say:

"The world's most widely grown genetically engineered crop contains some unexpected DNA next to its inserted gene, casting some doubts on the biotechnology industry's assertions that its technology is precise and predictable."

The mysterious DNA was discovered by Belgian government and university scientists. Last year, the Belgian scientists found that the soybeans contained not simply a single copy of the bacterial gene, as was expected, but two fragments of it. They commented:

"This is the second time that scientists have found something in Roundup Ready soybeans that Monsanto did not seem to know was there and had not cited at the time of the product's approval."

The Belgian scientists, led by Dr. Marc De Loose from the Centre for Agricultural Research, Melle, suggested that this unknown DNA was probably the plant's DNA that had been re-arranged or scrambled at the time of the original gene insertion. They also suggested it may be a portion of the plant's own DNA that was deleted. [780]

Apparently, Tony Combes of Monsanto defended the revelations of the DNA pieces by saying "It would have been a constituent of the Roundup Ready soybeans used in all the safety assessment studies." But, according to Arpad Pusztai, he hadn't seen *any* safety studies. Jeffrey Smith lists 14 items that he felt prudent to review, for safety considerations, but these were never undertaken to their knowledge. The fourteenth item, however, states that adequate testing for allergies in humans for their new soya has not been properly undertaken. Apparently this prompted Pusztai to label allergies as the "Achilles heel of GM food". All this followed the announcement in March 1999, when the York Nutritional Laboratory, reported, that soya allergies had skyrocketed over the previous 12 months to become one of the top ten allergies. This was no surprise to the British Medical Association, who had already warned that the new technology might well lead to new types of allergies. [781]

UNHEALTHY BETRAYAL

Unforeseen Changes to Our Food and the Rise of Food Allergies

According to the World Allergy Organization, the incidence of allergic diseases has been rising dramatically in both developed and developing countries over the past two decades. Typical cases include asthma, rhinitis, anaphylaxis, eczema, urticarial (hives), and angioedema (this is associated with swelling and build-up of fluid under the skin and is associated with immune problems). Children in particular, have been affected by this rising trend.[782]

Scientists in Australia, at the Commonwealth Science and Industrial Research Organisation (CSIRO), halted the commercialisation of genetically modified peas after their research had produced alarming results. The GM pea contained an added protein, found naturally in beans, which protects them from common pests such as the pea weevil. The protein, an alpha-amylase inhibitor, disrupts the enzyme that is necessary for starch digestion in the weevil, causing it to starve to death. However, when mice were fed these GM peas, they showed an immune response. Following a second exposure they suffered allergic-type reactions, asthma with narrowing of the airways, and inflammation of the airways with excessive mucus secretion. Following injections, swellings occurred. More disturbingly, it was discovered that when the mice were fed egg white protein at the same time as the GM peas, they also developed an immune response to the egg white protein—indicating that the new GM protein was priming the mice to react to other foods.[783]

In 2002, Professor David Schubert of the Salk Institute in La Jolla, California, added his concerns about GM food, in addition to the potential for allergies:

As a cell biologist, I am very discouraged by the nature of the ongoing "debate" on the introduction of genetically modified (GM) plants into the marketplace. This discussion has usually pitted irrational emotional arguments against the apparently rational notion that genetic engineering is just like traditional plant breeding, only more specific. In particular, I believe that insufficient attention has been paid to three important issues: first, introduction of the same gene into two different types of cells can produce two very distinct protein molecules; second, the introduction of any gene, whether from a different or the same species, usually significantly changes overall gene expression and therefore the phenotype of the recipient cell; and third, enzymatic pathways introduced to synthesize small molecules, such as vitamins, could interact with endogenous pathways to produce novel molecules. The potential consequence of all of these perturbations could be the biosynthesis of molecules that are toxic, allergenic, or carcinogenic. And there is no *a priori* way of predicting the outcome. In what follows I outline these concerns and argue that GM food is not a safe option, given our current lack of understanding of the consequences of recombinant technology. [784]

One of the concerns of GMO food, is not just the unknown factors of harmful substances, and allergy potential etc., it is also the worry about the changing nutritional content. As previously mentioned, Pusztai's experiments, showed that the nutritional content of some of the potatoes was considerably different in the GM group; some had 20% less protein than the parent line, even when they were grown in identical conditions. Even worse, their offspring produced different results from their parent. These concerns, of course, also apply to some of the new generation GM products, such as pharmaceuticals and others referred to as nutritionally enhanced plants (NEPs). These are supposed to deliver higher levels of vitamins or other supplements. One example would be golden rice which is engineered to produce higher levels of carotene, the precursor of retinol (vitamin A).

NEPs are designed to make molecules that are biologically active in animals. Professor Schubert worries:

"Given the transfection procedures used to make GM plants cause random mutations that can alter the already unpredictable plant metabolism, there will be unforeseen pleiotropic interactions between overproduced enzymes and normal plant metabolism."

He further expresses concern over the lack of discussion about safety, despite the fact that simple derivatives of carotene are known teratogens (teratogens are substances or environmental agents which cause the development of abnormal cell masses during foetal growth, resulting in physical defects in the foetus). He further cites the example of how the manipulation of the metabolic process by GM technology in yeast, to promote ethanol production, can have unexpected consequences. When three genes were introduced to yeast, there was a 30-fold increase in the synthesis of methylglyoxal (MG), which is a highly toxic mutagen that causes protein glycation and oxidative stress, and is associated with diabetes, neurodegenerative disease and a number of autoimmune diseases. [785]

It seems from reading much of the information that has become available in subsequent decades, that there appears to be a particular mind-set among many geneticists, Dr Mae-Wan Ho refers to this as a 'Neo-Darwinian determinism' which assumes three basic assumptions:

1. Genes determine characters in a straightforward additive (i.e., non-interactive) way.

2. Genes and genomes are stable and, except for rare random mutations, are passed on unchanged to the next generation.

3. Genes and genomes cannot be changed directly in response to the environment.

All of the above of course, is totally incorrect, and in her book *Genetic Engineering, Dream or Nightmare? The Brave New World of Bad Science and Big Business,* Dr Ho explains how, following the revelations of the past two decades, it has become obvious that the genome is a much more fluid structure than previously believed. It is a continuously changing population of sequences, with amplifications, deletions, inversions, exchanges and conversion of sequences creating an unexpected fluidity. It has also been discovered that there seemed to be far too much DNA, more than was required for coding all the proteins, and supplying all the signals for gene transcription. In fact, in some cases up to 99% of DNA in some genomes appears to have no known function, and some geneticists refer to this as 'junk DNA' or 'selfish DNA'. She also explains how sequences in the genome can be amplified or contracted a thousand-fold, or hundreds of thousands of times, as part of normal development, or as a result of environmental challenges.[786]

Dr Ho has many concerns about the way genetically modified products are being released into the environment, with little understanding of their effect on our health, or, indeed, the environment itself. Numerous websites dealing with these issues are given in the resource section in this book in addition to the sources that are annotated. Dr Ho's book I can highly recommend to those who would like more information on the science and ethics behind the industry.

The Dangers of Antibiotic Resistance

One of Dr Ho's concerns, shared by a great many scientists, regards horizontal gene transfer and recombination, which she considers are the most underestimated hazards of agricultural biotechnology. One of the problems faced, as a result of the industry using marker genes for antibiotics, such as ampicillin, which was used in Ciba-Geigy's transgenic maize; this was an antibiotic which is still in use. Zeneca's transgenic tomato paste and Calgene's transgenic tomatoes both used a marker gene for kanamycin resistance; whilst it was claimed that this antibiotic has been replaced by new generations of antibiotics, at least one kanamycin resistance gene, used as a genetic marker, had been found to have conferred cross-resistance on two of the newer aminoglycosides, amikacin and tobramycin. The worry is that use of these marker genes will confer antibiotic resistance to a new host of more virulent bacteria that will come back and haunt us. There are also serious concerns, that the way some transgenic crops, engineered for resistance to viral diseases, by incorporating the gene for the virus's coat protein—might generate new diseases. There are a number of ways this can happen:

by transcapsidation for example, which involves the DNA or RNA of one virus being wrapped up in the coat protein of another—which would enable viral genes into cells that would otherwise be excluded. Infectious viruses could be regenerated by recombination; it is now known that transgenic plants increase the frequency of viral recombination. [787]

You may be wondering how it is that we find ourselves in a situation in which we have released into the environment products that we are only now beginning to understand, and that may come back and haunt us even if we were to stop producing them right now. Dan Glickman, Bill Clinton's outgoing Secretary of Agriculture, made a revealing comment in an interview, in January 2001, as he was being replaced by Ann Veneman. He warned her that the agency's top issue was genetically modified food, and further revealed the pressure he was under to actively promote GM technology:

> "What I saw generically on the pro-biotech side was the attitude that the technology was good and that it was almost immoral to say that it wasn't good because it was going to solve the problems of the human race and feed the hungry and clothe the naked. And there was a lot of money that had been invested in this, and if you're against it, you're Luddites, you're stupid. There was rhetoric like that even here in this department. You felt like you were almost an alien, disloyal, by trying to present an open-minded view on some of the issues being raised. So I pretty much spouted the rhetoric that everybody else around here spouted; it was written into my speeches" **788**

This is an amazing revelation by the US Secretary of Agriculture. His successor, Ann Veneman, previously served on the board of Calgene, a company owned by Monsanto.

Genetically Modified Crops Contaminate Farmland

Considering there are few, if any, benefits to growing GM crops, you may be wondering why we continue to grow them—and whether farmers really do want them. So the Soil Association in the UK undertook a study to discover exactly that—and published their findings in September 2002. In this they confirmed that, except for a small increase in Bt maize yields, increased yields had not been realised. In fact, they found that the main GM variety of soya, Roundup Ready soya, yielded 6-11% *less* than the conventional crop. They also found that the new herbicide tolerant crops were, in fact, making farmers more reliant on herbicide use—so increasing costs and creating new weed problems.

Rogue GM oilseed rape plants (volunteers) have become a widespread problem in Canada. Such contamination is considered one of the most serious problems for farmers:

> Widespread GM contamination has occurred rapidly and caused major disruption at all levels of the agricultural industry, for seed resources, crop production, food processing and bulk commodity trading. It has undermined the viability of the whole North American farming industry:
>
> Contamination has caused the loss of nearly the whole organic oilseed rape sector in the province of Saskatchewan, at a potential cost of millions of dollars.
>
> Organic farmers are struggling practically and economically; many have been unable to sell their produce as organic due to contamination. [789]

Non-GM famers are finding it difficult, and in some cases impossible, to grow GM-free crops due to seed contamination and field contamination. In September 2000, just 1% of unapproved GM maize contaminated almost half the national maize supply and cost Aventis, the manufacturer, up to $1 billion in compensation claims. Following the introduction of GM crops, most of the $300 million annual US maize exports to the EU, as well as the $300 million annual Canadian rape exports to the EU, all totally disappeared. The US share of the world soya market also substantially decreased. One further result was a massive rise in government farm subsidies, estimated at $3-5 Billion annually in 2001/2002, and as much as $12 billion from 1999 -2001. [790]

Reduced Yields and the Rise of Birth Defects and Health Issues

The increase in use of herbicides is causing great concern, especially since the favoured product— Roundup, is causing the most worry. Research published by the University of Arkansas, in 2000, discovered that root development, nodulation, and nitrogen fixation were impaired by glyphosate, one of the main components of Roundup. It was found to be particularly destructive in dry or low fertility conditions where a sensitivity of the nitrogen fixing bacteria in the soil, reduced yields by up to 25%. The authors of the report lamented the fact that this information had only become available after 100 million acres had been sown with Monsanto Roundup Ready (RR) soya.[791]

The news gets worse; a recent report by a group of international scientists revealed that Roundup, also causes birth defects and that industry and regulators knew this back in the 1980s and 1990s. The industry's own studies had shown that glyphosate causes malformations in experimental animals at high doses since the 1980s, and since 1993, that these effects also occur at lower and mid-size doses. The German government has been aware of this problem since 1998, and the EU Commission's expert scientific review panel knew all about it in 1999. It has also been apparent to the EU Commission since 2002, the year they approved its use.[792]

Their report, had been prompted by an earlier Argentine study, published in August 2010, demonstrating how glyphosate, causes malformations in frog and chicken embryos at doses far lower than those used in agricultural spraying—and well below maximum residue levels in products presently approved in the European Union. Professor Andrés Carrasco, director of the Laboratory of Molecular Embryology at the University of Buenos Aires Medical School, and member of Argentina's National Council of Scientific and Technical Research, was led to do this research—following reports of high rates of birth defects in rural areas of Argentina where large areas of land were growing monocultures of Monsanto Roundup Ready (RR) soybeans, which are routinely sprayed from airplanes. Reports of human birth defects started in 2002—two years after the large scale introduction of RR soybeans in Argentina. The authors of the report concluded that the results raise "concerns about the clinical findings from human offspring in populations exposed to Roundup in agricultural fields." [793]

At the sixth European Conference of GMO Free Regions in the European Parliament, Professor Carrasco explained his position further, "The findings in the lab are compatible with malformations observed in humans exposed to glyphosate during pregnancy."[794]

One of the victims of the aerial spraying was Sofia Gatica, from the district of Ituzaingó, in Cordoba. Her daughter died from a kidney malformation just three days after she was born. Sofia has been actively opposing the aerial spraying, and despite threatening visits from the 'Pistoleros'—has tried to document just how many miscarriages, birth defects and cancer cases have occurred in her neighbourhood. Following is an account of some small success in her struggle for justice.

On September 5, 2012, the Criminal Court of Cordoba declared spraying with pesticides was a crime with a conditional prison sentence. After more than two months of legal wrangling, an agrarian producer and a crop spraying pilot were sentenced to three years of conditional prison term for pollution and harm to public health. Following the ruling, and the fact that the prison sentences were only conditional, the Mothers of Ituzaingó left the courtroom crying and shouting "They kill our children and they go home." Sofia Gatica challenged one of the members of the political establishment there, surrounded by cameras, "What would have happened if the children of the President, the Governor or the Mayor were sick or dead?" And he replied: "Certainly these guys would have gone to jail, but that did not happened today."

"They make our children sick and now bring Monsanto. Both, President, Governor, and Mayor govern for corporations, for Monsanto. They do not care about poor peasants, who are sprayed with agrochemicals and evicted from their lands" denounced Gatica. [795]

In Europe, alarming concentrations of glyphosate can be detected in the urine of citizens. Its use is also being increasingly associated with problems in animal husbandry. Nonetheless, a safety review of the world's best-selling herbicide, due in Europe, has been postponed by three years. At the same time, the maximum allowable quantities of this plant toxin in feed and food have been *increased.* [796] The maximum residue level (MRL) allowed for glyphosate in soy was increased 200-fold, from 0.1 mg/kg to 20 mg/kg, in 1997—after GM RR soy had been commercialized in Europe. [797]

Following the study undertaken by Professor Carrasco, the provincial government of Chaco province, issued a report on health statistics from Leonesa that found the childhood cancer rate tripled and the rate of birth defects increased fourfold between 2000 and 2009. The report said that those staggering increases had coincided with the expansion of soy and rice crops and the corresponding rise in agrochemical use. [798] Carrasco's report, galvanised action by other health professionals and doctors in the crop spraying regions, and a further study was undertaken with the University of Cordoba—which made further alarming discoveries:

> That the processes of soyization, monoculture, direct sowing, intense farming ... have affected our natural co-existence in the following order: Health: Reduction in the average age and height in crop-sprayed towns due to malnutrition, and a decrease of the body's natural defenses. Birth defects, mutagenesis, miscarriages, depression and suicide, disorders of the central nervous system and other neurological pathologies; disabilities, spina bifida, lupus, leukemia and other types of cancers; chloracne and other skin problems; asthma, allergies, and other respiratory and lung-related problems; male sterility and impotence; hormonal disruption and other hormonal disorders; diminished childhood development; prolonged febrile syndrome without focus; children's increased vulnerability to pollutants; anemia, multiple sclerosis, cerebral ischemia, death...[799]

The report listed how birth defects went from 19.1 per 100,000 live births to 28.1 per 100,000 in 2001—almost a 50% increase. Yet in 2008 this had skyrocketed to 85.5 per 100,000—a horrific 445% increase. At the same time, cancer incidence linked to chemical exposure increased dramatically. At La Leonesa, for example, three times the levels of cancer than in other towns less affected by agrochemicals were reported. The report added that the amount of glyphosate sprayed per hectare on the same plot of land increased annually. Where they had started with just 2 litres per hectare, most had to increase their usage to between 10 and 20 litres per hectare.

The report estimates that 12 million Argentineans are directly sprayed as a result of spray covering houses, schools, parks, water courses, sports fields and work areas. Child cancer cases in 1991 were just 8.03 per 100,000, but by 2007 they had virtually doubled to 15.7 per 100,000. According to Doctor Hugo Gomez Demaio, a paediatric surgeon who specialized in Neurosurgery from Cleveland, USA, the true extent of the congenital defects to human health caused by agrochemicals is yet to be accurately determined. His report also acknowledges that neurological problems are yet to be assessed.[800]

A 2009 study of the effects of agrochemicals on US congenital birth defects over a population of more than three million people reported a link with pesticides in drinking water. The study looked at the timing of pregnancy, related to the last menstruation period (LMP), and found that a significant correlation with mothers whose LMP was in the spring months when levels of agrochemicals (Atrazine, nitrates, and other pesticides) were higher—as was the level of birth defects—five times higher in this case.[801]

A further study, by Dr Schreinemacher, at the EPA, compared congenital defects in infants, in areas of high wheat production with significant quantities of 2.4D herbicide that were used on those crops and found a similar correlation with birth defects in sprayed areas as had been found when LMP occurred in spring.[802]

A further study by Dr Margaret Sanborn, Assistant Clinical Professor of family medicine at McMaster University in Canada, and member of Ontario College of Family Physicians Environmental Health Committee, undertook a systematic revision of 50 studies from 9 countries to see what other links she could find between pesticides and birth defects. This study was in the field of Evidence-Based Medicine (EBM) that was developed by McMaster University. The studies consistently showed an increase in risk for defects at birth due to exposure to pesticides in mothers which included: limb reduction, urogenital anomalies, CNS defects, orofacial clefts, heart conditions, and ocular defects. 9 out of 11 studies showed a positive association between exposure to pesticides and miscarriage, foetal death, stillbirth, and neonatal death. [803]

Dr Sanborn appeared before the Spring 2002 Parliamentary hearings, into the proposed new Pest Control Products Act, testifying to the serious and long-term health impacts of pesticides. She discussed the implications on neurodevelopment and reproduction, and cited studies that showed pesticide-exposed rats and mice had fewer brain cells—permanent changes in the levels of neurotransmitters (messenger chemicals) in the brain, defective cell-to-cell signalling, and hyperactive behaviour which persisted into adult life. These changes were found to occur at exposure levels which did not cause acute toxicity. They also occur from pesticides in current household use, such as chlorpyrifos and pyrethroids - substances previously thought to be much safer than the old organochlorine insecticides. She expressed concern for childhood development:

> It is clear that the brains of children are more susceptible to pesticide effects. For example, in pesticide poisonings, 25% of children present with seizures as a symptom; in adults only 2-3% present with seizures. In children, we are concerned about sharp increases in the rates of autism and attention deficit disorders (previously called hyperactivity). Health Canada has stated recently that 28% of Canadian children under the age of 12 have an identified learning or behaviour problem. Apart from these known clinical disorders, there is a spectrum of less severe problems which involve memory and attention, and affect learning ability and skills to socialize and form relationships.
>
> I would like to draw attention to the dramatic population effects caused by small reductions in brain function. A reduction of only 5 IQ points across the whole population causes a 57% increase in those classified as "mentally challenged", and a corresponding 57% decrease in those classified as "intellectually gifted". The economic and social costs of such a shift, both in increased health and social costs at the lower end, and reduced capacity for innovation and knowledge-based economic output at the upper end, are enormous. I believe these concepts deserve serious consideration when cost-benefit, or "health risk-value" analyses of pesticides are conducted.

She refers to a number of studies on birth defects and pesticide exposure in the US and Canada and the Ontario Farm Family Health Study. These documented a 40-50% increase in early spontaneous abortions in farm women exposed to 2,4-D or atrazine type herbicides before conception. She also refers to research, undertaken in Montreal, that showed that foetuses exposed to pesticides, from home and garden use during pregnancy, led to a 2-5 times increased risk of developing acute lymphocytic leukemia by age 9. The risk of leukemia is highest if the child has one of two genetic subtypes which cause an inability to break down pesticides. This genetic subtype is not a rare occurrence; in the Montreal study it was present in 35.5% of children. In other words, *about one-third of Canadian children are born with a specific inability to detoxify commonly used pesticides.* They also have a corresponding increased vulnerability to other adverse health effects—such as immune problems, susceptibility to disease and cancer. Cancer in Canadian children under the age of 15 has doubled in the last 25 years.[804]

THE GENIE IS OUT OF THE BOTTLE

EU Commission Ignores Birth Defects

These studies confirmed the Argentinian experience—yet were not drawn to the attention of European bureaucrats. Following the revelations of the Argentinian report, members of the European Parliament, and NGOs, both raised concerns about it. Yet the German Federal Office for Consumer Protection and Food Safety (BVL), apparently dismissed it, claiming that it had a huge database of studies on glyphosate showing no evidence of teratogenicity (the ability to cause birth defects). According to the European scientists, BVL cited as proof of their decision, the very same industry studies, that supplied the very evidence of teratogenicity. The BVL explained away the birth defects in the industry studies with some bizarre excuses—skeletal deformations became simply a 'variation', and they made important data simply 'disappear' using historical data instead of bona fide control data from the experiment in hand. The EU Commission's expert review panel followed Germany in dismissing the birth defects, and the Commission signed off final approval of glyphosate in 2002. They then passed a directive delaying any further review of glyphosate and 38 other dangerous pesticides, until 2015. The authors of the studies called on the Commission to cancel its delay in reviewing glyphosate and, in the meantime, to use its powers—to withdraw glyphosate and Roundup from the market. [805]

Monsanto, no doubt, will claim the studies that show problems with glyphosate are 'flawed'. Claire Robinson, one of the authors of the report, comments, 'as our report proves, studies that show glyphosate causes birth defects include industry's own studies, Monsanto's among them. Is Monsanto saying its own studies are flawed? If so, we have all the more reason to worry, as these are the studies on which the current approval of glyphosate rests'.[806]

Following a legal request by Friends of the Earth, the European Commission released a number of new documents that question the safety of genetically modified food. These documents form the basis of the scientific arguments made by the EU regarding its current trade dispute with the World Trade Organisation (WTO). The Friends of the Earth subsequently noted that, at the same time as these papers were written, the Commission, broke Europe's six year moratorium on new GM foods. They also commercialised 31 varieties of GM maize (since September 2004), and forced member states to vote twice on proposals that would require them to lift their national bans on certain GM products.

The report shows that although the Commission informed member states that GM foods and crops were safe, it was presenting evidence behind closed doors that expressed a far different view that:

- There are substantial scientific concerns about the safety of GM foods and crops.
- New and complex risks are emerging.
- The risks to human and animal health cannot be excluded.
- Serious concerns remain about the environmental safety of growing GM crops.
- The environmental risks of GM organisms (GMOs) will vary according to the region and its environment.
- Biotechnology companies provided poor quality applications and research in their applications to market GMOs.
- Commission had considerable reservations about the risk assessments conducted by the European Food Safety Authority (EFSA) which undertakes independent risk assessments of GM crops and foods as part of the approvals process.[807]

So, even though the reports of birth defects reached the EFSA and the EU Commission, it appears that soybeans in the EU now have residue levels of glyphosate as high as 17mg/kg—following the raising of the maximum residue limit (MRL) in 1997 by 200 percent. Professor Carrasco, found malformations in chicken and frogs, at doses ten times lower than the MRL. If you think that simply by avoiding eating soya or maize will protect you, you would be wrong. If you eat meat, you may be concerned to know that animal feed in the western world contains large amounts of soya—90% of the world's total harvest. The EU imported more than 23 million tons of soya in 2003. In the UK, imported soya and maize by-products account for 20% of raw materials used by feed manufacturers and farmers. [808]

An ICM opinion poll carried out for Greenpeace discovered that 95% of those questioned believed people should be given a choice as to whether or not they wished to consume meat and dairy products derived from animals fed on a GM diet. They also felt that GM products should be labelled. [809]

The Dangers of Horizontal Gene Transfer

Whilst not wishing to ignore the above issues, Dr Mae-Wan Ho's feels we may face a graver threat from GMOs through horizontal gene transfers.

THE GENIE IS OUT OF THE BOTTLE

She says:

'I do not think it is an exaggeration to say that horizontal gene transfer (and consequent recombination) is the greatest threat to public health facing us to-day—especially if commercial-scale genetic engineering biotechnology is allowed to continue unchecked.'

She cites the rapid rise in anti-biotic resistance, and the emergence of more virulent pathogens such as *S. enteritidis and S.* typhimurium—and the more than 20-fold increase of Salmonella infections over the last 20 years. She explains how the presence of antibiotics can actually increase the frequency of horizontal gene transfer 10 to-100 fold. She does not believe that all the increase in virulence, and all antibiotic resistance, is simply due to our overuse of antibiotics. Her concern is the very nature of genetic engineering:

"Although there is no direct evidence linking genetic engineering biotechnology, to the spread of virulence and antibiotic resistance, there is clear evidence, that horizontal gene transfer *is* responsible for both. And, there is no escaping the fact, that the *raison d'être,* and aspiration of genetic engineering, *is* to increase the facility of horizontal gene transfer, so as to create ever more exotic transgenic organisms."

Dr Ho cites a number of examples that raised her concerns: Australian scientists who engineered a virus that hopes to control mouse plagues in the wild—but stops mice from getting pregnant. Critics point out that such a contraceptive virus could cause an ecological disaster if released, and could infect and sterilise non-target species. She gives the example of a rabies vaccine used on dogs in Serengeti Wildlife Park to prevent spread of an outbreak of rabies. 34 animals were vaccinated and, within 10 months, four of them had been found dead—and there have been no sightings of any live dogs, since. She suggests that the rabies vaccine could have regenerated a live version—by recombination. It has been documented numerous times that amongst the human population there have been outbreaks of polio and measles amongst a *previously vaccinated* population. Dr Ho cites the mid-1980s outbreak in Corpus Christi, Texas as an example, and makes the following comment: 'Vaccines are, in any case, notoriously ineffective against viruses that mutate and recombine to generate new variants. Vaccines can cause the very diseases for which they are supposed to offer protection in immunologically-deficient individuals. Some vaccines are produced in transgenic plants for use in humans and animals. One method of doing this is by inserting pieces of animal viral coat protein genes into plant viruses such as cowpea mosaic virus. The chimaeric virus is then multiplied in susceptible plants. The plants are then fed to animals or humans for immunisation'. She concludes: 'Their ability to create more viruses that attack a wide range of species should not be underestimated.' Dr Ho further cites the example of the Pasteur Institute who lost six genetic engineering scientists, working on cancer-related oncogenes, who all contracted cancer. She believes that we may be facing a risk of new iatrogenic (doctor-caused) diseases from new generations of genetically engineered drugs and vaccines. What adds to the problem, is that it would be very difficult to discover the source of these new diseases, once released. Many people may not be aware that, when industry scientists report new outbreaks of measles, for example, the outbreak is more often than not due to the vaccination program—the infection is A-typical measles, which means it was generated by the vaccine—but this is rarely pointed out. [810]

Bush Administration Declares GMOs Safe

One of the major criticisms facing the regulatory authorities is their failure to adequately protect the general public, from the release of unproven and genetically hazardous products. This appears to be because politics plays a much more important role than science. In the USA, for example, the FDA declared that GM crops are covered under the terminology as 'generally recognised as safe' (GRAS), as long as their producers say they are (which of course they do enthusiastically). Given this unsound 'reassurance', the FDA does not require safety evaluations or labelling. In fact a company can even introduce a genetically modified food product without having to inform the FDA. However, according to internal memos at the FDA, the overwhelming consensus amongst its own agency scientists, is that GM crops have unpredictable and hard-to-detect side-effects. They urged their superiors to ask for long-term safety studies.[811]

The argument that there is more politics than science in the way genetically modified food has been foisted on the public was particularly brought home in an article in the *New York Times*, in 2001. This revealed the influence Monsanto wielded in the White House, following a meeting between four of their executives and George Bush. On that occasion, it appears they had come to ask for regulation of their industry to bolster the public's confidence in genetically modified products. The article elaborates:

THE GENIE IS OUT OF THE BOTTLE

In the weeks and months that followed, the White House complied, working behind the scenes to help Monsanto — long a political power with deep connections in Washington — get the regulations that it wanted.

It was an outcome that would be repeated, again and again, through three administrations. What Monsanto wished for from Washington, Monsanto—and, by extension, the biotechnology industry—got. If the company's strategy demanded regulations, rules favored by the industry were adopted. And when the company abruptly decided that it needed to throw off the regulations and speed its foods to market, the White House quickly ushered through an unusually generous policy of self-policing.

Even longtime Washington hands said that the control this nascent industry exerted over its own regulatory destiny — through the Environmental Protection Agency, the Agriculture Department and ultimately the Food and Drug Administration — was astonishing. [812]

The authors of the article go on to say that back in the early 1990s a new management team had taken over in Monsanto and initiated a new urgency to erase barriers and get products to market. The White House obliged on May 26, 1992, when the Vice President, Dan Quayle outlined the Bush administration's new policy on bioengineered food:

"The reforms we announce today will speed up and simplify the process of bringing better agricultural products, developed through biotech, to consumers, food processors and farmers," Mr Quayle went on to tell a crowd of executives and reporters in the Indian Treaty Room of the Old Executive Office Building. "We will ensure that biotech products will receive the same oversight as other products, instead of being hampered by unnecessary regulation." He further added his assurance, "We will not compromise safety one bit."

Not everyone was happy with this new approach, particularly some among the seventeen government scientists who had been working on policy for genetically modified food. One of these was Dr Louis Pribyl who was already aware that new toxins could be created when new genes were inserted into a plant's cell. He was aware the new government approach would mean there would be no oversight, and that biotech companies would not now require government approval to sell the foods they were developing. He made the following comment in a memo to the scientist overseeing the FDA's policy: "This is the industry's pet idea, namely that there are no unintended effects that will raise the F.D.A.'s level of concern. But time and time again, there is no data to back up their contention."

Dr. Gerald Guest, director of the Center of Veterinary Medicine, wrote that he and other scientists at the Center had concluded there was "ample scientific justification" to require tests and a government review of each genetically engineered food before it was sold.

Three toxicologists wrote, "The possibility of unexpected, accidental changes in genetically engineered plants justifies a limited traditional toxicological study." [813]

One more government scientist, Dr Suzanne Wuerthele, US Environmental Protection Agency (EPA) toxicologist expressed her concern thus:

"This technology is being promoted, in the face of concerns by respectable scientists and in the face of data to the contrary, by the very agencies which are supposed to be protecting human health and the environment. The bottom line in my view is that we are confronted with the most powerful technology the world has ever known, and it is being rapidly deployed with almost no thought whatsoever to its consequences." [814]

The warnings being voiced don't just come from people who might simply be against biotechnology, some enthusiasts for it express serious concerns too. Take David Suzuki, a geneticist: "I'm a geneticist, so I'm very excited by what's going on in terms of genetic engineering... What bothers me is we have governments that are supposed to be looking out for our health, for the safety of our environment, and they're acting like cheerleaders for this technology, which... is in its infancy, and we have no idea what the technology is going to do.

Anyone that says, 'Oh, we know that this is perfectly safe,' I say is either unbelievably stupid or deliberately lying. The reality is we don't know. The experiments simply haven't been done and we now have become the guinea pigs." [815]

There is also a lot of controversy not just about the lack of research, but the appalling quality of a lot of the so called trials, produced by the industry, some of which I have already referred to. I don't intend to go into this area a great deal further, those of you who would like more information about this I refer you to Jeffrey Smith's excellent book, *Genetic Roulette* that I have already referred to, I can also highly recommend his DVD by the same name. [816]

Dispossessed Farmers, Diversity, GMOs, & Agribusiness

There is no doubt that all this critical information has slowed down the momentum of North American GM agriculture. But it has not slowed the reckless development of the GM industry in South

America. GM soy is rapidly replacing rainforest and displacing vast numbers of people. The fastest growing areas are in Brazil and Argentina where soy grows fast and needs little input. More than 150 million hectares of land were planted with GM crops in 2010, 10% more than in 2009. In Paraguay, more than 2.6 million hectares of land have been planted with GM soy. According to the World Land trust more than 90 percent of the Atlantic Rainforest in the south has been lost to make way for such crops, robbing thousands of unique bird and plant species—and endangered animals such as the jaguar—of their natural habitat. It is of course, not just these animals and plants that are lost forever— the forest supported vast numbers of people who have been displaced by the robbing of their homes and lands. This 'displacement' generally means a mass migration of the population to more urban areas to look for work—which is rarely available. This creates further shanty towns on the outskirts of urban areas with the resulting problems of malnutrition, disease and further poverty. [817]

Vandana Shiva equates the shift from environmentally sound processes of production to technological processes that involve the dispossession of farmers and the drastic reduction of biological diversity as being due to a 'reductionist' mind-set—in which everything is reduced to inputs, outputs and profit margins. She sees this as the root cause of poverty and non-sustainability in agriculture. She compares this kind of mind-set with the one that drove European colonialism—which began when Queen Isabel and Kind Ferdinand granted Christopher Columbus the privileges of 'discovery and conquest' on April 17, 1492, and led to immense desecration. This was exacerbated by the Papal Bull of Donation granted by Pope Alexander VI on May 4, 1493, which granted to the Catholic monarchs Isabel of Castille and Ferdinand of Aragon all Islands and main-lands "discovered and to be discovered, one hundred leagues to the West and South of the Azores towards India"—and not already occupied or held by any Christian king or prince as of Christmas of 1492. Vandana Shiva quotes Walter Ullmann:

> The Pope as the vicar of God commanded the world as if it were a tool in his hands; the Pope, supported by the canonists, considered the world as his property to be disposed of according to his will. [818]

The charters and patents accordingly turned acts of piracy into divine will, and laid the judicial and moral foundation for the colonisation and partial extermination of non-European peoples. The decimation of the indigenous people was morally justified by asserting that they were not really human, but part of the fauna. Europeans were able to describe their invasions as discoveries, their piracy and theft as 'trade', and their extermination and enslavement as a civilising mission. Shiva equates the modern General Agreement on Tariffs and Trade (GATT) treaty, the massive use of patents, the introduction of Intellectual Property Rights (IPRs), and their enforced imposition by The World Trade Organisation (WTO) as simply the 'more secular version of the same project of colonization'; the second wave of colonialism, which she refers to as 'the second coming of Columbus'.

Engdahl describes how the WTO 'emerged as a new weapon which could force open various national barriers and which could thereby enhance the proliferation of the soon-to-be commercialized genetically modified crops'. He describes how it was the outcome of the Uruguay round of GATT talks which led to the founding of WTO. The Washington position on the Uruguay agricultural agenda had been drafted by Cargill Corporation of Minneapolis. Daniel Armstutz a former Cargill executive drew up the four-point Armstutz Plan, which he believes was really a Cargill plan, the then dominant US private agribusiness giant.

Armstutz's demands at the GATT talks focused on a ban of all government farm programs and price supports world-wide; a prohibition on countries who sought to impose import controls to defend their national agriculture production; a ban on all government export controls that affected agriculture, even in the time of famine; and, finally, a limit on the ability of countries to enforce strict food safety laws or restrictions on trade for safety or health concerns, and which would limit the right of a corporation to be able to trade its products. This list of demands worked uniquely to the benefit of US agribusiness, but was also to be welcomed by many other US corporations—including the tobacco industry. Currently, the tobacco industry argues that even though their products kill people (and even could be considered a form of genocide) that their right to trade is being infringed. Agribusiness interests also did not want any national concerns about health and safety to get in the way of marketing their genetically engineered crops.[819]

Vandana Shiva describes an event arranged by the Dag Hammarskjöld Foundation in 1987, called the "Laws of Life", which she describes as a 'watershed event' which identified the patenting of genetic engineering as a means of controlling agriculture. The meeting made it clear that although the giant chemical companies were rebranding themselves as "life sciences" companies, their goal was, in fact, the complete domination of agriculture.

Shiva relates a number of patents that set the agenda for the takeover of food production: the first was a patent on the maize plant, taken out by genetic scientist, Kenneth Hibbert. This included the tissue culture, seed and whole plant of a maize line selected from tissue, and gave Hibbert the right to 260 separate claims for maize while excluding others from the use of all 260 of them. Sungene, a US biotech company took out a patent on a high oleic acid content sunflower plant.

THE GENIE IS OUT OF THE BOTTLE

It gave notice than any breeders who bred a high oleic acid sunflower plant would be considered infringing their copyright. Shiva relates how, for over 2000 years, the neem tree has been part of Indian culture, used for many different treatments due to its medicinal and anti-bacterial properties. But, since 1985, a number of American and Japanese corporations have been taking out patents on the use of neem it being a part of Indian legacy. She reports that, of 120 active compounds studied, 75% had uses that were widely used in Western medicine. Such compounds had evolved through experimentation and the development of this knowledge over many generations by the indigenous population. Shiva considers the taking out of patents on them without any payment to the indigenous source to be a form of piracy. [820]

However, it is the patenting of seed that seems to draw the most ire and condemnation, particularly the use of terminator seed technology and traitor technologies. Monsanto bought out Delta and Pine, owners of the terminator patent, which allowed them to produce seed that would not replicate each year; instead a new batch of seeds would have to be purchased each year from the supplier. Farmers would, of course, also have to purchase the herbicide that the terminator plants were designed to be used with. In India, this had dire consequences, since extremely poor farmers had to buy both seeds and chemicals on credit from the same company. When there was a crop failure due to pest incidence or large-scale seed failure, many peasants committed suicide by consuming the same pesticides that had gotten them into such debt. In the Warangal district, almost four hundred cotton farmers committed suicide due to crop failure in 1997; in the following year, dozens more followed suit.

For millennia, farmers have traditionally saved their own seed and freely exchanged it amongst themselves, developing a rich diversity of seed and, consequently a rich diversity of plants. This stood them in good stead as there would sometimes be a failure of one particular species due to adverse weather conditions or pest problem. So, having a rich diversity of crops was an insurance against crop failure. The total failure of the potato crop in Ireland in the 1840s, due to potato blight, is well documented, but what is less well known is that the entire crop was just one susceptible species and there was no other to replace it with. In the Andes mountains alone, there are supposed to be approximately three thousand varieties of potato. Shiva makes the point that biodiversity, and the ability to save seed is essential to sustainable agriculture. She points out that the whole movement into biotechnology, relying mostly on monocultures that degrade the soils and require ever more expensive inputs of fertilizers, and herbicides is totally unsustainable. Many scientists agree with her.[821]

UNHEALTHY BETRAYAL

Dire Warnings by One of America's Leading Scientists

Don Huber, Emeritus Professor at Purdue University and senior scientist on USDA's National Plant Disease Recovery System, has been a plant physiologist and pathologist for over 50 years; he specialised in soil-borne diseases, microbial ecology and host parasitic relationships. For the past 20 years, he has conducted extensive research into the effects of glyphosate on crops. In the process, he and other scientists discovered some very alarming facts about glyphosate and Roundup, the most widely used herbicide worldwide.

In January 2011 he was so concerned by what they were finding that he wrote to the Secretary of Agriculture, Tom Vilsack warning of his findings, and particularly the discovery of a new, and currently unidentified organism. At precisely this time Vilsack, a known enthusiast for genetically modified crops and genetic engineering in general, was preparing to approve two new Roundup-Ready alfalfa applications. There was a concerted lobbying effort by the industry to push this through. There were even calls for his resignation by an article in *Forbes,* suggesting that his considering to implement separation of GMO crops by geographic restrictions and by imposing minimum separation distances from other crops would cripple an important and environmentally beneficial technology—the genetic engineering of crop plants. [822]

Following the approval by the Obama administration three weeks later, however, Huber's letter was leaked to the press. Because of the nature of some of the revelations, I feel justified in reproducing some of this correspondence below:

> Dear Secretary Vilsack:
>
> A team of senior plant and animal scientists have recently brought to my attention the discovery of an electron microscopic pathogen that appears to significantly impact the health of plants, animals, and probably human beings. Based on a review of the data, it is widespread, very serious, and is in much higher concentrations in Roundup Ready (RR) soybeans and corn—suggesting a link with the RR gene or more likely the presence of Roundup. This organism appears NEW to science!

He gives a little of the background to his expertise:

> For the past 40 years, I have been a scientist in the professional and military agencies that evaluate and prepare for natural and man made biological threats, including germ warfare and disease outbreaks. Based on this experience, I believe the threat we are facing from this

pathogen is unique and of a high risk status. In layman's terms, it should be treated as an emergency.

He goes on to call for an immediate moratorium on the deregulation of RR crops until the causal relationship with glyphosate and RR plants can be ascertained, and finishes with an ominous warning:

> I have studied plant pathogens for more than 50 years. We are now seeing an unprecedented trend of increasing plant and animal diseases and disorders. This pathogen may be instrumental to understanding and solving this problem. It deserves immediate attention with significant resources to avoid a general collapse of our critical agricultural infrastructure. [823]

It has to be said that you would have to go a long way to find anyone better qualified than Professor Huber. Following the approval, Huber was so concerned about the ramifications of his discoveries that he allowed himself to be interviewed on a number of occasions to bring this information into the public domain. To say that the subsequent revelations are explosive is an understatement. No doubt there will be a concerted campaign by the industry to downplay his revelations—expect the vast Monsanto PR machine to go into overdrive. Below is a summary of some of his consequential revelations in an interview with Dr Mercola, to whom I am thankful for permission to reproduce them:

> What you have to do is realize what an herbicide is, or a pesticide. They are metal chelators, in other words they are able to immobilize specific nutrients. That's how they perform their function as a pesticide, by immobilizing an essential nutrient that is required or kind of keyed for a specific enzyme...... By chelator, we mean it's a compound that can grab onto another element and change either its solubility or its availability for that critical function that it has physiologically. We have those herbicides and pesticides that are quite specific just for a particular essential micronutrient like copper, zinc, iron, or manganese.

He goes on to explain how glyphosate is quite unique in its ability to bind with any positively-charged cation (mineral element), which effectively immobilizes the bound minerals from being adequately used by the plant, rendering it so severely weakened that it dies. But he goes on to explain that this binding of the essential minerals affects more than the targeted weeds:

UNHEALTHY BETRAYAL

You have to realize all that mode of action is immobilizing a critical essential nutrient. Those nutrients aren't just required by the weed, but they're required by microorganisms. They're required by us for our own physiologic functions. So if it's immobilized, it may be present if we do a regular test. But it's not necessarily physiologically available in the same efficiency that would have been if it wasn't chelated with that glyphosate or other chemical chelator.

He further adds that even the glyphosate tolerant plant is impacted by the chelation, in that numerous enzymes are also affected and disrupt normal plant function. When asked whether this process affects the nutritional status of consumers of these GM plants he replied:

Well, it is well documented that the nutritional efficiency–just having that foreign gene inserted–reduces the capability of that plant to take up nutrients and to translocate nutrients.

Then when you apply the chemical, you have a further compounding effect in reducing the efficiency of the plants at rates as low as a half-pound per acre–12 grams per acre.... It's been demonstrated that you reduce the uptake and efficiency of iron by 50 percent of manganese that's critical for liver function and immune response by 80 percent. But then if you look at the translocation from roots to shoot, you also have a reduction in zinc, and all three of those critical elements, of 80 to 90%.

Greatly compromised is the nutritional efficiency, as well as the ability of that plant to accumulate and to store those nutrients not only for its own use, but also for us and for our animal's nutrition in that process.

He explains how the glyphosate is systemic in the plant and accumulates in most of the growth points:

It's going to be in your root tips, your shoot tips, your legume nodules, and in the food that we eat. Because it's in those reproductive structures, that's where it accumulates. The later it is supplied, now that they're using glyphosate—as ripening agents to kill a plant to kind of speed up its harvest process—the only place that it can go is right into the seed.

About 20% of it moves out of the roots, so it moves down out into the soil where it has the same effect on many of the beneficial soil microorganisms that it has on weeds, because they have that same critical, essential metabolic pathway.

These beneficial soil organisms are really important for nutrient up-take which he explains:

The plant can only utilize certain forms of all the nutrients. For instance, with manganese, most iron has been in reduced form. The way that it becomes reduced in the soil is through those beneficial microorganisms. We also have those microorganisms for legumes like soybeans, alfalfa, peas, or any of the other legumes that can fix up to 75% of their actual nitrogen for protein in amino acid synthesis that actually comes from the air through the microorganisms in the soil.

Glyphosate is extremely toxic to all of those organisms. What we see with our continued use and abuse of this powerful pesticide, this powerful weed killer, is it is also totally eliminating many of those organisms from the soil. We no longer have the same balance that we used to have.

Consequently, we see an increase of over 40 new diseases or 40 diseases that we used to have managed under fairly effective control, but all of a sudden are another serious problem for us.

Huber relates that a number of fungi seem to thrive with glyphosate application, such as fusaria, the fungi that causes sudden death syndrome on soybeans, showing a 500% increase in root colonization. He explains how they are seeing problems with the animals that he believes are due to the normal gut flora in the animals being affected by glyphosate:

The other thing we see is that the normal biological control organisms, even in the animal, are very sensitive to the residual glyphosate levels. I was just reviewing a paper—as I flew out here yesterday—on chronic botulism or toxic botulism type problem. This is where you have the Clostridium botulinum in the intestinal tract. It's a common soil organism everywhere.

But all of a sudden we're seeing cases now, especially in dairy and other situations, where the animals are dying and becoming impaired from the botulism toxin from the Clostridium in the intestinal tract, and rumen in the stomach. That normally didn't occur before, because you have all of those organisms that provided the natural biological control.

In this paper, what they show is that residues of glyphosate that are permitted in our feed and food products are high enough to kill those normal biological control organisms—your Lactobacillus, your Alcaligenes. The numbers of those organisms are very effective in preventing the toxin production by Clostridium that those organisms are eliminated by glyphosate levels that can be in our food and feed supply. Then the animals suffer the same effects as with giving them treatment of this very intense biological warfare chemical that is produced naturally in the intestine, without that balance again.... I saw again that there's enough residual glyphosate potential in our feed and food to all of a sudden make an extremely benign organism fatal or lethal in that process.

Dr Mercola asked professor Huber about an organism that he understood was causing serious worries in the agricultural community:

> We're not sure what it is. It was first identified by veterinarians who were confronted with very high reproductive failure in animals. This was probably in 1998 or 2000. It was a sporadic, kind of a limited situation. We initially thought that it might just be one of those bubbles that happen and never be able to really explain it, but it continues to increase in its severity...It's not a fungus. It's not bacteria. It's not a mycoplasma or a virus–about the same size of a small virus. You have to magnify it from 38 to 40,000 times.

He cites cases where in the dairy industry there are herds with 70% abortion rates and commented:

> You put that on top of 10 to 15%t of infertility to start with, and you're not going to have a dairy very long. In fact, a lot of our veterinarians are now becoming very concerned at the failure for being able to have to have replacement animals.
>   But what we do know is that it causes reproductive failure, infertility, as well as miscarriage for cattle, horses, pigs, sheep, and poultry. We can anticipate with that broad spectrum of animal species, which is extremely unusual, that it will also be with humans.
>   We see an increasing frequency of miscarriage and a dramatic increase in infertility in human populations in just the last eight to 10 years.
>   If you look at where this entity is–again, with the veterinarians when they have identified it and the American Cattlemen's Association testified to it before Congress in 2002– there were two conditions that were threatening the industry. One was this reproductive failure– as many as 40 to 50% of the pregnant animals losing their offspring. The other one was premature aging. [824]

Dr Huber describes how animals which were only two, or two and a half years old would be downgraded to that of a ten year old cow. He cites a bull breeder who had to pull 40% of his bulls out of service, because they couldn't get conception any more. As you can see, the ramifications for the agricultural industry would be catastrophic if this was to become widespread. I have quoted here from part one of two interviews by Dr Mercola. I recommend viewing both these interviews and a number of others online that can be viewed. [825]

Huber believes that we are overusing glyphosate, abusively. When asked to what level it is being used, he simply mentioned that in 2007, the USDA asked for permission not to have to record what the figure is. The growing of GM corn, cotton, and soybean in the USA is responsible for the eight-fold increase in glyphosate use between 1995 and 2005. It is believed to be the most heavily used pesticide in the world, with over 600 thousand tons used annually. [826]

Whilst Monsanto would wish us to believe that glyphosate is perfectly harmless, it is clear that this is not the case. But I'll leave this subject with a final comment from Professor Don Huber:

> The future historians aren't going to judge us by how many tons or pounds of pesticides we apply or don't apply, but how willing we are to sacrifice future generations, as well as jeopardize the very basis of our own existence, all based upon failed promises and flawed science.

> The only benefit is that it affects the bottom line of a few companies. There's no nutritional value. [827]

Genetically Modified Crops are Un-Sustainable and Unnecessary

The great tragedy about genetic modification, though, is that it is totally unnecessary. Most people believe the hype that modern agriculture, has to follow conventional lines of high chemical inputs of fertiliser and pesticides, as well as genetically modified crops to feed the growing population of the world—hardly surprising since the companies that will benefit from it spend huge sums on PR to promote it. However, many studies now show that organic agriculture, for example, can not only match the yields of conventional agriculture but in some cases exceed them. There are a number of studies around the world that show promising developments in this respect. In one, prepared for the Food and Agriculture Organisation (FAO), 25% of farmers in Ethiopia were able to reduce fertiliser inputs from approximately 14,000 tons to 8,000 tons a year—by replacing them with natural compost. Far from reducing yields, this enabled them to increase total grain yields from 714 to 1,354 thousand tonnes between 2003 and 2006. The study looked at a number of different crops switching to compost and, on average, the yields increased by an average of 30%. [828]

Researchers led by David Pimental, agricultural scientist at Cornell University, New York, looked at a number of long-term field trials and found there was no difference in yields between organic methods and chemical methods in normal growing conditions. During drought conditions however, yields for the organic systems far outpaced the chemical systems due to better water retention of the soil. The organic yields were, in fact, 31% higher. Organic soils, aside from having better retention of moisture, also have higher levels of nitrogen, and higher levels of carbon due to their ability to act as carbon sinks.[829]

UNHEALTHY BETRAYAL

According to a report that came out of the Food and Agricultural Organizations of the United Nations (FAO) International Conference on Organic Agriculture and Food Security, they acknowledged that the global food security community is shifting swiftly in support of an organic approach:

> Organic agriculture has the potential to secure a global food supply, just as conventional agriculture is today, but with reduced environmental impact.
>
> Agribusinesses have long clung to the rallying cry of needing to increase yields in order to feed the world. However, feeding the world is not simply a matter of yields. Organic agriculture has the potential to secure a global food supply, just as conventional agriculture is today, but with reduced environmental impact.
>
> Agroecological farming methods could double global food production in just 10 years, according to a report from the United Nations.
>
> Switching to organic methods in communities where people struggle to feed themselves and their families can lead to a harvest 180% larger than that produced by conventional method.
> 830

The prestigious Rodale Institute in the USA has been running a trial for over thirty years, comparing organic agriculture with chemical systems, and has come to the conclusion:

> The hallmark of a truly sustainable system is its ability to regenerate itself. When it comes to farming, the key to sustainable agriculture is healthy soil, since this is the foundation for present and future growth.
>
> Organic farming is far superior to conventional systems when it comes to building, maintaining and replenishing the health of the soil. For soil health alone, organic agriculture is more sustainable than conventional. When one also considers yields, economic viability, energy usage, and human health, it's clear that organic farming is sustainable, while current conventional practices are not.

It is clear, after thirty years of studying both conventional and organic systems, that our current system needs to change—and the Institute offers welcome observations:

> Today we produce food within a system that is broken. Within roughly seventy years, our current chemical-based agricultural system is already showing its weaknesses— depleted soil, poisoned water, negative impacts on human and environmental health, and dysfunctional rural communities. We should be directing our valuable time and resources working towards a truly sustainable food production system based on sound biological principles.

THE GENIE IS OUT OF THE BOTTLE

To repair our food system, we must focus on the basics—soil health and water quality—and how we can improve upon these natural resources so that we return as much as we take, thus ensuring our future. By building and improving soil health, utilizing organic practices to fix nutrients in the soil, encouraging biodiversity, and greatly minimizing synthetic inputs, organic producers are ensuring the sustainability of the system indefinitely. Not just feeding the world's growing population today, or tomorrow, but far into the foreseeable future.

After thirty years of a rigorous side-by-side comparison, the Rodale Institute confidently concludes organic methods are improving the quality of our food, improving the health of our soils and water, and improving our nation's rural areas. Organic agriculture is creating more jobs, providing a liveable income for farmers, and restoring America's confidence in our farming community and food system. [831]

André Lue, in his excellent book, *The Myths of Safe Pesticides,* lists a number of studies showing organic yields not just comparable with conventional agriculture, but, showing improved yields, not just in developing countries, but in developed countries such as the UK, and USA.[832]

An article in *Nature,* in 1998, referred to a number studies where organic systems were not just on a par with conventional yields, but also reported on a long running trial at the Rothamstead Experimental Station in the UK. This trial has been running for more than 150 years, and reported that yields of wheat on manured plots have consistently improved yields over the conventional systems (using complete nitrogen, phosphorous and potassium (NPK) fertilizer). Further that the soil organic matter and the total soil nitrogen levels increased by 120% over 150 years in the manured plots (the nitrogen levels in the NPK system were 20%). [833]

These are welcome reports. Sometimes it takes a long time to see the results of our actions, but they are coming home to roost now and we are coming to realise that there are no short-cuts or quick fixes available for agriculture and our food supply. I believe that, in time, the industrialisation of agriculture by large commercial interests will come to be seen an unsustainable disaster. When you add the numerous costs that the industry has managed to evade and externalize: the pollution of the water supplies, pollution of the sea, pesticide poisoning, degradation of the soil, pollution of the air, the loss of nutrients, loss of local farmers, bankruptcies etc., its costs will seem even higher. However, these costs to the environment and our health that are not included in the costs the industry currently bears, would make chemically-produced food not only less productive than organic farming, but also more expensive. Organic agriculture is sustainable; it can not only feed the world, it can also sustain both the earth, and our health.

UNHEALTHY BETRAYAL

In Third World countries this lesson is being learnt, and farmers are responding in a positive way. Mostly for them, however, industrialised agriculture is a costly venture, utilising expensive pesticides and fertilisers, whereas organic farming mostly involves a different and less-intensive approach.

You may be interested in the views of someone who we associate with the GMO or conventional approach to agriculture, for example Monsanto CEO Robert Shapiro:

"The commercial industrial technologies that are used in agriculture today to feed the world... are not inherently sustainable...Feeding the world sustainably is out of the question with current agricultural practice...Loss of topsoil, of salinity of soil as a result of irrigation, and ultimate reliance on petrochemicals...are, obviously, not renewable. That clearly isn't sustainable." [834]

Here are the views of yet another insider, Steve Smith, a director of the world's biggest biotechnology company, Novartis:

"If anyone tells you that GM is going to feed the world, tell them that it is not. To feed the world takes political and financial will – it's not about production and distribution."

Those comments were reported in an article in *The Guardian,* by George Monbiot in August 2000. His article also referred to a number of studies farming practices that produced better yields than conventional agriculture. One study showed improved yields by planting a number of mixed strains of rice together instead of one species, and produced yields 18% higher than previously. The authors of this study commented:

The experiment was so successful that fungicidal sprays were no longer applied by the end of the two-year programme. Our results support the view that intraspecific crop diversification provides an ecological approach to disease control that can be highly effective over a large area and contribute to the sustainability of crop production. [835]

The rice study showed how reverting back to the much older technique of crop diversification to overcome disease (in this case rice blast, a fungus that prior to sowing a diversified crop, need numerous applications with fungicide, to save the crop), provided a simple way of reducing fungicide use.

André Leu, makes the point that of the US $52 billion spent annually on agriculture research worldwide, less than 0.4% is spent on solutions specific to organic agriculture. [836] We can only guess at the likely outcome if a larger sum were to be devoted to this research. What, however, we can be sure of, is that we would undoubtedly improve yields further, reduce chemical use, improve the soil, and make the world a safer and better place for future generations.

Monbiot, makes the point that crop diversification threatens the biotech companies, who are currently buying up seed companies and trying through patents and controlling seed supplies, to achieve large profits. He makes the point:

> All this requires an unrelenting propaganda war against the tried and tested techniques of traditional farming, as the big companies and their biddable scientists dismiss them as unproductive, unsophisticated and unsafe. The truth, so effectively suppressed that it is now almost impossible to believe, is that organic farming is the key to feeding the world.[837]

Some farmers in western economies argue that they are simply producing what people can afford, and not everyone can afford to pay the cost of organic produce prices. To address this point, we have to understand one of the central issues that this book addresses—the cost of dealing with all the chronic health problems due to malnutrition, pesticides, herbicides, chemical exposure and soil degradation are a significant cost.

The main reason that public healthcare systems are collapsing under the weight of dealing with this ever-rising cost of treating the chronic health problems of society, is that the cost is mostly borne, indirectly, by the very people who cannot always afford healthier organic food. They may be paying less for the food which causes them health problems, over the long term, but they pay more, through taxation for the treatment of those problems. Whilst much of industry pays some tax, as I have already described, the majority of the cost of dealing with industry's pollution of the earth, soil and water, is *externalised*. They themselves rarely pay the cost of dealing with the clean-up— ordinary taxpayers do. If all these costs were absorbed, instead, by the industries that cause the problems organic farming would suddenly become cheap.

Chapter 17
Invisible Death

The number of children and grandchildren with cancer in their bones, with leukemia in their blood, or with poison in their lungs might seem statistically small to some, in comparison with natural health hazards, but this is not a natural hazard—and it is not a statistical issue. The loss of even one human life, or the malformation of even one baby—who may be born long after we are gone— should be of concern to us all. Our children and grandchildren are not merely statistics towards which we can be indifferent. President John F Kennedy

There is one thread that runs through this volume, chapter after chapter, and that is the way corporate interests have sought to manipulate the media, governments, scientists, public opinion—all in the interests of generating ever larger profits with little or no benefit to the wider community. And although they have spent vast sums on those efforts, they have universally failed to spend anything like the same amount funding measures that prevent pollution or provide accurate truthful research. Truthful research is becoming a rare commodity. The ability to actually carry it out is becoming harder by the day, particularly as our debt-based economy becomes ever more burdened by yet more debt.

In the previous chapter, I quoted Don Huber and his research into the effects of glyphosate on crops. When he was questioned about his letter to the Secretary of Agriculture, and the 130 peer reviewed papers he referred to, regarding a call from Risk Management who wanted more details about the papers—he made the following illuminating comment:

I didn't want to disclose names of scientists or details because of the retaliatory effect that we see with anyone researching this area—they can be either fired from their job or their program shut down. That's a real fact.

UNHEALTHY BETRAYAL

He was further questioned about the fact that a scientist with a dissenting opinion could be "squelched":

> I think that's fairly well-documented. All you have to do is look at the statement of what the 26 North Central entomologists wrote. This is where the scientists who were set up as a regional project to determine the biosafety of genetically engineered crops. As a point of frustration perhaps, they wanted to notify the EPA, which they did. That public document that they sent in, they asked that their names be withheld because all 26 of them said that their funding is dependent on industry support. [838]

In the document referred to, they complained that they could not even do their job effectively—if they did the research, they were not only prohibited from publishing it, but they were also denied access to the very materials they were appointed to determine the safety of. So they were totally unable conduct the proper research needed to carry out the objective science on which to base a regulatory decision.

Another common thread I have previously discussed is that, as debt levels rise even further, the rhetoric that there is 'a shortage of funds' or 'no money for independent research' will get even louder. Industry, of course, will take up the slack—as we have seen—but this will simply further stifle independent research, independent thought, and creativity.

A further thread is the way corporations seek to limit their overheads, and maximise their profits by reducing their exposure to the costs of their irresponsible actions, such as clearing up pollution, resolving health issues —and the costs of litigation. When, for example, they move their production base to countries with poor regulatory frameworks, that are desperate for a source of income to service their massive debts, they know they will not have to care about the consequences of pollution and ill health. These externalized costs are mostly passed on to the local people, at least initially. The trouble is that these debts, the financial debts, the health consequences and the environmental consequences, all add to our collective DEBT BURDEN.

In the West it may seem we don't need to worry about what the oil industry gets up to in Nigeria, or the massive destruction of the forests in Paraguay, Brazil, Malaysia and other countries. The levels of toxins in our bodies are testament to the fact we have disregarded their release into these other parts of the world. The growing health problems in our populations, and the overwhelming cost to our health services, not only in the west, but throughout the whole world, bears this out. This is our true DEBT. When we get to the situation where a woman breast-feeding her new born baby anywhere on the planet understands that a great part of the toxins she carries are being transferred to her new-born, we know we are in trouble. As I previously mentioned, and it is worth repeating, the levels of dioxin alone, considered so toxic that it is measured in parts per trillion, are so high that if the mother was a food product, her milk would be banned for far exceeding the levels allowed *for adults* in our society. This is not to say that women should be discouraged from breast-feeding, far from it (as bad as this may be—there is nothing nutritionally comparable to mother's milk). This surely is not the issue, this is just one contaminant of hundreds that we already know about that make up our man-made chemical body burden; surely it is long overdue that we change our ways and remove this toxic burden from humanity.

If all these industrial processes that involve secrecy, cover-ups, manipulation of data, lies and deceit give you cause for concern, you'll be horrified by what follows next about nuclear radiation. You cannot taste or smell it, you cannot see it or feel it, and they tell you it does not exist, what can you do about it? Where I have reported that scientists feel hampered by telling the truth, or offering an alternative view, there is nothing that compares with the closed ranks and the total lack of any real science as exists in the nuclear industry. This is by far the greatest corporate scam perpetrated anywhere, the supreme industry for externalising costs and manipulating public opinion.

Its advocates would love you to see nuclear power as a 'green' technology, a 'low-carbon' alternative to fossil fuels, a high-tech solution to our growing energy needs, but how much truth is there in that?

We know secrecy existed in the nuclear industry way back—because it started with the development of nuclear weapons and the strategic development of the arms race. So all information concerning anything to do with it was kept under strict control. Well, we are now in the twenty-first century, and it's time those secrets are more widely disseminated. This is particularly so in the light of more recent events such as the disasters at Chernoble and Fukushima—and the ever growing stockpiles of radioactive waste that the corporate interests would have us believe are not a problem. Read what follows, make your own mind up, and then tell your friends what you think.

Discovery of X-rays

In 1895 Wilhelm Roentgen discovered X-rays whilst experimenting with the passage of electricity through an evacuated glass tube. He observed a phosphorescent screen glow with an energy he had not seen before. Yet with it he was able to develop X-ray technology and take X-ray pictures of his wife's hand showing her bones and her wedding ring. This discovery led to the development of X-rays for medical use, culminating today in the use of such radiation technology as Computerised Tomography scanning.

Thomas Edison was one of the first to take up the new technology at the end of the 19th Century, and developed what became known as the fluoroscope, a device that produced an instantaneous X-ray image on a fluorescent screen. In March 1896 it was licensed for mass production. People queued up to see the device, and to see an X-ray image of their arms and legs. So much enthusiasm for the new technology existed that it was used to treat all manner of conditions: ringworm, acne, and female depression—for which the ovaries were irradiated. One textbook recommended it for inducing menopause. The editor of the *American X-ray Journal* stated that there were 100 named diseases that responded favourably to X-rays. One company, the Tricho Institute, founded by the New York physician Albert Geyser, leased X-ray machines to beauty parlours to be used to treat unwanted facial and body hair. However, it didn't take long before reports started coming in of a catalogue of injuries and illnesses resulting from their use: radiodermatitis, horrible burns, painful ulcerations, later cancer and eventually deaths. The number of cases was not recorded, but is believed to have been in the thousands. One of the first people known to have died from X-rays was Thomas Edison's assistant, Clarence Dally, who passed away at the age of 39, after suffering six years of increasing pain from burned, inflamed and ulcerated skin. Along the way he had had his left hand amputated and part of his right, followed by the whole of his right arm and his left arm up to his elbow.

Marie Curie Discovers "Radiation".

In the same year that Roentgen discovered X-rays, Henri Becquerel from Paris, discovered that the uranium containing ore, pitchblende, a naturally occurring mineral, gave off a weak but similar radiation that was capable of passing through metal and fogging sealed photographic plates. Three years later, Marie Curie was able to identify a further attribute of pitchblende that she called 'radon'. She later isolated the radium from which this emanated from thousands of kilograms of pitchblend, and went on to isolate and identify polonium, another radioactive isotope. She was responsible for calling this new form of energy "radiation".

However, the effects of radiation on human health were not immediately apparent. Marie Curie herself was one of the early casualties—she died in 1934 from aplastic anaemia, brought on by her exposure to it. This is a disease in which the bone marrow, and the blood stem cells that reside there, are damaged. It causes a deficiency of all three blood cell types: red blood cells (anaemia), white blood cells (leukopenia), and platelets (thrombocytopenia). Well before Marie Curie's death, though, when radium was still thought to be a wonderful discovery, it was used in toothpaste, health elixirs, hair restorers—in fact a cure-all for everything from infertility to arthritis. One company supplied radium-water, as 'liquid sunshine' to 150,000 customers. Another company, W. J. A. Bailey sold a product called Radithor during the 1920s, made of water pre-mixed with radium, that they enthusiastically advertised as "A Cure for the Living Dead". One of the users of this was the steel tycoon Eben Byers from Pittsburgh, who became so seriously ill from it that portions of his jaw were surgically removed before he died in 1931. His death made front page news in the *New York Times,* and contributed to growing concern that radiation carried hazards to our health that had not previously been apparent.[839]

Around this time the medical profession was also using intravenous injections and oral treatments which included radioactive substances. Thousands of patients were treated with radium for just about every conceivable disease, ranging from rheumatism, high blood pressure, menstrual irregularities, depression, waning sex drive and a whole host of other conditions. In 1932, 31 patients at St Elgin State Hospital in Illinois were injected with radium in the belief it would treat their schizophrenia. The American Medical Association had fully sanctioned its use since 1914.

The Dangers of Radon

One of the most tragic stories about radon is that of the radium painters from Orange, New Jersey, who became known as the Radium Girls. They were employed by the United States Radium Corporation to paint watch dials and compasses with luminescent paint. They were told the paint was harmless, and were encouraged by their managers to use their lips to sharpen the points of their brushes to get a finer brush stroke on the narrow dials they were painting.

Grace Fryer started working at US Radium Corporation in 1917, in a large dusty room with 70 other women; she worked there for three years but then left for a better job, working in a local bank. But 5 years later, in 1922, she started to become worried about her health; her teeth began to loosen and fall out for no reason, and her jaw became swollen and inflamed. Her doctor discovered serious bone decay that he had never seen before—her jawbone was riddled with small holes like a honeycomb. One local dentist came across other women with similar degeneration of the jawbone and teeth, and linked all of them with having previously worked in the same watch-painting factory.

UNHEALTHY BETRAYAL

Nevertheless, US Radium continued to assure the public that the radium quantities were so low as to be harmless. They were, however, not unfamiliar with the hazards of radioactivity. They knew, for example, that radium was approximately one million times more active than uranium. They issued lead screens, masks and tongs to company chemists when working with the paint, but did not supply either the same information or the same protection to the hundreds of women working there. Instead the company went even further to conceal the true nature of the hazard by sending for a supposed specialist from Columbia University, Frederick Flynn, to examine Grace Fryer, who had been complaining. However, Frederick Flynn turned out to be not a doctor, but a toxicologist on US Radium's payroll—who declared that that Grace was in firm health. His colleague who accompanied him, and confirmed her good health, was later revealed to be one of the vice-presidents of US Radium. Even when deaths began to occur among the workforce the company blamed them on syphilis to undermine the women's reputations.

In early 1924, the company hired Cecil Drinker, Professor of Physiology at Harvard University, to undertake a study of conditions in the factory to show that they were taking allegations about the company seriously. However, when Drinker presented his report to the management, describing a heavily contaminated workforce, unusual blood conditions, and advanced radium necrosis in several workers, they blocked its publication and threatened Drinker with legal action if he released it. They did however send a sanitised version of the report to the New Jersey Department of Labor, in which conditions at the factory were given glowing accolades. The recommendations made by Drinker were totally ignored. It was only thanks to a colleague of Drinker's that he found out his report had been doctored. He was so incensed by this that he released his report in a scientific journal despite the threat of legal action. In his study Drinker reported massive contamination of the workplace. All his dust samples had glowed in the dark—and he found that the hair, faces, hands, arms, necks, dresses and even underclothes of workers were luminous with radium paint.

Whilst he was preparing his report, Drinker had noticed that Edward Lehman, the company chemist, had lesions on his hands. But when he approached Lehman with his concerns about the careless and unprotected way the chemist worked with the radium, he just scoffed at him and waved his concerns aside. Yet, in the spring of 1925, Lehman died of acute anaemia. An autopsy found radioactive materials in his lungs, his bones and other organs. Although he had never swallowed any paint, Lehman had regularly breathed in dust contaminated with radium. His bones were found to be so radioactive that his body photographed itself when photographic plates were placed under his torso. This was the first major report indicating the dangers of swallowing dust particles contaminated with the radio isotope radium.

INVISIBLE DEATH

Grace Fryer herself had difficulty in getting a lawyer to take up her case, since US Radium was a defence contractor, but eventually she did succeed. She filed suit in 1927 with a number of other women who were seriously damaged.

The women's health deteriorated during the prolonged slow-moving court process to such a degree that when the court hearing began in January 1928, two were bedridden and none had the strength to raise their arms to take the oath. Grace, who was described as 'pretty' was unable to walk, and she needed a back brace to enable her to sit up. By this time she had lost all her teeth. The grim descriptions of the hopeless condition of the "Radium Girls" reached Marie Curie in Paris who offered support. She explained that "there is absolutely no means of destroying the substance once it has entered the human body."

The women were too ill to attend the next hearing in April, and despite strenuous objections from the ladies' lawyer, the judge adjourned the case until the following September—because many of US Radium's witnesses were holidaying in Europe. But there was such uproar about this that it had to be rescheduled. In the event, the company decided to settle out of court a few days prior to that hearing.[840]

I have indulged with this story to try to give a human face to the kind of tragedy that can often seem like too many statistics with little direct relevance. I also put it in because, far from being a simple isolated incident, a one-off quirky story, it is, in fact, very typical of the treatment handed out to victims of anything to do with nuclear radiation, as we shall see a little later.

Leukaemia in Children Link to X-rays Provokes Limiting Exposure

In 1955 Dr Alice Stewart, head of the Department of Preventative Medicine at Oxford University, became aware of a sharp rise in leukaemia in young children in the UK and the USA. A young statistician, David Hewitt had found that this form of cancer of the blood had risen over 50 percent in the UK and approximately 100 percent in the USA. It seemed to strike children just over two or three years of age—yet not younger ones, which was really puzzling—especially since it had only developed since the end of the WWII. Dr Stewart undertook a study with the help of health officers throughout England and Wales, and almost 1700 women were interviewed. They analysed data on cases of leukaemia, brain and kidney tumours and discovered that babies who had been born to mothers who had had a series of X-rays of the pelvic region during pregnancy were twice as likely to have developed leukaemia, or another form of cancer, as those born to mothers who had not been X-rayed. Dr Alice Stewart published her findings in 1958, and concluded that the chances of this being a statistical accident with a two-to-one ratio, were less than one in ten million. [841]

In the rush to exploit the new technologies, such as X-rays, there had been little real understanding of the harm. Visible harm from burning, or hair falling out, was attributed to an excessive dose. Eventually the dose required to make the skin red, the Erythermal Dose (ED) was used as a guide. In 1924 the X-ray manufacturer Arthur Mutscheller proposed to the American Roentgen Society to limit X-rays to 1/100th of the ED per month or 1/10th per year. The following year Rolf Sievert, from Sweden suggested linking the 'safe' dose to background radiation levels, and proposed that one tenth the ED dose ought to be a safe level. A few years later, two British physicists who had been studying individuals who had been working with radiation for six years, without any noticeable effect, proposed dividing the level by a factor of 25 to end up with a figure of 0.08ED per year. Whilst there was very little in the way of any real science behind these moves, this level became accepted—and probably saved many people from suffering damage from higher levels. Professor Chris Busby made the following comment about the development of such 'safety' levels:

> The similarity in these three numbers, though fortuitous, gave a spurious scientific validity to the choice of the first radiation protection standard. Since this was adopted, there have been developments in knowledge, but there have been developments in practice also. Any reassessment of risk has always had to contend with having to force change on people who have been functioning under a standard derived from this first standard. Thus there has never been a total rethink. All that has happened over the years, has been a minor reduction of each level of safe dose-limit against opposing choruses of wails from those in the industry who have been functioning on the previous rule, usually supported by their friends who are, alas, in these instances, employed to defend public safety. [842]

The trouble with public safety issues, though, was that much of the development of the understanding of its safety was undertaken by physicists and not biologists. When, in 1934, they came up with a new standard of a tolerance level for radiation of 0.1r per day (Roentgen), this was based on the unit of energy transfer, even though it was well known that human beings react very differently to all the various levels of exposure. Lauriston Taylor, chairman of the Committee on X-ray and Radiation Protection in 1933, was quoted as criticising the way the limit was arrived at by saying: 'This work is seriously flawed, and yet it is still the basis for our protection standard of today. It really is.'

INVISIBLE DEATH

Development of atomic theory, of course, was not just taken up by the medical industry. Splitting the atom led to the development of nuclear weapons and their use by the USA in World War Two—and the development of larger and larger bombs after the war ended. The USSR detonated its first bomb in 1949, and Britain followed in 1952. Atmospheric tests escalated in both size and volume in this period, with extremely large thermonuclear hydrogen bombs releasing vast quantities of radioactive fallout materials into the atmosphere. There were two particular periods of intense testing during the years 1952-58 and 1961-63. Throughout that time there was huge concern over the release of such vast quantities of radiation into the atmosphere, and public pressure led to the establishment of the United Nations Scientific Committee on the Effects of Atomic Radiation (UNSCEAR) in 1955 to try and allay panic.

In the USA, the Atomic Energy Commission (AEC) was created following the development of the Hiroshima bomb which itself was associated with developing the field of atomic energy for security purposes. Safety issues were left to the US Advisory Committee on X-Ray and Radium Protection which came to be called the National Council on Radiological Protection (NCRP). The NCRP was made up of eight representatives from medical societies, two representatives from X-ray manufacturers and nine representatives from government agencies, including the armed forces and the AEC.

From the very beginning, the AEC put pressure on the group to set dose-limits—and the X-ray limit was reduced from 0.1rem to 0.05rem per day, partly due to the discovery that even small radiation doses can cause genetic damage and mutated offspring. However, as the US military wanted to continue development of atomic weapons research, pressure was put on the NCRP to set dose limits that would not inhibit that work.

Meanwhile, the nuclear industry had funded the formation of the International Commission on Radiological Protection (ICRP) – and the NCRP subsequently canvassed the ICRP to help them come up with a new workable limit. The problem with this, though, is that both organisations are staffed by pro-nuclear people—even though both have the words 'Radiological Protection in their names. It's like one is just the overseas branch of the other – another revolving door between industry and regulators. Between them, they set dose limits considerably higher than what others consider to be safe.[843]

UNHEALTHY BETRAYAL

The Weapons Program

It is impossible to separate the development of nuclear weapons from nuclear reactors; the later were needed to create the material for making the former. The development of them for the generation of electricity helped justify their use for the development of atomic energy. It was also a means of making more money being made out of them by the nuclear industry. However, before we get into the effects of this development, and the subsequent investment of more than a billion billion dollars into this one method of energy production at the expense of virtually any other method-- let's examine the results of the atomic weapons program.

The Troy Incident

It has to be said that at the absolute height of the weapons testing program, few people had any idea of the effects on human health of the atomic fallout. Some of the cancers took between 10 and thirty years to show up.

So let's go back to April 27th 1953, one Monday morning, when Professor Herbert Clark was teaching a radiochemistry class high on a hill overlooking the city of Troy in upper New York State. His class was interrupted by the buzz of all the Geiger counters in the lab suddenly, registering high levels of radiation, the highest which came from those nearest to the outside walls. When portable counters were taken outside the levels were even higher over a wide area—levels thousands of times higher than the so called 'permitted levels' were recorded—far higher than Professor Clark's previous experience of bomb test fallout. He suspected fallout from a nuclear test—as there had been heavy rain during the night. He quickly called John Harley of the US Atomic Energy Commission's Health and Safety Laboratory in New York City for confirmation of whether or not this was the case.

He was told that there had indeed been a test, code-named 'Simon', detonated 300 hundred feet above the desert in Nevada two days earlier. The fallout, it turned out, drifted at an altitude of 30,000 feet for 2300 miles until it reached New York State and hit a thunderstorm with which it combined—and so poured down on the unsuspecting population below. Professor Clark then proceeded to document all the readings they found, testing water from the reservoirs and taking readings all over the state. However, New York State Health Department declared the readings were not high enough to be seriously concerned about. Nonetheless, Professor Clark continued to monitor the levels in the reservoirs and sent in a more detailed report—which was never released. It was classified as "secret" and the general public knew nothing of the incident. Professor Clark continued to monitor the reservoirs and surroundings and obtained numerous repeated high readings, especially following further rainfall. He eventually published his own report in the obscure, highly specialized *Journal of the American Water Works Association.* [844]

This incident was nevertheless forgotten initially—but subsequent discoveries were to give it far greater significance. It was already known that fallout was taken up by water, plants and animals. What was not known though, was how it was found to become concentrated in milk, for example, from cows exposed to the fallout. Little known at the time was how the various fallout isotopes seemed to concentrate in particular areas of the human body—Iodine-131 and iodine-132 for example were found to build up in the thyroid replacing the normal iodine; strontium-90 being similar to calcium. It was found to be taken up in the bones and teeth of animals as well as people; Caesium-134 and Caesium-137 were found in many parts of the body, particularly in the muscles. What was even more disturbing was the discovery that iodine-131, for example, would be concentrated in cow's milk--and further concentrated in that very small organ, the thyroid in *children.*

Interest in the Troy incident was re-awoken in 1962, with the publication in *Science* of a report by the nuclear physicist, Ralph Lapp who documented the very high levels of fallout that had rained down on Troy and a large part of New York State in April 1953. He suggested that this would be a very good place to undertake a study—as it was well documented and he believed the findings would be significant and far reaching.

The Discoveries of Professor Sternglass

Dr Ernest Sternglass, Professor of Radiation Physics at the University of Pittsburgh, was part of a group called the Federation of American Scientists—professionals who were actively studying the possibility of surviving a nuclear war. He was, at the time, researching ways of reducing the radiation dose from medical X-rays, and was a considered a specialist in the effects of low-level radiation. He was disturbed right from the start of this work that all the government agencies were basing all their calculations on the premise that an adult could tolerate an enormous dose of 200 rads, spread over a few days, and as much as 1000 rads over one year. He was already aware that a dose of only a few rads per year was found to decrease radiologist's lifespans—and to increase congenital defects in their children. He was also aware of research by Dr Stewart from Oxford

University in the UK, who reported on the increase in leukemia following pelvic X-rays of pregnant mothers. It was discovered that the timing of the X-ray had an even more significant affect: children whose mothers were X-rayed during the first third of their term in pregnancy were found to be ten times more likely to develop leukemia than mothers who had X-rays in the later part of their pregnancy. Research from the University of Michigan, published in 1960, found that levels of radiation in unborn children were studied up to 100 times higher than that of an adult.

Dr Sternglass was motivated to re-look at the Troy study—and came up with some very worrying conclusions. As time passed, reports of high cases of leukemia started to filter through. In the case of Troy, in New York State, reported leukemia cases quadrupled, beginning in the fourth and fifth years following exposure. Dr Sternglass had been informed of these amounts and wrote to the New York State Health Department for their data—but was refused point blank. That, though, was a typical response to a request for information on cancer, in a supposedly democratic society, even though the disease was endemic in the USA and most everywhere else. Dr Sternglass became more concerned as reports from Hiroshima were also showing growing numbers of congenital malformations and mental retardation. Of those unborn children who had been about one mile from the explosions, and had received estimated doses of 10-20 rads, nearly one third were found to have reduced brain size and mental retardation. Japanese leukemia rates for all of Japan rose 50 percent from 1946 to the early 1950s, with a further sharp rise in 1959.

Eventually Dr Sternglass got hold of the US Vital Statistics for the three counties of upstate New York, and found that leukemia had risen by over 300 percent. He also found disquieting numbers of still births and miscarriages. In 1960, for example foetal deaths were 50 percent higher than expected. In 1954, the numbers had jumped by an astonishing 1500 cases. Since the 1940s foetal deaths had been in decline, which had been generally assumed to be due to better nutrition and healthcare. But, as soon as the atomic testing started, the rates stopped declining and stayed high. Following the end of the testing, the rates dropped to an all-time low. Dr Sternglass continued his research, and whenever he was able to get hold of the data he needed, he discovered that each time the levels of the short-lived isotopes, such as iodine-131 and strontium-89 shot up to their highest peaks, there was a sharp rise in foetal mortality within a year. [845]

To date there have been no large-scale studies on cancer and fallout. The AEC itself refused to undertake any studies. Evidence from Congressional Hearings revealed that for every 100 megatons of hydrogen bombs tested, a dose of 200 - 400 millirads would be absorbed by every man women and child in Europe, North America, and Asia. This covered testing up until 1962, and led Dr Sternglass to conclude that there would be a 20% increase in cancer as a result. He published a paper detailing his study, and although it was largely ignored initially, the levels of radioactivity in milk were reaching alarming levels by the spring of 1963, and his paper was accepted and published in *Science*.

This issue had become so worrisome that it provoked the USA and USSR to agree a treaty to end all atmospheric testing. In July 1963, President John Kennedy delivered his address to the nation, urging ratification of the treaty and made reference to the threat from atomic fallout:

> The number of children and grandchildren with cancer in their bones, with leukemia in their blood, or with poison in their lungs might seem statistically small to some, in comparison with natural health hazards, but this is not a natural hazard—and it is not a statistical issue. The loss of even one human life, or the malformation of even one baby—who may be born long after we are gone—should be of concern to us all. Our children and grandchildren are not merely statistics towards which we can be indifferent.[846]

It has been estimated that in the seventeen-year period from 1945—1962, the equivalent of 40,000 Hiroshima-sized bombs were let off and released fallout of man-made radioisotopes that are to this day in every man woman and child. Just to contrast the situation with the nature of the chemical onslaught against humanity, some of which I have discussed in the previous chapters, the cumulative output of organic chemicals rose 42-fold from 1945—1965 from 7.5 million tons to 316 million tons. At the same time the cumulative yield of nuclear materials as fallout released into the stratosphere rose 13,000-fold, from 45 kilotons to 587 megatons.[847]

Other Scientists Warn of the Dangers of Nuclear Testing and the Radiation Fallout

There were, of course, numerous people who tried to warn of the perilous consequences of nuclear testing. The well-known author, marine biologist and environmentalist, Rachel Carson, immortalised her concern in her book, *Silent Spring*, with the following:

> The most alarming of all man's assaults upon the environment is the contamination of air, earth, rivers, and the sea with dangerous and even lethal materials. This pollution is for the most part irrecoverable; the chain of evil it initiates not only for the world that must support life but in living tissues is for the most part irreversible. In this now universal contamination of the environment, chemicals are the sinister and little recognised partners of radiation in changing the very nature of the world—the very nature of its life. Strontium-90 released through nuclear

explosions into the air, comes to earth in rain or drifts down as fallout, lodges in soil, enters into the grass or corn or wheat grown there, and in time takes up its abode in the bones of a human being, there to remain until his death. [848]

Andrei Sakharov, the renowned Soviet nuclear physicist, who participated in the Soviet weapons program, predicted that between four and eight million deaths would result from the estimated 400 megatons of bomb testing alone. He became a convert to the peace process, and published a number of works arguing against nuclear proliferation—also supporting a ban on testing. In 1958 he published a paper with some of his predictions:

> When any nuclear weapons are exploded, including the so called "clean" (fissionless) hydrogen bomb, a very large number of neutrons enter the atmosphere and they are captured by atmospheric nitrogen according to the reaction $n + N^{14} \rightarrow p + C^{14}$ which give rise to long lived radioactive carbon-14. This radioactive carbon enters human tissue, where it decays, causing radiation damage with a dose of $7.5 \ 10^{-14}$ r per megaton burst.

He goes on to explain that due to Carbon-14's half-life of 5,570 years that the effects will be experienced for countless generations. The half-life of an isotope is the time that it takes to decay to half of its level.

He adds the following caveat:

> We are adding to the world's toll of suffering and death...All the moral implications of this problem lie in the fact that the crime cannot be punished (since it is impossible to prove that any specific human death was caused by radiation) and in the defencelessness of future generations against our acts.[849]

The Marshall Islands Test

One of the problems with examining the whole nature of nuclear energy is that there is a paltry amount of data available. Most of it is hidden from our view. The case involving the Marshall Islanders is one rare situation that gives us a glimpse of what is really going on.

In 1954, more than 200 of the native islanders resident on four atolls in the Marshall islands were exposed to nuclear fallout from a US explosion of the first hydrogen bomb, on Bikini Atoll in the South Pacific. This had the power equivalent of a thousand Hiroshima bombs. The

Islanders were one of the very few populations who were monitored by the military. Following the blast, a fine white ash not only landed on the bare arms of the islanders, but also dissolved into their water supplies and drifted into their homes. Within 24 hours, the people of Rongelap showed symptoms of acute radiation sickness, intense nausea, vomiting, diarrhoea, skin burns, itching and around the eyes. Soon afterwards people began to lose their hair. Two days after the test, the US evacuated the people of Rongelap to another atoll for further monitoring. Scientists at the Brookhaven National Laboratory calculated that islanders had each received a whole body dose of 175 rems, 25 times the radiation level permitted for a whole lifetime exposure. In 1976, it was acknowledged that 18 out of 22 children under ten years of age had developed thyroid cancer. Mothers also suffered from stillbirths and miscarriages as high as 41%. Later studies, incorporating all the islands, found the incidence of thyroid cancer to be 1000 times the normal level. The locals talked of grotesquely formed babies, so deformed that they died within hours. [850]

In 1995, one of the surviving islanders, Lijon Eknilang, a quiet, unassuming woman also from the Pacific island of Rongelap, made what is probably the longest trip in the world for a court appearance—to the International Court of Justice in The Hague to report on the horrors experienced by the islanders. Here's what she said:

> Women have experienced many reproductive cancers and abnormal births. In privacy, they give birth, not to children as we like to think of them, but to things we could only describe as "octopuses," "apples," "turtles," and other things in our experience.
>
> The most common birth defects on Rongelap and nearby islands have been "jellyfish" babies. These babies are born with no bones in their bodies and with transparent skin. We can see their brains and hearts beating. The babies usually live for a day or two before they stop breathing. Many women die from abnormal pregnancies, and those who survive give birth to what looks like purple grapes which we quickly hide away and bury. [851]

Lijon—who was eight years old when the detonation occurred, never successfully achieved a live birth, but had eight miss-carriages, she was eight years old when the detonation occurred. She pleaded before the court that no other human being on this Earth should ever suffer what her people had had to suffer. The judges concluded that nuclear weapons were unique in their destructive potential, that their impact could not be contained in time or space, and that there is a universal obligation to abolish such weapons.

UNHEALTHY BETRAYAL

The Windscale Incident

In 1957 the first serious nuclear accident occurred in the UK at the Windscale reactor in Cumbria. This was the first major accident involving a fire in a reactor core. The number one reactor was an air-cooled, graphite moderated reactor, used for producing plutonium for the weapons program. The fire burned for more than two days, and radioactive smoke was dispersed over England, Wales, Ireland and Northern Europe. Considerable quantities of radioisotopes were dispersed, including Iodine-131, strontium-90, Caesium-137 and Xenon-133. The most pressing concern was to reduce the impact of the short-lived isotope Iodine-131, which has a half-life of 8 days. It was decided to limit its impact by imposing a ban on the sale of milk with iodine-131 levels above 3.7kBq per litre. This was in force for over a month. [852]

At this point it's worth giving a little information on the half-life of isotopes. A fuller explanation on half-lives and ionising radiation is in the appendix, along with the atomic measurement systems for those who would like more detailed information. But for now, suffice it to say that the half-life is important because the shorter the half-life the more active the isotope and the more dangerous it becomes. Iodine-131, with a half-life of eight days will decay to half its starting level in eight days, a further half in the next eight days and so on. When iodine-131 decays it gives off beta particles, dangerous to tissues, particularly human and animal tissues.

The Kyshtym Disaster

In the same year, 1957, there was another major radiation incident, at Kyshtym in the South Urals in the USSR. This was a level six disaster according to the International Nuclear Event Scale. Level six makes it the third most serious after Chernobyl and Fukushima, which were both level seven. Apparently a tank in the Mayak nuclear fuel reprocessing plant, containing 168 tons of radioactive waste, overheated and exploded—blowing a cloud of radioactive materials into the sky over 1000 metres high. It travelled 3000 kilometres and contaminated more than 1500 sq. km of land, affecting 270,000 people. The cloud contained strontium-90, caesium-137, zirconium-95, ruthenium-106 and cerium-144.

No information on the health effects of this was released at the time, and even now little is known of the effects on the population of Ozvorsk, a closed city surrounding Mayak, and one which is not even marked on the maps. It is, however, alleged that 10,000 people were evacuated without being told the true reason why they had to go. Many more people were eventually evacuated in total, how many is unknown. At the same time all western governments and nuclear regulatory authorities maintained a total silence on the incident—even though they were sure to have been aware of it. The disaster was eventually made public by Zhores Medvedev on 4ᵗʰ November 1976—and in the UK, the *New Scientist* published an article that revealed some of the story. His account was derided by the nuclear industry, but was confirmed by numerous sources, including Professor Leo Tumerman, former head of the Biophysics Laboratory at the Institute of Molecular Biology in Moscow. [853]

Rising Mortality Rates

Dr Sternglass spent a lot of time looking at data on births, deaths and rainfall after his experience with the New York fallout—and a lot of what he found was disturbing. He was troubled by the fact that American birth-weights (and those in other countries) had mysteriously declined in the beginning of the early 1950s, and it seemed to him to be related to rainfall. Hawaii, for example, is a place with very high rainfall and had been enjoying a continuous downward trend in infant mortality rates.Thses had dropped from approximately 80 per 100 births in the 1930s to 28 per 100 in 1945. But at this point the the trend suddenly stopped and actually rose during 1946-48—following the detonations of Hiroshima and Nagasaki and the tests at Bikini and Eniwetok, all located directly upwind of Hawaii. They rose to another peak between 1957 and 1960, following the large hydrogen tests in the Pacific. Following the end of large-scale atmospheric testing in 1962, Hawaii's infant mortality rate continued its decline, and even fell below 20 per 100, the lowest in its history. Dr Sternglass looked at other areas, including Mississippi, where the average rainfall is 49 inches, directly in the path of the Nevada tests. It, too, followed the decline from 1930 to 1945, and it too subsequently rose by 45% 1960. Once again, following cessation of the bomb testing it then began to decline again. He was unable to get any data after 1966 so we don't know how low it went. He found this same pattern all over the USA as well as in other countries.

What troubled him even further, though, was that when he looked at the figures for every single infant that had died in the first year of life, there were between five and ten who had died prior to birth. This indicated that if the excess foetal deaths, spontaneous abortions and still births, were included in the figures this would total two to three million in the USA alone. So Dr Sternglass also looked into maternal deaths over the same periods—and found that in 1963, at the height of the testing, deaths of mothers who died from complications of pregnancy and childbirth in the US totalled 1,466—more than a thousand higher than had been expected, had the previous the downward trend continued. He estimated that globally the total would have been ten times the US total. He tried to publish his findings to stimulate further research, but was stonewalled and his paper was turned down. He was also scheduled to appear on the local Pittsburgh TV station, KDKA but this was cancelled at the very last minute.

Dr Sternglass's full story is well documented in his book, *Secret Fallout, Low—Level Radiation From Hiroshima to Three Mile Island,* which I recommend to anyone wishing to find out something closer to the truth than the PR proclamations from the nuclear industry. The only thing I can say is that he is not alone in his judgement. The more the industry tried to cover their tracks by denying him access to data, and even stopping monitoring radiation levels and recording data in some instances, the more determined he became to get to the truth.

Fortunately for him, the statistics for the whole of the USA were much easier to obtain, and if these followed the same pattern, this would be even more significant than the smaller studies. Other people, it soon became clear, were finding similar patterns. Dr Moriama, for example, had found that the annual death rate for white males, aged seventy-five to eighty-four years, from respiratory diseases (excluding influenza and pneumonia) was close to 110 per 100,000 in 1934, and that by 1948 they had declined to an all-time low of 70. But that by 1960 it had shot up to 190. Moriama calculated that during the heavy Nevada testing from 1956-60 there were 85,000 excess deaths (1961) and 131,000 excess deaths (1962).

Sternglass contacted numerous people all around the world to see if he was in error—but found a similar picture wherever he looked. Dr Campbell in the UK, for example, found a tremendous rise in cases of leukemia in England and Wales, in both men and women, between 1947 and 1951—with the sharpest rises among the *very young and the very old.* By 1959, the rate had jumped by approximately 500%. This was the very rise that had prompted Dr Stewart's study that I have already mentioned.

The Hiroshima Study

One of the bones of contention between independent researchers, (who, I have to say, are few and far between), and the nuclear lobby, is that the latter cites the Hiroshima studies (the ones the US military produced) as evidence that low-level radiation is irrelevant and was responsible for hardly any ill-effects on human health hardly any ill effects after the initial casualties. Well, to express an opinion about the health of one group, has to be compared to a control group. So to say there 'was no significant increase in cancer in Hiroshima', for example, you have to show that compared to a population not exposed to the Hiroshima fallout, that there was no significant rise. The trouble is there were few places in Japan that were not exposed in some degree to the fallout of either Hiroshima or Nagasaki so the Japanese people, used as a control group, were not an ideal choice. This however was not the most serious concern.

A further criticism of the Hiroshima study was due to the way it was updated and manipulated by two controllers of the study, the Radiation Effects Research Foundation (RERF) in Japan, and the US Department of Energy. They did a revision of the doses and were severely criticised by Professor Gofman, who said:

> Now I don't have any objection to the revision of doses, provided that you obey the cardinal rules of medical research. The first cardinal rule of medical research is: never, but never change the input data once you know what the follow-up shows. So, because they had this idea of changing the doses, they didn't just change the doses, they shuffled all the people from one dose category to another, with a new dose. So there was no continuity with everything that had been done up to 1986. [854]

Gofman goes into this subject at great depth in his book *Radiation-Induced Cancer from Low-Dose Exposure: An Independent Analysis*. He wrote to Itsuzo Shigematsu, the Director of RERF in Japan to express his concerns about the changes to the database, but considered Shigematsu's reply a mere brushoff, commenting: "We do not think that the meaningful rules of research can be disregarded in this field." I'm sure you'll agree that seems a little inadequate considering the immensity of his critique. I can recommend his book for those who would like a more technical and informative discussion. Gofman further comments that using the new dataset on cancer incidence produces a gentle curve that starts to rise, then rises much more steeply—whereas the original dataset produced a more or less a diagonal line. During the above mentioned interview, he was asked whether the changes they made had the intention of making it look as if low-level radiation was acceptable, and he replied: "Exactly. Their ultimate goal is fulfilled." [855]

Gofman believes that the Hiroshima study is important and of unique value because of both its size and length. It involved the lifespan study of 91,231 atomic bomb survivors, half of whom were still alive in 1990, and contrary to what many people think, the majority were low-dose study victims; very few of the survivors at Hiroshima and Nagasaki received high doses. In his book he clearly expresses his concern:

The A-bomb database is so valuable that it would be a real blow against human welfare if its scientific worth were undermined by irregular handling.

He also discusses the ramifications. If the nuclear industry were ever to get acceptance that there was such a thing as a completely safe dose, that would more than likely open the floodgates to a massive rise in exposure for the general population by inviting ever more irresponsible dumping of the tons and tons of radioactive waste that the industry is stockpiling in our once un-polluted environment:

Proposals are pending to EXCLUDE very low-dose exposure of entire populations from consideration in risk-estimates, and also handle large share of radioactive waste as if it were NOT radioactive—in other words, to declare a threshold by using edict to over-rule evidence.

It is self-evident that if a mistaken notion about safe doses and dose-rates prevails in this field, human exposures to ionizing radiation will rise dramatically—from occupational, environmental, and medical doses. Quite aside from heritable genetic consequences....such a mistake would be far from trivial. Over time, it could mean cancer inflicted on a hundred million or more humans.[856]

Dr Sternglass decided to see for himself what happened in Japan but you won't come across what he found in the official US Military report. Research by Dr Sergi at the School of Public Health, Tohoku University, Japan, sponsored by the Japanese Cancer Society, showed how many types of cancer known to be caused by radiation rose sharply all over Japan, not just in Hiroshima and Nagasaki, beginning approximately five to seven years after the bombs were detonated. Pancreatic cancer, for example, had been fairly stable in the ten years prior to 1945, but by 1965 had shot up 1200%after which it began to decline again. Similar data for lung cancer and prostate cancer showed that prostate cancer rose 900% and lung cancer by 750%.[857]

Following the bombing of Hiroshima and Nagasaki, there were numerous reports of people dying days and weeks after the detonations on Japanese radio and other media outlets. According to Caufield, General Groves ordered a team of Manhattan Project doctors and technicians to go to the bombed cities to prove there was no trace of radioactivity in either city—and what radiation they found there was 'not considered to be of great importance'. Their objective was to dispel any public opinion that it was 'inhumane'. All American journalists were escorted around the sites by US military personnel. But, just before they arrived on 5th September, 30 days after the first atomic bomb, the London *Daily Express*, carried a report by Wilfred Burchett, the first newsman to enter Hiroshima without an army escort, and therefore able to see whatever he wished. The headline of the front page read:

'I WRITE THIS AS A WARNING TO THE WORLD' His story went on: 'In Hiroshima, 30 days after the first atomic bomb, people are still dying, mysteriously and horribly—people who were uninjured in the cataclysm from an unknown something which I can only describe as the atomic plague'. [858]

It seems pretty obvious that the nuclear industry is still in almost total denial about the true effects of radiation, but is able to spend massive amounts of money on its public relations campaign to control public opinion. Here are some of its problems it has to try and conceal: it is totally unable have the backing of any insurance industry anywhere it the world; it is totally unable to come up with a realistic way of dealing with massive amounts of radioactive waste that is hugely toxic to man and most life on the Earth; and it cannot even contemplate the huge financial and physical burden of containing that waste for more than 24,000 years (the half-life of plutonium-239 is 24,400 years). They want us to believe that everything is just fine—that *there is no problem*, that reactors are absolutely safe, and they are really fantastically economical. As far as the small emissions are concerned, again no need to worry there either, the emissions are so small that we can regard their existence as insignificant.

Let me make my own personal position clear here, I have no axe to grind. Most of what is being referred to here, is about mostly past actions. I have no wish to pass judgment on the way the initial decisions to develop atomic energy for weapons were made. My interest is in the decisions that we need to make now to lessen the impact of those past mistakes, and to enhance the future of all of us.

That withstanding, I do intend to continue this narrative to make sure you're fully informed to reach your own conclusion. My overriding desire is to encourage debate, a free and open debate. I sincerely believe that open transparent debate and discussion can only serve us well. What is the need for secrecy if all we seek is the truth? However, if it was considered important for strategic reasons during the War, and the period after, so be it. But does it justify continuing the secrecy, lies and deceit today?

UNHEALTHY BETRAYAL

Petkau's Discovery

It was Professor Sternglass who reported the startling discovery by Dr Abram Petkau, of the Canadian Atomic Energy Laboratories in Pinawa, Manitoba. Petkau had been studying the basic processes that enable chemicals to diffuse through cell membranes. At the same time, he was studying the effects of x-rays on these membranes—and found that they generally ruptured following the relatively large dose of 3500 rads. His next step was to try something that no-one had been known to try before—to add a small quantity of radioactive sodium salt to the water, as may occur with radioactive fallout. What he discovered, to his great surprise, was that even a very small amount caused the cell wall to rupture. Instead of requiring 3500 rads, all it took was three-quarters of a single rad. This prompted him to try even less—and he eventually discovered he was able to rupture the cell wall with an infinitesimally small dose of 5000 times less than one rad. This was a truly astounding discovery—if such a small dose could achieve that level of destruction it would mean that the 25-year old guidelines on safe levels of exposure to nuclear radiation were completely flawed.

Subsequent experiments led him to discover that a more highly toxic and unstable form of ordinary oxygen than was found in healthy cell fluids was created by the irradiation process. What was happening was that a dangerous "free radical" was created—which was attracted to the cell membrane, where it started a chain reaction that oxidised and weakened the molecules composing the cell membrane. What he also discovered was that the more free radicals present in the cell fluids, the more destructive was the process. Increasing the dose further showed a non-linear effect—which basically meant that a massively increased exposure was, surprisingly, not as damaging as a low-level dose. [859]

This research has since been confirmed by others and has had profound implications for the types of radiation exposure and the degree of exposure. Later research into the mechanism behind this led Petkau to discover how superoxide dismutase (SOD), an enzyme in the cell, could help restrict the damage caused by radiation. Raised levels of this same enzyme were found in the leukocytes (white blood cells) of radiation workers—which is believed to be one of the ways the body tries to protect itself from ionizing radiation. Petkau found that giving supplemental SOD to radiation patients helped reduce inflammatory lesions, all of which confirms his original discovery.[860]

INVISIBLE DEATH

Sternglass Makes His Findings Public

In the published reports of the hearings on the environmental effects of electric power generation, held by the Joint Committee on Atomic Energy in November 1969, there were tables listing the various amounts of radioactive discharge by various nuclear reactors in the US. This revealed a large difference in emissions from plant to plant. Two plants, for example, had released in excess of 700,000 curies, whilst others were recorded as low as 2.4 curies—300.000 times less that the larger emitting stations. According to Dr Sternglass, one curie of iodine-131 could make 10 billion quarts of milk unfit for consumption. Also listed were the *permissible* levels for the reactors, which seemed enormous to Dr Sternglass. For the Dresden plant, for example, located only fifty miles from Chicago, the actual radioactive emissions for 1967 were 260,000 curies but the permissible levels set by the AEC were 22,000,000 curies. What Dr Sternglass discovered was that many of the higher emitters were the boiling-water type reactors that he believed to have been cheaper to build. If you look at the Dresden plant when it first started operation, its emissions were quite low—in 1961 only 0.158 percent of the maximum allowable amount had been released. After approximately one year of use, this had increased to 284,000 curies, an almost 10% increase. In 1964 it increased again to 521,000 curies. Sternglass discovered that the infant mortality rates for Grundy County, where the reactor was located, and for the adjacent county of Livingston, had jumped 140% within a year of the higher emission rates (1966).

These findings made Dr Sternglass look at other places. He had his students look into the first commercial fuel reprocessing plant in West Valley, New York, where the infant mortality rate had jumped by 54% between 1966 and 1967—far more than New York State as a whole. The levels of radioactivity in the milk were checked throughout the US, only those in Pennsylvania showed iodine-131 in levels greater than 1 micromicrocurie (this represents a picocurie 10^{-9}). They also found that all along the Allegheny River, in Warren County and Vernango County—where it was believed radiation seeping from the plant could explain the high rate of infant mortality—levels had risen 56% in the first of the two, and 48% in the second.

Sternglass decided to investigate locations with higher density populations surrounding a reactor. Small college campus reactors such, as the TRIGA, were ideal for this because their emissions were well documented—and the first of these he looked at was at Pennsylvania State College. Here, he very quickly found precipitous rises and falls in mortality corresponding with rises and falls in emissions. So he next looked for a TRIGRA with an even larger surrounding population, and selected the University of Illinois campus in Urbana. From 1962 when this reactor commenced operation through 1965, the year it reached full power, infant mortality increased by 300%. Also available were the statistics for congenital malformations which showed an increase of 600% from 1962-65. After the reactor was shut down, the rates universally dropped from 23.5 per 100,000 to around 6.6.

Following the publication of his paper on these findings, and a follow-up article on the topic of radiation fallout and child mortality for *Esquire* magazine, Sternglass was invited to debate the subject with Dr Arthur Tamplin, a physicist from the Livermore Laboratory, who had written a critique of Sternglass' work soon to be published in the *Bulletin of the Atomic Scientists*. *Esquire* had meanwhile sent a copy of the issue to every US Congressman, and placed full-page advertisements in the *New York Times* and the *Washington Post,* with the title 'The Death of All Children', which carried a summary of the main aspects of Sterglass's report.

Sternglass agreed to the debate—at which someone in the audience asked why the AEC had never found evidence of any significance in mortality in animal studies fed strontium-90 for long periods of time. Dr John Gofman, Tamplin's immediate supervisor, stood up and offered to answer the question. As a previous Director of the Biomedical Division of Livermore and an Associate Director of the Laboratory, he had been in charge of all their radiobiological studies since 1963. He was both a physician and a nuclear chemist, and had worked with the AEC chairman Glenn Seaborg in the 1940s. Gofman had developed a way of cleanly separating plutonium from uranium and was able to give Robert Oppenheimer his first milligram of plutonium at a time when the total world's supply had previously been approximately 0.06 milligram. He addressed the audience and mentioned that he had investigated all the animal studies carried out by the AEC, saying that in no case had they been designed to detect the kind of small reductions in birth-weight, or the ability to fight infections, that Dr Sternglass was finding in the increased infant mortality in humans. He concluded by saying there had not been one single animal experiment to contradict Dr Sternglass's findings, that he was aware of.

Tamplin, however, had been chosen by the AEC to try and dampen the effect that Sternglass's findings had been having on the media. To start with, he had arrived at different figures from Sternglass's 400,000 infant deaths, claiming that the figure was more in the region of 8,000. However, the AEC wanted him to omit that figure altogether from his own paper, being unwilling to admit that fallout was responsible for significant numbers of deaths of American Infants. Tamplin refused to do this, and published his paper as it was. Gofman supported Tamplin's action, and the response by the AEC was to threaten to remove a quarter of a million dollars from Lawrence Livermore's budget if Gofman was allowed to continue his research there.

What is interesting here, is that, following Dr Stewart's findings on the effects of x-rays on the unborn, the AEC had decided in 1962 to set up its own study into the effects of radiation on plants, animals, and man—and Gofman had been the man chosen to head that work at Livermore, and where he was made an Associate Director of the lab. But when the AEC found out that his work was going to threaten the industry's development, he was basically dumped.

Subsequent to the debate, Dr Tamplin was forced to supress his work in which he had calculated that as many as 8,000 deaths in the USA had been caused by genetic damage due to nuclear testing. Dr Gofman himself resigned his position as Associate Director as a result of this. They both testified before congressional committees that in their view there was *no safe threshold of radiation exposure* (my empahasis). [861]

Gofman and Tamplin were initially considered to be industry men, but have since become very vocal about what they believe is an intense cover-up by the whole nuclear industry. For example, they point out that the Nuclear Regulatory Commission (NRC) permits giant nuclear plants to operate *without* having radiation monitors installed, even with populated areas just fifty miles from the plant. They say that policy is deliberate because it protects utilities from lawsuits. In their jointly authored book, *Poisoned Power—The Case Against Nuclear Power Plants Before and After Three Mile Island,* they reveal a lot of previously unpublished. They claim the approach has been to "expose people first; learn the effects later". They go on to say 'there is only one description for such mass experimentation on humans—moral depravity. And such experimentation with "low" doses of radiation can produce irreversible effects not only on this generation, but upon countless future generations who have no voice, no choice. If that is not a crime against humanity, what is?'[862]

Further Bomb Testing But No Monitoring

Bomb tests in Nevada were given meaningless code names. The third series was called Tumbler-Snapper, and turned out to cause unexpected anxiety. Strong winds on 7th May 1952 the day of 'Easy', the third 'shot'—as the detonations were referred to, carried heavy fallout well beyond the expected range. According to the AEC itself, this was the heaviest fallout over a populated area since 'Trinity', their very first test. In the Trinity test investigators were sent off in pursuit of the radioactive cloud—and came across livestock and pets burned and bleeding and suffering hair loss.

And although all those maimed animals were quickly bought up to try and hush up the incident little effort was made to gather information on the effect of the fallout on the people who had been exposed to it. It wasn't until three years later that they realized it had travelled at least 1000 miles when complaints were made to Eastman Kodak about totally fogged film – the packaging paper for which had processed in water extracted from the Wabash River, which had been contaminated with fallout. Further evidence of fallout was found by testing the wheat grown in Montana—which was also found to be contaminated. Yet information about the fallout only became public when a radio technician reported high levels of it in Salt Lake City, 400 mile northeast of the test site.

When asked at an AEC meeting where the fallout tended to go, Lewis Strauss ,the Wall Street banker who became AEC Commissioner, said 'East it goes.. over St George, which they usually plaster.' It was generally understood that efforts were made to avoid testing when the wind direction would be likely to send fallout over Los Angeles or Las Vegas. Most of the information we have from de-classified files reveals that, prior to 1958, the AEC did little monitoring of exposure, particularly of food and water supplies. Much of the information it obtained came from external sources. For example, we know that high levels of fallout from the first Nevada test in January 1951 hit Rochester New York thanks to Geiger counters going wild at the Eastman Kodak plant. Kodak executives found readings were 25 times the normal level, as a result of heavy snowfall bringing down high levels of radioactive fallout. Apparently, following this incident, AEC officials decided to provide Eastman Kodak and other photographic companies with prior warning of tests to forestall possible lawsuits.

Information about the effects on the residents of places in the path of the fallout clouds, like St George, came from the residents themselves, with high rates of rare diseases, cancers and leukemias reported. In an interview with *Life* magazine, St George resident Elmer Picket explained how they knew there was a major problem: 'My father and I were both morticians, and when these cancer cases started coming in I had to go into my books to study how to do the embalming, cancers were so rare. But all of a sudden, in '56 and '57 they were coming in all the time. By 1960 it was a regular flood.' [863]

In 1979, reflecting on the legacy of the atmospheric bomb tests Dr John Gofman was quoted saying:

> There is no way I can justify my failure to help sound an alarm over these activities many years sooner than I did. I feel that at least several hundred scientists trained in the biomedical aspect of atomic energy—myself included—are candidates for Nuremberg-type trials for crimes

against humanity for our gross negligence and irresponsibility. Now that we know the hazard of low-dose radiation, the crime is not experimentation its murder. [864]

Health Effects Not Just Due to Bomb Detonation Fallout

Health problems as a result of the weapons program were not solely due to bomb detonation fallout. There were also problems at nuclear power stations, and I have already mentioned the accident at Windscale in the UK. In the US, news of the nuclear accident at the government's Savannah River nuclear weapons plant in South Carolina only came to light 20 years after the event—in 1988. An article in the *New York Times* of, October 1st 1988 revealed that the Savannah River plant complex that produces fuel for nuclear weapons had experienced a number of serious reactor accidents, all of which had been kept secret for more than 30 years—according to the evidence by two Congressional committees.

Dr Jay M Gould, former member of the EPA's Science Advisory Board and author of a number of works on the nuclear industry, reported on the Savannah complex, and described it as one of the most radioactive places on earth, with approximately a billion curies of high-level nuclear waste stored there—at least half of the US government's total inventory. He subsequently investigated the available information on the levels of radioactive isotopes in the milk supply for the south-eastern area of South Carolina, and the mortality data. What he found was peaks in infant mortality and total mortality following peaks in radioactive releases, as well as disturbing long-term trends in total mortality in the region. Radioactivity in South Carolina's rain jumped six-fold in December 1970 as a result of the November-December accident. This was five times higher than the Northeast and West, and 70 times higher than the Midwest. Levels of strontium-90, just 25 miles north of the plant, were highest in the country. South Carolina's infant mortality rate in January leapt 24% higher than the previous January. Dr Gould found a second, more protracted peak in infant mortality in the summer of 1971 and again in 1973. In all, the region had over 20,000 more deaths than expected and a three-fold increase in lung cancer. The majority of the additional deaths from lung cancer occurred approximately ten years after the accidents. He also found that by far the greatest concentration of strontium-90 occurred in the local produce and game. The Fish from the Savannah River had two thousand times the concentrations of strontium-90 than there were in the water supply. High levels were also found in vegetables, grains and poultry grown within twenty-five miles of the plant. He makes the further comment, that due to the half-life of strontium-90 being 30 days, it will contaminate the soils, root vegetables, and deep-rooted fruit trees for decades.

He also notes that, following these awful strontium-90 readings, the government stopped publishing data on the levels in human bones.[865]

March 28th 1979 marked one of the most traumatic events in US history, with the nuclear disaster at the Three Mile Island (TMI) nuclear plant, near Harrisburg Pennsylvania, unfolding under the glare of media interest. Dr Sternglass went there and found levels of radiation 15 times above normal as soon as he arrived at the airport, thirty-six hours after the accident following the alarm being raised. He suggested to the authorities that pregnant women and children should be urged to leave the area and not to drink fresh milk or water for a few weeks until monitoring the levels indicated they were safe again. The governor of Pennsylvania however, Richard Thornburgh, failed to deliver these instructions for two days, by which time a lot of the damage had already been done. According to Dr Sternglass, most of the radiation had already been released, and the iodine-131 bulk was estimated at fourteen curies. The Metropolitan Edison Company, the owners of the reactor, revealed the level of quantities involved:

> Based on techniques used in this analysis, dose estimates are consistent with the release of seven million curies of noble gases in the first one and a half days of the accident, two million in the next three days, and a relatively small amount thereafter.

This basically confirmed Dr Sternglass's original understanding. [866] It has to be said, though, that this whole incident was downplayed, as soon as the situation had been brought under control, and the glare of the media faded. Infant mortality started to peak three to four months later, with the sharpest increases occurring amongst those who lived nearest to the plant. From the three months prior to the accident to the end of the four months following it, infant mortality rose in Pennsylvania by nearly 16%, and in Maryland by 41%. At the same time, New York City, well to the East of Harrisburg, and not affected by the exposure, recorded a decrease of infant mortality of 6%. Infant deaths from birth defects in Dauphin County, by contrast, following the disaster at TMI, increased by a staggering 44%.

Denials about the true extent of the health effects of this disaster raged because of the 2,500 lawsuits filed against Metropolitan Edison Company for a host of radiation induced illnesses including: birth defects, still births, spontaneous abortions, cancer, sterility, leukemia, heart failure, emphysema, hypothyroidism, hair loss and many more. What became absolutely clear is that the authorities and the utilities have a vested interest in downplaying the whole issue of biological effects of radiation damage. It is very much cheaper to trot out some industry 'experts', industry lawyers and industry PR, than it is to have to deal with expensive legal claims and the vast costs of clean-ups, decommissioning, investing in the best-designed reactors, or even expensive plant maintenance.

There is a lot more to this story that can be gone into here, but the simple fact is that there was rush into building cheaper reactors such as the boiling water ones developed by General Electric Company, because of the promise of greater profits. Sternglass confirms that the largest fallouts were all released by these boiling water reactors, and says that safety was sacrificed to save on build and running costs.

Chernobyl

No discussion of the nuclear story could be written without mention of Chernobyl, a name few knew before the massive accident in the Ukraine on Saturday April 29th 1986—when satellite imagery picked up reactor number four on fire. Considered the world's worst nuclear disaster to date, the massive concrete lid was blown from the reactor that fateful Saturday, sending a plume of radioactive debris two thousand metres into air. The explosion split the reactor core, set fire to surrounding buildings and continued to burn for two weeks. Yet this was another incident that was totally down-played being portrayed in Europe as no more than a local disaster, and in the US as a European phenomenon. However Jay Gould, a highly respected statistician, noted that there was a strong correlation between the accident and increased levels of radioactivity in some parts of the USA, with higher than expected death rates. Even ignoring the hot spots (some areas were affected more than others) he found national US government data showed a statistically significant increase in deaths of 5.3% in the US during May 1986, the highest annual increase in May deaths for more than 50 years. The Department of Energy's Environmental Measurement Laboratory, measured significant peaks of iodine-131 (remember this has a half-life of only eight days so it cannot be that old), and other isotopes including cesium-137, strontium-89, strontium-90, and barium-140. These were all found in fresh milk (cited in the New York-New Jersey area). [867]

In a more recent work, *The Enemy Within—The High Cost of Living Near Nuclear Reactors,* produced by Dr Jay Gould and members of the Radiation and Public Health Project, statistics about every reactor site in every part of the USA were examined. These revealed a massive rise in breast cancer that could be directly attributed to the radiation emanating from nuclear reactors of both the commercial and the government types. The highest levels of mortality were found to be in the states with the most reactors and the highest levels of rainfall. Women living near the oldest Department of Energy (DOE) reactors registered the highest long-term increases in breast cancer mortality. By the investigators' own calculations, if every state that had had the same low-incidence rate as the non-nuclear states there would have been 40,000 fewer cases of breast cancer each year. This, of course, does not include all the other problems associated with low-level radiation, such as the, immune system damage, septicaemia, lung cancer and stomach cancer. [868]

Information coming out of the Ukraine had initially been difficult to get hold of but much more is available now. According to Russian authorities, more than 90% of the liquidators (the clean-up workers) have become invalids (740,000). They have been found to be aging prematurely and to have a high incidence of cancer, leukemia and neurological illnesses. A very large number have cataracts. The German Affiliate of International Physicians for the Prevention of Nuclear War (IPPNW), has released a study on some of the effects of Chernobyl on various groups of people—the 830,000 liquidators, the 350,400 evacuees from the 30 km zone, the populations in the heavily irradiated zones (8.3 million people), and the lesser irradiated populations of Europe (600 million people). Following is a summary of some of their findings:

- Available studies estimated the number of fatalities amongst infants as a result of Chernobyl to be about 5,000.
- Genetic and teratogenic damage (malformations) have also risen significantly, not only in the three directly affected countries, but also in many European countries. In Bavaria alone, between 1000 and 3000 additional birth deformities have been found since Chernobyl. We fear that in Europe more than 10,000 severe abnormalities could have been radiation induced. The estimated figure of unreported cases is high, given that even the IAEA came to the conclusion that there were between 100,000 and 200,000 abortions in Western Europe because of the Chernobyl catastrophe.
- According to UNSCEAR, between 12,000 and 83,000 children were born with congenital deformations in the region of Chernobyl, and around 30,000 to 207,000 genetically damaged children worldwide. Only 10% of the overall expected damage can be seen in the first generation.
- In the aftermath of Chernobyl, not only was there an increase in the incidence of stillbirths and malformations in Europe, but there was also a shift in the ratio of male and female embryos. Significantly fewer girls were born after 1986.
- A paper by Kristina Voigt and Hagen Scherb also showed that after 1986, in the aftermath of Chernobyl, around 800,000 fewer children were born in Europe than one might have expected. Scherb estimated that, as the paper did not cover all countries, the overall number of "missing"

children after Chernobyl could be about one million. Similar effects have also been observed following above-ground nuclear weapons tests.

- In Belarus alone, over 12,000 people have developed thyroid cancer since the catastrophe (Pavel Bespalchuk, 2007). According to a WHO prognosis, in the Belarus region of Gomel alone, more than 50,000 children will develop thyroid cancer during their lives. If one adds together all age groups, then about 100,000 cases of thyroid cancer will have to be reckoned with in the Gomel region.

- After Chernobyl, infant mortality rates in Sweden, Finland and Norway increased by a significant 15.8 percent compared to the trend for the period 1976 to 2006. Alfred Körblein calculated that, for the period 1987 to 1992, an additional 1,209 (95% confidence interval: 875 to 1,556) infants had died.

- Orlov and Shaversky reported on a series of 188 brain tumours amongst children under three in Ukraine. Before Chernobyl (1981 to 1985) 9 cases were counted, not even two a year. In the period 1986-2002, the number rose to 179 children diagnosed with brain tumours – more than ten per year.

- In the more contaminated areas of South Germany a significant cluster of a very rare type of tumour was found in children, so-called neuroblastoma.

- A paper published by the Chernobyl Ministry in Ukraine registered a multiplication of the cases of disease of the endocrine system (25-fold from 1987 to 1992), the nervous system (6-fold), the circulatory system (44-fold), the digestive organs (60-fold), the cutaneous and subcutaneous tissue (50 times higher), the muscular-skeletal system and psychological dysfunctions (53-fold). The number of healthy people among evacuees sank between 1987 and 1996, from 59% to 18% - and, among the population of the contaminated areas from 52% to 21%. Even worse—among the children who were not directly affected by Chernobyl fallout, but whose parents were exposed to high levels of radiation, the numbers of healthy children sank from 81% to 30% in 1996.

- It has been reported for several years that type I diabetes (insulin-dependent diabetes mellitus) has risen sharply amongst children and adolescents.

- Non-cancerous diseases greatly outnumber the more spectacular cases of leukaemia and other cancers.

This is just an edited version of their numerous findings, but the whole document is accessible online for those who would like the complete study. I have, however, included some of their conclusions because I believe these raise a number of interesting points:

Even though the lack of large-scale independent long-term studies does not permit a complete picture to be made of the current situation, a number of trends can be shown: a high mortality rate and an almost 100% morbidity rate can be observed among people, such as liquidators, who were exposed to high radiation levels. 25 years after the reactor catastrophe, cancer and other diseases have emerged on a scale that, owing to the long latency period, might have appeared inconceivable immediately following the catastrophe.

The number of non-cancerous diseases is far more dramatic than had ever before been imagined. "New" symptoms, such as the premature aging of liquidators, raise questions that research is still unable to answer.

By 2050 thousands more cases of illnesses will be diagnosed that will have been caused by the Chernobyl nuclear catastrophe. The delay between cause and noticeable physical reaction is insidious. Chernobyl is far from over.

Particularly tragic is the fate of the thousands of children who were born dead or died in infancy, who were born with malformations and hereditary diseases, or who are forced to live with diseases they would not have developed under normal circumstances.

The genetic defects caused by Chernobyl will continue to trouble the world for a long time to come – most of the effects will not become apparent until the second or third generation.

Even if the extent of the health effects is not yet clear, it can still be predicted that the suffering brought about by the nuclear disaster in Fukushima is, and will be, of a similar magnitude. [869]

The Insidious Nature of Low-level Radiation

It is worth discussing some of those findings with regard to the future implications for our health. They mention that the level of non-cancerous diseases was much more dramatic than they had expected, and that they found premature aging in liquidators. If you leave aside the dramatic levels of cancers and leukaemias that were eventually revealed, the rise in these other problems hint at the more insidious nature of radiation, particularly low-level radiation. Whilst we know that Strontium-90, for example affects bones and destroys the body's ability produce red blood cells, it is also known that it damages white blood cells as well. As these cells are major players in our immune systems, it can only be expected that simple infections could become life-threatening if the immune system is severely compromised. Busby, in his book *Wings of Death,* discusses his other researchers' studies, particularly in the UK and Wales, on strontium-90 levels and the risk of heart disease, in infants as well as older people. He reviews studies of heart disease in different populations in England and Wales, such as from 1958-63 when a rise in heart disease correlated with a rise in strontium-90 levels. At the time those studies were used to support the theory linking saturated fat to heart disease that I discussed in earlier chapters. Busby suggests it was known that the majority of the fat intake in these populations was from dairy products, which we now know concentrated the levels of strontium-90 many-fold. We know from animal studies that strontium-90 intake has a dramatic effect on heart development, dependant to some degree on the timing of the exposure. In his population studies, particularly in Wales where heavier rainfall carried higher levels of Chernobyl fallout, there were much higher levels of infant death, not only in the infant population, but across the board. [870]

Staying with the radiation effect on heart disease for a moment, Gould also found a link between the two, but reckoned another pathway might be opened by the ability of radiation in the body to create free radical damage, oxidize low-density cholesterol (LDL) and readily deposit it in the arteries. Of course any radiation particles in the blood system could also cause direct damage to the arteries themselves, kick-starting the repair mechanism that is also associated with atherosclerosis.

What is of concern, though, is that by failing to investigate the effects of low-level radiation particularly the more subtle ones, many of the health consequences are being missed. In 1975, the *New York Times* reported the fact that Scholastic Aptitude Tests (SATs) results had mysteriously dropped nationwide by the largest amount in two decades. Professor Sternglass was concerned enough to look into this, since the findings of post-radiation exposure in groups such as the Marshall islanders show both reduced brain size and lowered mental abilities in the offspring that survived. So he teamed up with a number of other people and compared the highest fallout with low fallout areas. Wherever he was able to get the data, his theory seemed to be confirmed. Between 1974 and 1976, Ohio had registered both a drop in SAT's level of 2 and had some of the lowest readings for radioactive iodine in milk. Utah, on the other hand, had some of the highest readings of radioactivity in milk— and a drop in SAT scores of 26 points. Dr Sternglass presented his findings to the American Psychological Association in September 1979, and predicted that, once the above-ground testing stopped, the SAT levels should rise again—which they did. Some Navy psychologists who had been looking into problems with new recruits were able to confirm this; they also found the same link between Utah's low SATs scores and the high fallout levels. Following Chernobyl, a report in the German version of *Psychology Today,* expressed new concerns about the mental health of German children following their exposure, and urged a re-examination Sternglass's work. [871]

Whether you look at high-level radiation exposure or some of the lower-level exposure deaths, most researchers find that the very young and the old are the most vulnerable groups.

What is troubling, though, is that I have revealed numerous man-made chemicals that have the ability to degrade the immune system in various ways, yet all of which are very hard to trace when a patient presents symptoms. And with low-level radiation, the source of the problem is almost impossible to identify—in most cases, it is only by a statistical study that can give us any hope. Chernobyl does give us an opportunity to understand this problem, due to the massive numbers involved. On the other hand the very institutions supposedly there for our benefit, such as the World Health Organisation (WHO), the United Nations or national health agencies, have so far shown no interest in undertaking the task—perhaps out of an unwillingness to acknowledge the true scope of the catastrophe. If you do not actually look for any problems, it's true you will not find anything. The danger, though, is that we will continue to see a decline in our sperm counts, our fertility, our mental abilities and our health in general. What value do we put on this? If you add all these costs to the cost of developing nuclear electricity, how cost-effective is it then?

Costs Escalate and Far Outweigh Predictions

Alexey V. Yablokov, Ph.D., gives us some perspective on some of the cost:

> The human and economic costs are enormous: In the first 25 years, the direct economic damage to Belarus, Ukraine and Russia has exceeded $500 billion. To mitigate some of the consequences, Belarus spends about 20 percent of its national annual budget, Ukraine up to 6 percent and Russia up to 1 percent. Funding from other countries and from the U.N. is essential to continue scientific studies and to provide help to those who continue to live with significant radioactive contamination. . . .
>
> It is becoming clear that low-dose and low-dose rates of radiation have a profound effect upon fine structures of the nervous system, upon higher nervous system function and upon neuropsychiatry function. .
>
> The most serious effect of the Chernobyl radiation is to the brain and is a major medical, social and economic problem for the affected individual, the persons' family and society at large. . . . [872]

In 2009, the New York Academy of Sciences published its own report *Chernobyl— Consequences of the Catastrophe for People and the Environment,* which reviewed many of the health consequences twenty years after the disaster. They report that, from year to year, that there has been an increase in non-malignant disease and that the percentage of healthy children has continued to decline. They cite Kiev in the Ukraine where, prior to the disaster, 90% of the children were considered healthy, but only 20% were after it. In some areas there are no healthy children. They report increased cardiovascular disease, more heart attacks, ischemic disease and circulatory pathogenesis due to radioactive destruction of the endothelium, the internal lining of the blood vessels. They further document damage to the endocrine system, immune system, respiratory system, musculoskeletal system, central nervous system, the list goes on....

Besides describing the rise in evidence of cancer, which was predicated by many, they list many other conditions, too many to mention here, that are now all associated with radiation exposure. Aside from the leukaemias already reported, they list numerous eye conditions; cataracts, conjunctive disorders, refraction anomalies and vitreous destruction. On the scale of thyroid cancer, they say: "All forecasts concerning this cancer have been erroneous; Chernobyl-related thyroid cancers have rapid onset and aggressive development, striking both children and adults". They also report on the changes in the body's biological balance which has led to increasing numbers of serious illnesses, including bacterial infections, sepsis, intestinal toxicosis, viral hepatitis, respiratory viruses and numerous others. The most obvious observation regarding radiation exposure is the simple fact that the consequences to health are never immediately apparent. There are innumerable hidden pathways through which the body can be harmed by radiation damage. As we have seen, the damage can take years or even generations to manifest itself—so it is all too frequently reported as 'increased incidence of health disorders in children. This is especially the case in those irradiated *in utero*. Even worse, these disorders, involving practically all the body's organs and systems, also include genetic changes.

There are many conditions that are not immediately associated with radiation effects, such as chronic fatigue syndrome which the report describes as 'excessive and unrelieved fatigue, fatigue without obvious cause', and list it alongside mood changes, memory loss, muscular and joint pains, immune system dysfunction etc. Chernobyl represents a unique opportunity to study the effects of radiation, particularly the low-level ones that still prevail.

As for the environmental consequences, the report describes how the secondary contamination caused by radionuclides transported by water, wind and migrating animals is now being felt thousands of kilometres away from Chernobyl. It states that:

> All the initial forecasts of rapid clearance or decay of the Chernobyl radionuclides from ecosystems were wrong: it is taking much longer than predicted because they recirculate. The overall state of the contamination in water, air, and soil appears to fluctuate greatly, and the dynamics of Sr-90, Cs-137, Pu, and Am contamination still present surprises.

UNHEALTHY BETRAYAL

The authors go on to describe how, far from dissipating, that the radionuclides such as caesium-137, Strontium-90, plutonium and americium are accumulating in the root-soil layer, are building up in plants and (consequently in people), and in the process have been found to bioaccumulate 1000-fold compared to natural water and soil levels. Levels vary so much, even in the same species of plant, that only by direct monitoring can accurate levels be ascertained. They give a warning that needs a real response:

> For better understanding of the Chernobyl-contaminated areas, radiobiological and other scientific studies should not be stopped, as has happened everywhere in Belarus, Ukraine, and Russia, but must be extended and intensified to understand and help to mitigate expected and unexpected consequences. [873]

Professor Bandazhevsky, in his study of children who were born after Chernobyl and after the initial effects of iodine-131 had been observed, describes how he discovered that caesium-137 was causing much more of a problem, due to it being a longer lived isotope (30 day half-life compared to iodine-131's 8 day half-life) and was found in much higher concentrations in children than in adults. It was found at autopsy that the highest accumulation was found in the endocrine glands: the thyroid, adrenals, and pancreas. High levels were also found in the heart, thymus, and spleen. It was clear that new-borns took up caesium from maternal milk, while children accumulated it from cow's milk, wild berries, mushrooms and game—all important sources of food in poorer communities. [874]

Professor Busby also looked into the after-effects of Chernobyl in the UK and found that the cancer incidence that could be attributed to Chernobyl had risen by 20%. Gould, on the other hand, calculated that it caused approximately 40,000 extra deaths in the US. [875] The full health consequences of Chernobyl will probably never be known, but there is no doubt there is much more still to be learned from this tragedy. Our problem remains, though, the almost total reluctance of the UN and the World Health Organisation (WHO) to get involved in studying the true effects—and the disinterest of the media. In 1995 the Director of WHO, Dr Hiroshi Nakajima, was prevented from publishing a report on Chernobyl by an international conference of 700 experts and physicians, and from publishing its findings, by the International Atomic Energy Agency (IAEA). Busby blames the apparent agreement made between WHO and the IAEA back in 1959, when it was agreed that WHO scientists would not study radiation, because it was solely the remit of the IAEA. Busby does not mince his words when he describes the ramifications of this:

INVISIBLE DEATH

This agreement has prevented the emergence of what is probably the biggest public health cover-up and scandal of all time, the systematic genetic poisoning of the human race. It is still in force, as those who have studied the consequences of the Chernobyl accident or looked at the effects of Depleted Uranium in Iraq, will testify.[876]

Fukushima

It is inevitable that people will compare Chernobyl with the more recent Fukushima disaster that followed the earthquake and tsunami that hit Japan on 11th March 2011. Like Chernobyl, this was a level seven disaster on the International Nuclear Event Scale. Considered the worst nuclear accident globally in a quarter of a century, Fukushima caused three reactor cores to melt, released massive radiation leaks, and prompted the gradual shutdown of all Japan's nuclear reactors until there were none left operating by May 2012. That left the country without atomic power for the first time since 1970. The effect on the Japanese economy has been immeasurable.

Just shutting down the reactors forced the country to import more oil and gas—87.31 million metric tons of liquefied natural gas (LNG), more than a third of the entire global output, in 2012 alone—making it the worlds' top LNG importer.[877] A report by Professor Tessa Morris-Suzuki put the initial estimated costs at decommissioning Fukushima's six reactors at between $500-$600 billion. The owners of the plant, TEPCO, have already paid out almost $2 billion in compensation to affected citizens. The report makes the point that at some point the government will have to bail out TEPCO—which means Japanese taxpayers will be footing the bill. They make the following comment:

> It is staggering to witness how the nuclear industry managed to build up a system whereby polluters harvest large profits, while the moment things go wrong, they throw the responsibility to deal with losses and damages to the impacted citizens. [878]

According to the French Institute for Radiological Protection and Nuclear Safety, the level of radioactive cesium-137 that flowed into the Pacific Ocean following the disaster was more than 30 times the amount stated by Tokyo Electric Power Company, stating that the true amount from March 21st to mid-July reached an estimated 27.1 quadrillion becquerels (a quadrillion represents 1000 trillion), 80% of which flowed into the sea by April 8th.[879]

UNHEALTHY BETRAYAL

Whilst some may say that everything is under control, the revelations of Ambassador Mitsuhei Murata, Japan's former Ambassador to Switzerland, who appeared before the Public Hearing of the Budgetary Committee of the House of Councillors on March 22, 2012, tells a different story. Murata expressed his concern regarding the spent fuel pool in the building of reactor 4, containing 1,535 fuel assemblies housed 30 metres above the ground. His grave concern was that if the crippled building of reactor 4 were to collapse, it would both cause the shutdown of all six reactors and disturb the common spent pool of 6,375 fuel assemblies located 50 metres away. The fuel assemblies, it must be stressed, are not protected by a containment vessel—they are dangerously exposed to the open air. Such an occurrence would certainly cause a global catastrophe like we have never seen before. He stressed that the responsibility of Japan to the rest of the world was immeasurable.

Akio Matsumura asked top spent-fuel expert Robert Alvarez, former Senior Policy Adviser to the Secretary and Assistant Secretary for National Security and the Environment at the US Department of Energy, what the potential impact would be for the 11,000 plus fuel assemblies. Alvarez explained his understanding:

> In recent times, more information about the spent fuel situation at the Fukushima-Dai-Ichi site has become known. It is my understanding that of the 1,532 spent fuel assemblies in reactor No.3, 304 assemblies are fresh and unirradiated. This then leaves 1,231 irradiated spent fuel rods in pool No. 4, which contain roughly 37 million curies (~1.4E+18 Becquerel) of long-lived radioactivity. The No. 4 pool is about 100 feet above ground, is structurally damaged and is exposed to the open elements. If an earthquake or other event were to cause this pool to drain this could result in a catastrophic radiological fire involving nearly 10 times the amount of Cs-137 released by the Chernobyl accident.[880]

He goes on to explain that spent reactor fuel cannot simply be lifted in the air by a crane. In order to prevent severe radiation exposures, fires and possible explosions, it has to be transferred—in water and heavily shielded structures into dry casks. As that had never been done before, this would involve a major and time-consuming re-construction effort—in his words, they 'will be charting in unknown waters.' He goes on to estimate the extent of his concern, and describes the breadth of the issues facing the Japanese:

> Based on U.S. Energy Department data, assuming a total of 11,138 spent fuel assemblies are stored at the Dai-Ichi site, nearly all, which is in pools. There will be roughly 336 million curies (~1.2 E+19 Bq) of long-lived radioactivity there. About 134 million of these is Cesium-137 — **roughly 85**

times the amount of Cs-137 that was released at the Chernobyl accident—as estimated by the U.S. National Council on Radiation Protection (NCRP). The total spent reactor fuel inventory at the Fukushima-Daichi site contains nearly half of the total amount of Cs-137 (again estimated by the NCRP) to have been released by all atmospheric nuclear weapons testing, Chernobyl, and world-wide reprocessing plants (~270 million curies or ~9.9 E+18 Becquerel).

It is essential for everyone in the world to be aware that reactors which have been operating for decades, such as those at the Fukushima-Dai-Ichi site, have generated some of the largest concentrations of radioactivity on the planet.

Many of us may find it difficult to appreciate the actual meaning of the figure, yet we can at least get some idea of what 85 times more Cesium-137 than was emitted by the Chernobyl disaster would mean. That much would destroy the world environment and our civilization. This is not rocket science, nor does it connect to the pugilistic debate over nuclear power plants. ***This is an issue of human survival** [my emphasis].*[881]

Whilst this is a horrific possibility, that I no-way want to down-play, there are other scenarios which could be just as destructive. Here are just a few of them:

The architect of reactor 3 at the Daiichi plant at Fukushima was interviewed by the former President of Saga University, Uehara Haruo, about the status of the reactor. The architect explained that the owner TEPCO's report did not make sense to him. He said that since eight months had passed without any improvement, he feels that melted fuel must by this time have left the containment vessel and sunk underground, leading to what is commonly referred to as the 'China syndrome'.[882] The 'China syndrome' refers to the loss of coolant from the reactor, and the subsequent severe meltdown of its core components, burning through the containment without there being anything to stop it. The reference to China jokingly refers to China as being the recipient if it were to happen in the USA.

The Scope of This Disaster is Seriously Downplayed

The amount of radiation that has escaped from Fukushima has been severely downplayed. Professor Kodam Tatsuhiko, head of the Radioisotope Center at the Research Center for Advanced Science and Technology, the University of Tokyo, gave a report to the Committee on Welfare and Labor of the House of Representatives. As a physician of internal medicine, it was his responsibility to monitor both radiation and decontamination work. His own words describe the issues better than I could:

When we examine radiation poisoning, we look at the entire amount. TEPCO and the government have never clearly reported on the total amount of radiation doses resulting from the Fukushima nuclear accident. When we calculate on the basis of the knowledge available at our Radioisotope Center, in terms of the quantity of heat, the equivalent of 29.6 Hiroshima a-bombs leaked. Converted to uranium, an amount equivalent to 20 Hiroshima a-bombs is estimated to have leaked.

What is further dreadful is that, according to what we know so far, when we compare the amount of radiation that remained after the A-bomb and that of radiation from the nuclear plant, that of the former goes down to one-thousandth after one year whereas radioactive contaminants of the latter are reduced to only one-tenth.

In other words, in thinking about the Fukushima nuclear power plant disaster, the first premise is that, as in the case of Chernobyl, an amount of radiation equivalent to tens of A-bombs was released and far greater contamination remains afterward compared with the A-bomb. [883]

Later in his report, he brings up the problem of trying to examine risk by using the linear risk model that is used by both the nuclear industry and international bodies such as the International Commission on Radiological Protection (ICRP). The problem with this model is that it is outdated, inaccurate – and yet is still in existence. For example, after the disaster at Fukushima, the authorities used it to produce a plan view of the plant wth circles drawn around it to indicate the decreasing levels of radiation in the surrounding areas. This enabled them to give the impression that there was no serious problem. However, what they failed to admit was that radiation does not disperse in such a neat and tidy manner. The reality is that the pattern of exposure varies considerably within and between each and every circle—as do the consequent health problems.

In his report, Professor Kodam Tatsuhiko, shows how inadequate the linear risk model is by showing the same mainland area around Fukushma, with the same circles used by the authorities, but this time with the correct radiation levels shown as irregular 'blobs' overlapping the circles. Each radiation level is given its own specific colour – so you can see at a glance the level of severity in any particular area. These areas bear no correlation at all to the circles used on the official documents, but reveal the totally non-uniform way in which radiation is dispersed. You'll find a link on my website (www.fundamentalhealth.org) to the report and the coloured drawing of circles around Fukushima for those who would like to see it. Professor Tatsuhiko also explain another aspect of radiation that the ICRP and other international National bodies, even including the WHO, refuse to acknowledge. This is that is that—low level radiation is not just about electromagnetic wave effects, such as Gamma waves, but also about exposure to particles in the air we all breathe in.

INVISIBLE DEATH

Here's Professor Kodam Tatsuhiko's explanation of how there's far more radiation contamination from an accident such as Fukushima than there is from an atomic bomb:

> If such is the case—we work in the field of systems biology, which focuses on complex interactions in biological systems—where the total amount is low, it suffices to look at the density of radiation in an individual. Not where the total amount is gigantic. We are talking about particles here. Spread of particles belongs to the field of non-linear science, which is the most difficult area in hydrodynamic calculations. In other words, when nuclear fuel, which can be compared to sand grains embedded in something like synthetic resin, melts down and leaks out, a large amount of ultrafine particles is released.
>
> When particles are released, what will happen? The problem of rice straw that recently surfaced is exactly that. For example, the figure was 57,000 Bq/kg (becquerels per kilogram) in Fujiwara; in Iwate: 17,000; in Ōsaki in Miyagi: 106,000; in Minami-Sōma in Fukushima: 97,000; in Shirakawa, also in Fukushima: 64,000. The figures never hew to concentric circles. How much falls and where depends upon the weather at that time and whether the material has absorbed, for example, water.[884]

In June 2011, marine chemist Ken Buessler led a group of scientists from the USA, Japan and Europe on a two week research cruise to ascertain the effects of Fukushima on the ocean, collecting 3,000 litres of water for analysis. They found that the highest concentrations of cesium were around 70-100 kilometres off shore, rather than close to Fukushima—and was even found as far as 600 kilometres away. Buesseler believes that the Kuroshio current, a strong boundary current similar to the Gulf Stream, prevented the contaminated water from migrating further southward—and made some interesting observations:

> "It's [an] interesting thing to think about, as the concentrations vary by a factor of 3,000... With what we knew about transport prior to this work, you wouldn't know why it is so different."

They found both caesium-137 and caesium-134 in the marine life, sometimes at concentrations hundreds of times higher than the surrounding water. Bottom-dwelling fish consistently showed the highest levels of contamination. The levels of contamination in almost all classifications of fish were not declining.[885]

UNHEALTHY BETRAYAL

This information, from the Woods Hole Oceanographic Institute, further illustrates how radiation contamination can accumulate even in the sea where common sense tells us it should dilute and dissipate.

Whilst this catastrophe is being completely downplayed in all the main media outlets, there are reports sneaking out that give some indication of the health consequences that will inevitably follow. Initial reports of the extent of the radioactive release were put at 15,000 terabecquerels, then subsequent estimates suggested a more realistic figure of 36,000 terabecquerels. According to the French Institute for Radiological Protection and Nuclear Safety, France's nuclear monitor, in excess of 27 petabecquerels of caesium had entered the sea—which they reckoned was the biggest single outpouring of man-made radionuclides into the marine environment ever observed. [886] When the Japanese government raised the level of permissible exposure to children from 1 mSv/year to 20 mSv/year, a twenty-fold increase, one of the senior nuclear advisers to the Prime Minister resigned in protest. It soon became apparent that confidence in government pronouncements had reached an all-time low, and people took to monitoring radioactivity themselves. High spots were found in a number of places in Tokyo: at a Tokyo elementary school in the Adachi ward, a reading of 3.99 microsieverts (3.99 μSv [10^{-6}]) per hour was observed—and this is 210 kilometres from the Fukushima plant. Some Tokyo citizens formed the Radiation Defense Project and they shared their readings. Mr Hayashida collected readings of Caesium in his neighbourhood as high as 138,000 becquerels. Following testing in 132 areas of Tokyo, 22 were above 37,000 becquerels per square metre, *the same as the level that was considered contaminated at Chernobyl.* [887]

Readings of caesium-137, 40 km north of the Fukushima plant, were 163,000 becquerels per kilogram (Bq/kg), together with iodine-131 levels of 1,170,000 Bq/kg—according to the Japanese Science Ministry. Since the exclusion zone extends only thirty miles from the Fukushima plant, people who stay within affected areas will be subjected to considerable risk. There is also, of course, a lot of unpredictable ways that low level contaminants will be able to migrate to other areas and become concentrated in the food chain—with inevitable consequences for human health. Dr Busby predicts that there will be at least 400,000 cases of cancer among the population living within 200 kilometres of Fukushima. Cancers of the thyroid, leukaemia, the pancreas, prostate, lung, skin, and bone—just about every type of cancer that exists will be the occur. Plutonium from Fukushima has been detected by eight different monitoring stations in Korea; and plutonium is the most toxic substance on the planet. [888]

One of the problems with this Japanese disaster is that it took place in a densely populated area with important industries close by. To have declared these areas as uninhabitable would have had unimaginable political, social and economic consequences. So, just about the only option for the government was to bluff it out, and rely on other governments to also play down the consequences as much as possible. And that's exactly what they did. The alternative would have been to admit that the mad rush into nuclear power generation does have consequences that can come home to roost very suddenly. On the plus side, and despite its horrific outcomes, the disaster does at least offer an opportunity to monitor and understand the true effects of radiation. For example, in the USA Dr Janette Sherman draws attention to the 35% spike in infant death rates revealed by CDC reports covering eight cities in the northwest of the USA. That spike followed the releases from Fukushima. Approximating the data Dr Sherman surmises that there were almost 14,000 excess deaths and 822 excess infant deaths worthy, in their view, of further investigation.[889]

There is no doubt that there are many people in Japan living in areas with varying levels of contamination. Unfortunately for many, the consequences may not be revealed for many years, and will certainly have repercussions for generations to come.

Scientists Reveal Health Damage Due to Radiation as an On-going Catastrophe that is Seriously Underplayed By the Authorities

Professor Busby was instrumental in discovering the link between low-level radiation exposure in Wales, and the UK in general. Because of its higher rainfall, Wales was contaminated to a higher degree following the Chernobyl disaster—and this explained the rise in cancer of 20% already mentioned. He also looked at other areas that had recorded a high incidence of cancer and leukaemia after a nuclear accident such as, the massive outpourings from Sellafield (re-named after the Windscale disaster). Here, significant quantities of alpha emitters: Plutonium-239, Plutonium-240 and Americium-241, and the beta emitters: Caesium-137 and Strontium-90 were discharged into the Irish Sea through a pipe—and through a chimney. As regards the dangerous alpha emitters, Busby says: "The quantities are very large and comparable with all the fallout from weapons testing." More specifically, he says: "In terms of density or concentration, the material represents a much larger risk to people living near the Irish Sea than weapons fallout." [890]

His research prompted the Welsh Office to commission a radiological survey of Wales in 1984. This found plutonium contamination of sheep 10 kilometres from the Irish Sea coast. The isotopic signatures confirmed the origin of the plutonium as being from Sellafield. Post-mortem examinations of UK citizens showed high concentrations of plutonium in their trachea-bronchial lymph nodes with the highest readings in occupationally exposed Cumbrian workers. Following the discovery of plutonium in children's teeth all over the UK in the 1990s, Busby decided to look at other populations and discovered numerous cancer clusters linked to sedimentary dispersals, not just from Sellafield but also other nuclear reactors sites. Routine measurements of radioactivity undertaken by the Atomic Weapons Establishment at Aldermaston, UK, measured air filters in places like Reading and Basingstoke (eight miles from Aldermaston) and it found alpha activity as high as 2500Bq/kg, and beta activity as high as 60,000 Bq/kg. Over a 16-year period, Busby's investigations along the coastal strip facing the Irish Sea revealed that the risk of being diagnosed with cancer rose four times in the latter four years. At the same time, the risk of brain tumour increased by a factor of five over the national average. From 1974 to 1989, more than 3500 adults in that coastal strip died from cancer.

Busby reports that his journey of discovery was dogged by obfuscation, denial, hiding of evidence, and institutional cover-up to prevent the revelation of the true effect of nuclear policies on the health of its populace. He cites the frustration of being confronted by the people who dominate the industry: "I have sat on government committees on radiation effects and listened to the sly weasel words, specious arguments arising from a system of institutional chicanery."

The biggest obstacle in the UK to understanding the true effects on health of radiation is the absolute control over cancer data exercised by the 'health' authorities. In his books, Busby documents how at every turn he was denied data when requested, where available parts would be altered, go 'missing' or even deemed not to have been collected. Yet, without this vital data, there remains little chance of linking radiation damage to health consequences. [891]

In July 1995 Karl Morgan, first President of the Health Physics Society, and first President of the Radiological Protection Association, commented on the moral bankruptcy of his former colleagues:

> When I first took on myself these offices I was very proud of what I thought was an organisation of scientists and professional men in whom the first objective and the first requirement was to protect people. Nowadays it appears, in this country at least, ...the first requirement is to protect the industry; to protect the person who signs your paycheque; because if you don't do that you'll lose your job. [892]

Busby refers to a quotation from Sir Richard Southwood, Director of the British National Radiological Protection Board, speaking at a 1993 conference to the Royal College of Radiologists, regarding the risks with low levels of radiation:

With Nuclear power, there are additional factors...

Distrust, because neither the radiation nor the radionuclides can be detected without special equipment, reliance has to be placed on experts but they are not to be trusted because in the past they have been shown to be economical with the truth. [893]

There cannot be many people in the world better qualified to discuss the effects of low-level radiation than John Gofman, M.D., Ph.D., whose work we have previously discussed: he was Professor Emeritus of Molecular and Cell Biology, University of California at Berkeley, and also on the faculty of the University of California Medical School at San Francisco. He earned his Ph.D. under Seaborg in 1943, when he became co-discoverer of isotopes of protactinium, uranium-232 and uranium-233. He also proved that uranium 233 is fissionable with both slow and fast neutrons, and shared patents on two processes for separating plutonium. Much of his work on these projects was classified. He wrote extensively on the health effects of radiation, and published more than a hundred papers as well as numerous books. [894]

In his 1990 book *Radiation Induced Cancer from Low-Dose Exposure: An Independent Analysis*, Gofman makes the point:

> By any reasonable standard of biomedical proof, that there is no threshold level (no harmless dose) of ionizing radiation with respect to radiation mutagenesis and carcinogenesis.

What he is saying here, is that there is no such thing as a 'safe dose' or 'safe level', that, in fact—*any dose is harmful, any dose can cause cancer*. His conclusion was supported by a 1995 government radiation committee, and has never been refuted. He further calculates that with 400 nuclear plants operating globally, and even with 99.9% containment which would be considered PERFECT containment, and even with PERFECT disposal, this would result in Cesium-137 contamination over a twenty-five year period equivalent in curies to FOUR CHERNOBYLS every twenty-five years.[895]

Following AEC invitation to Gofman to establish a Biomedical Research Division at its Livermore laboratory for the purpose of evaluating the health effects of all types of nuclear activities, Gofman became convinced that human exposure to ionizing radiation was much more serious than previously recognised. As a result, both he and his colleague, Arthur R. Tamplin, both spoke out against two AEC programs which they had previously accepted. The first was Project Plowshare which was a program to explode hundreds of nuclear bombs in the Rocky Mountains to liberate natural gas. This would have involved the burning off of radioactive gas into the atmosphere. It also would have required the creation of harbours and canals using nuclear explosions (I previously mentioned a new Panama Canal). The second AEC program was a plan to license approximately 1,000 commercial nuclear power plants in the USA as quickly as possible. In 1970 Gofman and Tamplin proposed a five-year moratorium on this venture, until the health consequences could be fully evaluated. [896]

In 1999, Gofman published another book, *Radiation from Medical Procedures in the Pathogenesis of Cancer and Ischemic Heart Disease: Dose-Response Studies with Physicians per 100,000 Population*. In this he explores two hypotheses: the first, that medical radiation—primarily X-rays, fluoroscopies and CT scans—was a highly important cause—probably the principal cause—of cancer mortality in the United States during the Twentieth Century. The second hypothesis was that medical radiation, even in very low doses, is a very important cause of death from Ischemic heart disease. I briefly mentioned this work in the previous chapters on heart disease and cancer. However, due to ill health at the time, Gofman was unable to promote his book widely—and many people in the field remain unaware of it. As previously mentioned, he was by no means anti-X-rays, he simply believed that they were over-prescribed and, in many cases, taken at levels of exposure that were unnecessarily high. Part of his work he devoted to developing safer, yet still effective levels.

During an interview with Shobhit Arora and Fred Gardner in 1994, Gofman was asked about the Department of Energy (DOE) which took over from the Atomic Energy Commission (AEC); it was known that for years Gofman had been critical of the DOE:

> For 25 years the DOE has not shown any concern for the health of Americans. Their concern has been for the health of the DOE. Their falsehoods concerning the hazards of ionizing radiation have put not thousands of people at risk, not millions of people, but billions of people.
>
> .....Ever since its inception, the Atomic Energy Commission—then called ERDA, then called DOE—has had one thing in mind: "Our program is sacrosanct." And they recognize, as I've recognized, that their entire program will live or die based upon one thing. *If the public should come to learn the truth about ionizing radiation, nuclear energy and the atomic energy program of DOE is going to be dead* [my emphasis]. Because the people of this country—and other countries—are not going to tolerate what it implies. The key thing—it's everything in the DOE program—is: ***"We must prove that low doses of radiation are not harmful."*** [my emphasis] They have been conducting a Josef Goebels propaganda war, saying there's a safe dose when there has never been any valid evidence for a safe dose of radiation. Yet the DOE and others continue to talk about their "zero-risk model."

INVISIBLE DEATH

Following the Chernobyl disaster Gofman predicted that there would be at least 475,000 fatal cancers and a further 475,000 non-fatal cancers caused by the amount of Cesium fallout. He then notes the response from the DOE:

> The DOE put out a report in 1987 ...saying "our zero-risk model says that at these low doses, nothing will happen, because low doses are safe." [897]

He goes on to state that the idea of having such a thing as a safe threshold for radiation presumes that the body is able to repair any damage caused by it. But all the research shows that this is not the case:

> The problem, though, is that the repair mechanisms don't work perfectly. There are those lesions in DNA and chromosomes that are unrepairable. There are those where the repair mechanisms don't get to the site and so they go unrepaired. And there are those lesions where the repair mechanisms simply cause misrepair. We can say that between 50 and 90 percent of the damage done by ionizing radiation is repaired perfectly. What we are then seeing is harm done by the residual 10 or 40 or 50 percent that is not repaired perfectly.
>
> The evidence that the repair mechanism is not perfect is very solid today.

He was asked what the lowest dose was that would produce cancer and his answer is quite clear:

> The answer is this: ionizing radiation is not like a poison out of a bottle where you can dilute it and dilute it. The lowest dose of ionizing radiation is one nuclear track through one cell. You can't have a fraction of a dose of that sort. Either a track goes through the nucleus and affects it, or it doesn't. So I said "What evidence do we have concerning one, or two or three or four or six or 10 tracks?" And I came up with nine studies of cancer being produced where we're dealing with up to maybe eight or 10 tracks per cell. Four involved breast cancer. With those studies, as far as I'm concerned, it's not a question of "We don't know." The DOE has never refuted this evidence. They just ignore it, because it's inconvenient. We can now say, there cannot be a safe dose of radiation. There is no safe threshold. If this truth is known, then any permitted radiation is a permit to commit murder.

Later in the interview, Gofman makes the comment that medical radiation from X-ray machines is approximately twice as harmful per unit dose as Hiroshima-Nagasaki radiation, following is his explanation why this is so:

It's the effect of linear energy transfer. When gamma rays or x-rays set electrons in motion, the electrons are traveling at a lower speed than the electrons coming out of Cesium-137. And as a result, when they're traveling at a lower speed, they interact much more with each micrometer of path they travel. Therefore the local harm is much greater. So medical x-rays set in motion electrons that are traveling at a lower speed and hence producing about twice the linear energy transfer, and hence twice the biological effect. That's why alpha particles from radium or plutonium are so much more devastating than beta rays set in motion from x-rays. The alpha particles, with their heavy mass and plus-2 charge, just rip through tissue so strenuously that they don't go very far. A deception of the crassest sort are the lectures by pro-nuclear people showing a plutonium or radium source and putting up a piece of paper and showing that the alpha-particle radiation on the other side is zero. "You see, a piece of paper will stop those alpha particles, folks, there's no problem with plutonium." Except when that alpha particle is lodged next to an endosteal cell in the bone and producing a horrendous amount of interaction. Or that alpha particle is lodging on the surface of the bronchi—that's why we've got an epidemic of lung cancer among the uranium miners! The fact that they don't travel far is because they interact like hell!

Getting information like this is not the same as from a textbook; hence the reason I have included some of this interview. This next piece I have not edited, and I have included the interviewer's direct question:

Interviewer: *Do you think medical professionals really appreciate how much potential there is for damage? Regardless of who you are, you go into the hospital and you get a chest x-ray as a routine diagnostic procedure.*

Gofman: I'm sad to say, I don't think 90% of doctors in this country know a goddamned thing about ionizing radiation and its effect. Somebody polled some pediatricians recently and said, "Do you believe there's a safe dose of radiation?" And 45% said, "Yes." They weren't asked, "What papers have you ever read on this subject that led you to conclude there's a safe dose?" I think medical education on the hazard of radiation is atrocious.

....government studies show that most hospitals and most offices of radiologists didn't have the foggiest notion of what dose they were giving you for a procedure. Nor did they know that the procedure could be accomplished with a third or a tenth of the dose.

He discusses how some hospitals give radiation doses twenty times higher for the same procedure, that in fact many doses are excessive, he explains how it provoked him to publish a report on this:

So Egan and I, in The Health Effects of Common Exams, took the data on what the average doses were in the United States, versus what has been accomplished by some elegant work in Toronto to reduce the dose to one-third of what was the average practice in 1984, and found that about 50,000 fatal cancers per year could be prevented. That's a million and a half in a generation! So what is this stuff about "Most procedures don't hurt you, they're small?"

I want to add one final part of his interview, which is discussed in his 1990 book *Radiation-Induced Cancer from Low-Dose Exposure: an Independent Analysis*. This referred to the Hiroshima study I referred to earlier, and his criticism of how the dose data was manipulated. As this study is one much touted by the industry as one of the major studies supposedly refuting the idea that low-dose radiation is a cause of serious harm, Gofman offers his opinion of the manipulations:

Distance was the biggest factor, but also whether you were outdoors or indoors, whether you were in a concrete or wooden structure. They tried to do a lot of that. And they shouldn't keep changing the placement of people! You take people with cancer and say, "Well, I guess the dose they originally got must have been a lot higher. We'll put that person here [in this dose category] and this one there." And with that sort of approach, you can make truth whatever you want it to be. And there's a very important additional lesson. Humanity needs to insist on the immaculate construction of databases concerning any accident or major event. If a crook makes the database, Einstein will get the wrong answer out of it. And then what happens? The Einsteins, with the best credentials, using this lousy, fabricated, false database, will put their findings in the medical journals. And then they get into the textbooks. And then it's taught to medical students for the next 100 years. And what happens? Hundreds of millions of people will suffer from cancer and genetic diseases because the answer will be wrong. The key thing is getting an honest database. [898]

That seems a convenient point at which to leave this dialogue. The importance of its message, though, cannot be over emphasized: The complete lack of adequate data, or along with corrupt data, contribute to the continuing total lack of transparency regarding everything nuclear. In *The Enemy Within,* Jay Gould reveals how that the EPA stopped publishing monthly reports in 1991 on the radioactivity measurements in milk and said this:

The public and Congress are therefore deprived of information essential for understanding one of the major causes of the current rise in cancer, low birthweights, and immune deficiency diseases. Nor do we have independent means to detect radioactivity in our milk and water from another accident of the magnitude of Chernobyl, either from abroad or at home.

Apparently when Charles Petko, the man who replaced Charles Porter at the Montgomery radiation facility, was asked why this data was no longer being published, he replied that he was not aware of "any public interest" in such measures. Gould suggests that this is one of the more alarming of all the revelations in his book—and there are many. Some might consider his revelation of the National Cancer Institute (NCI) study (1990) to have been equally alarming. This was designed to investigate increased cancer incidence near nuclear reactors, but was so badly flawed that Gould referred to it as 'a scandalous degree of deception'. [899]

If nuclear power is so wonderful, so cheap, so clean, such a boon to mankind, then why all the secrecy? Why is all the cancer data hidden from view, why is there virtually zero radiation monitoring of radiation around nuclear sites or countrywide? Who really stands to gain from nuclear power, and who will carry the costs of all the waste produced, particularly the intensely radioactive waste from spent fuel assemblies and the radiation from heavily polluted reactors that will have to be decommissioned and maintained in a safe way for 24,000 years? Let's see the costing proposals for that. I can absolutely guarantee that this cost will be passed on to future generations, and that the industry creating it will simply take the profits now, passing on the 'externalised costs' of the long-term waste and health problems. As long as we all remain ignorant, that can be the only result.

Mixed Response to the Fukushima Disaster

In the wake of the disaster at Chernobyl, the Italian government closed the last two of its four reactors and, following the Fukushima disaster on 11th March 2011 (and a subsequent referendum in June 2011), plans to generate 25% of the country's electricity from nuclear fusion were rejected. [900]

In Germany, after the Fukushima Disaster, there were demonstrations by tens of thousands of people in the streets against nuclear power, urging immediate closure of all their reactors—no doubt greatly influenced by the large amounts of radioactivity that had descended on the country after the earlier Chernobyl disaster. This prompted an about-turn by Merkel's government which announced it would shut down all seventeen nuclear power plants in Germany by 2022. That was the response of the world's fourth largest economy, and the biggest in Europe.

INVISIBLE DEATH

Angela Merkel, the Chancellor of Germany who holds a Ph.D. in physics, had reportedly been greatly affected by a technologically advanced country like Japan finding itself so helpless in the face of the disaster—hence her about-turn. Matthias Kleiner, co-chairman of the commission mandated to look into the ethics of nuclear power, was quoted as saying: "Fukushima was a dramatic experience, seeing there that a high-technology nation can't cope with such a catastrophe... Nuclear power is a technology with too many inherent risks to inflict it on us or our children."

Switzerland followed suit and also announced plans to shut down its reactors, and not replace them. [901]

The response in the UK, the "dirty man" of Europe was very different. The government announced plans to press ahead with building the biggest nuclear programme for a generation, with eight new sites to be developed, despite the public's concern for safety and clean-up costs. Charles Hendry, the Energy Minister, explained the government's position: "Around a quarter of the UK's generating capacity is due to close by the end of this decade. We need to replace this with secure, low carbon, affordable energy. This will require over £100bn of investment in electricity generation alone, twice what was invested last decade. Industry needs as much certainty as possible to make such big investments."[902]

So nuclear power is regarded by the UK government as 'secure,' 'low carbon', and 'affordable' energy. This follows in the wake of the decision to scrap the proposal for a ten mile barrage across the River Severn that would have provided five percent of the country's energy needs. It was decided that the cost of £15 billion for it was too high. Instead, are faced with a projected cost of between £100 and £200 billion for nuclear power stations. This follows a 2007 review that was thrown out by the High Court (Feb 2007) after a successful challenge by the environmental group, Greenpeace. The judge ruled that the consultation process before the decision the previous year had been "misleading", "seriously flawed" and "procedurally unfair". But Tony Blair said that while the ruling would change the consultation process, "this won't affect the policy at all". [903] A change of government to the Conservative/Liberal Democrat alliance made little difference. The River Severn barrage project had been undermined by the machinations of lobbyist John Stevenson, of Freshwater Public Affairs, a PR company serving the interests of the Bristol Port Company who feared loss of business had it been built. Undercover reporters revealed that Stevenson boasted he wrote the speech for the Tory Peer, Lord Cope, the former Paymaster General, who addressed the House of Lords attacking the idea of the Severn barrage, saying he wished to see it strangled. He apparently gave an impassioned speech opposing the barrage, saying it would require legislation so absurd that it "attacked my blood pressure and my funny bone simultaneously". Undercover reporters found Stevenson openly boasted that he wrote the speech as part of a 'Trojan Horse' operation to block the building of the barrage, and that he had two further Lords primed to speak out against it. [904] This kind of thing is a real pity—and likely to be repeated as the debt-based economy further declines, and the money supply becomes ever more restricted.

The Hidden Costs and Subsidies of the Nuclear Power Industry

The issue of cost is the one area where there is so much hidden from the general public. For example, in March 2012 the Nuclear Decommissioning Authority estimated the total undiscounted cost of decommissioning all nuclear sites at £100 billion. [905]

In February 2011, the Union of Concerned Scientists in an article on the hidden costs of nuclear power titled *After 50 Years, Nuclear Power is Still Not Viable without Subsidies,* reveal that the US nuclear industry has been propped up for years by a generous array of government subsidies. It seems that without even further subsidies, the industry is still not viable. The report listed more than 30 subsidies that support the industry at every stage, from uranium mining, construction subsidies, liability protection, waste storage—and right through to decommissioning. Added together, all the costs exceed the average price of the power produced. As these costs escalate, and following Fukushima, the industry is demanding even more subsidy and protection:

"Despite the fact that the nuclear power industry has benefited from decades of government support, the technology is still uneconomic, so the industry is demanding a lot more from taxpayers to build new reactors," said Ellen Vancko, manager of UCS's Nuclear Energy and Climate Change Project. "The cost of this technology continues to escalate despite billions in subsidies to both existing and proposed plants. Instead of committing billions in new subsidies that would further distort the market in favour of nuclear power, we should focus on more cost-effective energy sources that will reduce carbon emissions more quickly and with less risk." [906]

According to the Obama administration's new budget proposal, it would provide an additional $36 billion in Federal loan guarantees to underwrite reactor construction. This would bring the nuclear loan guarantees alone to a staggering $58.5 billion—and leave the tax payer liable for any default on the loans. Whilst these key subsidies do not involve direct payments, they do transfer the risks of constructing and operating plants, including cost overruns, waste management, and accidents away from the operators. However, there are also hidden indemnity clauses protecting the industry from liabilities such as serious accidents and malfunctions—and further protections from decommissioning and the horrendous costs of containing highly contaminated waste. In their article, the Union of Concerned Scientists makes the point:

> The key subsidies for nuclear power do not involve cash payments, the report found. They shift the risks of constructing and operating plants—including cost overruns, loan defaults, accidents and waste management—from plant owners and investors to taxpayers and ratepayers. These hidden subsidies distort market choices that would otherwise favor less risky investments. [907]

In *Poisoned Power,* Gofman and Tamplin reveal that, following the *Brookhaven Report* (1957), commissioned by the Atomic Energy Commission (AEC), to look into the potential cost of a nuclear accident that such an event could result in monetary losses of up to seven billion dollars—over and above the losses of life. Insurance companies subsequently refused to insure the industry—which is the case still today. Realising that the expansion of the nuclear industry was then in total jeopardy, the AEC put forward the bill called the Price-Anderson Act. This removed individual liability in the event of a major accident and laid it at the door of the taxpayer. Without this law, which is continuously renewed, Gofman believes the industry would fold overnight. He has campaigned for a repeal of it for decades. [908]

The Future We Face

Where does this leave us you may ask? Well an article by Professor Busby titled "Scientific Dishonesty and Nuclear Power" attempts to answer that. It addresses not only the issue of nuclear power, but also it the more fundamental problem of scientific bias and integrity. He raises the fact that most politicians do not have science degrees, and have to rely on information from 'experts' to give them the information on which to base their judgements. He makes the point that the people in the places of authority, the so-called experts, are often not the best scientists or the best qualified, but people who have managed to get into their positions by other means.

> But the end result is that, because of their behaviour, scientific evidence is ignored or marginalised, or alternatively, incorrect scientific evidence is used as a basis for policy.

UNHEALTHY BETRAYAL

His own words also best summarise the major thrust of his article:

Let me begin by saying that those who think that there is a conspiracy to exclude the truth in various areas associated with environmental risk are quite correct....

I am going to present some cases to you that I have personal experience of. I am going to leave it to you to decide whether these people were dishonest or just stupid or maybe culturally biased, by which I mean, they honestly thought that they knew what the real picture was and could discount evidence which, for some defensible reason, they disagreed with. But whatever the decision you come to in each case, I want you to be aware that as a result of these actions, policies and laws remain in place that have resulted in and will result in the deaths of millions of people. This is not an exaggeration. The death yield from the radioactive contamination permitted by the behaviour of such people is in excess of 60 million and this issue is the greatest public health scandal of history. Much is said and written about Hitler and the gas chambers. The systematic poisoning of the human race by novel radioactive pollution and now by uranium particles makes the World War II death yields seem quite mild. [909]

The most recent information from the U.S. Department of Health and Human Services, in conjunction with the National Institute of Health (NIH) and the National Cancer Institute (NCI), reported by the President's Cancer Panel confirms their acceptance that radon gas is now considered the second leading cause of lung cancer in the United States—and the leading cause of lung cancer among people who have never smoked. They now also acknowledge that, as regards exposure limits, 'In fact no safe exposure level has been identified'. They further estimate that radon-induced lung cancer is responsible for an estimated average of 21,000 deaths annually.

With regard to weapons program exposure they add:

'Exposure to ionizing radiation related to nuclear weapons testing is an underappreciated issue worldwide'.

On the issue of the medical use of radiation they say:

Most health care providers are not aware of cancer and other latent radiation effects and therefore are unlikely to adequately monitor patients for these health conditions... Americans are now estimated to receive half their total radiation exposure from medical imaging and other medical sources, compared with only 15% in the early 1980s. The increase in medical radiation has nearly doubled the total average effective dose per individual in the United States. Computed tomography (CT) and nuclear medicine tests alone now contribute 36% of the total radiation exposure and 75% of the medical radiation exposure of the U.S.[910]

Different researchers have analysed tree ash to see to what levels of radioactive pollutants—if any, might exist in them. Stewart Farber is one who analysed samples of tree ash in the USA from 14 states and found both caesium and strontium signatures. The level of radioactivity was 100 times greater than the lab had previously recorded, while also exceeding 100-fold, in some cases, the levels of radioactive caesium that would be permissible from a nuclear reactor (about 100 picocuries per kilogram of sludge). The levels were found to be highest in the northeast of the USA. A particular problem with this is that a lot of wood ash is used as fertilizer. The irony, Farber notes, is that federal regulations require releases from nuclear plants to be disposed of as radioactive wastes if they contain even 1 percent of the caesium and strontium levels detected in the ash samples from New England. If ash were subject to the same regulations, he says, its disposal would cost U.S. wood burners more than $30 billion annually. [911]

Burrows and Chalmers took things a step further and looked at global contamination of trees to estimate the global distribution of fallout radioactivity. Here is what they had to say:

> The importance of determining the relative concentrations of Cesium-137 in the atmosphere and the soil and hence, in the food chain has been emphasized by the recent Chernobyl catastrophe. Furthermore a recent reaffirmation of the potential importance of low levels of ionizing radiation as a cause of cancer and other effects makes surveys of environmental contamination especially pertinent.... Firewood ashes were shown to be a relatively reliable way of measuring cesium-137/potassium-40 ratios, resulting from environmental contamination that might be reflected in living organisms that participate in the food chain including man.

They looked at the caesium-137/potassium-40 ratio which they found to be 100,000 times higher in the northern hemisphere than in the southern hemisphere. They also made the observation that deer eating the leaves of these trees were accumulating radiation in their bodies that would become meat in the human food chain. [912]

The question still remains remains-where does this leave us? We have on one side government 'experts' and international experts telling us that nuclear energy is the best thing since sliced-bread and on the other side we have supremely well-qualified people such as John Goffman warning us that there is no such thing as a safe dose of radiation.

UNHEALTHY BETRAYAL

The proponents of the industry will argue that we have no choice, that unless we build more reactors we will run out of power. What they don't say, however, is what might have occurred if we had invested the billions upon billions upon billions of dollars, pounds and francs into a safe renewable technology that was not harmful. Where would we be today? They might argue that it's too late to change, but is it?

Chapter 18
Future Health and Restorative Economics

We are at that point in time when a four hundred year old age is rattling in its deathbed and another is struggling to be born. A shifting of culture, science, society, and institutions enormously greater and swifter than the world has ever experienced. Ahead, lies the possibility of regeneration of individuality, liberty, community, and ethics such as the world has never known, and a harmony with nature, with one another and with the divine intelligence such as the world has never seen. It is the path to a livable future in the centuries ahead, as society evolves into ever-increasing diversity and complexity. [913]

—Dee Hock, CEO Emeritus of Visa International, (the largest business organization in the world with a turnover ten times that of Wal-Mart and market value more than double that of General Electric).

There is no doubt that the decisions we make today will affect us for generations to come—and our rush into nuclear power must be the most worrying example of this. Throughout this book I have given numerous examples of how real science has been shoved to one side in the rush for major corporations to make major profits. That this has been done with the collusion of various government agencies is, as we have seen, very well documented.

The fact most of the evidence reported in this book has focused significantly on the American experience is because there is much more available evidence in the public domain in the USA. The UK, by comparison, is a lot more secretive. Here, government bodies do not have to reveal the minutes of closed meetings. Nevertheless, this phenomenon is assuredly global—as are the industrial giants that so dominate our world.

In previous chapters we have discussed the failure of governments and industry to protect our health. However, information of how this failure is significantly contributing to the pandemic of chronic illness and neurological damage is now becoming harder to ignore. A clamour for change has arisen from a number of prestigious organisations. For example, on the problem of endocrine disruption, The Endocrine Society has called for timely action to prevent harm. The European Society for Paediatric Endocrinology and the Pediatric Endocrine society (based in the USA), put forward a joint call for action regarding endocrine disrupters and their effects. The World Health Organisation, in its report on the *State of the Science of Endocrine Disrupting Chemicals (2012)* concluded:

> EDCs [endocrine disrupting chemicals] have the capacity to interfere with tissue and organ development and function, and therefore they may alter susceptibility to different types of diseases throughout life. This is a global threat that needs to be resolved…It is critical to move beyond the piecemeal, one chemical at a time, one disease at a time, one dose approach currently used by scientists. Understanding the effects of the mixtures of chemicals to which humans and wildlife are exposed is increasingly important.
>
> There is also a need to stimulate new adaptive approaches that break down institutional and traditional scientific barriers and stimulate interdisciplinary and multidisciplinary team science.[914]

In the Annual Report to the U.S. President, *Reducing Environmental Cancer Risk,* it was recommended:

> A precautionary, prevention-orientated approach should replace current reactionary approaches to environmental contaminants in which human harm must be proven before action is taken to reduce or eliminate exposure…Optimally, it should shift the burden of proving safety to manufacturers prior to new chemical approval.

They further recommend:

> A more integrated, coordinated, and transparent system for promulgating and enforcing environmental contaminant policy and regulations driven by science and free of political or industry influence, must be developed to protect public health.[915]

Their comments are echoed by numerous other scientists and professionals, many of whom I have previously quoted. A lot of us, of course, will have heard similar requests for change before. But public awareness, of the toxic nature of the more than 8,000 chemicals unleashed on us globally is, however, now also growing. The question remains though, 'Will anything significant happen as a result—other than superficial responses from well-paid committees, issuing more reports calling for more action. Because, if not, the industries that created the problems will remain free to carry on generating massive profits - and leaving the general public to pay for treating the illnesses that we suffer as a result. As soon as a suggestion of curtailing the use of a chemical that is damaging to our health becomes widespread, the industry will mount a campaign to dispute it, in order to protect its profits. As we have seen, this is what the lead industry and other polluters have done before. But even in our current economic model, one that I argue is fundamentally flawed— the costs of improving our health status can still be justified. For example, the National Institutes of Health (NIH) estimated that, in 2009, cancer cost the nation (U.S.) $243 billion-$99 billion for direct medical costs, $19.6 billion for indirect morbidity costs (costs for lost productivity due to illness), and $124.8 billion for indirect mortality costs (costs of lost productivity due to premature death).[916]

Let's examine the story of lead a little further: one study examined by Professor Grandjean looked into the costs of the introduction of lead-free petrol and found that it had generated an economic benefit of $200 billion in each annual birth cohort since 1980—which equated to an aggregate benefit over the previous 30 years of over $3 trillion. Professor Grandjean adds that this success has since been repeated in more than 150 countries. Since one of his specialities is neurodevelopmental disorders, he documents how the loss of IQ as a result of exposure to lead can impact the ability of a person to progress in the world. This has been quantified as the loss of each single IQ point decreasing a person's lifetime earnings capacity by approximately €12,000 or US$18,000 in 2008 currencies. He suggests the most recent estimates regarding methylmercury toxicity to the US are roughly $5 billion. In the European Union methylmercury exposure is estimated to cause a loss of about 600,000 IQ points every year—equivalent to an economic loss of somewhere close to €10 billion.

He further cites that France estimated lead exposure associated with IQ losses to result in an annual loss of productivity in excess of €20 billion. He makes the point that, as IQ losses represent only one aspect of neurotoxicity, that the total costs could well be higher. [917]

In our current economic climate, with governments already over-burdened with debt, resources for all these studies will be severely limited without, in my view, a radical change in economic policy.

UNHEALTHY BETRAYAL

The Drawbacks of a Debt-based Private Banking System

In this chapter we'll examine some of the most significant future developments that will have a direct bearing on our health. The two most important of these for most of us would be the state of the economy, and corporate domination, not just of global business, but also of political and social institutions.

As we have seen, the state of the global economy at the moment is burdened with massive debt. At the same time, the power of global corporations is threatening the very nature of our democracies.

In previous chapters we looked at the current money system, under which money creation is in the hands of private corporate banking. This system of money creation benefits the banks, those who invest in them, and the high-paid executives who run them. This does not seem very democratic, so it is worth repeating that if this system was in the hands of a government-owned entity instead, one that was not debt-based, tremendous benefits would accrue to society at large. As mentioned earlier, in the five years leading up to the financial collapse of 2008/09, UK banks' lending was £2.9 trillion for non-commercial loans, i.e. just personal loans to households. This is money that was created out of nothing, simply by tapping keys on a computer. So why should we give this fantastic sum to a small number of private companies that are already super wealthy, enabling its shareholders to become even wealthier? If this was debt-free money produced by the government, it could be used either to pay down existing debts, improve infrastructure such as schools, hospitals or roads, or to reduce the tax burden.

Instead of benefitting the wider community, the debt-based system has other negative effects that are not immediately apparent to most of us. For a start, since that we now have deposit protection insurance, private banks no longer have to act prudently—they know they will be bailed out by the government with tax-payers money if they make imprudent investment decisions—which might otherwise lead to insolvency. This inevitably leads them to be more irresponsible with their investment decisions than they otherwise might be. One major drawback of this is the fact that there is little separation from their investment activity side with the personal banking side, so if a bank was to fail it would affect all its customers. This system supports a riskier short-term-profit-seeking approach by banks that is not looking at the long-term consequences of the health of businesses or the wider economy. As I write this, there are moves afoot to introduce a change to this, but, not in every country. As previously stated less *than 10%* of their lending is to businesses that contribute to the national GDP.

A further consequence is the destabilising effect of the ability to inflate prices and create price bubbles—as happened in the recent collapse stoked by the housing bubble. Mortgages are one area that has a direct bearing on most of us. By investing heavily in the property market, house prices rise steeply, making it almost impossible for younger people to enter the market and following the inevitable bust that follows a boom, creates a very unstable economic system. Bank failures are considered endemic to the banking industry, with serious crises occurring every fifteen years or so. This view was reiterated by Sir Mervyn King, Governor of the Bank of England in a speech delivered in October 2010:

"Banking crises are endemic to the market economy that has evolved since the Industrial Revolution. The words "banking" and "crises" are natural bedfellows... Unfortunately, such crises are occurring more frequently and on an ever larger scale." [918]

It is hard to overemphasize the negative consequences of the downturn following the collapse of a banking investment bubble—such as was responsible for the 2009 – 2014 depression. The banks subsequently had to cut back on lending which reduced the money supply and consequently reduced funding to business. In previous recessions, interest rates were also raised, which further added to the costs to business and to the public at large. In the current system the only solutions proffered are principally those that increase the debt levels further. An example of this is 'quantitative easing', which basically means banks are being bailed out with taxpayer money. Another consequence is the downturn phase—when jobs are put on the line, unemployment is growing, businesses are failing, households are faced with negative equity etc. This is usually the time when corporations start to blame job losses on too much red tape, too many regulations etc. It's also the time when environmental protection becomes a casualty, and all the progress made in protecting the environment can be lost at the stroke of a pen.

I have previously referred to the way the Reagan administration was responsible for a massive turn-around regarding environmental regulation, slashing budgets to the EPA, loosening environmental controls etc. So it's no surprise that when Reagan was elected, the economy was in a serious downturn, with the prime rate over 21%.

During that downturn, the solutions offered did not tackle the real causes in any significant way. Debates seemed to polarise around minor bank reforms and whether to increase spending or to cut it back to help reduce the overburdened national debt. This, of course, had some sympathy from many people, but this approach introduces austerity measures, cut-backs, reductions in services, higher taxes—a range of unpleasant measures that make life harder for all of us. The pro-spending group maintains that cutting back spending at a time of recession will result in serious depression and prolonged economic stagnation—or even deflation which will lead to more bankruptcies etc. The only way out of such a mess is to increase government spending to stimulate the economy. The problem is something of a paradox; both sides are right in some respects, and both sides are wrong. Increasing government spending means increasing government debt even more—and that will increase the level of interest payments (currently running at £120 million a day), which—even at the historically low rates we are currently experiencing—would be enough to build a new hospital every week in the UK. The total interest payments on the UK national debt for 2012 reached £32 billion, rising to £43 billion in 2013. Cutting back spending, slashing government programs and services, and paying off some of the debt will, however, as those who argue against it tell us, reduce the money supply even further, prolong the downturn, and more than likely lead to a deeper recession.

A Healthier Alternative to a Private Debt-based Money Supply

Neither of those 'solutions' are real solutions. But removing the ability of privately-owned banks to create money through debt is a fundamental alternative.

Following the 2008 banking crisis Sir Mervyn King, the Governor of the Bank of England made the following pertinent comment:

"Of all the many ways of organising banking, the worst is the one we have today." [919]

Certainly, the concept of giving away vast sums of money to a relatively small group of private banks, enabling them to amass global wealth, and effectively cause the rest of the community to 'rent' the monetary supply at vast sums of interest, seems somewhat unfair. Especially since they continue to gamble with this artificially created money willy-nilly, and pay themselves vast sums of money in the process. Restoring the right to create money to sovereign governments is an infinitely better alternative, as long as it is done correctly.

FUTURE HEALTH AND RESTORATIVE ECONOMICS

Jackson and Dyson, in their book, *Modernising Money—Why our Monetary System is Broken and How it Can Be Fixed,* make the observation that paying the banks £213 billion in interest charges (2008 in the UK) effectively transfers a massive amount of money to the already wealthy, when it could, instead contribute to debt reduction, tax cuts, better services or improved infrastructure that would benefit the wider community. They also discuss the very plausible alternative, already mentioned by which the creation of money is transferred away from private banks, and back to central government. In the UK, the Bank of England would take overall control. Although, in their proposal, Jackson and Dyson suggest a Money Creation Committee (MCC) that is completely independent from the banks and the Chancellor of the Exchequer, and is accountable to an all-party Treasury Select Committee. The MCC would be responsible for ensuring that money creation would be constrained to an inflation target to prevent irresponsible money creation and excess inflation. In this new system the investment side of banking would be separated from the current account or checking account side—which would effectively be owned by the customers and held at the Bank of England. There it would be totally unaffected by any bank failure, and would consequently not need insurance. In this model, investment banks that invested in high-risk enterprises would be allowed to fail, without affecting current account holders. Customers could choose the level of risk they wished to be exposed to and, in this system—unlike the old system would be able to have some direct influence on where their money is invested. Banks would effectively become brokers of the money supply not creators of it. [920]

The principals Jackson and Dyson suggest are sound, and could be adapted by any country as long as these—are properly adhered to. The Money Creation Committee, or whatever body is set up to authorise money creation, would have to be a fully public body, independent of any political manipulation—and inflation targets would have to be met. Any new money would be debt-free and would introduce a new stability to the economy. Small and medium-sized businesses that currently are unable to get access to capital would, for the first time, have direct access to capital, and retail banks would no longer be able to chase short-term profits—this activity would be left to the investment banks. Stephen Zarlenga, the Director of the American Monetary Institute, offers very similar reforms as Jackson and Dyson. Here are his three recommendations:

1. Incorporate the Federal Reserve System into the U.S. Treasury where all new money would be created by government as money, not interest-bearing debt; and be spent into circulation to promote the general welfare. The monetary system would be monitored to be neither inflationary nor deflationary

2. Halt the banks' privilege to create money by ending the fractional reserve system in a gentle and elegant way. All the past monetized private credit would be converted into U.S. government money. Banks would then act as intermediaries accepting savings deposits and loaning them out to borrowers. They would do what people think they do now. This Act nationalizes the money system, not the banking system. Banking is not a proper function of government, but providing the nation's money supply is a government prerogative!

Spend new money into circulation on a 21st century eco-friendly infrastructure and energy sources, including the education and healthcare needed for a growing and improving society, starting with the $2.2 trillion that the Civil Engineers estimate is needed over the next 5 years for infrastructure repair; creating good jobs across our nation, re-invigorating local economies and re-funding local government at all levels. [921]

There will no doubt be other people offering their solutions to the present financial issues facing us, as there were following the Great Depression; beware of any proposals that leave the banks with the power to create money. We were warned by numerous people throughout history that giving private banks the power to create money would lead to our downfall:

> The system of banking we have both equally and ever reprobated. I contemplate it as a blot left in all our constitutions, which, if not covered, will end in their destruction, which is already hit by the gamblers in corruption, and is sweeping away in its progress the fortunes and morals of our citizens. ... And I sincerely believe, with you, that banking establishments are more dangerous than standing armies; and that the principle of spending money to be paid by posterity, under the name of funding, is but swindling futurity on a large scale.
> Thomas Jefferson—Letter to John Taylor, May 26,1816

We are reaping the results of allowing private banks to create money from debt on a vast scale. They have been allowed to increase the money supply by trillions of dollars, leaving us with the debts of trillions of dollars for which they charge us interest. This artificially created money bears no relationship to real wealth, the creation of goods, the gross national product or the real business world. It has led to a fantastic dis-equilibrium of wealth and money distribution, leading to an even more fantastic increase in the 'financial sector' and further forms of financial speculation such as hedge funds, leading to economic instability and collapse. This imbalance in my view is no friend of capitalism; the result is the downturn that followed the huge speculation which precipitated the 2008 crisis.

FUTURE HEALTH AND RESTORATIVE ECONOMICS

I'll leave the aspect of money with one last quote by Vincent Vickers, former Director of the Bank of England, an insider and a man well qualified to inform the debate:

> The existing monetary standard is unworthy of our modern civilisation and a growing menace to the world....I am qualified to tell the public that in my view, it is entirely mistaken if it believes that the monetary system of this country is normally managed by 'recognised monetary experts' working in accordance with the most scientific and up to date methods known to modern economists... The Bank of England should no longer attempt to stifle the efforts of modern economists, nor persist in regarding all 'Monetary Reformers' as impertinent busybodies trying to usurp her authority...When we see great sections of the community clamouring for monetary reform then, surely, it is time for the government to seek advice elsewhere, and to encourage open discussion....It is not ,productive industry' with its new machinery which is the root cause of our unemployment and our uncertainty, but 'Finance', with its antiquated mechanism, which has failed to adapt itself to modern requirements. [922]

Michael Rowbotham in his excellent book, *Grip of Death—A Study of Modern Money, Debt Slavery and Destructive Economics,* reveals the views of Abraham Lincoln, and CH Douglas: both believed that the power of money creation should be with the government, not private banks. Here are Lincoln's words:

> Government possessing the power to create and issue currency and credit as money and enjoying the right to withdraw both currency and credit from circulation by taxation and otherwise, need not and should not borrow capital at interest as means of financing governmental work and public enterprise. The government should create, issue and circulate all the currency and credit needed to satisfy the spending power of the government and the buying power of consumers. The privilege of creating and issuing money is not only the supreme prerogative of government, but it is the government's greatest creative opportunity.
> Abraham Lincoln, Senate document 23, page 91. 1865 [923]

Rowbotham offers a similar solution to the economic crisis we are in, based on the ideas of CH Douglas, as well as Lincoln. I don't wish to dwell on the financial aspect of our current crisis. That it has a direct bearing on our health is in my view beyond doubt. Everything suffers when an economy crashes. The effect is global—people in economies that are facing restrictions because of debt are subjected to many problems; rising unemployment, falling real incomes, personal rising debt, bankruptcies etc. Third-world countries are even more burdened by their inability to meet payments on their national debt, because increasing amounts of food grown to feed their indigenous populations has to be sold to pay interest to the banks.

Following the Fukushima disaster energy prices rocketed as Japan has had to import massive amounts of gas. Whilst we are experiencing a major recession, prices will continue to rise, in the longer term (currently there is a drop in the oil price, but it will more than likely be short-lived), leading in tandem with falling spending power, and the inability of more and more people to be able to feed themselves with adequate quality foods. It is the quality foods that include meat, fish, vegetables, and fruit that attract the higher prices, leading many people to choose less nutritious foods in their diets.

The Rise of Corporate Dominance

In tandem with the massive growth of the private banking sector, as a result of their ability to create money out of debt, we also have a massive increase in the size of corporations. You could say that one feeds the other. These corporations have grown so powerful that they can avoid paying taxes on their massive earnings—I have documented a few examples in previous chapters. Corporations are so powerful that most governments are easily coerced by them; most pander to them and some ignore them at their peril. Many are regarded as "bad apples" due to the illegal acts committed, the pollution they create, the false accounting, false science etc. Joe Bakan, Professor of Law and author of the book *The Corporation – The Pathological Pursuit of profit and Power,* compares the activities of numerous corporations and believes that the way they behave is pathological—even comparing them with psychopaths. After being given Limited Liability status, which removes the possibility of people who invest in them from being sued for the corporation's activities, they had pretty much free rein. In the US, according to Bakan, their hijacking of the 14th Amendment to the American Constitution, has led to 'moral decay and lack of responsibility within corporate organisations'. [924]

Dr Robert Hare, consultant to the FBI on psychopaths, compiled a checklist for psychopathic behaviour and corporations ticked all the boxes:

- Callous unconcern for the feelings of others.
- Reckless disregard for the safety of others.

- Deceitfulness: repeated lying and conning others for profit.
- Incapacity to experience guilt.
- Failure to conform to social norms with respect to lawful behaviours.[925]

There have been a number of attempts to revoke corporations licenses, one of which in California was supported by the National Lawyers Guild and a number of other groups. Although this was refused by the California Attorney General, the appellants acknowledged that he did have the power to do this. So the question was 'Are there alternatives?'

Ray Anderson, was CEO of Interface, the world's largest carpet manufacturer, before he died in August 2011, said he had been very affected by reading Paul Hawken's book, *The Ecology of Commerce*—and it made him review the impact his company was having on the planet. This led him to investigate a way of making it more ecologically sustainable, and to reduce its footprint on the Earth. He then introduced changes that produced substantial reductions in the company's inputs (which are highly petroleum-based) and also cut energy and water use. He cut his company's greenhouse emissions by 71%, and used renewable energy to power eight out of ten factories. Yet, throughout this time, sales increased by two-thirds and earnings doubled. His profit margins expanded and, at the same time, greenhouse gas emissions declined, relative to sales by 82%.[926]

Anderson made numerous speeches and wrote a couple of books about his experience. In a speech to civic and business leaders at North Carolina State University, he expressed how he felt our current industrialisation was failing us:

'Do I know you well enough to call you fellow plunderers?
There is not an industrial company on earth, not an institution of any kind, not mine, not yours, not anyone's that is sustainable. I stand convicted by me, myself alone, not by anyone else, as a plunderer of the earth, but not by our civilisation's definition. By our civilisation's definition I am a captain of industry, in the eyes of many, a kind of modern day hero. But really, really the first industrial revolution is flawed, it is not working, it is unsustainable, it is a mistake, and we must move on to another and better industrial revolution and get it right this time'. [927]

Whilst Interface has reduced its global footprint by over one third, its stated goal is to be totally sustainable by 2020, referred to as "Mission Zero." He compares the challenge to climbing Mount Everest, only much harder. In his book, *Confessions of a Radical Industrialist: How*

Interface proved that you can build a successful business without destroying the planet, he expresses his view on the challenges facing industry:

> The point of my story is deceptively simple. Business and industry—not just American business and industry, but global business and industry—must change their ways to survive. Some people have been saying this for a long time. Many more are saying it today.
>
> I make no claim to prescience, only to conviction. And by survive I do not mean maintain identity and integrity within the context of a financial system in meltdown, either. By survive I mean business must be steered through a transition from an old and dangerously dysfunctional model to a far better one that will operate in balance and in harmony with nature—thrive in a carbon constrained world, and put down the threats of global climate disruption, species extinction, resource depletion, and environmental degradation. In a word develop a business model that is sustainable. [928]

Coming from a successful industrialist, these comments are very significant, they are the views of an insider. I will quote one more of his comments that expresses the simple choice we all have:

> 'We have a choice to make during our brief visit to this beautiful blue and green living planet, to hurt it or to help it'. [929]

Anderson referred to himself as a "radical industrialist," so the questions are: 'Is he alone? 'Will industry take up the challenge without significant coercion?' I'm not optimistic that industry will. He has proved it does not have to cost the earth to make a business work, even a billion dollar-plus corporation. *One thing is for sure: corporations have to be made accountable for their actions and their effect on our environment because those actions affect the health of all of us.*

Current Law Inhibits Corporations from Being Responsible Entities

Harry Glasbeek, a Canadian corporate lawyer in his book *Wealth by Stealth—Corporate Crime, Corporate Law, and the Perversion of Democracy,* describes how, in many ways, the legal system is skewed in favour of corporations: there are few criminal charges ever brought against corporations or their managers; when they are actually prosecuted, the fines are generally so small as to be insignificant; assigning responsibility for violations due to corporate structure, buck passing and secrecy also enables those responsible to evade punishment. He details numerous studies that reveal how corporate crime is endemic. In 1980 for example, a US study found 60% of the 582 largest industrial corporations were found to have engaged in illegal activity. In eighty-three cases they were found responsible for more than five violations.

Glasbeek also reveals how corporations basically dominate the business world and effectively transfer wealth to the minority super rich. In 1984 the leading five hundred non-financial corporations owned 67.7% of assets, had 54% of sales and 70.4% of all profits. The degree of monopoly by corporations varied by sector; in manufacturing for example 1.92 percent of corporations had 79.29% of the assets, 72.89% of sales and earned 76.79% of the sectors total profits. Following the 1988 free-trade elections, concentration of power continued increasing. In 1990, Statistics Canada reported that, by 1987, the top 1% of all enterprises controlled 86% of Canada's assets and made 75% of all profits. Glasbeek expresses the situation clearly: 'This left the remaining 14% of assets in the control of 99 percent of all enterprises, and that 99% of all enterprises shared a derisory 25% of all the profits made in Canada.' If you add the fact that the controlling interest in 80% of corporations is held by between one and two people. This means a very small group of people exert enormous influence over our economies and our governments.[930]

Concentrating the wealth of countries into the hands of corporate élites enables them to subvert individual governments' policies, dominate the media, manipulate the legal profession, and promote whatever agenda suits them. For example, in 1984 the National Citizens' Coalition (NCC)—an umbrella group for corporations—challenged the Canadian Government's legislation to limit the power of wealth to influence elections—so that those with the most wealth would not be able to drown out the voices of the rest of us. The NCC defeated the legislation arguing that the Charter of Rights and Freedoms to all Canadians should also be applied to corporations. It seems strange to equate wealthy corporations with the man in the street, but that's what happened. A Royal Commission of inquiry in 1990, established to look into the impact of third party spending on the 'pocket-book elections' found that the Charter decisions had "destroyed the overall effectiveness of the legislative framework... for promoting fairness", and further had diminished "the 'democratic' character of our society."[931]

Another corporate lawyer, Robert Hinckley believes that law in its current form actually inhibits corporate executives from being socially responsible. He describes the problem thus:

> After 23 years as a corporate securities attorney, advising large corporations on securities offerings and mergers and acquisitions, I left my position as partner at Skadden, Arps, Slate, Meagher & Flom because I was disturbed by the game. I realized that the many social ills created by

corporations *stem directly from corporate law*. It dawned on me that the law, in its current form, actually inhibits executives and corporations from being socially responsible. So in June 2000 I quit my job and decided to devote the next phase of my life to making people aware of this problem. My goal is to build consensus to change the law so it encourages good corporate citizenship, rather than inhibiting it.

He refers to the provision that exists in various forms throughout the world that focuses on a corporation's raison d'être.

The provision in the law I am talking about is the one that says the purpose of the corporation is simply to make money for shareholders... Although the wording of this provision differs from jurisdiction to jurisdiction, its legal effect does not. This provision is the motive behind all corporate actions everywhere in the world. Distilled to its essence, it says that the people who run corporations have a legal duty to shareholders, and that duty is to make money. Failing this duty can leave directors and officers open to being sued by shareholders. [932]

Glasbeek cites the example of Ford, and their failure to recall the Pinto model that they knew was dangerous. Evidence came to light that the Ford executives had made a cold-hearted calculated decision that:

Given the number of cars on the road, the number of accidents in which they would statistically be involved, the number of passengers and the amount of property likely to be burnt and destroyed, it was cheaper to keep the car on the road, unmodified, than recall all the vehicles out there and refit them so as to make them less explosive. The jury imposed punitive damages of $125 million that was eventually reduced on appeal to mere $3.8 million. [933]

Glasbeek points out that the fines are derisory, whereas the cost to consumers and taxpayers can be very significant. He cites the example of the Heavy Electrical Equipment Conspiracy, an anti-trust violation involving General Electric in 1960. It cost the tax-payers $1 billion (in 1960 money) and, following a vigorous denunciation by the Judge, GE were fined $437,500, equivalent to giving a $3 parking fine who is earning $175,000 a year. It has been calculated that, for a corporation earning sales of $300 million a year, receiving the average fine of $5,000 would be equivalent to a 2.4 cent fine for someone earning $15,000 a year. On top of this they are able to offset their tax against this cost anyway so it effectively costs them nothing, which is why they will continue to do it. Glasbeek points out the iniquity of the legal status of corporations:

> In Anglo-American jurisdictions, capitalists have been blessed by a form of corporate law that promotes irresponsibility, criminality, and the perversion of democracy to advance their goal: the maximization of their wealth and political power. The corporation makes it all seem normal: selfishness, avarice, disregard for others, impersonal, commodified relations, the subjugation of the majority to the whims and caprices of the few. The very normality of it makes the mediation of the impacts of unequally divided wealth, so characteristic of capitalist economies, all the more difficult to achieve. All of this is to be tolerated because it generates wealth. Greed is elevated to a moral value, supported by massive education campaigns and commercial advertising techniques perfected to wrought changes in expectations and wants. [934]

Many people may feel that the problems we face are insurmountable, that corporations are simply too powerful and too dominant in our economy and political system to open to change. In my view, we all have the power to generate change, particularly collectively. We all have various choices that we make every day and our choices directly affect the world we live in. Simply changing the way you shop, for example, could transform our world. I believe that the choice is simple, that we have to develop a way of living that is truly sustainable. The way we choose to produce food, for example, has profound implications for our future health, our children's health and the health of our planet. Once we return the right to create money to our elected governments we will have taken the first steps towards creating a food supply that really serves our needs.

The Failure of Industrial Agriculture and Our Modern Food System

Everything in our economy is linked. The corporate takeover of agriculture and the food supply has vast repercussions for global health, and is now seen to be totally unsustainable. Yet the solutions to the problem are not rocket science.

Let's first look at some aspects of our modern industrialised food and agriculture system. Globally, industrialized agriculture uses 1000 tons of water to produce one ton of grain. 17% of total energy use in the USA goes into food production and distribution—and accounts for 20% of all transport within the US. Approximately 20% of all greenhouse gas emissions come from agriculture, without including the increases caused by the loss of forests. Agriculture produces 60% of methane and 70% of nitrous oxide.

In 2002, $318 billion of tax-payers money was spent on subsidising agriculture in the OECD. Of this, approximately 90% of it, was in the form of subsidies to large corporations and big farmers that grew food for export. Subsidised food dumped on Third World countries simply causes more poverty and bankruptcies on a massive scale. In the USA, 500 family-run farms close down every week—these are some of the extra costs of the industrial food production system, on top of what we have already discussed.

The alternative is to encourage farming systems that have lower inputs of fertilizer and chemicals, such as organic agriculture, that nurture the soil that improve fertility, that increase the quality of food and therefore sustain the health of those who consume the food produced. One of the main arguments against organic agriculture is that it is too expensive, that common people could not afford it—but this viewpoint is firmly-based in our redundant economic model—where banks burden us with debt—yet create vast sums of money for themselves and corporations saddle us with all the externalised costs. Costs, such as, the pollution, the extra transport costs, nutritionally deficient produce, the consequential ill health, developmental problems due to pesticides and even deaths, are just some of the externalised costs.

To understand how this is unsustainable, we must also take into account, how the private-money creation system transfers money away from those in the lower income brackets to the top 1%, as has previously been discussed. This results in a much diminished spending power for most of us. Further, if all the costs that are currently externalised by industrialised agriculture were met by the industry, the cost would be phenomenal—and in this light organic food production would be very cheap.

On top of this, the need for high taxation to cover the massive interest on the national debts—would be greatly reduced, following paying down the debt—the end result of which would leave greater spending power in the hands of the majority of the population.

The rush to cut down forests to replace them with GM and other crops, destroys a vital resource, the carbon dioxide sink, as well as the oxygen that trees produce aside from all the other benefits that trees bring to indigenous people. Deforestation is responsible for 18% of global greenhouse emissions. On the other hand, organic farming is estimated to be able to sequester 4 tonnes of CO_2 per hectare per year. If the UK, for example, were to convert to being fully organic it could save 68 Mt (million tonnes) of CO_2 annually. The transport, distribution, storage and processing of food is responsible for 18.4% of national greenhouse emissions. The benefits to the quality of food, is a very important aspect of organic agriculture. Numerous studies have looked at the benefits of organic food including a £20 million four-year study undertaken by the EU. This found that organic vegetables and fruit contain as much as 40% more antioxidants. Antioxidants in organic milk were even as high as 90% more than that obtained from conventional herds. [935]

The Institute of Science in Society has produced a useful book titled *Food Futures Now—Organic-Sustainable-Fossil Fuel Free,* by Mae-Wan Ho and others, which looks into the differences between conventional and organic agriculture and reviews the benefits of numerous ventures into more sustainable agriculture around the world. The book also compares the nutrient levels recorded in a 1940 study by McCance and Widowson with their updated version in 1991, and reveal that there has been a significant decline in the mineral content of foods over that period. Calcium levels in meat have declined by 41% and their iron levels by 54%. Zinc levels in fruit have declined by 27%. [936] These declines do not include the further mineral declines reported by Professor Huber and others as a result of the use of Glyphosate and Roundup.

Virginia Worthington looked at 41 studies that evaluated the nutritional changes in agriculture in the USA and the UK. Prior to World War Two, very few synthetic chemicals were in use, but by 1995 more than 45 million tons of chemical fertilizers and 770 million pounds of synthetic chemical had been used in the USA alone. Synthetic chemicals and fertilizers are now regarded as the mainstay of conventional agriculture, so it's fair to say that the decline in nutrient levels in our food is a direct result of this move away from previously universal organic farming. All the studies show serious declines in calcium, magnesium, sodium, potassium, phosphorus, iron, and copper. The decline in the levels of calcium were 19% in the UK and 29% in the USA; magnesium down by 35% in the UK and 21% in the USA; sodium by 43% and potassium by 14% in the UK. The studies also found that organic crops contained significantly higher levels of vitamin C and, iron, and had significantly fewer nitrates than conventional agriculture. There were also much lower levels of heavy metals in organic crops compared to conventional crops. [937]

In the UK, more than 450 pesticide active ingredients are licensed for use in UK agriculture, and more than 25,000 tonnes were applied to UK crops in 2000. Many of these are persistent contaminants and permeate the soils, water courses, and water supplies. Approximately half (48%) of all fruit and vegetables in the UK contain detectable levels of pesticide residues. An American study still found detectable levels of DDT in 17% of carrots analysed, twenty years after the chemical had been banned. Many samples of other fresh produce contained multiple residue levels which could have profound implications for our health. Current regulations do not take into account the 'cocktail effect' of multiple residues—and little is known about the toxicological interactions between pesticides. In one American study, researchers combined three pesticides and found that toxicity multiplied more than a hundred times more than when their individual totals were added together. In UK studies, a significant number of fruits and vegetables were found with more than one residue: 29% of apples, 68% of pears, 14% of carrots, 72% of lettuce, 94% of oranges, and 42% of strawberries—to cite just a few.[938]

The *Soil Association,* which promotes organic agriculture in the UK, reviewed the evidence from more than 400 publications on both organic and conventional agriculture, paying particular attention to nutrient comparisons. A number were rejected for not meeting the strict criteria required, but all the rest showed that organic crops had higher levels of minerals, higher levels of vitamin C and higher levels of phytonutrients (plant compounds associated with anti-cancer effects). [939]

A great number of factors affect the quality of our diets and, consequently, the level of nutrients available to us. Different soil types and plant varieties all contribute to the variation in nutrient uptake. I have previously quoted from the 1971 *Department of Agriculture Report on Nutrition* which revealed that the highest death rates were mostly associated with depleted soils. Another significant factor has been the growth in the consumption of processed foods and the decline in consumption of fresh fruit and vegetables. In a US Department of Agriculture study in 1965 revealed that the nutrients most often found below the RDA (Recommended Daily Allowance) were vitamin A, ascorbic acid (vitamin C), and calcium. The decline in vitamin A was attributed to a decline in the consumption of sweet potatoes, and dark green and yellow vegetables. Lower consumption of fresh vegetables is also responsible for a 10% decline of thiamine and a 25% decline of vitamin B_6 and a 20% decline of magnesium.[940]

Another significant factor is the loss of nutrients through storage, handling and distribution. Green leafy vegetables and broccoli, in particular, lose vitamin C in this way. Broccoli stored for two days in a refrigerator, on the other hand, has little loss of vitamin C, retaining 92% of it. When stored at room temperature, the retention drops to 56%. Green beans picked on a warm day, and stored overnight without refrigeration, will lose 60% of their vitamin C content. Peeled potatoes, soaked for two hours, lose approximately 12% of thiamine; sweet potatoes soaked for five hours lost almost 22%. Retention of nutrients after cooking varies from 67-100% for thiamine, 55-100% for riboflavin, 39-100% for niacin and 24-100% for vitamin C.

FUTURE HEALTH AND RESTORATIVE ECONOMICS

Clearly, nutrient uptake varies considerably when we make the choice between eating pre-cooked processed foods and cooking fresh food for ourselves. Whether we eat raw foods, whether we steam or boil our vegetables are all personal choices. But how the food we buy reaches us is mostly beyond our control. What is evident is that the most advantageous system of food production is the one that is most local, that involves the least transportation with minimal handling, and which takes the shortest time from harvesting to purchase. This system not only supports local farmers, but also cuts down on greenhouse gas emissions. If the local farmer is organic, further benefits would include less pollution from pesticide and fertilizer inputs, and an increase in the health of the soil, the water supply and the local population.

Alternatives to Industrial Agriculture That are Truly Sustainable

Healthier alternatives to industrial agriculture are already well under way, some of them we have already reviewed—such as how diversifying crops reduced the need for fungicides and gave greater yields. Other measures will be reviewed in this chapter. The growth in farmers' markets is to be welcomed, not only because they allow farmers to get a fairer price, but also because they give us access to healthier food. Addressing the issue of monetary reform will also put more purchasing power in our hands and give us the freedom of choice to purchase more organic produce. Any economic system that does not return a fair income to farmers is unsustainable and has no future. Farmers need to be rewarded for looking after the soil, producing healthy crops and animals, and increasing nutritional value—the opposite of what the current conventional system does.

Robert Kenner, director of a film *Food, Inc.,* provides us with a lot of factual information, such as; it takes 75 gallons of oil to bring a steer to slaughter, and 1 in 3 Americans born after 2000 will likely contract early onset diabetes—among minorities 1 in 2—a phenomenal 50%! He reports that in 1998 the USDA implemented microbial testing for salmonella and E.coli 0157h7, so that if an industrial plant repeatedly failed these tests, the USDA could shut it down. However, after it was taken to court by the meat and poultry associations, the USDA no longer has that power. This is all the more chilling when Kenner also reports that where there used to be thousands of slaughter-houses in the USA, there are now *only thirteen for the whole country*, which would be unbelievable if it wasn't true. So now it's not just banks that are considered too big to fail—slaughterhouses almost are too.. The film reviews some other aspects of our food production, and interviews people who have lost children to E.coli 01257h7.

Other people interviewed include Joe Salatin, owner of Polyface Farms in Virginia. He says that when his family took over the farm fifty years ago. The soil was so thin, and there was so little grass, that the land there which now supports a hundred head of cattle, would have struggled to supported twenty. The soil was so thin it was mostly bare ground and could no longer support plant growth. Yet, without having used a disk, ploughed, or planted a seed, and never having used a single bag of fertilizer, he finds that the fertility of the land just gets better and better every year. It is now highly fertile and supports a range of livestock, including pigs, and chickens as well as cattle.

He takes us into a pasture and illustrates the 'salad bar' that his cattle get to feed on—and it's not just grass. He picks out nettle, that the chickens particularly like, and is considered a tonic for them. He also picks out wide-leaf plantain, which is considered a blood cleanser for cattle. He picks out red clover, 'queen of the clovers, queen of the legumes', dandelion, orchard grass, narrow leaf plantain, white clover and timothy. Clearly pleased with the bouquet, he explains:

> There's your salad bar, and so that's what the cow is being able to eat as she puts her mouth over that, she gets the legume, the medic, the grass and it's all adding something nutritionally to her, that's the salad bar.

He philosophises:
> So when I say regenerative, redemptive healing food systems, this is the ultimate, when you are building soil, building earthworms, covering the ground with green material that cools the air instead of heating it up, that doesn't absorb heat and radiate heat like ploughed ground. When you create that landscape it is, it is the antithesis of global warming, it is the antithesis of everything that is wrong, it is the epitome of everything that is right in food and in production in farming and it is beautiful, I mean it is beautiful, it is beautiful.

He laments the fact that everything that used to be considered an asset on the farm has now become a liability to conventional farming—such as the vast cattle effluent or pig effluent on the current vast feedlots or large pig farms. On his farm, these products are considered extremely essential assets, and he explains why. He waxes lyrical about how the pigs create some immensely rich humus in the cattle shed. All winter long, the cattle feed on the seeder gates and 'drop fifty pounds a day out of their back end'—which all gets compacted down with straw, shavings etc. He apparently throws corn in amongst this mix, which the pigs dig up and root out, expressing their 'pigness'—and so aerate the mix without having to use expensive machinery, oil or labour, providing him with a very rich fertile compost that is used to enrich the land. He says he honours and respects the 'pigness of the pig', and allows it to 'express its physiological distinctiveness fully'. Here's what he says to expand on this: 'It is in honouring and respecting the pig and its distinctiveness that creates the physiological building block for honouring and respecting your gifts and talents. I mean, a culture that just uses a pig as a pile of protoplasmic inanimate structure to be manipulated by whatever creative design the human can foist on that critter can probably view individuals within its community and other cultures in the community of nations with the same disdain and disrespect and controlling type mentality'. [941]

I have had a lot of dealings with farmers, and it seems appropriate to leave the view on agriculture to a farmer, like Joe Salatin. There is one other aspect that I feel is worth repeating—a point made in the film that we have a choice about food, three times a day. This is simply the fact that the choices that we make directly affect the world we live in. Whilst many of us could not afford to choose to eat organic food at every meal, there are times we can. Choosing to purchase food from sources other than supermarkets, perhaps a local vegetable shop or butchers, or farmer's market will have an effect. Every action we take, every decision we make can have significant repercussions. Every journey of a thousand miles begins with a single step.

In chapter 4 we introduced the work of Professor T Campbell, who had participated in the study of 880 million Chinese people who seemed to thrive on a plant-based whole food diet. Aside from the obvious health benefits that he suggests would accrue to people adopting this type of diet— in his view not just the reduction in heart disease, cancer and diabetes, but numerous other illnesses—it would also have a dramatic effect on agriculture and the food industry. Instead of a world where vast resources are wasted on treating chronic disease—consider the benefits that would accrue if these resources were diverted to provide quality organic unsprayed food for everyone: naturally good health for ourselves, our children and – not least – our planet.

We have the power to change this world simply by what we choose to put on our plates.

Lack of Accountability and Scientific Dishonesty

The most fundamental change needed is in ourselves. The more of us who realize our society is in peril, largely as a result of corporate greed, aided by politicians and the legal system—the more quickly we can address these issues. We can change the money supply by removing from private banks the power to create money, and transferring it to Central Banks. That, in itself, will have a huge impact on corporations. Their domination of politics and their manipulation of the legal system will also have to be addressed, as will their tax avoidance of tax and their externalising of the costs of the damage they cause to our health and the environment.

In this review of health, I have quoted numerous examples of dishonest science, manipulation of the truth, manipulation of data, and concealment of information—all for the furtherance of corporate profits. Dr Chris Busby in an apposite article about this very topic, *Scientific Dishonesty and nuclear Radiation,* made this point:

> Peer-review literature itself is often biased by the affiliation of the researchers, and the affiliations of the reviewer or the editor. In addition, peer-review literature may be biased by the choice of the research topic (therefore who funds the research). Peer review literature may in fact be so brushed and spun as to approach dishonesty; it may have false data and indeed be dishonest. There is currently no law against such dishonesty or biased advice and culprits are not seen as criminals nor are they punished in any way in the UK. There is currently no such thing as a Scientific Crime and in my view there should be.

This is a very valid point. If you shoot somebody dead, you are liable to be arrested and prosecuted. If you produce a report that shows low levels of radiation is completely harmless—when you know this not to be the case, and thousands die as a result—you are not held accountable. Nor would you be held accountable if you produced a report saying a drug is safe when you know, in fact, that it isn't.

No-one is better qualified than Dr John Goffman to comment on low-level radiation, so let's hear his views on the subject:

> The so-called permissible dose of radiation, for nuclear workers or the public at large, represents only a legalized permit for the nuclear industry to commit random, premeditated murders upon the American population...
>
> Experimenting on humans without their knowledge or consent is obviously a crime. Taking life without due process of law is obviously a crime. There can be no doubt that the promoters of nuclear power—be they engineers, politicians, or scientists—are indeed committing these crimes against humanity. Americans would be justified in demanding that Nuremberg-type trials be held for these individuals.
>
> The charge that nuclear power promotion represents a crime against humanity is a serious one indeed. We do not make this charge lightly. [942]

FUTURE HEALTH AND RESTORATIVE ECONOMICS

Accountability is essential in any business, economic, or social system. In his book *Prosperity Without Growth,* Professor Tim Jackson, Economics Commissioner for the Sustainable Development Commission, challenges the notion that growth is necessary for prosperity. He says that for all the rest of the world to achieve the level of affluence of the OECD, the worldwide economy would have to be 40 times bigger than today's economy. This is clearly unsustainable. Here's how he puts it:

> A spiral of recession looms. Questioning growth is deemed to be the act of lunatics, idealists and revolutionaries.
>
> But question it we must. The idea of a non-growing economy may be an anathema to an economist. But the idea of a continuing growing economy is an anathema to an ecologist. No subsystem of a finite system can grow indefinitely in physical terms. [943]

It's not just the fact that our current system, based on the idea of growth forever is unsustainable—the whole premise of the idea of a 'consumer society', in which we plunder the earth, create huge amounts of often toxic waste, cannot go on forever. So the question is: can we create something better?. Paul Hawken, one of America's green entrepreneurs, makes the point: 'To create an enduring society, we will need a system of commerce and production where each and every act is inherently sustainable and restorative'.

Restorative Economics

In his book *The Ecology of Commerce,* Hawken broaches the idea of restorative economics, based more on the cyclical processes of nature. Instead of the linear concept of plunder, make product, dump waste—it's someone else's problem now—this involves no waste. He makes the point that in the USA, in 1993, the average American produced twice their own weight in household, hazardous and industrial waste. On top of that, he or she was responsible for half a ton of gaseous waste—including, of course, carbon dioxide. He makes the obvious point that, to change this state of affairs, business will have to consider three issues: what it takes, what it makes, and what it wastes. Manufacturing business is the problem, it must also be a part of the solution.

Hawken makes the point that incinerating waste does not remove it—it simply changes its form. He cites the example of a state-of-the-art incinerator in New Jersey which, consuming 2,250 tons of garbage daily, would emit 5 tons of lead, 17 tons of mercury, 580 pounds of cadmium, 777 tons of hydrogen chloride, 87 tons of sulphuric acid, 18 tons of fluorides and 98 tons of particulate matter, small enough to lodge permanently in the lungs, would be released, along with numerous different types of dioxin.[944]

On top of this, 30 tons of fly ash are produced by every 100 tons of trash, which are contaminated with heavy metals and dioxin compounds This has to be enclosed in plastic liners (which at best are only supposed to last twenty years), and transported to landfill. In some places they don't even use liners.

Imagine, on the other hand, a system where production is designed to have no waste or, at worst, a tiny amount of it. Imagine a system where whoever creates waste is responsible for it, and bears the cost of recycling or safely disposing of it. Every business is responsible for the waste it creates. This is no fantasy, it is the future. This is the basis of restorative economics.

Already there are moves afoot amongst car companies—in Japan and Germany in particular—to recycle their cars when their useful life is over. They are designing into their cars the idea of recycling them right from the beginning. Germany used to be one of the most wasteful countries in Europe, but it is now it one of the leaders in recycling. Hawken reports on the Duales system where 600 German companies created a recycling system serving 90% of the German market—placing yellow recycling bins in homes, factories, and apartments throughout the country. Only waste products with a trademarked green dot are collected. Companies pay a small fee, but all the packaging is recycled. Hawken makes the point:

> Only when the incentives to continue the manufacture of waste are removed, and only when the risks and costs far outweigh the gains and profits, will designers, engineers, chemists, and investors turn their attention to safer alternatives. We use wasteful methods today because they are the "cheapest" solution. [945]

Jared Diamond in his excellent book *Collapse—How Societies Choose to Fail or Survive*, cites the example of mining companies in Montana. Following extraction of the various minerals, and the closing down of the mines, they simply abandoned the project leaving arsenic, copper and toxic acids, leaking out into the river and into water courses. Following the introduction of laws in 1971 to prevent this, they simply declared bankruptcy closed their mines, and left the clean-up to the local citizens—amounting at that time to around $500 million. CEOs of the mining companies awarded themselves high salaries and great bonuses, and moved on to another location.[946]

Diamond also reveals a fundamental principle about pollution that came from Chevron. This is an intriguing source, as the petroleum industry is considered one of the worst polluters on the planet. Diamond had personally visited Chevron's Kutuba oil field in Papua, New Guinea, and found it to be remarkably pollution-free. He was studying bird populations there, and recorded more birds in the oil-field area than in surrounding areas. A Chevron manager told him he had learnt in Texas that the average clean-up cost, even for a small pit, was $100,000 - and that prevention was significantly cheaper. Diamond makes the point that it's the same with health. It is cheaper to prevent illness in the first place than to operate a system that degrades health, and subsequently incurs the huge expense of treating the sicknesses that follow. [947]

Hardin Tibbs describes the approach of industrial ecology to the problem of waste this way:

> In essence, industrial ecology involves designing industrial infrastructures as if they were a series of inter-locking, man-made ecosystems interfacing with the natural global ecosystem. Industrial ecology takes the pattern of the natural environment as a model for solving environmental problems, creating a new paradigm for the industrial system in the process. This is "biomimetic" design on the largest scale, and represents a decisive reorientation from conquering nature—which we have effectively already done—to cooperating with it.

> The "extract and dump" pattern is at the root of our current environmental difficulties. The natural environment works very differently. From its early non-cyclic origins, it has evolved into a truly cyclic system, endlessly circulating and transforming materials, and managing to run almost entirely on ambient solar energy. There is no reason why the international economy could not be reframed along these lines as a continuous cyclic flow of materials requiring a significantly lower level of energy input, and a vastly lower level of raw materials input from, and waste output to, the natural environment. [948]

Michael Braungart and William McDonough in their book *Cradle to Cradle—Remaking the Way We Make Things,* ask the question who would want to design a system that :

- Puts billions of pounds of toxic materials into the air, water and soils every year.
- Produces enormous amounts of waste.
- Measures productivity by how few people are working.
- Puts valuable materials in holes in the ground where they can never be retrieved.
- Creates prosperity by digging up or cutting down natural resources and then burning or burying them.

- Requires thousands of complex regulations—not to keep people and natural systems safe, but to prevent them from being poisoned too quickly.

They again suggest that instead of the linear system (which they refer to as the cradle to grave approach), we need to employ a cradle to cradle circular approach, in which, instead of building in obsolescence and creating massive amounts of waste, systems could be designed that utilize the waste as food, much as nature does. They believe the key to sustainable industrial systems must be to design in a way that replenishes, restores and nourishes the world. In such a system productivity and expansion is not a problem. McDonough is an architect who designs buildings to meet these new criteria—and cites a number of examples where, in which factories were re-designed to function in this way, either by recycling all their own waste or not producing any—and ended up making more money.

In the future, Braungart and McDonough suggest, electrical goods may be rented from manufacturers and returned to them for recycling when they're no longer needed [949]

The foundation for restorative economics rests on a number of principals:

- The need to take the creation of money away from private banks and return it governments that represent the people.
- The development of agricultural systems that regenerate soils, do not pollute the air and water, and promote health.
- The manufacture of products that produce zero waste, with have truly recyclable components or fully biodegradable components.
- The provision of secure, stable, and meaningful employment for people everywhere.
- The protection and promotion of biological diversity.
- The restoration and promotion responsibility in all aspects of production and commerce.
- Abolishment of Third World Debt.
- The promotion of Green Chemistry.
- Restore a sense of responsibility to corporations—make them legally liable for their actions.

All these principals are, in my view fully achievable. The details of how it can be done will be found in the books I have quoted from. In this volume, I have concentrated on giving an overview of how our own personal health is directly linked to the *modus operandi* of modern industry, the failure of our international banking system, and the failings of our supposedly democratic governments which, all too often, dance to the tune of the richest 1%.

If we were to start again from scratch and design a system that truly serves the needs of humanity, would we include features that create massive debt, force us to stumble from crisis to crisis, allow poverty, starvation, massive pollution, unsustainable amounts of waste, engender conflict in the world, and is so destructive to the eco-system of the planet? Surely we can do better than that can't we?

Without radical change it is hard not to be pessimistic about humanity's future. But I am an optimist. I believe more and more people realise that our current industrial/economic model is seriously flawed, but are not sure what to do about it. I once heard the statement "If you are not part of the solution you are part of the problem". This is one of those universal truths we can apply to our current challenge. I believe that every action we take has an effect and that we can either be part of the problem or part of the solution. Every choice we make has a direct effect on the world we live in. Our actions are like ripples in a pond, they make waves and travel much further than we may realise. Collectively, we have the power to change this world—and change it for the better, we must.

Whatever your previous beliefs it is hoped that this book has made clear that inaction is not an option. What you chose to do after reading this volume will hopefully include you as part of the solution, not part of the problem.

Further Resources

Monetary Change

http://www.monetary.org/ The American Monetary Institute (AMI) is a publicly supported charity, founded in 1996 to present the results of our research in a manner understandable by the average citizen; leading to monetary reforms which bring forth a greater level of economic justice and a more equitable and efficient functioning of government.

http://www.comer.org/ Committee on Monetary and Economic Reform COMER is an international publishing and education resource based in Toronto, Canada.

http://www.debtbombshell.com/uk-national-debt.htm UK Debt information site that gives the interest on the national debt for the UK will be in excess of £42 billion in 2015.

http://douglassocialcredit.com/ The Social Credit Site, Books and resources.

http://www.gold-eagle.com/research/schichtndx.html Selection of Economic Papers by Hans Schicht

www.moneyasdebt.net Paul Grignon's site, an excellent site on money, with a range of useful CDs.

http://www.wfhummel.net/ W F Hummel's site on Money

http://www.atimes.com/atimes/others/Henry.html The complete writings of Henry C K Liu, Asia Times.

http://henryckliu.com/ Henry C K Liu's site

http://moneymyths.org.uk/ Money Myths is presented by Brian Leslie. He has spent a lifetime looking at the problems with the current money system. He has been the Editor of Sustainable Economics magazine for over 16 years. Sites have video presentations & DVDs available

General Health

http://www.ucsusa.org Union of Concerned Scientists.

http://www.ewg.org/ Environmental Working group – A Chemical Industry Watchdog: The mission of the Environmental Working Group (EWG) is to use the power of public information to protect public health and the environment. EWG is a non-profit organization, founded in 1993.

http://braindrain.dk/ How Environmental Pollution Impairs Brain Development — and How to Protect the Brains of the Next Generation. Site edited by Professor Grandjean.

http://psychrights.org Law Project for Psychiatric Rights

www.madinamerica.com   For those interested in rethinking psychiatric care

http://www.grassrootshealth.net/ A medical Public awareness site advocating increased vitamin D understanding.

http://thenhf.com The National Health Federation is an international non-profit, consumer-education, health-freedom organization working to protect individuals' rights to choose to consume healthy food, take supplements, and use alternative therapies without government restrictions the World's oldest health-freedom organization & the only one accredited by Codex to attend and speak out at meetings of the Codex Alimentarius Commission, the highest international body on food standards.

http://www.ifbb.org.uk/about-us The Institute for Food, Brain and Behaviour exists to conduct research into the link between food and behaviour

http://foodfreedomgroup.com/ assesses food safety, freedom, and sovereignty issues.

http://www.thincs.org/   The International Network of Cholesterol Skeptics (THINCS) is a steadily growing group of scientists, physicians, other academicians and science writers from various countries

http://www.grassrootshealth.net/ A medical Public awareness site advocating increased vitamin D understanding

http://www.nmrc.ca/ The Naturopathic Medical Research Clinic, an orthomolecular approach to treatment.

http://drsircus.com/international-medical-veritas-associatio/ The International Medical Veritas Association (IMVA) is dedicated to research and instruction of a new form of medicine to people and physicians around the world.

http://www.cholesterol-and-health.com/cholesterol-and-health.html Chris Masterjohn Ph.d., cholesterol information site.

http://www.chemicalbodyburden.org/ The chemical body burden and its health effects - known and unknown.

https://www.rxisk.org/default.aspx Report a drug risk, site devoted to consumer and doctor awareness on drug reactions.

http://www.healyprozac.com/ This website explores threats to public safety and academic freedom surrounding the SSRI group of drugs – Prozac, Zoloft (Lustral), Paxil (Seroxat/Aropax).

http://orthomolecular.org/library/jom/ Archive Articles for the *Journal of Orthomolecular Medicine* Browse 40 years of research articles for free.

http://www.mpwhi.com/main.htm Mission Possible World Health International- Primarily aspartame information site – founded by Dr Betty Martini D Hum., who has researched Aspartame for more than 20 years, this is the best informed site on aspartame.

http://www.doctoryourself.com/ Health information site by Andrew A Saul PhD

FURTHER RESOURCES

http://www.holisticmed.com/aspartame/scf2002-response.htm Independent Analysis of the

"Opinion of the European Commission, Scientific Committee on Food: Update on the Safety of Aspartame. by Mark D. Gold, February 3, 2003.

http://www.curethenhs.co.uk/ Cure the NHS following the Staffordshire Hospital's appalling revelations.

www.nhppa.org The Natural Health Products Protection Association is federally incorporated as a non-profit organization with the sole object of: Protecting access to Natural Health Products and Dietary Supplements.

http://charterofhealthfreedom.org/index.php?/interactive-charter Canadian Charter for health Freedom.

www.hans.org – Canadian Health Action Network

http://www.drcranton.com/ Dr Elmer Cranton's Website, EDTA Bible Author and Nutrition website and much more.

http://www.saveourherbs.org.uk/index.html Save our Herbs, UK Herbalist's site includes Henry VIII's Charter.

http://drrimatruthreports.com/ Health education charity

http://www.vitaminlawyernews.com/ Vitamin Lawyer –Codex info

http://www.icimed.com International College of Integrative Medicine. Chelation therapy and more.

http://www.healthy-eating-politics.com/dietary-guidelines.html Healthy Eating Politics

http://www.worstpills.org. Public Citizen page on prescription drugs & other health topics.

Sites of Interest

http://www.monbiot.com/category/farming/ George Monbiot's website

http://www.commondreams.org/ Common Dreams is a non-profit independent news center, To inform, to inspire, to ignite change for the common good.

http://earthopensource.org/about-earth-open-source/ Earth Open Source aims to restore the open source roots of the food system – collaboration, transparency, and shared knowledge and resources – to help feed humanity, increase equity, support self-reliance and foster healthy ecosystems.

http://www.ourstolenfuture.org/Industry/2006/2006-1103hardelletal.html this is the article on Our Stolen Future's Site about Richard Doll's dealings with Monsanto.

www.EnvironmentalHealthNews.org a not-for-profit organization founded in 2002 to help increase public understanding of emerging scientific links between environmental exposures and human health.

Farming and GMO sites

www.gmwatch.org GM Watch is an independent organisation that seeks to counter the enormous corporate political power and propaganda of the biotech industry and its supporters.

www.bangmfood.org A project established by GMWatch with guidance from scientists and other experts on genetic modification, food and farming.

http://www.i-sis.org.uk/list.php Institute of Science in SocietyOpen Letter from World Scientists to All Governments Concerning Genetically Modified Organisms (GMOs)- Signed by 828 scientists from 84 different countries. A call for the immediate suspension of all environmental releases of GM crops and products and more.This site also has The Independent Science Panel on GM Final Report – Four page summary of the report: http://www.i-sis.org.uk/ispr-summary.php

http://www.seedsofdeception.com/ Jeffrey Smith's site about Genetically engineered food.

http://responsibletechnology.org/ Site on GM Science

www.fooddemocracynow.org Food Democracy / Farming

http://tv.naturalnews.com/v.asp?v=E9B36B60EF3E646E65735F3E35D700C9 Cartoon on GMOs

http://www.responsibletechnology.org/ Founded by Jeffrey Smith GMO Author

http://scoopwithmysoup.com/about-me/ A mother's experience with GMOs

http://sustainablepulse.com/ A GMO information website.

http://gmoaction.org/about-us/ A loose international coalition of citizens concerned about GMOs.

http://www.gmfreecymru.org.uk/index.htm A community pressure group campaigning to keep Wales free of genetically-modified crops

http://www.biointegrity.org/ Preserving the Safety of Our Food, the Health of Our Environment, and the Harmony of Our Relationship with Nature

http://www.whatsonmyfood.org/index.jsp *What's On My Food?* is a searchable database designed to make the public problem of pesticide exposure visible and more understandable.

www.goodfoodgoodfarming.eu Good food good farming campaign

http://www.arc2020.eu/front/ ARC2020 is a multi-stakeholder platform of over 150 civil society networks and organisations within 22 EU Member States all pushing for a REAL REFORM of the EU's Common Agricultural Policy.

FURTHER RESOURCES

Radiation Information Sites

http://www.ratical.com/ rat haus reality press, dedicated to promulgating and promoting life-nurturing activities and awareness. This site has a tremendous resource of Nuclear information, Including "Chernobyl 25 years on" and Gofman & Tamplin's book "Poisoned Power" it also has Gofman's book "Radiation from Medical Procedures" all online.

http://fukushima-diary.com Fukushima Diary, Alternative News Source

http://www.beyondnuclear.org/ General information site on nuclear energy

www.ccnr.org. Canadian Coalition for Nuclear Responsibility.

http://www.nuclearreader.info Nuclear information site

http://www.x-raysandhealth.org/ Medical X-ray information site

http://www.energyfair.org.uk/financial-risks Gives the Financial risks of Nuclear Power.

http://www.naav.com/html/links.htm National Association of Atomic Veterans, Inc.

http://www.euradcom.org/ European Committee on Radiation Risk

http://www.llrc.org/ Low Level Radiation Campaign

http://www.sgiquarterly.org A Buddhist Forum for Peace. Some useful articles on nuclear issues.

http://www.lbl.gov/abc/Basic.html#Half information site on nuclear science, half-lives etc.

PR, Advertising & General Information Sites

http://www.spinwatch.org/ A UK-based charity: Spinwatch investigates the way that the public relations (PR) industry and corporate and government propaganda distort public debate and undermine democracy.

http://www.commercialalert.org/ Public Citizen's Commercial Alert: Commercial Alert's mission is to keep the commercial culture within its proper sphere, and to prevent it from exploiting children and subverting the higher values of family, community, environmental integrity and democracy.

http://concernforhealth.org/ The International Institute of Concern for Public Health is a Canadian-based non-profit organization dedicated to helping communities assess and improve their environmental health status. The IICPH alerts and informs the public of the health hazards of pesticides, nuclear industries and other commercial, military, and industrial products.

http://www.sgiquarterly.org A Buddhist Forum For Peace. Some useful articles on Nuclear Issues.

http://www.naturalnews.com/UK.html a source of great articles. The Natural News Network is a non-profit collection of public education websites covering topics that empower individuals to make positive changes in their health, environmental sensitivity, consumer choices and informed scepticism.

http://www.eea.europa.eu/ European Environment Agency – Some useful articles and reports.

http://www.mindfully.org/ A resource site for greater awareness

www.naturalnews.com A general information site.

http://candobetter.net/about Site to encourage ordinary people to engage themselves with the political process

http://www.opensecrets.org An independent, nonpartisan, nonprofit organization, the Center for Responsive Politics does not advocate for specific legislation or regulations–with one important exception: Transparency.

www.projectcensored.org Reports news that the mainstream press ignores.

http://www.naturalpedia.com The NaturalNews Network is a non-profit collection of public education websites.

http://www.takejusticeback.com/ Powerful corporations have spent billions to evade accountability when they hurt and kill Americans. Take Justice Back is a public education and grassroots campaign to restore accountability, promote safety and ensure Americans have access to justice.

www.citizen.org Public Citizen -consumer watchdog site.

http://www.bravenewfilms.org/ Free films that you may not see on your TV

http://www.uspirg.org/page/usp/about-us
U.S. PIRG, the federation of state Public Interest Research Groups (PIRGs), a public information site on issues, such as product safety, public health, political corruption, tax and budget reform and consumer protection, where these interests stand in the way of reform and progress.

http://www.nrdc.org/media/pressreleases/060118.asp Natural Resources Defense Council.

http://www.sourcewatch.org The Centre for Media Democracy. A great site, gives the lowdown on PR companies such as Ketchum: http://www.sourcewatch.org/index.php?title=Ketchum

See their page on the Atrazine papers recently unsealed from a court hearing:
http://www.sourcewatch.org/index.php?title=Portal:Atrazine_Exposed

http://globalleadnet.com/47/the-international-action-plan Global Lead Network.

http://www.tobaccoarchives.com/doc.html Tobacco Archives for loads of stuff.

http://www.tobaccofreekids.org A large information site on tobacco issues.

http://www.legacyforhealth.org/?o=4075# American Legacy Foundation tobacco education site.

FURTHER RESOURCES

http://www.rachel.org/ Archive up to Feb 2009 of over 1000 issues by The Environmental Research Foundation.

http://anh-europe.org/ Alliance for Natural health. Alliance for Natural Health, Founded by Dr Robert Verkerk, Codex information site.

www.iahf.com International Advocates for Health Freedom. Founded by John Hammell Codex information site

http://www.slingshotpublications.com/ Martin Walker's Site, author of "Dirty Medicine" many articles on alternative issues.

http://www.ecomed.org.uk/ British Society for Ecological Medicine. The principal aim of the Society is to promote the study and good practice of allergy, environmental and nutritional medicine, for the benefit of the public.

www.credence.org Philip Day's Health information and publication site.

www.vaccinenation.net Gary Null's website on vaccination

Appendix on Radiation

SI Units and Prefixes

The International System of Units has been given official status and recommended for universal use by the General Conference on Weights and Measures.

Radiation Measurements

	Radioactivity	Absorbed Dose	Dose Equivalent	Exposure
Common Units	curie (Ci)	rad	rem	roentgen (R)
SI Units	becquerel (Bq)	gray (Gy)	sievert (Sv)	Coulomb kilogram (C/kg)

Multiple	Prefix	Symbol
10^{12}	tera	T
10^{9}	giga	G
10^{6}	mega	M
10^{3}	kilo	k
10^{-2}	centi	c
10^{-3}	milli	m
10^{-6}	micro	μ
10^{-9}	nano	N
10^{-9}	pico	p

Conversion Factors

To convert from	To	Multiply by
Curies (Ci)	becquerels (Bq)	3.7×10^{10}
millicuries (mCi)	megabecquerels (MBq)	37
microcuries (μCi)	megabecquerels (MBq)	0.037
millirads (mrad)	milligrays (mGy)	0.01
millirems (mrem)	microsieverts (μSv)	10
milliroentgens (mR)	microcoulombs/kilogram (μC/kg)	0.258
becquerels (Bq)	curies (Ci)	2.7×10^{-11}
megabecquerels (MBq)	millicuries (mCi)	0.027
megabecquerels (MBq)	microcuries (μCi)	27
milligrays (mGy)	millirads (mrad)	100
microsieverts (μSv)	millrems (mrem)	0.1
microcoulombs/kilogram (μC/kg)	milliroentgens (mR)	3.88

References

[1] Honor Whiteman, "1 in 2 people will develop cancer in their lifetime", *Medical News Today,* Weds 4th Feb, 2014. https://www.medicalnewstoday.com/articles/288916.php

[2] Health Expenditures, National Center for Health Statistics. https://www.cdc.gov/nchs/fastats/health-expenditures.htm

[3] Quentin D. Young, M.D.President, American Public Health Association, quoted in The Politics of Cancer Revisited, Samuel S. Epstein, M.D. East Ridge Press, New York, 1998.

[4] http://info.cancerresearchuk.org/cancerstats/keyfacts/Allcancerscombined/

[5] ibid.

[6] Moss, Ralph W, *The Cancer Industry* 1989

[7] Ibid

[8] Griffin, Edward G, *World Without Cancer, The Story of Vitamin B17*

[9] Collins English Dictionary, 21st Century Edition

[10] Griffin, Edward G, *World Without Cancer, The Story of Vitamin B17*

[11] ibid.

[12] http://info.cancerresearchuk.org/news/archive/cancernews/2008-05-30-oestrogen-signalling-pathways-are-important-in-about-half-of-all-prostate-cancers

[13] http://en.wikipedia.org/wiki/Estradiol - cite_ref-9 Collins, P; Rosano, GM; Sarrel, PM; Ulrich, L; Adamopoulos, S; Beale, CM; McNeill, JG; Poole-Wilson, PA (1995). "17 beta-Estradiol attenuates acetylcholine-induced coronary arterial constriction in women but not men with coronary heart disease.". *Circulation* **92** (1): 24–30

[14] http://www.fda.gov/Drugs/DrugSafety/InformationbyDrugClass/ucm135339.htm

[15] Scott Peskin, Brian, B.S.E.E., M.I.T & Habib Amid, M.D., F.A.A.P., F.A.C.E., The Hidden Story of Cancer.

[16] ibid

[17] Finnegan, John, *The Facts About Fats*

[18] Enig, Mary G, Ph.D. *Know Your Fats.* Bethesda Press 2000

[19] Enig, Mary G, Ph.D. *Know Your Fats.* 2000

[20] Ibid.

[21] Joan M Lappe, Dianne Travers-Gustafson, K Michael Davies, Robert R Recker, & Robert P Heaney. Vitamin D and calcium supplementation reduces cancer risk: results of a randomized trial. *Am J Clin Nutr June 2007 vol. 85 no. 6 1586-159. See also:*
http://www.grassrootshealth.net/media/download/dip_with_numbers_8-24-12.pdf
Further: http://articles.mercola.com/sites/articles/archive/2013/05/12/vitamin-d-may-prevent-breastcancer.aspx?e_cid=20130512IRG_SNL_Art_1&utm_source=snl&utm_medium=email&utm_content=art1&utm_campaign=20130512IRG

[22] 1900-1970, U.S. Public Health Service, *Vital Statistics of the United States,* annual, Vol. I.

[23] http://www.preventcancer.com/about/epstein.htm

[24] Epstein, Samuel S, M.D., *The Politics of Cancer Revisited.*

[25] http://www.preventcancer.com/press/pdfs/Stop_Cancer_Book.pdf

[26] Ibid.

[27] Richard Doll and Richard Peto, *The Causes of Cancer*. Oxford University Press (Jan 1982).

[28] *The Stop Cancer Before It Starts Campaign: How to Win the Losing War Against Cancer.* 2003 by Samuel S. Epstein, M. D.
http://www.preventcancer.com/press/pdfs/Stop_Cancer_Book.pdf

[29] Landrigan, P. Commentary: Environmental Disease: A Preventable Epidemic. *Am. J. Pub. Health* 82 (7):941-943, 1992.

[30] John W. Gofman M.D., Arthur R. Tamplin, Ph.D., *Poisoned Power—The Case Against Nuclear Power Plants Before and After Three Mile Island,* Rodale Press 1980.

[31] John W. Gofman M.D., *Radiation Induced Cancer from Low-Dose Exposure: An Independent Analysis.* Committee for Nuclear Responsibility, 1990.

[32] John W. Gofman M.D., *Radiation from Medical Procedures in the Pathogenesis of Cancer and Ischemic Heart Disease: Dose—Response Studies with Physicians per 100,000 Population.* 1999

[33] 2010 Annual Report, President's Cancer Panel. *Reducing Environmental Risk.* *http://deainfo.nci.nih.gov/advisory/pcp/annualReports/*

[34] Taubes, Gary. *The Diet Delusion.* Vermillion, 2007

[35] Ibid

[36] Ibid

REFERENCES

[37] Kendrick, Dr. Malcolm. *The Great Cholesterol Con*. John Blake 2007

[38] Ibid.

[39] LANCET. 1965 Aug 7;2(7406):259–261. [PubMed]; Paul O, MacMillan A, McKean H ...

[40] Dayton S D, and *others* "A controlled Clinical Trial of a Diet High in Unsaturated Fat in Preventing Complications of Atherosclerosis." *Circulation,* July: 40(1): II.1.62, 1969.

[41] Taubes, Gary. *The Diet Delusion*. 2007

[42] Ibid.

[43] Jacobs et al: Report on the Conference of Low Blood Cholesterol: Mortality Associations. *Circulation* Vol 86 No3 Sept 1992

[44] Ulmer H, Kelleher C, Diem G, Prospective Follow up of 14965 Women & Men of Cholesterol & Other Risk Factors Related to Cardiovascular & All Cause Mortality. *J. Women's Health* 2004 Jan-Feb; 13(1): 41-53

[45] Kendrick, Dr. Malcolm, *The Great Cholesterol Con*. 2007

[46] Enig, Mary G, Ph.D., *Know Your Fats*. 2000

[47] Taubes, Gary. *The Diet Delusion*. 2007

[48] Enig, Mary G, Ph.D., *Know Your Fats*. 2000

[49] Taubes, Gary. *The Diet Delusion*. 2007

[50] Ibid.

[51] Taubes, Gary. *The Diet Delusion*. 2007

[52] Kendrick, Dr. Malcolm, *The Great Cholesterol Con*. 2007

[53] Taubes, Gary. *The Diet Delusion*. 2007

[54] http://www.ktl.fi/monica/public/intrep.htm

[55] http://www.framinghamheartstudy.org/

[56] Ibid

[57] Enig, Mary G, Ph.D., *Know Your Fats*. 2000 p85

[58] Ravnskov, Uffe, MD, PhD, *Fat and Cholesterol are Good For You!* GB Publishing 2009.

[59] Vredevoe DL and others, *Am J Cardiol* 82, 223-8, 1998.

[60] Bhakdi S, Tranum-Jensen J, Utermann G, Füssle R. Binding and partial inactivation of Staphylococcus aureus a-toxin by human plasma low density lipoprotein. J Biol Chem 1983; 258:5899-904.

[61] Netea NG and others, *J Clin Invest* 97, 1366-72, 1996

[62] Pesonen M and others, *Clin Exp Allergy* 2007

[63] Neil HAW and others, *Atherosclerosis* 179, 293-7, 2005.

[64] Ravnskov, Uffe, MD, PhD, *Fat and Cholesterol are Good For You!* 2009.

[65] Ravnskov, Uffe, MD, PhD, 2000

[66] The Coronary Drug Project Research Group. *Circulation 47,suppl. 1, 1-50, 1973*

[67] Ravnskov, Uffe, MD, PhD, 2000.

[68] The primary results from the WHO study can be found in *Br Heart J* 40, 1069-1118, 1978. Follow up results can be found in *Lancet* 2, 379-85, 1980.

[69] Frick M H and others, *Ann Med* 25, 41-45, 1993.

[70] Frick M H and others, 317, 1237-45, 1987.

[71] Duane Graveline M.D., *The Statin Damage Crisis,* 2009.

[72] Philips PS and others, *Ann Intern Med,* 137, 581-5, 2002

[73] Draeger a. and others, *J Pathol* 210, 94-102, 2006.

[74] Ravnskov, Uffe, MD, PhD, 2000.

[75] Pfrieger F. Brain researcher discovers bright side of ill-famed molecule. *Science*, 9 November, 2001.

[76] Muldoon M.F. and others. Effects of Lovestatin on cognitive functioning and psychological wellbeing. *Am J Med* 2000 May, : 108(7) 538-460.

[77] Duane Graveline M.D., *The Statin Damage Crisis,* 2009.

[78] Newman TB, Hulley SB, *JAMA,* 275, 55-60, 1996

[79] Ravnskov, Uffe, MD, PhD, 2000. The *4S* trial was the Scandinavian Simvastatin Survival Study Group, *Lancet* 344, 1383-9, 1994. The HPS trial was the MRC/BHF Heart Protection Study, *Lancet* 360: 7-22, 2002.

REFERENCES

[80] Ibid. The *PROSPER* Study see Shepherd J Blauw GJ, Murphy MB et al, Pravastatin in elderly individuals at risk of vascular disease (PROSPER): a randomised controlled trial, *Lancet* 360 (9346): 1623-30.

[81] Iwata H nad others, *Cancer Science* 97, 133-8, 2006

[82] Shepherd J, Cobbe SM, Ford I, et al. (1995) Prevention of coronary heart disease with prevastatin in men with hypercholesterolemia, *New England Journal Of Medicine*, 333:1301-7

[83] **www.spacedoc.net**

[84] Stamler J and others, *JAMA* 256, 2823-8, 1986.

[85] Krumholz HM and others, *JAMA* 257, 2176-80, 1987 as cited in Ravnskov, Uffe, MD, PhD, 2000.

[86] Gotto A M and others, Circulation 81, 1721-33, 1990.

[87] Kendrick, Dr. Malcolm, *The Great Cholesterol Con.* 2007. For the data on birth defects see: *New Eng J Med*, April 2004, Central nervous system and limb anomalies in case reports of first trimester statin exposure.

[88] Ibid.

[89] Agnell M, The truth about drug companies. How they deceive us and what to do about it. Random House, NY, 2004

[90] McCully, Kilmer, M.D., *The Heart Revolution.* Harper Collins 1999

[91] McCully, KS, Chemical pathology of homocysteine. IV. Excitotoxicity, oxidative stress, endothelial dysfunction, and inflammation. **Ann Clin Lab Sci.** 2009 Summer;39(3):219-32

[92] Linus Pauling PhD, Mattias Rath M.D., Lipoprotein(a) is a surrogate for ascorbate, *Proc. Nati. Acad. Sci. USA Vol. 87, pp. 6204-6207, August 1990*

[93] Matthias Rath M.D. *Why Animals Don't Get Heart Attacks – But People Do.* MP publishing 2000.

[94] Stephen T Sinatra, M.D., F.A.C.C. *The Sinatra Solution, Metabolic Cardiology*, Basic Health Publications Inc, 2011.

[95] Sinatra 2011

[96] Ibid.

[97] Joel M. Kauffman, PhD. *Malignant Medical Myths,* Infinity Publishing 2006.

[98] Smith, L. F., et al, *International Journal of Cardiology* 1986: 12:175-180.

[99] Rasmussen, H. Sandvod, et al, *Lancet* 1986: Feb 1, pp 234-236. See Also Parsons, R.S., et al, *Medical Proceedings* 1959; 5:487.

[100] Mamdani M, Juurlink D.N., Lee D.S., et al. Cyclo-oxygenase-2 inhibitors versus non-selective non-steroidal anti-inflammatory drugs and congestive heart failure outcomes in elderly patients: a population based study. *Lancet* 363: 1751-1756.

[101] Fored CM, Ejerblad EE, Lindblad P, et al. (2001). Acetaminophen, Aspirin, and chronic Renal Failure. *New England Journal of Medicine,* 345(25): 1801-1808.

[102] Pelton R, LaValle JB, (200). *The Nutritional Cost of Prescription Drugs,* Englewood, CO: Perspective/Morton, PHS89: Steeing Committee of the Physicians Health Study Research Group (1989). *New England Journal of Medicine* 321: 129-135.

[103] Stampfer MJ, et al, (1993). Vitamin E Consumption and the Risk of Coronary Disease in Women, *The New England Journal Of Medicine,* 328, 1444-92.

[104] Neustat J, Pizzorno J, (2005). Vitamin E and all cause mortality, *Integrative Medicine.* 4(1): 14-17.

[105] Joel M. Kauffman, PhD. *Malignant Medical Myths,* Infinity Publishing 2006.

[106] Stephen S Sinatra, M.D., James C Roberts, M.D. *Reverse Heart Disease Now,* Jiohn Wiley 2007.

[107] Cranton EM, *A textbook on EDTA Chelation Therapy,* 2nd Ed. Charlottesville, VA: Hampton Roads Publ. Co. 2001.

[108] Karppanen H et al, Minerals, coronary heart disease and sudden coronary heart death. *Adv Cardiol,* vol 25, pp 9 – 24, 1978.

Eisenberg MJ, Magnesium deficiency and sudden death. *Amer Heart J, vol 124, no 2 pp. 544 - 549, 1992.*

Altura BM, Sudden-death ischemic heart disease and dietary magnesium intake: is the target site coronary vascular smooth muscle? *Med Hypotheses,* vol 5, no. 8, pp. 843 -848, 1979.

Turlplaty PD, Altura BM, Magnesium deficiency produces spasms of coronary arteries: relationship to etiology of sudden death ischemic heart disease, *Science,* vol. 208, no 4440, pp. 198 – 200, 1980.

REFERENCES

[109] Teo KK, et al., Effects of intravenous magnesium in suspected acute myocardial infarction: overview of randomised trials. *Brit Med J,* vol. 303 pp. 1499 – 1503, 1991.
Teo Kk, Yusuf S, Role of magnesium in reducing mortality in acute myocardial infarction. A review of the evidence, *Drugs,* vol. 46, pp. 347 – 359, 1993.

[110]John W. Gofgman, M.D., Ph.D., *Radiation from Medical Procedures in the Pathogenesis of Cancer and Ischemic Heart Disease,* Committee for Nuclear Responsibility, 1999.
[111] Dr John Gofman Obituary, UC Berkeley. By Robert Sanders, Media Relations 4 September 2007. http://www.berkeley.edu/news/media/releases/2007/09/04_GofmanObit.shtml
[112] Weston A. Price, *Nutrition and Physical Degeneration,* Benediction Classics, Oxford, 2010

[113] Dufty, William. *Sugar Blues,* Warner Books 1975
[114] Ibid.
[115] Taubes, Gary. *The Diet Delusion*, Vermilion, London. 2007.
[116] Dufty, William. *Sugar Blues,* Warner Books. New York. 1975.
[117] Ibid
[118] Dufty, William. *Sugar Blues,,* Warner Books. New York 1975
[119] Taubes, Gary. *The Diet Delusion,* Vermilion, London.2007
[120] Doll R, Peto R. Mortality in relation to smoking: 20 years' observations on male British doctors. *Br Med J.* 1976 Dec 25;2(6051):1525-36
 See also: Armstrong B, Doll R, . Environmental factors and cancer incidence and mortality in different countries, with special reference to dietary practices. .*Int J Cancer.* 1975 Apr 15;15(4):617-31.

[121] Ibid.
[122] Weston Price, *Nutrition and Physical Degeneration.* Benediction Classics, Oxford, 2010.
[123] Ibid.
[124] See Price-Pottinger foundation: http://www.ppnf.org/catalog/ppnf/index.htm and also : http://www.westonaprice.org/

[125] Tim Lang & Michael Heasman, *Food Wars—The Global Battle for Mouths and Markets,* Earthscan, London, 2004.

[126] http://www.cdc.gov/obesity/childhood/data.html

[127] Early Identification of Mexican American children who are at risk of becoming Obese, *Int J Obes Relat Metab Disord.* 1999 Aug;23(8):823-9.

[128] NHS, *Statistics on Obesity, Physical Activity and Diet*: England, Feb 24, 2011

[129] http://www.cspinet.org/new/pdf/sdtaxes_obesity_factsheet.pdf

[130] The InterAct Consortium 'Consumption of sweet beverages and type 2 diabetes incidence in European adults: results from EPIC-InterAct' Diabetologia 2013. DOI 10.1007/s00125-013-2899-8 See also: Jo Wiley ."Diabetes Risk in Daily Fizzy Drink", *Daily Express.* Thursday April 25th 2013.

[131] Taubes, Gary. *The Diet Delusion.* Vermilion, London. 2007

[132] Ibid.

[133] Krauss RM, Lindgren FT, Ray RM. Interrelationships among subgroups of serum lipoproteins in normal human subjects. *Clin Chim Acta.* 1980 Jul 1;104(3):275-90.

[134] Sniderman A, Shapiro S, Marpole D, Skinner B, Teng B, Kwiterovich PO Jr. Association of coronary atherosclerosis with hyperapobetalipoproteinemia [increased protein but normal cholesterol levels in human plasma low density (beta) lipoproteins].
Proc Natl Acad Sci U S A. 1980 Jan;77(1):604-8.

[135] Taubes, Gary. *The Diet Delusion.* Vermilion, London. 2007

[136] Reaven GM. Banting lecture 1988. Role of insulin resistance in human disease. *Diabetes* 1988;37:1595-607. PMID 3056758.

[137] Taubes, Gary. *The Diet Delusion* . Vermilion, London. 2007

[138] http://www.diabetes.org.uk/Guide-to-diabetes/Food_and_recipes/The-Glycaemic-Index/

[139] http://www.glycemicindex.com

[140] Taubes, Gary. *The Diet Delusion.* Vermilion, London. 2007

[141] Ibid

[142] Dr David Perlmutter, *Grain Brain,* Hodder & Stoughton Ltd, London, 2014.

[143] http://content.onlinejacc.org/cgi/content/full/43/5/731

[144] Colin T Campbell, *The China Study,* BenBella Books, Dallas, 2004

REFERENCES

[145] Colin T Campbell, *The Low-Carb Fraud.* BenBella Books, Dallas, 2014

[146] John A McDougall, MD. *The Starch Solution.* Rodale 2012.

[147] Caldwell B Esselstyn, Jr., M.D. *Prevent and Reverse Heart Disease.* Penguin 2008. Dean Ornish, M.D. *The Spectrum.* Ballantine Books 2007.

[148] Geoffrey Cannon, *The Politics of Food,* Century Hutchinson Ltd., London, 1989.

[149] Andrew Hough. Britain facing food crisis as world's soil 'vanishes in 60 years'. *The Telegraph.* 03 Feb 2010.

[150] Tansey, G , Worsley, T, *The Food System.* Earthscan Publications Ltd, London. 1995.

[151] http://www.nao.org.uk/publications/0708/financial_management_in_the_eu.aspx

[152] http://www.pan-uk.org/agriculture/test

[153] Carson, Rachel, *Silent Spring.* Houghton Mifflin, 1962.

[154] Harvey, Graham, *The Killing of the Countryside.* Jonathan Cape, London, 1997.

[155] Ibid.

[156] Tansey, G , Worsley, T, *The Food System.* Earthscan Publications Ltd, London. 1995.

[157] Harvey, Graham, *The Killing of the Countryside.* Jonathan Cape, London, 1997

[158] Ib id.

[159] Schlosser, Eric, *Fast Food Nation.*

[160] Ibid

[161] Lawrence, Felicity, *Not On The Label.* Penguin Books, 2004

[162] Ibid.

[163] Schlosser, Eric, *Fast Food Nation.*

[164] http://www.viva.org.uk/pdfs/egg_factsheet.pdf

[165] http://www.viva.org.uk/campaigns/chickens/broilerfactsheet.htm

[166] http://www.food.gov.uk/multimedia/pdfs/chickenfoodchain

[167] Lawrence, Felicity, *Not On The Label.* Penguin Books, 2004

[168] http://www.medkb.com/Uwe/Forum.aspx/nutrition/3452/Toxic-Eggs-Poultry-UK

[169] http://www.soilassociation.org/LinkClick.aspx?fileticket=%2bmWBoFr348s%3d&tabid=385

[170] http://www.soilassociation.org/Whyorganic/Welfareandwildlife/Antibiotics/tabid/350/Default.aspx

[171] Harvey, Graham, *The Killing of the Countryside.* Jonathan Cape, London, 1997

[172] Michael Pollan, *The Omnivore's Dilema*, Bloomsbury, London, 2007.

[173] Theo Colborn, Dianne Dumanoski & John Peterson Myers. *Our Stolen Future*

[174] Joanna Blythman. *Bad Food Britain,* Fourth Estate, London, 2006.

[175] Felicity Lawrence. *Eat Your Heart Out.* Penguin Books. 2008.

[176] Sunday Telegraph December 3rd 2007

[177] http://www.canceractive.com/cancer-active-page-link.aspx?n=190

[178] Felicity Lawrence. *Eat Your Heart Out* Penguin Books, 2008

[179] Evidence for sugar addiction: Behavioural and neurochemical effects of intermittent, excessive sugar intake, Nicole M. Avena, Pedro Rada, and Bartley G. Hoebel, Neuroscience & Biobehavioral Reviews, Volume 32, Issue 1, 2008, Pages 20-39. See also: Wideman CH, Nadzam GR, Murphy HM.
Implications of an animal model of sugar addiction, withdrawal and relapse for human health.

[180] http://www.ukfg.org.uk/docs/UKFG-Foodinc-Nov03.pdf

[181] Felicity Lawrence. *Eat Your Heart Out* Penguin Books, 2008.

[182] http://en.wikipedia.org/wiki/Sucralose

[183] http://www.bmj.com/content/328/7433/185.1.extract

[184] http://www.fao.org/DOCREP/005/AC911E/AC911E00.HTM See also:
http://www.nationalreviewofmedicine.com/issue/2004_02_15/features06.html

[185] Tansey, G , Worsley, T, *The Food System*. Earthscan Publications Ltd, London. 1995.

[186] Ibid.

[187] Joanna Blythman. *Bad Food Britain.* Fourth Estate, London, 2006.

[188] Lawrence, Felicity, *Not On the Label.* Penguin Books, 2004.

[189] Dibb, Sue, *What the Label Doesn't Tell You.* Thorsons. London 1997

[190] Cohen, Robert, *Milk The Deadly Poison.* Argus Publishing Inc. Eaglewood Cliffs.1998

[191] Ibid.

[192] Sarah Knapton, Science Correspondent *The Telegraph*, Sugar is as dangerous as alcohol and tobacco, warn health experts. *The Telegraph*, 9 Jan 2014

[193] Russell L Blaylock M.D., *Excitotoxins – The Taste That Kills.* Health Press, Santa Fe, 1005.

[194] Starr Hull, Janet, *Sweet Poison, How the World's most popular Artificial Sweetener is Killing Us – My Story*. New Horizon Press Publishers Inc.,U.S. 1999.

[195] http://aspartamesafety.com

REFERENCES

[196] Starr Hull, Janet, *Sweet Poison, How the World's most popular Artificial Sweetener is Killing Us – My Story.* New Horizon Press Publishers Inc.,U.S. 1999.

[197] Ibid.

[198] Willatts P et al. Lancet. 1998 Aug 29;352(9129):688-91, see also LUCAS, A; MORLEY, R; COLE, T J BMJ. 317(7171):1481-1487, November 28, 1998.

[199] Blaylock 2002

[200] The Guardian, Friday 30th, 2005, Felicity Lawrence

[201] Blaylock, Russell L. M.D., *Health and Nutrition Secrets,* Health Press. Albuquerque, 2002.

[202] Dr Erik Millstone. 'Sweet and Sour: the Unanswered Questions about Aspartame'

The Ecologist, Vol. 24, No. 2, March/April 1994, pp. 71-74.

http://exacteditions.theecologist.org/browse/307/308/6239/3/33

[203] Ibid

[204] Bryson, Christopher, *The Fluoride Deception*, 2004.

[205] Roholm, E, K, Fluorine Intoxication: A Clinical-Hygienic Study, London.1937

[206] Yiamouyiannis, Dr. John, *Fluoride, The Aging Factor*, Ohio.1983.

[207] Ibid.

[208] The Case Against Fluoride, Paul Connett PhD, James Beck, MD, PhD, Micklem,H.S. DPhil, 2010, p117.

[209] Bigay,J, Deterre P, Pfister, C, Chabre, M, "Fluoroaluminates Activate Transducin-GDP by Mimicking the GammPhosphate of GTP in Its Binding Site". FEBS letters 191, no2 (1985): 181-85.

See also: Bigay,J, Deterre P, Pfister, C, Chabre, M, "Fluoride Complexes of Aluminium or Beryllium Act on G-Protiens as Reversibly Bound Analogues of the Gamma Phosphate of GTP," EMBO Journal 6, no.10 (1987): 2907-13.

[210] Paul Connett PhD, James Beck, MD, PhD, Micklem,H.S. DPhil. *The Case Against Fluoride* Chelsea Green Publishing Co. 2010.

[211] Bowman, W.C, Rand, M.J, "Textbook of Pharmacology" Blackwell.1980, 1.29

[212] Emsley, John, et al, "An unexpectedly Strong Hydrogen Bond: Ab Initio Calculations and Spectroscopic Studies of Amide-Fluoride Systems", Journal of The American Chemical Society, vol 103, 1981, pp 24-28

[213] Yiamouyiannis, Dr. John, *Fluoride, The Aging Factor*, Health Action Press .Ohio.1983.

[214] I. Golub et al, "The Effect of Sodium Fluoride on the Rates of Synthesis and Degradation of Bone Collagen in Tissue Culture" Proceedings of The Society for Experimental Biology and Medicine, Vol 129, pp 973-977, 1968.
See also : W.A.Peck et al , "Fluoride Inhibition of Bone Collagen Synthesis", Clinical Research, Vol 13, p 330, 1965.

[215] Kakuya Ishida, "The Effects of Fluoride on Bone Metabolism", Koku Eisei Gakkai Zasshi, Vol 31, no.2, pp 74-78, 1981.
Marain Drozdz et al " Studies on the influence of Fluoride Compounds upon connective tissue Metabolism in Growing rats" Toxilogical European Research, Vol 3, No5, pp 237 – 241, 1981.
A.K .Sushella and Mohan Jha, "Effect of Fluoride Ingestion on Cortical and Cancellous Bone Composition" IRCS Medical Sciences Library Compendium, Vol 9 , No 11, pp1021-1022, 1981.
Y.D.Sharma, " Effect of Sodium Fluoride on Collagen Cross-link Precursors" Toxicological Letters, Vol 10, pp97-100, 1982.
Y.D.Sharma, "Variations in the Metabolism and Maturation of Collagen after Fluoride Ingestion", Biochimica et Biophysica Acta, vol 715 pp137-141, 1982
A.K. Sushella & D Muskerjee, "Fluoride Poisoning and the Effect of Collagen Biosynthesis of Ossoeus and Nonosseous Tissues of the Rabbit", Toxicological European research, Vol 3, No2, pp 99-104, 1981.

[216] Paul Connett Phd, James Beck, MD.PhD, H.S.Micklem, DPhil, "The Case Against Fluoride", 2010.

[217] Brunelle JA, Carlos J, Recent trends in dental caries in US children and the effect of water fluoridation. J Dent Res, 1990;69: 723-7.

[218] Burt BA, et al, "The effects of a break in water fluoridation on the development of dental caries   and fluorosis". J Dent Res, 2000; 79: 761-9.

[219] Griffin SO et al, Esthetically objectionable fluorosis attributable to water fluoridation. Commun Dent Oral Epidemiol, 2002; 30: 199-209

[220] Beltran-Aguilar ED et al, Prevalence and trends in enamel fluorosis in the United States from the 1930s to the 1980s. J Am Dent assoc, 2002; 133: 157.

[221] Christopher Bryson, "The Fluoride deception", 2004.

[222] Ibid.

REFERENCES

223 Varner et al, "Chronic Administration of Aluminum-Fluoride or Sodium-Fluoride to Rats in Drinking Water: Alterations in Neuronal and Cerebrovascular Integrity," *Brain Research* 784, no 1-2 (1998): 284-98.

224 This section of the text was copied from chapter 7 of its report cited in "The Case Against Fluoride", Connett et al. http:/books.nap.edu/openbook.php?record_id=11571

225 Paul Connett Phd, James Beck, MD.PhD, H.S.Micklem, DPhil, "The Case Against Fluoride", 2010.

226 http://poisonfluoride.com/pfpc/html/thyroid_history.html

227 Dean Murphy DDS, *The Devil's Poison—How fluoride is killing you.* Trafford Publishing, 2008.

228 J. Caffey, "On Fibrous Defects in Cortical Walls: Their Radiological Appearance, Structure, Prevalence, Natural Course and Diagnostic Significance", *Advances in Pediatrics, 1955.*

229 M.T. Alarcón-Herrera, I.R. Martin-Dominguez, R. Trejo-Vázquez, et al, "Well Water Fluoride, Dental Fluorosis, Bone Fractures in the Guardiana Valley of Mexico, " *Fluoride 34, no.2 (2001): 139-49.* www.fluoride-journal.com/01-34-2/342-139.pdf.

230 Paul Connett Phd, James Beck, MD.PhD, H.S.Micklem, DPhil, "The Case Against Fluoride", 2010.

231 Ibid.

232 Public Health Investigation of Epidemiological data on Disease and Mortality in Ireland related to Water Fluoridation and Fluoride Exposure--Key findings and observations on Fluoride by the U.S National Research Council examined within the context of a comparison of population health and disease burdens between Fluoridated Republic of Ireland and Non-Fluoridated Northern Ireland and Europe. Report for: the Government of Ireland, the European Commission, and World Health Organisation. Prepared By Declan Waugh BSc. CEnv. MCIWEM. MIEMA. MCIWM February 2013

233 Following are a number of sites that have further information: www.nofluoride.com www.fluoridation.com http://rense.com/health/fluoride1.html http://poisonfluoride.com/pfpc/

234 Xenobiotic Compounds in Adipose Tissue of U.S. Citizens. US EPA National Adipose Tissue Survey 1982

235 Jacobson JL, Humphrey HE, Jacobson SW, et al. *Am J Public Health* 1989; 79: 1401-1404.

[236] Gunderson EL. FDA Total Diet Survey, April 1982-April 1986, Dietary intakes of pesticides, selected elements and other chemicals. Food and Drug Administration, Division of Contaminants Chemistry, Washington, DC 20204.

[237] EPA Atrazine public docket 25th April,1985.

[238] IARC Working Group on the Evaluation of Carcinogenic Risks to Humans, "Occupational Exposures in Insecticide Application, and some Pesticides: Atrazine," IARC monographs on the Evaluation of Carcinogenic Risks to Humans, vol 53 (Lyon, France: World Health Organisation, 1991): 449

[239] H Leon Bradlow et al., "Effects of Pesticides on the Ratio of 16 alpha/2-Hyroxyesterone: A Biologic Marker Of Breast Cancer Risk," Environmental Health Perspectives 103, sup. 7 October 1995: 147-50.

[240] EPA atrazine public docket, 11th January 1988.

[241] Laurie Moyer and Joel Cross, Pesticide Monitoring: Illinois EPA's Summary of Results 1985-1989, (n.p.:Illinois EPA 1990), 17.

[242] D.A.Goolsby et al., "Occurrence of Herbicides and Metabolites in Surface Water, Ground Water, and Rainwater in the Midwestern Unite States," Proceedings, 1995 Annual Conference: Water Research, American Water Works Association, 18-22 June 1995, 588.

[243] http://www.iwatchnews.org/2011/10/03/6858/many-private-wells-across-us-are-contaminated-arsenic-and-other-elements This article is on the web site for The Center For Public Integrity.

[244] Report of the Working Party on Pesticide Residues 1988-89 HMSO 1990

[245] Consumer Risk assessment of Insecticide Residues in Carrots, Pesticides Safety Directorate, 1995

[246] SAFE Alliance, 1992, cited in Peter Beaumont, Pesticides, Policies and People: a guide to the Issues, The Pesticides Trust, 1993.

[247] Dr Margaret Sanborn et al. "Ontario College of Family Physicians Pesticide Report".(April, 2004) http://www.ocfp.on.ca/docs/pesticides-paper/pesticides-paper.pdf

[248] Fred Pearce & Debora Mackenzie, "It's raining pesticides; The water falling from our skies is unfit to drink," New Scientist. April 3, 1999, pg. 23

REFERENCES

[249] Emmanouil Charizopoulos and Euphemia Papadopoulou-Mourkidou, "Occurrence of Pesticides in Rain of the Axios River Basin,Greece," *Environmental Science & Technology, ES&T]* Vol. 33, No.14 (July 15, 1999), pgs. 2363-2368.

[250] 2010 Annual Report, Presidents Cancer Panel. U.S. Department of Health and Human Services.

[251] The Fourth National Report on Human Exposure to Environmental Chemicals. Centers For Disease Control and Prevention. Available at: http://www.cdc.gov/exposurereport/

[252] Theo Colburn, Dianne Dumanoski, and John Peterson Myers, *Our Stolen Future,* Dutton Books, New York, 1996.

[253] Carol Van Strum, *A Bitter Fog,* The Sierra Club, 1983.

[254] Ibid

[255] *Toxic Deception, How the chemical industry manipulates science, bends the law and endangers your health,* Dan Fagin, Marianne Lavelle and the Center For Public Integrity, Common Courage Press, Maine 1999.

[256] William D Kerns et al., "Carcinogenicity of Formaldehyde in Rats and Mice After long-Term Inhalation Exposure," *Cancer Research* 43(September 1983): 4382
James A Swenberg et al., "Induction of Squamous Cell Carcinomas of the rat nasal cavity by Inhalation Exposure to Formaldehyde Vapor," *Cancer Research* 40 (September 1980):3398-402

[257] *Toxic Deception, How the chemical industry manipulates science, bends the law and endangers your health,* Dan Fagin, Marianne Lavelle and the Center For Public Integrity, Common Courage Press, Maine 1999.

[258] Ruder AM, Ward EM, Brown DP, "Cancer Mortality in Female and Male Dry-Cleaning Workers " *Journal of Occupational Medicine* Aug 1994 36 (8): 867-74.

[259] Ann Aschengrau et al., "Cancer Risk and Tetrachloroethylene-Contaminated Drinking Water in Massachusetts," *ASrchives of Environmental Health* 48, no5 (September/October 1993): 284-92.

[260] *Toxic Deception, How the chemical industry manipulates science, bends the law and endangers your health,* Dan Fagin, Marianne Lavelle and the Center For Public Integrity, Common Courage Press, Maine 1999.

[261] EPA Atrazine public docket, 13 January 1987

262 IARC Working Group on the Evaluation of Carcinogenic Risks to Humans, " Occupational Exposures in Insecticide Application, and some Pesticides: Atrazine," IARC Monographs on the Evaluation of Carcinogenic Risks to Humans, vol 53 (Lyon, France: World Health Organisation, 1990): 449.

263 H. Leon Bradlow et al., " Effects of Pesticides on the Ratio of 16 Alpha/2-Hydroxyesterone: A Biologic Marker of Breast Cancer Risks," *Environmental Health Perspectives* 103, sup. 7 (October1995): 147-50.

264 EPA Atrazine public docket , 11 January 1988

265 *Toxic Deception, How the chemical industry manipulates science, bends the law and endangers your health,* Dan Fagin, Marianne Lavelle and the Center For Public Integrity, Common Courage Press, Maine 1999.

266 Sandra Steingraber PhD, *Living Downstream,*Da Capo Press 2010.

267 Ibid.

268 Ibid.

269 Finalization of Atrazine IRED, and Completion of Tolerance Reassessment and Reregistration Eligibility Process (April 6, 2006) see http://www.epa.gov/oppsrrd1/REDs/atrazine_combined_docs.pdf

270 H. Bradlow et al, " Medical Hypothesis Xenoestrogens as Preventable Causes of Breast Cancer," *Environmental Health Perspectives* 101 (5): 372-77 (993).

271 The North-East and Mid-Atlantic Breast Cancer Study (NE/MA), July 2000 available at: http://epi.grants.cancer.gov/NEMA/Report0700.html?view=plain#partII

272 Mary S Wolff et al., "Blood Levels of Organochlorine Residues and Risk Of Breast Cancer" *Journal of the National Cancer Institute* 1993 Volume 85, Issue8 Pp. 648-652

273 Dr C Charlier, Laboratoire de Toxicologie clinique *Occup Environ Med 2003;60:348-351 doi:10.1136/oem.60.5.348*

274 Engel L S. et al., "Polychlorinated Biphenyl Levels in Peripheral Blood and Non-Hodgkin's Lymphoma. A Report from Three Cohorts." *Cancer Res* 2007; 67(11):5545–52

275 *Toxic Deception, How the chemical industry manipulates science, bends the law and endangers your health,* Dan Fagin, Marianne Lavelle and the Center For Public Integrity, Common Courage Press, Maine 1999.

276 Ibid

REFERENCES

277 Theo Colborn, Dianne Dumanoski & John Peterson Myers, "Our Stolen Future", Penguin Books, New York, 1996.

278 Ibid.

279 Wallace LA, Pellizzari ED, Hartwell TD, et al. Personal exposures, indoor-outdoor relationships, and breath levels of toxic air pollutants measured for 355 persons in New Jersey. EPA 0589. Referenced in Article by Walter J Crinnion, Environmental Medicine, Part 1: The Human Burden of Environmental Toxins and Their Common Health Effects , *Altern Med Rev.*2000: 5 (1): 52-63

280 Gunderson EL. FDA Total Diet Survey, April 1982-April 1986, Dietary intakes of pesticides, selected elements and other chemicals. Food and Drug Administration, Division of Contaminants Chemistry, Washington, DC 20204.

281 Walter J Crinnion, Environmental Medicine, Part 1: The Human Burden of Environmental Toxins and Their Common Health Effects , *Altern Med Rev.*2000: 5 (1): 52-63

282 Alistair Hay, *The Chemical Scythe, Lessons of 2,4,5-T and Dioxin,* Plenum Press, 1982.

283 Ibid

284 Robert Allen, *The Dioxin Wars- Truth and lies about a perfect poison, Pluto Press, London 2004.*

285 Theo Colborn, Dianne Dumanoski & John Peterson Myers, "Our Stolen Future", Penguin Books, New York, 1996.

286 Alistair Hay, *The Chemical Scythe, Lessons of 2,4,5-T and Dioxin,* Plenum Press, 1982.

287 Ibid

288 Robert Allen, *The Dioxin Wars- Truth and lies about a perfect poison, Pluto Press, London 2004.*

289 Sandra Steingraber PhD, *Living Downstream –An Ecologist's Personal Investigation of Cancer and the Environment,* Merloyd Lawrence Book, 2010.

290 Robert Allen, *The Dioxin Wars- Truth and lies about a perfect poison, Pluto Press, London 2004.*

291 Alistair Hay, *The Chemical Scythe, Lessons of 2,4,5-T and Dioxin,* Plenum Press, 1982.

[292] Generations At Risk, Reproductive Health and the Environment, Ted Shettler, M.D., Gina Soloman, M.D., Maria Valenti and Annette Huddle. MIT Press, 1999.

[293] Robert Allen, *The Dioxin Wars- Truth and lies about a perfect poison, Pluto Press, London 2004.*

[294] Alistair Hay, *The Chemical Scythe, Lessons of 2,4,5-T and Dioxin,* Plenum Press, 1982

[295] Thomas Whiteside, *The Pendulum and the Toxic Cloud –The course of dioxin contamination.* Yale University Press 1978.

[296] Thomas Whiteside, *Defoliation- What are out herbicides doing to us?* Ballantine Books, New York, 1970.

[297] Carol Van Strum, *A Bitter Fog,* The Sierra Club, 1983.

[298] Hardell, L., and Sandström, A., 'Case –control study: soft tissue sarcomas and exposure to the phenoxyacetic acids or chlorophenols' *Br J Cancer,* 39: 711 -717, 1979. The follow-up study was: 'Soft tissue sarcomas and exposure to chemical substances: a case reference study' Hardell et al, *Br J Ind Med* 38, 27-33, 1981.

[299] Sandra Steingraber PhD, *Living Downstream –An Ecologist's Personal Investigation of Cancer and the Environment,* Merloyd Lawrence Book, 2010.

[300] Lois Marie Gibbs and the Citizens Clearinghouse for Hazardous Waste. *Dying From Dioxin— A Citizen's Guide to Reclaiming Our Health and Rebuilding Democracy.* South End Press, Boston 1995.

[301] http://en.wikipedia.org/wiki/Fritz_Haber

[302] Robert Allen, *The Dioxin Wars- Truth and lies about a perfect poison, Pluto Press, London 2004.*

[303] Byron J, Richards, *Fight For Your Health, exposing the FDA's betrayal of America.*Truth In Wellness, 2006,

[304] Eric Francis, Sierra Magazine, September/October 1994

[305] Eric Francis," Conspiracy of Silence", *Sierra Magazine,* Sept-Oct 1994

[306] Ibid

REFERENCES

[307] Peter Montague, *Rachel's News* #327 - How We Got Here -- Part 1 The History Of Chlorinated Diphenyl (PCBs), 03-Mar-1993 Published March 3, 1993 available from: http://www.rachel.org/?q=en/node/4120

[308] Eric Francis," Conspiracy of Silence", *Sierra Magazine,* Sept-Oct 1994

[309] Michael Grunwald , "Monsanto Hid Decades Of Pollution, PCBs Drenched Ala. Town, But No One Was Ever Told" Washington Post, Tuesday, January 1, 2002; Page A01

[310] Ibid.

[311] Ibid.

[312] Michael Grunwald , "Monsanto Hid Decades Of Pollution, PCBs Drenched Ala. Town, But No One Was Ever Told" Washington Post, Tuesday, January 1, 2002; Page A01

[313] Eric Francis," Conspiracy of Silence", *Sierra Magazine,* Sept-Oct 1994.

[314] Ibid

[315] Ibid.

[316] Cate Jenkins, "Memo to Raymond Loehr: Newly Revealed Fraud by Monsanto in an Epidemiological Study Used by Epa to Assess Human health Effects from Dioxins," dated February 23, 1990. Jenkins is a chemist with the Waste Characterization Branch (OS 332), Characterization and Assessment Division, U.S. EPA, 401 M St., SW, Washington, DC 20460. Loehr is Chairperson of the Executive Committee of the Science Advisory Board (A-101), Office of the Administrator, U.S. EPA, 401 M St., SW, Washington, DC 20460. The Jenkins memo has attached to it 25 pages of a brief filed in Case No. 5-88-0420, in the Appellate Court of Illinois, Fifth District by attorneys suing Monsanto on behalf of plaintiffs who say they were harmed when a Norfolk and Western railroad tank car derailed, spilling 19,000 gallons of a Monsanto chemical called "ocp- crude" into the community of Sturgeon, Missouri the night of January 10, 1979. Chief attorney for the plaintiffs is Rex Carr, 412 Missouri Avenue, East St. Louis, Il 62201. Further info can be obtained at: Environmental Research Foundation, #171 - Dioxin -- Part 1: Dioxins And Cancer: Fraudulent Studies, 06-Mar-1990 Published March 6, 1990. http://www.rachel.org/?q=en/node/4284
Also see Robert Allen, *The Dioxin Wars- Truth and lies about a perfect poison, Pluto Press, London 2004.*

[317] Robert Allen, *The Dioxin Wars- Truth and lies about a perfect poison, Pluto Press, London 2004.*

[318] Stephanie Wanchinksi, "New Analysis links dioxin to cancer," *NEW SCIENTIST* October 28, 1989, pg. 24

[319] Ibid. For a more in-depth review of these cases see: : Environmental Research Foundation, #171 - Dioxin -- Part 1: Dioxins And Cancer: Fraudulent Studies, 06-Mar-1990 Published March 6, 1990. http://www.rachel.org/?q=en/node/4284

 Also see Robert Allen, *The Dioxin Wars- Truth and lies about a perfect poison, Pluto Press, London 2004.*

[320] Eric Francis," Conspiracy of Silence", *Sierra Magazine,* Sept-Oct 1994

[321] Ibid.

[322] Internal Memorandum summarizing findings of EPA/FDA inspection of IBT labs; and "Memorandum of Telecon Between Walter Hansen, S.I.S., HED-108 & David R Foltz, Supervisor Investigator, Springfield Resident Post." 14 March,1978, 22. I am relying on much of the info on IBT from *Toxic Deception, How the chemical industry manipulates science, bends the law and endangers your health,* Dan Fagin, Marianne Lavelle and the Center For Public Integrity, Common Courage Press, Maine 1999.

[323] *Toxic Deception, How the chemical industry manipulates science, bends the law and endangers your health,* Dan Fagin, Marianne Lavelle and the Center For Public Integrity, Common Courage Press, Maine 1999.

[324] Ibid.

[325] Ibid

[326] Ibid.

[327] 2010 Annual Report- President's Cancer Panel."Reducing Environmental Cancer Risk" U.S. Department of Health and Human Services.

[328] Allan M Brandt, *The Cigarette Century,* Basic Books, New York, 2007, Taken from the inside cover.

[329] Robert N. Proctor "Tobacco and Health" Expert Witness Report Filed on behalf of Plaintiffs in: "The United States of America, Plaintiff, v. Philip Morris, Inc., et al., Defendants," Civil Action No. 99-CV-02496 (GK (Federal case),* re-printed in *The Journal of Philosophy, Science & Law* 4 (March 2004)

REFERENCES

[330] Devra Davis, *The Secret History of the War on Cancer.* Basic Books, 2007, New York.

[331] Robert N. Proctor "Tobacco and Health" Expert Witness Report Filed on behalf of Plaintiffs in: "The United States of America, Plaintiff, v. Philip Morris, Inc., et al., Defendants," Civil Action No. 99-CV-02496 (GK (Federal case),* re-printed in *The Journal of Philosophy, Science & Law* 4 (March 2004).

[332] Ibid.

[333] Devra Davis, *The Secret History of the War on Cancer.* Basic Books, 2007, New York.

[334] Robert N. Proctor "Tobacco and Health" Expert Witness Report Filed on behalf of Plaintiffs in: "The United States of America, Plaintiff, v. Philip Morris, Inc., et al., Defendants," Civil Action No. 99-CV-02496 (GK (Federal case),* re-printed in *The Journal of Philosophy, Science & Law* 4 (March 2004). Proctor reviews the whole German period in this review.

[335] Doll, R, Hill, A, Smoking and carcinoma of the lung: Preliminary report, *BMJ,* 1950: 739-48.

Levin ML, Goldstein H, Gerhardt PR, Cancer and tobacco smoking: A preliminary report, *JAMA,* 1950; 143:336-38.

Schrek R, Baker LA, Ballard GP et al, Tobacco smoking as an etiologic factor in disease. Part 1: Cancer. *Cancer Research,* 1950; 10:49-58.

Wynder EL, Graham EA, Tobacco smoking as a possible etiologic factor in bronchiogenic carcinoma. *JAMA,* 1950; 143:329-36.

Mills CA, Porter MM, Tobacco smoking habits and cancer of the mouth and respiratory system, *Cancer Research,* 1950, 10:539-42.

[336] Richard Kluger, *Ashes To Ashes, America's hundred-year cigarette war, the public health and the unabashed triumph of Philip Morris,* Vintage Books, New York, 1997.

[337] Members of the Planning Committee- Forwarding Memorandum, EDF (Edwin F Dakin) Hill & Knowlton, 1953 available from John W. Hill Papers from the State Historical Society of Wisconsin site allocation: http://www.ttlaonline.com/HKWIS/hksplash.htm

[338] Dec 15 1953. Bert C Goss, Background Material on the Cigarette Industry Client. Hill & Knowlton: http://www.ttlaonline.com/HKWIS/hksplash.htm

[339] Preliminary Recommendations for Cigarette Manufacturers, Dec 24th 1953.Hill & Knowlton. available from John W. Hill Papers from the State Historical Society of Wisconsin site allocation: http://www.ttlaonline.com/HKWIS/hksplash.htm

[340] Stanton A. Glantz, John Slade, Lisa A. Bero, Peter Hanauer, and Deborah E. Barnes, *The Cigarette papers.* University of California Press, 1996 Berkeley, (p2)

[341] Ibid.

[342] David Michaels, *Doubt is Their Product-How industry's assault on science threatens your health.* Oxford University Press, 2008, New York.

[343] Brown and Williamson, *Smoking and Health Proposal,* Brown and Williamson document no. 680561778-1786, 1969. Available from 📖 http://legacy.library.ucsf.edu/tid/nvs40f00

[344] 1964—Smoking and Health: Report of the Advisory Committee to the Surgeon General of the Public Health Service, available on the CDC website at- http://www.cdc.gov/tobacco/data_statistics/sgr/pre_1994/index.htm   All the Surgeon General reports are available from the Centers for Disease Control and Prevention (CDC).

[345] Richard Kluger, *Ashes to Ashes, America's hundred-year cigarette war, public health, and unabashed triumph of Philip Morris.* Vintage Books, New York 1997.

[346] David Kessler, *A Question of Intent, A great American battle with a deadly industry,* Public Affairs, New York, 2001.

[347] Ibid.

[348] Bates no: TIOK0034667/4670. A Meeting in London with Dr Haselbach, 8th, 9th November 1961, Minutes- 15th Nov 1961.Tobacco Institute collection. Alternative no.30108362 Author Sir Charles Ellis. .Available from http://legacy.library.ucsf.edu/tid/diu91f00

[349] From British American Tobacco's website: www.bat.com.

[350] From Reynolds American Inc. website - http://www.reynoldsamerican.com/faq.cfm

[351] The Surgeon General's Report 1988, available on the CDC website at: http://www.cdc.gov/tobacco/data_statistics/sgr/1998/index.htm

[352] 1802.05. Yeaman A. Implications of Battelle Hippo I & II and the Griffith Filter, memo July 17, 1963. Available from - http://legacy.library.ucsf.edu/action/search/basic

[353] Allan M Brandt, *The Cigarette Century – The rise, fall, and deadly persistence of the product that defined America.* Basic Books, New York, 2007.

[354] 2302-05. Pepples E. Campaign Report-Proposition 5, California 1978, January 11, 1979. Available from the above website.

[355] Ibid.

REFERENCES

356 Stanton A. Glantz, John Slade, Lisa A. Bero, Peter Hanauer, and Deborah E. Barnes, *The Cigarette papers.* University of California Press, 1996 Berkeley.

357 Ernest Pepples: Ernest Pepples, B&W draft memo, "New Strategy on Smoking and Health," 1980, B&W ID 680051009-14.Available at http://legacy.library.ucsf.edu/tid/edz95a00 .

358 Christian Warren, *Brush with Death – A social history of lead poisoning,* The John Hopkins University Press, Baltimore, 2000.

359 Alice Hamilton, M.D., "Industrial Diseases, with Special Reference to the Trade in Which Women are Employed," *Charities and the Commons* 20 (September 5, 1908), 655 -658.

360 Gerald Markowitz& David Rosner, *Deceit and Denial – the deadly politics of industrial pollution,* University of California Press, Berkeley, 2002.

361 Christian Warren, *Brush with Death – A social history of lead poisoning,* The John Hopkins University Press, Baltimore, 2000.

362 New York Times, June 22, 1925, 3. See also Gerald Markowitz,PhD, and David Rosner PhD," A gift of God?" : The Public Health Controversy Over Leaded Gasoline in the 1920s, *Public Health- Then and Now.* Available at*:* http://www.ncbi.nlm.nih.gov/pmc/articles/PMC1646253/pdf/amjph00280-0026.pdf

363 Gerald Markowitz & David Rosner, *Deceit and Denial – the deadly politics of industrial pollution.* University of California Press, Berkeley, 2002.

364 Christian Warren, *Brush with Death – A social history of lead poisoning,* The John Hopkins University Press, Baltimore, 2000.

365 Gerald Markowitz & David Rosner, *Deceit and Denial – the deadly politics of industrial pollution.* University of California Press, Berkeley, 2002.

366 Christian Warren, *Brush with Death – A social history of lead poisoning,* The John Hopkins University Press, Baltimore, 2000.

367 Gerald Markowitz & David Rosner, *Deceit and Denial – the deadly politics of industrial pollution.* University of California Press, Berkeley, 2002.

368 "Dutch Boy Nominated for Packaging's Hall of Fame Because:" *Modern Packaging (April 1949), 126-30, 266, 268.*

369 Charles F. McKhann, "Lead Poisoning in Children," *The Archives of Neurology and Psychiatry* 27 (February 1932), 294-95.

[370] Edward Vogt, "Roentgenolic Diagnosis of Lead Poisoning of Infants and Children," *JAMA* 98 (January 9, 1932), 125.

[371] McKhann C., "Lead Poisoning in Children: The Cerebral Manifestations," *Archives of Neurology and Psychiatry 27* (1932): 294-304.

[372] Christian Warren, *Brush with Death – A social history of lead poisoning,* The John Hopkins University Press, Baltimore, 2000.

[373] William Kovarik PhD., "Ethyl-leaded Gasoline: How a classic Occupational Disease Became an International Public Health Disaster. *Int J Occup Environ Health 2005;11 384-307*

[374] Ibid.

[375] Gerald Markowitz & David Rosner, *Deceit and Denial – the deadly politics of industrial pollution.* University of California Press, Berkeley, 2002.

[376] Markowitz G., Rosner D.," A gift of God? : The Public Health Controversy Over Leaded Gasoline in the 1920s, Public Health- Then and Now" .*AJPH* 1985 vol 75 No4.

[377] William Kovarik PhD., "Ethyl-leaded Gasoline: How a classic Occupational Disease Became an International Public Health Disaster. *Int J Occup Environ Health 2005;11 384-307*

[378] Memorandum of the Surgeon General's Committee on Tetraethyl Lead to the Surgeon General, Jan 17, 1926. Box 101, Folder 1802, Winslow papers, Yale University Library, New Haven, CT.

[379] William Kovarik PhD., "Ethyl-leaded Gasoline: How a classic Occupational Disease Became an International Public Health Disaster. *Int J Occup Environ Health 2005;11 384-307*

[380] George R Tilton, " A Biographical Memoir of Clair Cameron Patterson 1922-1995", *National Academy of Sciences. National Academy Press, 1998.Washington DC.*

[381] Sandra Steingraber PhD, *Living Downstream –An Ecologist's Personal Investigation of Cancer and the Environment,* Merloyd Lawrence Book, 2010.

[382] William Kovarik PhD., "Ethyl-leaded Gasoline: How a classic Occupational Disease Became an International Public Health Disaster. *Int J Occup Environ Health 2005;11 384-307*

[383] Christian Warren, *Brush with Death – A social history of lead poisoning,* The John Hopkins University Press, Baltimore, 2000.

[384] Needleman HL, Gunnoe C, Leviton A et al. Deficits in psychologic and classroom performance of children with elevated dentine lead levels. *NEJM* 1979: 300 (13): 689-95.

REFERENCES

[385] Schwartz J, Low-level lead exposure and children's IQ: A meta-analysis and search for a threshold. *Environ* Res 1994;65 (1): 42-55.
See also: Lanphear BP, Hornung R, Khoury J et al. Low-level environmental lead exposure and children's intellectual function: An international pooled analysis. *Environ Health Perspect.* 2005; 113 (7): 894-99.

[386] Lead Toxicity: What Are the U.S. Standards for Lead Levels? CDC report Aug 2007 http://www.atsdr.cdc.gov/csem/csem.asp?csem=7&po=8

[387] Canfield RL, Henderson CR, Cory-Slechta DA, Cox C, Juski TA, Lanphear BP. 2003. Intellectual impairment in children with blood lead concentrations below 10 µg per Deciliter. New England Journal of Medicine. 348(16): 1517-1526.

See Also: Todd A. Jusko; Charles R. Henderson Jr.; Bruce P. Lanphear; Deborah A. Cory-Slechta; Patrick J. Parsons; Richard L. Canfield. Blood Lead Concentrations < 10 mug/dL and Child Intelligence at 6 Years of Age *Environmental Health Perspectives.* 2008;116(2):243-248. Available at: National Institute of Environmental Health Sciences-http://www.medscape.com/viewarticle/571058

[388] Lanphear BP, Dietrich K, Auinger P, Cox. C 2000. Cognitive deficits associated with BLLs <10 µg/dL in US children and adolescents. Public Health Rep. 115:521-529.

[389] Childhood Lead Poisoning- Information For Advocacy and Action, UNICEF 1997, available at: http://www.unicef.org/wash/files/lead_en.pdf

[390] Markowitz G., Rosner D.," A gift of God? : The Public Health Controversy Over Leaded Gasoline in the 1920s, Public Health- Then and Now" .*AJPH* 1985 vol 75 No4.

[391] Michael Peel, Legal Correspondent," Judge attacks SFO for handling of graft case." Financial Times, March 27 2010.

[392] Joe Thornton, *Pandora's Poison – Chlorine, health, and a new environmental strategy,* MIT Press, Cambridge 2000.

[393] Ibid

[394] Ibid.

[395] Ibd.

[396] Joe Thornton, Ph.D. Environmental Impacts of Polyvinyl Chloride (PVC) Building Materials - A briefing paper for the Healthy Building Network, Available at: http://mts.sustainableproducts.com/SMaRT/ThorntonRevised.pdf

[397] Ted Schettler, M.D., Gina Soloman, M.D., Maria Valenti, and Annette Huddle, *Generations at Risk,* Massachusetts Institute of Technology, 1999.

[398] Joe Thornton, Ph.D. Environmental Impacts of Polyvinyl Chloride (PVC) Building Materials - A briefing paper for the Healthy Building Network.

[399] Gerald Markowitz & David Rosner, *Deceit and Denial – the deadly politics of industrial pollution.* University of California Press, Berkeley, 2002.

[400] Linak E, Yagi K. 2003. Polyvinyl Chloride Resins. Menlo Park, CA: Chemical Economics Handbook Program, SRI Consulting.

[401] Viola PL, Bigotti A, Caputo A. Oncogenic response of rat skin, lungs, and bones to vinyl chloride. Cancer Res. 1971 May;31(5):516-22.

[402] Maltoni C. Liver angiosarcoma in workers exposed to vinyl chloride. Report on the 1st 2 cases encountered [in Italian] Med Lav. 1974;65(11–12):445–450. See also: Creech JL Jr, Johnson MN. Angiosarcoma of liver in the manufacture of polyvinyl chloride. *J Occup Med.* 1974 Mar;16(3):150-1.

[403] OSHA 1975. Regulations (Standards – 29 CFR). Vinyl Choride. – 1910.1017. Washington, DC:Occupational Safety and Health Administration. Available: http://www.osha.gov/pls/oshaweb/owadisp.show_document?p_table=STANDARDS& p_id=10021 [accessed Feb 20th 2012].

[404] Department of HEW, Food and Drug Administration, "Prior Sanctioned Poly Vinyl Chloride Resin," Notice of Proposed Rule Making, *Federal Register,* Vol 38, No 95 (May 17, 1973), 12931.

[405] Health Services and Mental Health Administration, Occupational Safety and Health, "Request for Information on Certain Chemical and Physical Agents," *Federal Register* (January 30, 1973), 2782.

[406] Gerald Markowitz & David Rosner, *Deceit and Denial – the deadly politics of industrial pollution.* University of California Press, Berkeley, 2002.

[407] Jennifer Beth Sass, Barry Castleman, and David Wallinga, Vinyl Chloride: A Case Study of Data Suppression and Misrepresentation, *Environ Health Perspect.* 2005 July; 113(7): 809–812.

REFERENCES

Published online 2005 March 24. doi: 10.1289/ehp.7716. Available at:
http://www.ncbi.nlm.nih.gov/pmc/articles/PMC1257639/ Accessed Feb 2012.

[408] US Department of Labor. OSHA, *Informal Fact-Finding Hearings on possible Hazards of Vinyl Chloride Manufacture and Use* (February 15, 1974), 26-34, MCA Papers. Available from: http://www.chemicalindustryarchives.org/search/pdfs/vinyl/19740215_001_00000495.PDF Accessed Feb 2012.

[409] Ibid. 125-128

[410] IARC (International Agency for Research on Cancer). . Vinyl chloride, polyvinyl chloride and vinyl chloride-vinyl acetate copolymers. IARC Monogr Eval Carcinog Risk Chem Hum. 1979;19:377–438.

IARC (International Agency for Research on Cancer). . Vinyl chloride. IARC Monogr Eval Carcinog Risks Hum Suppl. 1987;7:373.

[411] Joe Thornton, *Pandora's Poison – Chlorine, health, and a new environmental strategy,* MIT Press, Cambridge 2000.

[412] Gerald Markowitz & David Rosner, *Deceit and Denial – the deadly politics of industrial pollution.* University of California Press, Berkeley, 2002.

[413] Jennifer Beth Sass, Barry Castleman, and David Wallinga, Vinyl Chloride: A Case Study of Data Suppression and Misrepresentation, *Environ Health Perspect.* 2005 July; 113(7): 809–812. Published online 2005 March 24. doi: 10.1289/ehp.7716. Available at: http://www.ncbi.nlm.nih.gov/pmc/articles/PMC1257639/ Accessed Feb 2012.

[414] Joe Thornton, Ph.D. Environmental Impacts of Polyvinyl Chloride (PVC) Building Materials - A briefing paper for the Healthy Building Network. 2002. Available at: http://www.healthybuilding.net/pvc/Thornton_Enviro_Impacts_of_PVC.pdf Accessed Feb 2012

[415] Joe Thornton, *Pandora's Poison – Chlorine, health, and a new environmental strategy,* MIT Press, Cambridge 2000.

[416] Environmental fate and effects of bleached pulp mill effluents : proceedings of a SEPA Conference held at Grand Hotel Saltsjöbaden, Stockholm, Sweden 19-21 November 1991: ed. A. Södergren, *Rapport / Naturvårdsverket,* ISSN 0282-7298; 4031, 57 - 67.

[417] Fredrik Wulff, Lars Rahm, Per Jonsson, Lars Brydsten, Torsten Ahl and Åke Granmo . A Mass-Balance Model of Chlorinated Organic Matter for the Baltic Sea: A Challenge for Ecotoxicology. *Ambio.* Vol. 22, No. 1 (Feb., 1993), pp. 27-31

[418]Komulainen, H et al., Carcinogenicity of the Drinking Water mutagen 3-chloro-4-(dichloromethyl)-5-hydroxy-2(5H)-furanone in the rat, Journal of the National Cancer Institute, 89:848-856, 1997. See also:

 Akiyoshi Nishikawa, et al., Promoting Effects of 3-Chloro-4-(dichloromethyl)-5-hydroxy-2(5*H*)-furanone on Rat Glandular Stomach Carcinogenesis Initiated with *N*-Methyl-*N'*-nitro-*N*-nitrosoguanidine. *Cancer Res May 5, 1999 59; 2045-2049*

[419] Joe Thornton, *Pandora's Poison – Chlorine, health, and a new environmental strategy,* MIT Press, Cambridge 2000.

[420] See for example- The Response from International Society for Doctors for the Environment (ISDE) to the Green Paper on PVC (Com [2000] 469 Final, Brussels, 26.7.2000).

http://ec.europa.eu/environment/waste/pvc/public_hearing/pdf/drs.pdf

[421] Rachel's Environment & Health Weekly,*#586* **http://www.rachel.org/?q=en/node/3850** See also -

http://www.lmtf.org/FoLM/Plans/CompPlan/PrecautionaryPrinciple/wingspread_conference_on_the_precautionary_principle.h

[422] 2010 Annual Report. President's Cancer Panel. *Reducing Environmental Cancer Risk.*

http://deainfo.nci.nih.gov/advisory/pcp/annualReports/

[423] http://www.ketchum.com/facts

[424] Crisis Management Plan for the Clorox Company, 1991 Draft Prepared by Ketchum Public Relations. Available from: http://www.sourcewatch.org/images/e/e4/Clorox.pdf accessed Feb 2012.

[425] Memorandum to: Clyde Greenert/Brad Lienhart From: Jack Mongoven, PR Watch, Vol 3, No 2, 2nd Quarter 1996

[426] Memorandum to: Clyde Greenert/Brad Lienhart From: Jack Mongoven

Re: MBD Activist Report for August, Mongoven, Biscoe and Duchin, September 7, 1994.

available from: http://www.prwatch.org/prwissues/1996Q2/update.html

REFERENCES

[427] Sheldon Rampton and John Stauber's, *Trust Us We're Experts- How Industry Manipulates Science and Gambles With Your Future,* Center for Media Democracy, Putnam 2002.

[428] http://www.prwatch.org/

[429] Nancy Turner banks, M.D. *Aids, Opium, Diamonds and Empire, The Deadly Virus of International Greed,* iUniverse, New York 2010.

[430] Sheldon Rampton and John Stauber's, *Trust Us We're Experts- How Industry Manipulates Science and Gambles With Your Future,* Center for Media Democracy, Putnam 2002.

[431] S. Krimsky, L.S. Rothenberg, P. Stott, G. Kyle, Scientific Journals and Their Authors' Financial Interests: A Pilot Study, *Psychother Psychosom* 1998;67:194-201 (DOI: 10.1159/000012281).

[432] Lisa A. Bero, Ph.D., Alison Galbraith, B.A., and Drummond Rennie, M.D. The Publication of Sponsored Symposiums in Medical Journals. *N Engl J Med* 1992; 327:1135-1140 October 15, 1992.

[433] Statement of Mr Sheldon Rampton to the Subcommittee of Investigation and Oversight, Committee on Science and Technology, House of Representatives, March 28, 2007

[434] Sheldon Rampton and John Stauber's, *Trust Us We're Experts- How Industry Manipulates Science and Gambles With Your Future,* Center for Media Democracy, Putnam 2002.
Gerald Markowitz & David Rosner, *Deceit and Denial – the deadly politics of industrial pollution.* University of California Press, Berkeley, 2002.

David Michaels, *Doubt is Their Product-How Industry's Assault on Science Threatens Your Health,* Oxford University Press, New York, 2008.

[435] Elizabeth M. Whelan *Priorities* Vol 8 No 3, 1996, p32

[436] Theo Colborn, Diane Dumanoski and John Myers, *Our Stolen Future,* Dutton Books, 1996.

[437] Ted Schettler, MD, Gina Soloman, MD, Maria Valenti and Annette Huddle, *Generations at Risk- Reproductive Health and the Environment,* Massachusetts Institute of Technology, 1999.

[438] Devra Davis, *The Secret History of the War on Cancer,* Basic Books, 2007.

[439] Philip Knightley, Harold Evans, Elaine Potter and Marjorie Wallace, *Suffer the Children- The Story of Thalidomide,* Sunday Times Insight Team, Futura Publications, 1980, London.

[440] Theo Colborn, Diane Dumanoski and John Myers, *Our Stolen Future,* Dutton Books, 1996.

[441] Ted Schettler, M.D., M.P.H. Gina Solomon, M.D., Maria Valenti and Annette Huddle. *Generations At Risk- Reproductive Health and the Environment,* Massachusetts Institute of Technology, 1999.

[442] EPA National Human Adipose Tissue Survey (NHATS) 1982.

[443] Mount Sinai School of Medicine Body Burden study, New York, Environmental Working Group and Commonweal, Jan 30, 2003, available at:
http://www.ewg.org/sites/bodyburden1/es.php

[444] Body Burden: The Pollution in Newborns, *Environmental Working Group, July 14, 2005*
http://www.ewg.org/research/body-burden-pollution-newborns

[445] *Contamination,* World Wildlife Fund Biomonitoring Survey, November 2003

[446] *A Present For Life – Hazardous chemicals in the umbilical cord,* World Wildlife Fund –UK and Greenpeace, September 2005.

[447] *UK Royal Commission on Environmental Pollution (2003)*

[448] *A Present For Life – Hazardous chemicals in the umbilical cord,* World Wildlife Fund –UK and Greenpeace, September 2005.

[449] Council of Environmental Advisors ,1991.

[450] Nick Davies, *Flat Earth News,* Vintage Books, London, 2009.

[451] John Stauber and Sheldon Rampton, *Toxic Sludge Is Good For You – Lies damn lies and the Public Relations industry,* Center for Media Democracy, Common Courage Press, Monroe, 1995.

[452] *Reading At Risk: A Survey of Literary Reading in America, Research Division Report #46* National Endowment for the Arts, June 2004.

[453] Susan B Trento, *The Power House – Robert Keith Gray and the selling of Access and Influence in Washington,* St Martin's Press, New York, 1992.

[454] Nick Davies, *Flat Earth News,* Vintage Books, London, 2009.

[455] Thomas Huxley. *Geological Reform,* Quarterly Journal of the Geological Society of London, Vol. 25 (1869); as reprinted in Huxley, Discourses, Biological and Geological essays (1909), pp. 335–336

[456] Anne Martin et al.,Recession Contributes To Slowest Annual Rate Of Increase In Health Spending In Five Decades. doi: 10.1377/hlthaff.2010.1032 *Health Aff January 2011 vol. 30 no. 1 11-22.* Available at: http://content.healthaffairs.org/content/30/1/11.abstract

REFERENCES

[457] To Err is Human: Building a Safer Health System, Institute of Medicine, National Academy of Sciences November 1999. Available from: http://www.iom.edu/Reports/1999/To-Err-is-Human-Building-A-Safer-Health-System.aspx

[458] GaryNull, PhD, Martin Feldman, MD, Deborah Rasio, MD, and Carolyn Dean, MD, ND, *Death By Medicine,* Praktikos Books, 2010.

[459] Thomas J Moore, *Deadly Medicine – Why tens of thousands of heart patients died in America's worst drug disaster.* Simon and Shuster, New York, 1995.

[460] Ibid.

[461] Ibid.

[462] GaryNull, PhD, Martin Feldman, MD, Deborah Rasio, MD, and Carolyn Dean, MD, ND, *Death By Medicine,* Praktikos Books, 2010.

[463] Ivan T Borda and Raymond S Koff, NSIADS: *A profile of Adverse Effect,* Hanley & Belfus, Philadelphia, 1992. See also Thomas J Moore, *Prescription for Disaster- The hidden dangers in your medicine cabinet.* Simon & Schuster, New York, 1998

[464] Singh Gurkirpal, MD, "Recent Considerations in Nonsteroidal Anti-Inflammatory Drug Gastropathy", The American Journal of Medicine, July 27, 1998, p. 31S

[465] Wolfe M. MD, Lichtenstein D. MD, and Singh Gurkirpal, MD, "Gastrointestinal Toxicity of Nonsteroidal Anti-inflammatory Drugs", The New England Journal of Medicine, June 17, 1999, Vol. 340, No. 24, pp. 1888-1889.

[466] US Senate Finance Committee, Testimony of David J. Graham MD, MPH, November 18, 2004 http://finance.senate.gov/imo/media/doc/111804dgtest.pdf. Accessed March 2012.

[467] Anna Wilde Mathews and Barbara Martinez Warning Signs, E-Mails Suggest Merck Knew Vioxx's Dangers at Early Stage As Heart-Risk Evidence Rose, Officials Played Hardball; Internal Message: 'Dodge!' Company Says 'Out of Context', *Wall Street Journal*, November 1, 2004, pg. A1. Available from: http://www.marshall-attorneys.com/Press/2004_11_01_WSJ.htm

[468] Dean Murphy, *The Devil's Poison- How fluoride is killing you.*Trafford Publishing, Victoria 2008

[469] David Michaels, *Doubt Is Their Product,* Oxford University Press, New York, 2008

[470] Patel, A M A, "Crisis communication under transformative changes: The emerging context and notes of primary and secondary organisations."

School of Advertising, Marketing and Public Relations, QUT Business School, Queensland University of Technology, Australia.

[471] John Abramson, MD, *Overdosed America –The promise of American medicine: How the pharmaceutical companies are corrupting science, misleading doctors, and threatening your health.* Harper Perennial, 2005, New York.

[472] Marcia Angell, MD. *The Truth About the Drug Companies – How they deceive us and what to do about it.* Random House, 2004, New York.

[473] Ibid.

[474] Peter Lurie and Sidney M Wolfe, "FDA Medical Officers Report Lowers Standards Permit Dangerous Drug Approvals," Public Citizen Health Research Group, December 2, 1998 www.citizen.org/publications/release.cfm?ID=7104.

[475] Alicia Mundy, *Dispensing With the Truth – The victims, the drug companies and the dramatic story behind the battle over fen-phen.* St Martin's Press, New York, 2001.

[476] Ibid.

[477] Frontline Interview with Professor Stuart Rich, Nov. 19, 2002. Available at: http://www.pbs.org/wgbh/pages/frontline/shows/prescription/interviews/rich.html

[478] Alicia Mundy, *Dispensing With the Truth – The victims, the drug companies and the dramatic story behind the battle over fen-phen.* St Martin's Press, New York, 2001

[479] Mark EJ, Patalas ED, Chang HT, et al. Fatal pulmonary hypertension associated with short-term use of fenfluramine and phentermine. *N Engl J Med* 1997; 337:602–606.

[480] Frontline Interview with Professor Stuart Rich, Nov. 19, 2002. Available at: http://www.pbs.org/wgbh/pages/frontline/shows/prescription/interviews/rich.html

[481] Alicia Mundy, *Dispensing With the Truth – The victims, the drug companies and the dramatic story behind the battle over fen-phen.* St Martin's Press, New York, 2001

[482] Sheldon Rampton and John Stauber's, *Trust Us We're Experts- How Industry Manipulates Science and Gambles With Your Future,* Center for Media Democracy, Putnam 2002.

[483] Alicia Mundy, *Dispensing With the Truth – The victims, the drug companies and the dramatic story behind the battle over fen-phen.* St Martin's Press, New York, 2001

[484] Annette Flanagin, RN, MA; Lisa A. Carey, PhD; Phil B. Fontanarosa, MD; Stephanie G. Phillips, MS, PhD;

REFERENCES

Brian P. Pace, MA; George D. Lundberg, MD; Drummond Rennie, MD. Prevalence of Articles With Honorary Authors and Ghost Authors in Peer-Reviewed Medical Journals *JAMA,* 280: 222-224, 998 http://jama.ama-assn.org/content/280/3/222.full.pdf

[485] Melody Petersen, Madison Ave. Has Growing Role In the Business of Drug Research, *New York Times,* November 22, 2002

[486] Jennifer Corbett Dooren, FDA Advisers Bless Weight-Loss Pill, Wall St Journal 23rd Feb 2012.

[487] Lara Salahi, Weight Loss Drugs: Public Citizen Calls for Ban on Alli, Xenical, ABC News, April 14, 2011.

[488] Jennifer Corbett Dooren, FDA Advisers Bless Weight-Loss Pill, Wall St Journal 23rd Feb 2012.

[489]Joshua De Leon. "Many Diabetes Drugs Under FDA Review, Linked to Cancer" Ring of Fire TV/Radio show. Posted on May 8, 2013. Available at: http://www.ringoffireradio.com/2013/05/08/many-diabetes-drugs-under-fda-review-linked-to-cancer/# See also: Amy Corderoy "Australians to join multi-million dollar diabetes drug class action lawsuit" Sydney Morning Herald. May 20, 2013. Also: Thomas H. Maugh "Diabetes drug Actos increases the risk of bladder cancer, the FDA warns." Los Angeles Times. June 16, 2011.

[490] Derek Bok, "Universities in the Marketplace – The commercialisation of Higher Education, Princeton University Press, Princeton, 2003.

[491] Marcia Angell, MD. *The Truth About the Drug Companies – How they deceive us and what to do about it.* Random House, 2004, New York.

[492] Jerome P. Kassirer, M.D., "On the Take – How medicine's complicity with big business can endanger your health. Oxford University Press. New York, 2005.

[493] Richard Smith. Making progress with competing interests Still some way to go. *British Medical Journal*, 2002; 325: 1375-76 Obtained from http://www.ncbi.nlm.nih.gov/pmc/articles/PMC1124846/

[494] Jerome P. Kassirer, M.D., "On the Take – How medicine's complicity with big business can endanger your health. Oxford University Press. New York, 2005.

[495] Jerry Avorn, M.D., "Powerful Medicines – The Benefits, Risks, and Costs of Prescription Drugs," Vintage Books, New York, 2005.

[496] David Willman ,"The Rise and Fall of the Killer Drug Rezulin" LE Magazine September 2000.

[497] Edwin AM Gale, Troglitazone: the lesson that nobody learned? *Diabetologia*, 49 (1), January 2006, pp 1-6. Available also from http://www.troglitazone-story.net/Index.html#Ref16

[498] David Willman, "New FDA: Rezulin -Fast-Track Approval and a Slow Withdrawal." LA Times, December 20, 2000.

[499] Jerry Avorn, M.D., "Powerful Medicines – The Benefits, Risks, and Costs of Prescription Drugs," Vintage Books, New York, 2005.

[500] David Willman, *Los Angeles Times,* 2000. http://www.pulitzer.org/works/2001-Investigative-Reporting

[501] David Willman ,"The Rise and Fall of the Killer Drug Rezulin." LA Times June 4, 2000 reprinted in LE Magazine September 2000.

[502] Edwin AM Gale, Troglitazone: the lesson that nobody learned? *Diabetologia*, 49 (1), January 2006, pp 1-6. Available also from http://www.troglitazone-story.net/Index.html#Ref16

[503] David Willman ,"The Rise and Fall of the Killer Drug Rezulin" LA Times June 4, 2000 reprinted in LE Magazine September 2000.

[504] Jerry Avorn, M.D., "Powerful Medicines – The Benefits, Risks, and Costs of Prescription Drugs," Vintage Books, New York, 2005.

[505] David Willman ,"The Rise and Fall of the Killer Drug Rezulin." LA Times June 4, 2000 reprinted in LE Magazine September 2000.

[506] Jerry Avorn, M.D., "Powerful Medicines – The Benefits, Risks, and Costs of Prescription Drugs," Vintage Books, New York, 2005.

Australia New Zealand Therapeutic Products Authority, http://www.anztpa.org/about.htm

[507] Dennis Cauchon. FDA Advisers Tied To Industry.-*USA Today* Monday, September 25, 2000 *http://www.commondreams.org/headlines/092500-01.htm*

[508] Edwin AM Gale, Troglitazone: the lesson that nobody learned? *Diabetologia*, 49 (1), January 2006, pp 1-6. Available also from http://www.troglitazone-story.net/Index.html#Ref16

[509] John Abramson, MD, *Overdosed America –The promise of American medicine: How the pharmaceutical companies are corrupting science, misleading doctors, and threatening your health.* Harper Perennial, 2005, New York.

REFERENCES

510 Julie Schmit," Drug companies dodge ban from Medicare, Medicaid," *USA Today,* August 16, 2004.

511 "Bayer Pleads Guilty in Medicare Fraud Case,"17 *Corporate Crime Reporter* 16(1), April 21, 2003.

512 Peter Rost MD., "The Whistleblower- Confessions of a healthcare hitman," Soft Skull Press, New York, 2006.

513 Ibid.

514 Stephen Labaton,"S.E.C. to Require More Disclosure Of Executive Pay." *New York Times*, January 18, 2006.

515 Lawrence K Altman, "Even the Elite Hospitals Aren't Immune to Errors," New York Times, February 23, 2003.

516 Piero Impicciatore, Imti Choonara, Amanda Clarkson, Davide Provasi, Chiara Pandolfini,and Maurizio Bonati Incidence of adverse drug reactions in paediatric in/out-patients: a systematic review and meta-analysis of prospective studies, Br J Clin Pharmacol. 2001 July; 52(1): 77–83. doi: 10.1046/j.0306-5251.2001.01407.x

517 Barbara Starfield, "Is US Health Really the Best in the World?" JAMA,July 26, 2000, 284(4): 483-485.

518 Leape L L, Unnecessary Surgery. Health Serv Res, 1989, Aug 24, (3) : 351 – 407.

519 Annis Tircesimo Quarto and Tricesimo Quinto. Henry VIII Regis. Cap. VIII. An Act That Persons, Being No Common Surgeons, May Administer Outward Medicines. 1512. Available from: http://www.saveourherbs.org.uk/Charter.html

520 Montague Summers, "The History of Witchcraft and Demonology." Dover Publications, London, 1987.

521 Paul Starr, "The Social Transformation of American Medicine- The rise of a sovereign profession and the making of a vast industry." Basic Books, New York, 1982.

522 Ibid.

523 G. Edward Griffin, "World Without Cancer – The story of vitamin B17."American Media, 1999.

524 Ibid.

525 Ibid.

526 Paul Starr, "The Social Transformation of American Medicine- The rise of a sovereign profession and the making of a vast industry." Basic Books, New York, 1982.

527 Ibid.

[528] G. Edward Griffin, "World Without Cancer – The story of vitamin B17."American Media, 1999.

[529] Paul Starr, "The Social Transformation of American Medicine- The rise of a sovereign profession and the making of a vast industry." Basic Books, New York, 1982.

[530] William Trevor, "In the Public Interest", 1972

[531] Howard Wolinsky and Tom Brune, *The Serpent on the Staff—The Unhealthy Politics of the American Medical Association,* Putman & Sons, New York, 1994.

[532] Ibid.

[533] Elaine Feuer, *Innocent Casualties –The FDA's war against humanity.* Dorrance Publishing, Pittsburgh, 1996.

[534] James P Carter, MD., Dr, P.H. Racketeering In Medicine – The Suppression of Alternatives, Hampton Roads Publishing Company Inc.1992, Norfolk USA.

[535] Ibid

[536] Carolyn Dean, MD.,ND., *Death By Modern Medicine, - Seeking Safe Solutions,2010*

[537] Ibid.

[538] James P Carter, MD., Dr, P.H. Racketeering In Medicine – The Suppression of Alternatives, Hampton Roads Publishing Company Inc.1992, Norfolk USA.

[539] Carolyn Dean, MD.,ND., *Death By Modern Medicine, - Seeking Safe Solutions,2010*

[540] Helke Ferrie, *What Part of No Don't They Understand?--Rescuing Food and Medicine from Government Abuse, A Manifesto. Kos Publishing, June 2008.*

[541] Ibid.

[542] Elaine Feuer, *Innocent Casualties –The FDA's war against humanity.* Dorrance Publishing, Pittsburgh, 1996.

[543] Ibid

[544] GaryNull, PhD, Martin Feldman, MD, Deborah Rasio, MD, and Carolyn Dean, MD, ND, *Death By Medicine,* Praktikos Books, 2010.

[545] US Department of Agriculture, Human Nutrition Report No. 2 Benefits from Nutrition Research, August 1971.

[546] K-G Wenzel, M.D., & R.J. Pataracchia N.D., *The Earth's Gift To Medicine- Minerals in Health and Disease,2005.*

[547] US Department of Agriculture, Human Nutrition Report No. 2 Benefits from Nutrition Research, August 1971.

REFERENCES

[548] Chronic Disease Prevention and Health Promotion, CDC, 2009. http://www.cdc.gov/chronicdisease/overview/index.htm

[549] Marcia Angell, MD. *The Truth About the Drug Companies – How they deceive us and what to do about it.* Random House, 2004, New York.

[550] Carolyn Dean, MD.,ND., *Death By Modern Medicine, - Seeking Safe Solutions,2010.* See also: John W Gofman, M.D., Ph.D., *Radiation from Medical Procedures in the Pathogenesis of Cancer and Ischemic Heart Disease.* Committee for Nuclear Responsibility, San Francisco. 1999.

[551] Abram Hoffer MD, PhD, *Psychiatry- Yesterday (1950) and Today (2007), From Despair to Hope with Orthomolecular Psychiatry,* Trafford Publishing, 2008.

[552] Abram Hoffer MD., PhD., Andrew W. Saul, PhD., and Harold D. Foster, PhD. *Niacin, The Real Story,* Basic Health Publications, Inc., Laguna Beach, 2012.

[553] Abram Hoffer MD, PhD, *Psychiatry- Yesterday (1950) and Today (2007), From Despair to Hope with Orthomolecular Psychiatry,* Trafford Publishing, 2008.

[554] Carl C Pfeiffer, PhD., M.D., *Nutrition and Mental Illness, An Orthomolecular Approach to Balancing Body Chemistry,* Healing Arts Press, 1987.

[555] Abram Hoffer MD, PhD, *Psychiatry- Yesterday (1950) and Today (2007), From Despair to Hope with Orthomolecular Psychiatry,* Trafford Publishing, 2008. *The Journal of Orthomolecular Medicine, http://www.orthomed.org/jom/jom.html*

[556] Medawar, C. *Power and Dependence,* Social Audit. London,1992. I obtained this reference from: John Abraham & Julie Sheppard, *The Therapeutic Nightmare ,* Earthscan Publications, London, 1999.

[557] Chetley, A. *A Healthy Business? World Health and the Pharmaceutical Industry,* Zed Books, 1990 London. I obtained this reference from: John Abraham & Julie Sheppard, *The Therapeutic Nightmare ,* Earthscan Publications, London, 1999.

[558] Medawar, C. *Power and Dependence,* Social Audit. London,1992. I obtained this reference from: John Abraham & Julie Sheppard, *The Therapeutic Nightmare ,* Earthscan Publications, London, 1999.

[559] John Abraham & Julie Sheppard, *The Therapeutic Nightmare – The Battle over the World's Most Controversial Sleeping Pill,* Earthscan Publications, London, 1999.

[560] http://www.wikinvest.com/concept/Antidepressant_Drug_Market

[561] John Abraham & Julie Sheppard, *The Therapeutic Nightmare – The Battle over the World's Most Controversial Sleeping Pill,* Earthscan Publications, London, 1999

[562] Van der Kroef, K., 'Reactions to Triazolam', Lancet, Vol 314 Issue 8141, 8 September, 1979 p526

[563] Royal Courts of Justice (1994) Judgement between the Upjohn Company and Upjohn Ltd and Professor Ian Oswald and between Dr Royston Frederick Drucker and Professor Oswald and between the Upjohn Company and between and Upjohn Ltd and the BBC and Tom Mangold before Mr Justice May, Beverley F Nunnery, London 27 May.

[564] John Abraham, and Julie Sheppard, *The Therapeutic Nightmare- The Battle Over the World's Most Controversial Sleeping Pill.*Earthscan Publications Ltd,London, 1999.

[565] Kales, A., Soldatos, C.R., Bixler, E.O., and Kales, J.D., 'Early morning insomnia with rapidly eliminated benzodiazepines', *Science,*1987, vol 220 pp2295-97. See also: Morgan K, Oswald I. Anxiety caused by short-life hypnotic. *BMJ.* 1982; 284:942-944.
Adam K, Oswald I. Can a rapidly eliminated hypnotic cause daytime anxiety? *Pharmacopsychiatry.*1989;22:115-119.

[566] John Abraham, and Julie Sheppard, *The Therapeutic Nightmare- The Battle Over the World's Most Controversial Sleeping Pill.*Earthscan Publications Ltd,London, 1999.

[567] Peter Breggin, M.D., *Medication Madness, The Role of Psychiatric Drugs in Cases of Violence, Suicide, and Crime.*St Martin's Griffin, New York 2008.

[568] Peter Breggin, M.D., *Medication Madness, The Role of Psychiatric Drugs in Cases of Violence, Suicide, and Crime.*St Martin's Griffin, New York 2008.

[569] Peter R. Breggin, 'Analysis of Adverse Behavioural Effects of Benzodiazepines With a Discussion on Drawing Scientific Conclusions from the FDA's Spontaneous Reporting System'. The Journal of Mind and Behaviour, Winter 1998, Volume 19. Number 1 ps 21-50. Sourced at: http://www.brown.uk.com/brownlibrary/BREGGIN.htm

[570] Ibid.

[571] Peter Breggin, M.D., *Medication Madness, The Role of Psychiatric Drugs in Cases of Violence, Suicide, and Crime.*St Martin's Griffin, New York 2008.

[572] John Abraham, and Julie Sheppard, *The Therapeutic Nightmare- The Battle Over the World's Most Controversial Sleeping Pill.*Earthscan Publications Ltd,London, 1999.

REFERENCES

[573] Deseret News, Salt Lake City 'Utah Woman, Upjohn Settle Halcion suit out of court.' Saturday, Aug. 10 1991, Associated Press.

[574] G.E.Simon and M Korff, " Suicide Mortality among Patients Treated for Depression in an Insured Population," *American Journal of Epidemiology,* 147 (1998): 155-60.

[575] David Healy, *Let Them Eat Prozac- The Unhealthy Relationship between the Pharmaceutical Industry and Depression,* New York University Press, 2004.

[576] Alec Coppen, "The Biochemistry of Affective Disorders" *British Journal of Psychiatry* 113 (1967): 1237-64

[577] Julius Axelrod and Joseph K Inscoe, "The uptake and Binding of Circulating Serotonin and the effect of Drugs", *Journal of Pharmacology and Experimental Therapeutics,* 141, no 2 (1963): 161-65.

[578] The History of Neuroscience in Autobiography Volume 1, Edited by Larry R. Squire, *Society for Neuroscience* , Washington, D.C.1996

[579] Ruhé, H. G.,Mason, N.S. and Schene,A.H. "Mood Is Indirectly Related to Serotonin, Norpinephrine and Dopamine Levels in Humans: A Meta-Analysis of Monoamine Depletion Studies." *Molecular Psychiatry* 12 (2007): 331-59. Available on PubMed at: http://www.ncbi.nlm.nih.gov/pubmed/17389902

[580] Irving Kirsch, Guy Sapirstein, 'Listening To Prozac but Hearing Placebo: A Meta-Analysis of Antidepressant Medication', *Prevention & Treatment,* Article 0002a (1998). American Psychological Association.

[581] Irving Kirsch, *The Emperor's New Drugs – Exploding the Antidepressant Myth.* The Bodley Head, London, 2009.

[582] David Healy, *Let Them Eat Prozac- The Unhealthy Relationship between the Pharmaceutical Industry and Depression,* New York University Press, 2004.

[583] Wayne Kondro and Barbara Sibbald, 'Drug Company Experts Advised Staff to Withhold Data About SSRI Use in Children', *Canadian Medical Association Journal,* 170, no.5 (2004): 783.

[584] Irving Kirsch, *The Emperor's New Drugs – Exploding the Antidepressant Myth.* The Bodley Head, London, 2009.

[585] Peter R Breggin, M.D., *The Ritalin Fact Book, What you doctor won't tell you about ADHD and stimulant drugs.* Perseus Publishing, Cambridge MA, 2002.

[586] Ibid.

[587] R Mayes, " ADHD and the rise in stimulant use among children," *Harvard Review of Psychiatry* 16 (2008): 151-66

[588] Swanson JM, Cantwell D, Lerner M, McBurnett K, Hanna G," Effects of stimulant medication on learning in children with ADHD." *Journal of Learning Disabilities,* 24 (1991): 219-30

[589] Russell A. Barkley and Charles E. Cunningham, "Do stimulant drugs improve the academic performance of hyperkinetic children? A Review of Outcome Studies." *Clinical Pediatrics* Jan 1978 Vol 17 no 1 85-92

[590] Cheerland, E., and Fitzpatrick, R., "Psychotic side effects of psychostimulants: A 5-year review," *Canadian Journal of Psychiatry* 1999 44:811-813.

[591] Editorial "Depressing Research*", Lancet vol* 363 April 24, 2004: 1335

[592] Peter R Breggin, M.D., *The Ritalin Fact Book, What you doctor won't tell you about ADHD and stimulant drugs.* Perseus Publishing, Cambridge MA, 2002.

[593] Robinson, T.E., and Kolb, B. "Persistent structural modifications in the nucleus accumbens and prefrontal cortex neurons produced by previous experience with amphetamine. *Journal of Neuroscience* 1997, 17:8491-8497

[594] Louk J. M. J. Vanderschuren, E. Donné Schmidt,Taco J. De Vries, Caroline A. P. Van Moorsel, Fred J.H. Tilders, and Anton N. M. Schoffelmeer "A Single Exposure to Amphetamine Is Sufficient to Induce Long-Term Behavioral, Neuroendocrine, and Neurochemical Sensitization in Rats." *The Journal of Neuroscience*, 1 November 1999, 19(21): 9579-9586.

[595] Patricia K Sonsalla, Nina D Jochnowitz, Gail D Zeevalk, Jo A Oostveen, Edward D Hall "Treatment of mice with methamphetamine produces cell loss in the substantia nigra." *Brain Research* 738:172-175

[596] Peter R Breggin, M.D., *The Ritalin Fact Book, What you doctor won't tell you about ADHD and stimulant drugs.* Perseus Publishing, Cambridge MA, 2002.

[597] Robert Whitaker, *Anatomy of an Epidemic- Magic Bullets, Psychiatric Drugs and the Astonishing Rise in Mental Illness in America.* Broadway Paperbacks, New York 2010.

[598] Jon N Jureidini, Christopher J Doecke, Peter R Mansfield, Michelle M Haby, David B Menkes, and Anne L Tonkin, "Efficacy and safety of antidepressants for children and adolescents." *BMJ.* 2004 April 10; 328(7444): 879–883.

[599]E. Cherland, "Psychotic side effects of psychostimulants,"*Canadian Journal of Psychiatry,*44 (1999):811-13.

REFERENCES

600 . Faedda, "Pediatric onset bipolar disorder," *Harvard Review of Psychiatry* 3 (1995): 171-95

601 Geller, "Bipolar disorder at prospective follow-up of adults who had prepubertal major depressive disorder," *Amer J of Psychiatry* 158 (2001):125-7.

602 Robert Whitaker, *Anatomy of an Epidemic- Magic Bullets, Psychiatric Drugs and the Astonishing Rise in Mental Illness in America.* Broadway Paperbacks, New York 2010.

603 Fred A. Baughman Jr., M.D., *The ADHD Fraud: How Psychiatry Makes "Patients" of Normal Children.* Trafford Publishing 2006.

604 Daniel J. Carlat, MD., *Unhinged- The Trouble with Psychiatry—A Doctor's Revelations about a Profession in Crisis.* Simon and Schuster, 2010. See also Bruce Wiseman, *Psychiatry The Ultimate Betrayal,* Freedom Publishing, Los Angeles, 1995.

605 Ellen Hodgson Brown, J.D., *The Web of Debt-The shocking truth about our money system and how we can break free.* Third Millennium Press, 2010.

606 Ibid.

607 Murray N Rothbard, *The Mystery of Banking.* Terra Libertas, 2011 UK.

608 Andrew Jackson & Ben Dyson. *Modernising Money—Why our Monetary System is Broken and How it Can Be Fixed*, Positive Money, London, 2012.Check out their site for further information on banking: www.positivemoney.org.uk

609 Ibid.

610 Ibid

611 Alexander Del Mar. *A History of Money in Ancient Countries—From the Earliest Times to the Present.* George Bell and Sons, London 1885.

612 Steven Zarlenga, *The Lost Science of Money—The Mythology of Money—The Story of Power,* American Monetary Institute, New York, 2002

613 Ellen Hodgson Brown, J.D., *The Web of Debt-The shocking truth about our money system and how we can break free.* Third Millennium Press, 2010.

614 http://www.mailstar.net/money-masters.html

615 Ellen Hodgson Brown, J.D., *The Web of Debt-The shocking truth about our money system and how we can break free.* Third Millennium Press, 2010. Eustace Mullins, *The Secrets of The Federal Reserve,* Bridger House Publishers, Inc. 1991. Also available online at: http://www.barefootsworld.net/fedsecrets_00.html

616 Wikipedia.

[617] Eustace Mullins, *The Secrets of The Federal Reserve,* Bridger House Publishers, Inc. 1991. Also available online at: http://www.barefootsworld.net/fedsecrets_00.html

[618] E. C. Knuth, *The Empire of the "City" – The Secret History of British Financial Power.* The Book Tree, San Diego, 2006.

[619] Eustace Mullins, *The Secrets of The Federal Reserve,* Bridger House Publishers, Inc. 1991. Also available online at: http://www.barefootsworld.net/fedsecrets_00.html

[620] William Guy Carr, *Pawns in the Game,* Noontide Press, U.S. (31 Dec 1978) reprinted from 1956. See also Mullins.1991.

[621] Ellen Hodgson Brown, J.D., *The Web of Debt-The shocking truth about our money system and how we can break free.* Third Millennium Press, 2010.

[622] Alexander Del Mar, 1895. Quoted in Hodgson Brown 2010.

[623] Ellen Hodgson Brown, J.D., *The Web of Debt-The shocking truth about our money system and how we can break free.* Third Millennium Press, 2010

[624] Charles A. Beard, *Rise of American Civilization,* Macmillan 1930.

[625] Ellen Hodgson Brown, J.D., *The Web of Debt-The shocking truth about our money system and how we can break free.* Third Millennium Press, 2010.

[626] Ibid.

[627] Paul Grignon, Money as Debt CD. Also at www.moneyasdebt.net

[628] Ellen Hodgson Brown, J.D., *The Web of Debt-The shocking truth about our money system and how we can break free.* Third Millennium Press, 2010.

[629] Paul Grignon, Money as Debt CD. Also at www.moneyasdebt.net

[630] Otto Von Bismarck, - Ellen Hodgson Brown, J.D., *The Web of Debt-The shocking truth about our money system and how we can break free.* Third Millennium Press, 2010.

[631] William Bonner and Addison Wiggin, *The New Empire of Debt, The Rise and Fall of an Epic Financial Bubble,* John Wiley and Sons Inc., 2009

[632] Salmon P Chase, Treasury Secretary. Ibid.

[633] Eustace Mullins, *The Secrets of the Federal Reserve,* Bridger House Publishers, Inc. 1991.

[634] Wright Patman, *The Primer of Money, (U.S. House of Representatives. Committee on Banking and Currency. Subcommittee on Domestic Finance. Subcommittee Print), 1964.*

[635] Paul Grignon, Money as Debt CD. Also at www.moneyasdebt.net

REFERENCES

[636] Eustace Mullins, *The Secrets of the Federal Reserve,* Bridger House Publishers, Inc. 1991.

[637] Michael Rowbotham. *The Grip of Death- A Study of Modern Money, Debt Slavery and Destructive Economics. Jon Carpenter Publishing, 2009.*

[638] Lord Josiah Stamp, a public address ,Westminster, 1937. Ibid.

[639] King, M. Banking from Bagehot to Basel and Back again, speech presented at the second Bagehot Lecture, Buttonwood Gathering, October 25 2010. New York City

[640] Ibid.

[641] Andrew Jackson & Ben Dyson. *Modernising Money—Why our Monetary System is Broken and How it Can Be Fixed,* Positive Money, London, 2012.

[642] Ellen Hodgson Brown, J.D., *The Web of Debt-The shocking truth about our money system and how we can break free.* Third Millennium Press, 2010.

[643] David Knight, financial analyst, reported in Brown above.

[644] Wikipedia.

[645] George Soros, *The Crisis of Global Capitalism – Open Society Endangered,* Little, Brown and Company. London, 1998.

[646] Christopher White, and Richard Freeman, Testimony submitted on April 13, 1994 to the Committee on Banking, Finance and Urban Affairs, of the U.S. House of Representatives. Also available at http://www.textfiles.com/conspiracy/CN/cn1-11.txt Accessed June 2012

[647] Financial Stability Review, European Central Bank, June 2006. http://www.ecb.int/pub/pdf/other/financialstabilityreview200606en.pdf

[648] Michael Rowbotham, *The Grip of Death- A Study of Modern Money, Debt Slavery and Destructive Economics. Jon Carpenter Publishing, 2009.*

[649] Ibid.

[650] Noam Chomsky,"The people always pay", The Guardian, January 21, 1999

[651] Ibid.

[652] Ellen Hodgson Brown, J.D., *The Web of Debt-The shocking truth about our money system and how we can break free.* Third Millennium Press, 2010.

[653] John Perkins, *Confessions of an Economic Hit Man, The Shocking Story of How America Really Took Over the World,* Ebury Press, 2006.

[654] Ibid.

655 Reginald McKenna, American Bankers association, New York, October 4, 1922. Reported in *The Politics of Plenty,* H. Norman Smith, George Allen & Unwin Ltd, 1946.

656 H. Norman Smith, *The Politics of Plenty,* George Allen & Unwin Ltd, 1946.

657 Susan George, *The Debt Boomerang, How Third World Debt Harms Us All, Pluto Press, 1992*

658 Ibid

659 Michael Rowbotham, *Goodbye America, Globalisation, Debt and the Dollar Empire. Jon Carpenter Publishing, 2000.*

660 Susan George, *The Debt Boomerang, How Third World Debt Harms Us All, Pluto Press, 1992.*

661 Ibid.

662 Michael Rowbotham, *Goodbye America, Globalisation, Debt and the Dollar Empire. Jon Carpenter Publishing, 2000.*

663 Michael Rowbotham, *The Grip of Death- A Study of Modern Money, Debt Slavery and Destructive Economics. Jon Carpenter Publishing, 2009.*

664 Ibid.

665 Susan George, *The Debt Boomerang, How Third World Debt Harms Us All, Pluto Press, 1992.*

666 Michael Rowbotham, *Goodbye America, Globalisation, Debt and the Dollar Empire. Jon Carpenter Publishing, 2000*

667 H. Norman Smith M.P.,The Politics of Plenty. George Allen and Unwin Ltd, 1946

668 Ibid.

669 Susan George, *The Debt Boomerang, How Third World Debt Harms Us All, Pluto Press, 1992.*

670 Cheryl Payer, *The Debt Trap: The International Monetary Fund and the Third World.* Monthly Review Press, 1974.

671 Joseph E Stiglitz, *Globalization and its Discontents,* W W Norton & Company, New York, 2002.

672 Michael Rowbotham, *Goodbye America, Globalisation, Debt and the Dollar Empire. Jon Carpenter Publishing, 2000*

673 Joseph E Stiglitz, *Globalization and its Discontents,* W W Norton & Company, New York, 2002.

REFERENCES

[674] Vandana Shiva, *Stolen Harvest – The Hijacking of the Global Food Supply,* South End Press, Cambridge MA, 2000.

[675] President Luiz Inacio Lula da Silva, at the Havana Debt Conference in August 1985, quoted by Susan George, A Fate Worse Than Death p 238

[676] Christopher Huhne, Economics Editor, *The Independent on Sunday,* 25 February 1990.

[677] Michael Rowbotham, *Goodbye America, Globalisation, Debt and the Dollar Empire. Jon Carpenter Publishing, 2000*

[678] Joseph E Stiglitz, *Globalization and its Discontents,* W W Norton & Company, New York, 2002.

[679] Irwin Stelzer, American account, *The Sunday Times,* 12 October 1986.

[680] Michael Rowbotham, *Goodbye America, Globalisation, Debt and the Dollar Empire. Jon Carpenter Publishing, 2000*

[681] John Perkins, *Confessions of an Economic Hit Man, The Shocking Story of How America Really Took Over the World,* Ebury Press, 2006.

[682] Wikipedia, Distribution of wealth.

[683] Joseph E Stiglitz, *Globalization and its Discontents,* W W Norton & Company, New York, 2002.

[684] Joyce Nelson, *Sultans of Sleaze, Public Relations and the Media,* Common Courage Press, Monroe, Maine USA. 1989.

[685] William Greider, *Who Will Tell the People – The Betrayal of American Democracy.* Simon & Shuster, New York 1992.

[686] Joyce Nelson, *Sultans of Sleaze, Public Relations and the Media,* Common Courage Press, Monroe, Maine USA. 1989.

[687] Ibid.

[688] George Monbiot, *Captive State, The Corporate Takeover of Britain,* Macmillan, 2000.

[689] Wikipedia.

[690] Michael Rowbotham, *Goodbye America, Globalisation, Debt and the Dollar Empire. Jon Carpenter Publishing, 2000*

[691] Richard Thomson, Business News Analysis, *The Independent on Sunday,* 3 June 1990.

[692] Eustace Mullins, *The Secrets of the Federal Reserve,* Bridger House Publishers, Inc. 1991.

[693] Michael Rowbotham, *The Grip of Death- A Study of Modern Money, Debt Slavery and Destructive Economics. Jon Carpenter Publishing, 2009.*

[694] Ben Stein, "In Class Warfare, Guess Which Class Is Winning", *New York Times*, Nov. 26, 2006

[695] Wikipedia.

[696] Virginia Myers, Interview, Sir James Goldsmith, *The Independent on Sunday, 21 October 1990.*

[697] Gregory Mannarino, *The Politics of Money,* 2013

[698] Director of the Bank of England 1910-1919. Vincent C Vickers, *Economic Tribulation* John Lane, The Bodley Head 1941.Also available from: http://userpage.fu-berlin.de/roehrigw/vickers/

[699] Michael Rowbotham, *The Grip of Death- A Study of Modern Money, Debt Slavery and Destructive Economics. Jon Carpenter Publishing, 2009.*

[700] John Perkins, *Confessions of an Economic Hit Man, The Shocking Story of How America Really Took Over the World,* Ebury Press, 2006.

[701] Joel Bakan, *The Corporation –The Pathological Pursuit of Profit and Power,* Constable and Robinson, London, 2004.

[702] Ibid.

[703] George Anders, *Merchants of Debt – KKR and the Mortgaging of American Business,* Jonathan Cape, London,1992.

[704] Susan Faludi, "Safeway LBO Yields Vast Profits but Extracts a Heavy Human Toll." *Wall Street Journal.* May 16, 1990.

[705] Ibid.

[706] George Anders, *Merchants of Debt – KKR and the Mortgaging of American Business,* Jonathan Cape, London,1992.

[707] Wikipedia.

[708] BBC, 31 January 2012.

[709] David C Korten, *When Corporations Rule The World*, Earthscan Publications, London, 1996.

[710] Economist, January 27th, 2000.

[711] Charles Grey, "Corporate Goliaths- Sizing Up Corporations and Governments" *Multinational Monitor,* June 1999, vol 20 no 6. http://www.multinationalmonitor.org/mm1999/061999/gray.html

REFERENCES

[712] Andy Serwer, "The Waltons/ Inside America's Richest Family" *Fortune Magazine,* November 15, 2004

[713] Charles Grey, "Corporate Goliaths- Sizing Up Corporations and Governments" *Multinational Monitor,* June 1999, vol 20 no 6. http://www.multinationalmonitor.org/mm1999/061999/gray.html

[714] Sharon Beder, *Global Spin—The Corporate Assault on Environmentalism,* Green Books, Totnes, 2002

[715] Ibid.

[716] Federal Election Commission : http://www.fec.gov/press/paccnt_grph.html

[717] Andrew Rowell, *Green Backlash, Global Subversion of the Environment Movement.* Routledge 1996, New York.

[718] E.Bruce Harrison, *Going Green, How to Communicate you Company's Environmental Commitment,* Business One Irwin. 1993

[719] Sharon Beder, *Global Spin—The Corporate Assault on Environmentalism,* Green Books, Totnes, 2002

[720] Darcy Frey, *New York Times,* Dec 8 2002

[721] Edited by Eveline Lubbers, *Battling Big Business –Countering Greenwash, Infiltration and Other Forms of Corporate Bullying,* Green Books, 2002

[722] Sharon Beder, *Global Spin—The Corporate Assault on Environmentalism,* Green Books, Totnes, 2002

[723] Ibid.

[724] Andrew Rowell, *Green Backlash, Global Subversion of the Environment Movement.* Routledge 1996, New York.

[725] Sharon Beder, *Global Spin—The Corporate Assault on Environmentalism,* Green Books, Totnes, 2002

[726] *Why Poverty? Park Avenue, Money Power and the American Dream.* Democracy Pictures & Steps International, 2012. See also http://www.oilwatchdog.org/meet-koch-industries/

[727] Jane Meyer, A Reporter at Large -*Covert Operations.* The billionaire brothers who are waging a war against Obama. *August 30, 2010 - The New Yorker*

[728] Sharon Beder, *Global Spin—The Corporate Assault on Environmentalism,* Green Books, Totnes, 2002

[729] Ibid.

[730] Joyce Nelson, *Sultans of Sleaze, Public Relations and the Media,* Common Courage Press, Monroe, Maine USA. 1989.

[731] Joyce Nelson, *Sultans of Sleaze, Public Relations and the Media,* Common Courage Press, Monroe, Maine USA. 1989.

[732] http://en.wikipedia.org/wiki/NBC

[733] http://en.wikipedia.org/wiki/General_Electric

[734] http://www.peri.umass.edu/toxic100/

[735] William Greider, *Who Will Tell the People – The Betrayal of American Democracy,* Simon & Schuster, New York, 1992.

[736] Ibid.

[737] Sharon Beder, *Global Spin—The Corporate Assault on Environmentalism,* Green Books, Totnes, 2002

[738] Andrew Rowell, *Green Backlash, Global Subversion of the Environment Movement.* Routledge 1996, New York.

[739] BNA, " Bjerregaard calls anti-environmental drive in U.S. Congress blow to global leadership", Brussels, 27 July 1995. Obtained from Rowell above.

[740] Dr Mae-Wan Ho, *Genetic Engineering, Dream or Nightmare? – The Brave New World of Bad Science and Big Business,* Gateway Books, Bath UK, 1998.

[741] F William Engdahl, *Seeds of Destruction, The Hidden Agenda of Genetic Manipulation,* Global Research, 2007.

[742] Ibid.

[743] J B Neilands, from the editorial in *Against The Grain- The Genetic Transformation of Global Agriculture.* Marc Lappé and Britt Bailey, Earthscan Publications, London,1999.

[744]Molecular biology is undergoing its biggest shake-up in 50 years, as a hitherto little-regarded chemical called RNA acquires an unsuspected significance , *The Economist,* June 14, 2007

[745] Don Lotter, Ph.D, The Genetic Engineering of Food and the Failure of Science, Food First, Institute for Food and Development Policy, posted August 7th, 2009. Available at: http://www.foodfirst.org/en/genetic+engineering+of+food

[746] Ibid.

REFERENCES

[747] F William Engdahl, *Seeds of Destruction, The Hidden Agenda of Genetic Manipulation,* Global Research, 2007.

[748] Andrew Rowell "The Sinister Sacking of the World's Leading GM Expert- and the Trail that leads to Tony Blair and the White House. *The Daily Mail,* July 7,2003.

[749] F William Engdahl, *Seeds of Destruction, The Hidden Agenda of Genetic Manipulation,* Global Research, 2007

[750] Dr Mae-Wan Ho, Invited lecture at conference on TRADITIONAL SEEDS OUR NATIONAL TREASURE AND HERITAGE -Traditional and Organic Agriculture instead of GMO, 17 May 2008, Bewelder, Warsaw, Poland

[751] L B Mann Ph.D., The Selfish Commercial Gene. Available at: http://www.psrast.org/selfshgen.htm

[752] Steven M Drucker, *Altered Genes, Twisted Truth,* Clear River Press. 2015.

[753] Henryk Behr, *A Momentary Lapse of Reason – Living with L-Tryptophan Induced EMS and the Hidden Dangers of Genetic Modification of our Foods, Xlibris Publishing 2011.*

[754] Tomoko Inose & Kousaku Murata. "Enhanced accumulation of toxic compound in yeast cells having high glycolytic activity: a case study on the safety of genetically engineered yeast." International Journal of Food Science and Technology (1995) 30, 141-146 1 April 1995.

[755] Doug Gurian-Sherman, *Failure to Yield, Evaluating the Performance of Genetically Engineered Crops*, Union of Concerned Scientists April 2009

[756]Catherine Badgley,Jeremy Moghtader,Eileen Quintero,Emily Zakem,M. Jahi Chappell,Katia Avilés-Vázquez,Andrea Samulon and Ivette Perfecto. "Organic agriculture and the global food supply" *Renewable Agriculture and Food Systems*, Volume 22, Issue 02, June 2007 pp 86-108

[757] See also: Steven M. Druker. "The Poor Performance of Genetically Engineered Crops: Imposing New Risks on Consumers and the Environment While Failing to Improve the Farmers' Bottom Line." Alliance for Bio-Integrity June 3, 2003 www.biointegrity.org

[758] André Leu, The *Myths of Safe Pesticides,* Acres USA, Texas 2014

[759] *Global Food - Waste Not, Want Not- Feeding the 9 Billion*, Institution of Mechanical Engineers. Jan 2013.

[760] Ibid.

[761] Tim Lang & Michael Heasman, *Food Wars- The Global Battle for Mouths, Minds and Markets.* Earthscan, London, 2004.

762 http://finance.econsultant.com/monsanto-2009-revenue-profit-2010-fortune-500-rank/

763 F William Engdahl, Seeds of Destruction, The Hidden Agenda of Genetic Manipulation, Global Research, 2007

764 Henryk Behr, A Momentary Lapse of Reason – Living with L-Tryptophan Induced EMS and the Hidden Dangers of Genetic Modification of our Foods, Xlibris Publishing 2011

765 Ibid.

766 *The Poor Performance of Genetically Engineered Crops: Imposing New Risks on Consumers and the Environment While Failing to Improve the Farmers' Bottom Line,* Alliance for Bio-Integrity, June 3, 2003.

767 Jeffrey M. Smith, *Genetic Roulette, The Documented Health Risks of Genetically Engineered Foods,* Yes Books, 2007.

768 Amy Dean, D.O. and Jennifer Armstrong, M.D. Genetically Modified Foods, *American Academy of Environmental Medicine* , May 8, 2009.) Available at: http://aaemonline.org/gmopost.html

769 Jeffrey M. Smith, *Genetic Roulette, The Documented Health Risks of Genetically Engineered Foods,* Yes Books, 2007.

770 Amy Dean, D.O. and Jennifer Armstrong, M.D. Genetically Modified Foods, *American Academy of Environmental Medicine* , May 8, 2009.) Available at: http://aaemonline.org/gmopost.html

771 Ibid.

772 Elements of Precaution: Recommendations for the Regulation of Food Biotechnology in Canada, An Expert Panel Report on the Future of Food Biotechnology, *The Royal Society of Canada,* January 2001.

773 Health Risks of Genetically Modified Foods, *The Lancet,* Volume 353, Issue 9167, Page 1811, 29 May 1999. doi:10.1016/S0140-6736(99)00093-8

774 Susan Bardocz, as quoted in Jeffrey M. Smith, *Genetic Roulette, The Documented Health Risks of Genetically Engineered Foods,* Yes Books, 2007.

775 Jeffrey M Smith, *Seeds of Deception- Exposing Corporate and Government Lies about the Safety of Genetically Engineered Food,* Green Books, Totnes, 2004.

REFERENCES

[776] Jonathan R. Latham, Allison K. Wilson, and Ricarda A. Steinbrecher "The Mutational Consequences of Plant Transformation", *J Biomed Biotechnol.* 2006; 2006: 25376. Published online 2006 March 1. doi: 10.1155/JBB/2006/25376 Available at: http://www.ncbi.nlm.nih.gov/pmc/articles/PMC1559911/

[777] Ibid.

[778] Jeffrey M. Smith, *Genetic Roulette, The Documented Health Risks of Genetically Engineered Foods,* Yes Books, 2007.

[779] Jeffrey M Smith, *Seeds of Deception- Exposing Corporate and Government Lies about the Safety of Genetically Engineered Food,* Green Books, Totnes, 2004.

[780] Andrew Pollack, 'Mystery DNA Is Discovered in Soybeans by Scientists', *New York Times,* August 16, 2001. See Also: Pieter Windels , Isabel Taverniers, Ann Depicker, Erik Van Bockstaele, & Marc De Loose, "Characterisation of the Roundup Ready soybean insert," *Eur Food Res Technol* (2001) 213:107–112. DOI 10.1007/s002170100336

[781] Jeffrey M Smith, *Seeds of Deception- Exposing Corporate and Government Lies about the Safety of Genetically Engineered Food,* Green Books, Totnes, 2004

[782] World Allergy Organization, WAO White Book on Allergy 2011-2012: Executive Summary.

[783] Prescott VE, Campbell PM, Moore A, Mattes J, Rothenberg ME, Foster PS, Higgins TJV and Hogan SP (2005). *Transgenic expression of bean alpha-amylase inhibitor in peas results in altered structure and immunogenicity.* Journal of Agricultural and Food Chemistry 53:9023-30. See Also: Could GM foods cause allergies? A critique of current allergenicity testing in the light of new research on transgenic peas. Friends of the Earth Briefing, February 2006. Available at: http://www.foe.co.uk/resource/briefings/gm_alergies.pdf

[784] Schubert D, "A different perspective on GM food" Nature Biotechnology 20, 969 (2002) doi:10.1038/nbt1002-969

[785] David R. Schubert, "The Problem with Nutritionally Enhanced Plants." *Journal Med Food 11 (4) 2008.*

[786] Dr Mae-Wan Ho, *Genetic Engineering, Dream or Nightmare? The Brave New World of Bad Science and Big Business,* Gateway Books, Bath, UK,1998.

[787] Ibid.

[788] Bill Lambrecht, "Outgoing Secretary Says Agency's Top Issue is Genetically Modified Food." *St. Louis Post-Dispatch,* 25 Jan 2001. See article at http://www.mindfully.org/GE/Dan-Glickman-Outgoing.htm

[789] Soil Association, "Seeds of doubt North American farmers' experiences of GM crops" September 2002.

[790] Ibid..

[791] King C, Purcell L & Vories E, 'Plant growth and nitrogenase activity of glyphosate-tolerant soybeans in response to foliar application', *Agronomy Journal*, vol 93, p179–186, 2001 (abstract at http://biotech-info.net/ king_abstract.pdf

[792] Claire Robinson. "The inside story on Monsanto and the glyphosate birth defect data." *The Ecologist*, 13th June 2011. Main article :

Michael Antoniou, Mohamed Ezz El-Din Mostaffa Habib, C. Vyvyan Howard, Richard C. Jennings, Carlo Leifert, Rubens Onofre Nodari, Claire Robinson, & John Fagan. "Roundup and birth defects: Is the public being kept in the dark?" © Earth Open Source, 2011. Available online at: http://www.scribd.com/doc/57277946/RoundupandBirthDefectsv5

[793] Paganelli, A., Gnazzo, V., Acosta, H., López, S.L., Carrasco, A.E. 2010. Glyphosate-based herbicides produce teratogenic effects on vertebrates by impairing retinoic acid signalling. Chem. Res. Toxicol., August 9. http://pubs.acs.org/doi/abs/10.1021/tx1001749

[794] GM Watch, "Groundbreaking study shows Roundup link to birth defects
International scientists confirm dangers of Roundup at GMO-Free Regions Conference in Brussels"
Brussels 16 September 2010 Available at: http://www.gmwatch.org/latest-listing/1-news-items/12491-groundbreaking-study-shows-roundup-link-to-birth-defects

[795] http://www.juicioalafumigacion.com.ar/trial-against-use-of-agrochemicals-in-ituzaingo-argentina-spraying-is-a-crime/   Trial against use of agrochemicals in Ituzaingó (Argentina): Spraying is a crime. 6 septiembre, 2012 / 2 Comentarios

[796]GMO Free Europe, "Fatal Soya - The Mothers of Ituzaingó,"
http://www.gmo-free-regions.org/gmo-free-conference-2012/speakers/gatica.html

[797] GM Watch, "Groundbreaking study shows Roundup link to birth defects
International scientists confirm dangers of Roundup at GMO-Free Regions Conference in Brussels" Brussels 16 September 2010.

REFERENCES

[798]Claire Robinson, "Revealed: the glyphosate research the GM soy lobby doesn't want you to read"

The Ecologist, 24th November, 2010.

[799] Report from the 1st National Meeting of Physicians in the Crop-Sprayed Towns Faculty of Medical Sciences, National University of Cordoba. August 28th 2010

[800] Ibid.

[801] Winchester, PD., Huskins, J., Ying, J. (2009, April). "Agrichemicals in surface water and birth defects in the United States." *Acta Paediatrica,* 98(4), 664-9. PubMed PMID: 19183116; PubMed Central PMCID: PMC2667895

[802] Schreinemachers, DM. (2003, July)."Birth defects and other adverse perinatal outcomes in four U.S. Wheat-producing states." *Environmental Health Perspectives*, 111(9), 1259-64. PubMed PMID: 12842783; PubMed Central PMCID: PMC1241584.

[803] Sanborn, M., Kerr, KJ., Sanin, LH., Cole, DC., Bassil, KL., Vakil, C. "Non-cancer health effects of pesticides: systematic review and implications for family doctors." *Canadian Family Physician,* October 2007, 53(10), 1712-20. Review. PubMed PMID: 17934035; PubMedCentral PMCID: PMC2231436.

[804] Dr Margaret Sanborn, testimony to the House of Commons Standing Committee on Health on the Pest Control Products Act. Briefing notes -Bill C 53

Pest Control Products Act May 9, 2002

[805] Michael Antoniou, Mohamed Ezz El-Din Mostaffa Habib, C. Vyvyan Howard, Richard C. Jennings, Carlo Leifert, Rubens Onofre Nodari, Claire Robinson, & John Fagan. "Roundup and birth defects: Is the public being kept in the dark?" © Earth Open Source, 2011. Available online at: http://www.scribd.com/doc/57277946/RoundupandBirthDefectsv5

[806] Claire Robinson, "The inside story on Monsanto and the glyphosate birth defect data". *The Ecologist,* 13th June 2011.

[807] Friends of the Earth, Greenpeace ."Hidden Uncertainties: What the European Commission doesn't want us to know about the risks of GMOs". April 2006.

[808] Friends of the Earth, Briefing Paper: "Genetically modified animal feed" May 2006

[809] Ibid.

[810] Dr Mae-Wan Ho, *Genetic Engineering, Dream or Nightmare? The Brave New World of Bad Science and Big Business,* Gateway Books, Bath, UK,1998.

[811] Jeffrey M. Smith, *Genetic Roulette, The Documented Health Risks of Genetically Engineered Foods,* Yes Books, 2007.

[812] Kurt Eichenwald, Gina Kolata, and Melody Petersen,"Biotechnology Food: From the lab to a Debacle," *New York Times,* January 25, 2001

[813] Ibid.

[814] "Scientists and Government Regulators Speak Out Against Genetic Engineering." The Centre for Food Safety and The International Forum on Globalization. Available at: http://www.ifg.org/pdf/ind_ag-scient.pdf

[815] Dr David Suzuki, geneticist and broadcaster, quoted in Angela Hall, "Suzuki warns against hastily accepting GMOs", The Leader-Post (Canada), 26 April 2005.

[816] Jeffrey M. Smith, *Genetic Roulette, The Documented Health Risks of Genetically Engineered Foods,* Yes Books, 2007. Also see his website: http://www.responsibletechnology.org/

[817] Louise Gray "GM soy: the high cost of the quest for 'green gold'." *The Telegraph,* 17 May 2011.

[818] Vandana Shiva, *Biopiracy –The Plunder of Nature and Knowledge,* Green Books, Totnes, England 1998.

[819] F. William Engdahl, *Seeds of Destruction – The Hidden Agenda of Genetic Manipulation,* Global Research, 2007.

[820] Vandana Shiva, *Biopiracy –The Plunder of Nature and Knowledge,* Green Books, Totnes, England 1998.

[821] Vandana Shiva, *Stolen Harvest, The Hijacking of the Global Food Supply,* South End Press, Cambridge, MA. 2000

[822] Henry I. Miller and Gregory Conko, "The USDA secretary wants to cripple the genetic engineering of crop plants. Why that's a bad idea." Forbes, 5 Jan 2011

[823] Dr. Don Huber, Letter to Secretary of Agriculture, Tom Vilsack, January 17, 2011.

Available at: http://farmandranchfreedom.org/letter-dr-huber-roundup-animal-miscarriage-infertility/

REFERENCES

[824] Don Huber Interview with Dr Mercola, The Hidden Epidemic Destroying Your Gut Flora December 10, 2011. available at:

http://articles.mercola.com/sites/articles/archive/2012/01/15/dr-don-huber-interview-part-1.aspx

[825] See also the interview with David Murphy of Food Democracy Now at:

http://action.fooddemocracynow.org/sign/dr_hubers_warning/#research

[826] World Outlook of Glyphosate 2012-2016.CCM International Limited, December 2012. Available at: http://www.researchandmarkets.com/reportinfo.asp?report_id=649031. Also See: Glyphosate Monologue, November 2009, Pesticide Action Network available at:

http://www.panap.net/sites/default/files/monograph_glyphosate.pdf

[827] "Worse than DDT: When You Eat This, it Ends Up Lingering in Your Gut"

A One on One Interview with Dr Don Huber (Part 2) January 15, 2012. Available at:

http://articles.mercola.com/sites/articles/archive/2012/01/15/dr-don-huber-interview-part-2.aspx

[828] Sue Edwards, Arefayne Asmelash, Hailu Araya and Tewolde Berhan Gebre Egziabher. The Impact of Compost Use on Crop Yields in Tigray, Ethiopia, 2000-2006 inclusive. Paper prepared for the FAO international conference on Organic Agriculture and food security. Available at www.fao.org

[829] Pimental D, Hepperly P, Hanson J, Douds D, and Seidel R. Environmental, energetic, and economic comparisons of organic and conventional farming systems. *BioScience,* 2005, 55, 573-82.

[830] El-Hage Scialabba, N. 2007. Organic Agriculture and Food Safety. Food and Agriculture Organization of the United Nations. Web (ftp://ftp.fao.org/paia/organicag/ofs/OFS-2007-5.pdf). August 17, 2011

[831] The Rodale Farming Systems trial—Celebrating 30 Years. The Rodale Institute. http://rodaleinstitute.org/our-work/farming-systems-trial/farming-systems-trial-30-year-report/

[832] André Leu, *The Myths of Safe Pesticides,* Acres USA, Austin, Texas 2014.

[833] David Tillman, *Nature* 396, 211-212 (19 November 1998)

[834] Christos Vasilikiotis, Ph.D , Can Organic Farming "Feed the World"? University of California, Berkeley November 2000.

[835] Youyong Zhu et al. "Genetic diversity and disease control in rice". *Nature* 406, 718 - 722 (2000). See also George Monbiot, "Organic Farming Will Feed the World". *The Guardian* 24th August 2000.

[836] André Leu, *The Myths of Safe Pesticides,* Acres USA, Austin, Texas 2014.

[837] George Monbiot, "Organic Farming Will Feed the World". *The Guardian* 24th August 2000.

[838] "Worse than DDT: When You Eat This, it Ends Up Lingering in Your Gut"

A One on One Interview with Dr Don Huber (Part 2) January 15, 2012. Available at:

http://articles.mercola.com/sites/articles/archive/2012/01/15/dr-don-huber-interview-part-2.aspx

[839] Catherine Caufield, *Multiple Exposures—Chronicle of the Radiation Age,* Harper & Row, New York

[840] Ibid. See Also Bill Kovarik and Mark Neuzil, from Mass Media and Environmental Conflict (Sage, 1996), p. 32-52. Also available online at:

http://66.147.244.135/~enviror4/people/radiumgirls/

See also : Alan Bellows. "Undark and the Radium Girls" Article #241. Available at:

http://www.damninteresting.com/undark-and-the-radium-girls/

[841] Ernest Sternglass. *Secret Fallout – Low-Level Radiation from Hiroshima to Three-Mile Island,* McGraw-Hill, 1981.

[842] Chris Busby, *Wings of Death – Nuclear Pollution and Human Health.* Green Audit Books, Aberystwyth. 1995

[843] Catherine Caufield, *Multiple Exposures—Chronicle of the Radiation Age,* Harper & Row, New York.

[844] Ernest Sternglass. *Secret Fallout – Low-Level Radiation from Hiroshima to Three-Mile Island,* McGraw-Hill, 1981.

[845] Ernest Sternglass. *Secret Fallout – Low-Level Radiation from Hiroshima to Three-Mile Island,* McGraw-Hill, 1981.

[846] Ibid.

[847] Jay M Gould, Benjamin A Goldman, *Deadly Deceit—Low Level Radiation High Level Cover-Up,* Four Walls Eight Windows, New York, 1990.

[848] Rachel Carson. *Silent Spring.* Houghton Mifflin Company, New York, 1994.

[849] Andrei Sakharov, "Radioactive carbon from nuclear explosion and non-threshold biological effects," Soviet Journal of Atomic Energy, vol 4 no. 6, June 1958. Available at:

http://scienceandglobalsecurity.org/archive/sgs01sakharov.pdf

[850] Chris Busby, *Wings of Death – Nuclear Pollution and Human Health.* Green Audit Books, Aberystwyth. 1995. See also Catherine Caufield, *Multiple Exposures—Chronicle of the Radiation Age,* Harper & Row, New York.

REFERENCES

851 Alyn Ware. "The Human Factor--Revising Einstein" Marshall Islanders- Lijon Eknilang Testimony, SGI Quarterly, July 2007. Available at:
http://www.sgiquarterly.org/feature2007Jly-7.html

852 Chris Busby, *Wings of Death – Nuclear Pollution and Human Health.* Green Audit Books, Aberystwyth. 1995

853 Kyshtm Disaster, Wikipedia. http://en.wikipedia.org/wiki/Kyshtym_disaster

854 John Gofman. "There is no safe threshold--on the health effects of radiation" Interview with Shobhit Arora and Fred Gardner. 1994. Available at:
http://www.ratical.org/radiation/CNR/synapseP.html

855 John Goffman, *Radiation-Induced Cancer from Low-Dose Exposure: An Independent Analysis.* Committee for Nuclear Responsibility, Inc. San Francisco. 1990.

856 Ibid.

857 Ernest Sternglass. *Secret Fallout – Low-Level Radiation from Hiroshima to Three-Mile Island,* McGraw-Hill, 1981

858 Catherine Caufield, *Multiple Exposures—Chronicle of the Radiation Age,* Harper & Row, New York.

859 Ernest Sternglass. *Secret Fallout – Low-Level Radiation from Hiroshima to Three-Mile Island,* McGraw-Hill, 1981.

860 A Petkau, "Role of superoxide dismutase in the modification of radiation injury." (1985) *The British Journal of Cancer. Supplement.* **8**: 87–95. ISSN 0306-9443. PMC 2149491. PMID 3307878.

861 Ernest Sternglass. *Secret Fallout – Low-Level Radiation from Hiroshima to Three-Mile Island,* McGraw-Hill, 1981. See also Catherine Caufield, *Multiple Exposures—Chronicle of the Radiation Age,* Harper & Row, New York.

862 John W. Gofman, Ph.D., M.D. & Arthur R. Tamplin, Ph.D. *Poisoned Power—The Case Against Nuclear Power Plants Before and After Three Mile Island.* Rodal Press, Emmaus, Pa.1979.

863 Catherine Caufield, *Multiple Exposures—Chronicle of the Radiation Age,* Harper & Row, New York.

864 J Gofman, An Irreverent, Illustrated view of Nuclear Power, San Francisco, Ca: Committee for Nuclear Responsibility, 1979, pp227-228. Obtained from: Jay M Gould, Benjamin A

Goldman, *Deadly Deceit—Low Level Radiation High Level Cover-Up,* Four Walls Eight Windows, New York, 1990

[865] Jay M Gould, Benjamin A Goldman, *Deadly Deceit—Low Level Radiation High Level Cover-Up,* Four Walls Eight Windows, New York, 1990. For further information on the Savannah river see the following site: http://agreenroad.blogspot.co.uk/2012/11/savannah-river-site-most-severely.html

[866] Ernest Sternglass. *Secret Fallout – Low-Level Radiation from Hiroshima to Three-Mile Island,* McGraw-Hill, 1981.

[867] Ibid.

[868] Jay M. Gould, Ernest J. Sternglass, Joseph J. Mangano, & William McDonnell, *The Enemy Within—The High Cost of Living Near Nuclear Reactors,* Four Walls Eight Windows, New York. 1996.

[869] German Affiliate of International Physicians for the Prevention of Nuclear War (IPPNW). "Health Effects of Chernobyl 25 years after the reactor catastrophe." April 2011. Accessed from: http://ratical.org/radiation/Chernobyl/HEofC25yrsAC.html

[870] Chris Busby, *Wings of Death – Nuclear Pollution and Human Health.* Green Audit Books, Aberystwyth.

[871] Ernest Sternglass. *Secret Fallout – Low-Level Radiation from Hiroshima to Three-Mile Island,* McGraw-Hill, 1981. Jay M Gould, Benjamin A Goldman, *Deadly Deceit—Low Level Radiation High Level Cover-Up,* Four Walls Eight Windows, New York, 1990

[872] Janette D. Sherman, M.D., and Alexey V. Yablokov, Ph.D, "Chernobyl: Consequences of the catastrophe 25 years later", San Francisco Bay View, 27 April 2011.

[873] Alexey V. Yablokov, Vassily B. Nesterenko, & Alexey V. Nesterenko. "Chernobyl Consequences of the Catastrophe for People and the Environment" *Annals of the New York Academy of Sciences*, Vol 1181, 2009.

[874] Y. I. Bandazhevsky Chronic Cs-137 incorporation in children's organs. *Swiss Media Weekly* 2003;133:488–490

[875] Jay M Gould, Benjamin A Goldman, *Deadly Deceit—Low Level Radiation High Level Cover-Up,* Four Walls Eight Windows, New York, 1990

[876] Chris Busby, *Wolves of Water,* Green Audit, Aberystwyth 2006

REFERENCES

[877] Reuters. Aaron Sheldrick. "Japan faces nuclear shutdown for second time since Fukushima". Tokyo. Thu Jan 24, 2013.

[878] Tessa Morris-Suzuki et al. "Lessons from Fukushima, Executive Summary". Greenpeace. 2012

[879] "Cesium-137 flow into sea 30 times greater than stated by TEPCO: report" Mainichi Daily News October 29, 2011. Institut De Radioprotection et de Sûreté Nucléaire. "Accident nucléaire de Fukushima-Daiichi : l'IRSN publie une mise â jour de sa note d'information sur l'impact sur le milieu marin des rejets radioactifs consécutifs â l'accident", 10-27-11. See also http://www.ratical.org/radiation/Fukushima/Cs137-30timesHigher.html

[880] Akio Matsumura. "Fukushima Daiichi Site: Cesium-137 is 85 times greater than at Chernobyl Accident" April 3rd 2012. Available at: http://akiomatsumura.com/2012/04/682.html
See also: http://www.ratical.org/radiation/Fukushima/index.html

[881] Ibid.

[882] Architect of Reactor 3 warns of massive hydrovolcanic explosion. Posted by Mochizuki on November 19th, 2011 *Fukushima Diary*
Available at: http://www.ratical.org/radiation/Fukushima/UeharaHaruo.html

[883] Kodama Tatsuhiko "Radiation Effects on Health: Protect the Children of Fukushima " Translation by Kyoko Selden. The Asia-Pacific Journal Vol 9, Issue 32 No 4 August 8, 2011. Also available at http://www.ratical.org/radiation/Fukushima/index.html

[884] Ibid.

[885] Impacts of the Fukushima Dai-Ichi Nuclear Power Plants on the Ocean Tuesday, Feb. 21 Woods Hole Oceanographic Institute. Available at: media@whoi.edu.

[886] Danielle Demetriou. "Japan: Fukushima disaster released twice as much radiation as initially estimated." The Telegraph 28 Oct 2011.

[887] 2008 Jeffrey Hays. "Fear and high radiation levels from Fukushima" *Facts & Details,* 2008. Available at:
http://factsanddetails.com/japan.php?itemid=2230&catid=26&subcatid=162#1110

[888] Joe Giambrone. "Radiation: The Future Children of Fukushima." *Global Research* May 3, 2011 Available at: http://theglobalrealm.com/2011/05/03/radiation-the-future-children-of-fukushima/

[889] Joseph J. Mangano and Janette D. Sherman. "An un-expected mortality increase in the United States follows arrival of the radioactive plume from Fukushima: Is there a correlation?" *Journal of Health Services, Volume 42, Number 1, Pages 47–64, 2012.*

[890] Chris Busby, *Wolves of Water,* Green Audit, Aberystwyth 2006.

[891] Ibid & Chris Busby, *Wings of Death – Nuclear Pollution and Human Health.* Green Audit Books, Aberystwyth. 1995

[892] Geiger Sweet, Geiger Sour, BBC2 Broadcast 31 July 1995, obtained from Busby above.

[893] & Chris Busby, *Wings of Death – Nuclear Pollution and Human Health.* Green Audit Books., Aberystwyth. 1995.

[894] Dr John Gofman Obituary, UC Berkeley. Robert Sanders, Media Relations 4 September 2007. http://www.berkeley.edu/news/media/releases/2007/09/04_GofmanObit.shtml

[895] John Gofman, M.D., Ph.D., *Radiation Induced Cancer from Low-Dose Exposure: An Independent Analysis.* Committee for Nuclear Responsibility, Inc. San Francisco 1990.

[896] John Gofman, M.D., Ph.D., *Radiation from Medical Procedures in the Pathogenesis of Cancer and Ischemic Heart Disease: Dose-Response Studies with Physicians per 100,000 Population.* Committee for Nuclear Responsibility, Inc. San Francisco 1999.

[897] Interview with John Gofman by Shobhit Arora and Fred Gardner. On the health effects of radiation: "There is no safe threshold" 1994 available at: http://www.ratical.org/radiation/CNR/synapseP.html

[898] Ibid. See also University of California San Francisco, *Synapse Vol 38 Number 16, Jan 20 1994*

[899] Jay M. Gould, Ernest J. Sternglass, Joseph J. Mangano, & William McDonnell, *The Enemy Within—The High Cost of Living Near Nuclear Reactors.* Four Walls Eight Windows, New York. 1996.

[900] Nuclear Power in Italy. World Nuclear Association, November 2012. Available at: http://www.world-nuclear.org/info/Country-Profiles/Countries-G-N/Italy/#.UVc4kVcu2E8

[901] Juergen Baetz. "Germany decides to abandon nuclear power by 2022" Bloomberg Business Week. The Associated Press May 30, 2011, http://www.businessweek.com/ap/financialnews/D9NHTJM02.htm

REFERENCES

902 Nigel Morris ."UK Government names eight new sites for nuclear power plants". The Independent. Friday 24 June 2011

http://www.independent.co.uk/news/uk/politics/government-names-eight-new-sites-for-nuclear-power-plants-2302035.html

903 Nuclear review 'was misleading' BBC News. Thursday, 15 February 2007, 18:10 GMT

http://news.bbc.co.uk/1/hi/uk_politics/6364281.stm

904Puppetmaster lobbyists boast of pulling in 'sleeplike' MPs.*The Sunday Times.* Published: 23 June 2013 Insight Investigation: Heidi Blake & Jonathan Calvert, additional reporting Katie Gibbons and Cal Flyn.

905 House of Commons Committee of Public Accounts. Nuclear Decommissioning Authority: "Managing risk at Sellafield" Twenty-fourth Report of Session 2012–13.

http://www.publications.parliament.uk/pa/cm201213/cmselect/cmpubacc/746/746.pdf

906 "Nuclear Power is Still Not Viable without Subsidies." Union of Concerned Scientists. February 23, 2011.

http://www.ucsusa.org/nuclear_power/nuclear_power_and_global_warming/nuclear-power-subsidies-report.html

907 Ibid.

908 John W. Gofman, M.D., Ph.D., & Arthur R. Tamplin, Ph.D. *Poisoned Power—The case Against nuclear Power Plants Before and After Three Mile Island.* Rodale Press, Emmaus Pa. 1979.

909Dr Christopher Busby. Dishonesty and the Science Policy Interface--Scientific dishonesty and nuclear power. See Nexus, Vol 20, No1, January 2013. Also available at: http://candobetter.net/node/2744 .

910 "Reducing Environmental Cancer Risk" Annual Report 2010, President's Cancer Panel. U.S.Department of Health and Human Services.

911 Deane Rimerman. Editor "Your firewood ash is radioactive & wildfire is nuclear fallout". *Science News* – August 10, 1991.

912 Burrows BA, Chalmers TC. "Cesium-137/potassium-40 ratios in firewood ashes as a reflection of worldwide radioactive contamination of the environment". *Annals of the New York Academy of Sciences.* Volume 609, "Trends in Cancer Mortality in Industrial Countries", pages 334–337, November 1990.

[913] Dee Hock, *One from Many: VISA and the Rise of the Chaordic Organization.* Berrett-Koehler. 2005.

[914] State of the Science of Endocrine Disrupting Chemicals 2012 WHO

[915] *Reducing Environmental Cancer Risk,* 2010 Annual Report. Presidents Cancer Panel. U.S. Department of Health and Human Services.

[916] Ibid.

[917] Philippe Grandjean & Philip J Landrigan. "Neurobehavioural effects of developmental toxicity". *Lancet Neurol* 2014; 13: 330-38

[918] King, M. Banking from Bagehot to Basel and Back again, speech presented at the second Bagehot Lecture, Buttonwood Gathering, October 25 2010. New York City.

[919] Andrew Jackson & Ben Dyson, *Modernising Money—Why Our Monetary System is Broken and How It Can Be Fixed.* Positive Money, London 2012.

[920] Ibid.

[921] Presenting the American Monetary Act (as of July 18, 2010) American Monetary Institute. http://www.monetary.org/wp-content/uploads/2011/12/32-page-brochure-sept20111.pdf See also Stephen Zarlenga, *The Lost Science of Money, The Mythology of Money—The Story of Power,* American Monetary Institute, New York, 2002.

[922] Michael Rowbotham. *Grip of Death—A Study of Modern Money, Debt Slavery and Destructive Economics.* John Carpenter Publishing. Charlbury 2009.

[923] Ibid.

[924] Joe Bakan, *The Corporation – The Pathological Pursuit of profit and Power,* Constable, London, 2004.

[925] Robert Hare Ph.D., *The Corporation—A Film by Mark Achbar, Jennifer Abbott & Joel Bakan,* Big Picture Media Corporation.

[926] Ray Anderson, *Confessions of a Radical Industrialist: How Interface proved that you can build a successful business without destroying the planet.* Random House. 2010.

[927] Ray Anderson. Speech to civic and business leaders in North Carolina State University *The Corporation—A Film by Mark Achbar, Jennifer Abbott & Joel Bakan,* Big Picture Media Corporation.

[928] Ray Anderson, *Confessions of a Radical Industrialist: How Interface proved that you can build a successful business without destroying the planet.* Random House. 2010.

REFERENCES

929 Ibid.

930 Harry Glasbeek, *Wealth by Stealth—Corporate Crime, Corporate Law, and the Perversion of Democracy.* Between the Lines. Toronto, Canada. 2002.

931 Ibid.

932 Robert Hinkley. Corporate Social Responsibility Report--How Corporate Law Inhibits Social Responsibility. A Corporate Attorney Proposes a 'Code for Corporate Citizenship' in State Law. *Business Ethics*: January/February 2002. Also available at: www.commondreams.org?views02/0119.04.htm

933 Harry Glasbeek, *Wealth by Stealth—Corporate Crime, Corporate Law, and the Perversion of Democracy.* Between the Lines. Toronto, Canada. 2002.

934 Ibid.

935 Mae-Wan Ho, Sam Burcher, Lim Li Ching & others, *Food Futures Now-Organic-Sustainable-Fossil Fuel Free,* Institute of Science in Society. London 2008.

936 Ibid.

937 Worthington V. Nutritional quality of organic versus conventional fruits, vegetables, and grains. *Journal of Alternative and Complementary Medicine.* 2001, 7 (2), 161-173.

938 Heaton, S. Organic farming, food quality and human health: A review of the evidence. Soil Association, Bristol, 2001

939 Ibid.

940 *Nutritional Qualities of Fresh Fruits and Vegetables.* Edited by Philip L. White, Sc.D. & Nancy Selvey, R.D. Futura Publishing Company. New York,1974

941 Food, Inc. A film by Robert Kenner. Participant Media and River Road Entertainment.

942 John W. Gofman, Ph.D., M.D. & Arthur R. Tamplin, Ph.D. *Poisoned Power—The Case Against Nuclear Power Plants. Before and After Three Mile Island.* Rodale Press, Emmaus Pa.1979.

943 Tim Jackson. *Prosperity Without Growth.* Earthscan. 2009.

944 Paul Hawken, *The Ecology of Commerce.* Weidenfield and Nicholson. London.1993.

945 Ibid.

946 Jared Diamond. *Collapse—How Societies Choose to Fail or Survive.* Allen Lane, Penguin Books, 2005.

947 Ibid.

[948] Hardin Tibbs,"Industrial Ecology: An environmental Agenda for Industry," Global Business Network :

http://www.gbn.com/articles/pdfs/Industrial%20Ecology%20June%201993.pdf

[949] Michael Braungart and William McDonough. *Cradle to Cradle—Remaking the Way We Make Things*. Jonathan Cape, London.2008.

www.ingramcontent.com/pod-product-compliance
Lightning Source LLC
Chambersburg PA
CBHW050131290326
R18043500001B/R180435PG41927CBX00018B/13